THE
KOCH BOOK
OF TABLES

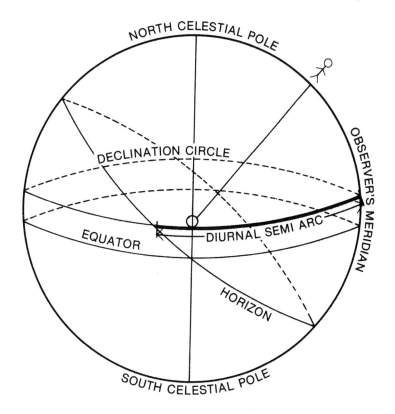

Koch Tables of Houses
Time Tables
Interpolation Tables
How to Cast a Natal Horoscope

Compiled and Programmed by
Neil F. Michelsen

Published by
ACS Publications, Inc.
P.O. Box 34487
San Diego, California 92103-0802

Library of Congress Catalog Card Number: 76-023547
International Standard Book Number 0-917086-79-1

Published by ACS Publications, Inc.
P.O. Box 34487
San Diego, CA 92103-0802

Printed in the United States of America

First printing, May 1985
Second printing, May 1987
Third printing, November 1989

Contents

How to Cast a Natal Horoscope

by Robert Hand and Joshua Brackett

These instructions consist of two parts: the worksheet, which is an outline used for casting a horoscope, and the notes, which explain the worksheet. The worksheet provides minimal directions for one method of casting an ordinary natal chart. The notes support the worksheet directions with theory, with alternative methods and with prescriptions for special cases. Each section of notes is headed by the lines from the worksheet to which the notes apply, with the spaces filled in with appropriate example values. A complete chart is cast as an example for the reader to follow.

We anticipate that the beginner will read through the entire text of the notes, perhaps casting a first chart as s/he goes. The experienced astrologer, on the other hand, will use the worksheet to cast charts and will select notes to read at leisure out of curiosity rather than necessity.

In the worksheet and in the notes, the order of operations is (1) time calculations, (2) locating the planets and (3) locating the house cusps. We know that astrologers usually do the house cusps before the planets, probably because the house cusps have to be put on the horoscope wheel first. We have changed the usual order so as to help the beginner by arranging the tasks in ascending order of difficulty. Locating the planets requires only a one-way interpolation whereas locating the house cusps requires two-way interpolation. If you prefer to calculate the house cusps first, there is nothing to prevent you from doing so.

The ephemeris referred to in the text and illustrations is *The American Ephemeris*, available in paperback decade volumes and the hardcover *American Ephemeris 1931 to 1980 and Book of Tables* (which includes this text) published by ACS Publications, Inc.

NATAL HOROSCOPE WORKSHEET

Name _____

TIME CALCULATIONS

1	**Born**	am/pm Zone		**Date**				
2	**Place**	Longitude		**Latitude**				
3	**Standard Time** (pm: +12h, DST: −1h)				3	h	m	
4	**Time Zone Number** (Table 1)				4	h		
5	**Universal Time** (West +, East −) **Greenwich Date**				5	h	m	**UT**

6	△T (5 date, Table IV)	6		s	
7	**Ephemeris Time** (add 5 + 6 = 7)	7	h m s		**ET**

8	**Greenwich Sidereal Time 00h** (Ephemeris)	8	h	m	s
9	**Solar-Sidereal Correction** (5, Table II)	9		m	s
10	**Greenwich Sidereal Time** (add 5 + 8 + 9 = 10)	10	h	m	s
11	**Longitude Correction** (Table III) **degrees: 11a** h m				
	minutes: 11b m s				
	total (add **11a** + **11b** = **11c**)	11c	h	m	s
	(West: subtract 10 − 11c = 12); East: add 10 + 11c = 12				
12	**Local Sidereal Time**	12	h	m	s **LST**

LOCATING THE PLANETS

13	☉ **Longitude 0h After Birth** (5 date + 1d, Ephemeris)	13	°	′	″	
14	☉ **Longitude 0h Before Birth** (5 date, Ephemeris)	14	°	′	″	
15	**24h Travel** (subtract 13 − 14 = 15)	15	°	′	″	
16	**ET Travel** (7, 15, Table V) minutes	16a		′	″	
	hours	16b	°	′	″	
17	☉ **Longitude at Birthtime** (add 14 + 16a + 16b =17)	17	°	′	″ ☉	

If ET (7) is less than 12h:				*If ET (7) is greater than 12h:*		
18	☽ **12h date of birth** (5 date) 18 ° ′ ″	18	☽ **next day** (5 date + 1d)	18	° ′ ″
19	☽ **date of birth** (5 date) 19 ° ′ ″	19	☽ **12h date of birth** (5 date)	19	° ′ ″
20	**12h Travel** (18 − 19 = 20) 20 ° ′ ″	20	**12h Travel** (18 − 19 = 20)	20	° ′ ″
21	**ET** (7) 21 h m s	21	**ET Since Noon** (7−12h=21)	21	h m s
22	☽ **Travel to Birthtime** (20, 21, Table VI)		minutes	22a	° ′ ″
			hours	22b	° ′ ″
23	☽ **Longitude at Birthtime** (add 19 + 22a + 22b = 23)	23	° ′ ″ ☽		

24 **Longitude 0h After Birth** (5 date + 1d, Ephemeris)
25 **Longitude 0h Before Birth** (5 date, Ephemeris)
26 **24h Travel** (subtract 24 − 25 = 26; if retrograde, subtract 25 − 24 = 26)
27 **ET Travel** (7, 26, Table VII: minutes 27a, hours 27b, 27a + 27b = 27c)
28 **Longitude At Birthtime** (25 + 27c = 28; if retrograde, 25 − 27c = 28)

	Mean ☊	True ☊	☿	♀	♂	♃	♄	♅	♆	♇
24										
25										
26										
27a										
27b										
27c										
28										
	Mean ☊	**True ☊**	**☿**	**♀**	**♂**	**♃**	**♄**	**♅**	**♆**	**♇**

LOCATING HOUSE CUSPS

29	**Local Sidereal Time** (12)	29	h	m	s
30	**Earlier LST** (Table of Houses)	30	h	m	s
31	**Later LST** (Table of Houses)	31	h	m	s
32	**LST Increment** (subtract 29 − 30 = 32)	32		m	s	△LST

33	**Midheaven at Later LST** (Table of Houses)	33	°	′
34	**Midheaven at Earlier LST** (Table of Houses)	34	°	′
35	**4m Midheaven Interval** (subtract 33 − 34 = 35)	35	°	′
36	**Midheaven Increment** (32, 35, Table XI)	36	°	′
37	**Midheaven at Birth LST** (add 34 + 36 = 37)	37	°	′	MC

38	**Lower Latitude** (Table of Houses)	38	°	′
39	**Higher Latitude** (Table of Houses)	39	°	′
40	**Latitude Increment** (subtract Birth Latitude − 38 = 40)	40	°	′	△Lat

41 **House Cusps at Later LST, Lower Latitude** (Table of Houses)
42 **House Cusps at Earlier LST, Lower Latitude** (Table of Houses)
43 **4m Cusp Intervals** (subtract 41 − 42 = 43)
44 **Cusp Increments** (32, 43, Table XI)
45 **House Cusps at Birth LST, Lower Latitude** (add 42 + 44 = 45)

	LST	Latitude	11	12	ASC	2	3
41	LATER	LOWER (38)					
42	EARLIER						
43	4m	°					
44	LINE 32						
45	BIRTH						

46 **House Cusps at Later LST, Higher Latitude** (Table of Houses)
47 **House Cusps at Earlier LST, Higher Latitude** (Table of Houses)
48 **4m Cusp Intervals** (subtract 46 − 47 = 48)
49 **Cusp Increments** (32, 48, Table XI)
50 **House Cusps at Birth LST, Higher Latitude** (add 47 + 49 = 50)

	LST	Latitude	11	12	ASC	2	3
46	LATER	HIGHER (39)					
47	EARLIER						
48	4m	°					
49	LINE 32						
50	BIRTH						

51 **1° Cusp Intervals**
   If **50** is greater than **45**, rewrite **45** below. Subtract **50 − 45 = 51**.
   If **50** is less than **45** mark **51** and **52** negative (−) for that house. Subtract **45 − 50 = 51**.
52 **Cusp Increments for Latitude** (40, 51, Table XII)
53 **House Cusps at Birth LST, Birth Latitude** (add 45 + 52 = 53)

	LST	Latitude	11	12	ASC	2	3
45	BIRTH (29)	LOWER					
51		1°					
52	h m s	LINE 40					
53		BIRTH					
			11	12	ASC	2	3

TIME CALCULATIONS

1 **Born** 8:22   (am)/pm **Zone** EASTERN   **Date** MARCH 25, 1970

Using the procedure outlined on the worksheet, you can cast a chart with Sun and Moon positions accurate to the nearest second of arc, planet positions accurate to the nearest minute of arc, and house cusps accurate to the nearest three minutes of arc. Such precision is futile, however, if the original birth information is in error. Birthtime should be verified by official records — a birth certificate or hospital file. Parents' memories are notoriously unreliable.

2 **Place** HYANNIS, MA   **Longitude** 70°W 15'   **Latitude** 41° N39'

If you do not find the longitude and latitude of the birthplace in the list of major cities at the back of this book, consult *The American Atlas or The International Atlas.*

3 **Standard Time** (pm: + 12h, DST: − 1h)   **3**   8 h 22m

h = hours
m = minutes

The recorded birthtime must be expressed as standard time, if it is not already, and in terms of the twenty-four-hour clock. This means you must add twelve hours if the birthtime is 1:00 pm or later, and also you must subtract one hour if Daylight Saving Time was in effect at the time of birth. Remember that during World War II, 1942-45, the United States was on year-round Daylight Saving Time, called War Time. When in doubt, consult *The American Atlas* or *The International Atlas.*

4 **Time Zone Number** (Table 1)   **4**   5 h
5 **Universal Time** (West +, East −) Greenwich Date   **5** 1 3 h 22 m   UT

Universal Time (UT) is the twenty-four-hour clock version of Greenwich Mean Time (GMT), the standard time of Great Britain, where the Greenwich Meridian, 0° longitude, is located. Time measurements in the earth sciences ordinarily use UT, as do astronomical tables.

Universal Time and all other standard times are forms of solar time in that they measure time by the changing relationship of the Sun to the meridian at a certain place on the Earth. The meridian of a place is the arc of the great circle that runs from the north point of the horizon to the zenith, directly overhead, to the south point of the horizon. At northern latitudes, when the Sun crosses the meridian, it is due south of the observer. In old books, the crossing of the meridian is called the Sun's "southing" and defines local noon.

The trouble with using the real Sun as the basis of timekeeping is that because of the elliptical shape of the Earth's orbit around the Sun, the Sun's apparent motion is not constant. Time measurements using the southing of the Sun can vary by as much as fifteen minutes from measurements that use a constant clock. This became a problem with the invention of the mechanical clock, which was constant and could not easily be adjusted to fit the Sun's variations. So astronomers created a fictitious "mean Sun," which moves along the celestial equator at a constant rate. Noon local mean time then, is the southing of the

4

mean Sun, which moves at the average rate of the true Sun and coincides with it twice a year.

In theory, every place on Earth could keep its own local mean time based on the angle between the local meridian and the mean Sun. In practice, the Earth has been divided into twenty-four time zones. Every place keeps the time of a nearby meridian of longitude, which is usually a multiple of 15° east or west of Greenwich. Most of these time zones are a whole number of hours ahead or behind Greenwich.

Table I gives the number of hours for each time zone. The time in zones to the west of Greenwich is earlier than Greenwich time; therefore you add to get Greenwich time. Conversely, in zones to the east of Greenwich, you subract the time-zone number given in Table I.

If a person is born near midnight standard time, adding or subtracting the time-zone number can put the birthtime into the preceding or following day. For example, if the birthtime is 11:15 pm Eastern Standard time or 23h 15m, when we add the time-zone number 5, we get 28h 15m UT. What does that figure mean? It actually means 4h 15m of the following day. In other words, we must subtract twenty-four hours from the time and add one day to the date. The date on line 5 would then be March 26, 1970, even though the date in line 1 was March 25, 1970. That would be the date at Greenwich at the time of birth in Hyannis, Massachusetts. The corrected date on line 5 would be used from then on when you are consulting the ephemeris.

| 6 | △T (5 date, Table IV) | 6 | | | 41 s | |
| 7 | Ephemeris Time (add 5 + 6 = 7) | 7 | 13h | 22m | 41 s | ET |

The abbreviated directions on the worksheet are meant to be read, "Line 6 is for △T. You get it by taking the information on line 5 and going to Table IV. Line 7 is for Ephemeris Time. Add the values on lines 5 and 6 and write the sum on line 7."

s = seconds

Universal Time, measured as it is by the angle between the mean Sun and the Greenwich Meridian, would be perfect for astronomical and astrological purposes if the Earth turned at a perfectly uniform rate. However, because of earthquakes and other disturbances, the Earth does not rotate uniformly. Thus UT clocks, especially the newer astronomical clocks that keep time extremely precisely by measuring the disintegration of atomic nuclei, have to be reset when the Earth is fast or slow. The astronomical calculations that go into an ephemeris presuppose a constant time, independent of the Earth's variations. So astronomers have created such a time. Ephemeris Time is Universal Time as it would be if the Earth had rotated uniformly since the beginning of the century. It is an ideal mean solar time, used in all modern ephemerides. The difference between ET and UT, △T, cannot be predicted exactly, because it is the result of observations. It can only be estimated for the future. Thus Table IV, which gives △T in this book ends with the year 1983, with ET differing from UT by about 53 seconds.

Planetary calculations should be done in ET because the planets move independently of the Earth. House cusps, on the other hand, are closely related to the rotation of the Earth and should, therefore, be calculated based on UT. Calculating an entire chart in ET is a common error, which results in slightly misplaced house cusps.

The difference between UT and ET is only worth bothering with if you are going to locate the Sun and Moon as accurately as possible, perhaps for the purpose of solar and lunar returns. If you are satisfied with accuracy to the nearest minute of arc, forty-odd seconds of birthtime is not significant.

	5	13h	22m		**UT**
	6			41s	
	7	13h	22m	41s	**ET**

8 Greenwich Sidereal Time 00h (Ephemeris)	8	12h	8m	9s
9 Solar-Sidereal Correction (5, Table II)	9		2m	12s
10 Greenwich Sidereal Time (add 5 + 8 + 9 = 10)	10	25h	32m	21s

Universal Time and Ephemeris Time are solar times, but to measure planetary motion, it is convenient to have a time that is related not to the Sun but to the zodiac: Sidereal Time. Instead of measuring the angle from the Sun to the meridian, Sidereal Time (ST) measures the angle from the vernal equinox (0° Aries) to the meridian. Thus at 0h 0m ST, 0° Aries is on the meridian or "southing." At 1h 0m ST, 0° Aries is 15° west of the meridian.

In the time it takes the Earth to revolve around the Sun once, a solar year, the Earth rotates on its axis 366.2422 times. Thus to us on Earth it appears that the zodiac and the vernal equinox, our reference point on the zodiac, go around the Earth 366.2422 times a year. The Sun, however, rises, crosses the meridian and sets only 365.2422 times a year. Why? The Sun's apparent yearly motion through the zodiac is opposed to its apparent daily motion across the sky. Thus one yearly motion "undoes" one daily motion. Consequently a year has 366.2422 sidereal days and only 365.2422 solar days, or exactly one less; a sidereal day is shorter than a solar day by 3 minutes 56 seconds; and a sidereal hour is shorter than a solar hour by 9.86 seconds. Universal Time and Sidereal Time are together on September 21 every year. Then ST pulls ahead of UT at the rate of 9.86 seconds per hour of UT until a year later on September 21, ST is exactly twenty-four hours ahead.

The ephemeris gives ST for 0h 0m 0s UT at the beginning of every day. Therefore, you must add 9.86 seconds for every hour of UT in order to find the correct ST. Table II gives this correction. Read across the top to find the column for the number of hours of UT; then read down that column to the line for the number of minutes of UT. Enter the correction on line 9.

MARCH 1970
LONGITUDE

DAY	SID. TIME			☉			☽	
	h	m	s	°	'	"	°	'
1 Su	10	33	32	9♓	59	12	8♐	38
2 M	10	37	29	10	59	25	22	25
3 Tu	10	41	25	11	59	37	6♑	34
4 W	10	45	22	12	59	47	21	3
5 Th	10	49	18	13	59	55	5♒	48
6 F	10	53	15	15	0	2	20	44
7 Sa	10	57	12	16	0	7	5♓	43
8 Su	11	1	8	17	0	10	20	37
9 M	11	5	5	18	0	11	5♈	18
10 Tu	11	9	1	19	0	10	19	39
11 W	11	12	58	20	0	7	3♉	36
12 Th	11	16	54	21	0	2	17	6
13 F	11	20	51	21	59	55	0♊	12
14 Sa	11	24	47	22	59	46	12	54
15 Su	11	28	44	23	59	34	25	16
16 M	11	32	41	24	59	21	7♋	22
17 Tu	11	36	37	25	59	5	19	18
18 W	11	40	34	26	58	46	1♌	8
19 Th	11	44	30	27	58	26	12	56
20 F	11	48	27	28	58	3	24	47
21 Sa	11	52	23	29	57	38	6♍	43
22 Su	11	56	20	0♈	57	11	18	48
23 M	12	0	16	1	56	42	1♎	3
24 Tu	12	4	13	2	56	11	13	30
25 W	12	8	9	3	55	38	26	10
26 Th	12	12	6	4	55	3	9♍	3
27 F	12	16	3	5	54	26	22	10
28 Sa	12	19	59	6	53	48	5♐	31
29 Su	12	23	56	7	53	7	19	5
30 M	12	27	52	8	52	25	2♑	53
31 Tu	12	31	49	9♈	51	41	16♑	53

The ephemeris gives Greenwich Sidereal Time at 0h 0m UT at the beginning of every day.

Table II Solar-Sidereal Correction

MIN	0h m s	1h m s	2h m s	3h m s	4h m s	5h m s	6h m s	7h m s	8h m s	9h m s	10h m s	11h m s	12h m s	13h m s	14h m s	15h m s	16h m s	17h m s	18h m s	19h m s	20h m s
21	0 3	0 13	0 23	0 33	0 43	0 53	1 3	1 12	1 22	1 32	1 42	1 52	2 2	2 12	2 21	2 31	2 41	2 51	3 1	3 11	3 21
22	0 4	0 13	0 23	0 33	0 43	0 53	1 3	1 13	1 22	1 32	1 42	1 52	2 2	2 12	2 22	2 31	2 41	2 51	3 1	3 11	3 21
23	0 4	0 14	0 23	0 33	0 43	0 53	1 3	1 13	1 23	1 32	1 42	1 52	2 2	2 12	2 22	2 31	2 41	2 51	3 1	3 11	3 21
24	0 4	0 14	0 24	0 34	0 43	0 53	1 3	1 13	1 23	1 33	1 43	1 52	2 2	2 12	2 22	2 32	2 42	2 52	3 1	3 11	3 21
25	0 4	0 14	0 24	0 34	0 44	0 53	1 3	1 13	1 23	1 33	1 43	1 53	2 2	2 12	2 22	2 32	2 42	2 52	3 2	3 11	3 21

Table II, Solar-Sidereal Correction, gives the difference between Solar and Sidereal Time since midnight UT before birth, 9.86 seconds per hour of UT.

		10	25h 32m 21s
11 Longitude Correction (Table III) degrees:	**11a** 4h 40m		
minutes:	**11b** 1m 0s		
total (add 11a + 11b = 11c)		**11c**	4h 41m 0s
(West: subtract 10 – 11c = 12; East: add 10 + 11c = 12)			
12 Local Sidereal Time		**12**	20h 51m 21s LST

Sidereal Time, because it measures the angle between the local meridian and 0° Aries, is different for different longitudes. Since Sidereal Time has no time zones, the difference between Sidereal Time at any place and Greenwich Sidereal Time depends on the longitude of the place. Longitude divides the Earth into 360°; time measurement divides its rotation into 24 hours. Therefore, 360° ÷ 24 or 15°, equals one hour. The longitude correction is given along with longitude and latitude for major cities of the United States and the world in the back of this book. If the birthplace is not listed there, use Table III. Table III gives the correction for each degree and each minute of longitude. If the longitude of birth is east of Greenwich, add the correction; if it is west, subtract it. The result is Local Sidereal Time of birth or LST.

Table III Longitude Correction

Degrees						Minutes	
°	h m	°	h m	°	h m	'	m s
1	0 4	61	4 4	121	8 4	1	0 4
2	0 8	62	4 8	122	8 8	2	0 8
3	0 12	63	4 12	123	8 12	3	0 12
4	0 16	64	4 16	124	8 16	4	0 16
5	0 20	65	4 20	125	8 20	5	0 20
6	0 24	66	4 24	126	8 24	6	0 24
7	0 28	67	4 28	127	8 28	7	0 28
8	0 32	68	4 32	128	8 32	8	0 32
9	0 36	69	4 36	129	8 36	9	0 36
10	0 40	70	4 40	130	8 40	10	0 40
11	0 44	71	4 44	131	8 44	11	0 44
12	0 48	72	4 48	132	8 48	12	0 48
13	0 52	73	4 52	133	8 52	13	0 52
14	0 56	74	4 56	134	8 56	14	0 56
15	1 0	75	5 0	135	9 0	15	1 0

Table III, Longitude Correction, gives the difference between Local Sidereal Time and Greenwich Sidereal Time, a function of the difference in longitude between the birthplace and Greenwich.

Direct Method

This method of calculating Local Sidereal Time, called the direct method because it dispenses with local mean time, was first worked out by Charles Carter. The more cumbersome traditional methods are holdovers from the days before standard time zones, when all times were local. The direct method can be used even when birthtime is given in local mean time: simply reverse the longitude correction to get back to UT and proceed with steps **6** through **12**.

7

Rounding Off

Although we began with a birthtime accurate only to the nearest minute, we now have a Local Sidereal Time accurate to the nearest second. In truth, 8:22 am means some time between 8:21:30 and 8:22:30. Consequently our LST is really some time between 20:50:51 and 20:51:51. Should LST then be rounded off to the nearst minute? No, because LST is only an intermediate value on the way to locating house cusps. Rounding off an intermediate value has the effect of increasing the error introduced by the approximation of birthtime. When you have the final house cusps, however, remember that they are accurate only to within ± seven minutes of arc, which is the average error caused by a one-minute error of birthtime. Only a rectified chart can be assumed to have house cusps accurate to the nearest minute of arc. Not even the chart of a birth timed with a stopwatch qualifies, because astrologers are still uncertain about what a precise moment of birth is. In spite of these uncertainties, our task here is to learn the techniques of calculation, so we will assume that birthtime is precisely 8:22:00 am EST.

Sexagesimal Arithmetic

In casting a horoscope, you often have to add or subtract sexagesimal numbers, quantities counted by sixties, in the form of hours, minutes and seconds, or degrees, minutes and seconds. It is a simple process that often can be done mentally. Perhaps the greatest problem is to overcome the habits of a lifetime and remember to do it correctly.

The principle involved is the same as that used in ordinary decimal addition and subtraction: if you add and subtract equal quantities to and from a quantity, the result is identical to the quantity you started with. In our example above, we had to do the following subtraction:

$$
\begin{array}{rrr}
25\text{h} & 32\text{m} & 21\text{s} \\
-\,4\text{h} & 41\text{m} & 0\text{s} \\
\end{array}
$$

How can we subtract 41m from 32m? By first adding and subtracting equal quantities.

$$
\begin{array}{rrr}
25\text{h} & 32\text{m} & 21\text{s} \\
 & +\,60\text{m} & \\
-\,1\text{h} & & \\
\hline
24\text{h} & 92\text{m} & 21\text{s} \\
\end{array}
$$

Because 1h = 60m, 25h 32m 21s = 24h 92m 21s. Now we can subtract.

$$
\begin{array}{rrr}
24\text{h} & 92\text{m} & 21\text{s} \\
-\,4\text{h} & 41\text{m} & 0\text{s} \\
\hline
20\text{h} & 51\text{m} & 21\text{s} \\
\end{array}
$$

You can see that the principle is the same as the one we use when we "borrow" in ordinary subtraction.

Suppose that instead of subtracting, we had to add 4h 41m 0s.

$$
\begin{array}{rrr}
25h & 32m & 21s \\
+\,4h & 41m & 0s \\
\hline
29h & 73m & 21s
\end{array}
$$

First we would deal with the 73m.

$$
\begin{array}{rrr}
29h & 73m & 21s \\
 & -\,60m & \\
+\,1h & & \\
\hline
30h & 13m & 21s
\end{array}
$$

Now what about the 30h?

$$
\begin{array}{rrrr}
 & 30h & 13m & 21s \\
 & -\,24h & & \\
+\,1d & & & \\
\hline
1d & 6h & 13m & 21s
\end{array}
$$

And now what about the extra day? If we are at line 5, Universal Time, or above, we have to add the one day to the date of birth so that we go into the ephemeris with the correct date. That date matters because Greenwich Sidereal Time and the positions of the planets are different on different days. But Sidereal Time is used only for locating house cusps, which are the same if the LST is the same, regardless of date. Therefore we discard the extra day and use 6h 31m 21s as our LST.

The identity principle applies to adding and subtracting angles as well. For example.

$$
\begin{array}{rrrr}
29° & \approx & 41' & 33'' \\
+\,2° & & 30' & 48'' \\
\hline
31° & \approx & 71' & 81'' \\
 & & +\,1' & -\,60'' \\
+\,1° & & -\,60' & \\
\hline
32° & \approx & 12' & 21''
\end{array}
$$

This result is satisfactory except for the fact that Aquarius has only 30 degrees. So we must subtract 30 degrees and add one sign. The result is 2° ⟋ 12′ 21″.

9

LOCATING THE PLANETS

The ephemeris gives the longtitudes of the Sun and the planets at midnight (0h) at the beginning of every day and the Moon at midnight and noon. The ephemeris does not give the position of any planet at any other time. So unless you are casting the chart for someone born at midnight, you have to interpolate.

The underlying principle of interpolation is quite simple. Assuming that any body, an automobile, an airplane or a planet, is moving at a constant speed, if you know how far it traveled in one period of time, you can deduce how far it traveled in another period of time. If in two hours a car goes 100 miles, in one hour it will go 50 miles because

$$\frac{1}{2} = \frac{50}{100}$$

The assumption of constant speed is much more realistic when applied to planets than to automobiles. Interpolation takes the form ''If Venus moved 1°14′ in twenty-four hours, how far did it move in nine hours and thirteen minutes?'' The answer is: twenty-eight minutes of arc because

$$\frac{9h \quad 13m}{24h} = \frac{28}{1° \quad 14′}$$

If Venus was at 8°⌭10′ at midnight, where was it at 9h 13m? Answer: 8°⌭38″ because 8°⌭10′ + 28′ = 8°⌭38′. In principle, that is all there is to it. The rest is details.

13 ☉ **Longitude** 0h **After Birth** (5 date + 1d, Ephemeris)	13	4°♈55′ 3″
14 ☉ **Longitude** 0h **Before Birth** (5 date, Ephemeris)	14	3°♈55′ 38″
15 24h **Travel** (subtract 13 − 14 = 15)	15	° 59′ 25″

d = day

By subtracting the Sun's 0h longitude at the beginning of the date of birth (given in the ephemeris) from its 0h longitude at the beginning of the following day, we find out how far the Sun traveled in twenty-four hours. Be sure to use the date from line 5 if it is different from the original birthdate.

Do not round off the Sun's twenty-four-hour travel. It is desirable to have the Sun's position accurate to within a second or two of arc in order to be able to calculate solar return charts.

MARCH 1970

LONGITUDE

DAY	SID. TIME	☉	☽	☽ 12 Hour	MEAN ☊	TRUE ☊	☿	♀	♂	♃	♄	♅	♆	♇
	h m s	° ′ ″	° ′ ″	° ′ ″	° ′	° ′	° ′	° ′	° ′	° ′	° ′	° ′	° ′	° ′
20 F	11 48 27	28 58 3	24 47 26	0♍ 44 36	11 9.3	11 50.6	25 26.3	12 9.1	9 12.9	4 45.7	6 44.2	7 5.8	0 48.9	25 58.9
21 Sa	11 52 23	29 57 38	6♍ 43 33	12 44 37	11 6.1	11R 51.3	27 22.9	13 23.5	9 55.3	4 40.7	6 50.9	7 3.3	0 48.4	25 57.3
22 Su	11 56 20	0♈ 57 11	18 48 6	24 54 12	11 2.9	11 51.3	29 20.5	14 38.0	10 37.7	4 35.5	6 57.6	7 0.7	0 47.8	25 55.7
23 M	12 0 16	1 56 42	1♎ 3 10	7♎ 15 7	10 59.7	11 50.3	1♈ 19.2	15 52.3	11 20.1	4 30.1	7 4.3	6 58.1	0 47.1	25 54.1
24 Tu	12 4 13	2 56 11	13 30 13	19 48 34	10 56.6	11 48.3	3 18.9	17 6.7	12 2.4	4 24.7	7 11.1	6 55.5	0 46.5	25 52.5
25 W	12 8 9	3 55 38	26 10 12	2♏ 35 13	10 53.4	11 45.3	5 19.4	18 21.0	12 44.7	4 19.0	7 18.0	6 52.9	0 45.8	25 50.8
26 Th	12 12 6	4 55 3	9♏ 3 36	15 35 24	10 50.2	11 41.9	7 20.7	19 35.3	13 26.9	4 13.3	7 24.9	6 50.3	0 45.1	25 49.2
27 F	12 16 3	5 54 26	22 10 36	28 49 13	10 47.0	11 38.3	9 22.5	20 49.6	14 9.1	4 7.4	7 31.8	6 47.7	0 44.4	25 47.6
28 Sa	12 19 59	6 53 48	5♐ 31 15	12♐ 16 40	10 43.9	11 35.1	11 24.9	22 3.9	14 51.2	4 1.4	7 38.8	6 45.1	0 43.6	25 46.0

The ephemeris gives the longitudes of the Sun, Moon and planets at 0h 0m 0s at the beginning of each day of the month.

16	ET Travel (7, 15, Table V)		minutes	16a	0′ 57″
			hours	16b	32′ 11″

Table V, Diurnal Motion of the Sun, has two parts. The upper part gives the Sun's motion for time changes of one to 60 minutes. The bottom part gives the same thing for one to twenty-four hours. The numbers at the head of each column across the top of the page show the twenty-four-hour motion of the Sun at intervals of two seconds of arc. In this section, we go down the column for 59′ 24″ that value being nearest to our actual twenty-four-hour travel of 59′ 25′. Then reading across the line for 23 minutes, which is closest to 22m 41s, we find 0′57″ and enter it on line **16a**. Continuing down the 59′24″ column into the hours section, we find the line for 13h and on it 32′11′. We enter that on line **16b**.

Table V Diurnal Motion of the Sun

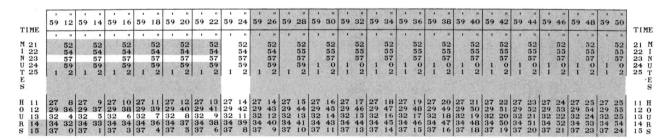

Table V, Diurnal Motion of the Sun, gives the motion of the Sun between 0h 0m 0s and birthtime.

Table V simply solves the following proportion for you.

$$\frac{\text{ET travel}}{24\text{h travel}} = \frac{\text{ET}}{24\text{h}}$$

In our example,

$$\frac{\text{ET travel}}{59'25''} = \frac{13\text{h } 22\text{m } 41\text{s}}{24\text{h}}$$

Direct Calculation

Some may prefer to do planetary positions on a calculator or by hand. First translate sexagesimal numbers into decimal numbers by dividing the appropriate parts by 60. $\simeq$ means "is approximately equal to."

$$25 \div 60 \simeq .42$$
$$59'25'' \simeq 59.42'$$
$$41 \div 60 \simeq .7$$
$$22m\ 41s \simeq 22.7m$$
$$22.7 \div 60 \simeq .38$$
$$13h\ 22.7m \simeq 13.38h$$

$$ET\ travel\ = \frac{13.38}{24} \times 59.42'$$
$$= .5575 \times 59.42'$$
$$\simeq 33.13'$$

$$.13 \times 60 \simeq 8$$
$$33.13' \simeq 33'8''$$

You will recall that using Table V we got $0'57''$ and $32'11''$. Together they add up to $33'8''$ or exactly the same result.

Logarithms

The traditional method of interpolating planetary positions is by means of logarithms or "logs." What logs do is convert all multiplications to additions and all divisions to subtractions.

To calculate the longitude of the Sun or of the other planets by means of logs, we must find the log of the time ratio, which is constant for all planets in a chart except the Moon, and add it to the log of the twenty-four-hour travel of the planet. We get the log of the time ratio from Table IX, Diurnal Motion Logarithms, 0 to 24 Hours. In our example ET is 13h 22m 41s. We read across to the column for 13h and down to the line for 23m, the closest value to 22m 41s. The number we find there is the log of 13h 23m ÷ 24h, .25365. We get the log of the twenty-four-hour travel of the Sun, 0°59'5'' in our example from Table X. Diurnal Motion Logarithms, 0 to 2 Hours/Degrees, by reading across the top to the column for 0°59' and down to the line for 25''. Where they meet we find 1.38445. Adding the two logs we get

$$log\ 13h\ 23m \div 24h = .25365$$
$$\underline{log\ 0°\ 59'25'' = 1.38445\ +}$$
$$1.63810$$

Working Table X backwards we find that 1.63810 is the log of 0° 33'8''. This is the same as the result we got using the two previous methods.

	14	3°T55'	38"	
	15	° 59'	25"	
minutes	16a	° 0'	57"	
hours	16b	° 32'	11"	
17 ☉ Longitude at Birthtime (add 14 + 16a + 16b = 17)	17	4°T28'	46"	☉

Whatever method you use to calculate the Sun's ET travel, you must add it to the Sun's 0h position before birth to get the Sun's birthtime position.

If ET (7) is less than 12h:				*If ET (7) is greater than 12h:*			
18 ☽ 12h **date of birth** (5 date) 18	°	'	"	18 ☽ **next day** (5 date + 1d)	18	9°♏ 3'	36"
19 ☽ **date of birth** (5 date) 19	°	'	"	19 ☽ 12h **date of birth** (5 date)	19	2°♏35'	13"
20 12h **Travel** (18 − 19 = 20) 20	°	'	"	20 12h **Travel** (18 − 19 = 20)	20	6° 28'	23"
21 **ET** (7) 21	h	m	s	21 **ET Since Noon** (7 − 12h = 21)	21	1h 22m	41s
22 ☽ **Travel to Birthtime** (20, 21, Table VI)				minutes 22a	°	12'	24"
				hours 22b	°	32'	20"

Because the apparent motion of the Moon is faster and more erratic than that of any other planets, the ephemeris gives the Moon's position at twelve-hour instead of twenty-four-hour intervals. To find the Moon's position at birth, we must interpolate between midnight and noon if the birth took place in the morning (Universal Time) or between noon and midnight for an afternoon birth. Otherwise, the process is exactly the same as the one we followed in determining the Sun's position.

The ☽ column of the ephemeris gives the 0h position of the Moon at the beginning of each day. The ☽ 12h column gives the Moon's noon position for that day. For a morning birth, ET less than 12h, use the left side of the worksheet. Go into Table VI with ET and the twelve-hour travel of the Moon between 0h and noon of the date of birth.

For an afternoon birth, ET greater than 12h, use the right side of the worksheet. Go into Table VI with the time elapsed betweed noon and ET (ET − 12h) and the twelve-hour travel of the Moon between noon and 0h of the following day.

In our example, ET is 13h 22m 41s, which is greater than 12h, so we use the right side of the worksheet.

Table VI Semidiurnal Motion of the Moon

TIME	6° 25'	6° 26'	6° 27'	6° 28'	6° 29'	6° 30'	6° 31'	6° 32'	6° 33'	6° 34'	6° 35'	6° 36'	6° 37'	6° 38'	6° 39'	TIME
	° ' "	° ' "	° ' "	° ' "	° ' "	° ' "	° ' "	° ' "	° ' "	° ' "	° ' "	° ' "	° ' "	° ' "	° ' "	
M 21	11 14	11 15	11 17	11 19	11 21	11 22	11 24	11 26	11 28	11 29	11 31	11 33	11 35	11 36	11 38	21 M
I 22	11 46	11 48	11 49	11 51	11 53	11 55	11 57	11 59	12 0	12 2	12 4	12 6	12 8	12 10	12 11	22 I
N 23	12 18	12 20	12 22	12 24	12 26	12 27	12 29	12 31	12 33	12 35	12 37	12 39	12 41	12 43	12 45	23 N
U 24	12 50	12 52	12 54	12 56	12 58	13 0	13 2	13 4	13 6	13 8	13 10	13 12	13 14	13 16	13 18	24 U
T 25	13 22	13 24	13 26	13 28	13 30	13 32	13 35	13 37	13 39	13 41	13 43	13 45	13 47	13 49	13 51	25 T
E S																E S
H 1	32 5	32 10	32 15	32 20	32 25	32 30	32 35	32 40	32 45	32 50	32 55	33 0	33 5	33 10	33 15	1 H
O 2	1 4 10	1 4 20	1 4 30	1 4 40	1 4 50	1 5 0	1 5 10	1 5 20	1 5 30	1 5 40	1 5 50	1 6 0	1 6 10	1 6 20	1 6 30	2 O
U 3	1 36 15	1 36 30	1 36 45	1 37 0	1 37 15	1 37 30	1 37 45	1 38 0	1 38 15	1 38 30	1 38 45	1 39 0	1 39 15	1 39 30	1 39 45	3 U
R 4	2 8 20	2 8 40	2 9 0	2 9 20	2 9 40	2 10 0	2 10 20	2 10 40	2 11 0	2 11 20	2 11 40	2 12 0	2 12 20	2 12 40	2 13 0	4 R
S 5	2 40 25	2 40 50	2 41 15	2 41 40	2 42 5	2 42 30	2 42 55	2 43 20	2 43 45	2 44 10	2 44 35	2 45 0	2 45 25	2 45 50	2 46 15	5 S

Table VI, Semidiurnal Motion of the Moon, gives the motion of the Moon from noon or midnight, whichever is most recent, to birthtime.

The Moon's travel to birthtime can be gotten from Table VI, Semidiurnal Motion of the Moon, or it can be calculated directly or by using logs. If you want to use logs, you must use a special log table based on twelve-hour instead of twenty-four-hour motion. No such log table is included in this book.

19	2°	35'	13"
20	6°	28'	23"
21	1h	22m	41s
22a	°	12'	24"
22b	°	32'	20"
23 ☽ **Longitude at Birthtime** (add **19 + 22a + 22b = 23**)	**23**	3° ♏ 19' 57" ☽	

After getting the Moon's travel to birthtime, we add it to the Moon's position before birth to get the Moon's position at birthtime. The result is accurate to the nearest minute of arc, and the original birth data does not allow any greater accuracy. The calculated result in our example was 3° ♏ 19'57", which rounds off to 3° ♏ 20'.

24 Longitude 0h After Birth (5 date + 1d, Ephemeris)
25 Longitude 0h Before Birth (5 date, Ephemeris)
26 24h Travel (subtract 24 − 25 = 26; if retrograde, subtract 25 − 24 = 26)
27 ET Travel (7, 26, Table VII: minutes 27a, hours 27b, 27a + 27b = 27c)
28 Longitude At Birthtime (25 + 27c = 28; if retrograde, 25 − 27c = 28)

	Mean ☋	True ☋	☿	♀	♂	♃	♄	♅	♆	♇
24	10♓50'	11♓42'	7♈21'	19♈35'	13♉27'	4♏13'	7♉25'	6≏50'	0♐45'	25♍49'
25	10♓53'	11♓45'	5♈19'	18♉21'	12♉45'	4♏19'	7♉18'	6≏53'	0♐46'	25♍51'
26	R 3'	R 3'	2°2'	1°14'	42'	R 6'	7'	R 3'	R 1'	R 2'
27a	0'3"	0'3"	1'57"	1'11"	40"	6"	7"	3"	1"	2"
27b	1'38"	1'38"	1°6'5"	40'5"	22'45"	3'15"	3'46"	1'38"	33'	1'5"
27c	1'41"	1'41"	1°8'2"	41'16"	23'25"	R 3'21"	3'55"	R 1'41"	R 34"	R 1'7"
28	10♓51'	11♓43'	6♈27'	19♈2'	13♉8'	4♏16'	7♉22'	6≏51'	0♐45'	25♍50'
	Mean ☋	True ☋	☿	♀	♂	♃	♄	♅	♆	♇

The positions of the Moon's nodes and the planets are calculated using Table VII, Diurnal Motion of the Planets, and the same interpolation methods used to calculate the positions of the Sun and the Moon.

There is only one consideration that applies to the planets and nodes and not to the Sun and Moon. When a planet is retrograde, its longitude is greater before birth than after birth. Retrograde planets are marked in the ephemeris with an R next to the planet's position on the day it goes retrograde or next to its position on the first of the month if it is already retrograde then. Its position on the day it goes direct is marked D. The mean node is, of course, always retrograde.

Whether or not a planet is retrograde, subtract the lesser longitude from the greater to get the twenty-four-hour travel. But in the case of a retrograde planet, mark the twenty-four-hour travel and the ET travel (lines **26** and **27c** with an R to remind you to subtract it from 0h longitude later instead of adding it. In our example, this has been done in the columns for Jupiter, Uranus, Neptune and Pluto.

Second Difference Interpolation of the Moon's Position

There are times when it is desirable to obtain a more accurate position of the Moon than can be gotten with the interpolation techniques described so far. In calculating lunar returns, for example, the natal Moon must be calculated to at least $\pm$ 1' of accuracy and even more accurately if the chart has been rectified or if you are using the precise position of the Moon in directions. Most ephemerides give the position of the Moon only every twenty-four hours, which can result in an error of $\pm$ 5' of arc. This ephemeris gives the Moon's position every twelve hours, which allows an accuracy by simple interpolation techniques of about $\pm$ 2' of arc.

Simple interpolation techniques assume that the speed of motion of a planet is constant over the period of time between two successive positions. If a body does not move at a constant speed, simple interpolation produces an error. To deal with this problem, a technique of higher-order interpolation has been developed which takes into consideration the change in the rate of motion and allows us to correct for it.

We find the Moon's position, using simple interpolation techniques but calculating directly rather than using tables. Then we apply a correction to that position based on the rate of change of the Moon's motion. We derive that correction as follows.

1. Find the two consecutive Moon positions in the ephemeris that come at twelve-hour intervals before birth and the two consecutive positions after birth.
2. Find the three twelve-hour travels between each of the three pairs of successive Moon positions. These are called the first differences.
3. Find the difference between the first two twelve-hour travels and the difference between the second and third. These are called the second differences.
4. Add the two second differences and divide by two. The result is the mean second difference.

The following array should make this clearer. Let us start with the times for which Moon positions are given in the ephemeris immediately before and after birth, the times associated with lines **18** and **19** on the worksheet. Let us call them t_2 and t_3. If birthtime was before noon, t_2 and t_3 will be 0h and 12h on the date of birth; if birthtime was after noon, t_2 and t_3 will be 12h on the date of birth and 0h the following day. Let us use t_1 for the time twelve hours before t_2 and t_4 for the time twelve hours after t_3. We will use L_1, L_2, L_3 and L_4 for the Moon longitudes give in the ephemeris for t_1, t_2, t_3 and t_4 respectively.

Times	Moon positions	First differences	Second differences	Mean second difference
t_1	L_1			
		$L_2 - L_1 = d_1$		
t_2	L_2		$d_2 - d_1 = D_1$	
		$L_3 - L_2 = d_2$		$\dfrac{D_1 + D_2}{2}$ = Mean D
t_3	L_3		$d_3 - d_2 = D_2$	
		$L_4 - L_3 = d_3$		
t_4	L_4			

We go into Table VIII with two values: the time elapsed from the ephemeris time just before birth to birthtime (birthtime $- t_2$, the time on line **21**) and the mean second difference. From the table we get a correction which we will add to or subtract from the Moon position we got by ordinary methods (line **23**).

If the second differences and the mean second difference are positive, it means that the Moon was accelerating. It had been moving slower before birthtime than at birthtime; therefore its true position was behind the position indicated by ordinary methods, which assume constant speed. So we must subtract the correction that we get from the tables in order to get the true position. Conversely, if the second differences and the mean second difference are negative, we know that the Moon was decelerating. It had been moving faster before birthtime than at birthtime; therefore its true position was ahead of the position indicated by ordinary methods which assume constant speed. So we must add the correction from the tables to get the true position.

Let us now apply this technique to our sample horoscope.

$$t_1 = 3/25/70 \quad 0h$$
$$t_2 = 3/25/70 \quad 12h$$
$$t_3 = 3/26/70 \quad 0h$$
$$t_4 = 3/26/70 \quad 12h$$

$L_1 = 26° \simeq 10'12''$

$\qquad\qquad d_1 = 6° 25' 1''$

$L_2 = 2° \, ♏ \, 35'13''$

$\qquad\qquad\qquad\qquad D_1 = 3'22''$

$\qquad\qquad d_2 = 6° 28'23'' \qquad\qquad$ Mean D $= 3'23.5''$

$L_3 = 9° \, ♏ \, 3'36''$

$\qquad\qquad\qquad\qquad D_2 = 3'25''$

$\qquad\qquad d_3 = 6° 31'48''$

$L_4 = 15° \, ♏ \, 35'24''$

Simple interpolation calculated directly:

$$1h\ 22m\ 41s\ =\ 1h\ 22.7\ =\ 1.3783h$$
$$6°28'23''\ =\ 6°\ 28.3833'\ =\ 6.4731°$$

$$1.3783h\ \div\ 12h\ =\ .11486$$
$$.11486\ \times\ 6.4731°\ =\ .7436°$$
$$=\ 44.616'$$
$$=\ 44'37''$$

$$2°\ \text{♏}\ 35'13''\ +\ 44'37''\ =\ 3°\ \text{♏}\ 19'50''$$

You will recall that using Table VI we got 3° ♏ 19'57", which we rounded off to 3° ♏ 20'. We can assume that 3° ♏ 19'50" is slightly more accurate because it was calculated directly. We now enter Table VIII with a time of 1h 22m 41s and a mean second difference of 3'23.5". In the table, correction values are given to the nearest second for every minute of mean second difference and every hour of time.

Table XIII Second Difference Interpolation for the Moon

TIME INTVL	MEAN SECOND DIFFERENCE																				TIME INTVL
	1'		2'		3'		4'		5'		6'		7'		8'		9'		10'		
	'	"	'	"	'	"	'	"	'	"	'	"	'	"	'	"	'	"	'	"	
0–1	0	1	0	2	0	4	0	5	0	6	0	7	0	8	0	10	0	11	0	12	11–12
1–2	0	3	0	7	0	10	0	13	0	16	0	20	0	23	0	26	0	30	0	33	10–11
2–3	0	5	0	10	0	15	0	20	0	25	0	30	0	35	0	40	0	45	0	49	9–10
3–4	0	6	0	12	0	19	0	25	0	31	0	37	0	43	0	50	0	56	1	2	8–9
4–5	0	7	0	14	0	21	0	28	0	35	0	42	0	49	0	56	1	3	1	10	7–8
5–6	0	7	0	15	0	22	0	30	0	37	0	45	0	52	0	60	1	7	1	14	6–7

We read across the top of the twelve-hour section of the table to the column for a mean second difference of 3', which is closest to 3'23.5", and read down to the line for a time interval of between one and two hours, which includes 1h 22m 41s. Where the column and line meet we find 0'10", which is our correction. The Moon was accelerating, so we subtract 0'10" from the constant-speed position of 3" ♏ 19'50". The result is 3° ♏ 19'40".

The above method can also be used with an ephemeris that gives Moon positions only at twenty-four-hour intervals. Simply read "twenty-four hours" for "twelve-hours" in the above instructions and use the twenty-four-hour section of Table VIII. The results will be slightly less accurate than those obtained with the help of a twelve-hour Moon ephemeris but much more accurate than with constant-speed interpolation only.

LOCATING HOUSE CUSPS

The Table of Houses in this book gives a complete set of house cusps for every four minutes of Sidereal Time for latitudes from 0° to 60°. For those readers who have access to a trigonometric calculator, the methods for extracting house cusps by trigonometry are given at the end of this section. Trigonometry gives the most accurate results, but the tables supplied here to assist in your calculations will suffice for most purposes.

Since the Tables give house cusps only for every four minutes of Sidereal Time and for whole degrees of latitude, we must either be satisfied with approximate house cusps, say to the nearest degree at best, or we must interpolate. But before we get to that, let us learn more about the layout of the Table of Houses.

As you thumb through the table, you will note that the Sidereal Time is given at the top of the page, along with a zodiacal longitude. There is only one Midheaven for each Sidereal Time because the Midheaven is independent of the latitude of the place. But beneath the Midheaven and the ST are five columns of positions, headed as follows: 11, 12, ASC, 2, 3. These are the cusps of the eleventh, twelfth, first, second and third houses. The first house cusp is also called the Ascendant. These house cusps are not independent of latitude and therefore must be listed for every degree of latitude. That makes finding house cusps other than the tenth (Midheaven) a bit complicated, but it doesn't require any mathematics beyond the high-school level.

The techniques outlined here for interpolating precise cusps from a table apply to any kind of house tables, even though the numbers may vary. The house division system of Koch is by no means the only system. A variety of other house systems exist, among them Placidus, Regiomontanus, Equal, Meridian, Topocentric, Porphyry and Alcabitius. You can order a report called *House Systems Comparison* from Astro Computing Services. The report lists house cusps for any horoscope in nine systems and specifies the house placements of the planets in each of the nine systems. A brief discussion of Koch's astronomical basis is given later on in this section.

Our birth LST of 20h 51m 21s falls between 20h 48m 0s and 20h 52m 0s. At these two times, 9° ≈ 34′ and 10° ≈ 33′, respectively, are on the Midheaven. Our birthtime Midheaven will fall between these two values. We can roughly estimate the house cusps by observing that our birth LST is nearer to 20h 52m than to 20h 48m and that our latitude, 41° N 39′, is about two thirds of the way from 41° N to 42° N. Our estimates would be: Midheaven: 10° ≈, eleventh: 19° ♓ twelfth: 1° ♉, first: 5° ♊, second: 0° ♋, third: 21° ♋. Many astrologers never go beyond this point, and you can do a great deal with approximate house cusps. If you don't like to calculate, this is a good shortcut to take until you are ready to do more. On the other hand, all predictive techniques involving directions or progressions require greater accuracy than this. So we will now find out how to get that accuracy.

Koch Table of Houses
for Latitudes 0° to 60° North

The Table of Houses gives zodiacal longitude and house cusps for every four minutes of Sidereal Time. The Midheaven, which is the same at all latitudes, is given at the top. The other house cusps are given for latitudes 0° to 60°.

| 20h 48m 0s   312° 0' 0"   09 ♒ 34 | | | | | | 20h 52m 0s   313° 0' 0"   10 ♒ 33 | | | | |
11	12	ASC	2	3	LAT.	11	12	ASC	2	3
10✠30	13♈03	14♉28	13♊24	11♋02	0	11✠34	14♈07	15♉28	14♊20	11♋58
10 57	14 09	15 58	14 50	12 00	5	12 03	15 16	16 59	15 47	12 56
11 27	15 22	17 34	16 20	12 58	10	12 34	16 31	18 37	17 17	13 54
12 00	16 44	19 19	17 54	13 56	15	13 09	17 55	20 24	18 52	14 53
12 38	18 18	21 15	19 34	14 57	20	13 49	19 31	22 21	20 33	15 54
12 47	18 38	21 40	19 55	15 09	21	13 58	19 51	22 46	20 55	16 07
12 56	18 59	22 06	20 17	15 22	22	14 07	20 13	23 12	21 16	16 19
13 05	19 21	22 32	20 39	15 35	23	14 17	20 35	23 38	21 38	16 32
13 14	19 44	22 59	21 01	15 48	24	14 27	20 59	24 06	22 00	16 45
13 24	20 07	23 26	21 23	16 01	25	14 37	21 23	24 33	22 23	16 58
13 34	20 31	23 55	21 46	16 14	26	14 48	21 48	25 02	22 46	17 11
13 45	20 57	24 24	22 10	16 27	27	14 59	22 13	25 32	23 10	17 25
13 56	21 23	24 54	22 34	16 41	28	15 11	22 40	26 02	23 34	17 38
14 08	21 50	25 25	22 59	16 54	29	15 23	23 08	26 33	23 59	17 52
14 20	22 19	25 57	23 24	17 08	30	15 36	23 38	27 06	24 24	18 06
14 33	22 49	26 31	23 50	17 23	31	15 49	24 08	27 39	24 50	18 20
14 47	23 20	27 05	24 16	17 37	32	16 04	24 40	28 14	25 16	18 35
15 01	23 53	27 41	24 43	17 52	33	16 19	25 14	28 50	25 43	18 49
15 16	24 28	28 17	25 11	18 07	34	16 34	25 49	29 27	26 11	19 04
15 32	25 04	28 56	25 39	18 22	35	16 51	26 26	00♊05	26 40	19 20
15 49	25 42	29 35	26 09	18 38	36	17 09	27 05	00 45	27 09	19 35
16 07	26 23	00♊17	26 39	18 54	37	17 28	27 46	01 27	27 39	19 51
16 27	27 05	01 00	27 10	19 10	38	17 48	28 29	02 10	28 10	20 08
16 47	27 50	01 45	27 42	19 27	39	18 10	29 15	02 55	28 43	20 25
17 10	28 38	02 32	28 15	19 44	40	18 33	00♋04	03 42	29 16	20 41
17 34	29 29	03 21	28 49	20 01	41	18 59	00 56	04 31	29 50	20 59
17 59	00♊24	04 12	29 25	20 19	42	19 26	01 51	05 22	00♋25	21 17
18 28	01 22	05 05	00♋01	20 38	43	19 55	02 50	06 16	01 01	21 35
18 58	02 24	06 02	00 39	20 57	44	20 27	03 53	07 12	01 49	21 54
19 32	03 31	07 01	01 19	21 16	45	21 02	05 00	08 11	02 18	22 14
20 09	04 43	08 03	01 59	21 37	46	21 41	06 13	09 13	02 59	22 34
20 49	06 00	09 08	02 42	21 57	47	22 24	07 31	10 18	03 41	22 54
21 35	07 24	10 17	03 26	22 19	48	23 11	08 56	11 26	04 25	23 16
22 26	08 55	11 29	04 12	22 41	49	24 04	10 27	12 38	05 10	23 38
23 23	10 34	12 46	04 59	23 04	50	25 03	12 07	13 54	05 58	24 01
24 28	12 22	14 07	05 49	23 28	51	26 11	13 55	15 15	06 47	24 24
25 42	14 20	15 33	06 42	23 52	52	27 28	15 53	16 40	07 39	24 49
27 08	16 29	17 03	07 36	24 18	53	28 58	18 01	18 10	08 33	25 14
28 48	18 50	18 40	08 33	24 45	54	00♈42	20 22	19 45	09 30	25 41
00♈46	21 26	20 22	09 33	25 13	55	02 44	22 57	21 26	10 29	26 09
03 08	24 17	22 11	10 36	25 42	56	05 11	25 47	23 13	11 31	26 37
06 01	27 26	24 06	11 43	26 12	57	08 08	28 53	25 07	12 37	27 07
09 34	00♊53	26 09	12 52	26 44	58	11 46	02♊17	27 08	13 46	27 39
14 01	04 40	28 19	14 06	27 18	59	16 19	06 00	29 16	14 58	28 12
19♈41	08♊49	00♋38	15♋23	27♋53	60	22♈03	10♊03	01♋32	16♋14	28♋47

Interpolation

Interpolation works because there is a constant proportional relationship between change of LST and change in the Midheaven and in the other house cusps. There is a similar relationship as well between change in latitude and change in house cusps.

29	**Local Sidereal Time** (12)	29	20h 51m 21s	
30	**Earlier LST** (Table of Houses)	30	20h 48m	
31	**Later LST** (Table of Houses)	31	20h 52m	
32	**LST Increment** (subtract 29 − 30 = 32)	32	3m 21s	△LST

We will call the times in the Table of Houses just before and just after birth "earlier LST" and "later LST" and enter them on lines **30** and **31** respectively. In order to interpolate, we need to know the LST increment or time change between earlier LST and birth LST. We get this by subtracting earlier LST from birth LST. The result goes on line **32**.

33 **Midheaven at Later LST** (Table of Houses)	33	10° ≈ 33'
34 **Midheaven at Earlier LST** (Table of Houses)	34	9° ≈ 34'
35 4m **Midheaven Interval** (subtract 33 − 34 = 35)	35	° 59'

Next we need to know how much the Midheaven changed in the four minutes between earlier LST and later LST. We find out by reading the Midheavens at the two times from the Table of Houses and subtracting.

36 **Midheaven Increment** (32, 35, Table XI)	36	° '

When we know how much time elapsed between earlier LST and birth LST (LST increment) and how much the Midheaven changed in the four minutes between earlier LST and later LST (Midheaven interval), we can deduce how much the Midheaven changed between earlier LST and birth LST (Midheaven increment), using Table XI. Read across the top to find the column closest to the LST increment, then read down to find the line for the Midheaven interval. Where they meet is the Midheaven increment. In our example, the 3m 20s column is closest to our LST increment of 3m 21s. The one-second difference is not significant. We read down to the 0° 59' line and find that our Midheaven increment is 49'.

Table XI House Cusp Interpolation Between Sidereal Times

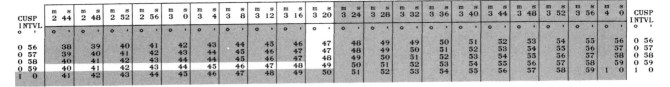

CUSP INTVL	m s 2 44	m s 2 48	m s 2 52	m s 2 56	m s 3 0	m s 3 4	m s 3 8	m s 3 12	m s 3 16	m s 3 20	m s 3 24	m s 3 28	m s 3 32	m s 3 36	m s 3 40	m s 3 44	m s 3 48	m s 3 52	m s 3 56	m s 4 0	CUSP INTVL
° '	° '	° '	° '	° '	° '	° '	° '	° '	° '	° '	° '	° '	° '	° '	° '	° '	° '	° '	° '	° '	° '
0 56	38	39	40	41	42	43	44	45	46	47	48	49	49	50	51	52	53	54	55	56	0 56
0 57	39	40	41	42	43	44	45	46	47	47	48	49	50	51	52	53	54	55	56	57	0 57
0 58	40	41	42	43	44	44	45	46	47	48	49	50	51	52	53	54	55	56	57	58	0 58
0 59	40	41	42	43	44	45	46	47	48	49	50	51	52	53	54	55	56	57	58	59	0 59
1 0	41	42	43	44	45	46	47	48	49	50	51	52	53	54	55	56	57	58	59	1 0	1 0

Table XI, House Cusp Interpolation Between Sidereal Times, gives the cusp increment, the amount by which the house cusp changed from earlier LST to birth LST.

What Table XI actually does is solve the following proportion for us.

$$\frac{\text{cusp increment}}{\text{cusp interval}} = \frac{\text{LST increment}}{\text{LST interval}}$$

In our example,

$$\frac{\text{cusp increment}}{59'} = \frac{3m\ 21s}{4m}$$

$$\text{cusp increment} = \frac{3m\ 21s}{4m} \times 59'$$

$$= 49'$$

Direct Calculation

If you have a calculator, or even if you do not, you may prefer to do this calculation directly instead of using Table XI. In this case, first translate the LST increment into decimal minutes to make the arithmetic easier. Do this by dividing the seconds portion by 60 and adding it to the whole minutes. For example.

$$21 \div 60 = .35$$
$$3m\ 21s = 3.35m$$

Then solve the proportion as above.

$$
\begin{aligned}
\text{cusp increment} &= (3.35 \div 4) \times 59' \\
&= 0.8375 \times 59' \\
&= 49.4125' \\
&\simeq 49' \text{ (rounded off)}
\end{aligned}
$$

Although cusp intervals are different for different houses, the LST increment and LST interval are the same for all houses in the chart. Therefore the time ratio, 0.8375 in our example, will be the same for all houses. Note it down for later use. If you have a calculator that stores a constant multiplier, this is an opportunity to use it.

Logarithms

House cusps can be interpolated using logarithms as well. You will recall that logs convert all multiplications into additions and all divisions into subtractions. In our example,

$$\frac{3m\ 21s}{4m} \times 59'$$

becomes

$$\log 3m\ 21s - \log 4m + \log 59'$$

In Table IX the numbers across the top are units that can be read either as hours, as degrees or even as minutes. The vertical column at the left refers to minutes if you are looking up degrees and minutes or hours and minutes, or it refers to seconds if you are looking up minutes and seconds. In other words, the column at the left gives sixtieths of the numbers along the top.

From Table IX, we get the following values. Log 3m 21s = .85517; log 4m = .77815. From Table X we get log 59' = 1.38751.

We calculate as follows.

$$
\begin{aligned}
&.85517 \\
&-.77815 \\
\hline
&= .07702 \\
&+1.38751 \\
\hline
&= 1.46453
\end{aligned}
$$

Working Table X backwards, we find that 1.46453 is the log of 49'25" + . This rounds off to 49', almost the same result we got by other methods.

		34	9° ♒ 34'
		35	° 59'
		36	° 49'
37 Midheaven at Birth LST (add 34 + 36 = 37)		37	10° ♒ 23'	MC

No matter which method we use to get the Midheaven increment, we must add the increment to the Midheaven at earlier time to get the Midheaven at birthtime. When we know the Midheaven, we also know the cusp of the fourth house, which is opposite, that is, exactly six signs away.

The IC [Imum Coeli], the cusp of the fourth house, is always exactly six signs away from the MC [Medium Coeli] or Midheaven, the cusp of the tenth house.

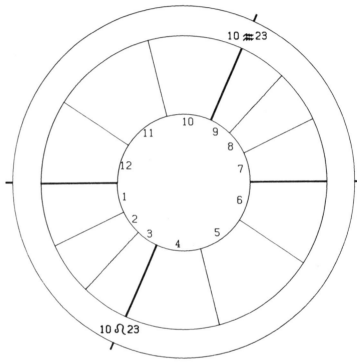

38 Lower Latitude (Table of Houses)		38	41°N '
39 Higher Latitude (Table of Houses)		39	42°N '
40 Latitude Increment (subtract **Birth Latitude** − 38 = 40)		40	° 39'	△Lat

The Midheaven at a given LST is the same at all latitudes, but the cusps of the other houses vary with latitude. The Table of Houses in this book gives the cusps of the eleventh, twelfth, first (Ascendant), second and third houses for 0°, 5°, 10°, 15° and every whole degree of latitude from 20° to 60°.

To find the house cusps at birth LST at birth latitude, our strategy will be to find the house cusps at birth LST at the two latitudes in the Table that are nearest the birth latitude, using exactly the same methods we used to find the Midheaven, and then to interpolate between latitudes. On lines **38, 39** and **40**, we locate those two latitudes and find the increment from the lower latitude to birth latitude, which we will need later in order to interpolate. It is a good idea at this point to fill in the **LST** and **Latitude** columns of lines **41** to **53** completely. All the values are now known, and they serve to label the lines and thereby avoid confusion.

41 House Cusps at Later LST, Lower Latitude (Table of Houses)
42 House Cusps at Earlier LST, Lower Latitude (Table of Houses)
43 4m Cusp Intervals (subtract 41 − 42 = 43)
44 Cusp Increments (32, 43, Table XI)
45 House Cusps at Birth LST, Lower Latitude (add 42 + 44 = 45)

	LST	Latitude	11	12	ASC	2	3
41	LATER 20:52	LOWER (38)	18♓59'	0♉56'	4♊31'	29♊50'	20♋59'
42	EARLIER 20:48		17♓34'	29♈29'	3♊21'	28♊49'	20♋01'
43	4m	41°N	1°25'	1°27'	1°10'	1°1'	0°58'
44	LINE 32 3:21		1°11'	1°13'	0°58'	0°51'	0°48'
45	BIRTH 20:51:21		18♓45'	0♉42'	4♊19'	29♊40'	20♋49'

Lines **41** to **45** of the worksheet are devoted to finding the house cusps at birth LST at the lower latitude. The method is exactly the same as that used in finding the Midheaven on lines **30** to **37**. Specific instructions for each line are given on the worksheet.

Koch Table of Houses for Latitudes 0° to 60° North

20h 48m 0s		312° 0' 0"			20h 52m 0s		313° 0' 0"			
		09 ♒ 34					10 ♒ 33			
11	12	ASC	2	3	11	12	ASC	2	3	LAT.
10♓30	13♈03	14♉28	13♊24	11♋02	11♓34	14♈07	15♉28	14♊20	11♋58	0
10 57	14 09	15 58	14 50	12 00	12 03	15 16	16 59	15 47	12 56	5
11 27	15 22	17 34	16 20	12 58	12 34	16 31	18 37	17 17	13 54	10
12 00	16 44	19 19	17 54	13 56	13 09	17 35	20 24	18 52	14 53	15
12 38	18 18	21 15	19 34	14 57	13 49	19 31	22 21	20 33	15 54	20
17 34	29 29	03 21	28 49	20 01	18 59	00♋56	04 31	29 50	20 59	41
17 59	00♉24	04 12	29 25	20 19	19 26	01 51	05 22	00♋25	21 17	42
18 28	01 22	05 05	00♋01	20 38	19 55	02 50	06 16	01 01	21 35	43
18 58	02 24	06 02	00 39	20 57	20 27	03 53	07 12	01 39	21 54	44
19 32	03 31	07 01	01 19	21 16	21 02	05 00	08 11	02 18	22 14	45

The Table of Houses gives house cusps for 0°, 5°, 10°, 15° and every whole degree of latitude from 20° to 60°.

This part of the process of casting a chart is by far the most subject to error, not because any link in the chain of calculation is especially difficult but because the chain is so long. It is important to check your work continually so that if you make an error you will catch it and correct it before it spoils further work.

For example, line **41** should be greater than line **42**. Subtracting, you should get a difference of less than two degrees in most cases, less than four degrees in extreme cases. If you do not, check to see that you have copied from the right place in the Table of Houses and have done the sexagesimal subtraction correctly.

Line **44** should be smaller than line **43** and in the same proportion to it as the LST increment is to the interval 4m. That is, in our example, 3m 21s is about three quarters of 4m. Therefore, each increment on line **44** should be about three quarters of the interval on line **43**.

Check to be sure that the cusp on line **45** for each house is between the cusps on lines **41** and **42** (greater than line **42** and less than line **41**.)

46 **House Cusps at Later LST, Higher Latitude** (Table of Houses)
47 **House Cusps at Earlier LST, Higher Latitude** (Table of Houses)
48 **4m Cusp Intervals** (subtract 46 − 47 = 48)
49 **Cusp Increments** (32, 48, Table XI)
50 **House Cusps at Birth LST, Higher Latitude** (add 47 + 49 = 50)

	LST	Latitude	11	12	ASC	2	3
46	LATER 20:52	HIGHER (38)	19°♓26'	1°♉51'	5°♊22'	0°♋25'	21°♋17'
47	EARLIER 20:48		17°♓59'	0°♉24'	4°♊12'	29°♊25'	20°♋19'
48	4m	42°N	1°27'	1°27'	1°10'	1°0'	0°58'
49	LINE 32 3:21		1°13'	1°13'	0°58'	0°50'	0°48'
50	BIRTH 20:51:21		19°♓12	1°♉37'	5°♊10'	0°♋15'	21°♋07'

Lines **46** to **50** of the worksheet are devoted to finding the house cusps at birthtime at the higher latitude. The method is exactly the same as that used for the lower latitude on lines **41** to **45**. Check your work in the same ways. Also, compare line **48** to line **43** and line **49** to line **44**. If for a given house they differ by more than a few minutes, something is wrong.

51 **1° Cusp Intervals**
If 50 is greater than 45, rewrite 45 below. Subtract 50 − 45 = 51.
If 50 is less than 45 mark 51 and 52 negative (−) for that house. Subtract 45 − 50 = 51.
52 **Cusp Increments for Latitude** (40, 51, Table XII)
53 **House Cusps at Birth LST, Birth Latitude** (add 45 + 52 = 53)

	LST	Latitude	11	12	ASC	2	3
45	BIRTH (29)	LOWER 41°N	18°♓45'	0°♉42'	4°♊19'	29°♊40'	20°♋49'
51		1°	0°27'	0°55'	0°51'	0°35'	0°18'
52	20h 51m 21s	LINE 40 0°39'	0°18'	0°36'	0°33'	0°23'	0°12'
53		BIRTH 41°N39'	19°♓03'	1°♉18'	4°♊52'	0°♋03'	21°♋01'

When we have the birthtime cusps at the two whole latitudes, we must interpolate between them to find birthtime cusps at birth latitude. We do this on lines **51**, **52** and **53**, using Table XII for the interpolation.*

Table XII House Cusp Interpolation between Latitudes

	HOUSE CUSP INTERVAL																														
LAT INCR	1	2	3	4	5	6	7	8	9	10	11	12	13	14	15	16	17	18	19	20	21	22	23	24	25	26	27	28	29	30	LAT INCR
36	1	1	2	2	3	4	4	5	5	6	7	7	8	8	9	10	10	11	11	12	13	13	14	14	15	16	16	17	17	18	36
37	1	1	2	2	3	4	4	5	5	6	7	7	8	9	9	10	10	11	12	12	13	13	14	15	15	16	16	17	18	18	37
38	1	1	2	3	3	4	4	5	6	6	7	8	8	9	9	10	11	11	12	13	13	14	15	15	16	16	17	18	18	19	38
39	1	1	2	3	3	4	5	5	6	6	7	8	8	9	10	10	11	11	12	12	13	14	14	15	16	16	17	18	19	19	39
40	1	1	2	3	3	4	5	5	6	7	7	8	9	9	10	11	11	12	13	13	14	15	15	16	17	17	18	19	19	20	40

Table XII, House Cusp Interpolation between Latitudes, gives the cusp increment for latitude, the amount by which the house cusp at the birth latitude differs from the cusp at the lower whole latitude.

* If birth latitude is less than 20°, the difference between the two whole latitudes will be 5° instead of 1° and the difference between the cusps of a house at those two latitudes will be a 5° cusp interval instead of a 1° cusp interval. Two extra steps are necessary (1) To get the 1° cusp interval for each house, divide the 5° cusp interval by five. Enter the quotient on line 51. (2) If the latitude increment on line 40 is greater than 1°, the largest argument in Table XII, go into Table XII with only the minutes part of the latitude increment. Add the cusp increment you get from Table XII to the product of the 1° cusp interval multiplied by the number of whole degrees in the latitude increment on line 40. The result of this calculation is the cusp increment for latitude and goes on line 52.

Sometimes house cusps *increase* as latitude increases. When they do, the cusp at the higher latitude (line **50**) is greater than the cusp at the lower latitude (line **45**). In that case, to get the cusp interval for latitude, (line **51**) you subtract line **45** from line **50**. To make this easier, we have provided a place on the worksheet to rewrite line **45** below line **50**. You should fill in a space on this line only if the cusp of that house is increasing, that is, if line **50** is greater than line **45** for that house. If it is, add the cusp increment from Table XII (line **52**) to the cusp at the lower latitude (line **45**) to get the final cusp (line **53**). This is the case with all the house cusps in our example.

Sometimes house cusps *decrease* as latitude increases, and the birthtime cusp at the higher latitude (line **50**) is less than the cusp at the lower latitude (line **45**). To get the cusp interval for latitude (line **52**), subtract line **50** from line **45**. Line **50** is already below line **45**, so there is no need to rewrite it. Mark the difference (line **51**) as negative with a minus sign too, to remind you to subtract it from line **45** later instead of adding it. (If you look in the Table of Houses at a LST of 12:32:00, you will note that all the house cusps are *decreasing* with latitude.)

Once you have found the eastern house cusps, the tenth through the third, it is simple to find the western cusps, the fourth through the ninth. Each of the western cusps is opposite, exactly six signs away from, one of the eastern cusps. The complete house cusps for our example are:

Midheaven	10°	♒	23′		fourth	10°	♌	23′
eleventh	19°	♓	3′		fifth	19°	♍	3′
twelfth	1°	♉	18′		sixth	1°	♏	18′
Ascendant	4°	♊	52′		seventh	4°	♐	52′
second	0°	♋	3′		eighth	0°	♑	3′
third	21°	♋	1′		ninth	21°	♑	1′

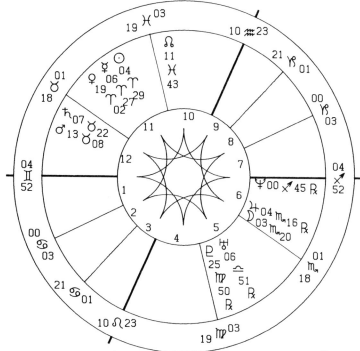

Our example chart completed.

South Latitudes

These Table of Houses are calculated for north latitudes only, but they can easily be used for casting charts of persons born in south latitudes. The technique is quite simple.

First find the LST that is twelve hours different from your LST of birth (line **12**). If LST of birth is less than 12h, add 12h; if it is greater than 12h, subtract 12h. Using the Table of Houses, calculate the Midheaven for that time. The Midheaven for that time is actually the IC (Imum Coeli), the cusp of the fourth house for your birth LST at south latitudes. Similarly, calculate the cusps of the eleventh through the third houses at birth LST ± 12h in the usual way. Actually you are calculating the cusps of the fifth through the nine houses for south latitude. In our example chart, if the native had been born at 41° S 39′ the cusps would have been:

fourth	10°	♌	23′	Midheaven	10°	♒	23′
fifth	7°	♍	57′	eleventh	7°	♓	57′
sixth	5°	♎	47′	twelfth	5°	♈	47′
seventh	3°	♏	31′	Ascendant	3°	♉	31′
eighth	1°	♐	8′	second	1°	♊	8′
ninth	1°	♑	1′	third	1°	♋	1′

Vertex and East Point

There are two other sensitive points that have become quite popular among astrological researchers, the Vertex and the East Point. The first of these, the Vertex, is the degree and minute of the ecliptic that is exactly due west of the observer at the time of the chart. Technically it is the intersection of the prime vertical and the ecliptic. The Vertex is considered a key to relationships with others, often denoting personal qualities we find mirrored by a partner. It is especially useful in synastry (comparing contacts between charts).* The method for determining this point from the Table of Houses is similar to the method of finding an Ascendant. Here is the procedure.

1. Add or subtract twelve hours to or from the LST of birth (line **12**) as with a south latitude birth. This is similar to the procedure for finding an Ascendant for south latitudes, but watch out for the difference.

2. Instead of using the latitude of birth, subtract the given latitude of birth from 90° to find the value known as the *colatitude*.

3. Now go into the Table of Houses and calculate an Ascendant for the colatitude using the new LST obtained in step 1. This "Ascendant" is actually the Vertex.

In our sample chart the colatitude is 48° 21′. If you perform the calculations correctly according to these rules, you should obtain a Vertex of 1° ♏ 16′.

The East Point, also called the Equatorial Ascendant, is the zodiacal longitude of the degree of the equator that is rising at birth. It is also what the Ascendant would have been if the native had been born at the equator, hence the name, Equatorial Ascendant. Since the Table of Houses in this book gives the Ascendants for 0° latitude, the East Point can be found without calculation.

---

* See also the booklet *The Eastpoint and the Anti-Vertex* available through ACS Publications, Inc.

The Koch House System

The Koch House System is one of several — including Placidus, derivatives of Placidus such as Dalton's, and Alcabitius — that use a trisection of a semi-arc as the basis for calculating the cusps. A semi-arc is a quadrant of a declination circle bounded by the horizon and the meridian as shown in figure 1.

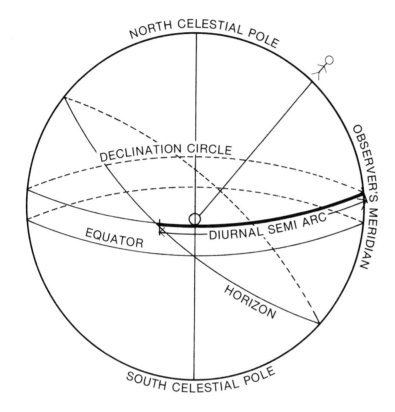

Figure 1

The Koch principles are:

1) Trisect the diurnal semi-arc of the MC. Call the result DSA/3.
2) Rotate the MC counter-clockwise to the horizon.
3) Then rotate the MC clockwise above the horizon by DSA/3 degrees. The Ascendant for this position is the 11th house cusp. Repeat this procedure by adding DSA/3 degrees to the MC to find, in turn, the 12th, 1st, 2nd and 3rd house cusps.

By following the above explanation, one can manually calculate the Koch cusps by using any table of houses that gives the MC and Ascendant positions.

1) Calculate the sidereal time for the given data.
2) Find the MC and Ascendant for the given latitude and calculated sidereal time.
3) Calculate the sidereal time as if the MC were the Ascendant.
4) Subtract the results of 3) from the results of 1) and divide by 3. Call this result DSA/3.

5a) Add DSA/3 to the result from 3).

  b) Calculate the Ascendant as if this were the sidereal time to get the 11th house cusp.

6a) Add DSA/3 to the result from 5a).

  b) Calculate the Ascendant as if this were the sidereal time to get the 12th house cusp.

7a) Add DSA/3 to the result from 6a).

  b) Calculate the Ascendant as if this were the sidereal time to get the Ascendant (which it is). This is obviously redundant but is inserted here to further clarify how the procedure works.

8a) Add DSA/3 to the result from 7a).

  b) Calculate the Ascendant as if this were the sidereal time to get the 2nd house cusp.

9a) Add DSA/3 to the result from 8a).

  b) Calculate the Ascendant as if this were the sidereal time to get the 3rd house cusp.

Direct Calculation of MC

Calculate the Midheaven (MC) as follows.

1) Find the right ascension of the Midheaven (RAMC) by converting ST of birth to angular measure (1h = 15°).

2) $MC = \arctan\left[\dfrac{\tan RAMC}{\cos OE}\right]$

The result may be 180° off. If so, subtract 180° to place the MC in the same quadrant as the RAMC.

Direct Calculation of the Ascendant

$$ASC = \arctan\left[\frac{\cos RAMC}{-(\sin OBLIQUITY \times \tan LATITUDE + \cos OBLIQUITY \times \sin RAMC)}\right]$$

The quadrant of the Ascendant and any other position determined by arctan is unambiguously determined as follows:

$$Longitude = \arctan(\;a\;/\;b\;)$$

Longitude	a	b
0- 90°	+	+
90-180°	+	−
180-270°	−	−
270-360°	−	+

Calculation of the Intermediate House Cusps

The calculator or computer calculation procedure is as follows:

1) Calculate the Ascensional Difference of the MC

     ADMC = arcsin(sin RAMC × tan OBLIQUITY × tan LATITUDE)

2) Calculate the Oblique Ascension of the MC

     OAMC = RAMC − ADMC

3) Calculate the diurnal semi-arc of the MC

     DSAMC = 90 + ADMC

4) Divide the DSAMC by 3

     ARC = DSAMC/3

5) Calculate the Oblique Ascension of the houses

$$OA(11) = OAMC + ARC$$
$$OA(12) = OAMC + ARC \times 2$$
$$OA(\ 1) = OAMC + ARC \times 3$$
$$OA(\ 2) = OAMC + ARC \times 4$$
$$OA(\ 3) = OAMC + ARC \times 5$$

6) Calculate the longitude from the OA

$$\text{Longitude} = \arctan\left[\frac{\sin OA}{\cos OA \cos OBLIQUITY - \tan LATITUDE \times \sin OBLIQUITY}\right]$$

Like the other semi-arc systems, the Ascendant is the 1st house cusp and the MC is the 10th house cusp. Like the other semi-arc systems, except for Alcabitius, the calculation procedure breaks down when the MC is circumpolar since the MC cannot then be rotated through its semi-arc to the horizon.

Since the house cusps are only clearly defined on the ecliptic, a planet off the ecliptic, i.e., with latitude greater than 0°, will not clearly fall in one house or another when it is close to a cusp. The greater the latitude, the more uncertain is the house position. In the current practice of astrology, when we construct a flat, two-dimensional chart we ignore the three-dimensional ramifications of house position determination.

If one draws curves from the north ecliptic pole to the south ecliptic pole through the points on the ecliptic determined by the Koch system, then the lunes defined in this way are implicitly the Koch house curves.

Supporters of the Koch system claim that the cusps are unusually sensitive to transits and directions particularly in mundane affairs. Indeed, the ''Winning'' system of Joyce Wehrman is based on transiting Koch house cusps aspecting natal planets and cusps. She claims that if one used Placidian cusps one would not enjoy as frequent trips to the cashier to cash in winning tickets as one does when using Koch cusps.

Walter Koch, who devised this system makes the misleading claim that his is the only method calculated for the ''exact birthplace''. Since most other systems whether using semi-arcs or not, are also latitude dependent, they are just as ''birthplace'' oriented as Koch's. From the interpretation point of view, the only basis for a claim of superiority of one house system over another would be convincing evidence that the house system explained more observable data than any other. No study has been published that supports any such claim for any house system.

Koch Table of Houses for Latitudes 0° to 60° North

0h 0m 0s — 0° 0' 0" — 00 ♈ 00

11	12	ASC	2	3
02♉11	02♊05	00♋00	27♋55	27♌49
03 21	03 55	02 00	29 41	28 55
04 37	05 50	04 01	01♌25	29 58
06 01	07 52	06 05	03 08	00♍59
07 35	10 05	08 14	04 52	01 58
07 55	10 32	08 41	05 13	02 10
08 16	11 01	09 08	05 35	02 22
08 38	11 30	09 35	05 56	02 34
09 00	11 59	10 03	06 17	02 46
09 23	12 30	10 31	06 39	02 58
09 47	13 00	10 59	07 00	03 10
10 12	13 32	11 28	07 22	03 22
10 37	14 04	11 57	07 44	03 34
11 04	14 37	12 26	08 07	03 47
11 31	15 11	12 56	08 29	03 59
12 00	15 46	13 27	08 52	04 11
12 29	16 22	13 58	09 14	04 23
13 00	16 59	14 29	09 38	04 36
13 32	17 36	15 01	10 01	04 48
14 06	18 15	15 34	10 25	05 01
14 41	18 55	16 07	10 49	05 14
15 18	19 36	16 41	11 13	05 27
15 57	20 19	17 16	11 38	05 40
16 38	21 02	17 52	12 03	05 53
17 21	21 48	18 28	12 28	06 06
18 06	22 35	19 05	12 54	06 20
18 54	23 23	19 43	13 20	06 33
19 44	24 13	20 21	13 46	06 47
20 38	25 05	21 01	14 14	07 01
21 35	25 59	21 42	14 41	07 15
22 35	26 55	22 24	15 09	07 29
23 39	27 53	23 06	15 38	07 44
24 48	28 53	23 50	16 07	07 59
26 02	29 56	24 36	16 37	08 14
27 21	01♋01	25 22	17 08	08 29
28 46	02 09	26 10	17 39	08 45
00♊18	03 20	26 59	18 11	09 01
01 56	04 34	27 50	18 44	09 17
03 43	05 52	28 42	19 17	09 34
05 39	07 12	29 36	19 52	09 51
07 45	08 37	00♌32	20 27	10 09
10 01	10 05	01 30	21 03	10 26
12 29	11 37	02 29	21 40	10 45
15 11	13 13	03 31	22 19	11 03
18♊06	14♋54	04♌34	22♌58	11♍23

0h 4m 0s — 1° 0' 0" — 01 ♈ 05

11	12	ASC	2	3	LAT.
03♉13	03♊03	00♋55	28♋52	28♌52	0
04 24	04 52	02 55	00♌38	29 57	5
05 40	06 47	04 56	02 22	01♍00	10
07 04	08 49	07 00	04 05	02 00	15
08 38	11 01	09 08	05 48	03 00	20
08 58	11 29	09 35	06 09	03 11	21
09 19	11 57	10 02	06 30	03 23	22
09 41	12 26	10 29	06 52	03 35	23
10 03	12 55	10 56	07 13	03 47	24
10 26	13 25	11 24	07 34	03 59	25
10 50	13 56	11 52	07 56	04 11	26
11 15	14 27	12 20	08 18	04 23	27
11 40	15 00	12 49	08 39	04 35	28
12 07	15 32	13 19	09 02	04 47	29
12 34	16 06	13 48	09 24	04 59	30
13 02	16 41	14 19	09 46	05 11	31
13 32	17 16	14 49	10 09	05 23	32
14 03	17 53	15 21	10 32	05 36	33
14 35	18 30	15 53	10 55	05 48	34
15 09	19 09	16 25	11 19	06 01	35
15 44	19 48	16 58	11 42	06 13	36
16 20	20 29	17 32	12 06	06 26	37
16 59	21 11	18 06	12 31	06 39	38
17 40	21 54	18 41	12 56	06 52	39
18 22	22 39	19 17	13 21	07 05	40
19 07	23 26	19 54	13 46	07 18	41
19 55	24 13	20 31	14 12	07 32	42
20 45	25 03	21 10	14 39	07 46	43
21 38	25 54	21 49	15 06	07 59	44
22 34	26 48	22 29	15 33	08 13	45
23 34	27 43	23 11	16 01	08 28	46
24 38	28 40	23 53	16 29	08 42	47
25 46	29 40	24 36	16 58	08 57	48
26 59	00♋42	25 21	17 28	09 12	49
28 17	01 46	26 07	17 58	09 27	50
29 41	02 53	26 54	18 29	09 43	51
01♊12	04 03	27 43	19 00	09 58	52
02 49	05 16	28 33	19 33	10 15	53
04 34	06 32	29 25	20 06	10 31	54
06 28	07 52	00♌18	20 40	10 48	55
08 32	09 15	01 13	21 15	11 05	56
10 46	10 42	02 10	21 50	11 23	57
13 12	12 12	03 08	22 27	11 41	58
15 50	13 47	04 09	23 05	11 59	59
18♊42	15♋26	05♌12	23♌44	12♍18	60

0h 8m 0s — 2° 0' 0" — 02 ♈ 11

11	12	ASC	2	3
04♉16	04♊00	01♋50	29♋49	29♌54
05 26	05 49	03 50	01♌35	00♍59
06 42	07 44	05 50	03 19	02 02
08 06	09 46	07 54	05 01	03 02
09 41	11 57	10 02	06 45	04 01
10 01	12 25	10 28	07 06	04 13
10 22	12 53	10 55	07 26	04 24
10 44	13 22	11 22	07 47	04 36
11 06	13 51	11 49	08 09	04 48
11 29	14 21	12 17	08 30	05 00
11 53	14 51	12 45	08 51	05 11
12 17	15 23	13 13	09 13	05 23
12 43	15 55	13 42	09 35	05 35
13 09	16 27	14 11	09 57	05 47
13 36	17 01	14 41	10 19	05 59
14 05	17 35	15 11	10 41	06 11
14 34	18 10	15 41	11 03	06 23
15 05	18 46	16 12	11 26	06 36
15 37	19 23	16 44	11 49	06 48
16 11	20 02	17 16	12 13	07 00
16 45	20 41	17 49	12 36	07 13
17 22	21 21	18 22	13 00	07 26
18 00	22 03	18 56	13 24	07 38
18 41	22 46	19 31	13 49	07 51
19 23	23 30	20 06	14 14	08 04
20 08	24 16	20 43	14 39	08 17
20 55	25 04	21 20	15 05	08 31
21 45	25 53	21 58	15 31	08 44
22 37	26 43	22 37	15 57	08 58
23 33	27 36	23 17	16 24	09 12
24 33	28 31	23 57	16 52	09 26
25 36	29 27	24 39	17 20	09 40
26 43	00♋26	25 22	17 49	09 55
27 55	01 27	26 06	18 18	10 10
29 13	02 31	26 52	18 48	10 25
00♊36	03 37	27 38	19 18	10 40
02 05	04 46	28 26	19 50	10 56
03 41	05 58	29 16	20 22	11 12
05 25	07 13	00♌07	20 54	11 28
07 17	08 31	00 59	21 28	11 45
09 19	09 53	01 54	22 02	12 02
11 30	11 18	02 50	22 38	12 19
13 54	12 47	03 47	23 14	12 37
16 29	14 20	04 47	23 51	12 55
19♊18	15♋58	05♌49	24♌30	13♍14

0h 12m 0s — 3° 0' 0" — 03 ♈ 16

11	12	ASC	2	3
05♉18	04♊57	02♋45	00♌47	00♍57
06 28	06 46	04 44	02 33	02 02
07 45	08 41	06 45	04 16	03 04
09 09	10 43	08 48	05 58	04 03
10 43	12 53	10 56	07 41	05 02
11 04	13 21	11 22	08 02	05 14
11 25	13 49	11 48	08 22	05 25
11 46	14 17	12 15	08 43	05 37
12 08	14 46	12 42	09 04	05 49
12 31	15 16	13 10	09 25	06 00
12 55	15 46	13 38	09 47	06 12
13 20	16 17	14 06	10 08	06 24
13 45	16 49	14 34	10 30	06 36
14 11	17 22	15 03	10 52	06 48
14 39	17 55	15 33	11 13	07 00
15 07	18 29	16 02	11 36	07 12
15 36	19 04	16 33	11 58	07 24
16 07	19 40	17 03	12 21	07 36
16 39	20 17	17 35	12 43	07 48
17 12	20 54	18 07	13 07	08 00
17 47	21 33	18 39	13 30	08 13
18 23	22 13	19 12	13 54	08 25
19 01	22 55	19 46	14 18	08 38
19 41	23 37	20 20	14 42	08 50
20 24	24 21	20 56	15 07	09 03
21 08	25 06	21 32	15 32	09 16
21 55	25 53	22 08	15 57	09 30
22 44	26 42	22 46	16 23	09 43
23 36	27 32	23 24	16 49	09 57
24 32	28 24	24 04	17 16	10 10
25 30	29 18	24 44	17 43	10 24
26 33	00♋14	25 25	18 11	10 38
27 40	01 12	26 08	18 40	10 53
28 51	02 12	26 52	19 08	11 07
00♊07	03 15	27 36	19 38	11 22
01 29	04 20	28 22	20 08	11 38
02 57	05 28	29 10	20 39	11 53
04 32	06 39	29 59	21 11	12 09
06 14	07 53	00♌49	21 43	12 25
08 05	09 10	01 41	22 16	12 41
10 04	10 30	02 34	22 50	12 58
12 14	11 54	03 29	23 25	13 15
14 35	13 22	04 26	24 01	13 33
17 08	14 54	05 25	24 38	13 51
19♊54	16♋29	06♌26	25♌15	14♍10

0h 16m 0s — 4° 0' 0" — 04 ♈ 22

11	12	ASC	2	3
06♉19	05♊54	03♋40	01♌45	02♍00
07 30	07 43	05 39	03 30	03 05
08 47	09 38	07 40	05 13	04 06
10 11	11 39	09 42	06 55	05 05
11 45	13 49	11 49	08 37	06 03
12 06	14 16	12 15	08 58	06 15
12 27	14 44	12 42	09 18	06 27
12 48	15 13	13 08	09 39	06 38
13 11	15 42	13 35	10 00	06 50
13 33	16 11	14 03	10 21	07 01
13 57	16 41	14 30	10 42	07 13
14 22	17 12	14 58	11 04	07 25
14 47	17 44	15 26	11 25	07 36
15 13	18 16	15 55	11 47	07 48
15 40	18 49	16 24	12 08	08 00
16 08	19 23	16 54	12 30	08 12
16 38	19 57	17 24	12 53	08 24
17 08	20 33	17 55	13 15	08 36
17 40	21 09	18 26	13 38	08 48
18 13	21 47	18 57	14 00	09 00
18 48	22 25	19 29	14 24	09 12
19 24	23 05	20 02	14 47	09 25
20 02	23 46	20 36	15 11	09 37
20 42	24 28	21 10	15 35	09 50
21 23	25 12	21 45	15 59	10 03
22 07	25 56	22 20	16 24	10 15
22 54	26 43	22 57	16 50	10 29
23 43	27 31	23 34	17 15	10 42
24 34	28 20	24 12	17 41	10 55
25 29	29 12	24 51	18 08	11 09
26 28	00♋05	25 31	18 35	11 23
27 30	01 00	26 11	19 02	11 37
28 36	01 57	26 53	19 30	11 51
29 46	02 57	27 37	19 59	12 05
01♊01	03 59	28 21	20 28	12 20
02 22	05 03	29 06	20 58	12 35
03 49	06 10	29 53	21 28	12 50
05 23	07 20	00♌41	22 00	13 06
07 03	08 32	01 31	22 32	13 22
08 52	09 48	02 22	23 04	13 38
10 50	11 07	03 15	23 38	13 55
12 57	12 30	04 09	24 12	14 12
15 16	13 56	05 05	24 48	14 29
17 46	15 27	06 03	25 24	14 47
20♊29	17♋01	07♌03	26♌01	15♍05

0h 20m 0s — 5° 0' 0" — 05 ♈ 27

11	12	ASC	2	3	LAT.
07♉21	06♊50	04♋35	02♌43	03♍03	0
08 32	08 40	06 34	04 28	04 07	5
09 49	10 34	08 34	06 10	05 08	10
11 13	12 35	10 36	07 52	06 07	15
12 47	14 44	12 43	09 33	07 05	20
13 08	15 12	13 09	09 54	07 16	21
13 29	15 39	13 35	10 15	07 28	22
13 50	16 08	14 02	10 35	07 39	23
14 12	16 36	14 28	10 56	07 51	24
14 35	17 06	14 55	11 17	08 02	25
14 59	17 36	15 23	11 38	08 14	26
15 23	18 06	15 51	11 59	08 25	27
15 48	18 38	16 19	12 20	08 37	28
16 14	19 10	16 47	12 42	08 49	29
16 41	19 42	17 16	13 03	09 00	30
17 10	20 16	17 45	13 25	09 12	31
17 39	20 50	18 15	13 47	09 24	32
18 09	21 26	18 46	14 09	09 36	33
18 41	22 02	19 16	14 32	09 48	34
19 14	22 39	19 48	14 54	10 00	35
19 48	23 17	20 20	15 17	10 12	36
20 24	23 56	20 52	15 41	10 24	37
21 02	24 37	21 25	16 04	10 37	38
21 41	25 19	21 59	16 28	10 49	39
22 23	26 02	22 33	16 52	11 02	40
23 06	26 46	23 09	17 17	11 15	41
23 52	27 32	23 45	17 42	11 27	42
24 41	28 19	24 21	18 07	11 41	43
25 32	29 08	24 59	18 33	11 54	44
26 27	29 59	25 38	18 59	12 07	45
27 24	00♋51	26 17	19 26	12 21	46
28 25	01 46	26 57	19 53	12 35	47
29 31	02 42	27 39	20 21	12 49	48
00♊40	03 41	28 21	20 49	13 03	49
01 55	04 42	29 05	21 18	13 18	50
03 15	05 46	29 50	21 48	13 33	51
04 40	06 52	00♌36	22 18	13 48	52
06 12	08 00	01 24	22 48	14 03	53
07 52	09 12	02 13	23 20	14 19	54
09 39	10 27	03 03	23 52	14 35	55
11 34	11 44	03 55	24 26	14 51	56
13 40	13 06	04 49	25 00	15 08	57
15 56	14 31	05 44	25 34	15 25	58
18 23	15 59	06 41	26 10	15 43	59
21♊03	17♋32	07♌40	26♌47	16♍01	60

0h 24m 0s — 6° 0' 0" — 06 ♈ 32

11	12	ASC	2	3
08♉23	07♊47	05♋30	03♌41	04♍07
09 34	09 36	07 29	05 26	05 10
10 51	11 30	09 29	07 08	06 11
12 15	13 31	11 31	08 49	07 09
13 49	15 40	13 36	10 30	08 06
14 09	16 07	14 02	10 50	08 18
14 30	16 34	14 28	11 11	08 29
14 52	17 02	14 55	11 31	08 40
15 14	17 31	15 21	11 52	08 52
15 37	18 00	15 48	12 12	09 03
16 00	18 30	16 15	12 33	09 15
16 24	19 00	16 43	12 54	09 26
16 49	19 31	17 11	13 15	09 38
17 15	20 03	17 39	13 37	09 49
17 42	20 36	18 08	13 58	10 01
18 10	21 09	18 37	14 20	10 12
18 39	21 43	19 06	14 42	10 24
19 10	22 18	19 36	15 04	10 36
19 41	22 54	20 07	15 26	10 48
20 14	23 31	20 38	15 48	11 00
20 48	24 09	21 10	16 11	11 12
21 24	24 47	21 42	16 34	11 24
22 01	25 28	22 15	16 58	11 36
22 40	26 09	22 48	17 21	11 48
23 21	26 51	23 22	17 45	12 01
24 05	27 35	23 57	18 10	12 14
24 50	28 21	24 33	18 34	12 26
25 38	29 07	25 09	18 59	12 39
26 29	29 56	25 46	19 25	12 52
27 23	00♋46	26 24	19 51	13 06
28 20	01 38	27 03	20 17	13 19
29 21	02 31	27 43	20 44	13 33
00♊25	03 27	28 24	21 12	13 47
01 34	04 25	29 06	21 40	14 01
02 48	05 25	29 49	22 08	14 15
04 06	06 28	00♌34	22 37	14 30
05 31	07 33	01 19	23 07	14 45
07 01	08 41	02 06	23 37	15 00
08 39	09 51	02 54	24 09	15 16
10 24	11 05	03 44	24 41	15 32
12 18	12 21	04 35	25 13	15 48
14 22	13 41	05 28	25 47	16 05
16 35	15 05	06 23	26 21	16 22
19 00	16 32	07 19	26 57	16 39
21♊37	18♋03	08♌17	27♌33	16♍57

0h 28m 0s — 7° 0' 0" — 07 ♈ 37

11	12	ASC	2	3
09♉24	08♊43	06♋26	04♌39	05♍10
10 35	10 33	08 24	06 24	06 13
11 52	12 26	10 23	08 06	07 13
13 16	14 26	12 25	09 46	08 11
14 50	16 35	14 30	11 26	09 08
15 10	17 02	14 55	11 47	09 19
15 31	17 29	15 21	12 07	09 30
15 53	17 57	15 47	12 27	09 42
16 15	18 25	16 14	12 48	09 53
16 37	18 54	16 41	13 08	10 04
17 01	19 24	17 08	13 29	10 16
17 25	19 54	17 35	13 50	10 27
17 50	20 25	18 03	14 11	10 38
18 16	20 56	18 31	14 32	10 50
18 43	21 29	18 59	14 53	11 01
19 11	22 02	19 28	15 14	11 13
19 40	22 35	19 57	15 36	11 24
20 10	23 10	20 27	15 58	11 36
20 41	23 46	20 58	16 20	11 48
21 13	24 22	21 28	16 42	11 59
21 47	25 00	22 00	17 05	12 11
22 23	25 38	22 31	17 28	12 23
23 00	26 18	23 04	17 51	12 36
23 39	26 59	23 37	18 14	12 48
24 20	27 41	24 11	18 38	13 00
25 03	28 24	24 45	19 02	13 13
25 48	29 09	25 21	19 27	13 25
26 36	29 55	25 56	19 51	13 38
27 26	00♋43	26 33	20 17	13 51
28 19	01 32	27 11	20 42	14 04
29 16	02 24	27 49	21 08	14 18
00♊15	03 17	28 29	21 35	14 31
01 19	04 12	29 09	22 02	14 45
02 27	05 09	29 51	22 30	14 59
03 40	06 08	00♌33	22 58	15 13
04 57	07 10	01 17	23 27	15 28
06 21	08 14	02 02	23 56	15 42
07 50	09 20	02 48	24 26	15 57
09 26	10 30	03 36	24 57	16 13
11 10	11 42	04 25	25 29	16 29
13 02	12 58	05 16	26 01	16 45
15 03	14 16	06 08	26 34	17 01
17 14	15 39	07 01	27 08	17 18
19 36	17 04	07 57	27 43	17 35
22♊10	18♋34	08♌54	28♌19	17♍53

Koch Table of Houses for Latitudes 0° to 60° North

0h 32m 0s — 8° 0' 0" — 08 ♈ 43

LAT.	11	12	ASC	2	3
0	10♉25	09♊40	07♋21	05♌38	06♍14
5	11 36	11 29	09 19	07 22	07 17
10	12 53	13 22	11 18	09 03	08 16
15	14 17	15 22	13 19	10 43	09 13
20	15 51	17 29	15 23	12 23	10 09
21	16 11	17 56	15 49	12 43	10 21
22	16 32	18 24	16 14	13 03	10 32
23	16 54	18 51	16 40	13 23	10 43
24	17 16	19 19	17 07	13 44	10 54
25	17 38	19 48	17 33	14 04	11 05
26	18 02	20 18	18 00	14 25	11 17
27	18 26	20 48	18 27	14 45	11 28
28	18 51	21 18	18 55	15 06	11 39
29	19 16	21 49	19 22	15 27	11 50
30	19 43	22 21	19 51	15 48	12 02
31	20 11	22 54	20 19	16 09	12 13
32	20 39	23 28	20 48	16 31	12 25
33	21 09	24 02	21 18	16 52	12 36
34	21 40	24 37	21 48	17 14	12 48
35	22 13	25 13	22 18	17 36	12 59
36	22 46	25 51	22 49	17 59	13 11
37	23 22	26 29	23 21	18 21	13 23
38	23 58	27 08	23 53	18 44	13 35
39	24 37	27 48	24 26	19 07	13 47
40	25 18	28 30	24 59	19 31	13 59
41	26 00	29 13	25 33	19 55	14 12
42	26 45	29 57	26 08	20 19	14 24
43	27 32	00♋43	26 44	20 44	14 37
44	28 22	01 30	27 20	21 08	14 50
45	29 15	02 19	27 57	21 34	15 03
46	00♊10	03 09	28 35	22 00	15 16
47	01 10	04 02	29 14	22 26	15 29
48	02 13	04 56	29 54	22 53	15 43
49	03 20	05 52	00♌35	23 20	15 57
50	04 31	06 51	01 17	23 48	16 11
51	05 48	07 51	02 01	24 16	16 25
52	07 10	08 55	02 45	24 46	16 40
53	08 38	10 00	03 31	25 15	16 55
54	10 12	11 09	04 18	25 46	17 10
55	11 54	12 20	05 06	26 17	17 25
56	13 45	13 34	05 56	26 49	17 41
57	15 44	14 52	06 47	27 21	17 57
58	17 52	16 12	07 40	27 55	18 14
59	20 12	17 37	08 35	28 29	18 31
60	22♊43	19♋05	09♌31	29♌05	18♍48

0h 36m 0s — 9° 0' 0" — 09 ♈ 48

LAT.	11	12	ASC	2	3
0	11♉26	10♊36	08♋16	06♌37	07♍18
5	12 37	12 25	10 14	08 20	08 20
10	13 54	14 18	12 12	10 01	09 19
15	15 18	16 17	14 13	11 40	10 16
20	16 52	18 24	16 16	13 19	11 11
21	17 12	18 51	16 42	13 39	11 22
22	17 33	19 18	17 07	13 59	11 33
23	17 54	19 45	17 33	14 19	11 44
24	18 16	20 13	17 59	14 40	11 55
25	18 38	20 42	18 26	15 00	12 06
26	19 02	21 11	18 52	15 20	12 18
27	19 26	21 41	19 19	15 41	12 29
28	19 51	22 11	19 46	16 01	12 40
29	20 16	22 42	20 14	16 22	12 51
30	20 43	23 14	20 42	16 43	13 02
31	21 10	23 46	21 10	17 04	13 13
32	21 39	24 20	21 39	17 25	13 25
33	22 08	24 54	22 09	17 47	13 36
34	22 39	25 29	22 38	18 08	13 48
35	23 11	26 04	23 08	18 30	13 59
36	23 45	26 41	23 39	18 52	14 11
37	24 20	27 19	24 10	19 15	14 23
38	24 56	27 58	24 42	19 38	14 35
39	25 35	28 38	25 15	20 00	14 46
40	26 15	29 19	25 48	20 24	14 59
41	26 57	00♋01	26 21	20 47	15 11
42	27 41	00 45	26 56	21 11	15 23
43	28 28	01 30	27 31	21 36	15 36
44	29 17	02 17	28 07	22 00	15 48
45	00♊09	03 05	28 44	22 25	16 01
46	01 05	03 55	29 21	22 51	16 14
47	02 03	04 46	00♌00	23 17	16 28
48	03 05	05 40	00 39	23 43	16 41
49	04 11	06 35	01 20	24 10	16 55
50	05 22	07 33	02 01	24 38	17 09
51	06 38	08 33	02 44	25 06	17 23
52	07 58	09 35	03 28	25 35	17 37
53	09 25	10 40	04 13	26 04	17 52
54	10 58	11 47	04 59	26 34	18 07
55	12 39	12 57	05 47	27 05	18 22
56	14 27	14 10	06 36	27 36	18 38
57	16 24	15 26	07 26	28 09	18 54
58	18 30	16 46	08 19	28 42	19 10
59	20 47	18 09	09 12	29 16	19 27
60	23♊16	19♋35	10♌08	29♌51	19♍44

0h 40m 0s — 10° 0' 0" — 10 ♈ 53

LAT.	11	12	ASC	2	3
0	12♉27	11♊32	09♋11	07♌35	08♍22
5	13 38	13 21	11 09	09 19	09 23
10	14 55	15 13	13 07	10 59	10 22
15	16 19	17 12	15 07	12 38	11 18
20	17 52	19 18	17 10	14 16	12 13
21	18 12	19 45	17 35	14 36	12 24
22	18 33	20 12	18 00	14 56	12 35
23	18 54	20 39	18 26	15 16	12 46
24	19 16	21 07	18 52	15 36	12 57
25	19 38	21 35	19 18	15 56	13 08
26	20 02	22 04	19 44	16 16	13 19
27	20 25	22 34	20 11	16 36	13 30
28	20 50	23 04	20 38	16 57	13 41
29	21 16	23 35	21 06	17 17	13 52
30	21 42	24 06	21 33	17 38	14 03
31	22 09	24 38	22 01	17 59	14 14
32	22 38	25 11	22 30	18 20	14 25
33	23 07	25 45	22 59	18 41	14 36
34	23 38	26 20	23 28	19 03	14 48
35	24 10	26 55	23 58	19 24	14 59
36	24 43	27 31	24 29	19 46	15 11
37	25 18	28 09	25 00	20 08	15 22
38	25 54	28 47	25 31	20 31	15 34
39	26 32	29 27	26 03	20 54	15 46
40	27 12	00♋07	26 36	21 17	15 58
41	27 53	00 49	27 09	21 40	16 10
42	28 37	01 32	27 43	22 04	16 22
43	29 24	02 17	28 18	22 28	16 34
44	00♊12	03 03	28 54	22 52	16 47
45	01 04	03 51	29 30	23 17	17 00
46	01 58	04 40	00♌07	23 42	17 13
47	02 56	05 31	00 45	24 08	17 26
48	03 57	06 24	01 24	24 34	17 39
49	05 03	07 18	02 04	25 01	17 52
50	06 12	08 15	02 45	25 28	18 06
51	07 27	09 14	03 27	25 56	18 20
52	08 46	10 15	04 10	26 24	18 34
53	10 12	11 19	04 55	26 53	18 49
54	11 43	12 25	05 40	27 23	19 04
55	13 22	13 34	06 27	27 53	19 19
56	15 09	14 46	07 16	28 24	19 34
57	17 03	16 01	08 06	28 56	19 50
58	19 08	17 19	08 57	29 29	20 06
59	21 22	18 41	09 50	00♍02	20 23
60	23♊48	20♋06	10♌45	00♍37	20♍40

0h 44m 0s — 11° 0' 0" — 11 ♈ 58

LAT.	11	12	ASC	2	3
0	13♉27	12♊28	10♋07	08♌34	09♍26
5	14 39	14 17	12 04	10 17	10 27
10	15 56	16 09	14 02	11 57	11 24
15	17 19	18 07	16 01	13 35	12 20
20	18 52	20 13	18 03	15 13	13 15
21	19 12	20 39	18 28	15 32	13 26
22	19 33	21 06	18 53	15 52	13 36
23	19 54	21 33	19 19	16 12	13 47
24	20 16	22 00	19 44	16 32	13 58
25	20 38	22 29	20 10	16 52	14 09
26	21 01	22 57	20 36	17 12	14 20
27	21 25	23 27	21 03	17 32	14 30
28	21 49	23 57	21 30	17 52	14 41
29	22 15	24 27	21 57	18 12	14 52
30	22 41	24 58	22 25	18 33	15 03
31	23 08	25 30	22 52	18 54	15 14
32	23 36	26 03	23 21	19 14	15 25
33	24 06	26 36	23 49	19 36	15 37
34	24 36	27 10	24 19	19 57	15 48
35	25 08	27 45	24 48	20 18	15 59
36	25 41	28 21	25 18	20 40	16 10
37	26 15	28 58	25 49	21 02	16 22
38	26 51	29 36	26 20	21 24	16 34
39	27 29	00♋15	26 52	21 47	16 45
40	28 08	00 56	27 24	22 09	16 57
41	28 49	01 37	27 57	22 33	17 09
42	29 33	02 20	28 31	22 56	17 21
43	00♊19	03 04	29 05	23 20	17 33
44	01 07	03 49	29 40	23 44	17 46
45	01 58	04 36	00♌16	24 08	17 58
46	02 52	05 25	00 53	24 33	18 11
47	03 49	06 15	01 30	24 59	18 24
48	04 49	07 07	02 09	25 25	18 37
49	05 54	08 01	02 48	25 51	18 50
50	07 02	08 57	03 29	26 18	19 04
51	08 16	09 55	04 10	26 45	19 18
52	09 34	10 55	04 53	27 13	19 32
53	10 58	11 58	05 37	27 42	19 46
54	12 28	13 03	06 22	28 11	20 01
55	14 05	14 11	07 08	28 41	20 16
56	15 50	15 22	07 56	29 12	20 31
57	17 43	16 35	08 45	29 43	20 47
58	19 45	17 52	09 35	00♍15	21 03
59	21 57	19 13	10 28	00 48	21 19
60	24♊20	20♋36	11♌22	01♍22	21♍36

0h 48m 0s — 12° 0' 0" — 13 ♈ 03

LAT.	11	12	ASC	2	3
0	14♉28	13♊24	11♋02	09♌34	10♍30
5	15 39	15 12	12 59	11 16	11 30
10	16 56	17 04	14 56	12 55	12 27
15	18 19	19 02	16 55	14 32	13 23
20	19 52	21 07	18 56	16 09	14 16
21	20 12	21 33	19 21	16 29	14 27
22	20 33	21 59	19 46	16 48	14 38
23	20 54	22 26	20 11	17 08	14 49
24	21 15	22 54	20 37	17 28	14 59
25	21 37	23 22	21 02	17 48	15 10
26	22 00	23 50	21 28	18 07	15 21
27	22 24	24 19	21 55	18 27	15 31
28	22 48	24 49	22 21	18 47	15 42
29	23 14	25 19	22 48	19 08	15 53
30	23 40	25 50	23 16	19 28	16 04
31	24 07	26 22	23 43	19 48	16 15
32	24 35	26 54	24 11	20 09	16 26
33	25 04	27 27	24 40	20 30	16 37
34	25 34	28 01	25 09	20 51	16 48
35	26 05	28 36	25 38	21 12	16 59
36	26 38	29 11	26 08	21 34	17 10
37	27 12	29 48	26 38	21 55	17 22
38	27 48	00♋25	27 09	22 17	17 33
39	28 25	01 04	27 40	22 40	17 45
40	29 04	01 44	28 12	23 02	17 56
41	29 45	02 25	28 45	23 25	18 08
42	00♊28	03 07	29 18	23 48	18 20
43	01 13	03 50	29 52	24 12	18 32
44	02 01	04 35	00♌27	24 36	18 44
45	02 51	05 21	01 02	25 00	18 57
46	03 44	06 09	01 39	25 25	19 09
47	04 41	06 59	02 16	25 50	19 22
48	05 40	07 50	02 54	26 15	19 35
49	06 44	08 43	03 33	26 41	19 48
50	07 52	09 38	04 12	27 08	20 02
51	09 04	10 36	04 53	27 35	20 15
52	10 21	11 35	05 35	28 02	20 29
53	11 44	12 37	06 19	28 31	20 43
54	13 12	13 41	07 03	29 00	20 58
55	14 48	14 48	07 49	29 29	21 13
56	16 31	15 57	08 36	29 59	21 28
57	18 21	17 10	09 24	00♍30	21 43
58	20 21	18 25	10 14	01 02	21 59
59	22 31	19 44	11 05	01 35	22 15
60	24♊51	21♋07	11♌58	02♍08	22♍32

0h 52m 0s — 13° 0' 0" — 14 ♈ 07

LAT.	11	12	ASC	2	3
0	15♉28	14♊20	11♋58	10♌33	11♍34
5	16 39	16 08	13 54	12 15	12 34
10	17 56	17 59	15 51	13 53	13 31
15	19 19	19 56	17 48	15 30	14 25
20	20 52	22 00	19 49	17 06	15 18
21	21 11	22 26	20 14	17 26	15 29
22	21 32	22 53	20 39	17 45	15 40
23	21 53	23 20	21 04	18 04	15 50
24	22 14	23 47	21 29	18 24	16 01
25	22 36	24 15	21 55	18 43	16 11
26	22 59	24 43	22 20	19 03	16 22
27	23 23	25 12	22 47	19 23	16 32
28	23 47	25 41	23 13	19 43	16 43
29	24 12	26 11	23 40	20 03	16 54
30	24 38	26 42	24 07	20 23	17 04
31	25 05	27 13	24 34	20 43	17 15
32	25 32	27 45	25 02	21 04	17 26
33	26 01	28 18	25 30	21 24	17 37
34	26 31	28 51	25 59	21 45	17 48
35	27 02	29 25	26 28	22 06	17 59
36	27 35	00♋01	26 57	22 28	18 10
37	28 09	00 37	27 27	22 49	18 21
38	28 44	01 14	27 58	23 11	18 33
39	29 21	01 52	28 29	23 33	18 44
40	29 59	02 31	29 00	23 55	18 55
41	00♊40	03 12	29 33	24 18	19 07
42	01 22	03 53	00♌05	24 41	19 19
43	02 07	04 36	00 39	25 04	19 31
44	02 54	05 21	01 13	25 27	19 43
45	03 44	06 06	01 48	25 51	19 55
46	04 36	06 54	02 24	26 16	20 08
47	05 32	07 42	03 01	26 41	20 20
48	06 31	08 33	03 38	27 06	20 33
49	07 34	09 25	04 17	27 31	20 46
50	08 40	10 20	04 56	27 58	20 59
51	09 51	11 16	05 36	28 24	21 13
52	11 07	12 15	06 18	28 52	21 26
53	12 29	13 15	07 00	29 20	21 40
54	13 56	14 18	07 44	29 48	21 55
55	15 30	15 24	08 29	00♍17	22 09
56	17 11	16 33	09 15	00 47	22 24
57	19 00	17 44	10 03	01 18	22 39
58	20 57	18 58	10 52	01 49	22 55
59	23 04	20 16	11 43	02 21	23 11
60	25♊22	21♋37	12♌35	02♍54	23♍27

0h 56m 0s — 14° 0' 0" — 15 ♈ 12

LAT.	11	12	ASC	2	3
0	16♉28	15♊16	12♋53	11♌32	12♍39
5	17 39	17 03	14 49	13 14	13 38
10	18 56	18 54	16 45	14 52	14 34
15	20 19	20 51	18 42	16 28	15 28
20	21 51	22 54	20 42	18 03	16 20
21	22 11	23 20	21 07	18 22	16 31
22	22 31	23 46	21 32	18 42	16 41
23	22 52	24 13	21 56	19 01	16 52
24	23 13	24 40	22 21	19 20	17 02
25	23 35	25 07	22 47	19 40	17 12
26	23 58	25 35	23 12	19 59	17 23
27	24 21	26 04	23 38	20 19	17 33
28	24 45	26 33	24 04	20 38	17 44
29	25 10	27 03	24 31	20 58	17 54
30	25 36	27 33	24 58	21 18	18 05
31	26 02	28 04	25 25	21 38	18 16
32	26 30	28 35	25 52	21 58	18 26
33	26 58	29 08	26 20	22 19	18 37
34	27 28	29 41	26 49	22 39	18 48
35	27 59	00♋15	27 17	23 00	18 59
36	28 31	00 50	27 46	23 21	19 10
37	29 05	01 26	28 16	23 43	19 21
38	29 40	02 02	28 46	24 04	19 32
39	00♊16	02 40	29 17	24 26	19 43
40	00 54	03 19	29 48	24 48	19 55
41	01 34	03 59	00♌20	25 10	20 06
42	02 16	04 40	00 53	25 33	20 18
43	03 01	05 22	01 26	25 56	20 30
44	03 47	06 06	02 00	26 19	20 41
45	04 36	06 51	02 34	26 43	20 54
46	05 28	07 38	03 10	27 07	21 06
47	06 23	08 26	03 46	27 31	21 18
48	07 21	09 16	04 23	27 56	21 31
49	08 23	10 07	05 01	28 22	21 44
50	09 29	11 01	05 39	28 48	21 57
51	10 39	11 56	06 19	29 14	22 10
52	11 53	12 54	07 00	29 41	22 24
53	13 13	13 54	07 42	00♍08	22 37
54	14 39	14 56	08 25	00 37	22 52
55	16 11	16 00	09 10	01 05	23 06
56	17 51	17 08	09 55	01 35	23 21
57	19 38	18 18	10 42	02 05	23 36
58	21 33	19 31	11 30	02 36	23 51
59	23 38	20 47	12 20	03 08	24 07
60	25♊53	22♋07	13♌12	03♍40	24♍23

1h 0m 0s — 15° 0' 0" — 16 ♈ 17

LAT.	11	12	ASC	2	3
0	17♉28	16♊11	13♋49	12♌32	13♍43
5	18 39	17 59	15 44	14 13	14 42
10	19 55	19 49	17 40	15 50	15 37
15	21 18	21 45	19 36	17 25	16 30
20	22 50	23 47	21 35	19 00	17 22
21	23 09	24 13	22 00	19 19	17 32
22	23 30	24 39	22 24	19 38	17 43
23	23 50	25 05	22 49	19 57	17 53
24	24 12	25 32	23 14	20 16	18 03
25	24 33	26 00	23 39	20 36	18 14
26	24 56	26 27	24 04	20 55	18 24
27	25 19	26 56	24 30	21 14	18 34
28	25 43	27 24	24 56	21 34	18 45
29	26 08	27 54	25 22	21 53	18 55
30	26 33	28 24	25 49	22 13	19 06
31	27 00	28 55	26 16	22 33	19 16
32	27 27	29 26	26 43	22 53	19 27
33	27 55	29 58	27 10	23 13	19 37
34	28 25	00♋31	27 38	23 34	19 48
35	28 55	01 05	28 07	23 54	19 59
36	29 27	01 39	28 36	24 15	20 10
37	00♊00	02 14	29 05	24 36	20 20
38	00 35	02 51	29 35	24 57	20 31
39	01 11	03 28	00♌05	25 19	20 43
40	01 49	04 06	00 36	25 41	20 54
41	02 29	04 46	01 08	26 03	21 05
42	03 10	05 26	01 40	26 25	21 17
43	03 54	06 08	02 13	26 48	21 28
44	04 40	06 51	02 46	27 11	21 40
45	05 28	07 36	03 20	27 34	21 52
46	06 19	08 22	03 55	27 58	22 04
47	07 13	09 09	04 31	28 22	22 16
48	08 11	09 58	05 07	28 47	22 29
49	09 12	10 49	05 45	29 12	22 41
50	10 16	11 42	06 23	29 37	22 54
51	11 25	12 36	07 02	00♍04	23 07
52	12 39	13 33	07 42	00 30	23 21
53	13 58	14 32	08 24	00 57	23 35
54	15 22	15 33	09 06	01 25	23 48
55	16 53	16 37	09 50	01 53	24 03
56	18 30	17 43	10 35	02 22	24 17
57	20 15	18 52	11 21	02 52	24 32
58	22 08	20 04	12 09	03 23	24 47
59	24 11	21 19	12 58	03 54	25 03
60	26♊23	22♋37	13♌49	04♍26	25♍19

Koch Table of Houses for Latitudes 0° to 60° North

1h 4m 0s — 16° 0' 0" — 17 ♈ 21

LAT.	11	12	ASC	2	3
0	18♉28	17♊07	14♋44	13♌32	14♍48
5	19 39	18 54	16 40	15 12	15 46
10	20 55	20 44	18 35	16 49	16 40
15	22 17	22 39	20 30	18 23	17 33
20	23 48	24 41	22 29	19 57	18 24
21	24 08	25 06	22 53	20 16	18 34
22	24 28	25 32	23 17	20 35	18 44
23	24 49	25 58	23 41	20 54	18 55
24	25 10	26 25	24 06	21 13	19 05
25	25 31	26 52	24 31	21 32	19 15
26	25 54	27 19	24 56	21 51	19 25
27	26 17	27 47	25 22	22 10	19 35
28	26 41	28 16	25 47	22 29	19 46
29	27 05	28 45	26 13	22 49	19 56
30	27 30	29 15	26 40	23 08	20 06
31	27 57	29 45	27 06	23 28	20 17
32	28 24	00♋16	27 33	23 48	20 27
33	28 52	00 48	28 00	24 08	20 37
34	29 21	01 20	28 28	24 28	20 48
35	29 51	01 54	28 56	24 48	20 59
36	00♊23	02 28	29 25	25 09	21 09
37	00 56	03 03	29 54	25 30	21 20
38	01 30	03 39	00♌23	25 51	21 31
39	02 06	04 15	00 53	26 12	21 42
40	02 43	04 53	01 24	26 34	21 53
41	03 22	05 32	01 55	26 55	22 04
42	04 03	06 12	02 27	27 17	22 15
43	04 46	06 53	02 59	27 40	22 27
44	05 32	07 36	03 32	28 03	22 39
45	06 20	08 20	04 06	28 26	22 50
46	07 10	09 05	04 40	28 49	23 02
47	08 03	09 52	05 15	29 13	23 14
48	09 00	10 40	05 51	29 37	23 27
49	10 00	11 30	06 28	00♍02	23 39
50	11 04	12 22	07 06	00 27	23 52
51	12 12	13 16	07 45	00 53	24 05
52	13 24	14 12	08 25	01 19	24 18
53	14 41	15 10	09 05	01 46	24 32
54	16 04	16 10	09 47	02 13	24 45
55	17 33	17 13	10 30	02 41	24 59
56	19 09	18 18	11 15	03 10	25 14
57	20 52	19 26	12 00	03 39	25 28
58	22 43	20 36	12 47	04 10	25 43
59	24 43	21 50	13 35	04 40	25 59
60	26♊53	23♋07	14♌25	05♍12	26♍15

1h 8m 0s — 17° 0' 0" — 18 ♈ 26

LAT.	11	12	ASC	2	3
0	19♉27	18♊02	15♋40	14♌32	15♍53
5	20 38	19 49	17 35	16 11	16 50
10	21 54	21 39	19 29	17 47	17 44
15	23 16	23 33	21 24	19 21	18 35
20	24 47	25 34	23 22	20 54	19 26
21	25 06	25 59	23 46	21 13	19 36
22	25 26	26 25	24 10	21 32	19 46
23	25 47	26 51	24 34	21 50	19 56
24	26 08	27 17	24 58	22 09	20 06
25	26 29	27 44	25 23	22 28	20 16
26	26 51	28 11	25 48	22 47	20 26
27	27 14	28 39	26 13	23 06	20 36
28	27 38	29 07	26 39	23 25	20 46
29	28 02	29 36	27 04	23 44	20 57
30	28 27	00♋06	27 30	24 03	21 07
31	28 53	00 36	27 57	24 23	21 17
32	29 20	01 06	28 23	24 43	21 27
33	29 48	01 38	28 50	25 02	21 38
34	00♊17	02 10	29 18	25 22	21 48
35	00 47	02 43	29 46	25 42	21 58
36	01 18	03 16	00♌14	26 03	22 09
37	01 51	03 51	00 43	26 23	22 20
38	02 24	04 26	01 12	26 44	22 30
39	03 00	05 03	01 41	27 05	22 41
40	03 37	05 40	02 12	27 26	22 52
41	04 16	06 19	02 42	27 48	23 03
42	04 56	06 58	03 14	28 10	23 14
43	05 39	07 39	03 46	28 32	23 26
44	06 23	08 21	04 18	28 54	23 37
45	07 11	09 04	04 52	29 17	23 49
46	08 00	09 49	05 26	29 40	24 00
47	08 53	10 35	06 00	00♍04	24 12
48	09 49	11 22	06 36	00 28	24 24
49	10 48	12 12	07 12	00 52	24 37
50	11 51	13 03	07 49	01 17	24 49
51	12 57	13 56	08 28	01 43	25 02
52	14 09	14 51	09 07	02 08	25 15
53	15 25	15 48	09 47	02 35	25 28
54	16 46	16 47	10 28	03 02	25 42
55	18 14	17 48	11 11	03 30	25 56
56	19 48	18 52	11 54	03 58	26 10
57	21 29	19 59	12 39	04 27	26 25
58	23 18	21 09	13 25	04 56	26 39
59	25 16	22 21	14 13	05 27	26 55
60	27♊23	23♋36	15♌02	05♍58	27♍10

1h 12m 0s — 18° 0' 0" — 19 ♈ 30

LAT.	11	12	ASC	2	3
0	20♉26	18♊58	16♋36	15♌32	16♍57
5	21 37	20 44	18 30	17 11	17 54
10	22 53	22 33	20 24	18 46	18 47
15	24 15	24 27	22 18	20 19	19 38
20	25 45	26 27	24 15	21 51	20 28
21	26 04	26 52	24 38	22 10	20 38
22	26 24	27 17	25 02	22 28	20 48
23	26 44	27 43	25 26	22 47	20 58
24	27 05	28 09	25 51	23 05	21 08
25	27 27	28 36	26 15	23 24	21 18
26	27 49	29 03	26 40	23 43	21 27
27	28 11	29 30	27 05	24 02	21 37
28	28 35	29 58	27 30	24 21	21 47
29	28 59	00♋27	27 55	24 40	21 57
30	29 24	00 56	28 21	24 59	22 07
31	29 50	01 26	28 47	25 18	22 17
32	00♊16	01 56	29 14	25 37	22 28
33	00 44	02 27	29 40	25 57	22 38
34	01 12	02 59	00♌08	26 17	22 48
35	01 42	03 32	00 35	26 36	22 58
36	02 13	04 05	01 03	26 57	23 09
37	02 45	04 39	01 31	27 17	23 19
38	03 19	05 14	02 00	27 37	23 30
39	03 54	05 50	02 30	27 58	23 40
40	04 30	06 27	02 59	28 19	23 51
41	05 08	07 05	03 30	28 40	24 02
42	05 48	07 44	04 01	29 02	24 13
43	06 31	08 24	04 32	29 24	24 24
44	07 15	09 05	05 04	29 46	24 35
45	08 01	09 48	05 37	00♍09	24 47
46	08 50	10 32	06 11	00 31	24 58
47	09 42	11 17	06 45	00 55	25 10
48	10 37	12 04	07 20	01 18	25 22
49	11 35	12 53	07 56	01 42	25 34
50	12 37	13 43	08 33	02 07	25 47
51	13 43	14 35	09 10	02 32	25 59
52	14 53	15 29	09 49	02 58	26 12
53	16 08	16 25	10 28	03 24	26 25
54	17 28	17 24	11 09	03 50	26 39
55	18 53	18 24	11 51	04 18	26 52
56	20 26	19 27	12 34	04 45	27 06
57	22 05	20 33	13 18	05 14	27 21
58	23 52	21 41	14 03	05 43	27 35
59	25 48	22 52	14 50	06 13	27 51
60	27♊53	24♋06	15♌39	06♍44	28♍06

1h 16m 0s — 19° 0' 0" — 20 ♈ 34

LAT.	11	12	ASC	2	3
0	21♉26	19♊53	17♋32	16♌33	18♍02
5	22 36	21 39	19 26	18 11	18 58
10	23 52	23 28	21 19	19 45	19 50
15	25 13	25 20	23 12	21 17	20 41
20	26 43	27 20	25 08	22 49	21 30
21	27 02	27 44	25 31	23 07	21 40
22	27 22	28 10	25 55	23 25	21 50
23	27 42	28 35	26 19	23 43	21 59
24	28 03	29 01	26 43	24 02	22 09
25	28 24	29 27	27 07	24 20	22 19
26	28 46	29 54	27 32	24 39	22 29
27	29 08	00♋22	27 56	24 57	22 38
28	29 31	00 49	28 21	25 16	22 48
29	29 55	01 18	28 46	25 35	22 58
30	00♊20	01 46	29 12	25 54	23 08
31	00 46	02 16	29 38	26 13	23 18
32	01 12	02 46	00♌04	26 32	23 28
33	01 39	03 17	00 30	26 51	23 38
34	02 08	03 48	00 57	27 11	23 48
35	02 37	04 20	01 24	27 31	23 58
36	03 08	04 53	01 52	27 50	24 08
37	03 39	05 27	02 20	28 10	24 19
38	04 12	06 01	02 49	28 31	24 29
39	04 47	06 37	03 17	28 51	24 39
40	05 23	07 13	03 47	29 12	24 50
41	06 01	07 51	04 17	29 33	25 01
42	06 40	08 29	04 47	29 54	25 12
43	07 22	09 09	05 19	00♍16	25 23
44	08 06	09 49	05 50	00 38	25 34
45	08 51	10 32	06 23	01 00	25 45
46	09 40	11 15	06 56	01 23	25 57
47	10 31	12 00	07 30	01 45	26 08
48	11 25	12 46	08 04	02 09	26 20
49	12 22	13 34	08 40	02 33	26 32
50	13 23	14 23	09 16	02 57	26 44
51	14 28	15 15	09 53	03 22	26 57
52	15 37	16 08	10 31	03 47	27 09
53	16 50	17 03	11 10	04 12	27 22
54	18 09	18 00	11 50	04 39	27 35
55	19 33	19 00	12 31	05 06	27 49
56	21 04	20 02	13 13	05 33	28 03
57	22 41	21 06	13 57	06 01	28 17
58	24 26	22 13	14 42	06 30	28 31
59	26 19	23 23	15 28	07 00	28 46
60	28♊22	24♋36	16♌15	07♍30	29♍02

1h 20m 0s — 20° 0' 0" — 21 ♈ 38

LAT.	11	12	ASC	2	3
0	22♉25	20♊49	18♋28	17♌33	19♍07
5	23 35	22 34	20 21	19 10	20 02
10	24 50	24 22	22 13	20 44	20 54
15	26 11	26 14	24 06	22 15	21 43
20	27 40	28 12	26 01	23 46	22 32
21	27 59	28 37	26 24	24 04	22 42
22	28 19	29 02	26 48	24 22	22 51
23	28 39	29 27	27 11	24 40	23 01
24	29 00	29 53	27 35	24 58	23 10
25	29 21	00♋19	27 59	25 17	23 20
26	29 42	00 46	28 23	25 35	23 30
27	00♊05	01 13	28 48	25 53	23 39
28	00 28	01 40	29 12	26 12	23 49
29	00 51	02 08	29 37	26 30	23 59
30	01 16	02 37	00♌03	26 49	24 08
31	01 41	03 06	00 28	27 08	24 18
32	02 07	03 35	00 54	27 27	24 28
33	02 34	04 06	01 20	27 46	24 38
34	03 02	04 37	01 47	28 05	24 48
35	03 32	05 09	02 14	28 25	24 58
36	04 02	05 41	02 41	28 44	25 08
37	04 33	06 14	03 09	29 04	25 18
38	05 06	06 49	03 37	29 24	25 28
39	05 40	07 24	04 05	29 44	25 39
40	06 16	07 59	04 34	00♍05	25 49
41	06 53	08 36	05 04	00 25	26 00
42	07 32	09 14	05 34	00 46	26 10
43	08 13	09 53	06 05	01 08	26 21
44	08 56	10 34	06 36	01 29	26 32
45	09 41	11 15	07 08	01 51	26 43
46	10 29	11 58	07 41	02 14	26 55
47	11 19	12 42	08 14	02 36	27 06
48	12 13	13 27	08 48	02 59	27 18
49	13 09	14 15	09 23	03 23	27 29
50	14 09	15 03	09 59	03 47	27 42
51	15 12	15 54	10 35	04 11	27 54
52	16 20	16 46	11 13	04 36	28 06
53	17 32	17 40	11 51	05 01	28 19
54	18 49	18 37	12 31	05 27	28 32
55	20 12	19 35	13 11	05 54	28 45
56	21 41	20 36	13 53	06 21	28 59
57	23 17	21 39	14 36	06 48	29 13
58	25 00	22 45	15 20	07 17	29 27
59	26 51	23 54	16 05	07 46	29 42
60	28♊51	25♋05	16♌52	08♍16	29♍57

1h 24m 0s — 21° 0' 0" — 22 ♈ 42

LAT.	11	12	ASC	2	3
0	23♉23	21♊44	19♋24	18♌34	20♍12
5	24 34	23 29	21 17	20 10	21 06
10	25 48	25 16	23 08	21 43	21 57
15	27 09	27 08	25 00	23 14	22 46
20	28 38	29 05	26 54	24 43	23 34
21	28 57	29 29	27 17	25 01	23 43
22	29 16	29 54	27 40	25 19	23 53
23	29 36	00♋19	28 04	25 37	24 02
24	29 56	00 45	28 27	25 55	24 12
25	00♊17	01 10	28 51	26 13	24 21
26	00 39	01 37	29 15	26 31	24 31
27	01 01	02 03	29 39	26 49	24 40
28	01 24	02 31	00♌04	27 08	24 50
29	01 47	02 58	00 28	27 26	24 59
30	02 11	03 27	00 53	27 44	25 09
31	02 36	03 55	01 19	28 03	25 18
32	03 02	04 25	01 44	28 22	25 28
33	03 29	04 55	02 10	28 40	25 38
34	03 57	05 26	02 36	29 00	25 48
35	04 26	05 57	03 03	29 19	25 57
36	04 56	06 29	03 30	29 38	26 07
37	05 27	07 02	03 57	29 58	26 17
38	05 59	07 36	04 25	00♍17	26 28
39	06 33	08 10	04 53	00 37	26 38
40	07 08	08 46	05 22	00 58	26 48
41	07 45	09 22	05 51	01 18	26 58
42	08 23	09 59	06 21	01 39	27 09
43	09 04	10 38	06 51	02 00	27 20
44	09 46	11 18	07 22	02 21	27 30
45	10 31	11 58	07 54	02 43	27 41
46	11 18	12 40	08 26	03 05	27 52
47	12 07	13 24	08 59	03 27	28 04
48	13 00	14 09	09 32	03 50	28 15
49	13 55	14 55	10 07	04 13	28 27
50	14 54	15 43	10 42	04 36	28 39
51	15 56	16 33	11 18	05 00	28 51
52	17 03	17 24	11 55	05 25	29 03
53	18 14	18 18	12 33	05 50	29 16
54	19 30	19 13	13 11	06 15	29 29
55	20 51	20 10	13 51	06 42	29 42
56	22 18	21 10	14 32	07 08	29 55
57	23 52	22 12	15 14	07 36	00♎09
58	25 33	23 17	15 58	08 04	00 23
59	27 22	24 24	16 42	08 33	00 38
60	29♊20	25♋35	17♌28	09♍02	00♎53

1h 28m 0s — 22° 0' 0" — 23 ♈ 46

LAT.	11	12	ASC	2	3
0	24♉22	22♊39	20♋20	19♌35	21♍17
5	25 32	24 24	22 12	21 11	22 11
10	26 46	26 10	24 03	22 42	23 01
15	28 07	28 01	25 54	24 12	23 49
20	29 35	29 57	27 47	25 41	24 36
21	29 54	00♋22	28 10	25 58	24 45
22	00♊13	00 46	28 33	26 16	24 55
23	00 33	01 11	28 56	26 34	25 04
24	00 53	01 36	29 19	26 51	25 13
25	01 14	02 02	29 43	27 09	25 22
26	01 35	02 28	00♌07	27 27	25 32
27	01 57	02 54	00 31	27 45	25 41
28	02 19	03 21	00 55	28 03	25 50
29	02 43	03 49	01 19	28 21	26 00
30	03 07	04 16	01 44	28 40	26 09
31	03 32	04 45	02 09	28 58	26 19
32	03 57	05 14	02 34	29 16	26 28
33	04 24	05 44	03 00	29 35	26 38
34	04 51	06 14	03 26	29 54	26 47
35	05 20	06 45	03 52	00♍13	26 57
36	05 49	07 17	04 19	00 32	27 07
37	06 20	07 49	04 46	00 51	27 17
38	06 52	08 22	05 13	01 11	27 27
39	07 25	08 56	05 41	01 30	27 37
40	08 00	09 31	06 09	01 50	27 47
41	08 36	10 07	06 38	02 11	27 57
42	09 14	10 44	07 08	02 31	28 07
43	09 54	11 22	07 38	02 52	28 18
44	10 36	12 01	08 08	03 13	28 29
45	11 20	12 42	08 39	03 34	28 39
46	12 06	13 23	09 11	03 56	28 50
47	12 55	14 06	09 43	04 18	29 01
48	13 46	14 50	10 16	04 40	29 13
49	14 41	15 36	10 50	05 03	29 24
50	15 39	16 23	11 25	05 26	29 36
51	16 40	17 12	12 00	05 50	29 48
52	17 46	18 02	12 37	06 14	00♎00
53	18 55	18 55	13 14	06 39	00 12
54	20 10	19 49	13 52	07 04	00 25
55	21 30	20 46	14 31	07 30	00 38
56	22 55	21 44	15 12	07 56	00 51
57	24 27	22 45	15 53	08 23	01 05
58	26 06	23 49	16 36	08 51	01 19
59	27 53	24 55	17 20	09 19	01 33
60	29♊49	26♋04	18♌05	09♍48	01♎48

1h 32m 0s — 23° 0' 0" — 24 ♈ 50

LAT.	11	12	ASC	2	3
0	25♉21	23♊34	21♋17	20♌36	22♍23
5	26 30	25 18	23 08	22 11	23 15
10	27 44	27 04	24 58	23 42	24 04
15	29 04	28 54	26 48	25 10	24 52
20	00♊32	00♋50	28 40	26 38	25 38
21	00 50	01 14	29 03	26 55	25 47
22	01 09	01 38	29 26	27 13	25 56
23	01 29	02 02	29 49	27 31	26 05
24	01 49	02 27	00♌12	27 48	26 14
25	02 10	02 53	00 35	28 06	26 24
26	02 31	03 19	00 58	28 23	26 33
27	02 53	03 45	01 22	28 41	26 42
28	03 15	04 11	01 46	28 59	26 51
29	03 38	04 39	02 10	29 17	27 00
30	04 02	05 06	02 35	29 35	27 10
31	04 26	05 34	02 59	29 53	27 19
32	04 52	06 03	03 24	00♍11	27 28
33	05 18	06 32	03 50	00 30	27 38
34	05 45	07 02	04 15	00 48	27 47
35	06 13	07 33	04 41	01 07	27 57
36	06 42	08 04	05 08	01 26	28 06
37	07 13	08 36	05 34	01 45	28 16
38	07 44	09 09	06 01	02 04	28 26
39	08 17	09 43	06 29	02 23	28 36
40	08 51	10 17	06 57	02 43	28 46
41	09 27	10 53	07 25	03 03	28 56
42	10 05	11 29	07 54	03 23	29 06
43	10 44	12 06	08 24	03 44	29 16
44	11 25	12 45	08 54	04 04	29 27
45	12 09	13 25	09 25	04 25	29 37
46	12 54	14 05	09 56	04 47	29 48
47	13 42	14 48	10 28	05 08	29 59
48	14 33	15 31	11 00	05 31	00♎10
49	15 26	16 16	11 34	05 53	00 22
50	16 23	17 02	12 08	06 16	00 33
51	17 24	17 50	12 43	06 39	00 45
52	18 28	18 40	13 19	07 03	00 57
53	19 36	19 32	13 55	07 27	01 09
54	20 49	20 25	14 33	07 52	01 22
55	22 08	21 21	15 12	08 18	01 34
56	23 32	22 18	15 51	08 44	01 47
57	25 02	23 18	16 32	09 10	02 01
58	26 39	24 21	17 14	09 37	02 15
59	28 24	25 26	17 57	10 05	02 29
60	00♋17	26♋33	18♌42	10♍34	02♎44

Koch Table of Houses for Latitudes 0° to 60° North

1h 36m 0s 25 ♈ 53 **24° 0' 0"**

LAT.	11	12	ASC	2	3
0	26♉19	24♊30	22♋13	21♌37	23♍28
5	27 28	26 13	24 04	23 11	24 19
10	28 42	27 58	25 53	24 41	25 08
15	00♊01	29 47	27 42	26 09	25 54
20	01 28	01♋42	29 33	27 36	26 40
21	01 47	02 06	29 56	27 53	26 49
22	02 06	02 30	00♌18	28 10	26 58
23	02 25	02 54	00 41	28 27	27 07
24	02 45	03 19	01 04	28 45	27 16
25	03 05	03 44	01 27	29 02	27 25
26	03 26	04 09	01 50	29 20	27 34
27	03 48	04 35	02 14	29 37	27 43
28	04 10	05 02	02 37	29 55	27 52
29	04 33	05 28	03 01	00♍12	28 01
30	04 56	05 56	03 25	00 30	28 10
31	05 21	06 24	03 50	00 48	28 19
32	05 46	06 52	04 14	01 06	28 28
33	06 12	07 21	04 39	01 24	28 38
34	06 38	07 51	05 05	01 43	28 47
35	07 06	08 21	05 30	02 01	28 56
36	07 35	08 52	05 56	02 20	29 06
37	08 05	09 23	06 23	02 38	29 15
38	08 36	09 56	06 49	02 57	29 25
39	09 09	10 29	07 17	03 16	29 35
40	09 43	11 03	07 44	03 36	29 44
41	10 18	11 38	08 12	03 56	29 54
42	10 55	12 14	08 41	04 15	00♎04
43	11 34	12 50	09 10	04 36	00 15
44	12 14	13 28	09 40	04 56	00 25
45	12 57	14 07	10 10	05 17	00 35
46	13 42	14 48	10 41	05 38	00 46
47	14 29	15 29	11 12	05 59	00 57
48	15 19	16 12	11 44	06 21	01 08
49	16 12	16 56	12 17	06 43	01 19
50	17 08	17 42	12 51	07 06	01 30
51	18 07	18 29	13 25	07 29	01 42
52	19 10	19 18	14 00	07 52	01 54
53	20 17	20 09	14 37	08 16	02 06
54	21 29	21 01	15 14	08 41	02 18
55	22 46	21 56	15 52	09 06	02 31
56	24 08	22 52	16 31	09 31	02 43
57	25 36	23 51	17 11	09 57	02 57
58	27 12	24 52	17 52	10 24	03 10
59	28 54	25 56	18 35	10 52	03 24
60	00♋45	27♋03	19♌18	11♍20	03♎39

1h 40m 0s 26 ♈ 57 **25° 0' 0"**

LAT.	11	12	ASC	2	3
0	27♉17	25♊25	23♋10	22♌39	24♍33
5	28 26	27 07	25 00	24 12	25 24
10	29 39	28 52	26 48	25 41	26 11
15	00♊58	00♋40	28 37	27 08	26 57
20	02 25	02 34	00♌26	28 33	27 42
21	02 43	02 57	00 49	28 50	27 50
22	03 02	03 21	01 11	29 07	27 59
23	03 21	03 45	01 33	29 24	28 08
24	03 41	04 10	01 56	29 42	28 17
25	04 01	04 35	02 19	29 59	28 26
26	04 22	05 00	02 42	00♍16	28 35
27	04 43	05 26	03 05	00 33	28 44
28	05 05	05 52	03 28	00 51	28 52
29	05 28	06 18	03 52	01 08	29 01
30	05 51	06 45	04 16	01 26	29 10
31	06 15	07 13	04 40	01 43	29 19
32	06 40	07 41	05 04	02 01	29 28
33	07 05	08 09	05 29	02 19	29 37
34	07 32	08 39	05 54	02 37	29 47
35	07 59	09 08	06 19	02 55	29 56
36	08 28	09 39	06 45	03 13	00♎05
37	08 57	10 10	07 11	03 32	00 14
38	09 28	10 42	07 38	03 51	00 24
39	10 00	11 15	08 04	04 10	00 33
40	10 34	11 48	08 32	04 29	00 43
41	11 08	12 23	08 59	04 48	00 53
42	11 45	12 58	09 27	05 08	01 03
43	12 23	13 34	09 56	05 27	01 13
44	13 03	14 12	10 25	05 48	01 23
45	13 45	14 50	10 55	06 08	01 33
46	14 29	15 30	11 26	06 29	01 44
47	15 16	16 11	11 57	06 50	01 54
48	16 05	16 53	12 28	07 11	02 05
49	16 56	17 36	13 01	07 33	02 16
50	17 51	18 21	13 34	07 55	02 27
51	18 50	19 07	14 08	08 18	02 38
52	19 52	19 55	14 42	08 41	02 50
53	20 58	20 45	15 18	09 05	03 02
54	22 08	21 37	15 54	09 29	03 14
55	23 23	22 30	16 32	09 53	03 27
56	24 44	23 26	17 10	10 19	03 39
57	26 11	24 24	17 50	10 44	03 52
58	27 44	25 24	18 30	11 11	04 06
59	29 25	26 27	19 12	11 38	04 20
60	01♋13	27♋32	19♌55	12♍06	04♎34

1h 44m 0s 28 ♈ 00 **26° 0' 0"**

LAT.	11	12	ASC	2	3
0	28♉15	26♊20	24♋06	23♌41	25♍38
5	29 24	28 02	25 56	25 13	26 28
10	00♊37	29 46	27 43	26 41	27 15
15	01 55	01♋33	29 31	28 06	28 00
20	03 21	03 26	01♌19	29 31	28 43
21	03 39	03 49	01 41	29 48	28 52
22	03 57	04 13	02 04	00♍04	29 01
23	04 17	04 37	02 26	00 21	29 10
24	04 36	05 01	02 48	00 38	29 18
25	04 56	05 25	03 11	00 55	29 27
26	05 17	05 50	03 34	01 12	29 36
27	05 38	06 16	03 56	01 29	29 44
28	06 00	06 42	04 20	01 46	29 53
29	06 22	07 08	04 43	02 04	00♎02
30	06 45	07 34	05 07	02 21	00 11
31	07 09	08 02	05 30	02 38	00 19
32	07 33	08 29	05 54	02 56	00 28
33	07 59	08 58	06 19	03 13	00 37
34	08 25	09 26	06 44	03 31	00 46
35	08 52	09 56	07 08	03 49	00 55
36	09 20	10 26	07 34	04 07	01 04
37	09 49	10 57	07 59	04 26	01 13
38	10 20	11 28	08 26	04 44	01 23
39	10 51	12 01	08 52	05 03	01 32
40	11 24	12 34	09 19	05 21	01 42
41	11 58	13 08	09 46	05 40	01 51
42	12 34	13 42	10 14	06 00	02 01
43	13 12	14 18	10 42	06 19	02 11
44	13 51	14 55	11 11	06 39	02 21
45	14 33	15 33	11 40	06 59	02 31
46	15 16	16 12	12 10	07 20	02 41
47	16 02	16 52	12 41	07 41	02 52
48	16 50	17 33	13 12	08 02	03 02
49	17 41	18 16	13 44	08 23	03 13
50	18 35	19 00	14 17	08 45	03 24
51	19 32	19 46	14 50	09 07	03 35
52	20 33	20 33	15 24	09 30	03 47
53	21 38	21 22	15 59	09 53	03 58
54	22 47	22 13	16 35	10 17	04 10
55	24 01	23 05	17 12	10 41	04 23
56	25 20	24 00	17 49	11 06	04 35
57	26 45	24 57	18 28	11 32	04 48
58	28 16	25 56	19 08	11 58	05 01
59	29 55	26 57	19 49	12 24	05 15
60	01♋41	28♋01	20♌32	12♍52	05♎29

1h 48m 0s 29 ♈ 03 **27° 0' 0"**

LAT.	11	12	ASC	2	3
0	29♉13	27♊15	25♋03	24♌42	26♍44
5	00♊21	28 56	26 52	26 13	27 32
10	01 34	00♋40	28 39	27 41	28 18
15	02 52	02 26	00♌25	29 05	29 02
20	04 17	04 18	02 13	00♍28	29 45
21	04 35	04 41	02 34	00 45	29 54
22	04 53	05 04	02 56	01 02	00♎02
23	05 12	05 28	03 18	01 18	00 11
24	05 31	05 52	03 40	01 35	00 19
25	05 51	06 16	04 03	01 52	00 28
26	06 11	06 41	04 25	02 09	00 36
27	06 32	07 06	04 48	02 25	00 45
28	06 54	07 31	05 11	02 42	00 53
29	07 16	07 57	05 34	02 59	01 02
30	07 39	08 24	05 57	03 16	01 11
31	08 02	08 50	06 21	03 33	01 19
32	08 26	09 18	06 44	03 51	01 28
33	08 52	09 46	07 09	04 08	01 37
34	09 17	10 14	07 33	04 26	01 46
35	09 44	10 43	07 58	04 43	01 55
36	10 12	11 13	08 23	05 01	02 03
37	10 41	11 43	08 48	05 19	02 13
38	11 11	12 14	09 14	05 37	02 22
39	11 42	12 46	09 40	05 56	02 31
40	12 14	13 19	10 06	06 14	02 40
41	12 48	13 52	10 33	06 33	02 50
42	13 24	14 27	11 00	06 52	02 59
43	14 01	15 02	11 28	07 11	03 09
44	14 39	15 38	11 57	07 31	03 19
45	15 20	16 15	12 26	07 51	03 28
46	16 03	16 54	12 55	08 11	03 39
47	16 48	17 33	13 25	08 31	03 49
48	17 35	18 14	13 56	08 52	03 59
49	18 25	18 56	14 27	09 13	04 10
50	19 18	19 39	14 59	09 35	04 21
51	20 14	20 24	15 32	09 57	04 32
52	21 14	21 10	16 06	10 19	04 43
53	22 18	21 59	16 40	10 42	04 55
54	23 25	22 48	17 15	11 05	05 06
55	24 38	23 40	17 52	11 29	05 18
56	25 55	24 34	18 29	11 54	05 31
57	27 18	25 29	19 07	12 19	05 44
58	28 48	26 27	19 46	12 44	05 57
59	00♋25	27 28	20 27	13 11	06 10
60	02♋09	28♋30	21♌08	13♍38	06♎24

1h 52m 0s 00 ♉ 06 **28° 0' 0"**

LAT.	11	12	ASC	2	3
0	00♊11	28♊10	26♋00	25♌44	27♍49
5	01 19	29 51	27 48	27 14	28 37
10	02 31	01♋33	29 34	28 40	29 22
15	03 48	03 19	01♌19	00♍04	00♎05
20	05 12	05 10	03 06	01 26	00 47
21	05 30	05 32	03 27	01 43	00 55
22	05 48	05 56	03 49	01 59	01 04
23	06 07	06 19	04 11	02 15	01 12
24	06 26	06 43	04 33	02 32	01 20
25	06 46	07 07	04 55	02 48	01 29
26	07 06	07 31	05 17	03 05	01 37
27	07 27	07 56	05 39	03 22	01 46
28	07 48	08 21	06 02	03 38	01 54
29	08 10	08 47	06 25	03 55	02 02
30	08 32	09 13	06 48	04 12	02 11
31	08 56	09 39	07 11	04 29	02 19
32	09 20	10 06	07 34	04 46	02 28
33	09 44	10 34	07 58	05 03	02 36
34	10 10	11 02	08 22	05 20	02 45
35	10 36	11 31	08 47	05 37	02 54
36	11 04	12 00	09 11	05 55	03 03
37	11 32	12 30	09 36	06 13	03 11
38	12 02	13 00	10 02	06 31	03 20
39	12 32	13 32	10 27	06 49	03 29
40	13 04	14 04	10 53	07 07	03 39
41	13 38	14 37	11 20	07 25	03 48
42	14 13	15 11	11 47	07 44	03 57
43	14 49	15 45	12 14	08 03	04 07
44	15 27	16 21	12 42	08 22	04 16
45	16 07	16 58	13 11	08 42	04 26
46	16 49	17 35	13 40	09 02	04 36
47	17 33	18 14	14 10	09 22	04 46
48	18 20	18 54	14 40	09 42	04 56
49	19 09	19 35	15 11	10 03	05 07
50	20 01	20 18	15 42	10 24	05 17
51	20 56	21 02	16 14	10 46	05 28
52	21 55	21 48	16 48	11 08	05 39
53	22 57	22 35	17 21	11 31	05 51
54	24 04	23 24	17 56	11 54	06 02
55	25 15	24 15	18 32	12 17	06 14
56	26 30	25 07	19 08	12 41	06 27
57	27 52	26 02	19 46	13 06	06 39
58	29 20	26 59	20 24	13 31	06 52
59	00♋54	27 58	21 04	13 57	07 05
60	02♋37	29♋00	21♌45	14♍24	07♎19

1h 56m 0s 01 ♉ 08 **29° 0' 0"**

LAT.	11	12	ASC	2	3
0	01♊08	29♊05	26♋57	26♌47	28♍55
5	02 16	00♋45	28 44	28 16	29 41
10	03 28	02 27	00♌29	29 41	00♎25
15	04 44	04 12	02 14	01♍03	01 08
20	06 08	06 01	03 59	02 24	01 49
21	06 25	06 24	04 20	02 40	01 57
22	06 43	06 47	04 42	02 56	02 05
23	07 02	07 10	05 03	03 13	02 13
24	07 21	07 33	05 25	03 29	02 21
25	07 40	07 57	05 47	03 45	02 30
26	08 00	08 21	06 09	04 01	02 38
27	08 21	08 46	06 31	04 18	02 46
28	08 42	09 11	06 53	04 34	02 54
29	09 03	09 36	07 16	04 51	03 03
30	09 26	10 02	07 38	05 07	03 11
31	09 49	10 28	08 01	05 24	03 19
32	10 12	10 54	08 24	05 41	03 28
33	10 37	11 22	08 48	05 57	03 36
34	11 02	11 49	09 12	06 14	03 44
35	11 28	12 18	09 36	06 31	03 53
36	11 55	12 47	10 00	06 49	04 02
37	12 23	13 16	10 25	07 06	04 10
38	12 52	13 46	10 50	07 24	04 19
39	13 23	14 17	11 15	07 42	04 28
40	13 54	14 49	11 41	08 00	04 37
41	14 27	15 21	12 07	08 18	04 46
42	15 01	15 54	12 33	08 36	04 55
43	15 37	16 29	13 00	08 55	05 04
44	16 15	17 04	13 28	09 14	05 14
45	16 54	17 40	13 56	09 33	05 23
46	17 35	18 17	14 25	09 53	05 33
47	18 19	18 55	14 54	10 12	05 43
48	19 05	19 34	15 24	10 33	05 53
49	19 53	20 15	15 54	10 53	06 03
50	20 44	20 57	16 25	11 14	06 14
51	21 38	21 40	16 57	11 35	06 25
52	22 35	22 25	17 29	11 57	06 36
53	23 36	23 11	18 03	12 19	06 47
54	24 42	23 59	18 37	12 42	06 58
55	25 51	24 49	19 12	13 05	07 10
56	27 06	25 41	19 47	13 29	07 22
57	28 25	26 34	20 24	13 53	07 34
58	29 51	27 30	21 02	14 18	07 47
59	01♋24	28 28	21 41	14 43	08 00
60	03♋04	29♋29	22♌21	15♍10	08♎14

2h 0m 0s 02 ♉ 11 **30° 0' 0"**

LAT.	11	12	ASC	2	3
0	02♊05	00♋00	27♋55	27♌49	00♎00
5	03 13	01 40	29 41	29 17	00 46
10	04 24	03 21	01♌25	00♍41	01 29
15	05 40	05 05	03 08	02 02	02 10
20	07 03	06 53	04 52	03 22	02 50
21	07 20	07 15	05 13	03 38	02 58
22	07 38	07 38	05 35	03 54	03 06
23	07 57	08 01	05 56	04 10	03 14
24	08 16	08 24	06 17	04 26	03 22
25	08 35	08 47	06 39	04 42	03 30
26	08 54	09 11	07 00	04 58	03 38
27	09 15	09 36	07 22	05 14	03 46
28	09 35	10 00	07 44	05 30	03 55
29	09 57	10 25	08 07	05 46	04 03
30	10 19	10 50	08 29	06 03	04 11
31	10 41	11 16	08 52	06 19	04 19
32	11 05	11 43	09 14	06 35	04 27
33	11 29	12 09	09 38	06 52	04 35
34	11 54	12 37	10 01	07 09	04 44
35	12 20	13 05	10 25	07 26	04 52
36	12 46	13 33	10 49	07 43	05 00
37	13 14	14 02	11 13	08 00	05 09
38	13 43	14 32	11 38	08 17	05 18
39	14 13	15 02	12 03	08 35	05 26
40	14 44	15 34	12 28	08 52	05 35
41	15 16	16 06	12 54	09 10	05 44
42	15 50	16 38	13 20	09 28	05 53
43	16 25	17 12	13 46	09 47	06 02
44	17 02	17 46	14 14	10 05	06 11
45	17 41	18 22	14 41	10 24	06 21
46	18 21	18 58	15 09	10 43	06 30
47	19 04	19 36	15 38	11 03	06 40
48	19 49	20 15	16 07	11 23	06 50
49	20 36	20 55	16 37	11 43	07 00
50	21 26	21 36	17 08	12 04	07 10
51	22 19	22 18	17 39	12 24	07 21
52	23 16	23 02	18 11	12 46	07 32
53	24 16	23 48	18 44	13 08	07 43
54	25 19	24 35	19 17	13 30	07 54
55	26 28	25 24	19 52	13 53	08 06
56	27 40	26 14	20 27	14 16	08 17
57	28 59	27 07	21 03	14 40	08 30
58	00♋23	28 02	21 40	15 04	08 42
59	01 53	28 59	22 19	15 30	08 55
60	03♋31	29♋58	22♌58	15♍56	09♎09

2h 4m 0s 03 ♉ 13 **31° 0' 0"**

LAT.	11	12	ASC	2	3
0	03♊03	00♋55	28♋52	28♌52	01♎05
5	04 10	02 34	00♌37	00♍18	01 50
10	05 20	04 14	02 20	01 41	02 32
15	06 36	05 57	04 03	03 01	03 13
20	07 58	07 45	05 46	04 20	03 52
21	08 15	08 07	06 06	04 36	04 00
22	08 33	08 29	06 27	04 51	04 08
23	08 51	08 52	06 48	05 07	04 16
24	09 10	09 15	07 10	05 23	04 23
25	09 29	09 38	07 31	05 38	04 31
26	09 48	10 01	07 52	05 54	04 39
27	10 08	10 25	08 14	06 10	04 47
28	10 29	10 50	08 36	06 26	04 55
29	10 50	11 14	08 57	06 42	05 03
30	11 12	11 39	09 20	06 58	05 11
31	11 34	12 05	09 42	07 14	05 19
32	11 57	12 31	10 04	07 30	05 27
33	12 21	12 57	10 27	07 47	05 35
34	12 45	13 24	10 50	08 03	05 43
35	13 11	13 52	11 14	08 20	05 51
36	13 37	14 20	11 37	08 36	05 59
37	14 04	14 48	12 01	08 53	06 08
38	14 33	15 18	12 25	09 10	06 16
39	15 02	15 48	12 50	09 28	06 25
40	15 33	16 18	13 15	09 45	06 33
41	16 05	16 50	13 40	10 03	06 42
42	16 38	17 22	14 06	10 20	06 51
43	17 13	17 55	14 32	10 39	07 00
44	17 49	18 29	14 59	10 57	07 09
45	18 27	19 04	15 26	11 15	07 18
46	19 07	19 40	15 54	11 34	07 27
47	19 49	20 17	16 22	11 53	07 37
48	20 33	20 55	16 51	12 13	07 47
49	21 19	21 34	17 20	12 33	07 57
50	22 09	22 14	17 50	12 53	08 07
51	23 01	22 56	18 21	13 14	08 17
52	23 56	23 39	18 53	13 35	08 28
53	24 54	24 24	19 25	13 56	08 38
54	25 57	25 10	19 58	14 18	08 50
55	27 04	25 58	20 31	14 40	09 01
56	28 15	26 48	21 06	15 03	09 13
57	29 32	27 39	21 42	15 27	09 25
58	00♋54	28 33	22 18	15 51	09 37
59	02 23	29 29	22 56	16 16	09 50
60	03♋59	00♌27	23♌35	16♍41	10♎04

Koch Table of Houses for Latitudes 0° to 60° North

2h 8m 0s — 32° 0' 0" — 04 ♉ 16

LAT.	11	12	ASC	2	3
0	04♊00	01♋50	29♋49	29♌54	02♎11
5	05 07	03 28	01♌34	01♍20	02 54
10	06 17	05 08	03 16	02 41	03 36
15	07 31	06 50	04 57	04 00	04 15
20	08 53	08 36	06 39	05 18	04 54
21	09 10	08 58	07 00	05 33	05 01
22	09 28	09 20	07 20	05 49	05 09
23	09 45	09 42	07 41	06 04	05 17
24	10 04	10 05	08 02	06 20	05 24
25	10 23	10 28	08 23	06 35	05 32
26	10 42	10 51	08 44	06 51	05 39
27	11 02	11 15	09 05	07 06	05 47
28	11 22	11 39	09 27	07 22	05 55
29	11 43	12 03	09 48	07 38	06 03
30	12 04	12 28	10 10	07 53	06 10
31	12 26	12 53	10 32	08 09	06 18
32	12 49	13 19	10 54	08 25	06 26
33	13 13	13 45	11 17	08 41	06 34
34	13 37	14 11	11 40	08 57	06 42
35	14 02	14 38	12 03	09 14	06 50
36	14 28	15 06	12 26	09 30	06 58
37	14 55	15 34	12 50	09 47	07 06
38	15 23	16 03	13 13	10 04	07 14
39	15 52	16 33	13 38	10 21	07 23
40	16 22	17 03	14 02	10 38	07 31
41	16 53	17 34	14 27	10 55	07 40
42	17 26	18 06	14 53	11 13	07 48
43	18 00	18 38	15 18	11 30	07 57
44	18 36	19 12	15 45	11 48	08 06
45	19 13	19 46	16 11	12 07	08 15
46	19 52	20 21	16 39	12 25	08 24
47	20 33	20 57	17 06	12 44	08 34
48	21 17	21 35	17 35	13 03	08 43
49	22 02	22 13	18 04	13 23	08 53
50	22 50	22 53	18 33	13 43	09 03
51	23 42	23 34	19 03	14 03	09 13
52	24 36	24 16	19 34	14 23	09 23
53	25 33	25 00	20 06	14 45	09 34
54	26 34	25 46	20 38	15 06	09 45
55	27 40	26 33	21 11	15 28	09 56
56	28 50	27 21	21 45	15 51	10 08
57	00♋05	28 12	22 20	16 14	10 20
58	01 25	29 04	22 56	16 38	10 32
59	02 52	29 59	23 33	17 02	10 45
60	04♋26	00♌56	24♌11	17♍27	10♎58

2h 12m 0s — 33° 0' 0" — 05 ♉ 18

LAT.	11	12	ASC	2	3
0	04♊57	02♋45	00♌47	00♍57	03♎16
5	06 03	04 23	02 31	02 21	03 59
10	07 13	06 01	04 12	03 42	04 39
15	08 27	07 42	05 52	04 59	05 17
20	09 47	09 27	07 32	06 16	05 55
21	10 04	09 49	07 53	06 31	06 03
22	10 22	10 11	08 13	06 46	06 10
23	10 40	10 33	08 34	07 01	06 17
24	10 58	10 55	08 54	07 17	06 25
25	11 16	11 18	09 15	07 32	06 32
26	11 35	11 41	09 36	07 47	06 40
27	11 55	12 04	09 57	08 02	06 47
28	12 15	12 28	10 18	08 18	06 55
29	12 36	12 52	10 39	08 33	07 02
30	12 57	13 16	11 01	08 49	07 10
31	13 19	13 41	11 23	09 04	07 18
32	13 41	14 07	11 44	09 20	07 25
33	14 04	14 32	12 07	09 36	07 33
34	14 28	14 58	12 29	09 52	07 41
35	14 53	15 25	12 52	10 08	07 49
36	15 18	15 52	13 15	10 24	07 57
37	15 45	16 20	13 38	10 40	08 05
38	16 12	16 49	14 01	10 57	08 13
39	16 41	17 18	14 25	11 13	08 21
40	17 10	17 48	14 49	11 30	08 29
41	17 41	18 18	15 14	11 47	08 37
42	18 13	18 49	15 39	12 05	08 46
43	18 47	19 21	16 04	12 22	08 54
44	19 22	19 54	16 30	12 40	09 03
45	19 59	20 28	16 57	12 58	09 12
46	20 37	21 02	17 23	13 16	09 21
47	21 18	21 38	17 51	13 34	09 30
48	22 00	22 15	18 18	13 53	09 40
49	22 45	22 53	18 47	14 12	09 49
50	23 32	23 32	19 16	14 32	09 59
51	24 22	24 12	19 46	14 52	10 09
52	25 15	24 53	20 16	15 12	10 19
53	26 12	25 36	20 47	15 33	10 30
54	27 12	26 21	21 19	15 54	10 40
55	28 16	27 07	21 51	16 16	10 51
56	29 24	27 55	22 25	16 38	11 03
57	00♋37	28 44	22 59	17 01	11 15
58	01 56	29 36	23 34	17 24	11 27
59	03 21	00♌29	24 11	17 48	11 39
60	04♋53	01♌25	24♌48	18♍13	11♎53

2h 16m 0s — 34° 0' 0" — 06 ♉ 19

LAT.	11	12	ASC	2	3
0	05♊54	03♋40	01♌45	02♍00	04♎22
5	07 00	05 17	03 27	03 23	05 03
10	08 09	06 55	05 07	04 42	05 42
15	09 22	08 35	06 47	05 59	06 20
20	10 42	10 19	08 26	07 14	06 56
21	10 59	10 40	08 46	07 29	07 04
22	11 16	11 02	09 06	07 44	07 11
23	11 33	11 24	09 26	07 59	07 18
24	11 51	11 46	09 47	08 14	07 26
25	12 10	12 08	10 07	08 29	07 33
26	12 29	12 31	10 28	08 44	07 40
27	12 48	12 54	10 48	08 59	07 47
28	13 08	13 17	11 09	09 14	07 55
29	13 28	13 41	11 30	09 29	08 02
30	13 49	14 05	11 51	09 44	08 10
31	14 10	14 29	12 13	10 00	08 17
32	14 33	14 54	12 34	10 15	08 25
33	14 55	15 20	12 56	10 31	08 32
34	15 19	15 46	13 18	10 46	08 40
35	15 43	16 12	13 41	11 02	08 47
36	16 09	16 39	14 03	11 18	08 55
37	16 35	17 06	14 26	11 34	09 03
38	17 02	17 34	14 49	11 50	09 11
39	17 30	18 03	15 13	12 06	09 19
40	17 59	18 32	15 37	12 23	09 27
41	18 29	19 02	16 01	12 40	09 35
42	19 01	19 33	16 25	12 57	09 43
43	19 34	20 04	16 50	13 14	09 52
44	20 08	20 36	17 16	13 31	10 00
45	20 44	21 10	17 42	13 49	10 09
46	21 22	21 44	18 08	14 07	10 18
47	22 02	22 19	18 35	14 25	10 27
48	22 43	22 55	19 02	14 43	10 36
49	23 27	23 32	19 30	15 02	10 45
50	24 14	24 10	19 59	15 21	10 55
51	25 03	24 50	20 28	15 41	11 05
52	25 55	25 30	20 58	16 01	11 15
53	26 50	26 13	21 28	16 21	11 25
54	27 49	26 56	21 59	16 42	11 36
55	28 51	27 41	22 31	17 04	11 47
56	29 58	28 28	23 04	17 25	11 58
57	01♋10	29 17	23 38	17 48	12 09
58	02 27	00♌07	24 12	18 11	12 21
59	03 50	00 59	24 48	18 34	12 34
60	05♋19	01♌54	25♌25	18♍59	12♎47

2h 20m 0s — 35° 0' 0" — 07 ♉ 21

LAT.	11	12	ASC	2	3
0	06♊50	04♋35	02♌43	03♍03	05♎27
5	07 56	06 11	04 24	04 25	06 07
10	09 04	07 48	06 03	05 43	06 45
15	10 17	09 27	07 41	06 58	07 22
20	11 36	11 10	09 19	08 12	07 58
21	11 53	11 31	09 39	08 27	08 05
22	12 10	11 53	09 59	08 41	08 12
23	12 27	12 14	10 19	08 56	08 19
24	12 45	12 36	10 39	09 11	08 26
25	13 03	12 58	10 59	09 25	08 33
26	13 22	13 21	11 20	09 40	08 40
27	13 41	13 43	11 40	09 55	08 47
28	14 00	14 06	12 00	10 10	08 55
29	14 20	14 30	12 21	10 25	09 02
30	14 41	14 53	12 42	10 40	09 09
31	15 02	15 18	13 03	10 55	09 16
32	15 24	15 42	13 24	11 10	09 24
33	15 47	16 07	13 46	11 25	09 31
34	16 10	16 33	14 08	11 41	09 38
35	16 34	16 58	14 30	11 56	09 46
36	16 59	17 25	14 52	12 12	09 53
37	17 24	17 52	15 14	12 27	10 01
38	17 51	18 19	15 37	12 43	10 09
39	18 18	18 48	16 00	12 59	10 17
40	18 47	19 16	16 24	13 15	10 24
41	19 17	19 46	16 48	13 32	10 32
42	19 48	20 16	17 12	13 49	10 41
43	20 20	20 47	17 36	14 05	10 49
44	20 54	21 19	18 01	14 22	10 57
45	21 30	21 51	18 27	14 40	11 06
46	22 07	22 25	18 53	14 57	11 14
47	22 46	22 59	19 19	15 15	11 23
48	23 27	23 34	19 46	15 33	11 32
49	24 10	24 11	20 13	15 52	11 41
50	24 55	24 48	20 41	16 11	11 51
51	25 43	25 27	21 10	16 30	12 00
52	26 34	26 07	21 39	16 50	12 10
53	27 28	26 49	22 09	17 10	12 20
54	28 25	27 31	22 40	17 30	12 31
55	29 27	28 16	23 11	17 51	12 41
56	00♋32	29 01	23 43	18 13	12 53
57	01 42	29 49	24 16	18 35	13 04
58	02 58	00♌38	24 50	18 57	13 16
59	04 19	01 30	25 25	19 21	13 28
60	05♋46	02♌23	26♌01	19♍45	13♎41

2h 24m 0s — 36° 0' 0" — 08 ♉ 23

LAT.	11	12	ASC	2	3
0	07♊47	05♋30	03♌41	04♍07	06♎32
5	08 52	07 06	05 22	05 27	07 11
10	10 00	08 42	06 59	06 44	07 48
15	11 12	10 20	08 36	07 58	08 24
20	12 30	12 01	10 13	09 10	08 59
21	12 47	12 22	10 33	09 25	09 06
22	13 03	12 43	10 52	09 39	09 13
23	13 21	13 05	11 12	09 53	09 20
24	13 38	13 26	11 32	10 08	09 27
25	13 56	13 48	11 51	10 22	09 33
26	14 14	14 10	12 11	10 37	09 40
27	14 33	14 33	12 32	10 51	09 47
28	14 53	14 55	12 52	11 06	09 54
29	15 12	15 18	13 12	11 20	10 01
30	15 33	15 42	13 33	11 35	10 08
31	15 54	16 06	13 54	11 50	10 16
32	16 15	16 30	14 14	12 05	10 23
33	16 37	16 54	14 36	12 20	10 30
34	17 00	17 19	14 57	12 35	10 37
35	17 24	17 45	15 19	12 50	10 44
36	17 48	18 11	15 41	13 05	10 52
37	18 14	18 38	16 03	13 21	10 59
38	18 40	19 05	16 25	13 36	11 07
39	19 07	19 32	16 48	13 52	11 14
40	19 35	20 01	17 11	14 08	11 22
41	20 04	20 30	17 34	14 24	11 30
42	20 35	20 59	17 58	14 40	11 38
43	21 07	21 30	18 22	14 57	11 46
44	21 40	22 01	18 47	15 14	11 54
45	22 15	22 33	19 12	15 31	12 02
46	22 51	23 06	19 37	15 48	12 11
47	23 29	23 40	20 03	16 06	12 19
48	24 09	24 14	20 30	16 23	12 28
49	24 52	24 50	20 56	16 42	12 37
50	25 36	25 27	21 24	17 00	12 46
51	26 23	26 05	21 52	17 19	12 56
52	27 13	26 44	22 21	17 38	13 06
53	28 06	27 25	22 50	17 58	13 15
54	29 02	28 07	23 20	18 18	13 26
55	00♋02	28 50	23 51	18 39	13 36
56	01 06	29 35	24 23	19 00	13 47
57	02 15	00♌21	24 55	19 21	13 58
58	03 28	01 10	25 28	19 44	14 10
59	04 47	02 00	26 03	20 07	14 22
60	06♋13	02♌52	26♌38	20♍30	14♎35

2h 28m 0s — 37° 0' 0" — 09 ♉ 24

LAT.	11	12	ASC	2	3
0	08♊43	06♋26	04♌39	05♍10	07♎37
5	09 48	08 00	06 19	06 29	08 16
10	10 55	09 35	07 56	07 45	08 52
15	12 07	11 12	09 31	08 57	09 26
20	13 24	12 53	11 07	10 08	10 00
21	13 40	13 13	11 26	10 22	10 07
22	13 57	13 34	11 45	10 37	10 13
23	14 14	13 55	12 05	10 51	10 20
24	14 31	14 16	12 24	11 05	10 27
25	14 49	14 38	12 44	11 19	10 34
26	15 07	15 00	13 03	11 33	10 40
27	15 26	15 22	13 23	11 48	10 47
28	15 45	15 44	13 43	12 02	10 54
29	16 04	16 07	14 03	12 16	11 01
30	16 24	16 30	14 23	12 31	11 08
31	16 45	16 54	14 44	12 45	11 15
32	17 06	17 17	15 05	13 00	11 22
33	17 28	17 42	15 25	13 14	11 29
34	17 51	18 06	15 46	13 29	11 36
35	18 14	18 31	16 08	13 44	11 43
36	18 38	18 57	16 29	13 59	11 50
37	19 03	19 23	16 51	14 14	11 57
38	19 29	19 50	17 13	14 29	12 04
39	19 55	20 17	17 35	14 45	12 12
40	20 23	20 45	17 58	15 01	12 19
41	20 52	21 13	18 21	15 16	12 27
42	21 22	21 43	18 44	15 32	12 35
43	21 53	22 12	19 08	15 49	12 43
44	22 26	22 43	19 32	16 05	12 51
45	23 00	23 14	19 57	16 22	12 59
46	23 35	23 47	20 22	16 39	13 07
47	24 13	24 20	20 47	16 56	13 15
48	24 52	24 54	21 13	17 13	13 24
49	25 34	25 29	21 40	17 31	13 33
50	26 17	26 05	22 07	17 49	13 42
51	27 03	26 42	22 34	18 08	13 51
52	27 52	27 21	23 02	18 27	14 01
53	28 44	28 01	23 31	18 46	14 10
54	29 39	28 42	24 01	19 06	14 21
55	00♋37	29 24	24 31	19 26	14 31
56	01 40	00♌08	25 02	19 47	14 42
57	02 47	00 54	25 34	20 08	14 53
58	03 59	01 41	26 07	20 30	15 04
59	05 16	02 30	26 40	20 53	15 16
60	06♋40	03♌21	27♌15	21♍16	15♎29

2h 32m 0s — 38° 0' 0" — 10 ♉ 25

LAT.	11	12	ASC	2	3
0	09♊40	07♋21	05♌38	06♍14	08♎43
5	10 44	08 55	07 16	07 32	09 20
10	11 51	10 29	08 52	08 45	09 55
15	13 01	12 05	10 26	09 57	10 28
20	14 18	13 44	12 00	11 06	11 01
21	14 34	14 04	12 19	11 20	11 08
22	14 50	14 25	12 38	11 34	11 14
23	15 07	14 46	12 57	11 48	11 21
24	15 24	15 07	13 17	12 02	11 27
25	15 42	15 28	13 36	12 16	11 34
26	16 00	15 49	13 55	12 30	11 40
27	16 18	16 11	14 15	12 44	11 47
28	16 37	16 33	14 34	12 58	11 53
29	16 56	16 56	14 54	13 12	12 00
30	17 16	17 18	15 14	13 26	12 07
31	17 36	17 41	15 34	13 40	12 14
32	17 57	18 05	15 55	13 55	12 20
33	18 19	18 29	16 15	14 09	12 27
34	18 41	18 53	16 36	14 23	12 34
35	19 04	19 18	16 57	14 38	12 41
36	19 27	19 43	17 18	14 53	12 48
37	19 52	20 09	17 39	15 08	12 55
38	20 17	20 35	18 01	15 23	13 02
39	20 43	21 02	18 23	15 38	13 09
40	21 11	21 29	18 45	15 53	13 17
41	21 39	21 57	19 08	16 09	13 24
42	22 08	22 26	19 31	16 24	13 32
43	22 39	22 55	19 54	16 40	13 39
44	23 11	23 25	20 18	16 56	13 47
45	23 44	23 56	20 42	17 13	13 55
46	24 19	24 28	21 06	17 29	14 03
47	24 56	25 00	21 31	17 46	14 11
48	25 35	25 34	21 57	18 03	14 20
49	26 15	26 08	22 23	18 21	14 28
50	26 58	26 43	22 49	18 39	14 37
51	27 43	27 20	23 16	18 57	14 46
52	28 31	27 58	23 44	19 15	14 56
53	29 21	28 37	24 12	19 34	15 05
54	00♋15	29 17	24 41	19 54	15 15
55	01 12	29 58	25 11	20 14	15 25
56	02 13	00♌41	25 41	20 34	15 36
57	03 19	01 26	26 13	20 55	15 47
58	04 29	02 12	26 45	21 16	15 58
59	05 45	03 00	27 17	21 39	16 10
60	07♋06	03♌50	27♌51	22♍02	16♎23

2h 36m 0s — 39° 0' 0" — 11 ♉ 26

LAT.	11	12	ASC	2	3
0	10♊36	08♋16	06♌37	07♍18	09♎48
5	11 40	09 49	08 14	08 34	10 24
10	12 46	11 22	09 48	09 46	10 57
15	13 56	12 57	11 21	10 56	11 30
20	15 11	14 35	12 54	12 05	12 02
21	15 27	14 55	13 13	12 18	12 08
22	15 44	15 15	13 31	12 32	12 15
23	16 00	15 36	13 50	12 46	12 21
24	16 17	15 57	14 09	12 59	12 27
25	16 34	16 18	14 28	13 13	12 34
26	16 52	16 39	14 47	13 26	12 40
27	17 10	17 00	15 07	13 40	12 46
28	17 29	17 22	15 26	13 54	12 53
29	17 48	17 44	15 45	14 08	12 59
30	18 07	18 07	16 05	14 21	13 06
31	18 27	18 29	16 25	14 35	13 12
32	18 48	18 52	16 45	14 49	13 19
33	19 09	19 16	17 05	15 04	13 25
34	19 31	19 40	17 25	15 18	13 32
35	19 53	20 04	17 46	15 32	13 39
36	20 16	20 29	18 07	15 46	13 46
37	20 41	20 54	18 28	16 01	13 53
38	21 05	21 20	18 49	16 16	14 00
39	21 31	21 46	19 11	16 30	14 07
40	21 58	22 13	19 32	16 45	14 14
41	22 26	22 41	19 55	17 01	14 21
42	22 55	23 09	20 17	17 16	14 28
43	23 25	23 38	20 40	17 32	14 36
44	23 56	24 07	21 03	17 47	14 43
45	24 29	24 38	21 27	18 03	14 51
46	25 03	25 09	21 51	18 20	14 59
47	25 39	25 41	22 16	18 36	15 07
48	26 17	26 13	22 41	18 53	15 15
49	26 57	26 47	23 06	19 10	15 24
50	27 39	27 22	23 32	19 28	15 32
51	28 23	27 58	23 59	19 46	15 41
52	29 09	28 34	24 26	20 04	15 51
53	29 59	29 13	24 53	20 22	16 00
54	00♋51	29 52	25 22	20 41	16 10
55	01 47	00♌33	25 51	21 01	16 20
56	02 47	01 15	26 21	21 21	16 30
57	03 51	01 58	26 51	21 42	16 41
58	04 59	02 44	27 23	22 03	16 52
59	06 13	03 31	27 55	22 25	17 04
60	07♋33	04♌19	28♌28	22♍47	17♎16

Koch Table of Houses for Latitudes 0° to 60° North

2h 40m 0s — 40° 0' 0" — 12 ♉ 27

LAT.	11	12	ASC	2	3
0	11♊32	09♋11	07♌35	08♍22	10♎53
5	12 35	10 43	09 11	09 36	11 27
10	13 41	12 16	10 45	10 47	12 00
15	14 50	13 50	12 16	11 56	12 32
20	16 05	15 26	13 48	13 03	13 03
21	16 21	15 46	14 06	13 16	13 09
22	16 37	16 06	14 25	13 30	13 15
23	16 53	16 26	14 43	13 43	13 21
24	17 10	16 47	15 02	13 56	13 27
25	17 27	17 07	15 21	14 10	13 34
26	17 44	17 28	15 39	14 23	13 40
27	18 02	17 50	15 58	14 36	13 46
28	18 20	18 11	16 17	14 50	13 52
29	18 39	18 33	16 36	15 03	13 58
30	18 58	18 55	16 56	15 17	14 05
31	19 18	19 17	17 15	15 31	14 11
32	19 38	19 40	17 35	15 44	14 17
33	19 59	20 03	17 55	15 58	14 24
34	20 20	20 27	18 15	16 12	14 30
35	20 43	20 51	18 35	16 26	14 37
36	21 06	21 15	18 55	16 40	14 43
37	21 29	21 40	19 16	16 54	14 50
38	21 54	22 05	19 37	17 09	14 57
39	22 19	22 31	19 58	17 23	15 04
40	22 45	22 57	20 20	17 38	15 11
41	23 13	23 24	20 41	17 53	15 18
42	23 41	23 52	21 04	18 08	15 25
43	24 10	24 20	21 26	18 23	15 32
44	24 41	24 49	21 49	18 39	15 40
45	25 13	25 19	22 12	18 54	15 47
46	25 47	25 49	22 36	19 10	15 55
47	26 22	26 21	23 00	19 26	16 03
48	26 59	26 53	23 24	19 43	16 11
49	27 38	27 26	23 49	20 00	16 19
50	28 19	28 00	24 15	20 17	16 28
51	29 02	28 35	24 41	20 34	16 36
52	29 48	29 11	25 07	20 52	16 45
53	00♋36	29 48	25 34	21 10	16 54
54	01 28	00♌27	26 02	21 29	17 04
55	02 22	01 07	26 31	21 48	17 14
56	03 21	01 48	27 00	22 08	17 24
57	04 23	02 31	27 30	22 28	17 35
58	05 30	03 15	28 01	22 49	17 46
59	06 42	04 01	28 32	23 10	17 57
60	07♋59	04♌48	29♌05	23♍33	18♎10

2h 44m 0s — 41° 0' 0" — 13 ♉ 27

LAT.	11	12	ASC	2	3
0	12♊28	10♋07	08♌34	09♍26	11♎58
5	13 31	11 38	10 09	10 39	12 31
10	14 36	13 09	11 41	11 49	13 03
15	15 44	14 42	13 11	12 56	13 34
20	16 58	16 17	14 42	14 01	14 03
21	17 14	16 37	15 00	14 14	14 09
22	17 29	16 57	15 18	14 27	14 15
23	17 46	17 17	15 36	14 40	14 21
24	18 02	17 37	15 55	14 53	14 27
25	18 19	17 57	16 13	15 06	14 33
26	18 36	18 18	16 31	15 20	14 39
27	18 54	18 39	16 50	15 33	14 45
28	19 12	19 00	17 09	15 46	14 51
29	19 30	19 21	17 28	15 59	14 57
30	19 49	19 43	17 47	16 12	15 03
31	20 08	20 05	18 06	16 26	15 10
32	20 28	20 27	18 25	16 39	15 16
33	20 49	20 50	18 44	16 53	15 22
34	21 10	21 13	19 04	17 06	15 28
35	21 32	21 37	19 24	17 20	15 35
36	21 54	22 01	19 44	17 34	15 41
37	22 18	22 25	20 04	17 48	15 48
38	22 42	22 50	20 25	18 02	15 54
39	23 07	23 16	20 46	18 16	16 01
40	23 32	23 41	21 07	18 30	16 08
41	23 59	24 08	21 28	18 45	16 14
42	24 27	24 35	21 50	19 00	16 21
43	24 56	25 03	22 12	19 14	16 28
44	25 26	25 31	22 34	19 30	16 36
45	25 58	26 00	22 57	19 45	16 43
46	26 31	26 30	23 20	20 01	16 51
47	27 05	27 01	23 44	20 16	16 58
48	27 41	27 32	24 08	20 33	17 06
49	28 19	28 05	24 32	20 49	17 14
50	28 59	28 38	24 57	21 06	17 22
51	29 42	29 13	25 23	21 23	17 31
52	00♋26	29 48	25 49	21 41	17 40
53	01 14	00♌24	26 16	21 58	17 49
54	02 04	01 02	26 43	22 17	17 58
55	02 57	01 41	27 11	22 36	18 08
56	03 54	02 21	27 39	22 55	18 18
57	04 55	03 03	28 09	23 15	18 28
58	06 00	03 46	28 39	23 35	18 39
59	07 10	04 31	29 10	23 56	18 51
60	08♋26	05♌18	29♌41	24♍18	19♎03

2h 48m 0s — 42° 0' 0" — 14 ♉ 28

LAT.	11	12	ASC	2	3
0	13♊24	11♋02	09♌34	10♍30	13♎03
5	14 26	12 32	11 07	11 42	13 35
10	15 30	14 03	12 38	12 50	14 06
15	16 38	15 34	14 07	13 55	14 35
20	17 51	17 09	15 36	15 00	15 04
21	18 07	17 28	15 53	15 12	15 10
22	18 22	17 47	16 11	15 25	15 16
23	18 38	18 07	16 29	15 38	15 21
24	18 54	18 27	16 47	15 51	15 27
25	19 11	18 47	17 05	16 03	15 33
26	19 28	19 07	17 24	16 16	15 39
27	19 45	19 28	17 42	16 29	15 44
28	20 03	19 49	18 00	16 42	15 50
29	20 21	20 10	18 19	16 55	15 56
30	20 40	20 31	18 37	17 08	16 02
31	20 59	20 53	18 56	17 21	16 08
32	21 18	21 15	19 15	17 34	16 14
33	21 39	21 37	19 34	17 47	16 20
34	22 00	22 00	19 54	18 00	16 26
35	22 21	22 23	20 13	18 14	16 32
36	22 43	22 47	20 33	18 27	16 38
37	23 06	23 11	20 53	18 41	16 45
38	23 30	23 35	21 13	18 55	16 51
39	23 54	24 00	21 33	19 09	16 58
40	24 19	24 26	21 54	19 23	17 04
41	24 46	24 52	22 15	19 37	17 11
42	25 13	25 18	22 36	19 51	17 18
43	25 41	25 45	22 58	20 06	17 24
44	26 11	26 13	23 20	20 21	17 32
45	26 42	26 42	23 42	20 36	17 39
46	27 14	27 11	24 05	20 51	17 46
47	27 48	27 41	24 28	21 07	17 54
48	28 23	28 12	24 52	21 22	18 01
49	29 01	28 44	25 16	21 38	18 09
50	29 40	29 16	25 40	21 55	18 17
51	00♋21	29 50	26 05	22 12	18 25
52	01 05	00♌25	26 31	22 29	18 34
53	01 51	01 00	26 57	22 46	18 43
54	02 40	01 37	27 23	23 04	18 52
55	03 32	02 15	27 51	23 23	19 02
56	04 27	02 55	28 19	23 42	19 11
57	05 27	03 35	28 47	24 01	19 22
58	06 30	04 18	29 17	24 21	19 33
59	07 39	05 01	29 47	24 42	19 44
60	08♋53	05♌47	00♍18	25♍03	19♎56

2h 52m 0s — 43° 0' 0" — 15 ♉ 28

LAT.	11	12	ASC	2	3
0	14♊20	11♋58	10♌33	11♍34	14♎07
5	15 21	13 27	12 05	12 44	14 39
10	16 25	14 56	13 34	13 51	15 08
15	17 32	16 27	15 02	14 55	15 37
20	18 44	18 00	16 30	15 58	16 04
21	18 59	18 19	16 47	16 10	16 10
22	19 15	18 38	17 05	16 23	16 16
23	19 30	18 57	17 22	16 35	16 21
24	19 46	19 17	17 40	16 48	16 27
25	20 03	19 37	17 58	17 00	16 32
26	20 20	19 57	18 16	17 13	16 38
27	20 37	20 17	18 34	17 25	16 43
28	20 54	20 37	18 52	17 38	16 49
29	21 12	20 58	19 10	17 50	16 55
30	21 30	21 19	19 28	18 03	17 00
31	21 49	21 40	19 47	18 16	17 06
32	22 08	22 02	20 05	18 29	17 12
33	22 28	22 24	20 24	18 42	17 18
34	22 49	22 46	20 43	18 55	17 24
35	23 10	23 09	21 02	19 08	17 30
36	23 32	23 32	21 21	19 21	17 36
37	23 54	23 56	21 41	19 34	17 42
38	24 17	24 20	22 01	19 48	17 48
39	24 41	24 45	22 21	20 01	17 54
40	25 06	25 10	22 41	20 15	18 01
41	25 32	25 35	23 02	20 29	18 07
42	25 59	26 01	23 23	20 43	18 14
43	26 27	26 28	23 44	20 57	18 20
44	26 56	26 55	24 05	21 12	18 27
45	27 26	27 23	24 27	21 26	18 34
46	27 57	27 52	24 49	21 41	18 41
47	28 31	28 21	25 12	21 56	18 49
48	29 05	28 52	25 35	22 12	18 56
49	29 42	29 23	25 59	22 28	19 04
50	00♋20	29 55	26 23	22 44	19 12
51	01 00	00♌28	26 47	23 00	19 20
52	01 43	01 01	27 12	23 17	19 28
53	02 28	01 36	27 38	23 34	19 37
54	03 16	02 12	28 04	23 52	19 46
55	04 06	02 50	28 31	24 10	19 55
56	05 01	03 28	28 58	24 28	20 05
57	05 58	04 08	29 26	24 48	20 15
58	07 00	04 49	29 55	25 07	20 26
59	08 07	05 32	00♍25	25 28	20 37
60	09♋19	06♌16	00♍55	25♍49	20♎49

2h 56m 0s — 44° 0' 0" — 16 ♉ 28

LAT.	11	12	ASC	2	3
0	15♊16	12♋53	11♌32	12♍39	15♎12
5	16 17	14 22	13 03	13 47	15 42
10	17 20	15 50	14 31	14 52	16 11
15	18 26	17 19	15 58	15 55	16 38
20	19 37	18 51	17 24	16 56	17 05
21	19 52	19 10	17 41	17 08	17 10
22	20 07	19 29	17 58	17 20	17 15
23	20 23	19 48	18 16	17 33	17 21
24	20 39	20 07	18 33	17 45	17 26
25	20 55	20 26	18 50	17 57	17 32
26	21 11	20 46	19 08	18 09	17 37
27	21 28	21 06	19 26	18 21	17 42
28	21 45	21 26	19 43	18 34	17 48
29	22 03	21 46	20 01	18 46	17 53
30	22 21	22 07	20 19	18 58	17 59
31	22 39	22 28	20 37	19 11	18 04
32	22 58	22 49	20 55	19 23	18 10
33	23 18	23 11	21 14	19 36	18 16
34	23 38	23 33	21 32	19 49	18 21
35	23 59	23 55	21 51	20 01	18 27
36	24 20	24 18	22 10	20 14	18 33
37	24 42	24 41	22 29	20 27	18 39
38	25 05	25 05	22 49	20 40	18 45
39	25 28	25 29	23 08	20 54	18 51
40	25 53	25 54	23 28	21 07	18 57
41	26 18	26 19	23 49	21 21	19 03
42	26 44	26 44	24 09	21 34	19 10
43	27 12	27 10	24 30	21 48	19 16
44	27 40	27 37	24 51	22 03	19 23
45	28 10	28 05	25 12	22 17	19 30
46	28 41	28 33	25 34	22 32	19 36
47	29 13	29 02	25 56	22 46	19 44
48	29 47	29 31	26 19	23 01	19 51
49	00♋22	00♌02	26 42	23 17	19 58
50	01 00	00 33	27 05	23 33	20 06
51	01 39	01 05	27 29	23 49	20 14
52	02 21	01 38	27 54	24 05	20 22
53	03 05	02 12	28 19	24 22	20 31
54	03 51	02 47	28 44	24 39	20 39
55	04 41	03 24	29 11	24 57	20 49
56	05 34	04 01	29 37	25 15	20 58
57	06 30	04 40	00♍05	25 34	21 08
58	07 31	05 20	00 33	25 53	21 19
59	08 35	06 02	01 02	26 13	21 30
60	09♋46	06♌45	01♍32	26♍34	21♎41

3h 0m 0s — 45° 0' 0" — 17 ♉ 28

LAT.	11	12	ASC	2	3
0	16♊11	13♋49	12♌32	13♍43	16♎17
5	17 12	15 16	14 02	14 50	16 46
10	18 14	16 43	15 28	15 54	17 13
15	19 20	18 12	16 53	16 55	17 39
20	20 30	19 42	18 18	17 54	18 05
21	20 45	20 00	18 35	18 06	18 10
22	21 00	20 19	18 52	18 18	18 15
23	21 15	20 38	19 09	18 30	18 20
24	21 30	20 57	19 26	18 42	18 26
25	21 46	21 16	19 43	18 54	18 31
26	22 02	21 35	20 00	19 06	18 36
27	22 19	21 55	20 17	19 18	18 41
28	22 36	22 15	20 35	19 30	18 46
29	22 53	22 35	20 52	19 42	18 52
30	23 11	22 55	21 10	19 54	18 57
31	23 29	23 16	21 28	20 06	19 02
32	23 48	23 37	21 46	20 18	19 08
33	24 07	23 58	22 04	20 30	19 13
34	24 27	24 20	22 22	20 43	19 19
35	24 47	24 42	22 40	20 55	19 24
36	25 08	25 04	22 59	21 08	19 30
37	25 30	25 27	23 18	21 20	19 36
38	25 52	25 50	23 37	21 33	19 41
39	26 15	26 13	23 56	21 46	19 47
40	26 39	26 37	24 16	21 59	19 53
41	27 04	27 02	24 35	22 13	19 59
42	27 30	27 27	24 55	22 26	20 05
43	27 57	27 53	25 16	22 40	20 12
44	28 24	28 19	25 36	22 53	20 18
45	28 53	28 46	25 57	23 07	20 25
46	29 24	29 13	26 19	23 22	20 31
47	29 55	29 42	26 40	23 36	20 38
48	00♋28	00♌11	27 03	23 51	20 45
49	01 03	00 40	27 25	24 06	20 53
50	01 40	01 11	27 48	24 21	21 00
51	02 18	01 42	28 11	24 37	21 08
52	02 59	02 15	28 35	24 53	21 16
53	03 42	02 48	29 00	25 10	21 24
54	04 27	03 23	29 25	25 27	21 33
55	05 16	03 58	29 50	25 44	21 42
56	06 07	04 35	00♍17	26 02	21 51
57	07 02	05 13	00 44	26 20	22 01
58	08 01	05 52	01 11	26 39	22 11
59	09 04	06 32	01 39	26 59	22 22
60	10♋12	07♌14	02♍09	27♍19	22♎34

3h 4m 0s — 46° 0' 0" — 18 ♉ 28

LAT.	11	12	ASC	2	3
0	17♊07	14♋44	13♌32	14♍48	17♎21
5	18 07	16 11	15 00	15 53	17 49
10	19 08	17 37	16 26	16 55	18 15
15	20 13	19 04	17 49	17 55	18 40
20	21 23	20 33	19 12	18 53	19 05
21	21 37	20 51	19 29	19 04	19 10
22	21 52	21 10	19 45	19 16	19 15
23	22 07	21 28	20 02	19 28	19 20
24	22 22	21 47	20 19	19 39	19 25
25	22 38	22 06	20 36	19 51	19 30
26	22 54	22 25	20 52	20 02	19 35
27	23 10	22 44	21 09	20 14	19 40
28	23 27	23 04	21 27	20 26	19 45
29	23 44	23 23	21 44	20 37	19 50
30	24 01	23 43	22 01	20 49	19 55
31	24 19	24 04	22 18	21 01	20 00
32	24 38	24 24	22 36	21 13	20 05
33	24 56	24 45	22 54	21 25	20 11
34	25 16	25 06	23 12	21 37	20 16
35	25 36	25 28	23 30	21 49	20 21
36	25 56	25 50	23 48	22 01	20 27
37	26 18	26 12	24 06	22 14	20 32
38	26 40	26 35	24 25	22 26	20 38
39	27 02	26 58	24 44	22 39	20 43
40	27 26	27 21	25 03	22 51	20 49
41	27 50	27 46	25 22	23 04	20 55
42	28 15	28 10	25 42	23 17	21 01
43	28 41	28 35	26 02	23 31	21 07
44	29 09	29 01	26 22	23 44	21 13
45	29 37	29 27	26 42	23 58	21 20
46	00♋07	29 54	27 03	24 12	21 26
47	00 38	00♌22	27 25	24 26	21 33
48	01 10	00 50	27 46	24 40	21 40
49	01 44	01 19	28 08	24 55	21 47
50	02 20	01 49	28 31	25 10	21 54
51	02 57	02 20	28 54	25 25	22 02
52	03 37	02 52	29 17	25 41	22 10
53	04 19	03 24	29 41	25 57	22 18
54	05 03	03 58	00♍05	26 14	22 26
55	05 50	04 32	00 30	26 31	22 35
56	06 40	05 08	00 56	26 48	22 44
57	07 34	05 45	01 22	27 06	22 54
58	08 31	06 23	01 49	27 25	23 04
59	09 32	07 03	02 17	27 44	23 15
60	10♋39	07♌44	02♍45	28♍04	23♎26

3h 8m 0s — 47° 0' 0" — 19 ♉ 27

LAT.	11	12	ASC	2	3
0	18♊02	15♋40	14♌32	15♍53	18♎26
5	19 02	17 06	15 59	16 56	18 52
10	20 03	18 31	17 23	17 56	19 17
15	21 07	19 57	18 45	18 54	19 41
20	22 15	21 24	20 06	19 51	20 05
21	22 29	21 42	20 23	20 02	20 10
22	22 44	22 00	20 39	20 14	20 14
23	22 59	22 18	20 55	20 25	20 19
24	23 14	22 37	21 12	20 36	20 24
25	23 29	22 55	21 28	20 47	20 29
26	23 45	23 14	21 45	20 59	20 33
27	24 01	23 33	22 01	21 10	20 38
28	24 17	23 52	22 18	21 21	20 43
29	24 34	24 12	22 35	21 33	20 48
30	24 51	24 31	22 52	21 44	20 53
31	25 09	24 51	23 09	21 56	20 58
32	25 27	25 11	23 26	22 07	21 03
33	25 46	25 32	23 44	22 19	21 08
34	26 05	25 53	24 01	22 31	21 13
35	26 24	26 14	24 19	22 43	21 18
36	26 44	26 35	24 37	22 55	21 23
37	27 05	26 57	24 55	23 07	21 29
38	27 27	27 20	25 13	23 19	21 34
39	27 49	27 42	25 31	23 31	21 39
40	28 12	28 05	25 50	23 43	21 45
41	28 36	28 29	26 09	23 56	21 51
42	29 00	28 53	26 28	24 09	21 56
43	29 26	29 18	26 48	24 22	22 02
44	29 53	29 43	27 07	24 35	22 08
45	00♋21	00♌09	27 28	24 48	22 15
46	00 49	00 35	27 48	25 02	22 21
47	01 20	01 02	28 09	25 16	22 27
48	01 51	01 30	28 30	25 30	22 34
49	02 25	01 58	28 51	25 44	22 41
50	02 59	02 27	29 13	25 59	22 48
51	03 36	02 57	29 36	26 14	22 55
52	04 15	03 28	29 59	26 29	23 03
53	04 55	04 00	00♍22	26 45	23 11
54	05 39	04 33	00 46	27 01	23 19
55	06 24	05 07	01 10	27 18	23 28
56	07 13	05 42	01 35	27 35	23 37
57	08 05	06 18	02 01	27 52	23 46
58	09 01	06 55	02 27	28 11	23 56
59	10 01	07 33	02 54	28 30	24 07
60	11♋05	08♌13	03♍22	28♍49	24♎18

Koch Table of Houses for Latitudes 0° to 60° North

3h 12m 0s — 20 ♉ 26 — 48° 0' 0"

LAT.	11	12	ASC	2	3
0	18♊58	16♋36	15♌32	16♍57	19♎30
5	19 57	18 00	16 58	17 59	19 55
10	20 57	19 24	18 20	18 58	20 19
15	22 00	20 49	19 41	19 54	20 42
20	23 07	22 16	21 01	20 50	21 05
21	23 22	22 33	21 17	21 00	21 09
22	23 36	22 51	21 33	21 11	21 14
23	23 51	23 09	21 49	21 22	21 18
24	24 05	23 27	22 05	21 33	21 23
25	24 21	23 45	22 21	21 44	21 27
26	24 36	24 04	22 37	21 55	21 32
27	24 52	24 22	22 54	22 06	21 37
28	25 08	24 41	23 10	22 17	21 41
29	25 24	25 00	23 26	22 28	21 46
30	25 41	25 19	23 43	22 40	21 51
31	25 59	25 39	24 00	22 51	21 55
32	26 16	25 59	24 17	23 02	22 00
33	26 35	26 19	24 34	23 13	22 05
34	26 53	26 39	24 51	23 25	22 10
35	27 13	27 00	25 08	23 36	22 15
36	27 32	27 21	25 26	23 48	22 20
37	27 53	27 43	25 43	24 00	22 25
38	28 14	28 04	26 01	24 11	22 30
39	28 36	28 27	26 19	24 23	22 35
40	28 58	28 49	26 37	24 35	22 41
41	29 21	29 12	26 56	24 48	22 46
42	29 46	29 36	27 15	25 00	22 52
43	00♋11	00♌00	27 34	25 13	22 57
44	00 37	00 25	27 53	25 26	23 03
45	01 04	00 50	28 13	25 39	23 09
46	01 32	01 16	28 33	25 52	23 15
47	02 02	01 42	28 53	26 05	23 22
48	02 33	02 09	29 14	26 19	23 28
49	03 05	02 37	29 35	26 33	23 35
50	03 39	03 06	29 56	26 47	23 42
51	04 15	03 35	00♍18	27 02	23 49
52	04 52	04 05	00 40	27 17	23 56
53	05 32	04 36	01 03	27 32	24 04
54	06 14	05 08	01 27	27 48	24 12
55	06 59	05 41	01 50	28 04	24 20
56	07 46	06 15	02 15	28 21	24 29
57	08 37	06 50	02 40	28 38	24 38
58	09 31	07 26	03 06	28 56	24 48
59	10 29	08 04	03 32	29 15	24 59
60	11♋32	08♌43	03♍59	29♍34	25♎10

3h 16m 0s — 21 ♉ 26 — 49° 0' 0"

LAT.	11	12	ASC	2	3
0	19♊53	17♋32	16♌33	18♍02	20♎34
5	20 51	18 55	17 57	19 03	20 58
10	21 51	20 18	19 18	19 59	21 21
15	22 53	21 42	20 37	20 54	21 43
20	24 00	23 07	21 55	21 48	22 04
21	24 14	23 24	22 11	21 58	22 09
22	24 28	23 42	22 26	22 09	22 13
23	24 42	23 59	22 42	22 20	22 17
24	24 57	24 17	22 58	22 30	22 22
25	25 12	24 35	23 14	22 41	22 26
26	25 27	24 53	23 30	22 52	22 30
27	25 42	25 11	23 46	23 02	22 35
28	25 58	25 30	24 02	23 13	22 39
29	26 15	25 48	24 18	23 24	22 44
30	26 31	26 07	24 34	23 35	22 48
31	26 48	26 27	24 51	23 46	22 53
32	27 06	26 46	25 07	23 57	22 57
33	27 23	27 06	25 24	24 08	23 02
34	27 42	27 26	25 40	24 19	23 07
35	28 01	27 46	25 57	24 30	23 11
36	28 20	28 07	26 14	24 41	23 16
37	28 40	28 28	26 32	24 52	23 21
38	29 01	28 49	26 49	25 04	23 26
39	29 22	29 11	27 07	25 16	23 31
40	29 44	29 33	27 25	25 27	23 36
41	00♋07	29 56	27 43	25 39	23 41
42	00 31	00♌19	28 01	25 51	23 47
43	00 55	00 43	28 20	26 04	23 52
44	01 21	01 07	28 39	26 16	23 58
45	01 47	01 31	28 58	26 29	24 04
46	02 15	01 57	29 17	26 42	24 10
47	02 44	02 22	29 37	26 55	24 16
48	03 14	02 49	29 57	27 08	24 22
49	03 46	03 16	00♍18	27 22	24 28
50	04 19	03 44	00 39	27 36	24 35
51	04 54	04 13	01 00	27 50	24 42
52	05 30	04 42	01 22	28 05	24 49
53	06 09	05 12	01 44	28 20	24 57
54	06 50	05 43	02 07	28 35	25 04
55	07 33	06 16	02 30	28 51	25 13
56	08 20	06 49	02 54	29 07	25 21
57	09 09	07 23	03 19	29 24	25 31
58	10 01	07 58	03 44	29 42	25 40
59	10 58	08 35	04 09	00♎00	25 51
60	11♋59	09♌12	04♍36	00♎19	26♎02

3h 20m 0s — 22 ♉ 25 — 50° 0' 0"

LAT.	11	12	ASC	2	3
0	20♊49	18♋28	17♌33	19♍07	21♎38
5	21 46	19 50	18 56	20 06	22 01
10	22 45	21 12	20 15	21 01	22 23
15	23 47	22 34	21 33	21 54	22 43
20	24 52	23 58	22 50	22 46	23 04
21	25 06	24 15	23 05	22 56	23 08
22	25 20	24 32	23 20	23 07	23 12
23	25 34	24 50	23 36	23 17	23 16
24	25 48	25 07	23 51	23 27	23 20
25	26 03	25 25	24 07	23 38	23 24
26	26 18	25 42	24 22	23 48	23 29
27	26 33	26 00	24 38	23 58	23 33
28	26 49	26 19	24 54	24 09	23 37
29	27 05	26 37	25 09	24 19	23 41
30	27 21	26 55	25 25	24 30	23 46
31	27 38	27 14	25 41	24 40	23 50
32	27 55	27 33	25 57	24 51	23 54
33	28 12	27 53	26 14	25 02	23 59
34	28 30	28 12	26 30	25 12	24 03
35	28 49	28 32	26 47	25 23	24 08
36	29 08	28 53	27 03	25 34	24 12
37	29 27	29 13	27 20	25 45	24 17
38	29 48	29 34	27 37	25 57	24 22
39	00♋09	29 56	27 54	26 08	24 27
40	00 30	00♌17	28 12	26 19	24 32
41	00 53	00 39	28 30	26 31	24 37
42	01 16	01 02	28 48	26 43	24 42
43	01 40	01 25	29 06	26 54	24 47
44	02 05	01 49	29 24	27 07	24 52
45	02 31	02 13	29 43	27 19	24 58
46	02 58	02 37	00♍02	27 31	25 04
47	03 26	03 03	00 21	27 44	25 09
48	03 55	03 29	00 41	27 57	25 15
49	04 26	03 55	01 01	28 10	25 22
50	04 58	04 22	01 22	28 24	25 28
51	05 32	04 50	01 42	28 38	25 35
52	06 08	05 19	02 04	28 52	25 42
53	06 46	05 48	02 25	29 07	25 49
54	07 26	06 19	02 48	29 22	25 57
55	08 08	06 50	03 10	29 37	26 05
56	08 53	07 22	03 34	29 53	26 13
57	09 40	07 56	03 58	00♎10	26 22
58	10 32	08 30	04 22	00 27	26 32
59	11 26	09 05	04 47	00 45	26 42
60	12♋25	09♌42	05♍13	01♎04	26♎53

3h 24m 0s — 23 ♉ 23 — 51° 0' 0"

LAT.	11	12	ASC	2	3
0	21♊44	19♋24	18♌34	20♍12	22♎42
5	22 41	20 45	19 55	21 09	23 04
10	23 39	22 06	21 13	22 03	23 24
15	24 40	23 27	22 29	22 54	23 44
20	25 44	24 49	23 44	23 44	24 03
21	25 58	25 06	23 59	23 54	24 07
22	26 11	25 23	24 14	24 04	24 11
23	26 25	25 40	24 29	24 14	24 15
24	26 39	25 57	24 44	24 24	24 19
25	26 54	26 14	25 00	24 34	24 23
26	27 09	26 32	25 15	24 44	24 27
27	27 24	26 49	25 30	24 55	24 31
28	27 39	27 07	25 45	25 05	24 35
29	27 55	27 25	26 01	25 15	24 39
30	28 11	27 44	26 16	25 25	24 43
31	28 27	28 02	26 32	25 35	24 47
32	28 44	28 21	26 48	25 45	24 51
33	29 01	28 40	27 04	25 56	24 55
34	29 19	28 59	27 20	26 06	25 00
35	29 37	29 19	27 36	26 17	25 04
36	29 55	29 38	27 52	26 27	25 08
37	00♋15	29 59	28 09	26 38	25 13
38	00 34	00♌19	28 25	26 49	25 17
39	00 55	00 40	28 42	27 00	25 22
40	01 16	01 01	28 59	27 11	25 27
41	01 38	01 23	29 17	27 22	25 31
42	02 01	01 45	29 34	27 34	25 36
43	02 24	02 08	29 52	27 45	25 41
44	02 48	02 31	00♍10	27 57	25 47
45	03 14	02 54	00 28	28 09	25 52
46	03 40	03 18	00 47	28 21	25 57
47	04 08	03 43	01 06	28 34	26 03
48	04 36	04 08	01 25	28 46	26 09
49	05 06	04 34	01 44	28 59	26 15
50	05 38	05 01	02 04	29 12	26 21
51	06 11	05 28	02 25	29 26	26 28
52	06 46	05 56	02 45	29 40	26 34
53	07 22	06 25	03 07	29 54	26 42
54	08 01	06 54	03 28	00♎09	26 49
55	08 42	07 25	03 50	00 24	26 57
56	09 26	07 56	04 13	00 40	27 05
57	10 12	08 28	04 36	00 56	27 14
58	11 02	09 02	05 00	01 13	27 23
59	11 55	09 36	05 25	01 30	27 34
60	12♋52	10♌11	05♍50	01♎49	27♎44

3h 28m 0s — 24 ♉ 22 — 52° 0' 0"

LAT.	11	12	ASC	2	3
0	22♊39	20♋20	19♌35	21♍17	23♎46
5	23 35	21 41	20 54	22 12	24 06
10	24 33	23 00	22 11	23 04	24 25
15	25 33	24 20	23 25	23 54	24 44
20	26 36	25 41	24 39	24 43	25 02
21	26 50	25 57	24 53	24 52	25 06
22	27 03	26 14	25 08	25 02	25 10
23	27 17	26 30	25 23	25 12	25 13
24	27 31	26 47	25 38	25 21	25 17
25	27 45	27 04	25 53	25 31	25 21
26	27 59	27 21	26 07	25 41	25 25
27	28 14	27 39	26 22	25 51	25 28
28	28 29	27 56	26 37	26 00	25 32
29	28 44	28 14	26 52	26 10	25 36
30	29 00	28 32	27 08	26 20	25 40
31	29 16	28 50	27 23	26 30	25 44
32	29 33	29 08	27 38	26 40	25 48
33	29 50	29 27	27 54	26 50	25 52
34	00♋07	29 46	28 09	27 00	25 56
35	00 25	00♌05	28 25	27 10	26 00
36	00 43	00 24	28 41	27 20	26 04
37	01 02	00 44	28 57	27 31	26 08
38	01 21	01 04	29 14	27 41	26 13
39	01 41	01 24	29 30	27 52	26 17
40	02 02	01 45	29 47	28 03	26 22
41	02 23	02 06	00♍03	28 14	26 26
42	02 45	02 28	00 21	28 25	26 31
43	03 08	02 50	00 38	28 36	26 36
44	03 32	03 13	00 55	28 47	26 41
45	03 57	03 36	01 13	28 59	26 46
46	04 23	03 59	01 31	29 11	26 51
47	04 49	04 23	01 50	29 23	26 56
48	05 17	04 48	02 09	29 35	27 02
49	05 47	05 13	02 28	29 48	27 08
50	06 17	05 39	02 47	00♎00	27 14
51	06 50	06 05	03 07	00 14	27 20
52	07 24	06 33	03 27	00 27	27 27
53	07 59	07 01	03 48	00 41	27 34
54	08 37	07 30	04 09	00 55	27 41
55	09 17	07 59	04 30	01 10	27 49
56	09 59	08 30	04 53	01 25	27 57
57	10 44	09 01	05 15	01 41	28 05
58	11 32	09 33	05 38	01 58	28 15
59	12 24	10 07	06 02	02 15	28 25
60	13♋19	10♌41	06♍27	02♎33	28♎35

3h 32m 0s — 25 ♉ 21 — 53° 0' 0"

LAT.	11	12	ASC	2	3
0	23♊34	21♋17	20♌36	22♍23	24♎50
5	24 30	22 36	21 54	23 16	25 09
10	25 27	23 54	23 09	24 06	25 27
15	26 26	25 12	24 21	24 54	25 44
20	27 28	26 32	25 33	25 41	26 01
21	27 41	26 48	25 48	25 50	26 05
22	27 55	27 04	26 02	26 00	26 08
23	28 08	27 21	26 17	26 09	26 12
24	28 22	27 37	26 31	26 18	26 15
25	28 36	27 54	26 46	26 28	26 19
26	28 50	28 11	27 00	26 37	26 22
27	29 04	28 28	27 15	26 47	26 26
28	29 19	28 45	27 29	26 56	26 29
29	29 34	29 02	27 44	27 05	26 33
30	29 50	29 20	27 59	27 15	26 37
31	00♋05	29 38	28 14	27 25	26 40
32	00 21	29 56	28 29	27 34	26 44
33	00 38	00♌14	28 44	27 44	26 48
34	00 55	00 32	28 59	27 54	26 52
35	01 12	00 51	29 15	28 04	26 56
36	01 30	01 10	29 30	28 13	27 00
37	01 49	01 29	29 46	28 24	27 04
38	02 08	01 49	00♍02	28 34	27 08
39	02 27	02 09	00 18	28 44	27 12
40	02 48	02 29	00 34	28 54	27 16
41	03 09	02 50	00 50	29 05	27 21
42	03 30	03 11	01 07	29 16	27 25
43	03 53	03 33	01 24	29 27	27 30
44	04 16	03 55	01 41	29 38	27 35
45	04 40	04 17	01 58	29 49	27 39
46	05 05	04 40	02 16	00♎00	27 44
47	05 31	05 03	02 34	00 12	27 50
48	05 59	05 28	02 52	00 24	27 55
49	06 27	05 52	03 11	00 36	28 01
50	06 57	06 17	03 30	00 49	28 07
51	07 28	06 43	03 49	01 01	28 13
52	08 01	07 10	04 09	01 15	28 19
53	08 36	07 37	04 29	01 28	28 26
54	09 13	08 05	04 49	01 42	28 33
55	09 51	08 34	05 10	01 56	28 40
56	10 32	09 03	05 32	02 11	28 48
57	11 16	09 34	05 54	02 27	28 57
58	12 03	10 05	06 17	02 43	29 06
59	12 52	10 38	06 40	03 00	29 16
60	13♋46	11♌11	07♍04	03♎17	29♎26

3h 36m 0s — 26 ♉ 19 — 54° 0' 0"

LAT.	11	12	ASC	2	3
0	24♊30	22♋13	21♌37	23♍28	25♎53
5	25 24	23 31	22 54	24 19	26 11
10	26 20	24 48	24 07	25 07	26 28
15	27 19	26 05	25 18	25 54	26 44
20	28 20	27 23	26 28	26 39	27 00
21	28 33	27 39	26 42	26 48	27 03
22	28 46	27 55	26 56	26 57	27 07
23	28 59	28 11	27 10	27 06	27 10
24	29 13	28 27	27 24	27 15	27 13
25	29 26	28 44	27 39	27 24	27 17
26	29 40	29 00	27 53	27 33	27 20
27	29 55	29 17	28 07	27 42	27 23
28	00♋09	29 34	28 21	27 52	27 27
29	00 24	29 51	28 36	28 01	27 30
30	00 39	00♌08	28 50	28 10	27 34
31	00 54	00 25	29 05	28 19	27 37
32	01 10	00 43	29 19	28 28	27 41
33	01 27	01 01	29 34	28 38	27 44
34	01 43	01 19	29 49	28 47	27 48
35	02 00	01 37	00♍04	28 57	27 51
36	02 18	01 56	00 19	29 06	27 55
37	02 36	02 15	00 34	29 16	27 59
38	02 54	02 34	00 50	29 26	28 03
39	03 14	02 53	01 06	29 36	28 07
40	03 33	03 13	01 21	29 46	28 11
41	03 54	03 34	01 37	29 56	28 15
42	04 15	03 54	01 54	00♎07	28 19
43	04 37	04 15	02 10	00 17	28 24
44	04 59	04 37	02 27	00 28	28 28
45	05 23	04 59	02 44	00 39	28 33
46	05 47	05 21	03 01	00 50	28 38
47	06 13	05 44	03 18	01 01	28 43
48	06 40	06 07	03 36	01 13	28 48
49	07 07	06 31	03 54	01 24	28 53
50	07 36	06 56	04 13	01 37	28 59
51	08 07	07 21	04 31	01 49	29 05
52	08 39	07 47	04 51	02 02	29 11
53	09 13	08 13	05 10	02 15	29 17
54	09 48	08 41	05 30	02 28	29 24
55	10 26	09 09	05 51	02 42	29 31
56	11 06	09 37	06 11	02 57	29 39
57	11 48	10 07	06 33	03 12	29 47
58	12 33	10 37	06 55	03 28	29 56
59	13 21	11 09	07 17	03 44	00♏06
60	14♋13	11♌41	07♍40	04♎02	00♏17

3h 40m 0s — 27 ♉ 17 — 55° 0' 0"

LAT.	11	12	ASC	2	3
0	25♊25	23♋10	22♌39	24♍33	26♎57
5	26 19	24 27	23 54	25 22	27 13
10	27 14	25 42	25 05	26 09	27 29
15	28 11	26 58	26 14	26 54	27 44
20	29 12	28 15	27 23	27 37	27 59
21	29 25	28 30	27 37	27 46	28 02
22	29 37	28 46	27 50	27 55	28 05
23	29 50	29 02	28 04	28 04	28 08
24	00♋04	29 18	28 18	28 12	28 11
25	00 17	29 34	28 32	28 21	28 14
26	00 31	29 50	28 46	28 30	28 17
27	00 45	00♌06	28 59	28 38	28 20
28	00 59	00 23	29 13	28 47	28 24
29	01 13	00 39	29 27	28 56	28 27
30	01 28	00 56	29 42	29 05	28 30
31	01 43	01 13	29 56	29 14	28 33
32	01 59	01 30	00♍10	29 23	28 37
33	02 15	01 48	00 24	29 32	28 40
34	02 31	02 05	00 39	29 41	28 43
35	02 48	02 23	00 53	29 50	28 47
36	03 05	02 42	01 08	29 59	28 50
37	03 23	03 00	01 23	00♎09	28 54
38	03 41	03 19	01 38	00 18	28 58
39	04 00	03 38	01 53	00 28	29 01
40	04 19	03 57	02 09	00 37	29 05
41	04 39	04 17	02 24	00 47	29 09
42	05 00	04 37	02 40	00 57	29 13
43	05 21	04 58	02 56	01 07	29 17
44	05 43	05 19	03 12	01 18	29 22
45	06 06	05 40	03 29	01 28	29 26
46	06 30	06 02	03 46	01 39	29 31
47	06 55	06 24	04 03	01 50	29 36
48	07 21	06 47	04 20	02 01	29 40
49	07 48	07 10	04 37	02 13	29 46
50	08 16	07 34	04 55	02 24	29 51
51	08 46	07 59	05 14	02 36	29 57
52	09 17	08 24	05 32	02 49	00♏03
53	09 49	08 50	05 51	03 02	00 09
54	10 24	09 16	06 11	03 15	00 15
55	11 00	09 43	06 31	03 28	00 23
56	11 39	10 11	06 51	03 43	00 30
57	12 20	10 40	07 12	03 57	00 38
58	13 04	11 09	07 33	04 13	00 47
59	13 50	11 40	07 55	04 29	00 56
60	14♋40	12♌11	08♍17	04♎46	01♏07

Koch Table of Houses for Latitudes 0° to 60° North

3h 44m 0s — 28 ♉ 15 — 56° 0' 0"

LAT.	11	12	ASC	2	3
0	26♊20	24♋06	23♌41	25♍38	28♎00
5	27 13	25 22	24 53	26 26	28 15
10	28 08	26 37	26 03	27 11	28 29
15	29 04	27 51	27 11	27 54	28 43
20	00♋04	29 06	28 18	28 36	28 57
21	00 16	29 22	28 31	28 44	29 00
22	00 29	29 37	28 45	28 52	29 03
23	00 42	29 52	28 58	29 01	29 06
24	00 55	00♌08	29 11	29 09	29 09
25	01 08	00 24	29 25	29 17	29 12
26	01 21	00 39	29 38	29 26	29 15
27	01 35	00 55	29 52	29 34	29 18
28	01 49	01 12	00♍06	29 43	29 20
29	02 03	01 28	00 19	29 51	29 23
30	02 18	01 44	00 33	00♎00	29 26
31	02 32	02 01	00 47	00 08	29 30
32	02 48	02 18	01 01	00 17	29 33
33	03 03	02 35	01 15	00 26	29 36
34	03 19	02 52	01 29	00 34	29 39
35	03 36	03 10	01 43	00 43	29 42
36	03 52	03 28	01 57	00 52	29 46
37	04 10	03 46	02 12	01 01	29 49
38	04 27	04 04	02 26	01 10	29 52
39	04 46	04 23	02 41	01 19	29 56
40	05 05	04 41	02 56	01 29	00♏00
41	05 24	05 01	03 11	01 38	00 03
42	05 44	05 20	03 27	01 48	00 07
43	06 05	05 40	03 42	01 58	00 11
44	06 27	06 01	03 58	02 08	00 15
45	06 49	06 22	04 14	02 18	00 19
46	07 12	06 43	04 30	02 28	00 24
47	07 36	07 05	04 47	02 39	00 28
48	08 02	07 27	05 04	02 50	00 33
49	08 28	07 50	05 21	03 01	00 38
50	08 55	08 13	05 38	03 12	00 43
51	09 24	08 37	05 56	03 24	00 48
52	09 54	09 01	06 14	03 36	00 54
53	10 26	09 26	06 32	03 48	01 00
54	11 00	09 52	06 51	04 01	01 06
55	11 35	10 18	07 11	04 14	01 13
56	12 12	10 45	07 30	04 28	01 21
57	12 52	11 13	07 51	04 43	01 29
58	13 34	11 42	08 11	04 58	01 37
59	14 19	12 11	08 33	05 13	01 47
60	15♋08	12♌41	08♍54	05♎30	01♏57

3h 48m 0s — 29 ♉ 13 — 57° 0' 0"

LAT.	11	12	ASC	2	3
0	27♊15	25♋03	24♌42	26♍44	29♎03
5	28 08	26 18	25 54	27 29	29 17
10	29 01	27 31	27 02	28 12	29 30
15	29 57	28 44	28 08	28 53	29 43
20	00♋56	29 58	29 13	29 34	29 56
21	01 08	00♌13	29 26	29 42	29 58
22	01 20	00 28	29 39	29 50	00♏01
23	01 33	00 43	29 52	29 58	00 04
24	01 45	00 58	00♍05	00♎06	00 06
25	01 58	01 14	00 18	00 14	00 09
26	02 12	01 29	00 31	00 22	00 12
27	02 25	01 45	00 44	00 30	00 14
28	02 39	02 01	00 58	00 38	00 17
29	02 53	02 17	01 11	00 46	00 20
30	03 07	02 33	01 24	00 54	00 23
31	03 21	02 49	01 38	01 03	00 26
32	03 36	03 05	01 51	01 11	00 28
33	03 52	03 22	02 05	01 19	00 31
34	04 07	03 39	02 19	01 28	00 34
35	04 23	03 56	02 32	01 36	00 37
36	04 40	04 13	02 46	01 45	00 40
37	04 56	04 31	03 00	01 53	00 44
38	05 14	04 49	03 15	02 02	00 47
39	05 32	05 07	03 29	02 11	00 50
40	05 50	05 26	03 44	02 20	00 54
41	06 09	05 44	03 58	02 29	00 57
42	06 29	06 04	04 13	02 39	01 01
43	06 49	06 23	04 28	02 48	01 04
44	07 10	06 43	04 44	02 58	01 08
45	07 32	07 03	04 59	03 07	01 12
46	07 55	07 24	05 15	03 17	01 16
47	08 18	07 45	05 31	03 28	01 21
48	08 43	08 07	05 47	03 38	01 25
49	09 08	08 29	06 04	03 49	01 30
50	09 35	08 51	06 21	04 00	01 35
51	10 03	09 15	06 38	04 11	01 40
52	10 32	09 38	06 56	04 23	01 45
53	11 03	10 03	07 14	04 35	01 51
54	11 35	10 28	07 32	04 47	01 57
55	12 10	10 53	07 51	05 00	02 04
56	12 46	11 19	08 10	05 14	02 11
57	13 24	11 46	08 30	05 28	02 19
58	14 05	12 14	08 50	05 42	02 27
59	14 49	12 42	09 10	05 58	02 36
60	15♋35	13♌11	09♍31	06♎14	02♏47

3h 52m 0s — 00 ♊ 11 — 58° 0' 0"

LAT.	11	12	ASC	2	3
0	28♊10	26♋00	25♌44	27♍49	00♏06
5	29 02	27 13	26 54	28 33	00 18
10	29 55	28 25	28 00	29 14	00 30
15	00♋50	29 37	29 05	29 53	00 42
20	01 47	00♌49	00♍08	00♎32	00 54
21	01 59	01 04	00 21	00 40	00 56
22	02 11	01 19	00 33	00 47	00 59
23	02 24	01 34	00 46	00 55	01 01
24	02 36	01 49	00 59	01 03	01 04
25	02 49	02 04	01 11	01 10	01 06
26	03 02	02 19	01 24	01 18	01 09
27	03 15	02 34	01 37	01 26	01 11
28	03 28	02 50	01 50	01 33	01 14
29	03 42	03 05	02 03	01 41	01 16
30	03 56	03 21	02 16	01 49	01 19
31	04 10	03 37	02 29	01 57	01 21
32	04 25	03 53	02 42	02 05	01 24
33	04 40	04 09	02 55	02 13	01 27
34	04 55	04 26	03 08	02 21	01 29
35	05 11	04 42	03 22	02 29	01 32
36	05 27	04 59	03 35	02 37	01 35
37	05 43	05 17	03 49	02 46	01 38
38	06 00	05 34	04 03	02 54	01 41
39	06 18	05 52	04 17	03 03	01 44
40	06 36	06 10	04 31	03 11	01 47
41	06 54	06 28	04 45	03 20	01 51
42	07 13	06 47	05 00	03 29	01 54
43	07 33	07 06	05 15	03 38	01 57
44	07 54	07 25	05 29	03 47	02 01
45	08 15	07 45	05 44	03 57	02 05
46	08 37	08 05	06 00	04 06	02 09
47	09 00	08 26	06 15	04 16	02 13
48	09 24	08 47	06 31	04 26	02 17
49	09 49	09 08	06 47	04 37	02 21
50	10 14	09 30	07 04	04 47	02 26
51	10 42	09 53	07 20	04 58	02 31
52	11 10	10 16	07 38	05 10	02 36
53	11 40	10 39	07 55	05 21	02 42
54	12 11	11 03	08 13	05 33	02 48
55	12 44	11 28	08 31	05 46	02 54
56	13 19	11 54	08 49	05 59	03 01
57	13 57	12 20	09 08	06 12	03 09
58	14 36	12 46	09 28	06 27	03 17
59	15 18	13 14	09 48	06 42	03 26
60	16♋03	13♌42	10♍08	06♎58	03♏36

3h 56m 0s — 01 ♊ 08 — 59° 0' 0"

LAT.	11	12	ASC	2	3
0	29♊05	26♋57	26♌47	28♍55	01♏08
5	29 56	28 09	27 54	29 36	01 20
10	00♋48	29 20	28 59	00♎15	01 31
15	01 42	00♌30	00♍02	00 53	01 41
20	02 39	01 41	01 03	01 30	01 52
21	02 51	01 56	01 16	01 37	01 54
22	03 03	02 10	01 28	01 45	01 56
23	03 15	02 24	01 40	01 52	01 59
24	03 27	02 39	01 52	01 59	02 01
25	03 39	02 54	02 05	02 07	02 03
26	03 52	03 09	02 17	02 14	02 05
27	04 05	03 24	02 30	02 21	02 08
28	04 18	03 39	02 42	02 29	02 10
29	04 31	03 54	02 55	02 36	02 12
30	04 45	04 09	03 07	02 44	02 15
31	04 59	04 25	03 20	02 51	02 17
32	05 13	04 41	03 33	02 59	02 19
33	05 28	04 56	03 46	03 07	02 22
34	05 43	05 13	03 58	03 14	02 24
35	05 58	05 29	04 11	03 22	02 27
36	06 14	05 45	04 25	03 30	02 30
37	06 30	06 02	04 38	03 38	02 32
38	06 47	06 19	04 51	03 46	02 35
39	07 04	06 37	05 05	03 54	02 38
40	07 21	06 54	05 19	04 03	02 41
41	07 39	07 12	05 32	04 11	02 44
42	07 58	07 30	05 46	04 20	02 47
43	08 17	07 49	06 01	04 28	02 50
44	08 37	08 07	06 15	04 37	02 54
45	08 58	08 27	06 30	04 46	02 57
46	09 19	08 46	06 45	04 55	03 01
47	09 42	09 06	07 00	05 05	03 05
48	10 05	09 27	07 15	05 15	03 09
49	10 29	09 48	07 31	05 25	03 13
50	10 54	10 09	07 47	05 35	03 17
51	11 20	10 31	08 03	05 45	03 22
52	11 48	10 53	08 19	05 56	03 27
53	12 17	11 16	08 36	06 07	03 32
54	12 47	11 39	08 53	06 19	03 38
55	13 19	12 03	09 11	06 31	03 44
56	13 53	12 28	09 29	06 44	03 51
57	14 29	12 53	09 47	06 57	03 58
58	15 07	13 19	10 06	07 11	04 06
59	15 47	13 45	10 26	07 26	04 15
60	16♋31	14♌12	10♍46	07♎41	04♏25

4h 0m 0s — 02 ♊ 05 — 60° 0' 0"

LAT.	11	12	ASC	2	3
0	00♋00	27♋55	27♌49	00♎00	02♏11
5	00 51	29 05	28 55	00 40	02 21
10	01 42	00♌15	29 58	01 17	02 31
15	02 35	01 23	00♍59	01 53	02 40
20	03 31	02 33	01 58	02 28	02 50
21	03 42	02 47	02 10	02 35	02 52
22	03 54	03 01	02 22	02 42	02 54
23	04 06	03 15	02 34	02 49	02 56
24	04 18	03 30	02 46	02 56	02 58
25	04 30	03 44	02 58	03 03	03 00
26	04 42	03 58	03 10	03 10	03 02
27	04 55	04 13	03 22	03 17	03 04
28	05 08	04 28	03 34	03 24	03 06
29	05 21	04 43	03 47	03 31	03 08
30	05 34	04 58	03 59	03 38	03 10
31	05 48	05 13	04 11	03 46	03 12
32	06 02	05 28	04 23	03 53	03 15
33	06 16	05 44	04 36	04 00	03 17
34	06 31	05 59	04 48	04 07	03 19
35	06 46	06 15	05 01	04 15	03 22
36	07 01	06 31	05 14	04 22	03 24
37	07 17	06 48	05 27	04 30	03 26
38	07 33	07 04	05 40	04 38	03 29
39	07 49	07 21	05 53	04 46	03 32
40	08 07	07 38	06 06	04 54	03 34
41	08 24	07 56	06 20	05 02	03 37
42	08 42	08 13	06 33	05 10	03 40
43	09 01	08 31	06 47	05 18	03 43
44	09 21	08 50	07 01	05 27	03 46
45	09 41	09 09	07 15	05 35	03 49
46	10 02	09 28	07 29	05 44	03 53
47	10 23	09 47	07 44	05 53	03 56
48	10 46	10 07	07 59	06 03	04 00
49	11 09	10 27	08 14	06 12	04 04
50	11 34	10 48	08 29	06 22	04 08
51	11 59	11 09	08 45	06 32	04 13
52	12 26	11 31	09 01	06 43	04 18
53	12 54	11 53	09 17	06 54	04 23
54	13 23	12 15	09 34	07 05	04 28
55	13 54	12 39	09 51	07 17	04 34
56	14 27	13 02	10 09	07 29	04 41
57	15 01	13 27	10 26	07 42	04 48
58	15 38	13 51	10 45	07 55	04 56
59	16 17	14 17	11 03	08 10	05 04
60	16♋59	14♌43	11♍23	08♎25	05♏14

4h 4m 0s — 03 ♊ 03 — 61° 0' 0"

LAT.	11	12	ASC	2	3
0	00♋55	28♋52	28♌52	01♎05	03♏13
5	01 45	00♌01	29 56	01 43	03 22
10	02 35	01 09	00♍57	02 18	03 31
15	03 28	02 17	01 56	02 53	03 39
20	04 22	03 25	02 54	03 26	03 48
21	04 33	03 38	03 05	03 33	03 49
22	04 45	03 52	03 17	03 39	03 51
23	04 56	04 06	03 28	03 46	03 53
24	05 08	04 20	03 40	03 52	03 55
25	05 20	04 34	03 52	03 59	03 56
26	05 32	04 48	04 03	04 06	03 58
27	05 45	05 03	04 15	04 12	04 00
28	05 57	05 17	04 27	04 19	04 02
29	06 10	05 32	04 39	04 26	04 04
30	06 23	05 46	04 50	04 33	04 06
31	06 37	06 01	05 02	04 40	04 08
32	06 50	06 16	05 14	04 47	04 10
33	07 04	06 31	05 26	04 54	04 12
34	07 18	06 46	05 38	05 01	04 14
35	07 33	07 02	05 51	05 08	04 16
36	07 48	07 18	06 03	05 15	04 18
37	08 03	07 34	06 15	05 22	04 20
38	08 19	07 50	06 28	05 29	04 23
39	08 35	08 06	06 41	05 37	04 25
40	08 52	08 23	06 54	05 45	04 28
41	09 09	08 40	07 07	05 52	04 30
42	09 27	08 57	07 20	06 00	04 33
43	09 45	09 14	07 33	06 08	04 36
44	10 04	09 32	07 47	06 16	04 38
45	10 24	09 50	08 00	06 24	04 41
46	10 44	10 09	08 14	06 33	04 45
47	11 05	10 28	08 28	06 42	04 48
48	11 27	10 47	08 43	06 51	04 51
49	11 50	11 07	08 57	07 00	04 55
50	12 13	11 27	09 12	07 09	04 59
51	12 38	11 47	09 27	07 19	05 03
52	13 04	12 08	09 43	07 29	05 08
53	13 31	12 30	09 59	07 40	05 13
54	13 59	12 51	10 15	07 50	05 18
55	14 29	13 14	10 31	08 02	05 24
56	15 01	13 37	10 48	08 14	05 30
57	15 34	14 00	11 05	08 26	05 37
58	16 09	14 24	11 23	08 39	05 44
59	16 47	14 48	11 41	08 53	05 53
60	17♋27	15♌13	12♍00	09♎08	06♏03

4h 8m 0s — 04 ♊ 00 — 62° 0' 0"

LAT.	11	12	ASC	2	3
0	01♋50	29♋49	29♌54	02♎11	04♏16
5	02 39	00♌58	00♍56	02 46	04 23
10	03 29	02 04	01 56	03 20	04 31
15	04 20	03 10	02 53	03 52	04 38
20	05 14	04 17	03 49	04 24	04 45
21	05 25	04 30	04 00	04 30	04 47
22	05 36	04 44	04 12	04 36	04 48
23	05 47	04 57	04 23	04 43	04 50
24	05 59	05 11	04 34	04 49	04 51
25	06 11	05 24	04 45	04 55	04 53
26	06 23	05 38	04 56	05 02	04 54
27	06 35	05 52	05 08	05 08	04 56
28	06 47	06 06	05 19	05 14	04 58
29	07 00	06 20	05 31	05 21	04 59
30	07 12	06 35	05 42	05 27	05 01
31	07 25	06 49	05 54	05 34	05 03
32	07 39	07 04	06 05	05 40	05 05
33	07 52	07 18	06 17	05 47	05 06
34	08 06	07 33	06 28	05 54	05 08
35	08 21	07 49	06 40	06 00	05 10
36	08 35	08 04	06 52	06 07	05 12
37	08 50	08 19	07 04	06 14	05 14
38	09 05	08 35	07 16	06 21	05 16
39	09 21	08 51	07 29	06 28	05 18
40	09 38	09 07	07 41	06 35	05 21
41	09 54	09 24	07 54	06 43	05 23
42	10 11	09 40	08 06	06 50	05 25
43	10 29	09 57	08 19	06 58	05 28
44	10 48	10 15	08 32	07 06	05 30
45	11 07	10 32	08 46	07 13	05 33
46	11 26	10 50	08 59	07 22	05 36
47	11 47	11 09	09 13	07 30	05 39
48	12 08	11 27	09 27	07 38	05 42
49	12 30	11 46	09 41	07 47	05 46
50	12 53	12 06	09 55	07 56	05 50
51	13 17	12 26	10 10	08 06	05 54
52	13 42	12 46	10 25	08 15	05 58
53	14 08	13 07	10 40	08 25	06 02
54	14 36	13 28	10 56	08 36	06 07
55	15 04	13 49	11 11	08 47	06 13
56	15 35	14 11	11 28	08 58	06 19
57	16 07	14 34	11 44	09 10	06 26
58	16 41	14 57	12 01	09 23	06 33
59	17 17	15 20	12 19	09 37	06 41
60	17♋55	15♌44	12♍37	09♎51	06♏51

4h 12m 0s — 04 ♊ 57 — 63° 0' 0"

LAT.	11	12	ASC	2	3
0	02♋45	00♌47	00♍57	03♎16	05♏18
5	03 34	01 54	01 57	03 50	05 24
10	04 22	02 59	02 55	04 21	05 30
15	05 13	04 04	03 50	04 52	05 36
20	06 05	05 09	04 45	05 22	05 43
21	06 16	05 22	04 55	05 28	05 44
22	06 27	05 35	05 06	05 33	05 45
23	06 38	05 48	05 17	05 39	05 46
24	06 50	06 01	05 28	05 45	05 48
25	07 01	06 15	05 39	05 51	05 49
26	07 13	06 28	05 50	05 57	05 51
27	07 25	06 42	06 01	06 03	05 52
28	07 37	06 56	06 12	06 09	05 53
29	07 49	07 09	06 23	06 15	05 55
30	08 01	07 23	06 34	06 22	05 56
31	08 14	07 37	06 45	06 28	05 58
32	08 27	07 52	06 56	06 34	05 59
33	08 40	08 06	07 07	06 40	06 01
34	08 54	08 20	07 19	06 46	06 02
35	09 08	08 35	07 30	06 53	06 04
36	09 22	08 50	07 42	06 59	06 06
37	09 37	09 05	07 53	07 06	06 08
38	09 52	09 20	08 05	07 13	06 09
39	10 07	09 36	08 17	07 19	06 11
40	10 23	09 52	08 29	07 26	06 13
41	10 39	10 08	08 41	07 33	06 15
42	10 56	10 24	08 53	07 40	06 18
43	11 13	10 40	09 06	07 47	06 20
44	11 31	10 57	09 18	07 55	06 22
45	11 50	11 14	09 31	08 02	06 25
46	12 09	11 32	09 44	08 10	06 27
47	12 29	11 49	09 57	08 18	06 30
48	12 49	12 08	10 11	08 26	06 33
49	13 10	12 26	10 24	08 35	06 37
50	13 33	12 45	10 38	08 43	06 40
51	13 56	13 04	10 52	08 52	06 44
52	14 20	13 24	11 07	09 01	06 48
53	14 45	13 44	11 21	09 11	06 52
54	15 12	14 04	11 36	09 21	06 57
55	15 40	14 25	11 52	09 32	07 02
56	16 09	14 46	12 07	09 43	07 08
57	16 40	15 08	12 23	09 55	07 14
58	17 12	15 30	12 40	10 07	07 21
59	17 47	15 52	12 57	10 20	07 30
60	18♋23	16♌15	13♍14	10♎34	07♏39

Koch Table of Houses for Latitudes 0° to 60° North

4h 16m 0s — 64° 0' 0" — 05 ♊ 54

LAT.	11	12	ASC	2	3
0	03♋40	01♌45	02♍00	04♎22	06♏19
5	04 28	02 50	02 58	04 53	06 25
10	05 16	03 54	03 54	05 23	06 30
15	06 05	04 57	04 47	05 51	06 35
20	06 57	06 01	05 40	06 19	06 40
21	07 07	06 13	05 50	06 25	06 41
22	07 18	06 26	06 01	06 31	06 42
23	07 29	06 39	06 11	06 36	06 43
24	07 40	06 52	06 22	06 42	06 44
25	07 51	07 05	06 32	06 47	06 45
26	08 03	07 18	06 43	06 53	06 46
27	08 14	07 32	06 53	06 59	06 48
28	08 26	07 45	07 04	07 04	06 49
29	08 38	07 58	07 15	07 10	06 50
30	08 50	08 12	07 25	07 16	06 51
31	09 03	08 26	07 36	07 22	06 52
32	09 16	08 40	07 47	07 27	06 54
33	09 29	08 53	07 58	07 33	06 55
34	09 42	09 08	08 09	07 39	06 56
35	09 55	09 22	08 20	07 45	06 58
36	10 09	09 36	08 31	07 51	06 59
37	10 23	09 51	08 42	07 58	07 01
38	10 38	10 06	08 53	08 04	07 03
39	10 53	10 21	09 05	08 10	07 04
40	11 08	10 36	09 16	08 17	07 06
41	11 24	10 52	09 28	08 23	07 08
42	11 41	11 08	09 40	08 30	07 10
43	11 57	11 24	09 52	08 37	07 12
44	12 15	11 40	10 04	08 44	07 14
45	12 33	11 56	10 16	08 51	07 16
46	12 51	12 13	10 29	08 58	07 19
47	13 10	12 30	10 42	09 06	07 21
48	13 30	12 48	10 54	09 14	07 24
49	13 51	13 06	11 08	09 22	07 27
50	14 13	13 24	11 21	09 30	07 30
51	14 35	13 43	11 35	09 39	07 33
52	14 58	14 01	11 48	09 47	07 37
53	15 23	14 21	12 03	09 57	07 41
54	15 48	14 40	12 17	10 06	07 46
55	16 15	15 00	12 32	10 17	07 51
56	16 43	15 21	12 47	10 27	07 56
57	17 13	15 42	13 02	10 39	08 02
58	17 44	16 03	13 18	10 51	08 09
59	18 17	16 24	13 34	11 03	08 17
60	18♋52	16♌46	13♍51	11♎17	08♏27

4h 20m 0s — 65° 0' 0" — 06 ♊ 50

LAT.	11	12	ASC	2	3
0	04♋35	02♌43	03♍03	05♎27	07♏21
5	05 22	03 47	04 00	05 56	07 25
10	06 09	04 49	04 53	06 24	07 29
15	06 58	05 51	05 45	06 51	07 33
20	07 48	06 53	06 36	07 17	07 37
21	07 59	07 05	06 46	07 22	07 38
22	08 09	07 18	06 56	07 27	07 39
23	08 20	07 30	07 06	07 33	07 39
24	08 31	07 43	07 16	07 38	07 40
25	08 42	07 56	07 26	07 43	07 41
26	08 53	08 09	07 36	07 49	07 42
27	09 04	08 21	07 46	07 54	07 43
28	09 16	08 34	07 57	07 59	07 44
29	09 28	08 48	08 07	08 05	07 45
30	09 39	09 01	08 17	08 10	07 46
31	09 52	09 14	08 27	08 15	07 47
32	10 04	09 27	08 38	08 21	07 48
33	10 17	09 41	08 48	08 26	07 49
34	10 30	09 55	08 59	08 32	07 50
35	10 43	10 09	09 09	08 38	07 52
36	10 56	10 23	09 20	08 43	07 53
37	11 10	10 37	09 31	08 49	07 54
38	11 24	10 51	09 42	08 55	07 55
39	11 39	11 06	09 53	09 01	07 57
40	11 54	11 21	10 04	09 07	07 58
41	12 09	11 36	10 15	09 13	08 00
42	12 25	11 51	10 27	09 20	08 02
43	12 41	12 07	10 38	09 26	08 03
44	12 58	12 22	10 50	09 33	08 05
45	13 16	12 39	11 02	09 40	08 07
46	13 34	12 55	11 14	09 47	08 09
47	13 52	13 11	11 26	09 54	08 12
48	14 12	13 28	11 38	10 01	08 14
49	14 32	13 46	11 51	10 09	08 17
50	14 52	14 03	12 04	10 17	08 20
51	15 14	14 21	12 17	10 25	08 23
52	15 37	14 39	12 30	10 33	08 26
53	16 00	14 58	12 44	10 42	08 30
54	16 25	15 17	12 58	10 51	08 35
55	16 51	15 36	13 12	11 01	08 39
56	17 18	15 56	13 26	11 11	08 44
57	17 46	16 16	13 41	11 22	08 50
58	18 16	16 36	13 57	11 34	08 57
59	18 48	16 57	14 12	11 46	09 05
60	19♋21	17♌17	14♍28	12♎00	09♏14

4h 24m 0s — 66° 0' 0" — 07 ♊ 47

LAT.	11	12	ASC	2	3
0	05♋30	03♌41	04♍07	06♎32	08♏23
5	06 17	04 44	05 01	06 59	08 25
10	07 03	05 45	05 53	07 25	08 28
15	07 50	06 45	06 42	07 50	08 31
20	08 40	07 45	07 31	08 15	08 34
21	08 50	07 57	07 41	08 20	08 34
22	09 00	08 09	07 51	08 24	08 35
23	09 11	08 22	08 00	08 29	08 36
24	09 21	08 34	08 10	08 34	08 36
25	09 32	08 46	08 20	08 39	08 37
26	09 43	08 59	08 30	08 44	08 38
27	09 54	09 11	08 39	08 49	08 38
28	10 05	09 24	08 49	08 54	08 39
29	10 17	09 37	08 59	08 59	08 40
30	10 28	09 50	09 09	09 04	08 41
31	10 40	10 02	09 19	09 09	08 41
32	10 52	10 16	09 29	09 14	08 42
33	11 05	10 29	09 39	09 19	08 43
34	11 17	10 42	09 49	09 25	08 44
35	11 30	10 56	09 59	09 30	08 45
36	11 43	11 09	10 10	09 35	08 46
37	11 57	11 23	10 20	09 41	08 47
38	12 11	11 37	10 30	09 46	08 48
39	12 25	11 51	10 41	09 52	08 49
40	12 39	12 06	10 52	09 58	08 51
41	12 54	12 20	11 02	10 04	08 52
42	13 10	12 35	11 13	10 09	08 53
43	13 26	12 50	11 24	10 16	08 55
44	13 42	13 05	11 36	10 22	08 57
45	13 59	13 21	11 47	10 28	08 58
46	14 16	13 37	11 59	10 35	09 00
47	14 34	13 53	12 10	10 42	09 02
48	14 53	14 09	12 22	10 49	09 04
49	15 12	14 26	12 34	10 56	09 07
50	15 32	14 43	12 47	11 03	09 09
51	15 53	15 00	12 59	11 11	09 12
52	16 15	15 17	13 12	11 19	09 16
53	16 38	15 35	13 25	11 27	09 19
54	17 01	15 54	13 39	11 36	09 23
55	17 26	16 12	13 52	11 46	09 27
56	17 52	16 31	14 06	11 56	09 32
57	18 19	16 50	14 20	12 06	09 38
58	18 48	17 10	14 35	12 17	09 45
59	19 18	17 29	14 50	12 29	09 52
60	19♋50	17♌49	15♍05	12♎43	10♏01

4h 28m 0s — 67° 0' 0" — 08 ♊ 43

LAT.	11	12	ASC	2	3
0	06♋26	04♌39	05♍10	07♎37	09♏24
5	07 11	05 41	06 02	08 03	09 25
10	07 56	06 40	06 52	08 27	09 27
15	08 43	07 39	07 40	08 50	09 29
20	09 31	08 37	08 27	09 12	09 30
21	09 41	08 49	08 36	09 17	09 31
22	09 51	09 01	08 46	09 21	09 31
23	10 02	09 13	08 55	09 26	09 32
24	10 12	09 25	09 04	09 30	09 32
25	10 23	09 37	09 14	09 35	09 32
26	10 33	09 49	09 23	09 39	09 33
27	10 44	10 01	09 32	09 44	09 33
28	10 55	10 14	09 42	09 49	09 34
29	11 06	10 26	09 51	09 53	09 34
30	11 17	10 38	10 01	09 58	09 35
31	11 29	10 51	10 10	10 03	09 36
32	11 41	11 04	10 20	10 07	09 36
33	11 53	11 16	10 30	10 12	09 37
34	12 05	11 29	10 39	10 17	09 37
35	12 18	11 43	10 49	10 22	09 38
36	12 31	11 56	10 59	10 27	09 39
37	12 44	12 09	11 09	10 32	09 40
38	12 57	12 23	11 19	10 37	09 41
39	13 11	12 36	11 29	10 43	09 42
40	13 25	12 50	11 39	10 48	09 43
41	13 40	13 04	11 50	10 53	09 44
42	13 54	13 19	12 00	10 59	09 45
43	14 10	13 33	12 11	11 05	09 46
44	14 26	13 48	12 22	11 11	09 48
45	14 42	14 03	12 32	11 17	09 49
46	14 59	14 18	12 44	11 23	09 51
47	15 16	14 34	12 55	11 29	09 52
48	15 34	14 50	13 06	11 36	09 54
49	15 53	15 06	13 18	11 43	09 56
50	16 12	15 22	13 30	11 50	09 59
51	16 33	15 39	13 42	11 57	10 01
52	16 54	15 56	13 54	12 05	10 04
53	17 15	16 13	14 07	12 13	10 08
54	17 38	16 30	14 19	12 21	10 11
55	18 02	16 48	14 32	12 30	10 15
56	18 27	17 06	14 46	12 39	10 20
57	18 53	17 25	14 59	12 49	10 25
58	19 20	17 43	15 13	13 00	10 32
59	19 49	18 02	15 28	13 12	10 39
60	20♋20	18♌20	15♍42	13♎25	10♏48

4h 32m 0s — 68° 0' 0" — 09 ♊ 40

LAT.	11	12	ASC	2	3
0	07♋21	05♌38	06♍14	08♎43	10♏25
5	08 05	06 38	07 04	09 06	10 25
10	08 50	07 36	07 52	09 28	10 26
15	09 36	08 33	08 38	09 49	10 26
20	10 23	09 30	09 23	10 10	10 27
21	10 33	09 41	09 32	10 14	10 27
22	10 43	09 53	09 41	10 18	10 27
23	10 53	10 04	09 50	10 22	10 27
24	11 03	10 16	09 58	10 26	10 28
25	11 13	10 28	10 07	10 31	10 28
26	11 23	10 40	10 16	10 35	10 28
27	11 34	10 51	10 25	10 39	10 28
28	11 45	11 03	10 34	10 43	10 29
29	11 55	11 15	10 43	10 48	10 29
30	12 07	11 27	10 53	10 52	10 29
31	12 18	11 40	11 02	10 56	10 30
32	12 29	11 52	11 11	11 01	10 30
33	12 41	12 04	11 20	11 05	10 30
34	12 53	12 17	11 29	11 10	10 31
35	13 05	12 30	11 39	11 14	10 31
36	13 18	12 42	11 48	11 19	10 32
37	13 30	12 55	11 58	11 24	10 32
38	13 43	13 08	12 07	11 28	10 33
39	13 57	13 22	12 17	11 33	10 34
40	14 11	13 35	12 27	11 38	10 34
41	14 25	13 49	12 37	11 43	10 35
42	14 39	14 03	12 47	11 48	10 36
43	14 54	14 17	12 57	11 54	10 37
44	15 09	14 31	13 07	11 59	10 38
45	15 25	14 46	13 18	12 05	10 40
46	15 42	15 00	13 29	12 11	10 41
47	15 58	15 15	13 39	12 17	10 42
48	16 16	15 30	13 50	12 23	10 44
49	16 34	15 46	14 01	12 29	10 46
50	16 53	16 02	14 13	12 36	10 48
51	17 12	16 18	14 24	12 43	10 50
52	17 32	16 34	14 36	12 50	10 53
53	17 53	16 50	14 48	12 58	10 56
54	18 15	17 07	15 00	13 06	10 59
55	18 38	17 24	15 13	13 14	11 03
56	19 02	17 42	15 25	13 23	11 07
57	19 27	17 59	15 38	13 33	11 13
58	19 53	18 17	15 52	13 43	11 19
59	20 20	18 34	16 06	13 55	11 26
60	20♋49	18♌52	16♍20	14♎07	11♏34

4h 36m 0s — 69° 0' 0" — 10 ♊ 36

LAT.	11	12	ASC	2	3
0	08♋16	06♌37	07♍18	09♎48	11♏26
5	09 00	07 35	08 06	10 09	11 25
10	09 44	08 31	08 51	10 29	11 24
15	10 28	09 27	09 35	10 48	11 24
20	11 15	10 22	10 18	11 07	11 23
21	11 24	10 34	10 27	11 11	11 23
22	11 34	10 45	10 36	11 15	11 23
23	11 43	10 56	10 44	11 18	11 23
24	11 53	11 07	10 53	11 22	11 23
25	12 03	11 19	11 01	11 26	11 23
26	12 13	11 30	11 10	11 30	11 23
27	12 24	11 42	11 18	11 34	11 23
28	12 34	11 53	11 27	11 38	11 23
29	12 45	12 05	11 36	11 42	11 23
30	12 56	12 16	11 44	11 46	11 23
31	13 07	12 28	11 53	11 50	11 23
32	13 18	12 40	12 02	11 54	11 24
33	13 29	12 52	12 11	11 58	11 24
34	13 41	13 04	12 20	12 02	11 24
35	13 53	13 17	12 29	12 06	11 24
36	14 05	13 29	12 38	12 10	11 24
37	14 17	13 42	12 47	12 15	11 25
38	14 30	13 54	12 56	12 19	11 25
39	14 43	14 07	13 05	12 24	11 26
40	14 56	14 20	13 15	12 28	11 26
41	15 10	14 33	13 24	12 33	11 27
42	15 24	14 47	13 34	12 38	11 27
43	15 38	15 00	13 44	12 43	11 28
44	15 53	15 14	13 53	12 48	11 29
45	16 08	15 28	14 03	12 53	11 30
46	16 24	15 42	14 13	12 58	11 31
47	16 41	15 57	14 24	13 04	11 32
48	16 57	16 11	14 34	13 10	11 33
49	17 15	16 26	14 45	13 16	11 35
50	17 33	16 41	14 56	13 22	11 37
51	17 52	16 57	15 07	13 28	11 39
52	18 11	17 12	15 18	13 35	11 41
53	18 31	17 28	15 29	13 42	11 44
54	18 52	17 44	15 41	13 50	11 47
55	19 14	18 01	15 53	13 58	11 50
56	19 37	18 17	16 05	14 07	11 55
57	20 01	18 34	16 18	14 16	11 59
58	20 26	18 51	16 30	14 26	12 05
59	20 52	19 07	16 43	14 37	12 12
60	21♋19	19♌24	16♍57	14♎49	12♏20

4h 40m 0s — 70° 0' 0" — 11 ♊ 32

LAT.	11	12	ASC	2	3
0	09♋11	07♌35	08♍22	10♎53	12♏27
5	09 54	08 32	09 08	11 12	12 25
10	10 37	09 27	09 51	11 30	12 23
15	11 21	10 21	10 33	11 47	12 21
20	12 06	11 15	11 14	12 04	12 19
21	12 15	11 26	11 23	12 08	12 19
22	12 25	11 37	11 31	12 11	12 19
23	12 34	11 48	11 39	12 15	12 19
24	12 44	11 59	11 47	12 18	12 18
25	12 54	12 10	11 55	12 22	12 18
26	13 04	12 21	12 03	12 25	12 18
27	13 14	12 32	12 12	12 29	12 18
28	13 24	12 43	12 20	12 32	12 17
29	13 34	12 54	12 28	12 36	12 17
30	13 45	13 06	12 36	12 39	12 17
31	13 55	13 17	12 45	12 43	12 17
32	14 06	13 29	12 53	12 47	12 17
33	14 17	13 40	13 02	12 50	12 17
34	14 29	13 52	13 10	12 54	12 17
35	14 40	14 04	13 19	12 58	12 17
36	14 52	14 16	13 27	13 02	12 17
37	15 04	14 28	13 36	13 06	12 17
38	15 16	14 40	13 45	13 10	12 17
39	15 29	14 53	13 53	13 14	12 17
40	15 42	15 05	14 02	13 18	12 18
41	15 55	15 18	14 11	13 23	12 18
42	16 09	15 31	14 21	13 27	12 18
43	16 23	15 44	14 30	13 32	12 19
44	16 37	15 57	14 39	13 36	12 19
45	16 52	16 11	14 49	13 41	12 20
46	17 07	16 24	14 58	13 46	12 21
47	17 23	16 38	15 08	13 51	12 22
48	17 39	16 52	15 18	13 57	12 23
49	17 56	17 07	15 28	14 02	12 24
50	18 13	17 21	15 39	14 08	12 25
51	18 31	17 36	15 49	14 14	12 27
52	18 50	17 51	16 00	14 20	12 29
53	19 09	18 06	16 11	14 27	12 31
54	19 29	18 21	16 22	14 34	12 34
55	19 50	18 37	16 33	14 42	12 37
56	20 12	18 53	16 45	14 50	12 41
57	20 35	19 09	16 57	14 59	12 46
58	20 59	19 25	17 09	15 08	12 51
59	21 23	19 40	17 21	15 19	12 58
60	21♋49	19♌56	17♍34	15♎31	13♏06

4h 44m 0s — 71° 0' 0" — 12 ♊ 28

LAT.	11	12	ASC	2	3
0	10♋07	08♌34	09♍26	11♎58	13♏27
5	10 49	09 30	10 10	12 15	13 24
10	11 31	10 23	10 51	12 31	13 21
15	12 14	11 15	11 31	12 46	13 18
20	12 58	12 08	12 10	13 02	13 15
21	13 07	12 18	12 18	13 05	13 15
22	13 16	12 29	12 26	13 08	13 14
23	13 25	12 39	12 34	13 11	13 14
24	13 35	12 50	12 41	13 14	13 13
25	13 44	13 01	12 49	13 17	13 13
26	13 54	13 11	12 57	13 20	13 13
27	14 04	13 22	13 05	13 23	13 12
28	14 14	13 33	13 13	13 26	13 12
29	14 24	13 44	13 20	13 30	13 11
30	14 34	13 55	13 28	13 33	13 11
31	14 44	14 06	13 36	13 36	13 11
32	14 55	14 17	13 44	13 40	13 10
33	15 06	14 28	13 52	13 43	13 10
34	15 17	14 40	14 00	13 46	13 10
35	15 28	14 51	14 08	13 50	13 09
36	15 39	15 03	14 17	13 53	13 09
37	15 51	15 14	14 25	13 57	13 09
38	16 03	15 26	14 33	14 01	13 09
39	16 15	15 38	14 42	14 04	13 09
40	16 28	15 50	14 50	14 08	13 09
41	16 40	16 03	14 59	14 12	13 09
42	16 54	16 15	15 07	14 16	13 09
43	17 07	16 28	15 16	14 20	13 09
44	17 21	16 40	15 25	14 24	13 09
45	17 35	16 53	15 34	14 29	13 10
46	17 50	17 07	15 43	14 33	13 10
47	18 05	17 20	15 53	14 38	13 11
48	18 21	17 33	16 02	14 43	13 12
49	18 37	17 47	16 12	14 48	13 13
50	18 54	18 01	16 22	14 54	13 14
51	19 11	18 15	16 32	14 59	13 15
52	19 29	18 30	16 42	15 05	13 17
53	19 48	18 44	16 52	15 12	13 19
54	20 07	18 59	17 03	15 18	13 21
55	20 27	19 14	17 13	15 26	13 24
56	20 48	19 29	17 24	15 33	13 28
57	21 09	19 44	17 36	15 42	13 32
58	21 32	19 59	17 47	15 51	13 37
59	21 55	20 14	17 59	16 01	13 43
60	22♋20	20♌28	18♍11	16♎12	13♏51

Koch Table of Houses for Latitudes 0° to 60° North

4h 48m 0s — 72° 0' 0" — 13 ♊ 24

LAT.	11	12	ASC	2	3
0	11♋02	09♌34	10♍30	13♎03	14♏28
5	11 43	10 27	11 12	13 18	14 23
10	12 24	11 19	11 51	13 32	14 19
15	13 06	12 10	12 29	13 45	14 15
20	13 49	13 01	13 06	13 59	14 11
21	13 58	13 11	13 14	14 01	14 10
22	14 07	13 21	13 21	14 04	14 10
23	14 16	13 31	13 28	14 07	14 09
24	14 25	13 41	13 36	14 10	14 08
25	14 35	13 52	13 43	14 12	14 08
26	14 44	14 02	13 51	14 15	14 07
27	14 54	14 13	13 58	14 18	14 06
28	15 03	14 23	14 05	14 21	14 06
29	15 13	14 34	14 13	14 24	14 05
30	15 23	14 44	14 20	14 26	14 04
31	15 33	14 55	14 28	14 29	14 04
32	15 43	15 06	14 35	14 32	14 03
33	15 54	15 16	14 43	14 35	14 03
34	16 04	15 27	14 51	14 38	14 02
35	16 15	15 39	14 58	14 41	14 02
36	16 26	15 50	15 06	14 45	14 01
37	16 38	16 01	15 14	14 48	14 01
38	16 49	16 12	15 22	14 51	14 00
39	17 01	16 24	15 30	14 54	14 00
40	17 13	16 36	15 38	14 58	14 00
41	17 26	16 47	15 46	15 01	14 00
42	17 38	16 59	15 54	15 05	13 59
43	17 52	17 11	16 03	15 09	13 59
44	18 05	17 24	16 11	15 13	13 59
45	18 19	17 36	16 20	15 17	13 59
46	18 33	17 49	16 28	15 21	14 00
47	18 48	18 02	16 37	15 25	14 00
48	19 03	18 15	16 46	15 30	14 00
49	19 18	18 28	16 55	15 34	14 01
50	19 34	18 41	17 05	15 39	14 02
51	19 51	18 55	17 14	15 45	14 03
52	20 08	19 08	17 24	15 50	14 04
53	20 26	19 22	17 33	15 56	14 06
54	20 44	19 36	17 43	16 02	14 08
55	21 04	19 50	17 54	16 09	14 11
56	21 23	20 05	18 04	16 16	14 14
57	21 44	20 19	18 15	16 24	14 18
58	22 05	20 33	18 26	16 33	14 23
59	22 27	20 47	18 37	16 43	14 29
60	22♋50	21♌01	18♍48	16♎54	14♏36

4h 52m 0s — 73° 0' 0" — 14 ♊ 20

LAT.	11	12	ASC	2	3
0	11♋58	10♌33	11♍34	14♎07	15♏28
5	12 38	11 25	12 14	14 20	15 22
10	13 18	12 15	12 51	14 32	15 17
15	13 59	13 04	13 27	14 44	15 12
20	14 41	13 54	14 02	14 56	15 07
21	14 50	14 03	14 09	14 58	15 06
22	14 58	14 13	14 16	15 00	15 05
23	15 07	14 23	14 23	15 03	15 04
24	15 16	14 33	14 30	15 05	15 03
25	15 25	14 43	14 37	15 08	15 02
26	15 34	14 53	14 44	15 10	15 01
27	15 44	15 03	14 51	15 12	15 00
28	15 53	15 13	14 58	15 15	14 59
29	16 02	15 23	15 05	15 17	14 59
30	16 12	15 34	15 12	15 20	14 58
31	16 22	15 44	15 19	15 22	14 57
32	16 32	15 54	15 27	15 25	14 56
33	16 42	16 05	15 34	15 28	14 55
34	16 52	16 15	15 41	15 30	14 55
35	17 03	16 26	15 48	15 33	14 54
36	17 14	16 37	15 56	15 36	14 53
37	17 25	16 48	16 03	15 39	14 52
38	17 36	16 59	16 11	15 41	14 52
39	17 47	17 10	16 18	15 44	14 51
40	17 59	17 21	16 26	15 47	14 51
41	18 11	17 32	16 33	15 51	14 50
42	18 23	17 44	16 41	15 54	14 50
43	18 36	17 55	16 49	15 57	14 49
44	18 49	18 07	16 57	16 01	14 49
45	19 02	18 19	17 05	16 04	14 49
46	19 16	18 31	17 13	16 08	14 49
47	19 30	18 44	17 22	16 12	14 49
48	19 45	18 56	17 30	16 16	14 49
49	20 00	19 09	17 39	16 20	14 49
50	20 15	19 21	17 48	16 25	14 50
51	20 31	19 34	17 57	16 30	14 51
52	20 47	19 47	18 06	16 35	14 52
53	21 05	20 00	18 15	16 40	14 53
54	21 22	20 14	18 24	16 46	14 55
55	21 40	20 27	18 34	16 52	14 57
56	21 59	20 41	18 44	16 59	15 00
57	22 19	20 54	18 54	17 07	15 03
58	22 39	21 08	19 04	17 15	15 08
59	23 00	21 21	19 15	17 24	15 13
60	23♋21	21♌34	19♍26	17♎35	15♏21

4h 56m 0s — 74° 0' 0" — 15 ♊ 16

LAT.	11	12	ASC	2	3
0	12♋53	11♌32	12♍39	15♎12	16♏28
5	13 33	12 23	13 16	15 23	16 21
10	14 12	13 11	13 51	15 33	16 15
15	14 52	13 59	14 25	15 43	16 08
20	15 33	14 47	14 58	15 53	16 02
21	15 41	14 56	15 05	15 55	16 01
22	15 50	15 06	15 12	15 57	16 00
23	15 58	15 15	15 18	15 59	15 59
24	16 07	15 25	15 25	16 01	15 58
25	16 16	15 34	15 31	16 03	15 57
26	16 25	15 44	15 38	16 05	15 55
27	16 34	15 54	15 44	16 07	15 54
28	16 43	16 03	15 51	16 09	15 53
29	16 52	16 13	15 58	16 11	15 52
30	17 01	16 23	16 04	16 13	15 51
31	17 11	16 33	16 11	16 15	15 50
32	17 21	16 43	16 18	16 17	15 49
33	17 30	16 53	16 25	16 20	15 48
34	17 40	17 03	16 31	16 22	15 47
35	17 51	17 14	16 38	16 24	15 46
36	18 01	17 24	16 45	16 27	15 45
37	18 12	17 34	16 52	16 29	15 44
38	18 23	17 45	16 59	16 32	15 43
39	18 34	17 56	17 06	16 34	15 42
40	18 45	18 06	17 14	16 37	15 41
41	18 57	18 17	17 21	16 40	15 40
42	19 09	18 28	17 28	16 43	15 40
43	19 21	18 39	17 36	16 45	15 39
44	19 33	18 51	17 43	16 49	15 39
45	19 46	19 02	17 51	16 52	15 38
46	19 59	19 14	17 58	16 55	15 38
47	20 13	19 26	18 06	16 59	15 37
48	20 27	19 37	18 14	17 02	15 37
49	20 41	19 49	18 22	17 06	15 37
50	20 56	20 02	18 31	17 10	15 37
51	21 11	20 14	18 39	17 15	15 38
52	21 27	20 26	18 48	17 19	15 39
53	21 43	20 39	18 56	17 24	15 40
54	22 00	20 52	19 05	17 30	15 41
55	22 17	21 04	19 14	17 35	15 43
56	22 35	21 17	19 24	17 42	15 45
57	22 54	21 30	19 33	17 49	15 49
58	23 13	21 42	19 43	17 57	15 53
59	23 33	21 55	19 53	18 06	15 58
60	23♋53	22♌06	20♍03	18♎16	16♏05

5h 0m 0s — 75° 0' 0" — 16 ♊ 11

LAT.	11	12	ASC	2	3
0	13♋49	12♌32	13♍43	16♎17	17♏28
5	14 27	13 21	14 18	16 25	17 20
10	15 06	14 08	14 51	16 34	17 12
15	15 45	14 54	15 23	16 42	17 05
20	16 25	15 40	15 54	16 49	16 58
21	16 33	15 49	16 01	16 51	16 56
22	16 41	15 58	16 07	16 53	16 55
23	16 49	16 07	16 13	16 54	16 54
24	16 58	16 17	16 19	16 56	16 52
25	17 06	16 26	16 25	16 58	16 51
26	17 15	16 35	16 32	16 59	16 49
27	17 24	16 44	16 38	17 01	16 48
28	17 33	16 54	16 44	17 03	16 47
29	17 42	17 03	16 50	17 04	16 45
30	17 51	17 13	16 57	17 06	16 44
31	18 00	17 22	17 03	17 08	16 43
32	18 09	17 32	17 09	17 10	16 41
33	18 19	17 42	17 15	17 12	16 40
34	18 29	17 51	17 22	17 14	16 39
35	18 38	18 01	17 28	17 16	16 38
36	18 49	18 11	17 35	17 18	16 36
37	18 59	18 21	17 41	17 20	16 35
38	19 09	18 31	17 48	17 22	16 34
39	19 20	18 42	17 55	17 24	16 33
40	19 31	18 52	18 01	17 26	16 32
41	19 42	19 02	18 08	17 29	16 31
42	19 54	19 13	18 15	17 31	16 30
43	20 05	19 24	18 22	17 34	16 29
44	20 17	19 34	18 29	17 36	16 28
45	20 30	19 45	18 36	17 39	16 27
46	20 43	19 56	18 43	17 42	16 26
47	20 56	20 08	18 51	17 45	16 26
48	21 09	20 19	18 58	17 48	16 25
49	21 23	20 30	19 06	17 52	16 25
50	21 37	20 42	19 14	17 55	16 25
51	21 52	20 54	19 22	17 59	16 25
52	22 07	21 06	19 30	18 04	16 25
53	22 22	21 17	19 38	18 08	16 26
54	22 38	21 29	19 46	18 13	16 27
55	22 55	21 41	19 55	18 18	16 29
56	23 12	21 53	20 03	18 24	16 31
57	23 29	22 05	20 12	18 31	16 34
58	23 47	22 17	20 21	18 38	16 37
59	24 06	22 29	20 31	18 47	16 42
60	24♋24	22♌39	20♍40	18♎56	16♏49

5h 4m 0s — 76° 0' 0" — 17 ♊ 07

LAT.	11	12	ASC	2	3
0	14♋44	13♌32	14♍48	17♎21	18♏28
5	15 22	14 19	15 21	17 28	18 18
10	16 00	15 05	15 52	17 34	18 10
15	16 38	15 49	16 21	17 40	18 01
20	17 16	16 33	16 51	17 46	17 53
21	17 24	16 42	16 56	17 47	17 51
22	17 32	16 51	17 02	17 49	17 50
23	17 41	17 00	17 08	17 50	17 48
24	17 49	17 08	17 14	17 51	17 46
25	17 57	17 17	17 20	17 53	17 45
26	18 05	17 26	17 25	17 54	17 43
27	18 14	17 35	17 31	17 55	17 42
28	18 22	17 44	17 37	17 57	17 40
29	18 31	17 53	17 43	17 58	17 38
30	18 40	18 02	17 49	17 59	17 37
31	18 49	18 12	17 54	18 01	17 35
32	18 58	18 21	18 00	18 02	17 34
33	19 07	18 30	18 06	18 04	17 32
34	19 17	18 40	18 12	18 05	17 31
35	19 26	18 49	18 18	18 07	17 29
36	19 36	18 58	18 24	18 08	17 28
37	19 46	19 08	18 31	18 10	17 26
38	19 56	19 18	18 37	18 12	17 25
39	20 06	19 28	18 43	18 14	17 23
40	20 17	19 38	18 49	18 16	17 22
41	20 28	19 48	18 56	18 18	17 21
42	20 39	19 58	19 02	18 20	17 19
43	20 50	20 08	19 08	18 22	17 18
44	21 02	20 18	19 15	18 24	17 17
45	21 14	20 29	19 22	18 26	17 16
46	21 26	20 39	19 29	18 29	17 15
47	21 38	20 50	19 35	18 31	17 14
48	21 51	21 01	19 42	18 34	17 13
49	22 04	21 12	19 49	18 37	17 12
50	22 18	21 23	19 57	18 40	17 12
51	22 32	21 34	20 04	18 44	17 12
52	22 46	21 45	20 12	18 48	17 12
53	23 01	21 56	20 19	18 52	17 12
54	23 16	22 07	20 27	18 56	17 13
55	23 32	22 19	20 35	19 01	17 14
56	23 48	22 30	20 43	19 07	17 16
57	24 05	22 41	20 51	19 13	17 18
58	24 22	22 52	21 00	19 20	17 21
59	24 39	23 03	21 09	19 27	17 26
60	24♋56	23♌13	21♍17	19♎37	17♏32

5h 8m 0s — 77° 0' 0" — 18 ♊ 02

LAT.	11	12	ASC	2	3
0	15♋40	14♌32	15♍53	18♎26	19♏27
5	16 17	15 17	16 23	18 30	19 17
10	16 54	16 01	16 52	18 34	19 07
15	17 30	16 44	17 20	18 39	18 57
20	18 08	17 26	17 47	18 43	18 48
21	18 16	17 35	17 52	18 44	18 46
22	18 24	17 43	17 58	18 45	18 44
23	18 32	17 52	18 03	18 45	18 42
24	18 40	18 00	18 08	18 46	18 41
25	18 48	18 09	18 14	18 47	18 39
26	18 56	18 18	18 19	18 48	18 37
27	19 04	18 26	18 24	18 49	18 35
28	19 12	18 35	18 30	18 50	18 33
29	19 21	18 44	18 35	18 51	18 31
30	19 29	18 52	18 41	18 52	18 30
31	19 38	19 01	18 46	18 53	18 28
32	19 47	19 10	18 52	18 54	18 26
33	19 56	19 19	18 57	18 56	18 24
34	20 05	19 28	19 03	18 57	18 22
35	20 14	19 37	19 08	18 58	18 21
36	20 24	19 46	19 14	18 59	18 19
37	20 33	19 55	19 20	19 00	18 17
38	20 43	20 04	19 25	19 02	18 15
39	20 53	20 14	19 31	19 03	18 14
40	21 03	20 23	19 37	19 05	18 12
41	21 14	20 33	19 43	19 06	18 10
42	21 24	20 42	19 49	19 08	18 09
43	21 35	20 52	19 55	19 10	18 07
44	21 46	21 02	20 01	19 11	18 06
45	21 58	21 12	20 07	19 13	18 04
46	22 09	21 22	20 14	19 15	18 03
47	22 21	21 32	20 20	19 18	18 02
48	22 34	21 42	20 26	19 20	18 01
49	22 46	21 53	20 33	19 23	18 00
50	22 59	22 03	20 40	19 25	17 59
51	23 13	22 14	20 47	19 28	17 58
52	23 26	22 24	20 54	19 32	17 58
53	23 41	22 35	21 01	19 35	17 58
54	23 55	22 46	21 08	19 39	17 58
55	24 10	22 56	21 15	19 44	17 59
56	24 25	23 07	21 23	19 49	18 00
57	24 41	23 17	21 30	19 54	18 02
58	24 56	23 27	21 38	20 01	18 05
59	25 12	23 37	21 46	20 08	18 09
60	25♋28	23♌46	21♍55	20♎17	18♏15

5h 12m 0s — 78° 0' 0" — 18 ♊ 58

LAT.	11	12	ASC	2	3
0	16♋36	15♌32	16♍57	19♎30	20♏26
5	17 12	16 16	17 26	19 32	20 15
10	17 48	16 58	17 52	19 35	20 04
15	18 23	17 39	18 18	19 37	19 53
20	19 00	18 20	18 43	19 39	19 43
21	19 08	18 28	18 48	19 40	19 41
22	19 15	18 36	18 53	19 40	19 39
23	19 23	18 44	18 58	19 41	19 37
24	19 31	18 53	19 03	19 41	19 34
25	19 39	19 01	19 08	19 42	19 32
26	19 46	19 09	19 13	19 43	19 30
27	19 54	19 17	19 18	19 43	19 28
28	20 02	19 25	19 23	19 44	19 26
29	20 11	19 34	19 28	19 44	19 24
30	20 19	19 42	19 33	19 45	19 22
31	20 27	19 51	19 38	19 46	19 20
32	20 36	19 59	19 43	19 46	19 18
33	20 44	20 08	19 48	19 47	19 16
34	20 53	20 16	19 53	19 48	19 14
35	21 02	20 25	19 58	19 49	19 12
36	21 11	20 34	20 04	19 50	19 10
37	21 21	20 42	20 09	19 51	19 08
38	21 30	20 51	20 14	19 52	19 06
39	21 40	21 00	20 20	19 53	19 04
40	21 49	21 09	20 25	19 54	19 02
41	21 59	21 18	20 30	19 55	19 00
42	22 10	21 27	20 36	19 56	18 58
43	22 20	21 37	20 41	19 57	18 56
44	22 31	21 46	20 47	19 59	18 55
45	22 42	21 56	20 53	20 00	18 53
46	22 53	22 05	20 59	20 02	18 51
47	23 05	22 15	21 05	20 04	18 50
48	23 16	22 24	21 11	20 06	18 48
49	23 28	22 34	21 17	20 08	18 47
50	23 41	22 44	21 23	20 10	18 46
51	23 54	22 54	21 29	20 13	18 45
52	24 07	23 04	21 36	20 16	18 44
53	24 20	23 14	21 42	20 19	18 44
54	24 34	23 24	21 49	20 22	18 43
55	24 48	23 34	21 56	20 26	18 44
56	25 02	23 44	22 03	20 31	18 45
57	25 17	23 53	22 10	20 36	18 46
58	25 31	24 03	22 17	20 42	18 49
59	25 46	24 12	22 24	20 49	18 52
60	26♋01	24♌20	22♍32	20♎57	18♏58

5h 16m 0s — 79° 0' 0" — 19 ♊ 53

LAT.	11	12	ASC	2	3
0	17♋32	16♌33	18♍02	20♎34	21♏26
5	18 07	17 15	18 28	20 35	21 13
10	18 42	17 55	18 53	20 35	21 01
15	19 17	18 35	19 16	20 35	20 49
20	19 52	19 14	19 39	20 36	20 37
21	20 00	19 21	19 44	20 36	20 35
22	20 07	19 29	19 48	20 36	20 33
23	20 14	19 37	19 53	20 36	20 31
24	20 22	19 45	19 58	20 36	20 28
25	20 29	19 53	20 02	20 37	20 26
26	20 37	20 00	20 07	20 37	20 24
27	20 45	20 08	20 11	20 37	20 21
28	20 53	20 16	20 16	20 37	20 19
29	21 00	20 24	20 20	20 37	20 17
30	21 08	20 32	20 25	20 38	20 14
31	21 17	20 40	20 30	20 38	20 12
32	21 25	20 48	20 34	20 38	20 10
33	21 33	20 56	20 39	20 39	20 08
34	21 42	21 05	20 44	20 39	20 05
35	21 50	21 13	20 49	20 40	20 03
36	21 59	21 21	20 53	20 40	20 01
37	22 08	21 30	20 58	20 41	19 58
38	22 17	21 38	21 03	20 41	19 56
39	22 26	21 46	21 08	20 42	19 54
40	22 36	21 55	21 13	20 43	19 52
41	22 45	22 04	21 18	20 43	19 49
42	22 55	22 12	21 23	20 44	19 47
43	23 05	22 21	21 28	20 45	19 45
44	23 16	22 30	21 33	20 46	19 43
45	23 26	22 39	21 38	20 47	19 41
46	23 37	22 48	21 44	20 48	19 39
47	23 48	22 57	21 49	20 50	19 37
48	23 59	23 06	21 55	20 51	19 35
49	24 11	23 16	22 00	20 53	19 34
50	24 22	23 25	22 06	20 55	19 32
51	24 35	23 34	22 12	20 57	19 31
52	24 47	23 44	22 18	20 59	19 30
53	25 00	23 53	22 24	21 02	19 29
54	25 13	24 03	22 30	21 05	19 28
55	25 26	24 12	22 36	21 08	19 28
56	25 39	24 21	22 42	21 12	19 29
57	25 53	24 30	22 49	21 17	19 30
58	26 07	24 38	22 55	21 22	19 32
59	26 21	24 47	23 02	21 29	19 35
60	26♋34	24♌54	23♍09	21♎36	19♏40

Koch Table of Houses for Latitudes 0° to 60° North

5h 20m 0s — 80° 0' 0" — 20 ♊ 49

LAT.	11	12	ASC	2	3
0	18♋28	17♌33	19♍07	21♎38	22♏25
5	19 02	18 14	19 31	21 37	22 11
10	19 36	18 52	19 53	21 35	21 58
15	20 10	19 30	20 15	21 33	21 45
20	20 44	20 07	20 36	21 32	21 32
21	20 51	20 15	20 40	21 32	21 30
22	20 59	20 22	20 44	21 32	21 27
23	21 06	20 30	20 48	21 31	21 24
24	21 13	20 37	20 52	21 31	21 22
25	21 20	20 45	20 56	21 31	21 19
26	21 28	20 52	21 01	21 31	21 17
27	21 35	21 00	21 05	21 31	21 14
28	21 43	21 07	21 09	21 31	21 12
29	21 50	21 15	21 13	21 30	21 09
30	21 58	21 22	21 17	21 30	21 07
31	22 06	21 30	21 21	21 30	21 04
32	22 14	21 38	21 26	21 30	21 02
33	22 22	21 45	21 30	21 30	20 59
34	22 30	21 53	21 34	21 30	20 56
35	22 38	22 01	21 39	21 30	20 54
36	22 47	22 09	21 43	21 30	20 51
37	22 55	22 17	21 47	21 31	20 49
38	23 04	22 25	21 52	21 31	20 46
39	23 13	22 33	21 56	21 31	20 44
40	23 22	22 41	22 01	21 31	20 41
41	23 31	22 49	22 05	21 32	20 39
42	23 41	22 58	22 10	21 32	20 36
43	23 51	23 06	22 14	21 32	20 34
44	24 00	23 14	22 19	21 33	20 31
45	24 10	23 23	22 24	21 34	20 29
46	24 21	23 31	22 29	21 35	20 27
47	24 31	23 40	22 34	21 35	20 24
48	24 42	23 49	22 39	21 36	20 22
49	24 53	23 57	22 44	21 38	20 20
50	25 04	24 06	22 49	21 39	20 18
51	25 16	24 15	22 54	21 41	20 17
52	25 28	24 24	23 00	21 43	20 15
53	25 40	24 33	23 05	21 45	20 14
54	25 52	24 41	23 11	21 47	20 13
55	26 04	24 50	23 16	21 50	20 12
56	26 17	24 58	23 22	21 54	20 12
57	26 30	25 06	23 28	21 58	20 13
58	26 42	25 14	23 34	22 03	20 15
59	26 55	25 22	23 40	22 09	20 18
60	27♋07	25♌28	23♍47	22♎16	20♏22

5h 24m 0s — 81° 0' 0" — 21 ♊ 44

LAT.	11	12	ASC	2	3
0	19♋24	18♌34	20♍12	22♎42	23♏23
5	19 57	19 13	20 34	22 38	23 09
10	20 30	19 50	20 54	22 35	22 54
15	21 03	20 26	21 13	22 31	22 40
20	21 37	21 01	21 32	22 28	22 26
21	21 43	21 08	21 36	22 28	22 24
22	21 50	21 15	21 40	22 27	22 21
23	21 57	21 22	21 43	22 26	22 18
24	22 04	21 30	21 47	22 26	22 15
25	22 11	21 37	21 51	22 25	22 13
26	22 18	21 44	21 54	22 25	22 10
27	22 26	21 51	21 58	22 24	22 07
28	22 33	21 58	22 02	22 24	22 04
29	22 40	22 05	22 06	22 23	22 01
30	22 48	22 13	22 10	22 23	21 59
31	22 55	22 20	22 13	22 22	21 56
32	23 03	22 27	22 17	22 22	21 53
33	23 11	22 35	22 21	22 22	21 50
34	23 19	22 42	22 25	22 21	21 47
35	23 27	22 49	22 29	22 21	21 45
36	23 35	22 57	22 33	22 21	21 42
37	23 43	23 04	22 37	22 20	21 39
38	23 51	23 12	22 41	22 20	21 36
39	24 00	23 20	22 45	22 20	21 33
40	24 09	23 27	22 49	22 20	21 30
41	24 18	23 35	22 53	22 20	21 28
42	24 27	23 43	22 57	22 20	21 25
43	24 36	23 51	23 01	22 20	21 22
44	24 45	23 59	23 05	22 20	21 19
45	24 55	24 07	23 10	22 20	21 17
46	25 05	24 15	23 14	22 21	21 14
47	25 15	24 23	23 18	22 21	21 11
48	25 25	24 31	23 23	22 22	21 09
49	25 36	24 39	23 27	22 22	21 07
50	25 46	24 47	23 32	22 23	21 04
51	25 57	24 56	23 37	22 25	21 02
52	26 08	25 04	23 42	22 26	21 00
53	26 20	25 12	23 46	22 28	20 59
54	26 31	25 20	23 51	22 30	20 57
55	26 43	25 28	23 57	22 32	20 56
56	26 55	25 36	24 02	22 35	20 56
57	27 07	25 43	24 07	22 39	20 56
58	27 18	25 50	24 13	22 43	20 57
59	27 30	25 57	24 18	22 49	20 59
60	27♋41	26♌02	24♍24	22♎55	21♏03

5h 28m 0s — 82° 0' 0" — 22 ♊ 39

LAT.	11	12	ASC	2	3
0	20♋20	19♌35	21♍17	23♎46	24♏22
5	20 53	20 12	21 36	23 40	24 06
10	21 24	20 47	21 54	23 35	23 51
15	21 56	21 21	22 12	23 29	23 36
20	22 29	21 55	22 28	23 24	23 21
21	22 35	22 02	22 32	23 23	23 18
22	22 42	22 09	22 35	23 22	23 15
23	22 49	22 15	22 38	23 21	23 12
24	22 56	22 22	22 42	23 20	23 09
25	23 02	22 29	22 45	23 20	23 06
26	23 09	22 36	22 48	23 19	23 03
27	23 16	22 42	22 52	23 18	23 00
28	23 23	22 49	22 55	23 17	22 57
29	23 30	22 56	22 58	23 16	22 54
30	23 38	23 03	23 02	23 15	22 51
31	23 45	23 10	23 05	23 14	22 47
32	23 52	23 17	23 09	23 14	22 44
33	24 00	23 24	23 12	23 13	22 41
34	24 07	23 31	23 15	23 12	22 38
35	24 15	23 38	23 19	23 11	22 35
36	24 23	23 45	23 22	23 11	22 32
37	24 31	23 52	23 26	23 10	22 29
38	24 39	23 59	23 29	23 09	22 26
39	24 47	24 06	23 33	23 09	22 23
40	24 55	24 14	23 36	23 08	22 20
41	25 04	24 21	23 40	23 08	22 17
42	25 13	24 28	23 44	23 07	22 13
43	25 21	24 36	23 48	23 07	22 10
44	25 30	24 43	23 51	23 07	22 07
45	25 40	24 51	23 55	23 07	22 04
46	25 49	24 58	23 59	23 07	22 01
47	25 59	25 06	24 03	23 07	21 58
48	26 08	25 14	24 07	23 07	21 55
49	26 18	25 21	24 11	23 07	21 53
50	26 28	25 29	24 15	23 07	21 50
51	26 39	25 36	24 19	23 08	21 47
52	26 49	25 44	24 24	23 09	21 45
53	27 00	25 52	24 28	23 10	21 43
54	27 11	25 59	24 32	23 12	21 41
55	27 22	26 06	24 37	23 14	21 40
56	27 33	26 14	24 42	23 16	21 39
57	27 44	26 20	24 46	23 19	21 39
58	27 55	26 27	24 51	23 23	21 39
59	28 05	26 32	24 56	23 28	21 41
60	28♋15	26♌37	25♍01	23♎34	21♏44

5h 32m 0s — 83° 0' 0" — 23 ♊ 34

LAT.	11	12	ASC	2	3
0	21♋17	20♌36	22♍23	24♎50	25♏21
5	21 48	21 11	22 39	24 42	25 04
10	22 19	21 45	22 55	24 34	24 47
15	22 50	22 17	23 10	24 27	24 31
20	23 21	22 49	23 25	24 20	24 15
21	23 28	22 56	23 28	24 19	24 12
22	23 34	23 02	23 31	24 18	24 08
23	23 40	23 08	23 34	24 16	24 05
24	23 47	23 15	23 36	24 15	24 02
25	23 54	23 21	23 39	24 14	23 59
26	24 00	23 28	23 42	24 12	23 55
27	24 07	23 34	23 45	24 11	23 52
28	24 14	23 40	23 48	24 10	23 49
29	24 21	23 47	23 51	24 09	23 46
30	24 27	23 53	23 54	24 07	23 42
31	24 34	24 00	23 57	24 06	23 39
32	24 42	24 07	24 00	24 05	23 36
33	24 49	24 13	24 03	24 04	23 32
34	24 56	24 20	24 06	24 03	23 29
35	25 03	24 26	24 09	24 02	23 26
36	25 11	24 33	24 12	24 01	23 22
37	25 19	24 40	24 15	24 00	23 19
38	25 26	24 46	24 18	23 59	23 15
39	25 34	24 53	24 21	23 58	23 12
40	25 42	25 00	24 24	23 57	23 09
41	25 50	25 07	24 28	23 56	23 05
42	25 59	25 14	24 31	23 55	23 02
43	26 07	25 21	24 34	23 54	22 58
44	26 16	25 28	24 37	23 53	22 55
45	26 24	25 35	24 41	23 53	22 52
46	26 33	25 42	24 44	23 52	22 48
47	26 42	25 49	24 48	23 52	22 45
48	26 52	25 56	24 51	23 52	22 42
49	27 01	26 03	24 55	23 51	22 39
50	27 11	26 10	24 58	23 51	22 36
51	27 20	26 17	25 02	23 52	22 33
52	27 30	26 25	25 06	23 52	22 30
53	27 40	26 31	25 09	23 53	22 27
54	27 51	26 38	25 13	23 54	22 25
55	28 01	26 45	25 17	23 55	22 23
56	28 11	26 51	25 21	23 57	22 22
57	28 21	26 57	25 26	24 00	22 21
58	28 31	27 03	25 30	24 03	22 21
59	28 41	27 08	25 34	24 07	22 22
60	28♋50	27♌12	25♍39	24♎13	22♏25

5h 36m 0s — 84° 0' 0" — 24 ♊ 30

LAT.	11	12	ASC	2	3
0	22♋13	21♌37	23♍28	25♎53	26♏19
5	22 43	22 11	23 42	25 43	26 01
10	23 13	22 42	23 56	25 34	25 43
15	23 43	23 13	24 09	25 25	25 26
20	24 14	23 43	24 21	25 16	25 09
21	24 20	23 50	24 24	25 14	25 05
22	24 26	23 56	24 26	25 13	25 02
23	24 32	24 02	24 29	25 11	24 58
24	24 38	24 08	24 31	25 09	24 55
25	24 45	24 14	24 34	25 08	24 51
26	24 51	24 20	24 36	25 06	24 48
27	24 58	24 26	24 39	25 04	24 44
28	25 04	24 32	24 41	25 03	24 41
29	25 11	24 38	24 44	25 01	24 37
30	25 17	24 44	24 46	25 00	24 34
31	25 24	24 50	24 49	24 58	24 30
32	25 31	24 56	24 51	24 57	24 27
33	25 38	25 03	24 54	24 55	24 23
34	25 45	25 09	24 56	24 53	24 20
35	25 52	25 15	24 59	24 52	24 16
36	25 59	25 21	25 02	24 50	24 12
37	26 06	25 28	25 04	24 49	24 09
38	26 14	25 34	25 07	24 48	24 05
39	26 21	25 40	25 10	24 46	24 01
40	26 29	25 47	25 12	24 45	23 57
41	26 37	25 53	25 15	24 44	23 54
42	26 45	26 00	25 18	24 42	23 50
43	26 53	26 06	25 21	24 41	23 46
44	27 01	26 13	25 23	24 40	23 43
45	27 09	26 19	25 26	24 39	23 39
46	27 18	26 26	25 29	24 38	23 35
47	27 26	26 32	25 32	24 37	23 31
48	27 35	26 39	25 35	24 36	23 28
49	27 44	26 46	25 38	24 36	23 24
50	27 53	26 52	25 41	24 35	23 21
51	28 02	26 59	25 44	24 35	23 17
52	28 12	27 05	25 48	24 35	23 14
53	28 21	27 11	25 51	24 35	23 11
54	28 31	27 18	25 54	24 36	23 09
55	28 40	27 24	25 58	24 36	23 06
56	28 50	27 29	26 01	24 38	23 04
57	28 59	27 35	26 05	24 40	23 03
58	29 08	27 40	26 08	24 43	23 02
59	29 17	27 44	26 12	24 46	23 03
60	29♋25	27♌47	26♍16	24♎51	23♏05

5h 40m 0s — 85° 0' 0" — 25 ♊ 25

LAT.	11	12	ASC	2	3
0	23♋10	22♌39	24♍33	26♎57	27♏17
5	23 39	23 10	24 45	26 45	26 58
10	24 08	23 40	24 56	26 33	26 39
15	24 37	24 09	25 07	26 22	26 21
20	25 06	24 38	25 18	26 12	26 03
21	25 12	24 44	25 20	26 10	25 59
22	25 18	24 49	25 22	26 08	25 55
23	25 24	24 55	25 24	26 06	25 52
24	25 30	25 01	25 26	26 04	25 48
25	25 36	25 06	25 28	26 02	25 44
26	25 42	25 12	25 30	26 00	25 40
27	25 49	25 18	25 32	25 58	25 37
28	25 55	25 23	25 34	25 56	25 33
29	26 01	25 29	25 36	25 54	25 29
30	26 07	25 35	25 39	25 52	25 25
31	26 14	25 41	25 41	25 50	25 21
32	26 20	25 46	25 43	25 48	25 18
33	26 27	25 52	25 45	25 46	25 14
34	26 34	25 58	25 47	25 44	25 10
35	26 41	26 04	25 49	25 42	25 06
36	26 47	26 10	25 51	25 40	25 02
37	26 54	26 15	25 54	25 38	24 58
38	27 02	26 21	25 56	25 37	24 54
39	27 09	26 27	25 58	25 35	24 50
40	27 16	26 33	26 00	25 33	24 46
41	27 23	26 39	26 03	25 31	24 42
42	27 31	26 45	26 05	25 30	24 38
43	27 39	26 51	26 07	25 28	24 34
44	27 46	26 57	26 10	25 26	24 30
45	27 54	27 04	26 12	25 25	24 26
46	28 02	27 10	26 14	25 23	24 22
47	28 11	27 16	26 17	25 22	24 18
48	28 19	27 22	26 19	25 21	24 14
49	28 27	27 28	26 22	25 20	24 10
50	28 36	27 34	26 24	25 19	24 06
51	28 45	27 40	26 27	25 18	24 02
52	28 53	27 46	26 30	25 17	23 58
53	29 02	27 52	26 32	25 17	23 55
54	29 11	27 57	26 35	25 17	23 52
55	29 20	28 03	26 38	25 18	23 49
56	29 29	28 08	26 41	25 18	23 46
57	29 37	28 12	26 44	25 20	23 45
58	29 45	28 17	26 47	25 22	23 44
59	29 53	28 20	26 50	25 25	23 44
60	00♌00	28♌23	26♍53	25♎30	23♏45

5h 44m 0s — 86° 0' 0" — 26 ♊ 20

LAT.	11	12	ASC	2	3
0	24♋06	23♌41	25♍38	28♎00	28♏15
5	24 35	24 10	25 48	27 46	27 55
10	25 03	24 38	25 57	27 32	27 35
15	25 31	25 06	26 06	27 20	27 16
20	25 59	25 32	26 14	27 07	26 56
21	26 04	25 38	26 16	27 05	26 52
22	26 10	25 43	26 17	27 03	26 48
23	26 16	25 48	26 19	27 00	26 45
24	26 22	25 54	26 21	26 58	26 41
25	26 28	25 59	26 22	26 55	26 37
26	26 34	26 04	26 24	26 53	26 33
27	26 39	26 10	26 26	26 51	26 29
28	26 45	26 15	26 27	26 48	26 25
29	26 52	26 20	26 29	26 46	26 21
30	26 58	26 26	26 31	26 44	26 17
31	27 04	26 31	26 32	26 41	26 13
32	27 10	26 36	26 34	26 39	26 08
33	27 16	26 42	26 36	26 37	26 04
34	27 23	26 47	26 38	26 34	26 00
35	27 29	26 53	26 39	26 32	25 56
36	27 36	26 58	26 41	26 30	25 52
37	27 43	27 04	26 43	26 28	25 47
38	27 49	27 09	26 45	26 25	25 43
39	27 56	27 15	26 46	26 23	25 39
40	28 03	27 20	26 48	26 21	25 35
41	28 10	27 26	26 50	26 19	25 30
42	28 17	27 31	26 52	26 17	25 26
43	28 25	27 37	26 54	26 15	25 21
44	28 32	27 42	26 56	26 13	25 17
45	28 40	27 48	26 58	26 11	25 13
46	28 47	27 54	26 59	26 09	25 08
47	28 55	27 59	27 01	26 07	25 04
48	29 03	28 05	27 03	26 05	24 59
49	29 11	28 10	27 05	26 04	24 55
50	29 19	28 16	27 08	26 02	24 51
51	29 27	28 21	27 10	26 01	24 46
52	29 35	28 27	27 12	26 00	24 42
53	29 43	28 32	27 14	25 59	24 38
54	29 52	28 37	27 16	25 59	24 35
55	00♌00	28 42	27 18	25 58	24 31
56	00 08	28 46	27 21	25 59	24 28
57	00 16	28 50	27 23	26 00	24 26
58	00 23	28 54	27 26	26 01	24 24
59	00 30	28 56	27 28	26 04	24 24
60	00♌36	28♌58	27♍31	26♎08	24♏24

5h 48m 0s — 87° 0' 0" — 27 ♊ 15

LAT.	11	12	ASC	2	3
0	25♋03	24♌42	26♍44	29♎03	29♏13
5	25 31	25 10	26 51	28 47	28 52
10	25 58	25 36	26 58	28 32	28 31
15	26 24	26 02	27 04	28 17	28 10
20	26 51	26 27	27 11	28 03	27 50
21	26 57	26 32	27 12	28 00	27 46
22	27 02	26 37	27 13	27 57	27 42
23	27 08	26 42	27 14	27 54	27 37
24	27 14	26 47	27 16	27 52	27 33
25	27 19	26 52	27 17	27 49	27 29
26	27 25	26 57	27 18	27 46	27 25
27	27 31	27 02	27 19	27 43	27 21
28	27 36	27 07	27 21	27 41	27 16
29	27 42	27 12	27 22	27 38	27 12
30	27 48	27 17	27 23	27 35	27 08
31	27 54	27 22	27 24	27 33	27 03
32	28 00	27 27	27 26	27 30	26 59
33	28 06	27 32	27 27	27 27	26 55
34	28 12	27 37	27 28	27 25	26 50
35	28 18	27 42	27 30	27 22	26 46
36	28 25	27 47	27 31	27 19	26 41
37	28 31	27 52	27 32	27 17	26 37
38	28 37	27 57	27 33	27 14	26 32
39	28 44	28 02	27 35	27 11	26 28
40	28 50	28 07	27 36	27 09	26 23
41	28 57	28 12	27 38	27 06	26 18
42	29 04	28 17	27 39	27 04	26 13
43	29 11	28 22	27 40	27 01	26 09
44	29 18	28 28	27 42	26 59	26 04
45	29 25	28 33	27 43	26 56	25 59
46	29 32	28 38	27 45	26 54	25 54
47	29 39	28 43	27 46	26 52	25 50
48	29 47	28 48	27 48	26 50	25 45
49	29 54	28 53	27 49	26 47	25 40
50	00♌02	28 58	27 51	26 46	25 35
51	00 09	29 03	27 52	26 44	25 31
52	00 17	29 08	27 54	26 42	25 26
53	00 25	29 12	27 55	26 41	25 22
54	00 32	29 17	27 57	26 40	25 17
55	00 40	29 21	27 59	26 39	25 13
56	00 47	29 25	28 01	26 39	25 10
57	00 54	29 28	28 02	26 39	25 07
58	01 01	29 31	28 04	26 40	25 05
59	01 07	29 33	28 06	26 42	25 03
60	01♌12	29♌34	28♍08	26♎45	25♏03

Koch Table of Houses for Latitudes 0° to 60° North

5h 52m 0s — 88° 0' 0" — 28 ♊ 10

LAT.	11	12	ASC	2	3
0	26♋00	25♌44	27♍49	00♏06	00♐11
5	26 27	26 10	27 54	29♎48	29♏48
10	26 53	26 35	27 58	29 31	29 26
15	27 18	26 58	28 03	29 14	29 05
20	27 44	27 22	28 07	28 58	28 43
21	27 50	27 26	28 08	28 55	28 39
22	27 55	27 31	28 09	28 52	28 35
23	28 00	27 35	28 10	28 49	28 30
24	28 05	27 40	28 10	28 46	28 26
25	28 11	27 45	28 11	28 42	28 21
26	28 16	27 49	28 12	28 39	28 17
27	28 22	27 54	28 13	28 36	28 12
28	28 27	27 58	28 14	28 33	28 08
29	28 33	28 03	28 15	28 30	28 03
30	28 38	28 08	28 15	28 27	27 59
31	28 44	28 12	28 16	28 24	27 54
32	28 50	28 17	28 17	28 21	27 50
33	28 56	28 21	28 18	28 18	27 45
34	29 01	28 26	28 19	28 15	27 40
35	29 07	28 31	28 20	28 12	27 35
36	29 13	28 35	28 21	28 09	27 31
37	29 19	28 40	28 21	28 06	27 26
38	29 25	28 45	28 22	28 02	27 21
39	29 32	28 49	28 23	27 59	27 16
40	29 38	28 54	28 24	27 56	27 11
41	29 44	28 59	28 25	27 53	27 06
42	29 51	29 03	28 26	27 50	27 01
43	29 57	29 08	28 27	27 48	26 56
44	00♌04	29 13	28 28	27 45	26 51
45	00 11	29 18	28 29	27 42	26 46
46	00 17	29 22	28 30	27 39	26 40
47	00 24	29 27	28 31	27 36	26 35
48	00 31	29 31	28 32	27 34	26 30
49	00 38	29 36	28 33	27 31	26 25
50	00 45	29 40	28 34	27 29	26 20
51	00 52	29 45	28 35	27 26	26 14
52	00 59	29 49	28 36	27 24	26 09
53	01 06	29 53	28 37	27 22	26 04
54	01 13	29 57	28 38	27 21	26 00
55	01 20	00♍01	28 39	27 20	25 55
56	01 27	00 04	28 40	27 19	25 51
57	01 33	00 07	28 42	27 18	25 47
58	01 39	00 09	28 43	27 19	25 45
59	01 44	00 10	28 44	27 20	25 43
60	01♌48	00♍10	28♍45	27♎23	25♏42

5h 56m 0s — 89° 0' 0" — 29 ♊ 05

LAT.	11	12	ASC	2	3
0	26♋57	26♌47	28♍55	01♏08	01♐08
5	27 23	27 11	28 57	00 48	00 45
10	27 48	27 33	28 59	00 29	00 22
15	28 12	27 55	29 01	00 11	29♏59
20	28 37	28 17	29 04	29♎53	29 37
21	28 42	28 21	29 04	29 50	29 32
22	28 47	28 25	29 04	29 46	29 27
23	28 52	28 29	29 05	29 43	29 23
24	28 57	28 33	29 05	29 39	29 18
25	29 03	28 38	29 06	29 36	29 13
26	29 08	28 42	29 06	29 32	29 09
27	29 13	28 46	29 06	29 29	29 04
28	29 18	28 50	29 07	29 25	28 59
29	29 24	28 55	29 07	29 22	28 55
30	29 29	28 59	29 08	29 19	28 50
31	29 34	29 03	29 08	29 15	28 45
32	29 40	29 07	29 09	29 12	28 40
33	29 45	29 11	29 09	29 08	28 35
34	29 51	29 16	29 09	29 05	28 30
35	29 56	29 20	29 10	29 01	28 25
36	00♌02	29 24	29 10	28 58	28 20
37	00 08	29 28	29 11	28 54	28 15
38	00 14	29 33	29 11	28 51	28 10
39	00 19	29 37	29 12	28 47	28 04
40	00 25	29 41	29 12	28 44	27 59
41	00 31	29 46	29 13	28 41	27 54
42	00 38	29 50	29 13	28 37	27 48
43	00 44	29 54	29 13	28 34	27 43
44	00 50	29 58	29 14	28 30	27 37
45	00 56	00♍03	29 14	28 27	27 32
46	01 03	00 07	29 15	28 24	27 26
47	01 09	00 11	29 15	28 21	27 21
48	01 16	00 15	29 16	28 18	27 15
49	01 22	00 19	29 16	28 15	27 09
50	01 29	00 23	29 17	28 12	27 04
51	01 35	00 27	29 17	28 09	26 58
52	01 42	00 30	29 18	28 06	26 53
53	01 48	00 34	29 18	28 04	26 47
54	01 55	00 37	29 19	28 02	26 42
55	02 01	00 40	29 20	28 00	26 37
56	02 07	00 43	29 20	27 58	26 32
57	02 13	00 45	29 21	27 57	26 28
58	02 18	00 46	29 21	27 57	26 24
59	02 22	00 47	29 22	27 58	26 21
60	02♌25	00♍47	29♍23	28♎00	26♏20

6h 0m 0s — 90° 0' 0" — 00 ♋ 00

LAT.	11	12	ASC	2	3
0	27♋55	27♌49	00♎00	02♏11	02♐05
5	28 19	28 11	00 00	01 49	01 41
10	28 43	28 32	00 00	01 28	01 17
15	29 06	28 52	00 00	01 08	00 54
20	29 30	29 11	00 00	00 49	00 30
21	29 35	29 15	00 00	00 45	00 25
22	29 40	29 19	00 00	00 41	00 20
23	29 45	29 23	00 00	00 37	00 15
24	29 50	29 27	00 00	00 33	00 10
25	29 55	29 31	00 00	00 29	00 05
26	29 59	29 35	00 00	00 25	00 01
27	00♌04	29 39	00 00	00 21	29♏56
28	00 09	29 42	00 00	00 18	29 51
29	00 14	29 46	00 00	00 14	29 46
30	00 20	29 50	00 00	00 10	29 40
31	00 25	29 54	00 00	00 06	29 35
32	00 30	29 58	00 00	00 02	29 30
33	00 35	00♍02	00 00	29♎58	29 25
34	00 40	00 05	00 00	29 55	29 20
35	00 46	00 09	00 00	29 51	29 14
36	00 51	00 13	00 00	29 47	29 09
37	00 56	00 17	00 00	29 43	29 04
38	01 02	00 21	00 00	29 39	28 58
39	01 08	00 25	00 00	29 35	28 52
40	01 13	00 29	00 00	29 31	28 47
41	01 19	00 32	00 00	29 28	28 41
42	01 25	00 36	00 00	29 24	28 35
43	01 30	00 40	00 00	29 20	28 30
44	01 36	00 44	00 00	29 16	28 24
45	01 42	00 48	00 00	29 12	28 18
46	01 48	00 51	00 00	29 09	28 12
47	01 54	00 55	00 00	29 05	28 06
48	02 00	00 59	00 00	29 01	28 00
49	02 06	01 02	00 00	28 58	27 54
50	02 12	01 06	00 00	28 54	27 48
51	02 18	01 09	00 00	28 51	27 42
52	02 25	01 12	00 00	28 48	27 35
53	02 30	01 15	00 00	28 45	27 30
54	02 36	01 18	00 00	28 42	27 24
55	02 42	01 20	00 00	28 40	27 18
56	02 47	01 22	00 00	28 38	27 13
57	02 52	01 24	00 00	28 36	27 08
58	02 57	01 24	00 00	28 36	27 03
59	03 00	01 24	00 00	28 36	27 00
60	03♌02	01♍23	00♎00	28♎37	26♏58

6h 4m 0s — 91° 0' 0" — 00 ♋ 55

LAT.	11	12	ASC	2	3
0	28♋52	28♌52	01♎05	03♏13	03♐03
5	29 15	29 12	01 03	02 49	02 37
10	29 38	29 31	01 01	02 27	02 12
15	00♌01	29 49	00 59	02 05	01 48
20	00 23	00♍07	00 56	01 43	01 23
21	00 28	00 10	00 56	01 39	01 18
22	00 33	00 14	00 56	01 35	01 13
23	00 37	00 17	00 55	01 31	01 08
24	00 42	00 21	00 55	01 27	01 03
25	00 47	00 24	00 54	01 22	00 57
26	00 51	00 28	00 54	01 18	00 52
27	00 56	00 31	00 54	01 14	00 47
28	01 01	00 35	00 53	01 10	00 42
29	01 05	00 38	00 53	01 05	00 36
30	01 10	00 41	00 52	01 01	00 31
31	01 15	00 45	00 52	00 57	00 26
32	01 20	00 48	00 51	00 53	00 20
33	01 25	00 52	00 51	00 49	00 15
34	01 30	00 55	00 51	00 44	00 09
35	01 35	00 59	00 50	00 40	00 04
36	01 40	01 02	00 50	00 36	29♏58
37	01 45	01 06	00 49	00 32	29 52
38	01 50	01 09	00 49	00 27	29 46
39	01 56	01 13	00 48	00 23	29 41
40	02 01	01 16	00 48	00 19	29 35
41	02 06	01 19	00 47	00 14	29 29
42	02 12	01 23	00 47	00 10	29 22
43	02 17	01 26	00 47	00 06	29 16
44	02 23	01 30	00 46	00 02	29 10
45	02 28	01 33	00 46	29♎57	29 04
46	02 34	01 36	00 45	29 53	28 57
47	02 39	01 39	00 45	29 49	28 51
48	02 45	01 42	00 44	29 45	28 44
49	02 51	01 45	00 44	29 41	28 38
50	02 56	01 48	00 43	29 37	28 31
51	03 02	01 51	00 43	29 33	28 25
52	03 07	01 54	00 42	29 30	28 18
53	03 13	01 56	00 42	29 26	28 12
54	03 18	01 58	00 41	29 23	28 05
55	03 23	02 00	00 40	29 20	27 59
56	03 28	02 02	00 40	29 17	27 53
57	03 32	02 03	00 39	29 15	27 47
58	03 36	02 03	00 39	29 14	27 42
59	03 39	02 02	00 38	29 13	27 38
60	03♌40	02♍00	00♎37	29♎13	27♏35

6h 8m 0s — 92° 0' 0" — 01 ♋ 50

LAT.	11	12	ASC	2	3
0	29♋49	29♌54	02♎11	04♏16	04♐00
5	00♌12	00♍12	02 06	03 50	03 33
10	00 34	00 29	02 02	03 25	03 07
15	00 55	00 46	01 57	03 02	02 42
20	01 17	01 02	01 53	02 38	02 16
21	01 21	01 05	01 52	02 34	02 10
22	01 25	01 08	01 51	02 29	02 05
23	01 30	01 11	01 50	02 25	02 00
24	01 34	01 14	01 50	02 20	01 55
25	01 39	01 18	01 49	02 15	01 49
26	01 43	01 21	01 48	02 11	01 44
27	01 48	01 24	01 47	02 06	01 38
28	01 52	01 27	01 46	02 02	01 33
29	01 57	01 30	01 45	01 57	01 27
30	02 01	01 33	01 45	01 52	01 22
31	02 06	01 36	01 44	01 48	01 16
32	02 10	01 39	01 43	01 43	01 10
33	02 15	01 42	01 42	01 39	01 04
34	02 20	01 45	01 41	01 34	00 59
35	02 25	01 48	01 40	01 29	00 53
36	02 29	01 51	01 39	01 25	00 47
37	02 34	01 54	01 39	01 20	00 41
38	02 39	01 58	01 38	01 15	00 35
39	02 44	02 01	01 37	01 11	00 28
40	02 49	02 04	01 36	01 06	00 22
41	02 54	02 07	01 35	01 01	00 16
42	02 59	02 10	01 34	00 57	00 09
43	03 04	02 12	01 33	00 52	00 03
44	03 09	02 15	01 32	00 47	29♏56
45	03 14	02 18	01 31	00 42	29 49
46	03 20	02 21	01 30	00 38	29 43
47	03 25	02 24	01 29	00 33	29 36
48	03 30	02 26	01 28	00 29	29 29
49	03 35	02 29	01 27	00 24	29 22
50	03 40	02 31	01 26	00 20	29 15
51	03 46	02 34	01 25	00 15	29 08
52	03 51	02 36	01 24	00 11	29 01
53	03 56	02 38	01 23	00 07	28 54
54	04 00	02 39	01 22	00 03	28 47
55	04 05	02 40	01 21	29♎59	28 40
56	04 09	02 41	01 20	29 56	28 33
57	04 13	02 42	01 18	29 53	28 27
58	04 15	02 41	01 17	29 51	28 21
59	04 17	02 40	01 16	29 50	28 16
60	04♌18	02♍37	01♎15	29♎50	28♏12

6h 12m 0s — 93° 0' 0" — 02 ♋ 45

LAT.	11	12	ASC	2	3
0	00♌47	00♍57	03♎16	05♏18	04♐57
5	01 08	01 13	03 09	04 50	04 29
10	01 29	01 28	03 02	04 24	04 02
15	01 50	01 43	02 56	03 58	03 36
20	02 10	01 57	02 49	03 33	03 09
21	02 14	02 00	02 48	03 28	03 03
22	02 18	02 03	02 47	03 23	02 58
23	02 23	02 06	02 46	03 18	02 52
24	02 27	02 08	02 44	03 13	02 46
25	02 31	02 11	02 43	03 08	02 41
26	02 35	02 14	02 42	03 03	02 35
27	02 39	02 17	02 41	02 58	02 29
28	02 44	02 19	02 39	02 53	02 24
29	02 48	02 22	02 38	02 48	02 18
30	02 52	02 25	02 37	02 43	02 12
31	02 57	02 27	02 36	02 38	02 06
32	03 01	02 30	02 34	02 33	02 00
33	03 05	02 33	02 33	02 28	01 54
34	03 10	02 35	02 32	02 23	01 48
35	03 14	02 38	02 30	02 18	01 42
36	03 19	02 41	02 29	02 13	01 35
37	03 23	02 43	02 28	02 08	01 29
38	03 28	02 46	02 27	02 03	01 23
39	03 32	02 49	02 25	01 58	01 16
40	03 37	02 51	02 24	01 53	01 10
41	03 42	02 54	02 22	01 48	01 03
42	03 47	02 56	02 21	01 43	00 56
43	03 51	02 59	02 20	01 38	00 49
44	03 56	03 01	02 18	01 32	00 42
45	04 01	03 04	02 17	01 27	00 35
46	04 06	03 06	02 15	01 22	00 28
47	04 10	03 08	02 14	01 17	00 21
48	04 15	03 10	02 12	01 12	00 13
49	04 20	03 13	02 11	01 07	00 06
50	04 25	03 14	02 09	01 02	29♏58
51	04 29	03 16	02 08	00 57	29 51
52	04 34	03 18	02 06	00 52	29 43
53	04 38	03 19	02 05	00 48	29 35
54	04 43	03 20	02 03	00 43	29 28
55	04 47	03 21	02 01	00 39	29 20
56	04 50	03 21	01 59	00 35	29 13
57	04 53	03 21	01 58	00 32	29 06
58	04 55	03 20	01 56	00 29	28 59
59	04 57	03 18	01 54	00 27	28 53
60	04♌57	03♍15	01♎52	00♏26	28♏48

6h 16m 0s — 94° 0' 0" — 03 ♋ 40

LAT.	11	12	ASC	2	3
0	01♌45	02♍00	04♎22	06♏19	05♐54
5	02 05	02 14	04 12	05 50	05 25
10	02 25	02 28	04 03	05 22	04 57
15	02 44	02 40	03 54	04 54	04 29
20	03 04	02 53	03 46	04 28	04 01
21	03 08	02 55	03 44	04 22	03 56
22	03 12	02 57	03 43	04 17	03 50
23	03 15	03 00	03 41	04 12	03 44
24	03 19	03 02	03 39	04 06	03 38
25	03 23	03 05	03 38	04 01	03 32
26	03 27	03 07	03 36	03 56	03 26
27	03 31	03 09	03 34	03 50	03 21
28	03 35	03 12	03 33	03 45	03 15
29	03 39	03 14	03 31	03 40	03 08
30	03 43	03 16	03 29	03 34	03 02
31	03 47	03 19	03 28	03 29	02 56
32	03 52	03 21	03 26	03 24	02 50
33	03 56	03 23	03 24	03 18	02 44
34	04 00	03 26	03 23	03 13	02 37
35	04 04	03 28	03 21	03 07	02 31
36	04 08	03 30	03 19	03 02	02 24
37	04 13	03 32	03 17	02 56	02 17
38	04 17	03 35	03 15	02 51	02 11
39	04 21	03 37	03 14	02 45	02 04
40	04 25	03 39	03 12	02 40	01 57
41	04 30	03 41	03 10	02 34	01 50
42	04 34	03 43	03 08	02 29	01 43
43	04 39	03 45	03 06	02 23	01 35
44	04 43	03 47	03 04	02 18	01 28
45	04 47	03 49	03 02	02 12	01 20
46	04 52	03 51	03 01	02 06	01 13
47	04 56	03 53	02 59	02 01	01 05
48	05 01	03 55	02 57	01 55	00 57
49	05 05	03 56	02 55	01 50	00 49
50	05 09	03 58	02 52	01 44	00 41
51	05 14	03 59	02 50	01 39	00 33
52	05 18	04 00	02 48	01 33	00 25
53	05 22	04 01	02 46	01 28	00 17
54	05 25	04 01	02 44	01 23	00 08
55	05 29	04 02	02 42	01 18	00 00
56	05 32	04 01	02 39	01 14	29♏52
57	05 34	04 00	02 37	01 10	29 44
58	05 36	03 59	02 34	01 06	29 37
59	05 36	03 56	02 32	01 04	29 30
60	05♌36	03♍52	02♎29	01♏02	29♏24

6h 20m 0s — 95° 0' 0" — 04 ♋ 35

LAT.	11	12	ASC	2	3
0	02♌43	03♍03	05♎27	07♏21	06♐50
5	03 02	03 15	05 15	06 50	06 21
10	03 21	03 27	05 04	06 20	05 52
15	03 39	03 38	04 53	05 51	05 23
20	03 57	03 48	04 42	05 22	04 54
21	04 01	03 50	04 40	05 16	04 48
22	04 05	03 52	04 38	05 11	04 42
23	04 08	03 54	04 36	05 05	04 36
24	04 12	03 56	04 34	04 59	04 30
25	04 16	03 58	04 32	04 54	04 24
26	04 20	04 00	04 30	04 48	04 18
27	04 23	04 02	04 28	04 42	04 11
28	04 27	04 04	04 26	04 37	04 05
29	04 31	04 06	04 24	04 31	03 59
30	04 35	04 08	04 21	04 25	03 53
31	04 39	04 10	04 19	04 19	03 46
32	04 42	04 12	04 17	04 14	03 40
33	04 46	04 14	04 15	04 08	03 33
34	04 50	04 16	04 13	04 02	03 26
35	04 54	04 18	04 11	03 56	03 19
36	04 58	04 20	04 09	03 50	03 13
37	05 02	04 22	04 06	03 45	03 06
38	05 06	04 23	04 04	03 39	02 58
39	05 10	04 25	04 02	03 33	02 51
40	05 14	04 27	04 00	03 27	02 44
41	05 18	04 29	03 57	03 21	02 37
42	05 22	04 30	03 55	03 15	02 29
43	05 26	04 32	03 53	03 09	02 21
44	05 30	04 34	03 50	03 03	02 14
45	05 34	04 35	03 48	02 56	02 06
46	05 38	04 37	03 46	02 50	01 58
47	05 42	04 38	03 43	02 44	01 49
48	05 46	04 39	03 41	02 38	01 41
49	05 50	04 40	03 38	02 32	01 33
50	05 54	04 41	03 36	02 26	01 24
51	05 58	04 42	03 33	02 20	01 15
52	06 02	04 43	03 30	02 14	01 07
53	06 05	04 43	03 28	02 08	00 58
54	06 08	04 43	03 25	02 03	00 49
55	06 11	04 42	03 22	01 57	00 40
56	06 14	04 42	03 19	01 52	00 31
57	06 15	04 40	03 16	01 48	00 23
58	06 16	04 38	03 13	01 43	00 15
59	06 16	04 35	03 10	01 40	00 07
60	06♌15	04♍30	03♎07	01♏37	00♐00

Koch Table of Houses for Latitudes 0° to 60° North

6h 24m 0s — 96° 0' 0" — 05 ♋ 30

LAT.	11	12	ASC	2	3
0	03♌41	04♍07	06♎32	08♏23	07♐47
5	03 59	04 17	06 18	07 49	07 17
10	04 17	04 26	06 04	07 18	06 47
15	04 34	04 35	05 51	06 47	06 17
20	04 51	04 44	05 39	06 17	05 46
21	04 55	04 46	05 36	06 10	05 40
22	04 58	04 47	05 34	06 04	05 34
23	05 02	04 49	05 31	05 58	05 28
24	05 05	04 51	05 29	05 52	05 22
25	05 09	04 52	05 26	05 46	05 15
26	05 12	04 54	05 24	05 40	05 09
27	05 16	04 56	05 21	05 34	05 02
28	05 19	04 57	05 19	05 28	04 56
29	05 23	04 59	05 16	05 22	04 49
30	05 26	05 00	05 14	05 16	04 43
31	05 30	05 02	05 11	05 10	04 36
32	05 33	05 03	05 09	05 04	04 29
33	05 37	05 05	05 06	04 57	04 22
34	05 40	05 07	05 04	04 51	04 15
35	05 44	05 08	05 01	04 45	04 08
36	05 48	05 10	04 58	04 39	04 01
37	05 51	05 11	04 56	04 32	03 54
38	05 55	05 12	04 53	04 26	03 46
39	05 59	05 14	04 50	04 20	03 39
40	06 03	05 15	04 48	04 13	03 31
41	06 06	05 16	04 45	04 07	03 23
42	06 10	05 18	04 42	04 00	03 15
43	06 14	05 19	04 39	03 54	03 07
44	06 17	05 20	04 37	03 47	02 59
45	06 21	05 21	04 34	03 41	02 51
46	06 25	05 22	04 31	03 34	02 42
47	06 29	05 23	04 28	03 28	02 34
48	06 32	05 24	04 25	03 21	02 25
49	06 36	05 24	04 22	03 14	02 16
50	06 39	05 25	04 19	03 08	02 07
51	06 43	05 25	04 16	03 01	01 58
52	06 46	05 25	04 12	02 55	01 48
53	06 49	05 25	04 09	02 49	01 39
54	06 51	05 24	04 06	02 42	01 29
55	06 54	05 24	04 02	02 36	01 20
56	06 56	05 22	03 59	02 31	01 10
57	06 57	05 20	03 55	02 25	01 01
58	06 58	05 17	03 52	02 20	00 52
59	06 57	05 14	03 48	02 16	00 43
60	06♌55	05♍09	03♎44	02♏13	00♐35

6h 28m 0s — 97° 0' 0" — 06 ♋ 26

LAT.	11	12	ASC	2	3
0	04♌39	05♍10	07♎37	09♏24	08♐43
5	04 56	05 18	07 21	08 49	08 12
10	05 13	05 26	07 05	08 15	07 41
15	05 29	05 33	06 50	07 43	07 10
20	05 45	05 40	06 35	07 11	06 39
21	05 48	05 41	06 32	07 04	06 32
22	05 52	05 42	06 29	06 58	06 26
23	05 55	05 44	06 26	06 52	06 20
24	05 58	05 45	06 24	06 45	06 13
25	06 01	05 46	06 21	06 39	06 06
26	06 05	05 48	06 18	06 32	06 00
27	06 08	05 49	06 15	06 26	05 53
28	06 11	05 50	06 12	06 20	05 46
29	06 14	05 51	06 09	06 13	05 39
30	06 18	05 53	06 06	06 07	05 33
31	06 21	05 54	06 03	06 00	05 26
32	06 24	05 55	06 00	05 53	05 18
33	06 28	05 56	05 57	05 47	05 11
34	06 31	05 57	05 54	05 40	05 04
35	06 34	05 58	05 51	05 34	04 57
36	06 38	05 59	05 48	05 27	04 49
37	06 41	06 00	05 45	05 20	04 41
38	06 45	06 01	05 42	05 14	04 34
39	06 48	06 02	05 39	05 07	04 26
40	06 51	06 03	05 36	05 00	04 18
41	06 55	06 04	05 32	04 53	04 10
42	06 58	06 05	05 29	04 46	04 01
43	07 02	06 06	05 26	04 39	03 53
44	07 05	06 07	05 23	04 32	03 44
45	07 08	06 07	05 19	04 25	03 36
46	07 12	06 08	05 16	04 18	03 27
47	07 15	06 08	05 12	04 11	03 18
48	07 18	06 08	05 09	04 04	03 08
49	07 21	06 09	05 05	03 57	02 59
50	07 24	06 09	05 02	03 50	02 49
51	07 27	06 08	04 58	03 43	02 40
52	07 30	06 08	04 54	03 35	02 30
53	07 33	06 07	04 51	03 29	02 20
54	07 35	06 06	04 47	03 22	02 09
55	07 37	06 05	04 43	03 15	01 59
56	07 38	06 03	04 39	03 09	01 49
57	07 39	06 00	04 34	03 03	01 39
58	07 39	05 57	04 30	02 57	01 29
59	07 38	05 53	04 26	02 52	01 19
60	07♌35	05♍47	04♎21	02♏48	01♐10

6h 32m 0s — 98° 0' 0" — 07 ♋ 21

LAT.	11	12	ASC	2	3
0	05♌38	06♍14	08♎43	10♏25	09♐40
5	05 54	06 20	08 24	09 48	09 07
10	06 09	06 25	08 06	09 13	08 36
15	06 24	06 31	07 48	08 39	08 04
20	06 39	06 36	07 32	08 05	07 31
21	06 42	06 37	07 28	07 58	07 25
22	06 45	06 38	07 25	07 51	07 18
23	06 48	06 39	07 22	07 45	07 11
24	06 51	06 40	07 18	07 38	07 04
25	06 54	06 40	07 15	07 31	06 58
26	06 57	06 41	07 12	07 24	06 51
27	07 00	06 42	07 08	07 18	06 44
28	07 03	06 43	07 05	07 11	06 37
29	07 06	06 44	07 02	07 04	06 30
30	07 09	06 45	06 58	06 57	06 22
31	07 13	06 46	06 55	06 50	06 15
32	07 16	06 46	06 51	06 43	06 08
33	07 19	06 47	06 48	06 36	06 00
34	07 22	06 48	06 45	06 29	05 53
35	07 25	06 49	06 41	06 22	05 45
36	07 28	06 49	06 38	06 15	05 37
37	07 31	06 50	06 34	06 08	05 29
38	07 34	06 51	06 31	06 01	05 21
39	07 37	06 51	06 27	05 54	05 13
40	07 40	06 52	06 24	05 46	05 05
41	07 43	06 52	06 20	05 39	04 56
42	07 47	06 53	06 16	05 32	04 47
43	07 50	06 53	06 12	05 24	04 39
44	07 53	06 53	06 09	05 17	04 30
45	07 56	06 53	06 05	05 09	04 20
46	07 59	06 53	06 01	05 02	04 11
47	08 02	06 53	05 57	04 54	04 01
48	08 05	06 53	05 53	04 46	03 52
49	08 07	06 53	05 49	04 39	03 42
50	08 10	06 53	05 45	04 31	03 32
51	08 13	06 52	05 41	04 24	03 21
52	08 15	06 51	05 36	04 16	03 11
53	08 17	06 50	05 32	04 08	03 00
54	08 19	06 48	05 28	04 01	02 49
55	08 20	06 46	05 23	03 54	02 38
56	08 21	06 44	05 18	03 46	02 27
57	08 21	06 41	05 14	03 40	02 16
58	08 21	06 37	05 09	03 33	02 05
59	08 19	06 32	05 04	03 28	01 55
60	08♌16	06♍26	04♎59	03♏23	01♐45

6h 36m 0s — 99° 0' 0" — 08 ♋ 16

LAT.	11	12	ASC	2	3
0	06♌37	07♍18	09♎48	11♏26	10♐36
5	06 51	07 22	09 26	10 47	10 03
10	07 06	07 25	09 06	10 10	09 30
15	07 20	07 29	08 47	09 34	08 57
20	07 34	07 32	08 28	08 59	08 23
21	07 36	07 32	08 24	08 52	08 17
22	07 39	07 33	08 20	08 45	08 10
23	07 42	07 34	08 17	08 38	08 03
24	07 45	07 34	08 13	08 30	07 56
25	07 47	07 35	08 09	08 23	07 49
26	07 50	07 35	08 06	08 16	07 42
27	07 53	07 36	08 02	08 09	07 34
28	07 56	07 36	07 58	08 02	07 27
29	07 59	07 37	07 54	07 55	07 20
30	08 01	07 37	07 50	07 47	07 12
31	08 04	07 38	07 47	07 40	07 05
32	08 07	07 38	07 43	07 33	06 57
33	08 10	07 38	07 39	07 25	06 49
34	08 13	07 39	07 35	07 18	06 41
35	08 15	07 39	07 31	07 11	06 33
36	08 18	07 39	07 27	07 03	06 25
37	08 21	07 40	07 23	06 56	06 17
38	08 24	07 40	07 19	06 48	06 09
39	08 27	07 40	07 15	06 40	06 00
40	08 30	07 40	07 11	06 33	05 51
41	08 32	07 40	07 07	06 25	05 42
42	08 35	07 40	07 03	06 17	05 33
43	08 38	07 40	06 59	06 09	05 24
44	08 41	07 40	06 55	06 01	05 15
45	08 43	07 40	06 50	05 53	05 05
46	08 46	07 39	06 46	05 45	04 55
47	08 49	07 39	06 42	05 37	04 45
48	08 51	07 38	06 37	05 29	04 35
49	08 53	07 38	06 33	05 21	04 24
50	08 56	07 37	06 28	05 13	04 14
51	08 58	07 35	06 23	05 04	04 03
52	09 00	07 34	06 18	04 56	03 52
53	09 01	07 32	06 14	04 48	03 40
54	09 03	07 30	06 09	04 40	03 29
55	09 04	07 28	06 03	04 32	03 17
56	09 04	07 25	05 58	04 24	03 05
57	09 04	07 21	05 53	04 17	02 53
58	09 03	07 17	05 47	04 10	02 42
59	09 01	07 11	05 42	04 03	02 30
60	08♌57	07♍05	05♎36	03♏58	02♐19

6h 40m 0s — 100° 0' 0" — 09 ♋ 11

LAT.	11	12	ASC	2	3
0	07♌35	08♍22	10♎53	12♏27	11♐32
5	07 49	08 23	10 29	11 46	10 58
10	08 02	08 25	10 07	11 08	10 24
15	08 15	08 27	09 45	10 30	09 50
20	08 28	08 28	09 24	09 53	09 16
21	08 30	08 28	09 20	09 45	09 09
22	08 33	08 28	09 16	09 38	09 01
23	08 36	08 29	09 12	09 30	08 54
24	08 38	08 29	09 08	09 23	08 47
25	08 41	08 29	09 04	09 15	08 40
26	08 43	08 29	08 59	09 08	08 32
27	08 46	08 29	08 55	09 00	08 25
28	08 48	08 29	08 51	08 53	08 17
29	08 51	08 30	08 47	08 45	08 10
30	08 53	08 30	08 43	08 38	08 02
31	08 56	08 30	08 39	08 30	07 54
32	08 58	08 30	08 34	08 22	07 46
33	09 01	08 30	08 30	08 15	07 38
34	09 04	08 30	08 26	08 07	07 30
35	09 06	08 30	08 21	07 59	07 22
36	09 09	08 30	08 17	07 51	07 13
37	09 11	08 29	08 13	07 43	07 05
38	09 14	08 29	08 08	07 35	06 56
39	09 16	08 29	08 04	07 27	06 47
40	09 19	08 29	07 59	07 19	06 38
41	09 21	08 28	07 55	07 11	06 29
42	09 24	08 28	07 50	07 02	06 19
43	09 26	08 28	07 46	06 54	06 09
44	09 29	08 27	07 41	06 46	06 00
45	09 31	08 26	07 36	06 37	05 50
46	09 33	08 25	07 31	06 29	05 39
47	09 36	08 25	07 26	06 20	05 29
48	09 38	08 24	07 21	06 11	05 18
49	09 40	08 22	07 16	06 03	05 07
50	09 42	08 21	07 11	05 54	04 56
51	09 43	08 19	07 06	05 45	04 44
52	09 45	08 17	07 00	05 36	04 32
53	09 46	08 15	06 55	05 27	04 20
54	09 47	08 13	06 49	05 19	04 08
55	09 48	08 10	06 44	05 10	03 56
56	09 48	08 06	06 38	05 02	03 43
57	09 47	08 02	06 32	04 54	03 30
58	09 45	07 57	06 26	04 46	03 18
59	09 42	07 51	06 20	04 38	03 05
60	09♌38	07♍44	06♎13	04♏32	02♐53

6h 44m 0s — 101° 0' 0" — 10 ♋ 07

LAT.	11	12	ASC	2	3
0	08♌34	09♍26	11♎58	13♏27	12♐28
5	08 47	09 25	11 32	12 45	11 53
10	08 59	09 25	11 07	12 05	11 18
15	09 11	09 25	10 44	11 25	10 43
20	09 23	09 24	10 21	10 46	10 08
21	09 25	09 24	10 16	10 39	10 00
22	09 27	09 24	10 12	10 31	09 53
23	09 29	09 24	10 07	10 23	09 46
24	09 32	09 24	10 02	10 15	09 38
25	09 34	09 23	09 58	10 07	09 31
26	09 36	09 23	09 53	10 00	09 23
27	09 39	09 23	09 49	09 52	09 15
28	09 41	09 23	09 44	09 44	09 07
29	09 43	09 23	09 40	09 36	09 00
30	09 46	09 22	09 35	09 28	08 52
31	09 48	09 22	09 30	09 20	08 43
32	09 50	09 22	09 26	09 12	08 35
33	09 52	09 21	09 21	09 04	08 27
34	09 55	09 21	09 16	08 55	08 18
35	09 57	09 20	09 11	08 47	08 10
36	09 59	09 20	09 07	08 39	08 01
37	10 02	09 19	09 02	08 30	07 52
38	10 04	09 19	08 57	08 22	07 43
39	10 06	09 18	08 52	08 14	07 34
40	10 08	09 17	08 47	08 05	07 24
41	10 11	09 17	08 42	07 56	07 15
42	10 13	09 16	08 37	07 48	07 05
43	10 15	09 15	08 32	07 39	06 55
44	10 17	09 14	08 27	07 30	06 44
45	10 19	09 13	08 22	07 21	06 34
46	10 21	09 12	08 16	07 12	06 23
47	10 23	09 10	08 11	07 03	06 12
48	10 25	09 09	08 05	06 54	06 01
49	10 26	09 07	08 00	06 44	05 49
50	10 28	09 05	07 54	06 35	05 38
51	10 29	09 03	07 48	06 26	05 25
52	10 30	09 01	07 42	06 16	05 13
53	10 31	08 58	07 36	06 07	05 00
54	10 32	08 55	07 30	05 57	04 47
55	10 32	08 52	07 24	05 48	04 34
56	10 31	08 48	07 18	05 39	04 21
57	10 30	08 43	07 11	05 30	04 07
58	10 28	08 38	07 05	05 22	03 53
59	10 25	08 31	06 58	05 13	03 39
60	10♌20	08♍24	06♎51	05♏06	03♐26

6h 48m 0s — 102° 0' 0" — 11 ♋ 02

LAT.	11	12	ASC	2	3
0	09♌34	10♍30	13♎03	14♏28	13♐24
5	09 45	10 28	12 34	13 44	12 48
10	09 56	10 25	12 08	13 02	12 12
15	10 07	10 23	11 42	12 21	11 37
20	10 17	10 21	11 17	11 40	11 00
21	10 19	10 20	11 12	11 32	10 52
22	10 21	10 20	11 07	11 24	10 45
23	10 23	10 19	11 02	11 16	10 37
24	10 26	10 19	10 57	11 07	10 29
25	10 28	10 18	10 52	10 59	10 21
26	10 30	10 17	10 47	10 51	10 14
27	10 32	10 17	10 42	10 43	10 06
28	10 34	10 16	10 37	10 35	09 58
29	10 36	10 16	10 32	10 26	09 49
30	10 38	10 15	10 27	10 18	09 41
31	10 40	10 14	10 22	10 09	09 33
32	10 42	10 14	10 17	10 01	09 24
33	10 44	10 13	10 12	09 52	09 16
34	10 46	10 12	10 07	09 44	09 07
35	10 48	10 11	10 02	09 35	08 58
36	10 50	10 10	09 56	09 26	08 49
37	10 52	10 09	09 51	09 18	08 39
38	10 54	10 08	09 46	09 09	08 30
39	10 56	10 07	09 40	09 00	08 20
40	10 58	10 06	09 35	08 51	08 11
41	11 00	10 05	09 30	08 42	08 01
42	11 02	10 04	09 24	08 33	07 50
43	11 04	10 03	09 19	08 23	07 40
44	11 05	10 01	09 13	08 14	07 29
45	11 07	10 00	09 07	08 04	07 18
46	11 09	09 58	09 01	07 55	07 07
47	11 10	09 56	08 55	07 45	06 55
48	11 12	09 54	08 49	07 36	06 44
49	11 13	09 52	08 43	07 26	06 32
50	11 14	09 50	08 37	07 16	06 19
51	11 15	09 47	08 31	07 06	06 06
52	11 16	09 44	08 24	06 56	05 53
53	11 16	09 41	08 18	06 46	05 40
54	11 17	09 38	08 11	06 36	05 26
55	11 16	09 34	08 04	06 26	05 12
56	11 15	09 29	07 57	06 16	04 58
57	11 14	09 24	07 50	06 07	04 43
58	11 11	09 18	07 43	05 57	04 29
59	11 08	09 11	07 36	05 48	04 14
60	11♌02	09♍03	07♎28	05♏40	03♐59

6h 52m 0s — 103° 0' 0" — 11 ♋ 58

LAT.	11	12	ASC	2	3
0	10♌33	11♍34	14♎07	15♏28	14♐20
5	10 43	11 30	13 37	14 43	13 43
10	10 53	11 26	13 08	13 59	13 06
15	11 03	11 21	12 40	13 16	12 30
20	11 12	11 17	12 13	12 34	11 52
21	11 14	11 16	12 08	12 25	11 44
22	11 16	11 15	12 02	12 17	11 36
23	11 18	11 15	11 57	12 08	11 28
24	11 19	11 14	11 52	12 00	11 20
25	11 21	11 13	11 46	11 51	11 12
26	11 23	11 12	11 41	11 42	11 04
27	11 25	11 11	11 36	11 34	10 56
28	11 27	11 10	11 30	11 25	10 48
29	11 29	11 09	11 25	11 16	10 39
30	11 30	11 08	11 19	11 08	10 31
31	11 32	11 07	11 14	10 59	10 22
32	11 34	11 06	11 08	10 50	10 13
33	11 36	11 04	11 03	10 41	10 04
34	11 38	11 03	10 57	10 32	09 55
35	11 39	11 02	10 52	10 23	09 46
36	11 41	11 01	10 46	10 14	09 36
37	11 43	11 00	10 40	10 05	09 27
38	11 45	10 58	10 35	09 56	09 17
39	11 46	10 57	10 29	09 46	09 07
40	11 48	10 55	10 23	09 37	08 57
41	11 50	10 54	10 17	09 27	08 46
42	11 51	10 52	10 11	09 18	08 36
43	11 53	10 50	10 05	09 08	08 25
44	11 54	10 49	09 59	08 58	08 14
45	11 56	10 47	09 53	08 48	08 02
46	11 57	10 45	09 46	08 38	07 51
47	11 58	10 42	09 40	08 28	07 39
48	11 59	10 40	09 34	08 18	07 26
49	12 00	10 37	09 27	08 07	07 14
50	12 01	10 35	09 20	07 57	07 01
51	12 02	10 32	09 13	07 46	06 47
52	12 02	10 28	09 06	07 36	06 34
53	12 02	10 25	08 59	07 25	06 19
54	12 02	10 21	08 52	07 14	06 05
55	12 01	10 16	08 45	07 04	05 50
56	12 00	10 11	08 37	06 53	05 35
57	11 58	10 06	08 30	06 43	05 19
58	11 55	09 59	08 22	06 33	05 04
59	11 51	09 52	08 14	06 23	04 48
60	11♌45	09♍43	08♎05	06♏14	04♐32

Koch Table of Houses for Latitudes 0° to 60° North

6h 56m 0s — 104° 0' 0" — 12 ♋ 53

LAT.	11	12	ASC	2	3
0	11♌32	12♍39	15♎12	16♏28	15♐16
5	11 42	12 32	14 39	15 41	14 38
10	11 50	12 26	14 08	14 55	14 00
15	11 59	12 20	13 39	14 11	13 22
20	12 07	12 14	13 09	13 27	12 44
21	12 09	12 13	13 04	13 18	12 36
22	12 10	12 11	12 58	13 09	12 28
23	12 12	12 10	12 52	13 00	12 19
24	12 14	12 09	12 46	12 52	12 11
25	12 15	12 07	12 40	12 43	12 03
26	12 17	12 06	12 35	12 34	11 55
27	12 18	12 05	12 29	12 25	11 46
28	12 20	12 03	12 23	12 16	11 38
29	12 22	12 02	12 17	12 07	11 29
30	12 23	12 01	12 11	11 58	11 20
31	12 25	11 59	12 06	11 48	11 11
32	12 26	11 58	12 00	11 39	11 02
33	12 28	11 56	11 54	11 30	10 53
34	12 29	11 55	11 48	11 20	10 43
35	12 31	11 53	11 42	11 11	10 34
36	12 32	11 52	11 36	11 02	10 24
37	12 34	11 50	11 29	10 52	10 14
38	12 35	11 48	11 23	10 42	10 04
39	12 37	11 46	11 17	10 32	09 54
40	12 38	11 44	11 11	10 22	09 43
41	12 39	11 42	11 04	10 12	09 32
42	12 41	11 40	10 58	10 02	09 21
43	12 42	11 38	10 52	09 52	09 10
44	12 43	11 36	10 45	09 42	08 58
45	12 44	11 34	10 38	09 31	08 46
46	12 45	11 31	10 31	09 21	08 34
47	12 46	11 29	10 25	09 10	08 22
48	12 47	11 26	10 18	08 59	08 09
49	12 48	11 23	10 11	08 48	07 56
50	12 48	11 20	10 03	08 37	07 42
51	12 48	11 16	09 56	08 26	07 28
52	12 48	11 12	09 48	08 15	07 14
53	12 48	11 08	09 41	08 04	06 59
54	12 47	11 04	09 33	07 53	06 44
55	12 46	10 59	09 25	07 41	06 28
56	12 44	10 53	09 17	07 30	06 12
57	12 42	10 47	09 09	07 19	05 55
58	12 39	10 40	09 00	07 08	05 38
59	12 34	10 33	08 51	06 57	05 21
60	12♌28	10♍23	08♎43	06♏47	05♐04

7h 0m 0s — 105° 0' 0" — 13 ♋ 49

LAT.	11	12	ASC	2	3
0	12♌32	13♍43	16♎17	17♏28	16♐11
5	12 40	13 35	15 42	16 39	15 33
10	12 48	13 26	15 09	15 52	14 54
15	12 55	13 18	14 37	15 06	14 15
20	13 02	13 11	14 06	14 20	13 35
21	13 04	13 09	13 59	14 11	13 27
22	13 05	13 07	13 53	14 02	13 19
23	13 06	13 06	13 47	13 53	13 11
24	13 08	13 04	13 41	13 43	13 02
25	13 09	13 02	13 35	13 34	12 54
26	13 11	13 01	13 28	13 25	12 45
27	13 12	12 59	13 22	13 16	12 36
28	13 13	12 57	13 16	13 06	12 27
29	13 15	12 56	13 10	12 57	12 18
30	13 16	12 54	13 03	12 47	12 09
31	13 17	12 52	12 57	12 38	12 00
32	13 19	12 50	12 51	12 28	11 51
33	13 20	12 48	12 45	12 18	11 41
34	13 21	12 46	12 38	12 09	11 31
35	13 22	12 44	12 32	11 59	11 22
36	13 24	12 42	12 25	11 49	11 11
37	13 25	12 40	12 19	11 39	11 01
38	13 26	12 38	12 12	11 29	10 51
39	13 27	12 36	12 05	11 18	10 40
40	13 28	12 34	11 59	11 08	10 29
41	13 29	12 31	11 52	10 58	10 18
42	13 30	12 29	11 45	10 47	10 06
43	13 31	12 26	11 38	10 36	09 55
44	13 32	12 24	11 31	10 26	09 43
45	13 33	12 21	11 24	10 15	09 30
46	13 34	12 18	11 17	10 04	09 17
47	13 34	12 15	11 09	09 52	09 04
48	13 35	12 12	11 02	09 41	08 51
49	13 35	12 08	10 54	09 30	08 37
50	13 35	12 05	10 46	09 18	08 23
51	13 35	12 01	10 38	09 06	08 08
52	13 35	11 56	10 30	08 54	07 53
53	13 34	11 52	10 22	08 43	07 38
54	13 33	11 47	10 14	08 31	07 22
55	13 31	11 42	10 05	08 19	07 05
56	13 29	11 36	09 57	08 07	06 48
57	13 26	11 29	09 48	07 55	06 31
58	13 23	11 22	09 39	07 43	06 13
59	13 18	11 13	09 29	07 31	05 54
60	13♌11	11♍04	09♎20	07♏21	05♐36

7h 4m 0s — 106° 0' 0" — 14 ♋ 44

LAT.	11	12	ASC	2	3
0	13♌32	14♍48	17♎21	18♏28	17♐07
5	13 39	14 37	16 44	17 37	16 27
10	13 45	14 27	16 09	16 49	15 48
15	13 52	14 17	15 35	16 01	15 08
20	13 58	14 07	15 02	15 13	14 27
21	13 59	14 05	14 55	15 04	14 19
22	14 00	14 03	14 48	14 54	14 10
23	14 01	14 01	14 42	14 45	14 02
24	14 02	13 59	14 35	14 35	13 53
25	14 03	13 57	14 29	14 26	13 44
26	14 05	13 55	14 22	14 16	13 35
27	14 06	13 53	14 16	14 06	13 26
28	14 07	13 51	14 09	13 57	13 17
29	14 08	13 49	14 02	13 47	13 08
30	14 09	13 47	13 56	13 37	12 59
31	14 10	13 45	13 49	13 27	12 49
32	14 11	13 43	13 42	13 17	12 39
33	14 12	13 40	13 35	13 07	12 30
34	14 13	13 38	13 29	12 57	12 20
35	14 14	13 36	13 22	12 46	12 09
36	14 15	13 33	13 15	12 36	11 59
37	14 16	13 31	13 08	12 26	11 48
38	14 17	13 28	13 01	12 15	11 37
39	14 18	13 26	12 54	12 04	11 26
40	14 19	13 23	12 46	11 54	11 15
41	14 20	13 20	12 39	11 43	11 03
42	14 20	13 17	12 32	11 32	10 51
43	14 21	13 15	12 24	11 21	10 39
44	14 21	13 11	12 17	11 09	10 27
45	14 22	13 08	12 09	10 58	10 14
46	14 22	13 05	12 02	10 46	10 01
47	14 23	13 01	11 54	10 34	09 47
48	14 23	12 58	11 46	10 23	09 33
49	14 23	12 54	11 38	10 11	09 19
50	14 23	12 50	11 29	09 58	09 04
51	14 22	12 45	11 21	09 46	08 49
52	14 21	12 41	11 12	09 34	08 33
53	14 20	12 36	11 04	09 21	08 17
54	14 19	12 30	10 55	09 08	08 00
55	14 17	12 25	10 46	08 56	07 43
56	14 15	12 18	10 36	08 43	07 25
57	14 11	12 11	10 27	08 30	07 06
58	14 07	12 03	10 17	08 18	06 47
59	14 02	11 54	10 07	08 05	06 27
60	13♌55	11♍44	09♎57	07♏54	06♐07

7h 8m 0s — 107° 0' 0" — 15 ♋ 40

LAT.	11	12	ASC	2	3
0	14♌32	15♍53	18♎26	19♏27	18♐02
5	14 38	15 40	17 46	18 35	17 22
10	14 43	15 28	17 09	17 45	16 42
15	14 48	15 16	16 33	16 56	16 01
20	14 53	15 04	15 58	16 06	15 19
21	14 54	15 02	15 51	15 57	15 10
22	14 55	15 00	15 44	15 47	15 02
23	14 56	14 57	15 37	15 37	14 53
24	14 57	14 55	15 30	15 27	14 44
25	14 58	14 52	15 23	15 17	14 35
26	14 59	14 50	15 16	15 07	14 26
27	15 00	14 48	15 09	14 57	14 16
28	15 01	14 45	15 02	14 47	14 07
29	15 01	14 43	14 55	14 37	13 58
30	15 02	14 40	14 48	14 26	13 48
31	15 03	14 38	14 41	14 16	13 38
32	15 04	14 35	14 33	14 06	13 28
33	15 05	14 32	14 26	13 55	13 18
34	15 05	14 30	14 19	13 45	13 08
35	15 06	14 27	14 12	13 34	12 57
36	15 07	14 24	14 04	13 23	12 46
37	15 08	14 21	13 57	13 12	12 35
38	15 08	14 19	13 49	13 01	12 24
39	15 09	14 16	13 42	12 50	12 13
40	15 09	14 13	13 34	12 39	12 01
41	15 10	14 09	13 27	12 28	11 49
42	15 10	14 06	13 19	12 16	11 37
43	15 11	14 03	13 11	12 05	11 24
44	15 11	13 59	13 03	11 53	11 11
45	15 11	13 56	12 55	11 41	10 58
46	15 11	13 52	12 47	11 29	10 44
47	15 11	13 48	12 38	11 16	10 30
48	15 11	13 44	12 30	11 04	10 15
49	15 11	13 40	12 21	10 51	10 00
50	15 10	13 35	12 12	10 39	09 45
51	15 09	13 30	12 03	10 26	09 29
52	15 08	13 25	11 54	10 13	09 13
53	15 07	13 20	11 45	10 00	08 55
54	15 05	13 14	11 36	09 46	08 38
55	15 03	13 08	11 26	09 33	08 20
56	15 00	13 01	11 16	09 19	08 01
57	14 57	12 53	11 06	09 06	07 41
58	14 52	12 45	10 56	08 52	07 21
59	14 47	12 36	10 45	08 39	07 00
60	14♌39	12♍25	10♎34	08♏26	06♐39

7h 12m 0s — 108° 0' 0" — 16 ♋ 36

LAT.	11	12	ASC	2	3
0	15♌32	16♍57	19♎30	20♏26	18♐58
5	15 37	16 42	18 48	19 33	18 17
10	15 41	16 28	18 09	18 41	17 36
15	15 45	16 15	17 31	17 50	16 54
20	15 49	16 01	16 54	16 59	16 11
21	15 50	15 59	16 46	16 49	16 02
22	15 50	15 56	16 39	16 39	15 53
23	15 51	15 53	16 32	16 29	15 44
24	15 52	15 50	16 24	16 19	15 35
25	15 52	15 48	16 17	16 08	15 25
26	15 53	15 45	16 09	15 58	15 16
27	15 54	15 42	16 02	15 47	15 06
28	15 54	15 39	15 55	15 37	14 57
29	15 55	15 36	15 47	15 26	14 47
30	15 56	15 34	15 40	15 16	14 37
31	15 56	15 31	15 32	15 05	14 27
32	15 57	15 28	15 25	14 54	14 17
33	15 57	15 25	15 17	14 44	14 06
34	15 58	15 22	15 09	14 33	13 56
35	15 58	15 19	15 02	14 21	13 45
36	15 59	15 15	14 54	14 10	13 34
37	15 59	15 12	14 46	13 59	13 22
38	16 00	15 09	14 38	13 48	13 11
39	16 00	15 06	14 30	13 36	12 59
40	16 00	15 02	14 22	13 24	12 47
41	16 00	14 59	14 14	13 13	12 34
42	16 01	14 55	14 06	13 01	12 22
43	16 01	14 51	13 57	12 49	12 08
44	16 01	14 47	13 49	12 36	11 55
45	16 01	14 43	13 40	12 24	11 41
46	16 00	14 39	13 32	12 11	11 27
47	16 00	14 35	13 23	11 58	11 12
48	16 00	14 30	13 14	11 45	10 57
49	15 59	14 26	13 05	11 32	10 42
50	15 58	14 21	12 55	11 19	10 26
51	15 57	14 15	12 46	11 05	10 09
52	15 56	14 10	12 36	10 52	09 52
53	15 54	14 04	12 27	10 38	09 34
54	15 52	13 58	12 17	10 24	09 16
55	15 49	13 51	12 06	10 10	08 56
56	15 46	13 44	11 56	09 55	08 37
57	15 42	13 36	11 45	09 41	08 16
58	15 37	13 27	11 34	09 27	07 55
59	15 31	13 17	11 23	09 13	07 33
60	15♌24	13♍06	11♎12	08♏59	07♐10

7h 16m 0s — 109° 0' 0" — 17 ♋ 32

LAT.	11	12	ASC	2	3
0	16♌33	18♍02	20♎34	21♏26	19♐53
5	16 36	17 45	19 50	20 30	19 11
10	16 39	17 29	19 09	19 37	18 29
15	16 42	17 14	18 29	18 45	17 46
20	16 45	16 58	17 50	17 52	17 02
21	16 45	16 55	17 42	17 42	16 53
22	16 46	16 52	17 34	17 31	16 44
23	16 46	16 49	17 26	17 21	16 35
24	16 47	16 46	17 19	17 10	16 25
25	16 47	16 43	17 11	16 59	16 16
26	16 47	16 40	17 03	16 49	16 06
27	16 48	16 37	16 55	16 38	15 56
28	16 48	16 34	16 47	16 27	15 46
29	16 49	16 30	16 40	16 16	15 36
30	16 49	16 27	16 32	16 05	15 26
31	16 49	16 24	16 24	15 54	15 16
32	16 50	16 20	16 16	15 43	15 05
33	16 50	16 17	16 08	15 32	14 54
34	16 50	16 14	16 00	15 20	14 43
35	16 51	16 10	15 52	15 09	14 32
36	16 51	16 07	15 43	14 57	14 21
37	16 51	16 03	15 35	14 46	14 09
38	16 51	15 59	15 27	14 34	13 57
39	16 51	15 56	15 18	14 22	13 45
40	16 51	15 52	15 10	14 10	13 32
41	16 51	15 48	15 01	13 57	13 20
42	16 51	15 44	14 53	13 45	13 06
43	16 51	15 40	14 44	13 32	12 53
44	16 51	15 36	14 35	13 20	12 39
45	16 50	15 31	14 26	13 07	12 25
46	16 50	15 27	14 17	12 53	12 10
47	16 49	15 22	14 07	12 40	11 55
48	16 48	15 17	13 58	12 27	11 39
49	16 47	15 12	13 48	12 13	11 23
50	16 46	15 06	13 38	11 59	11 06
51	16 45	15 01	13 28	11 45	10 49
52	16 43	14 55	13 18	11 30	10 31
53	16 41	14 48	13 08	11 16	10 12
54	16 39	14 42	12 57	11 01	09 53
55	16 36	14 34	12 47	10 46	09 33
56	16 32	14 27	12 36	10 31	09 12
57	16 28	14 18	12 24	10 16	08 51
58	16 23	14 09	12 13	10 01	08 28
59	16 17	13 59	12 01	09 46	08 05
60	16♌09	13♍48	11♎49	09♏32	07♐40

7h 20m 0s — 110° 0' 0" — 18 ♋ 28

LAT.	11	12	ASC	2	3
0	17♌33	19♍07	21♎38	22♏25	20♐49
5	17 35	18 48	20 52	21 28	20 06
10	17 37	18 30	20 09	20 33	19 23
15	17 39	18 13	19 27	19 39	18 39
20	17 41	17 56	18 46	18 45	17 54
21	17 41	17 52	18 37	18 34	17 45
22	17 41	17 49	18 29	18 23	17 35
23	17 41	17 45	18 21	18 12	17 26
24	17 42	17 42	18 13	18 01	17 16
25	17 42	17 38	18 05	17 50	17 06
26	17 42	17 35	17 57	17 39	16 56
27	17 42	17 31	17 48	17 28	16 46
28	17 43	17 28	17 40	17 17	16 36
29	17 43	17 24	17 32	17 06	16 26
30	17 43	17 21	17 24	16 54	16 15
31	17 43	17 17	17 15	16 43	16 05
32	17 43	17 13	17 07	16 31	15 54
33	17 43	17 10	16 58	16 20	15 43
34	17 43	17 06	16 50	16 08	15 31
35	17 43	17 02	16 41	15 56	15 20
36	17 43	16 58	16 33	15 44	15 08
37	17 43	16 54	16 24	15 32	14 56
38	17 43	16 50	16 15	15 20	14 44
39	17 43	16 46	16 07	15 07	14 31
40	17 42	16 42	15 58	14 55	14 18
41	17 42	16 37	15 49	14 42	14 05
42	17 42	16 33	15 39	14 29	13 51
43	17 41	16 28	15 30	14 16	13 37
44	17 41	16 24	15 21	14 03	13 23
45	17 40	16 19	15 11	13 49	13 08
46	17 39	16 14	15 02	13 36	12 53
47	17 38	16 09	14 52	13 22	12 37
48	17 37	16 03	14 42	13 08	12 21
49	17 36	15 58	14 32	12 53	12 04
50	17 35	15 52	14 21	12 39	11 47
51	17 33	15 46	14 11	12 24	11 29
52	17 31	15 40	14 00	12 09	11 10
53	17 29	15 33	13 49	11 54	10 51
54	17 26	15 26	13 38	11 39	10 31
55	17 23	15 18	13 27	11 23	10 10
56	17 19	15 10	13 15	11 07	09 48
57	17 14	15 01	13 03	10 51	09 25
58	17 09	14 52	12 51	10 35	09 01
59	17 02	14 41	12 39	10 20	08 37
60	16♌54	14♍29	12♎26	10♏04	08♐11

7h 24m 0s — 111° 0' 0" — 19 ♋ 24

LAT.	11	12	ASC	2	3
0	18♌34	20♍12	22♎42	23♏23	21♐44
5	18 35	19 51	21 54	22 25	21 00
10	18 36	19 31	21 09	21 29	20 16
15	18 36	19 12	20 25	20 33	19 32
20	18 37	18 53	19 42	19 38	18 45
21	18 37	18 49	19 33	19 26	18 36
22	18 37	18 45	19 24	19 15	18 26
23	18 37	18 42	19 16	19 04	18 17
24	18 37	18 38	19 07	18 53	18 07
25	18 37	18 34	18 59	18 41	17 57
26	18 37	18 30	18 50	18 30	17 47
27	18 37	18 26	18 42	18 18	17 36
28	18 37	18 22	18 33	18 07	17 26
29	18 37	18 18	18 24	17 55	17 15
30	18 37	18 14	18 16	17 44	17 04
31	18 37	18 10	18 07	17 32	16 53
32	18 36	18 06	17 58	17 20	16 42
33	18 36	18 02	17 49	17 08	16 31
34	18 36	17 58	17 40	16 56	16 19
35	18 36	17 54	17 31	16 43	16 07
36	18 36	17 50	17 22	16 31	15 55
37	18 35	17 45	17 13	16 18	15 43
38	18 35	17 41	17 04	16 06	15 30
39	18 34	17 36	16 55	15 53	15 17
40	18 34	17 32	16 45	15 40	15 04
41	18 33	17 27	16 36	15 27	14 50
42	18 33	17 22	16 26	15 13	14 36
43	18 32	17 17	16 16	15 00	14 22
44	18 31	17 12	16 07	14 46	14 07
45	18 30	17 07	15 57	14 32	13 52
46	18 29	17 02	15 47	14 18	13 36
47	18 28	16 56	15 36	14 03	13 19
48	18 27	16 50	15 26	13 49	13 03
49	18 25	16 44	15 15	13 34	12 45
50	18 23	16 38	15 04	13 19	12 27
51	18 21	16 32	14 53	13 03	12 08
52	18 19	16 25	14 42	12 48	11 49
53	18 16	16 18	14 31	12 32	11 29
54	18 13	16 10	14 19	12 16	11 08
55	18 10	16 02	14 07	11 59	10 46
56	18 05	15 53	13 55	11 43	10 23
57	18 01	15 44	13 42	11 26	09 59
58	17 55	15 34	13 30	11 09	09 34
59	17 48	15 23	13 17	10 53	09 08
60	17♌40	15♍11	13♎03	10♏36	08♐41

Koch Table of Houses for Latitudes 0° to 60° North

7h 28m 0s	20 ♋ 20	112° 0' 0"			
LAT.	11	12	ASC	2	3
0	19♌35	21♍17	23♎46	24♏22	22♐39
5	19 35	20 54	22 56	23 22	21 55
10	19 34	20 32	22 08	22 24	21 10
15	19 34	20 11	21 22	21 27	20 24
20	19 33	19 50	20 37	20 30	19 37
21	19 33	19 46	20 28	20 19	19 27
22	19 33	19 42	20 19	20 07	19 17
23	19 33	19 38	20 10	19 56	19 07
24	19 32	19 34	20 02	19 44	18 57
25	19 32	19 29	19 53	19 32	18 47
26	19 32	19 25	19 44	19 20	18 37
27	19 32	19 21	19 35	19 09	18 26
28	19 31	19 17	19 26	18 57	18 15
29	19 31	19 12	19 17	18 45	18 05
30	19 31	19 08	19 07	18 33	17 53
31	19 30	19 04	18 58	18 20	17 42
32	19 30	18 59	18 49	18 08	17 31
33	19 30	18 55	18 40	17 56	17 19
34	19 29	18 50	18 31	17 43	17 07
35	19 29	18 46	18 21	17 30	16 55
36	19 28	18 41	18 12	17 18	16 42
37	19 28	18 36	18 02	17 05	16 30
38	19 27	18 32	17 53	16 52	16 17
39	19 26	18 27	17 43	16 38	16 03
40	19 26	18 22	17 33	16 25	15 49
41	19 25	18 17	17 23	16 11	15 35
42	19 24	18 12	17 13	15 57	15 21
43	19 23	18 06	17 03	15 43	15 06
44	19 22	18 01	16 53	15 29	14 51
45	19 20	17 55	16 42	15 14	14 35
46	19 19	17 49	16 31	15 00	14 18
47	19 18	17 43	16 21	14 45	14 02
48	19 16	17 37	16 10	14 30	13 44
49	19 14	17 31	15 59	14 14	13 26
50	19 12	17 24	15 47	13 58	13 07
51	19 10	17 17	15 36	13 42	12 48
52	19 07	17 10	15 24	13 26	12 28
53	19 04	17 02	15 12	13 10	12 07
54	19 01	16 54	15 00	12 53	11 45
55	18 57	16 46	14 47	12 36	11 22
56	18 53	16 37	14 35	12 18	10 58
57	18 47	16 27	14 22	12 01	10 33
58	18 41	16 17	14 08	11 43	10 07
59	18 34	16 05	13 54	11 26	09 40
60	18♌26	15♍53	13♎40	11♏08	09♐11

7h 32m 0s	21 ♋ 17	113° 0' 0"			
LAT.	11	12	ASC	2	3
0	20♌36	22♍23	24♎50	25♏21	23♐34
5	20 35	21 57	23 58	24 19	22 49
10	20 33	21 33	23 08	23 20	22 04
15	20 31	21 10	22 20	22 21	21 17
20	20 30	20 48	21 33	21 23	20 29
21	20 29	20 43	21 24	21 11	20 19
22	20 29	20 39	21 14	20 59	20 09
23	20 28	20 34	21 05	20 47	19 58
24	20 28	20 30	20 56	20 35	19 48
25	20 28	20 25	20 46	20 23	19 37
26	20 27	20 21	20 37	20 11	19 27
27	20 27	20 16	20 28	19 59	19 16
28	20 26	20 11	20 18	19 46	19 05
29	20 26	20 07	20 09	19 34	18 54
30	20 25	20 02	19 59	19 22	18 43
31	20 24	19 57	19 50	19 09	18 31
32	20 24	19 53	19 40	18 56	18 19
33	20 23	19 48	19 30	18 44	18 07
34	20 23	19 43	19 21	18 31	17 55
35	20 22	19 38	19 11	18 17	17 42
36	20 21	19 33	19 01	18 04	17 29
37	20 20	19 28	18 51	17 51	17 16
38	20 19	19 23	18 41	17 37	17 03
39	20 18	19 17	18 31	17 24	16 49
40	20 17	19 12	18 21	17 10	16 35
41	20 16	19 07	18 10	16 56	16 20
42	20 15	19 01	18 00	16 41	16 06
43	20 14	18 55	17 49	16 27	15 50
44	20 12	18 49	17 38	16 12	15 34
45	20 11	18 43	17 28	15 57	15 18
46	20 09	18 37	17 16	15 42	15 01
47	20 08	18 31	17 05	15 26	14 44
48	20 06	18 24	16 54	15 10	14 26
49	20 04	18 17	16 42	14 54	14 07
50	20 01	18 10	16 30	14 38	13 48
51	19 59	18 03	16 18	14 21	13 27
52	19 56	17 55	16 06	14 04	13 06
53	19 52	17 47	15 53	13 47	12 45
54	19 49	17 39	15 41	13 30	12 22
55	19 45	17 30	15 28	13 12	11 58
56	19 40	17 21	15 14	12 54	11 33
57	19 35	17 11	15 01	12 35	11 07
58	19 28	17 00	14 47	12 17	10 40
59	19 21	16 48	14 32	11 58	10 11
60	19♌12	16♍35	14♎18	11♏40	09♐40

7h 36m 0s	22 ♋ 13	114° 0' 0"			
LAT.	11	12	ASC	2	3
0	21♌37	23♍28	25♎53	26♏19	24♐30
5	21 35	23 01	24 59	25 16	23 43
10	21 32	22 35	24 07	24 15	22 57
15	21 29	22 10	23 18	23 15	22 10
20	21 26	21 45	22 29	22 15	21 20
21	21 26	21 40	22 19	22 03	21 10
22	21 25	21 36	22 09	21 51	21 00
23	21 24	21 31	22 00	21 38	20 49
24	21 24	21 26	21 50	21 26	20 39
25	21 23	21 21	21 40	21 14	20 28
26	21 22	21 16	21 30	21 01	20 17
27	21 22	21 11	21 21	20 49	20 06
28	21 21	21 06	21 11	20 36	19 55
29	21 20	21 01	21 01	20 23	19 43
30	21 19	20 56	20 51	20 10	19 32
31	21 19	20 51	20 41	19 58	19 20
32	21 18	20 46	20 31	19 44	19 08
33	21 17	20 41	20 21	19 31	18 55
34	21 16	20 35	20 11	19 18	18 43
35	21 15	20 30	20 01	19 04	18 30
36	21 14	20 25	19 50	18 51	18 17
37	21 13	20 19	19 40	18 37	18 03
38	21 12	20 14	19 30	18 23	17 49
39	21 11	20 08	19 19	18 09	17 35
40	21 09	20 02	19 08	17 54	17 21
41	21 08	19 56	18 58	17 40	17 06
42	21 07	19 51	18 47	17 25	16 50
43	21 05	19 44	18 36	17 10	16 34
44	21 03	19 38	18 24	16 55	16 18
45	21 02	19 32	18 13	16 39	16 01
46	21 00	19 25	18 01	16 23	15 44
47	20 58	19 18	17 50	16 07	15 26
48	20 56	19 11	17 38	15 51	15 07
49	20 53	19 04	17 26	15 34	14 48
50	20 51	18 57	17 13	15 17	14 28
51	20 48	18 49	17 01	15 00	14 07
52	20 44	18 41	16 48	14 43	13 45
53	20 41	18 33	16 35	14 25	13 22
54	20 37	18 24	16 21	14 06	12 59
55	20 33	18 14	16 08	13 48	12 34
56	20 28	18 04	15 54	13 29	12 08
57	20 22	17 54	15 40	13 10	11 41
58	20 15	17 43	15 25	12 50	11 12
59	20 08	17 31	15 10	12 31	10 42
60	19♌59	17♍17	14♎55	12♏11	10♐10

7h 40m 0s	23 ♋ 10	115° 0' 0"			
LAT.	11	12	ASC	2	3
0	22♌39	24♍33	26♎57	27♏17	25♐25
5	22 35	24 04	26 00	26 13	24 38
10	22 31	23 36	25 07	25 11	23 51
15	22 27	23 09	24 15	24 09	23 02
20	22 23	22 43	23 24	23 07	22 12
21	22 22	22 38	23 14	22 55	22 01
22	22 21	22 33	23 04	22 42	21 51
23	22 21	22 27	22 54	22 30	21 40
24	22 20	22 22	22 44	22 17	21 29
25	22 19	22 17	22 34	22 04	21 18
26	22 18	22 11	22 24	21 51	21 07
27	22 17	22 06	22 14	21 39	20 56
28	22 16	22 01	22 03	21 26	20 44
29	22 15	21 55	21 53	21 12	20 32
30	22 14	21 50	21 43	20 59	20 21
31	22 13	21 45	21 33	20 46	20 08
32	22 12	21 39	21 22	20 33	19 56
33	22 11	21 34	21 12	20 19	19 43
34	22 10	21 28	21 01	20 05	19 30
35	22 08	21 22	20 51	19 51	19 17
36	22 07	21 17	20 40	19 37	19 04
37	22 06	21 11	20 29	19 23	18 50
38	22 05	21 05	20 18	19 09	18 36
39	22 03	20 59	20 07	18 54	18 21
40	22 02	20 53	19 56	18 39	18 06
41	22 00	20 47	19 45	18 24	17 51
42	21 58	20 40	19 33	18 09	17 35
43	21 57	20 34	19 22	17 53	17 19
44	21 55	20 27	19 10	17 38	17 02
45	21 53	20 20	18 58	17 21	16 44
46	21 51	20 13	18 46	17 05	16 26
47	21 48	20 06	18 34	16 49	16 08
48	21 46	19 59	18 22	16 32	15 48
49	21 43	19 51	18 09	16 14	15 28
50	21 40	19 43	17 56	15 57	15 08
51	21 37	19 35	17 43	15 39	14 46
52	21 34	19 27	17 30	15 21	14 23
53	21 30	19 18	17 16	15 02	14 00
54	21 25	19 09	17 02	14 43	13 35
55	21 21	18 59	16 48	14 24	13 09
56	21 16	18 49	16 34	14 04	12 42
57	21 10	18 38	16 19	13 44	12 14
58	21 03	18 26	16 03	13 24	11 44
59	20 55	18 14	15 48	13 03	11 12
60	20♌46	18♍00	15♎32	12♏43	10♐39

7h 44m 0s	24 ♋ 06	116° 0' 0"			
LAT.	11	12	ASC	2	3
0	23♌41	25♍38	28♎00	28♏15	26♐20
5	23 35	25 07	27 02	27 10	25 32
10	23 30	24 37	26 06	26 06	24 44
15	23 25	24 09	25 13	25 03	23 55
20	23 20	23 41	24 20	23 59	23 03
21	23 19	23 35	24 10	23 47	22 53
22	23 18	23 29	23 59	23 34	22 42
23	23 17	23 24	23 49	23 21	22 31
24	23 16	23 18	23 38	23 08	22 20
25	23 15	23 13	23 28	22 55	22 09
26	23 14	23 07	23 17	22 42	21 57
27	23 12	23 01	23 07	22 28	21 46
28	23 11	22 56	22 56	22 15	21 34
29	23 10	22 50	22 45	22 02	21 22
30	23 09	22 44	22 35	21 48	21 10
31	23 08	22 38	22 24	21 34	20 57
32	23 06	22 33	22 13	21 20	20 44
33	23 05	22 27	22 02	21 07	20 31
34	23 04	22 21	21 51	20 52	20 18
35	23 02	22 15	21 40	20 38	20 05
36	23 01	22 09	21 29	20 24	19 51
37	22 59	22 02	21 18	20 09	19 37
38	22 57	21 56	21 07	19 54	19 22
39	22 56	21 50	20 55	19 39	19 07
40	22 54	21 43	20 44	19 24	18 52
41	22 52	21 37	20 32	19 08	18 36
42	22 50	21 30	20 20	18 52	18 19
43	22 48	21 23	20 08	18 36	18 03
44	22 46	21 16	19 56	18 20	17 45
45	22 44	21 09	19 44	18 04	17 27
46	22 41	21 02	19 31	17 47	17 09
47	22 39	20 54	19 18	17 30	16 50
48	22 36	20 46	19 06	17 12	16 30
49	22 33	20 38	18 52	16 54	16 09
50	22 30	20 30	18 39	16 36	15 47
51	22 27	20 21	18 25	16 17	15 25
52	22 23	20 13	18 12	15 59	15 02
53	22 19	20 03	17 57	15 39	14 37
54	22 14	19 54	17 43	15 20	14 12
55	22 09	19 43	17 28	15 00	13 45
56	22 04	19 33	17 13	14 39	13 17
57	21 58	19 21	16 58	14 18	12 47
58	21 51	19 09	16 42	13 57	12 16
59	21 43	18 57	16 26	13 36	11 43
60	21♌33	18♍43	16♎09	13♏14	11♐08

7h 48m 0s	25 ♋ 03	117° 0' 0"			
LAT.	11	12	ASC	2	3
0	24♌42	26♍44	29♎03	29♏13	27♐15
5	24 36	26 10	28 03	28 06	26 26
10	24 30	25 39	27 05	27 01	25 38
15	24 24	25 08	26 10	25 56	24 47
20	24 17	24 38	25 15	24 51	23 55
21	24 16	24 32	25 05	24 38	23 44
22	24 15	24 27	24 54	24 25	23 33
23	24 14	24 21	24 43	24 12	23 22
24	24 12	24 15	24 32	23 59	23 10
25	24 11	24 09	24 21	23 45	22 59
26	24 09	24 03	24 10	23 32	22 47
27	24 08	23 57	23 59	23 18	22 35
28	24 07	23 51	23 48	23 04	22 23
29	24 05	23 45	23 37	22 51	22 11
30	24 04	23 38	23 26	22 37	21 59
31	24 02	23 32	23 15	22 23	21 46
32	24 01	23 26	23 04	22 08	21 33
33	23 59	23 20	22 53	21 54	21 20
34	23 58	23 14	22 41	21 40	21 06
35	23 56	23 07	22 30	21 25	20 52
36	23 54	23 01	22 18	21 10	20 38
37	23 52	22 54	22 07	20 55	20 23
38	23 51	22 47	21 55	20 40	20 08
39	23 49	22 41	21 43	20 24	19 53
40	23 47	22 34	21 31	20 08	19 37
41	23 45	22 27	21 19	19 52	19 21
42	23 42	22 20	21 07	19 36	19 04
43	23 40	22 13	20 54	19 20	18 47
44	23 38	22 05	20 42	19 03	18 29
45	23 35	21 58	20 29	18 46	18 10
46	23 33	21 50	20 16	18 28	17 51
47	23 30	21 42	20 03	18 11	17 31
48	23 27	21 34	19 49	17 52	17 11
49	23 23	21 25	19 36	17 34	16 50
50	23 20	21 17	19 22	17 15	16 27
51	23 16	21 08	19 08	16 56	16 04
52	23 12	20 59	18 53	16 36	15 40
53	23 08	20 49	18 39	16 16	15 15
54	23 03	20 39	18 24	15 56	14 48
55	22 58	20 28	18 08	15 35	14 20
56	22 52	20 17	17 53	15 14	13 51
57	22 46	20 05	17 37	14 52	13 20
58	22 39	19 53	17 20	14 30	12 48
59	22 30	19 40	17 03	14 08	12 13
60	22♌21	19♍26	16♎46	13♏45	11♐37

7h 52m 0s	26 ♋ 00	118° 0' 0"			
LAT.	11	12	ASC	2	3
0	25♌44	27♍49	00♏06	00♐11	28♐10
5	25 37	27 14	29♎04	29♏02	27 21
10	25 29	26 40	28 04	27 56	26 31
15	25 22	26 08	27 07	26 50	25 40
20	25 15	25 36	26 11	25 43	24 46
21	25 13	25 30	26 00	25 30	24 35
22	25 12	25 24	25 48	25 16	24 24
23	25 10	25 17	25 37	25 03	24 13
24	25 09	25 11	25 26	24 49	24 01
25	25 07	25 05	25 15	24 36	23 49
26	25 06	24 58	25 04	24 22	23 37
27	25 04	24 52	24 52	24 08	23 25
28	25 02	24 46	24 41	23 54	23 13
29	25 01	24 39	24 29	23 40	23 00
30	24 59	24 33	24 18	23 25	22 48
31	24 57	24 26	24 06	23 11	22 35
32	24 55	24 20	23 55	22 56	22 21
33	24 54	24 13	23 43	22 42	22 08
34	24 52	24 06	23 32	22 27	21 54
35	24 50	24 00	23 20	22 11	21 39
36	24 48	23 53	23 08	21 56	21 25
37	24 46	23 46	22 56	21 41	21 10
38	24 44	23 39	22 44	21 25	20 55
39	24 42	23 32	22 31	21 09	20 39
40	24 39	23 25	22 19	20 53	20 22
41	24 37	23 17	22 06	20 36	20 06
42	24 35	23 10	21 54	20 20	19 49
43	24 32	23 02	21 41	20 03	19 31
44	24 30	22 54	21 28	19 45	19 12
45	24 27	22 47	21 14	19 28	18 53
46	24 24	22 38	21 01	19 10	18 34
47	24 21	22 30	20 47	18 51	18 13
48	24 18	22 22	20 33	18 33	17 52
49	24 14	22 13	20 19	18 14	17 30
50	24 10	22 04	20 05	17 54	17 07
51	24 06	21 54	19 50	17 34	16 43
52	24 02	21 45	19 35	17 14	16 18
53	23 58	21 35	19 20	16 53	15 52
54	23 53	21 24	19 04	16 32	15 24
55	23 47	21 13	18 49	16 11	14 56
56	23 41	21 02	18 32	15 49	14 25
57	23 34	20 50	18 16	15 26	13 53
58	23 27	20 37	17 59	15 03	13 19
59	23 19	20 23	17 41	14 40	12 43
60	23♌09	20♍09	17♎23	14♏16	12♐05

7h 56m 0s	26 ♋ 57	119° 0' 0"			
LAT.	11	12	ASC	2	3
0	26♌47	28♍55	01♏08	01♐08	29♐05
5	26 38	28 17	00 04	29♏59	28 15
10	26 29	27 42	29♎03	28 51	27 25
15	26 21	27 07	28 04	27 43	26 32
20	26 12	26 34	27 06	26 35	25 38
21	26 11	26 27	26 55	26 22	25 27
22	26 09	26 21	26 43	26 08	25 15
23	26 07	26 14	26 32	25 54	25 04
24	26 05	26 08	26 20	25 40	24 52
25	26 04	26 01	26 08	25 26	24 40
26	26 02	25 54	25 57	25 12	24 28
27	26 00	25 48	25 45	24 57	24 15
28	25 58	25 41	25 33	24 43	24 03
29	25 56	25 34	25 21	24 28	23 50
30	25 54	25 27	25 10	24 14	23 37
31	25 52	25 20	24 58	23 59	23 23
32	25 50	25 13	24 46	23 44	23 10
33	25 48	25 06	24 34	23 29	22 56
34	25 46	24 59	24 22	23 14	22 42
35	25 44	24 52	24 09	22 58	22 27
36	25 42	24 45	23 57	22 42	22 12
37	25 40	24 38	23 45	22 26	21 57
38	25 37	24 31	23 32	22 10	21 41
39	25 35	24 23	23 19	21 54	21 25
40	25 32	24 15	23 06	21 37	21 08
41	25 30	24 08	22 53	21 20	20 51
42	25 27	24 00	22 40	21 03	20 33
43	25 24	23 52	22 27	20 46	20 15
44	25 22	23 44	22 13	20 28	19 56
45	25 19	23 36	22 00	20 10	19 36
46	25 15	23 27	21 46	19 51	19 16
47	25 12	23 18	21 32	19 32	18 55
48	25 09	23 09	21 17	19 13	18 33
49	25 05	23 00	21 03	18 53	18 10
50	25 01	22 51	20 48	18 33	17 47
51	24 57	22 41	20 33	18 13	17 22
52	24 52	22 31	20 17	17 52	16 56
53	24 47	22 20	20 01	17 30	16 29
54	24 42	22 10	19 45	17 09	16 01
55	24 36	21 58	19 29	16 46	15 31
56	24 30	21 46	19 12	16 23	14 59
57	24 23	21 34	18 55	16 00	14 26
58	24 16	21 21	18 37	15 36	13 51
59	24 07	21 07	18 19	15 12	13 13
60	23♌57	20♍52	18♎00	14♏47	12♐33

Koch Table of Houses for Latitudes 0° to 60° North

8h 0m 0s — 120° 0' 0" — 27 ♋ 55

LAT.	11	12	ASC	2	3
0	27♌49	00♎00	02♏11	02♐05	00♑00
5	27 39	29♍20	01 05	00 55	29♐09
10	27 29	28 43	00 02	29♏45	28 18
15	27 20	28 07	29♎01	28 37	27 25
20	27 10	27 32	28 02	27 27	26 29
21	27 08	27 25	27 50	27 13	26 18
22	27 06	27 18	27 38	26 59	26 06
23	27 04	27 11	27 26	26 45	25 54
24	27 02	27 04	27 14	26 30	25 42
25	27 00	26 57	27 02	26 16	25 30
26	26 58	26 50	26 50	26 02	25 18
27	26 56	26 43	26 38	25 47	25 05
28	26 54	26 36	26 26	25 32	24 52
29	26 52	26 29	26 13	25 17	24 39
30	26 50	26 22	26 01	25 02	24 26
31	26 48	26 14	25 49	24 47	24 12
32	26 45	26 07	25 37	24 32	23 58
33	26 43	26 00	25 24	24 16	23 44
34	26 41	25 53	25 12	24 01	23 29
35	26 38	25 45	24 59	23 45	23 14
36	26 36	25 38	24 46	23 29	22 59
37	26 34	25 30	24 33	23 12	22 43
38	26 31	25 22	24 20	22 56	22 27
39	26 28	25 14	24 07	22 39	22 11
40	26 26	25 06	23 54	22 22	21 53
41	26 23	24 58	23 40	22 04	21 36
42	26 20	24 50	23 27	21 47	21 18
43	26 17	24 42	23 13	21 29	20 59
44	26 14	24 33	22 59	21 10	20 39
45	26 11	24 25	22 45	20 51	20 19
46	26 07	24 16	22 31	20 32	19 58
47	26 04	24 07	22 16	20 13	19 37
48	26 00	23 57	22 01	19 53	19 14
49	25 56	23 48	21 46	19 33	18 51
50	25 52	23 38	21 31	19 12	18 26
51	25 47	23 28	21 15	18 51	18 01
52	25 42	23 17	20 59	18 29	17 34
53	25 37	23 06	20 43	18 07	17 06
54	25 32	22 55	20 26	17 45	16 37
55	25 26	22 43	20 09	17 21	16 06
56	25 19	22 31	19 51	16 58	15 33
57	25 12	22 18	19 34	16 33	14 59
58	25 04	22 05	19 15	16 09	14 22
59	24 56	21 50	18 57	15 43	13 43
60	24♌46	21♍35	18♎37	15♏17	13♐01

8h 4m 0s — 121° 0' 0" — 28 ♋ 52

LAT.	11	12	ASC	2	3
0	28♌52	01♎05	03♏13	03♐03	00♑55
5	28 40	00 24	02 06	01 51	00 04
10	28 29	29♍45	01 01	00 40	29♐12
15	28 19	29 07	29♎58	29♏30	28 18
20	28 08	28 30	28 57	28 19	27 21
21	28 06	28 23	28 44	28 04	27 09
22	28 04	28 15	28 32	27 50	26 57
23	28 01	28 08	28 20	27 36	26 45
24	27 59	28 01	28 08	27 21	26 33
25	27 57	27 53	27 55	27 06	26 21
26	27 55	27 46	27 43	26 51	26 08
27	27 52	27 39	27 30	26 36	25 55
28	27 50	27 31	27 18	26 21	25 42
29	27 48	27 24	27 05	26 06	25 29
30	27 45	27 16	26 53	25 51	25 15
31	27 43	27 09	26 40	25 35	25 01
32	27 41	27 01	26 27	25 19	24 47
33	27 38	26 53	26 14	25 04	24 32
34	27 36	26 46	26 02	24 47	24 17
35	27 33	26 38	25 49	24 31	24 02
36	27 30	26 30	25 35	24 15	23 46
37	27 28	26 22	25 22	23 58	23 30
38	27 25	26 14	25 09	23 41	23 13
39	27 22	26 06	24 55	23 23	22 56
40	27 19	25 57	24 41	23 06	22 39
41	27 16	25 49	24 28	22 48	22 21
42	27 13	25 40	24 14	22 30	22 02
43	27 10	25 32	23 59	22 11	21 43
44	27 06	25 23	23 45	21 53	21 23
45	27 03	25 14	23 30	21 33	21 02
46	26 59	25 05	23 15	21 14	20 41
47	26 55	24 55	23 00	20 54	20 18
48	26 51	24 45	22 45	20 33	19 55
49	26 47	24 35	22 29	20 12	19 31
50	26 43	24 25	22 13	19 51	19 06
51	26 38	24 15	21 57	19 29	18 40
52	26 33	24 04	21 41	19 07	18 12
53	26 28	23 53	21 24	18 44	17 43
54	26 22	23 41	21 07	18 21	17 13
55	26 16	23 29	20 49	17 57	16 41
56	26 09	23 16	20 31	17 32	16 07
57	26 02	23 03	20 13	17 07	15 31
58	25 54	22 49	19 54	16 41	14 53
59	25 45	22 34	19 34	16 15	14 13
60	25♌35	22♍19	19♎14	15♏48	13♐29

8h 8m 0s — 122° 0' 0" — 29 ♋ 49

LAT.	11	12	ASC	2	3
0	29♌54	02♎11	04♏16	04♐00	01♑50
5	29 42	01 27	03 06	02 47	00 58
10	29 30	00 46	02 00	01 35	00 05
15	29 18	00 07	00 55	00 23	29♐10
20	29 06	29♍28	29♎52	29♏11	28 13
21	29 04	29 20	29 39	28 56	28 01
22	29 01	29 13	29 27	28 41	27 49
23	28 59	29 05	29 14	28 26	27 36
24	28 56	28 57	29 01	28 11	27 24
25	28 54	28 50	28 49	27 56	27 11
26	28 51	28 42	28 36	27 41	26 58
27	28 49	28 34	28 23	27 26	26 45
28	28 46	28 27	28 10	27 10	26 32
29	28 44	28 19	27 57	26 55	26 18
30	28 41	28 11	27 44	26 39	26 04
31	28 39	28 03	27 31	26 23	25 50
32	28 36	27 55	27 18	26 07	25 35
33	28 33	27 47	27 05	25 51	25 20
34	28 31	27 39	26 52	25 34	25 05
35	28 28	27 31	26 38	25 18	24 49
36	28 25	27 23	26 25	25 01	24 33
37	28 22	27 14	26 11	24 43	24 17
38	28 19	27 06	25 57	24 26	24 00
39	28 16	26 57	25 43	24 08	23 42
40	28 13	26 49	25 29	23 50	23 24
41	28 09	26 40	25 15	23 32	23 06
42	28 06	26 31	25 00	23 13	22 47
43	28 03	26 22	24 45	22 54	22 27
44	27 59	26 13	24 31	22 35	22 06
45	27 55	26 03	24 16	22 15	21 45
46	27 51	25 54	24 00	21 55	21 23
47	27 47	25 44	23 45	21 34	21 00
48	27 43	25 34	23 29	21 13	20 36
49	27 39	25 23	23 13	20 52	20 11
50	27 34	25 13	22 56	20 30	19 46
51	27 29	25 02	22 40	20 07	19 18
52	27 24	24 50	22 22	19 44	18 50
53	27 18	24 39	22 05	19 21	18 20
54	27 12	24 27	21 47	18 57	17 49
55	27 06	24 14	21 29	18 32	17 16
56	26 59	24 01	21 11	18 06	16 41
57	26 51	23 48	20 52	17 40	16 03
58	26 43	23 33	20 32	17 14	15 24
59	26 34	23 18	20 12	16 46	14 42
60	26♌24	23♍02	19♎52	16♏18	13♐57

8h 12m 0s — 123° 0' 0" — 00 ♌ 47

LAT.	11	12	ASC	2	3
0	00♍57	03♎16	05♏18	04♐57	02♑45
5	00 43	02 31	04 06	03 42	01 52
10	00 30	01 48	02 58	02 29	00 59
15	00 17	01 07	01 52	01 16	00 03
20	00 04	00 26	00 47	00 02	29♐04
21	00 02	00 18	00 34	29♏47	28 52
22	29♌59	00 10	00 21	29 32	28 40
23	29 56	00 02	00 08	29 17	28 27
24	29 54	29♍54	29♎55	29 02	28 15
25	29 51	29 46	29 42	28 46	28 02
26	29 48	29 38	29 29	28 31	27 48
27	29 46	29 30	29 16	28 15	27 35
28	29 43	29 22	29 02	27 59	27 21
29	29 40	29 14	28 49	27 43	27 07
30	29 37	29 06	28 36	27 27	26 53
31	29 34	28 57	28 22	27 11	26 39
32	29 32	28 49	28 09	26 55	26 24
33	29 29	28 41	27 55	26 38	26 08
34	29 26	28 32	27 41	26 21	25 53
35	29 23	28 24	27 28	26 04	25 37
36	29 20	28 15	27 14	25 47	25 20
37	29 16	28 07	27 00	25 29	25 04
38	29 13	27 58	26 45	25 11	24 46
39	29 10	27 49	26 31	24 53	24 28
40	29 06	27 40	26 16	24 34	24 10
41	29 03	27 31	26 02	24 16	23 51
42	28 59	27 21	25 47	23 56	23 31
43	28 56	27 12	25 32	23 37	23 11
44	28 52	27 02	25 16	23 17	22 50
45	28 48	26 53	25 01	22 57	22 28
46	28 44	26 43	24 45	22 36	22 05
47	28 39	26 32	24 29	22 15	21 42
48	28 35	26 22	24 13	21 53	21 17
49	28 30	26 11	23 56	21 31	20 52
50	28 25	26 00	23 39	21 09	20 25
51	28 20	25 49	23 22	20 45	19 57
52	28 15	25 37	23 04	20 22	19 28
53	28 09	25 25	22 46	19 57	18 57
54	28 03	25 13	22 28	19 32	18 25
55	27 56	25 00	22 09	19 07	17 50
56	27 49	24 46	21 50	18 41	17 14
57	27 41	24 32	21 30	18 14	16 36
58	27 33	24 18	21 10	17 46	15 55
59	27 24	24 02	20 50	17 18	15 11
60	27♌13	23♍46	20♎29	16♏49	14♐25

8h 16m 0s — 124° 0' 0" — 01 ♌ 45

LAT.	11	12	ASC	2	3
0	02♍00	04♎22	06♏19	05♐54	03♑40
5	01 45	03 34	05 07	04 38	02 47
10	01 31	02 49	03 57	03 23	01 52
15	01 17	02 06	02 49	02 09	00 56
20	01 03	01 24	01 42	00 54	29♐56
21	01 00	01 16	01 29	00 38	29 44
22	00 57	01 08	01 15	00 23	29 31
23	00 54	00 59	01 02	00 08	29 18
24	00 51	00 51	00 49	29♏52	29 05
25	00 48	00 43	00 35	29 36	28 52
26	00 45	00 34	00 22	29 21	28 39
27	00 42	00 26	00 08	29 05	28 25
28	00 40	00 17	29♎54	28 48	28 11
29	00 37	00 09	29 41	28 32	27 57
30	00 34	00 00	29 27	28 16	27 42
31	00 30	29♍52	29 13	27 59	27 28
32	00 27	29 43	28 59	27 42	27 12
33	00 24	29 34	28 45	27 25	26 57
34	00 21	29 26	28 31	27 08	26 41
35	00 18	29 17	28 17	26 50	26 24
36	00 14	29 08	28 03	26 32	26 08
37	00 11	28 59	27 48	26 14	25 50
38	00 08	28 50	27 34	25 56	25 33
39	00 04	28 41	27 19	25 37	25 14
40	00 00	28 31	27 04	25 19	24 55
41	29♌57	28 22	26 49	24 59	24 36
42	29 53	28 12	26 33	24 40	24 16
43	29 49	28 02	26 18	24 20	23 55
44	29 45	27 52	26 02	23 59	23 33
45	29 41	27 42	25 46	23 38	23 11
46	29 36	27 32	25 30	23 17	22 48
47	29 32	27 21	25 13	22 55	22 24
48	29 27	27 10	24 56	22 33	21 58
49	29 22	26 59	24 39	22 10	21 32
50	29 17	26 48	24 22	21 47	21 05
51	29 12	26 36	24 04	21 23	20 36
52	29 06	26 24	23 46	20 59	20 06
53	29 00	26 12	23 28	20 34	19 34
54	28 54	25 59	23 09	20 08	19 00
55	28 47	25 46	22 49	19 42	18 25
56	28 39	25 32	22 30	19 15	17 48
57	28 31	25 17	22 09	18 47	17 08
58	28 23	25 02	21 49	18 18	16 26
59	28 13	24 47	21 27	17 49	15 41
60	28♌03	24♍30	21♎06	17♏19	14♐52

8h 20m 0s — 125° 0' 0" — 02 ♌ 43

LAT.	11	12	ASC	2	3
0	03♍03	05♎27	07♏21	06♐50	04♑35
5	02 47	04 38	06 06	05 33	03 41
10	02 31	03 51	04 55	04 18	02 46
15	02 16	03 06	03 46	03 02	01 49
20	02 01	02 23	02 37	01 45	00 48
21	01 58	02 14	02 23	01 30	00 35
22	01 55	02 05	02 10	01 14	00 23
23	01 52	01 56	01 56	00 58	00 10
24	01 49	01 48	01 42	00 42	29♐56
25	01 46	01 39	01 28	00 26	29 43
26	01 43	01 30	01 14	00 10	29 29
27	01 40	01 22	01 01	29♏54	29 15
28	01 36	01 13	00 47	29 37	29 01
29	01 33	01 04	00 33	29 21	28 47
30	01 30	00 55	00 18	29 04	28 32
31	01 27	00 46	00 04	28 47	28 17
32	01 23	00 37	29♎50	28 30	28 01
33	01 20	00 28	29 36	28 12	27 45
34	01 17	00 19	29 21	27 55	27 29
35	01 13	00 10	29 07	27 37	27 12
36	01 10	00 01	28 52	27 18	26 55
37	01 06	29♍51	28 37	27 00	26 37
38	01 02	29 42	28 22	26 41	26 19
39	00 59	29 32	28 07	26 22	26 00
40	00 55	29 23	27 51	26 03	25 41
41	00 51	29 13	27 36	25 43	25 21
42	00 47	29 03	27 20	25 23	25 00
43	00 43	28 53	27 04	25 02	24 39
44	00 38	28 42	26 48	24 41	24 17
45	00 34	28 32	26 31	24 20	23 54
46	00 29	28 21	26 14	23 58	23 30
47	00 24	28 10	25 57	23 36	23 05
48	00 20	27 59	25 40	23 13	22 39
49	00 14	27 47	25 23	22 50	22 12
50	00 09	27 36	25 05	22 26	21 44
51	00 03	27 24	24 46	22 01	21 14
52	29♌57	27 11	24 28	21 36	20 43
53	29 51	26 58	24 09	21 10	20 11
54	29 45	26 45	23 49	20 44	19 36
55	29 37	26 32	23 29	20 17	19 00
56	29 30	26 17	23 09	19 49	18 21
57	29 22	26 03	22 48	19 20	17 40
58	29 13	25 47	22 27	18 51	16 56
59	29 04	25 31	22 05	18 20	16 10
60	28♌53	25♍14	21♎43	17♏49	15♐20

8h 24m 0s — 126° 0' 0" — 03 ♌ 41

LAT.	11	12	ASC	2	3
0	04♍07	06♎32	08♏23	07♐47	05♑30
5	03 49	05 41	07 06	06 29	04 36
10	03 32	04 53	05 53	05 12	03 40
15	03 16	04 06	04 42	03 55	02 41
20	03 00	03 21	03 32	02 37	01 40
21	02 57	03 12	03 18	02 21	01 27
22	02 53	03 03	03 04	02 05	01 14
23	02 50	02 54	02 50	01 49	01 01
24	02 47	02 45	02 36	01 33	00 47
25	02 43	02 36	02 21	01 16	00 34
26	02 40	02 27	02 07	01 00	00 20
27	02 37	02 18	01 53	00 43	00 05
28	02 33	02 08	01 39	00 26	29♐51
29	02 30	01 59	01 24	00 09	29 36
30	02 26	01 50	01 10	29♏52	29 21
31	02 23	01 41	00 55	29 35	29 06
32	02 19	01 32	00 41	29 17	28 50
33	02 16	01 22	00 26	28 59	28 33
34	02 12	01 13	00 11	28 41	28 17
35	02 09	01 03	29♎56	28 23	28 00
36	02 05	00 54	29 41	28 04	27 42
37	02 01	00 44	29 26	27 45	27 24
38	01 57	00 34	29 10	27 26	27 06
39	01 53	00 24	28 54	27 07	26 46
40	01 49	00 14	28 39	26 47	26 27
41	01 45	00 04	28 23	26 26	26 06
42	01 41	29♍53	28 06	26 06	25 45
43	01 36	29 43	27 50	25 45	25 23
44	01 32	29 32	27 33	25 23	25 01
45	01 27	29 21	27 16	25 01	24 37
46	01 22	29 10	26 59	24 39	24 13
47	01 17	28 59	26 42	24 16	23 47
48	01 12	28 47	26 24	23 53	23 20
49	01 07	28 36	26 06	23 29	22 53
50	01 01	28 23	25 47	23 04	22 24
51	00 55	28 11	25 29	22 39	21 53
52	00 49	27 58	25 09	22 13	21 21
53	00 43	27 45	24 50	21 47	20 47
54	00 36	27 32	24 30	21 19	20 12
55	00 29	27 18	24 09	20 51	19 34
56	00 21	27 03	23 49	20 23	18 54
57	00 13	26 48	23 27	19 53	18 12
58	00 04	26 32	23 05	19 23	17 27
59	29♌54	26 16	22 43	18 51	16 39
60	29♌43	25♍58	22♎20	18♏19	15♐47

8h 28m 0s — 127° 0' 0" — 04 ♌ 39

LAT.	11	12	ASC	2	3
0	05♍10	07♎37	09♏24	08♐43	06♑26
5	04 51	06 44	08 06	07 24	05 30
10	04 33	05 54	06 51	06 06	04 33
15	04 16	05 06	05 39	04 48	03 34
20	03 59	04 19	04 27	03 28	02 32
21	03 55	04 10	04 12	03 12	02 19
22	03 52	04 00	03 58	02 56	02 05
23	03 48	03 51	03 43	02 39	01 52
24	03 45	03 42	03 29	02 23	01 38
25	03 41	03 32	03 14	02 06	01 24
26	03 38	03 23	03 00	01 49	01 10
27	03 34	03 13	02 45	01 32	00 56
28	03 31	03 04	02 31	01 15	00 41
29	03 27	02 55	02 16	00 58	00 26
30	03 23	02 45	02 01	00 40	00 10
31	03 20	02 35	01 46	00 22	29♐55
32	03 16	02 26	01 31	00 04	29 39
33	03 12	02 16	01 16	29♏46	29 22
34	03 08	02 06	01 01	29 28	29 05
35	03 04	01 56	00 45	29 09	28 48
36	03 00	01 47	00 30	28 50	28 30
37	02 56	01 36	00 14	28 31	28 11
38	02 52	01 26	29♎58	28 11	27 52
39	02 48	01 16	29 42	27 51	27 33
40	02 44	01 06	29 26	27 31	27 12
41	02 39	00 55	29 10	27 10	26 51
42	02 35	00 44	28 53	26 49	26 30
43	02 30	00 33	28 36	26 27	26 07
44	02 25	00 22	28 19	26 05	25 44
45	02 21	00 11	28 02	25 43	25 20
46	02 16	00 00	27 44	25 20	24 55
47	02 10	29♍48	27 26	24 57	24 29
48	02 05	29 36	27 08	24 32	24 01
49	01 59	29 24	26 49	24 08	23 33
50	01 53	29 11	26 30	23 43	23 03
51	01 47	28 59	26 11	23 17	22 32
52	01 41	28 45	25 51	22 50	21 59
53	01 34	28 32	25 31	22 23	21 24
54	01 27	28 18	25 11	21 55	20 47
55	01 20	28 04	24 50	21 26	20 09
56	01 12	27 49	24 28	20 57	19 28
57	01 03	27 33	24 06	20 26	18 44
58	00 54	27 17	23 43	19 55	17 57
59	00 44	27 00	23 20	19 22	17 08
60	00♍34	26♍43	22♎56	18♏49	16♐14

Koch Table of Houses for Latitudes 0° to 60° North

8h 32m 0s — 128° 0' 0" — 05 ♌ 38

LAT.	11	12	ASC	2	3
0	06♍14	08♎43	10♏25	09♐40	07♑21
5	05 54	07 48	09 06	08 19	06 25
10	05 35	06 56	07 49	07 00	05 27
15	05 16	06 06	06 35	05 40	04 27
20	04 58	05 17	05 21	04 19	03 24
21	04 54	05 08	05 07	04 03	03 10
22	04 50	04 58	04 52	03 46	02 57
23	04 47	04 48	04 37	03 30	02 43
24	04 43	04 39	04 22	03 13	02 29
25	04 39	04 29	04 07	02 56	02 15
26	04 35	04 19	03 53	02 39	02 01
27	04 32	04 09	03 38	02 21	01 46
28	04 28	04 00	03 23	02 04	01 31
29	04 24	03 50	03 08	01 46	01 16
30	04 20	03 40	02 52	01 28	01 00
31	04 16	03 30	02 37	01 10	00 44
32	04 12	03 20	02 22	00 52	00 27
33	04 08	03 10	02 06	00 33	00 10
34	04 04	03 00	01 51	00 14	29♐53
35	04 00	02 50	01 35	29♏55	29 35
36	03 56	02 40	01 19	29 36	29 17
37	03 52	02 29	01 03	29 16	28 58
38	03 47	02 19	00 46	28 56	28 39
39	03 43	02 08	00 30	28 36	28 19
40	03 38	01 57	00 13	28 15	27 58
41	03 34	01 46	29♎57	27 54	27 37
42	03 29	01 35	29 39	27 32	27 15
43	03 24	01 24	29 22	27 10	26 52
44	03 19	01 13	29 05	26 47	26 28
45	03 14	01 01	28 47	26 24	26 03
46	03 09	00 49	28 29	26 01	25 37
47	03 04	00 37	28 10	25 37	25 11
48	02 58	00 25	27 51	25 12	24 43
49	02 52	00 12	27 32	24 47	24 13
50	02 46	00 00	27 13	24 21	23 43
51	02 40	29♍46	26 53	23 55	23 10
52	02 33	29 33	26 33	23 27	22 36
53	02 26	29 19	26 12	22 59	22 01
54	02 19	29 05	25 51	22 30	21 23
55	02 11	28 50	25 30	22 01	20 43
56	02 03	28 35	25 07	21 30	20 01
57	01 55	28 19	24 45	20 59	19 16
58	01 45	28 02	24 22	20 27	18 28
59	01 35	27 45	23 58	19 53	17 36
60	01♍25	27♍27	23♎33	19♏19	16♐41

8h 36m 0s — 129° 0' 0" — 06 ♌ 37

LAT.	11	12	ASC	2	3
0	07♍18	09♎48	11♏26	10♐36	08♑16
5	06 56	08 51	10 05	09 15	07 19
10	06 36	07 57	08 47	07 54	06 21
15	06 16	07 06	07 31	06 33	05 20
20	05 57	06 16	06 16	05 11	04 16
21	05 53	06 06	06 01	04 54	04 02
22	05 49	05 56	05 46	04 37	03 49
23	05 45	05 46	05 31	04 20	03 35
24	05 41	05 36	05 16	04 03	03 21
25	05 37	05 26	05 00	03 46	03 06
26	05 33	05 16	04 45	03 28	02 51
27	05 29	05 05	04 30	03 11	02 36
28	05 25	04 55	04 15	02 53	02 21
29	05 21	04 45	03 59	02 35	02 05
30	05 17	04 35	03 44	02 16	01 49
31	05 13	04 25	03 28	01 58	01 33
32	05 09	04 15	03 12	01 39	01 16
33	05 05	04 04	02 56	01 20	00 59
34	05 00	03 54	02 40	01 01	00 41
35	04 56	03 43	02 24	00 41	00 23
36	04 52	03 33	02 08	00 22	00 05
37	04 47	03 22	01 51	00 01	29♐45
38	04 43	03 11	01 35	29♏41	29 26
39	04 38	03 00	01 18	29 20	29 05
40	04 33	02 49	01 01	28 59	28 44
41	04 29	02 38	00 43	28 37	28 22
42	04 24	02 26	00 26	28 15	27 59
43	04 19	02 15	00 08	27 52	27 36
44	04 13	02 03	29♎50	27 29	27 12
45	04 08	01 51	29 32	27 06	26 46
46	04 03	01 39	29 13	26 42	26 20
47	03 57	01 26	28 54	26 17	25 52
48	03 51	01 14	28 35	25 52	25 24
49	03 45	01 01	28 16	25 26	24 54
50	03 39	00 48	27 56	24 59	24 22
51	03 32	00 34	27 35	24 32	23 49
52	03 26	00 20	27 15	24 04	23 14
53	03 18	00 06	26 53	23 35	22 38
54	03 11	29♍51	26 32	23 06	21 59
55	03 03	29 36	26 10	22 35	21 18
56	02 55	29 20	25 47	22 04	20 34
57	02 46	29 04	25 24	21 32	19 48
58	02 37	28 47	25 00	20 58	18 58
59	02 26	28 30	24 35	20 24	18 05
60	02♍16	28♍11	24♎10	19♏49	17♐08

8h 40m 0s — 130° 0' 0" — 07 ♌ 35

LAT.	11	12	ASC	2	3
0	08♍22	10♎53	12♏27	11♐32	09♑11
5	07 59	09 54	11 04	10 10	08 14
10	07 37	08 59	09 45	08 48	07 15
15	07 17	08 06	08 27	07 26	06 13
20	06 56	07 14	07 10	06 02	05 08
21	06 52	07 04	06 55	05 45	04 54
22	06 48	06 53	06 40	05 28	04 40
23	06 44	06 43	06 24	05 10	04 26
24	06 40	06 33	06 09	04 53	04 12
25	06 36	06 22	05 53	04 35	03 57
26	06 31	06 12	05 38	04 18	03 42
27	06 27	06 02	05 22	04 00	03 27
28	06 23	05 51	05 06	03 41	03 11
29	06 19	05 41	04 51	03 23	02 55
30	06 14	05 30	04 35	03 05	02 39
31	06 10	05 20	04 19	02 46	02 22
32	06 06	05 09	04 03	02 27	02 05
33	06 01	04 58	03 46	02 07	01 48
34	05 57	04 48	03 30	01 48	01 30
35	05 52	04 37	03 13	01 28	01 11
36	05 48	04 26	02 57	01 07	00 52
37	05 43	04 15	02 40	00 47	00 33
38	05 38	04 03	02 23	00 26	00 12
39	05 33	03 52	02 06	00 04	29♐51
40	05 28	03 41	01 48	29♏43	29 30
41	05 23	03 29	01 30	29 21	29 07
42	05 18	03 17	01 12	28 58	28 44
43	05 13	03 06	00 54	28 35	28 20
44	05 08	02 53	00 36	28 11	27 55
45	05 02	02 41	00 17	27 47	27 29
46	04 56	02 29	29♎58	27 23	27 02
47	04 51	02 16	29 39	26 57	26 34
48	04 45	02 03	29 19	26 31	26 05
49	04 38	01 50	28 59	26 05	25 34
50	04 32	01 36	28 38	25 38	25 02
51	04 25	01 22	28 18	25 10	24 28
52	04 18	01 08	27 56	24 41	23 52
53	04 11	00 53	27 35	24 12	23 14
54	04 03	00 38	27 12	23 41	22 34
55	03 55	00 23	26 50	23 10	21 52
56	03 47	00 07	26 26	22 38	21 07
57	03 38	29♍50	26 02	22 04	20 20
58	03 28	29 33	25 38	21 30	19 28
59	03 18	29 15	25 13	20 55	18 34
60	03♍07	28♍56	24♎47	20♏18	17♐35

8h 44m 0s — 131° 0' 0" — 08 ♌ 34

LAT.	11	12	ASC	2	3
0	09♍26	11♎58	13♏27	12♐28	10♑07
5	09 02	10 57	12 03	11 05	09 09
10	08 39	10 01	10 42	09 42	08 09
15	08 17	09 06	09 23	08 18	07 07
20	07 56	08 12	08 05	06 53	06 00
21	07 51	08 02	07 49	06 36	05 46
22	07 47	07 51	07 34	06 18	05 32
23	07 43	07 40	07 18	06 01	05 18
24	07 38	07 30	07 02	05 43	05 03
25	07 34	07 19	06 46	05 25	04 48
26	07 30	07 08	06 30	05 07	04 33
27	07 25	06 58	06 14	04 49	04 18
28	07 21	06 47	05 58	04 30	04 02
29	07 16	06 36	05 42	04 12	03 45
30	07 12	06 25	05 26	03 53	03 29
31	07 07	06 14	05 09	03 33	03 12
32	07 03	06 03	04 53	03 14	02 54
33	06 58	05 52	04 36	02 54	02 37
34	06 53	05 41	04 20	02 34	02 18
35	06 49	05 30	04 03	02 14	01 59
36	06 44	05 19	03 46	01 53	01 40
37	06 39	05 08	03 28	01 32	01 20
38	06 34	04 56	03 11	01 11	00 59
39	06 29	04 44	02 53	00 49	00 38
40	06 24	04 33	02 35	00 27	00 16
41	06 19	04 21	02 17	00 04	29♐53
42	06 13	04 09	01 59	29♏41	29 29
43	06 08	03 56	01 40	29 17	29 05
44	06 02	03 44	01 21	28 53	28 39
45	05 56	03 31	01 02	28 29	28 13
46	05 50	03 18	00 43	28 03	27 45
47	05 44	03 05	00 23	27 38	27 16
48	05 38	02 52	00 03	27 11	26 46
49	05 32	02 38	29♎42	26 44	26 14
50	05 25	02 24	29 21	26 16	25 41
51	05 18	02 10	29 00	25 47	25 06
52	05 11	01 55	28 38	25 18	24 30
53	05 03	01 40	28 16	24 48	23 51
54	04 56	01 25	27 53	24 17	23 10
55	04 47	01 09	27 30	23 44	22 27
56	04 39	00 53	27 06	23 11	21 40
57	04 29	00 36	26 41	22 37	20 51
58	04 20	00 18	26 16	22 02	19 59
59	04 09	00 00	25 51	21 25	19 02
60	03♍58	29♍41	25♎24	20♏48	18♐01

8h 48m 0s — 132° 0' 0" — 09 ♌ 34

LAT.	11	12	ASC	2	3
0	10♍30	13♎03	14♏28	13♐24	11♑02
5	10 05	12 01	13 02	12 00	10 03
10	09 41	11 02	11 40	10 36	09 03
15	09 18	10 06	10 19	09 11	08 00
20	08 55	09 10	08 59	07 44	06 53
21	08 51	09 00	08 43	07 27	06 38
22	08 46	08 49	08 27	07 09	06 24
23	08 42	08 38	08 11	06 51	06 09
24	08 37	08 27	07 55	06 33	05 55
25	08 33	08 16	07 39	06 15	05 39
26	08 28	08 05	07 23	05 56	05 24
27	08 23	07 54	07 06	05 38	05 08
28	08 19	07 43	06 50	05 19	04 52
29	08 14	07 32	06 34	05 00	04 36
30	08 09	07 20	06 17	04 41	04 19
31	08 05	07 09	06 00	04 21	04 01
32	08 00	06 58	05 43	04 01	03 44
33	07 55	06 47	05 26	03 41	03 25
34	07 50	06 35	05 09	03 21	03 07
35	07 45	06 24	04 52	03 00	02 47
36	07 40	06 12	04 34	02 39	02 28
37	07 35	06 00	04 17	02 17	02 07
38	07 30	05 49	03 59	01 56	01 46
39	07 25	05 37	03 41	01 33	01 24
40	07 19	05 25	03 23	01 11	01 02
41	07 14	05 12	03 04	00 48	00 39
42	07 08	05 00	02 45	00 24	00 14
43	07 03	04 47	02 26	00 00	29♐49
44	06 57	04 34	02 07	29♏35	29 23
45	06 51	04 21	01 47	29 10	28 56
46	06 45	04 08	01 27	28 44	28 28
47	06 38	03 55	01 07	28 18	27 58
48	06 32	03 41	00 46	27 51	27 27
49	06 25	03 27	00 25	27 23	26 55
50	06 18	03 13	00 04	26 54	26 21
51	06 11	02 58	29♎42	26 25	25 45
52	06 04	02 43	29 20	25 55	25 08
53	05 56	02 28	28 57	25 24	24 28
54	05 48	02 12	28 33	24 52	23 46
55	05 40	01 56	28 10	24 19	23 01
56	05 31	01 39	27 45	23 45	22 14
57	05 22	01 22	27 20	23 10	21 23
58	05 12	01 04	26 54	22 34	20 29
59	05 01	00 45	26 28	21 56	19 31
60	04♍50	00♎26	26♎01	21♏17	18♐28

8h 52m 0s — 133° 0' 0" — 10 ♌ 33

LAT.	11	12	ASC	2	3
0	11♍34	14♎07	15♏28	14♐20	11♑58
5	11 08	13 04	14 01	12 54	10 58
10	10 43	12 04	12 37	11 29	09 57
15	10 19	11 06	11 15	10 03	08 53
20	09 55	10 09	09 54	08 36	07 45
21	09 50	09 58	09 37	08 18	07 31
22	09 46	09 46	09 21	08 00	07 16
23	09 41	09 35	09 05	07 42	07 01
24	09 36	09 24	08 48	07 23	06 46
25	09 31	09 13	08 32	07 05	06 31
26	09 27	09 01	08 15	06 46	06 15
27	09 22	08 50	07 59	06 27	05 59
28	09 17	08 39	07 42	06 08	05 43
29	09 12	08 27	07 25	05 48	05 26
30	09 07	08 16	07 08	05 29	05 09
31	09 02	08 04	06 51	05 09	04 51
32	08 57	07 53	06 34	04 49	04 33
33	08 52	07 41	06 16	04 28	04 14
34	08 47	07 29	05 59	04 07	03 55
35	08 42	07 17	05 41	03 46	03 36
36	08 37	07 05	05 23	03 25	03 16
37	08 31	06 53	05 05	03 03	02 55
38	08 26	06 41	04 47	02 40	02 33
39	08 21	06 29	04 29	02 18	02 11
40	08 15	06 17	04 10	01 55	01 48
41	08 09	06 04	03 51	01 31	01 24
42	08 04	05 51	03 32	01 07	01 00
43	07 58	05 38	03 12	00 42	00 34
44	07 52	05 25	02 53	00 17	00 07
45	07 45	05 12	02 32	29♏51	29♐39
46	07 39	04 58	02 12	29 25	29 11
47	07 33	04 44	01 51	28 58	28 40
48	07 26	04 30	01 30	28 30	28 09
49	07 19	04 16	01 09	28 02	27 35
50	07 12	04 01	00 47	27 33	27 01
51	07 05	03 46	00 24	27 03	26 24
52	06 57	03 31	00 01	26 32	25 45
53	06 49	03 15	29♎38	26 00	25 05
54	06 41	02 59	29 14	25 27	24 21
55	06 32	02 42	28 50	24 53	23 36
56	06 23	02 25	28 25	24 18	22 47
57	06 14	02 08	27 59	23 42	21 55
58	06 04	01 49	27 33	23 05	20 59
59	05 53	01 30	27 06	22 27	19 59
60	05♍42	01♎11	26♎38	21♏47	18♐55

8h 56m 0s — 134° 0' 0" — 11 ♌ 32

LAT.	11	12	ASC	2	3
0	12♍39	15♎12	16♏28	15♐16	12♑53
5	12 11	14 07	15 00	13 49	11 53
10	11 45	13 05	13 34	12 23	10 52
15	11 20	12 05	12 11	10 56	09 47
20	10 55	11 07	10 48	09 27	08 37
21	10 50	10 56	10 31	09 09	08 23
22	10 45	10 44	10 15	08 50	08 08
23	10 40	10 32	09 58	08 32	07 53
24	10 35	10 21	09 41	08 13	07 38
25	10 30	10 09	09 24	07 54	07 22
26	10 25	09 58	09 08	07 35	07 06
27	10 20	09 46	08 51	07 16	06 50
28	10 15	09 34	08 33	06 56	06 33
29	10 10	09 23	08 16	06 37	06 16
30	10 05	09 11	07 59	06 17	05 59
31	10 00	08 59	07 42	05 56	05 41
32	09 55	08 47	07 24	05 36	05 22
33	09 49	08 35	07 06	05 15	05 04
34	09 44	08 23	06 48	04 54	04 44
35	09 39	08 11	06 30	04 32	04 24
36	09 33	07 59	06 12	04 10	04 04
37	09 28	07 46	05 54	03 48	03 42
38	09 22	07 34	05 35	03 25	03 20
39	09 17	07 21	05 16	03 02	02 58
40	09 11	07 09	04 57	02 39	02 34
41	09 05	06 56	04 38	02 14	02 10
42	08 59	06 43	04 18	01 50	01 45
43	08 53	06 29	03 58	01 25	01 19
44	08 47	06 16	03 38	00 59	00 51
45	08 40	06 02	03 18	00 33	00 23
46	08 34	05 48	02 57	00 06	29♐53
47	08 27	05 34	02 35	29♏38	29 22
48	08 20	05 20	02 14	29 10	28 50
49	08 13	05 05	01 52	28 41	28 16
50	08 06	04 50	01 29	28 11	27 40
51	07 58	04 35	01 06	27 40	27 03
52	07 50	04 19	00 43	27 08	26 23
53	07 42	04 03	00 19	26 36	25 41
54	07 34	03 46	29♎55	26 02	24 57
55	07 25	03 29	29 30	25 28	24 10
56	07 16	03 12	29 04	24 52	23 20
57	07 06	02 54	28 38	24 15	22 26
58	06 56	02 35	28 11	23 37	21 29
59	06 45	02 16	27 43	22 57	20 28
60	06♍34	01♎56	27♎15	22♏16	19♐21

9h 0m 0s — 135° 0' 0" — 12 ♌ 32

LAT.	11	12	ASC	2	3
0	13♍43	16♎17	17♏28	16♐11	13♑49
5	13 14	15 10	15 58	14 44	12 48
10	12 47	14 06	14 32	13 17	11 46
15	12 21	13 05	13 07	11 48	10 40
20	11 55	12 06	11 42	10 18	09 30
21	11 50	11 54	11 25	10 00	09 15
22	11 45	11 42	11 08	09 41	09 00
23	11 40	11 30	10 51	09 22	08 45
24	11 34	11 18	10 34	09 03	08 30
25	11 29	11 06	10 17	08 44	08 14
26	11 24	10 54	10 00	08 25	07 58
27	11 19	10 42	09 43	08 05	07 41
28	11 14	10 30	09 25	07 45	07 24
29	11 08	10 18	09 08	07 25	07 07
30	11 03	10 06	08 50	07 05	06 49
31	10 58	09 54	08 32	06 44	06 31
32	10 52	09 42	08 14	06 23	06 12
33	10 47	09 30	07 56	06 02	05 53
34	10 41	09 17	07 38	05 40	05 33
35	10 36	09 05	07 20	05 18	05 13
36	10 30	08 52	07 01	04 56	04 52
37	10 24	08 40	06 42	04 33	04 30
38	10 19	08 27	06 23	04 10	04 08
39	10 13	08 14	06 04	03 47	03 45
40	10 07	08 01	05 44	03 23	03 21
41	10 01	07 47	05 25	02 58	02 56
42	09 55	07 34	05 05	02 33	02 30
43	09 48	07 20	04 44	02 07	02 03
44	09 42	07 07	04 24	01 41	01 36
45	09 35	06 53	04 03	01 14	01 07
46	09 29	06 38	03 41	00 47	00 36
47	09 22	06 24	03 20	00 18	00 05
48	09 15	06 09	02 57	29♏49	29♐32
49	09 07	05 54	02 35	29 20	28 57
50	09 00	05 39	02 12	28 49	28 20
51	08 52	05 23	01 49	28 18	27 42
52	08 44	05 07	01 25	27 45	27 01
53	08 36	04 50	01 00	27 12	26 18
54	08 27	04 33	00 35	26 37	25 33
55	08 18	04 16	00 10	26 02	24 44
56	08 09	03 58	29♎43	25 25	23 53
57	07 59	03 40	29 16	24 47	22 58
58	07 49	03 21	28 49	24 08	21 59
59	07 38	03 01	28 21	23 28	20 56
60	07♍26	02♎41	27♎51	22♏46	19♐48

Koch Table of Houses for Latitudes 0° to 60° North

9h 4m 0s — 136° 0' 0" — 13 ♌ 32

LAT.	11	12	ASC	2	3
0	14♍48	17♎21	18♏28	17♐07	14♑44
5	14 18	16 13	16 57	15 38	13 43
10	13 49	15 08	15 29	14 10	12 40
15	13 22	14 05	14 02	12 41	11 34
20	12 55	13 04	12 36	11 09	10 23
21	12 50	12 52	12 19	10 50	10 08
22	12 45	12 40	12 02	10 31	09 53
23	12 39	12 27	11 44	10 12	09 37
24	12 34	12 15	11 27	09 53	09 21
25	12 28	12 03	11 10	09 34	09 05
26	12 23	11 51	10 52	09 14	08 49
27	12 18	11 39	10 34	08 54	08 32
28	12 12	11 26	10 17	08 34	08 15
29	12 07	11 14	09 59	08 14	07 57
30	12 01	11 02	09 41	07 53	07 39
31	11 56	10 49	09 23	07 32	07 21
32	11 50	10 37	09 05	07 11	07 02
33	11 44	10 24	08 46	06 49	06 42
34	11 39	10 11	08 28	06 27	06 22
35	11 33	09 59	08 09	06 05	06 01
36	11 27	09 46	07 50	05 42	05 40
37	11 21	09 33	07 31	05 19	05 18
38	11 15	09 20	07 11	04 55	04 55
39	11 09	09 06	06 52	04 31	04 32
40	11 03	08 53	06 32	04 06	04 07
41	10 57	08 39	06 11	03 41	03 42
42	10 50	08 26	05 51	03 16	03 16
43	10 44	08 12	05 30	02 50	02 48
44	10 37	07 57	05 09	02 23	02 20
45	10 30	07 43	04 48	01 55	01 50
46	10 24	07 28	04 26	01 27	01 19
47	10 16	07 14	04 04	00 58	00 47
48	10 09	06 59	03 41	00 29	00 13
49	10 02	06 43	03 18	29♏58	29♐38
50	09 54	06 27	02 55	29 27	29 00
51	09 46	06 11	02 31	28 55	28 21
52	09 38	05 55	02 06	28 22	27 39
53	09 29	05 38	01 41	27 48	26 55
54	09 21	05 21	01 16	27 13	26 09
55	09 11	05 03	00 49	26 36	25 19
56	09 02	04 45	00 23	25 59	24 26
57	08 52	04 26	29♎55	25 20	23 30
58	08 41	04 07	29 27	24 40	22 29
59	08 30	03 47	28 58	23 58	21 25
60	08♍19	03♎26	28♎28	23♏15	20♐14

9h 8m 0s — 137° 0' 0" — 14 ♌ 32

LAT.	11	12	ASC	2	3
0	15♍53	18♎26	19♏27	18♐02	15♑40
5	15 21	17 16	17 55	16 33	14 39
10	14 52	16 09	16 26	15 04	13 35
15	14 23	15 05	14 58	13 33	12 28
20	13 56	14 02	13 30	12 00	11 16
21	13 50	13 50	13 13	11 41	11 01
22	13 44	13 37	12 55	11 22	10 45
23	13 39	13 25	12 38	11 03	10 30
24	13 33	13 12	12 20	10 43	10 14
25	13 28	13 00	12 02	10 23	09 57
26	13 22	12 47	11 44	10 03	09 40
27	13 17	12 35	11 26	09 43	09 23
28	13 11	12 22	11 08	09 23	09 06
29	13 05	12 10	10 50	09 02	08 48
30	13 00	11 57	10 32	08 41	08 30
31	12 54	11 44	10 13	08 20	08 11
32	12 48	11 31	09 55	07 58	07 52
33	12 42	11 18	09 36	07 36	07 32
34	12 36	11 05	09 17	07 14	07 11
35	12 30	10 52	08 58	06 51	06 50
36	12 24	10 39	08 39	06 28	06 28
37	12 18	10 26	08 19	06 04	06 06
38	12 12	10 12	07 59	05 40	05 43
39	12 06	09 59	07 39	05 15	05 19
40	11 59	09 45	07 19	04 50	04 54
41	11 53	09 31	06 58	04 25	04 28
42	11 46	09 17	06 37	03 59	04 01
43	11 40	09 03	06 16	03 32	03 33
44	11 33	08 48	05 55	03 05	03 04
45	11 26	08 34	05 33	02 37	02 34
46	11 19	08 19	05 11	02 08	02 03
47	11 11	08 04	04 48	01 39	01 29
48	11 04	07 48	04 25	01 08	00 55
49	10 56	07 32	04 01	00 37	00 18
50	10 48	07 16	03 37	00 05	29♐40
51	10 40	07 00	03 13	29♏32	29 00
52	10 32	06 43	02 48	28 59	28 17
53	10 23	06 26	02 22	28 24	27 32
54	10 14	06 08	01 56	27 48	26 44
55	10 05	05 50	01 29	27 10	25 54
56	09 55	05 32	01 02	26 32	24 59
57	09 45	05 12	00 34	25 52	24 02
58	09 34	04 53	00 05	25 11	23 00
59	09 23	04 32	29♎35	24 28	21 53
60	09♍11	04♎11	29♎05	23♏44	20♐41

9h 12m 0s — 138° 0' 0" — 15 ♌ 32

LAT.	11	12	ASC	2	3
0	16♍57	19♎30	20♏26	18♐58	16♑36
5	16 25	18 18	18 53	17 28	15 34
10	15 54	17 10	17 22	15 57	14 30
15	15 25	16 05	15 53	14 26	13 22
20	14 56	15 00	14 24	12 51	12 09
21	14 50	14 48	14 07	12 32	11 53
22	14 44	14 35	13 49	12 13	11 38
23	14 39	14 22	13 31	11 53	11 22
24	14 33	14 09	13 13	11 33	11 06
25	14 27	13 57	12 55	11 13	10 49
26	14 21	13 44	12 36	10 53	10 32
27	14 16	13 31	12 18	10 32	10 15
28	14 10	13 18	12 00	10 11	09 57
29	14 04	13 05	11 41	09 50	09 39
30	13 58	12 52	11 23	09 29	09 20
31	13 52	12 39	11 04	09 07	09 01
32	13 46	12 26	10 45	08 45	08 42
33	13 40	12 13	10 26	08 23	08 21
34	13 34	12 00	10 06	08 00	08 00
35	13 28	11 46	09 47	07 37	07 39
36	13 22	11 33	09 27	07 13	07 17
37	13 15	11 19	09 07	06 49	06 54
38	13 09	11 05	08 47	06 25	06 30
39	13 02	10 51	08 27	06 00	06 06
40	12 56	10 37	08 06	05 34	05 41
41	12 49	10 23	07 45	05 08	05 14
42	12 42	10 09	07 24	04 42	04 47
43	12 36	09 54	07 02	04 15	04 19
44	12 28	09 39	06 40	03 47	03 49
45	12 21	09 24	06 18	03 18	03 18
46	12 14	09 09	05 55	02 49	02 46
47	12 06	08 53	05 32	02 19	02 12
48	11 59	08 38	05 08	01 48	01 37
49	11 51	08 22	04 44	01 16	00 59
50	11 43	08 05	04 20	00 44	00 20
51	11 35	07 48	03 55	00 10	29♐39
52	11 26	07 31	03 29	29♏35	28 55
53	11 17	07 14	03 03	29 00	28 09
54	11 08	06 56	02 37	28 23	27 20
55	10 58	06 37	02 09	27 45	26 28
56	10 49	06 18	01 41	27 05	25 33
57	10 38	05 59	01 13	26 25	24 33
58	10 27	05 39	00 43	25 42	23 30
59	10 16	05 18	00 13	24 59	22 21
60	10♍04	04♎57	29♎42	24♏13	21♐07

9h 16m 0s — 139° 0' 0" — 16 ♌ 33

LAT.	11	12	ASC	2	3
0	18♍02	20♎34	21♏26	19♐53	17♑32
5	17 29	19 21	19 51	18 22	16 29
10	16 57	18 11	18 19	16 51	15 24
15	16 26	17 04	16 49	15 18	14 16
20	15 57	15 59	15 18	13 43	13 02
21	15 51	15 46	15 00	13 23	12 46
22	15 45	15 33	14 42	13 03	12 31
23	15 39	15 20	14 24	12 43	12 14
24	15 33	15 07	14 05	12 23	11 58
25	15 27	14 54	13 47	12 03	11 41
26	15 21	14 40	13 29	11 42	11 24
27	15 15	14 27	13 10	11 21	11 06
28	15 09	14 14	12 51	11 00	10 48
29	15 03	14 01	12 32	10 39	10 30
30	14 57	13 48	12 13	10 17	10 11
31	14 50	13 34	11 54	09 55	09 52
32	14 44	13 21	11 35	09 33	09 32
33	14 38	13 07	11 16	09 10	09 11
34	14 32	12 54	10 56	08 47	08 50
35	14 25	12 40	10 36	08 23	08 28
36	14 19	12 26	10 16	07 59	08 06
37	14 12	12 12	09 56	07 35	07 42
38	14 06	11 58	09 35	07 10	07 18
39	13 59	11 44	09 14	06 44	06 53
40	13 52	11 30	08 53	06 19	06 28
41	13 46	11 15	08 32	05 52	06 01
42	13 39	11 00	08 10	05 25	05 33
43	13 32	10 46	07 48	04 57	05 04
44	13 24	10 30	07 26	04 29	04 34
45	13 17	10 15	07 03	04 00	04 02
46	13 09	09 59	06 40	03 30	03 29
47	13 02	09 44	06 16	02 59	02 55
48	12 54	09 27	05 52	02 28	02 19
49	12 46	09 11	05 28	01 55	01 41
50	12 38	08 54	05 03	01 22	01 01
51	12 29	08 37	04 37	00 47	00 18
52	12 20	08 19	04 11	00 12	29♐34
53	12 11	08 02	03 44	29♏36	28 46
54	12 02	07 43	03 17	28 58	27 56
55	11 52	07 24	02 49	28 19	27 03
56	11 42	07 05	02 21	27 39	26 06
57	11 32	06 45	01 51	26 57	25 05
58	11 21	06 25	01 21	26 14	24 00
59	11 09	06 04	00 50	25 29	22 50
60	10♍57	05♎42	00♏19	24♏42	21♐34

9h 20m 0s — 140° 0' 0" — 17 ♌ 33

LAT.	11	12	ASC	2	3
0	19♍07	21♎38	22♏25	20♐49	18♑28
5	18 33	20 24	20 49	19 17	17 25
10	18 00	19 13	19 15	17 44	16 19
15	17 28	18 04	17 44	16 10	15 10
20	16 57	16 57	16 12	14 34	13 55
21	16 51	16 44	15 54	14 14	13 39
22	16 45	16 30	15 35	13 54	13 23
23	16 39	16 17	15 17	13 34	13 07
24	16 33	16 04	14 58	13 13	12 50
25	16 26	15 50	14 39	12 53	12 33
26	16 20	15 37	14 21	12 32	12 16
27	16 14	15 24	14 02	12 10	11 58
28	16 08	15 10	13 43	11 49	11 40
29	16 02	14 57	13 24	11 27	11 21
30	15 55	14 43	13 04	11 05	11 02
31	15 49	14 29	12 45	10 43	10 42
32	15 43	14 16	12 25	10 20	10 22
33	15 36	14 02	12 05	09 57	10 01
34	15 30	13 48	11 45	09 33	09 40
35	15 23	13 34	11 25	09 09	09 17
36	15 17	13 20	11 05	08 45	08 54
37	15 10	13 06	10 44	08 20	08 31
38	15 03	12 51	10 23	07 55	08 06
39	14 56	12 37	10 02	07 29	07 41
40	14 49	12 22	09 40	07 03	07 15
41	14 42	12 07	09 19	06 36	06 47
42	14 35	11 52	08 56	06 08	06 19
43	14 28	11 37	08 34	05 40	05 50
44	14 20	11 21	08 11	05 11	05 19
45	14 13	11 06	07 48	04 41	04 47
46	14 05	10 50	07 24	04 11	04 13
47	13 57	10 34	07 00	03 39	03 38
48	13 49	10 17	06 36	03 07	03 01
49	13 41	10 00	06 11	02 34	02 22
50	13 32	09 43	05 45	02 00	01 41
51	13 24	09 26	05 19	01 25	00 58
52	13 15	09 08	04 53	00 49	00 12
53	13 06	08 50	04 26	00 12	29♐24
54	12 56	08 31	03 58	29♏33	28 32
55	12 46	08 12	03 29	28 53	27 38
56	12 36	07 52	03 00	28 12	26 39
57	12 25	07 32	02 30	27 29	25 37
58	12 14	07 11	01 59	26 45	24 30
59	12 03	06 50	01 28	25 59	23 18
60	11♍50	06♎27	00♏55	25♏12	22♐01

9h 24m 0s — 141° 0' 0" — 18 ♌ 34

LAT.	11	12	ASC	2	3
0	20♍12	22♎42	23♏23	21♐44	19♑24
5	19 36	21 26	21 46	20 11	18 20
10	19 03	20 14	20 12	18 38	17 14
15	18 30	19 04	18 39	17 03	16 04
20	17 58	17 55	17 06	15 25	14 49
21	17 52	17 42	16 47	15 05	14 33
22	17 45	17 28	16 29	14 45	14 16
23	17 39	17 14	16 10	14 24	14 00
24	17 33	17 01	15 51	14 03	13 43
25	17 26	16 47	15 32	13 42	13 26
26	17 20	16 34	15 13	13 21	13 08
27	17 14	16 20	14 53	13 00	12 50
28	17 07	16 06	14 34	12 38	12 31
29	17 01	15 52	14 15	12 16	12 12
30	16 54	15 39	13 55	11 53	11 53
31	16 48	15 25	13 35	11 31	11 33
32	16 41	15 11	13 15	11 08	11 12
33	16 35	14 56	12 55	10 44	10 51
34	16 28	14 42	12 35	10 20	10 29
35	16 21	14 28	12 14	09 56	10 07
36	16 14	14 14	11 53	09 31	09 44
37	16 07	13 59	11 32	09 06	09 19
38	16 00	13 44	11 11	08 40	08 55
39	15 53	13 30	10 49	08 14	08 29
40	15 46	13 15	10 28	07 47	08 02
41	15 39	12 59	10 05	07 19	07 34
42	15 32	12 44	09 43	06 51	07 05
43	15 24	12 28	09 20	06 22	06 35
44	15 17	12 13	08 57	05 53	06 04
45	15 09	11 57	08 33	05 22	05 31
46	15 01	11 40	08 09	04 51	04 57
47	14 53	11 24	07 44	04 19	04 21
48	14 45	11 07	07 19	03 47	03 43
49	14 36	10 50	06 54	03 13	03 03
50	14 28	10 32	06 28	02 38	02 21
51	14 19	10 14	06 01	02 02	01 37
52	14 09	09 56	05 34	01 26	00 51
53	14 00	09 38	05 07	00 47	00 01
54	13 50	09 19	04 38	00 08	29♐09
55	13 40	08 59	04 09	29♏27	28 13
56	13 30	08 39	03 39	28 45	27 13
57	13 19	08 18	03 09	28 02	26 09
58	13 08	07 57	02 37	27 16	25 01
59	12 56	07 35	02 05	26 29	23 47
60	12♍44	07♎13	01♏32	25♏41	22♐27

9h 28m 0s — 142° 0' 0" — 19 ♌ 35

LAT.	11	12	ASC	2	3
0	21♍17	23♎46	24♏22	22♐39	20♑20
5	20 40	22 28	22 44	21 05	19 16
10	20 05	21 15	21 08	19 31	18 09
15	19 32	20 03	19 34	17 55	16 59
20	18 59	18 54	18 00	16 16	15 42
21	18 52	18 40	17 41	15 56	15 26
22	18 46	18 26	17 22	15 35	15 10
23	18 39	18 12	17 03	15 14	14 53
24	18 33	17 58	16 43	14 53	14 36
25	18 26	17 44	16 24	14 32	14 18
26	18 20	17 30	16 05	14 11	14 00
27	18 13	17 16	15 45	13 49	13 42
28	18 07	17 02	15 26	13 27	13 23
29	18 00	16 48	15 06	13 04	13 04
30	17 53	16 34	14 46	12 42	12 44
31	17 46	16 20	14 26	12 19	12 24
32	17 40	16 05	14 05	11 55	12 03
33	17 33	15 51	13 45	11 31	11 41
34	17 26	15 37	13 24	11 07	11 19
35	17 19	15 22	13 03	10 42	10 56
36	17 12	15 07	12 42	10 17	10 33
37	17 05	14 52	12 21	09 51	10 08
38	16 58	14 37	11 59	09 25	09 43
39	16 51	14 22	11 37	08 58	09 17
40	16 43	14 07	11 15	08 31	08 49
41	16 36	13 51	10 52	08 03	08 21
42	16 28	13 36	10 29	07 34	07 52
43	16 21	13 20	10 06	07 05	07 21
44	16 13	13 04	09 42	06 35	06 49
45	16 05	12 47	09 18	06 04	06 16
46	15 57	12 31	08 54	05 32	05 41
47	15 49	12 14	08 29	05 00	05 04
48	15 40	11 57	08 03	04 26	04 25
49	15 32	11 39	07 37	03 52	03 45
50	15 23	11 21	07 11	03 17	03 02
51	15 14	11 03	06 44	02 40	02 17
52	15 04	10 45	06 16	02 02	01 29
53	14 55	10 26	05 48	01 23	00 39
54	14 45	10 06	05 19	00 43	29♐45
55	14 35	09 46	04 49	00 02	28 48
56	14 24	09 26	04 19	29♏19	27 47
57	14 13	09 05	03 47	28 34	26 41
58	14 02	08 44	03 15	27 48	25 31
59	13 50	08 21	02 43	27 00	24 15
60	13♍37	07♎58	02♏09	26♏10	22♐54

9h 32m 0s — 143° 0' 0" — 20 ♌ 36

LAT.	11	12	ASC	2	3
0	22♍23	24♎50	25♏21	23♐34	21♑17
5	21 44	23 31	23 41	22 00	20 12
10	21 08	22 15	22 04	20 25	19 05
15	20 34	21 03	20 29	18 48	17 53
20	20 00	19 52	18 53	17 07	16 36
21	19 53	19 38	18 34	16 47	16 20
22	19 47	19 23	18 15	16 26	16 03
23	19 40	19 09	17 55	16 05	15 46
24	19 33	18 55	17 36	15 44	15 29
25	19 26	18 41	17 16	15 22	15 11
26	19 20	18 27	16 57	15 00	14 53
27	19 13	18 12	16 37	14 38	14 34
28	19 06	17 58	16 17	14 16	14 15
29	18 59	17 44	15 57	13 53	13 56
30	18 52	17 29	15 37	13 30	13 36
31	18 45	17 15	15 16	13 06	13 15
32	18 38	17 00	14 55	12 43	12 54
33	18 31	16 46	14 35	12 18	12 32
34	18 24	16 31	14 14	11 54	12 09
35	18 17	16 16	13 52	11 29	11 46
36	18 10	16 01	13 31	11 03	11 22
37	18 03	15 46	13 09	10 37	10 57
38	17 56	15 31	12 47	10 10	10 31
39	17 48	15 15	12 25	09 43	10 05
40	17 41	14 59	12 02	09 15	09 37
41	17 33	14 44	11 39	08 47	09 08
42	17 25	14 28	11 16	08 17	08 38
43	17 17	14 11	10 52	07 48	08 07
44	17 09	13 55	10 28	07 17	07 34
45	17 01	13 38	10 03	06 46	07 00
46	16 53	13 21	09 38	06 13	06 25
47	16 45	13 04	09 13	05 40	05 47
48	16 36	12 47	08 47	05 06	05 08
49	16 27	12 29	08 20	04 31	04 26
50	16 18	12 11	07 53	03 55	03 43
51	16 09	11 52	07 26	03 18	02 57
52	15 59	11 33	06 58	02 39	02 08
53	15 50	11 14	06 29	01 59	01 16
54	15 39	10 54	05 59	01 18	00 21
55	15 29	10 34	05 29	00 36	29♐23
56	15 18	10 13	04 58	29♏52	28 20
57	15 07	09 52	04 26	29 06	27 13
58	14 56	09 30	03 53	28 19	26 01
59	14 44	09 07	03 20	27 30	24 44
60	14♍31	08♎44	02♏45	26♏39	23♐20

Koch Table of Houses for Latitudes 0° to 60° North

9h 36m 0s — 21 ♌ 37 — 144° 0' 0"

LAT.	11	12	ASC	2	3
0	23♍28	25♎53	26♏19	24♐30	22♑13
5	22 49	24 33	24 38	22 54	21 08
10	22 12	23 16	23 01	21 18	20 00
15	21 36	22 02	21 24	19 40	18 48
20	21 01	20 50	19 47	17 59	17 30
21	20 54	20 35	19 27	17 38	17 13
22	20 47	20 21	19 08	17 17	16 57
23	20 40	20 07	18 48	16 55	16 39
24	20 33	19 52	18 28	16 34	16 22
25	20 27	19 38	18 09	16 12	16 04
26	20 20	19 23	17 49	15 50	15 46
27	20 13	19 09	17 28	15 27	15 27
28	20 06	18 54	17 08	15 05	15 07
29	19 59	18 40	16 48	14 42	14 48
30	19 52	18 25	16 27	14 18	14 27
31	19 44	18 10	16 06	13 54	14 06
32	19 37	17 55	15 46	13 30	13 45
33	19 30	17 40	15 24	13 06	13 23
34	19 23	17 25	15 03	12 41	13 00
35	19 16	17 10	14 41	12 15	12 36
36	19 08	16 55	14 19	11 49	12 12
37	19 01	16 39	13 57	11 22	11 46
38	18 53	16 24	13 35	10 55	11 20
39	18 46	16 08	13 12	10 28	10 53
40	18 38	15 52	12 49	09 59	10 25
41	18 30	15 36	12 26	09 30	09 56
42	18 22	15 20	12 02	09 01	09 25
43	18 14	15 03	11 38	08 30	08 53
44	18 06	14 46	11 13	07 59	08 20
45	17 58	14 29	10 48	07 27	07 45
46	17 49	14 12	10 23	06 54	07 09
47	17 41	13 54	09 57	06 20	06 31
48	17 32	13 37	09 30	05 46	05 51
49	17 23	13 18	09 04	05 10	05 08
50	17 14	13 00	08 36	04 33	04 24
51	17 04	12 41	08 08	03 55	03 37
52	16 54	12 22	07 39	03 16	02 47
53	16 45	12 02	07 10	02 35	01 54
54	16 34	11 42	06 40	01 53	00 58
55	16 24	11 21	06 09	01 10	29♐58
56	16 13	11 00	05 37	00 25	28 54
57	16 02	10 39	05 05	29♏39	27 45
58	15 50	10 16	04 32	28 50	26 32
59	15 38	09 53	03 57	28 00	25 13
60	15♍25	09♎30	03♏22	27♏08	23♐47

9h 40m 0s — 22 ♌ 39 — 145° 0' 0"

LAT.	11	12	ASC	2	3
0	24♍33	26♎57	27♏17	25♐25	23♑10
5	23 53	25 35	25 36	23 49	22 04
10	23 15	24 17	23 57	22 12	20 56
15	22 38	23 02	22 19	20 33	19 43
20	22 02	21 48	20 41	18 50	18 24
21	21 55	21 33	20 21	18 29	18 07
22	21 48	21 19	20 01	18 07	17 50
23	21 41	21 04	19 41	17 46	17 33
24	21 34	20 49	19 21	17 24	17 15
25	21 27	20 35	19 01	17 02	16 57
26	21 20	20 20	18 40	16 39	16 38
27	21 13	20 05	18 20	16 17	16 19
28	21 05	19 50	18 00	15 54	16 00
29	20 58	19 35	17 39	15 30	15 40
30	20 51	19 20	17 18	15 07	15 19
31	20 44	19 05	16 57	14 42	14 58
32	20 36	18 50	16 36	14 18	14 36
33	20 29	18 35	16 14	13 53	14 13
34	20 22	18 19	15 52	13 27	13 50
35	20 14	18 04	15 30	13 02	13 26
36	20 07	17 48	15 08	12 35	13 01
37	19 59	17 33	14 46	12 08	12 36
38	19 51	17 17	14 23	11 41	12 09
39	19 43	17 01	14 00	11 12	11 42
40	19 36	16 45	13 36	10 44	11 13
41	19 28	16 28	13 12	10 14	10 43
42	19 19	16 11	12 48	09 44	10 12
43	19 11	15 55	12 24	09 13	09 40
44	19 03	15 38	11 59	08 41	09 06
45	18 54	15 20	11 33	08 09	08 30
46	18 46	15 03	11 07	07 35	07 53
47	18 37	14 45	10 41	07 01	07 14
48	18 28	14 27	10 14	06 26	06 33
49	18 19	14 08	09 47	05 49	05 50
50	18 09	13 49	09 19	05 12	05 05
51	18 00	13 30	08 50	04 33	04 17
52	17 50	13 10	08 21	03 53	03 26
53	17 40	12 50	07 51	03 11	02 32
54	17 29	12 30	07 20	02 29	01 35
55	17 19	12 09	06 49	01 44	00 33
56	17 07	11 47	06 17	00 59	29♐28
57	16 56	11 25	05 44	00 11	28 18
58	16 44	11 03	05 10	29♏22	27 02
59	16 32	10 39	04 35	28 30	25 41
60	16♍19	10♎15	03♏59	27♏37	24♐14

9h 44m 0s — 23 ♌ 41 — 146° 0' 0"

LAT.	11	12	ASC	2	3
0	25♍38	28♎00	28♏15	26♐20	24♑06
5	24 57	26 37	26 33	24 43	23 00
10	24 18	25 18	24 53	23 05	21 51
15	23 40	24 01	23 13	21 25	20 38
20	23 04	22 46	21 34	19 41	19 18
21	22 56	22 31	21 14	19 20	19 01
22	22 49	22 16	20 54	18 58	18 44
23	22 42	22 01	20 34	18 36	18 27
24	22 34	21 46	20 13	18 14	18 09
25	22 27	21 31	19 53	17 52	17 50
26	22 20	21 16	19 32	17 29	17 31
27	22 13	21 01	19 12	17 06	17 12
28	22 05	20 46	18 51	16 43	16 52
29	21 58	20 31	18 30	16 19	16 32
30	21 50	20 16	18 09	15 55	16 11
31	21 43	20 00	17 47	15 31	15 50
32	21 35	19 45	17 26	15 06	15 27
33	21 28	19 29	17 04	14 40	15 05
34	21 20	19 14	16 42	14 14	14 41
35	21 13	18 58	16 19	13 48	14 17
36	21 05	18 42	15 57	13 21	13 51
37	20 57	18 26	15 34	12 54	13 25
38	20 49	18 10	15 11	12 26	12 58
39	20 41	17 54	14 47	11 57	12 30
40	20 33	17 37	14 23	11 28	12 01
41	20 25	17 20	13 59	10 58	11 31
42	20 17	17 03	13 35	10 27	10 59
43	20 08	16 46	13 10	09 56	10 26
44	20 00	16 29	12 44	09 24	09 52
45	19 51	16 11	12 18	08 50	09 16
46	19 42	15 53	11 52	08 16	08 38
47	19 33	15 35	11 25	07 41	07 58
48	19 24	15 17	10 58	07 05	07 17
49	19 15	14 58	10 30	06 28	06 33
50	19 05	14 39	10 01	05 50	05 46
51	18 55	14 19	09 32	05 10	04 57
52	18 45	13 59	09 02	04 30	04 05
53	18 35	13 39	08 32	03 47	03 10
54	18 24	13 18	08 01	03 04	02 11
55	18 13	12 56	07 29	02 19	01 09
56	18 02	12 35	06 56	01 32	00 02
57	17 51	12 12	06 22	00 43	28♐50
58	17 39	11 49	05 48	29♏53	27 33
59	17 26	11 26	05 12	29 01	26 10
60	17♍13	11♎01	04♏35	28♏06	24♐41

9h 48m 0s — 24 ♌ 42 — 147° 0' 0"

LAT.	11	12	ASC	2	3
0	26♍44	29♎03	29♏13	27♐15	25♑03
5	26 01	27 39	27 29	25 37	23 57
10	25 21	26 18	25 48	23 59	22 47
15	24 43	25 01	24 08	22 18	21 33
20	24 05	23 44	22 28	20 33	20 13
21	23 57	23 29	22 07	20 11	19 56
22	23 50	23 14	21 47	19 49	19 38
23	23 43	22 59	21 26	19 27	19 20
24	23 35	22 43	21 06	19 05	19 02
25	23 28	22 28	20 45	18 42	18 44
26	23 20	22 13	20 24	18 19	18 25
27	23 13	21 58	20 03	17 56	18 05
28	23 05	21 42	19 42	17 32	17 45
29	22 58	21 27	19 21	17 08	17 24
30	22 50	21 11	18 59	16 44	17 03
31	22 42	20 56	18 37	16 19	16 41
32	22 35	20 40	18 16	15 53	16 19
33	22 27	20 24	17 53	15 28	15 56
34	22 19	20 08	17 31	15 02	15 32
35	22 11	19 52	17 08	14 35	15 07
36	22 03	19 36	16 45	14 08	14 42
37	21 55	19 20	16 22	13 40	14 15
38	21 47	19 03	15 59	13 11	13 48
39	21 39	18 47	15 35	12 42	13 19
40	21 31	18 30	15 11	12 12	12 50
41	21 23	18 13	14 46	11 42	12 19
42	21 14	17 55	14 21	11 11	11 47
43	21 06	17 38	13 56	10 39	11 13
44	20 57	17 20	13 30	10 06	10 38
45	20 48	17 02	13 03	09 32	10 01
46	20 39	16 44	12 37	08 58	09 23
47	20 30	16 26	12 09	08 22	08 42
48	20 20	16 07	11 42	07 45	08 00
49	20 11	15 48	11 13	07 07	07 15
50	20 01	15 28	10 44	06 28	06 28
51	19 51	15 08	10 14	05 48	05 38
52	19 41	14 48	09 44	05 07	04 45
53	19 30	14 27	09 13	04 24	03 48
54	19 20	14 06	08 41	03 39	02 48
55	19 09	13 44	08 09	02 53	01 44
56	18 57	13 22	07 35	02 05	00 36
57	18 45	12 59	07 01	01 16	29♐23
58	18 33	12 36	06 26	00 24	28 04
59	18 21	12 12	05 49	29♏31	26 39
60	18♍07	11♎47	05♏12	28♏35	25♐07

9h 52m 0s — 25 ♌ 44 — 148° 0' 0"

LAT.	11	12	ASC	2	3
0	27♍49	00♏06	00♐11	28♐10	26♑00
5	27 06	28♎40	28♏26	26 32	24 53
10	26 24	27 19	26 44	24 52	23 43
15	25 45	26 00	25 03	23 10	22 29
20	25 06	24 42	23 21	21 24	21 07
21	24 59	24 27	23 00	21 02	20 50
22	24 51	24 11	22 40	20 40	20 32
23	24 43	23 56	22 19	20 18	20 15
24	24 36	23 40	21 58	19 55	19 56
25	24 28	23 25	21 37	19 32	19 37
26	24 21	23 09	21 16	19 09	19 18
27	24 13	22 54	20 55	18 45	18 58
28	24 05	22 38	20 33	18 21	18 38
29	23 57	22 22	20 12	17 57	18 17
30	23 50	22 07	19 50	17 32	17 56
31	23 42	21 51	19 28	17 07	17 34
32	23 34	21 35	19 06	16 41	17 11
33	23 26	21 19	18 43	16 15	16 47
34	23 18	21 03	18 20	15 49	16 23
35	23 10	20 46	17 57	15 22	15 58
36	23 02	20 30	17 34	14 54	15 32
37	22 54	20 13	17 10	14 26	15 05
38	22 46	19 56	16 47	13 57	14 37
39	22 37	19 39	16 22	13 27	14 08
40	22 29	19 22	15 58	12 57	13 38
41	22 20	19 05	15 33	12 26	13 07
42	22 12	18 47	15 07	11 54	12 34
43	22 03	18 30	14 42	11 22	12 00
44	21 54	18 12	14 15	10 48	11 24
45	21 45	17 53	13 49	10 14	10 47
46	21 36	17 35	13 21	09 39	10 08
47	21 26	17 16	12 54	09 03	09 27
48	21 17	16 57	12 25	08 25	08 43
49	21 07	16 37	11 56	07 47	07 58
50	20 57	16 17	11 27	07 07	07 10
51	20 47	15 57	10 57	06 26	06 18
52	20 37	15 37	10 26	05 44	05 24
53	20 26	15 15	09 54	05 00	04 27
54	20 15	14 54	09 22	04 14	03 26
55	20 04	14 32	08 49	03 27	02 20
56	19 52	14 09	08 15	02 39	01 10
57	19 40	13 46	07 40	01 48	29♐55
58	19 28	13 22	07 04	00 56	28 35
59	19 15	12 58	06 27	00 01	27 08
60	19♍02	12♎33	05♏49	29♏04	25♐34

9h 56m 0s — 26 ♌ 47 — 149° 0' 0"

LAT.	11	12	ASC	2	3
0	28♍55	01♏08	01♐08	29♐05	26♑57
5	28 10	29♎42	29♏23	27 26	25 50
10	27 28	28 19	27 40	25 46	24 40
15	26 47	26 59	25 57	24 03	23 24
20	26 08	25 40	24 14	22 15	22 02
21	26 00	25 24	23 54	21 53	21 45
22	25 52	25 09	23 33	21 31	21 27
23	25 44	24 53	23 12	21 08	21 09
24	25 37	24 37	22 50	20 45	20 50
25	25 29	24 22	22 29	20 22	20 31
26	25 21	24 06	22 08	19 59	20 12
27	25 13	23 50	21 46	19 35	19 52
28	25 05	23 34	21 24	19 10	19 31
29	24 57	23 18	21 03	18 46	19 10
30	24 49	23 02	20 40	18 21	18 48
31	24 41	22 46	20 18	17 55	18 26
32	24 33	22 30	19 56	17 29	18 03
33	24 25	22 13	19 33	17 03	17 39
34	24 17	21 57	19 10	16 36	17 15
35	24 09	21 40	18 46	16 08	16 49
36	24 01	21 24	18 23	15 40	16 23
37	23 52	21 07	17 59	15 12	15 56
38	23 44	20 50	17 35	14 42	15 27
39	23 35	20 32	17 10	14 12	14 58
40	23 27	20 15	16 45	13 42	14 27
41	23 18	19 57	16 20	13 10	13 55
42	23 09	19 40	15 54	12 38	13 22
43	23 00	19 21	15 28	12 05	12 47
44	22 51	19 03	15 01	11 31	12 11
45	22 42	18 45	14 34	10 56	11 33
46	22 33	18 26	14 06	10 20	10 53
47	22 23	18 07	13 38	09 43	10 11
48	22 13	17 47	13 09	09 05	09 27
49	22 03	17 27	12 40	08 26	08 41
50	21 53	17 07	12 10	07 46	07 51
51	21 43	16 46	11 39	07 04	06 59
52	21 32	16 25	11 07	06 21	06 04
53	21 22	16 04	10 35	05 36	05 06
54	21 10	15 42	10 02	04 50	04 03
55	20 59	15 20	09 29	04 02	02 56
56	20 47	14 57	08 54	03 12	01 45
57	20 35	14 33	08 18	02 21	00 28
58	20 23	14 09	07 42	01 27	29♐06
59	20 10	13 44	07 04	00 31	27 37
60	19♍56	13♎19	06♏25	29♏33	26♐01

10h 0m 0s — 27 ♌ 49 — 150° 0' 0"

LAT.	11	12	ASC	2	3
0	00♎00	02♏11	02♐05	00♑00	27♑55
5	29♍14	00 43	00 19	28♐20	26 47
10	28 31	29♎19	28♏35	26 39	25 36
15	27 50	27 58	26 52	24 55	24 20
20	27 10	26 38	25 08	23 07	22 57
21	27 02	26 22	24 47	22 45	22 40
22	26 54	26 06	24 25	22 22	22 22
23	26 46	25 50	24 04	21 59	22 03
24	26 38	25 34	23 43	21 36	21 44
25	26 30	25 18	23 21	21 13	21 25
26	26 22	25 02	23 00	20 49	21 06
27	26 14	24 46	22 38	20 24	20 45
28	26 05	24 30	22 16	20 00	20 25
29	25 57	24 14	21 53	19 35	20 03
30	25 49	23 57	21 31	19 10	19 41
31	25 41	23 41	21 08	18 44	19 19
32	25 33	23 25	20 46	18 17	18 55
33	25 25	23 08	20 22	17 51	18 31
34	25 16	22 51	19 59	17 23	18 06
35	25 08	22 34	19 35	16 55	17 40
36	25 00	22 17	19 11	16 27	17 14
37	24 51	22 00	18 47	15 58	16 46
38	24 42	21 43	18 22	15 28	16 17
39	24 34	21 25	17 57	14 58	15 47
40	24 25	21 08	17 32	14 26	15 16
41	24 16	20 50	17 06	13 54	14 44
42	24 07	20 32	16 40	13 22	14 10
43	23 58	20 13	16 14	12 48	13 35
44	23 49	19 55	15 46	12 14	12 58
45	23 39	19 36	15 19	11 38	12 19
46	23 30	19 17	14 51	11 02	11 39
47	23 20	18 57	14 22	10 24	10 56
48	23 10	18 37	13 53	09 45	10 11
49	23 00	18 17	13 23	09 05	09 24
50	22 50	17 56	12 52	08 24	08 34
51	22 39	17 36	12 21	07 42	07 41
52	22 28	17 14	11 49	06 58	06 44
53	22 17	16 52	11 16	06 12	05 44
54	22 06	16 30	10 43	05 25	04 41
55	21 54	16 07	10 08	04 36	03 32
56	21 43	15 44	09 33	03 46	02 20
57	21 30	15 20	08 57	02 53	01 01
58	21 18	14 56	08 20	01 58	29♐37
59	21 05	14 30	07 41	01 01	28 07
60	20♍51	14♎04	07♏02	00♐02	26♐29

10h 4m 0s — 28 ♌ 52 — 151° 0' 0"

LAT.	11	12	ASC	2	3
0	01♎05	03♏13	03♐03	00♑55	28♑52
5	00 19	01 44	01 16	29♐15	27 44
10	29♍35	00 19	29♏31	27 33	26 32
15	28 52	28♎57	27 46	25 48	25 16
20	28 11	27 36	26 01	23 59	23 52
21	28 03	27 20	25 40	23 36	23 35
22	27 55	27 04	25 18	23 13	23 17
23	27 47	26 47	24 57	22 50	22 58
24	27 39	26 31	24 35	22 27	22 39
25	27 30	26 15	24 13	22 03	22 20
26	27 22	25 59	23 51	21 39	22 00
27	27 14	25 42	23 29	21 14	21 39
28	27 06	25 26	23 07	20 49	21 18
29	26 57	25 09	22 44	20 24	20 57
30	26 49	24 53	22 22	19 58	20 34
31	26 41	24 36	21 59	19 32	20 11
32	26 32	24 19	21 36	19 06	19 48
33	26 24	24 03	21 12	18 38	19 23
34	26 16	23 46	20 48	18 11	18 58
35	26 07	23 29	20 24	17 42	18 32
36	25 58	23 11	20 00	17 13	18 05
37	25 50	22 54	19 35	16 44	17 37
38	25 41	22 36	19 10	16 14	17 08
39	25 32	22 18	18 45	15 43	16 37
40	25 23	22 00	18 19	15 11	16 06
41	25 14	21 42	17 53	14 39	15 33
42	25 05	21 24	17 27	14 06	14 59
43	24 56	21 05	17 00	13 31	14 23
44	24 46	20 46	16 32	12 56	13 45
45	24 37	20 27	16 04	12 20	13 06
46	24 27	20 07	15 35	11 43	12 25
47	24 17	19 48	15 06	11 05	11 41
48	24 07	19 27	14 36	10 26	10 55
49	23 57	19 07	14 06	09 45	10 07
50	23 46	18 46	13 35	09 03	09 16
51	23 35	18 25	13 03	08 20	08 22
52	23 24	18 03	12 31	07 35	07 25
53	23 13	17 41	11 57	06 49	06 24
54	23 02	17 18	11 23	06 01	05 18
55	22 50	16 55	10 48	05 11	04 09
56	22 38	16 31	10 13	04 19	02 54
57	22 26	16 07	09 36	03 26	01 35
58	22 13	15 42	08 58	02 30	00 09
59	22 00	15 17	08 19	01 32	28♐36
60	21♍46	14♎50	07♏39	00♐31	26♐56

Koch Table of Houses for Latitudes 0° to 60° North

10h 8m 0s — 152° 0' 0" — 29 ♌ 54

LAT.	11	12	ASC	2	3
0	02♎11	04♏16	04♐00	01♑50	29♑49
5	01 23	02 46	02 12	00 09	28 41
10	00 38	01 20	00 26	28♐27	27 29
15	29♍55	29♎56	28♏41	26 41	26 12
20	29 13	28 34	26 54	24 50	24 48
21	29 05	28 17	26 33	24 28	24 30
22	28 56	28 01	26 11	24 04	24 12
23	28 48	27 45	25 49	23 41	23 53
24	28 40	27 28	25 27	23 17	23 34
25	28 31	27 12	25 05	22 53	23 14
26	28 23	26 55	24 43	22 29	22 54
27	28 14	26 38	24 21	22 04	22 33
28	28 06	26 22	23 58	21 39	22 12
29	27 58	26 05	23 35	21 13	21 50
30	27 49	25 48	23 12	20 47	21 28
31	27 41	25 31	22 49	20 21	21 04
32	27 32	25 14	22 26	19 54	20 40
33	27 24	24 57	22 02	19 26	20 16
34	27 15	24 40	21 38	18 58	19 50
35	27 06	24 23	21 13	18 29	19 24
36	26 57	24 05	20 49	18 00	18 56
37	26 49	23 47	20 24	17 30	18 28
38	26 40	23 29	19 58	17 00	17 58
39	26 31	23 11	19 33	16 28	17 28
40	26 21	22 53	19 07	15 56	16 56
41	26 12	22 35	18 40	15 23	16 22
42	26 03	22 16	18 13	14 49	15 47
43	25 53	21 57	17 46	14 15	15 11
44	25 44	21 38	17 18	13 39	14 33
45	25 34	21 18	16 49	13 02	13 53
46	25 24	20 58	16 20	12 25	13 11
47	25 14	20 38	15 50	11 46	12 27
48	25 04	20 18	15 20	11 06	11 40
49	24 53	19 57	14 49	10 25	10 51
50	24 43	19 36	14 18	09 42	09 59
51	24 32	19 14	13 46	08 58	09 04
52	24 21	18 52	13 12	08 12	08 05
53	24 09	18 29	12 39	07 25	07 03
54	23 58	18 06	12 04	06 36	05 56
55	23 46	17 43	11 28	05 45	04 45
56	23 33	17 19	10 52	04 53	03 30
57	23 21	16 54	10 14	03 58	02 08
58	23 08	16 29	09 36	03 01	00 40
59	22 55	16 03	08 56	02 02	29♐06
60	22♍41	15♎36	08♏15	01♐00	27♐23

10h 12m 0s — 153° 0' 0" — 00 ♍ 57

LAT.	11	12	ASC	2	3
0	03♎16	05♏18	04♐57	02♑45	00♒47
5	02 28	03 47	03 08	01 04	29♑39
10	01 42	02 19	01 21	29♐20	28 26
15	00 58	00 55	29♏35	27 34	27 08
20	00 15	29♎32	27 47	25 42	25 43
21	00 06	29 15	27 26	25 19	25 25
22	29♍58	28 58	27 04	24 56	25 07
23	29 49	28 42	26 42	24 32	24 48
24	29 41	28 25	26 20	24 08	24 29
25	29 32	28 08	25 57	23 44	24 09
26	29 24	27 51	25 35	23 19	23 49
27	29 15	27 35	25 12	22 54	23 28
28	29 07	27 18	24 49	22 29	23 06
29	28 58	27 01	24 26	22 03	22 44
30	28 49	26 44	24 03	21 36	22 21
31	28 41	26 27	23 39	21 10	21 58
32	28 32	26 09	23 16	20 42	21 34
33	28 23	25 52	22 51	20 14	21 08
34	28 14	25 34	22 27	19 46	20 43
35	28 05	25 17	22 02	19 17	20 16
36	27 57	24 59	21 37	18 47	19 48
37	27 47	24 41	21 12	18 17	19 19
38	27 38	24 23	20 46	17 46	18 49
39	27 29	24 04	20 20	17 14	18 18
40	27 20	23 46	19 54	16 41	17 46
41	27 10	23 27	19 27	16 08	17 12
42	27 01	23 08	19 00	15 33	16 36
43	26 51	22 49	18 32	14 58	15 59
44	26 41	22 29	18 03	14 22	15 21
45	26 32	22 09	17 34	13 45	14 40
46	26 21	21 49	17 05	13 06	13 57
47	26 11	21 29	16 35	12 27	13 12
48	26 01	21 08	16 04	11 46	12 25
49	25 50	20 47	15 33	11 04	11 35
50	25 39	20 25	15 01	10 21	10 42
51	25 28	20 03	14 28	09 36	09 46
52	25 17	19 41	13 54	08 50	08 46
53	25 05	19 18	13 20	08 01	07 42
54	24 54	18 55	12 45	07 12	06 35
55	24 42	18 31	12 08	06 20	05 22
56	24 29	18 06	11 31	05 26	04 05
57	24 16	17 41	10 53	04 31	02 42
58	24 03	17 16	10 14	03 33	01 12
59	23 50	16 49	09 33	02 32	29♐35
60	23♍36	16♎22	08♏52	01♐30	27♐51

10h 16m 0s — 154° 0' 0" — 02 ♍ 00

LAT.	11	12	ASC	2	3
0	04♎22	06♏19	05♐54	03♑40	01♒45
5	03 32	04 47	04 04	01 58	00 36
10	02 45	03 19	02 17	00 14	29♑23
15	02 00	01 54	00 29	28♐27	28 05
20	01 17	00 29	28♏41	26 34	26 39
21	01 08	00 12	28 19	26 11	26 21
22	00 59	29♎56	27 56	25 47	26 03
23	00 50	29 39	27 34	25 23	25 43
24	00 42	29 22	27 12	24 59	25 24
25	00 33	29 05	26 49	24 35	25 04
26	00 24	28 48	26 26	24 10	24 43
27	00 16	28 31	26 04	23 44	24 22
28	00 07	28 14	25 40	23 18	24 00
29	29♍58	27 56	25 17	22 52	23 38
30	29 49	27 39	24 53	22 26	23 15
31	29 41	27 22	24 30	21 58	22 51
32	29 32	27 04	24 06	21 31	22 27
33	29 23	26 47	23 41	21 02	22 01
34	29 14	26 29	23 16	20 34	21 35
35	29 05	26 11	22 52	20 04	21 08
36	28 56	25 53	22 26	19 34	20 40
37	28 47	25 34	22 01	19 03	20 11
38	28 37	25 16	21 34	18 32	19 40
39	28 28	24 57	21 08	17 59	19 09
40	28 18	24 39	20 41	17 26	18 36
41	28 09	24 20	20 14	16 52	18 02
42	27 59	24 00	19 46	16 18	17 26
43	27 49	23 41	19 18	15 42	16 48
44	27 39	23 21	18 49	15 05	16 09
45	27 29	23 01	18 20	14 27	15 27
46	27 19	22 40	17 50	13 48	14 44
47	27 08	22 19	17 19	13 08	13 58
48	26 58	21 58	16 48	12 27	13 10
49	26 47	21 37	16 16	11 44	12 19
50	26 36	21 15	15 43	11 00	11 25
51	26 25	20 53	15 10	10 14	10 28
52	26 13	20 30	14 36	09 27	09 27
53	26 02	20 07	14 01	08 38	08 22
54	25 50	19 43	13 25	07 47	07 13
55	25 37	19 19	12 48	06 55	05 59
56	25 25	18 54	12 11	06 00	04 40
57	25 12	18 28	11 32	05 03	03 15
58	24 59	18 02	10 52	04 04	01 44
59	24 45	17 36	10 11	03 03	00 05
60	24♍31	17♎08	09♏28	01♐59	28♐19

10h 20m 0s — 155° 0' 0" — 03 ♍ 03

LAT.	11	12	ASC	2	3
0	05♎27	07♏21	06♐50	04♑35	02♒43
5	04 36	05 48	05 00	02 53	01 34
10	03 49	04 19	03 12	01 08	00 21
15	03 03	02 52	01 23	29♐20	29♑02
20	02 18	01 27	29♏34	27 26	27 35
21	02 10	01 10	29 11	27 03	27 17
22	02 01	00 53	28 49	26 39	26 58
23	01 52	00 36	28 27	26 15	26 39
24	01 43	00 18	28 04	25 50	26 19
25	01 34	00 01	27 41	25 25	25 59
26	01 25	29♎44	27 18	25 00	25 38
27	01 16	29 27	26 55	24 34	25 17
28	01 08	29 09	26 32	24 08	24 55
29	00 59	28 52	26 08	23 42	24 32
30	00 50	28 34	25 44	23 15	24 09
31	00 41	28 17	25 20	22 47	23 45
32	00 32	27 59	24 56	22 19	23 20
33	00 23	27 41	24 31	21 51	22 55
34	00 13	27 23	24 06	21 21	22 28
35	00 04	27 05	23 41	20 52	22 01
36	29♍55	26 47	23 15	20 21	21 32
37	29 46	26 28	22 49	19 50	21 03
38	29 36	26 09	22 22	19 18	20 32
39	29 27	25 50	21 56	18 45	20 00
40	29 17	25 31	21 28	18 12	19 26
41	29 07	25 12	21 01	17 37	18 52
42	28 57	24 52	20 33	17 02	18 15
43	28 47	24 33	20 04	16 26	17 37
44	28 37	24 12	19 35	15 48	16 57
45	28 27	23 52	19 05	15 10	16 15
46	28 16	23 31	18 34	14 30	15 31
47	28 06	23 10	18 03	13 49	14 44
48	27 55	22 49	17 32	13 07	13 55
49	27 44	22 27	16 59	12 24	13 04
50	27 33	22 05	16 26	11 39	12 09
51	27 22	21 42	15 52	10 53	11 10
52	27 10	21 19	15 18	10 05	10 08
53	26 58	20 55	14 42	09 15	09 02
54	26 46	20 31	14 06	08 23	07 52
55	26 33	20 07	13 28	07 30	06 37
56	26 21	19 41	12 50	06 34	05 16
57	26 08	19 16	12 10	05 36	03 49
58	25 54	18 49	11 30	04 36	02 16
59	25 40	18 22	10 48	03 33	00 35
60	25♍26	17♎54	10♏05	02♐28	28♐47

10h 24m 0s — 156° 0' 0" — 04 ♍ 07

LAT.	11	12	ASC	2	3
0	06♎32	08♏23	07♐47	05♑30	03♒41
5	05 41	06 49	05 56	03 47	02 32
10	04 52	05 19	04 07	02 02	01 18
15	04 06	03 51	02 18	00 13	29♑59
20	03 20	02 24	00 27	28♐18	28 32
21	03 11	02 07	00 04	27 54	28 13
22	03 02	01 50	29♏42	27 30	27 54
23	02 53	01 33	29 19	27 06	27 35
24	02 44	01 15	28 56	26 41	27 15
25	02 35	00 58	28 33	26 16	26 55
26	02 26	00 40	28 10	25 51	26 34
27	02 17	00 23	27 46	25 25	26 12
28	02 08	00 05	27 23	24 58	25 50
29	01 59	29♎48	26 59	24 32	25 27
30	01 50	29 30	26 35	24 04	25 04
31	01 41	29 12	26 10	23 36	24 39
32	01 32	28 54	25 46	23 08	24 14
33	01 22	28 36	25 21	22 39	23 48
34	01 13	28 17	24 55	22 09	23 22
35	01 04	27 59	24 30	21 39	22 54
36	00 54	27 40	24 04	21 08	22 25
37	00 45	27 22	23 37	20 37	21 55
38	00 35	27 03	23 11	20 04	21 24
39	00 25	26 44	22 43	19 31	20 51
40	00 16	26 24	22 16	18 57	20 17
41	00 06	26 04	21 48	18 22	19 42
42	29♍56	25 45	21 19	17 46	19 05
43	29 45	25 24	20 50	17 10	18 26
44	29 35	25 04	20 20	16 32	17 46
45	29 25	24 43	19 50	15 53	17 03
46	29 14	24 22	19 19	15 12	16 18
47	29 03	24 01	18 48	14 31	15 31
48	28 52	23 39	18 16	13 48	14 41
49	28 41	23 17	17 43	13 04	13 48
50	28 30	22 54	17 09	12 18	12 52
51	28 18	22 31	16 35	11 31	11 53
52	28 06	22 08	16 00	10 42	10 50
53	27 54	21 44	15 23	09 51	09 43
54	27 42	21 19	14 46	08 59	08 31
55	27 29	20 54	14 08	08 04	07 14
56	27 17	20 29	13 29	07 08	05 52
57	27 03	20 03	12 49	06 09	04 24
58	26 50	19 36	12 08	05 08	02 48
59	26 36	19 08	11 25	04 04	01 06
60	26♍21	18♎40	10♏42	02♐57	29♐15

10h 28m 0s — 157° 0' 0" — 05 ♍ 10

LAT.	11	12	ASC	2	3
0	07♎37	09♏24	08♐43	06♑26	04♒39
5	06 45	07 49	06 52	04 42	03 30
10	05 56	06 18	05 02	02 56	02 16
15	05 08	04 50	03 12	01 06	00 56
20	04 22	03 22	01 20	29♐10	29♑28
21	04 13	03 05	00 57	28 46	29 10
22	04 04	02 47	00 34	28 22	28 51
23	03 55	02 29	00 11	27 58	28 31
24	03 46	02 12	29♏48	27 33	28 11
25	03 36	01 54	29 25	27 07	27 50
26	03 27	01 37	29 02	26 41	27 29
27	03 18	01 19	28 38	26 15	27 07
28	03 09	01 01	28 14	25 49	26 45
29	03 00	00 43	27 50	25 21	26 22
30	02 50	00 25	27 25	24 54	25 58
31	02 41	00 07	27 01	24 26	25 34
32	02 32	29♎49	26 36	23 57	25 08
33	02 22	29 30	26 10	23 28	24 42
34	02 13	29 12	25 45	22 58	24 15
35	02 03	28 53	25 19	22 27	23 47
36	01 54	28 34	24 52	21 56	23 18
37	01 44	28 15	24 26	21 24	22 47
38	01 34	27 56	23 59	20 51	22 16
39	01 24	27 37	23 31	20 17	21 43
40	01 14	27 17	23 03	19 43	21 09
41	01 04	26 57	22 35	19 07	20 33
42	00 54	26 37	22 06	18 31	19 55
43	00 44	26 16	21 36	17 54	19 16
44	00 33	25 56	21 06	17 15	18 35
45	00 23	25 35	20 35	16 35	17 51
46	00 12	25 13	20 04	15 55	17 06
47	00 01	24 52	19 32	15 12	16 18
48	29♍50	24 29	19 00	14 29	15 27
49	29 38	24 07	18 26	13 44	14 34
50	29 27	23 44	17 52	12 58	13 37
51	29 15	23 21	17 17	12 10	12 36
52	29 03	22 57	16 41	11 20	11 32
53	28 51	22 33	16 05	10 28	10 24
54	28 38	22 08	15 27	09 35	09 11
55	28 26	21 42	14 48	08 39	07 52
56	28 13	21 16	14 09	07 42	06 28
57	27 59	20 50	13 28	06 42	04 58
58	27 45	20 23	12 46	05 39	03 21
59	27 31	19 55	12 03	04 34	01 36
60	27♍16	19♎26	11♏18	03♐27	29♐43

10h 32m 0s — 158° 0' 0" — 06 ♍ 14

LAT.	11	12	ASC	2	3
0	08♎43	10♏25	09♐40	07♑21	05♒38
5	07 49	08 49	07 48	05 36	04 28
10	06 59	07 18	05 57	03 50	03 14
15	06 11	05 48	04 06	01 59	01 53
20	05 24	04 19	02 13	00 03	00 25
21	05 15	04 02	01 50	29♐38	00 06
22	05 05	03 44	01 27	29 14	29♑47
23	04 56	03 26	01 04	28 49	29 27
24	04 47	03 09	00 41	28 24	29 07
25	04 38	02 51	00 17	27 58	28 46
26	04 28	02 33	29♏53	27 32	28 25
27	04 19	02 15	29 29	27 06	28 03
28	04 10	01 57	29 05	26 39	27 41
29	04 00	01 39	28 41	26 11	27 17
30	03 51	01 20	28 16	25 44	26 53
31	03 41	01 02	27 51	25 15	26 28
32	03 32	00 44	27 26	24 46	26 03
33	03 22	00 25	27 00	24 16	25 36
34	03 13	00 06	26 34	23 46	25 09
35	03 03	29♎47	26 08	23 15	24 40
36	02 53	29 28	25 41	22 43	24 11
37	02 43	29 09	25 14	22 11	23 40
38	02 33	28 49	24 47	21 38	23 08
39	02 23	28 30	24 19	21 04	22 35
40	02 13	28 10	23 51	20 29	22 00
41	02 03	27 49	23 22	19 53	21 24
42	01 53	27 29	22 52	19 16	20 46
43	01 42	27 08	22 22	18 38	20 06
44	01 31	26 47	21 52	17 59	19 24
45	01 21	26 26	21 21	17 18	18 40
46	01 10	26 04	20 49	16 37	17 54
47	00 59	25 42	20 17	15 54	17 05
48	00 47	25 20	19 44	15 10	16 14
49	00 36	24 57	19 10	14 24	15 19
50	00 24	24 34	18 35	13 37	14 21
51	00 12	24 10	18 00	12 48	13 20
52	00 00	23 46	17 23	11 58	12 14
53	29♍48	23 21	16 46	11 05	11 05
54	29 35	22 56	16 08	10 11	09 50
55	29 22	22 30	15 29	09 14	08 30
56	29 09	22 04	14 48	08 16	07 05
57	28 55	21 37	14 07	07 15	05 33
58	28 41	21 09	13 24	06 11	03 54
59	28 27	20 41	12 40	05 05	02 07
60	28♍12	20♎12	11♏55	03♐56	00♑11

10h 36m 0s — 159° 0' 0" — 07 ♍ 18

LAT.	11	12	ASC	2	3
0	09♎48	11♏26	10♐36	08♑16	06♒37
5	08 54	09 50	08 43	06 31	05 26
10	08 03	08 17	06 52	04 44	04 12
15	07 14	06 46	05 00	02 52	02 51
20	06 26	05 17	03 06	00 55	01 22
21	06 17	04 59	02 43	00 31	01 03
22	06 07	04 41	02 20	00 06	00 44
23	05 58	04 23	01 56	29♐41	00 24
24	05 48	04 05	01 33	29 15	00 04
25	05 39	03 47	01 09	28 50	29♑43
26	05 29	03 29	00 45	28 23	29 21
27	05 20	03 11	00 21	27 57	28 59
28	05 10	02 52	29♏56	27 29	28 36
29	05 01	02 34	29 32	27 02	28 13
30	04 51	02 16	29 07	26 33	27 49
31	04 42	01 57	28 41	26 05	27 24
32	04 32	01 38	28 16	25 35	26 58
33	04 22	01 20	27 50	25 05	26 31
34	04 12	01 00	27 24	24 34	26 03
35	04 03	00 41	26 57	24 03	25 34
36	03 53	00 22	26 30	23 31	25 04
37	03 43	00 02	26 03	22 58	24 33
38	03 32	29♎43	25 35	22 24	24 01
39	03 22	29 23	25 07	21 50	23 27
40	03 12	29 02	24 38	21 14	22 52
41	03 02	28 42	24 09	20 38	22 15
42	02 51	28 21	23 39	20 01	21 37
43	02 40	28 00	23 09	19 22	20 56
44	02 30	27 39	22 38	18 42	20 14
45	02 19	27 17	22 06	18 02	19 29
46	02 08	26 55	21 34	17 20	18 42
47	01 56	26 33	21 01	16 36	17 53
48	01 45	26 10	20 28	15 51	17 00
49	01 33	25 47	19 53	15 05	16 05
50	01 21	25 24	19 18	14 17	15 06
51	01 09	25 00	18 42	13 27	14 04
52	00 57	24 35	18 05	12 36	12 57
53	00 44	24 10	17 27	11 42	11 46
54	00 31	23 45	16 49	10 47	10 30
55	00 18	23 18	16 09	09 50	09 09
56	00 05	22 52	15 28	08 50	07 42
57	29♍51	22 24	14 46	07 48	06 08
58	29 37	21 56	14 02	06 43	04 27
59	29 22	21 27	13 18	05 36	02 38
60	29♍07	20♎58	12♏32	04♐25	00♑40

Koch Table of Houses for Latitudes 0° to 60° North

10h 40m 0s — 160° 0' 0" — 08 ♍ 22

LAT.	11	12	ASC	2	3
0	10♎53	12♏27	11♐32	09♑11	07♒35
5	09 58	10 50	09 39	07 26	06 25
10	09 06	09 16	07 47	05 38	05 10
15	08 17	07 45	05 54	03 46	03 49
20	07 28	06 14	03 59	01 48	02 20
21	07 18	05 56	03 36	01 23	02 01
22	07 09	05 38	03 12	00 58	01 41
23	06 59	05 20	02 49	00 33	01 21
24	06 50	05 02	02 25	00 07	01 00
25	06 40	04 43	02 01	29♐41	00 39
26	06 30	04 25	01 37	29 14	00 18
27	06 21	04 07	01 12	28 47	29♑55
28	06 11	03 48	00 48	28 20	29 32
29	06 01	03 30	00 23	27 52	29 09
30	05 52	03 11	29♏57	27 23	28 44
31	05 42	02 52	29 32	26 54	28 19
32	05 32	02 33	29 06	26 25	27 53
33	05 22	02 14	28 40	25 54	27 26
34	05 12	01 55	28 13	25 23	26 58
35	05 02	01 35	27 46	24 51	26 28
36	04 52	01 16	27 19	24 19	25 58
37	04 42	00 56	26 51	23 46	25 27
38	04 32	00 36	26 23	23 11	24 54
39	04 21	00 16	25 55	22 36	24 20
40	04 11	29♎55	25 26	22 01	23 44
41	04 00	29 35	24 56	21 24	23 07
42	03 50	29 14	24 26	20 46	22 28
43	03 39	28 52	23 55	20 07	21 47
44	03 28	28 31	23 24	19 26	21 04
45	03 17	28 09	22 52	18 45	20 19
46	03 05	27 46	22 19	18 02	19 31
47	02 54	27 24	21 46	17 18	18 41
48	02 42	27 01	21 12	16 33	17 47
49	02 31	26 37	20 37	15 45	16 51
50	02 18	26 13	20 01	14 57	15 51
51	02 06	25 49	19 25	14 06	14 48
52	01 54	25 24	18 47	13 14	13 40
53	01 41	24 59	18 09	12 20	12 28
54	01 28	24 33	17 29	11 23	11 11
55	01 15	24 06	16 49	10 25	09 48
56	01 01	23 39	16 07	09 24	08 19
57	00 47	23 12	15 24	08 21	06 43
58	00 33	22 43	14 40	07 15	05 00
59	00 18	22 14	13 55	06 06	03 09
60	00♎03	21♎44	13♏08	04♐55	01♑09

10h 44m 0s — 161° 0' 0" — 09 ♍ 26

LAT.	11	12	ASC	2	3
0	11♎58	13♏27	12♐28	10♑07	08♒34
5	11 02	11 49	10 34	08 21	07 24
10	10 10	10 15	08 41	06 32	06 08
15	09 19	08 43	06 48	04 40	04 47
20	08 30	07 11	04 52	02 40	03 17
21	08 20	06 53	04 29	02 16	02 58
22	08 10	06 35	04 05	01 50	02 38
23	08 01	06 17	03 41	01 25	02 18
24	07 51	05 58	03 17	00 59	01 57
25	07 41	05 40	02 53	00 33	01 36
26	07 31	05 21	02 28	00 06	01 14
27	07 22	05 03	02 04	29♐38	00 52
28	07 12	04 44	01 39	29 11	00 29
29	07 02	04 25	01 14	28 42	00 05
30	06 52	04 06	00 48	28 14	29♑40
31	06 42	03 47	00 22	27 44	29 14
32	06 32	03 28	29♏56	27 14	28 48
33	06 22	03 09	29 30	26 43	28 21
34	06 12	02 49	29 03	26 12	27 52
35	06 02	02 29	28 36	25 40	27 23
36	05 52	02 10	28 08	25 07	26 52
37	05 41	01 50	27 40	24 33	26 21
38	05 31	01 29	27 11	23 59	25 48
39	05 21	01 09	26 43	23 23	25 13
40	05 10	00 48	26 13	22 47	24 37
41	04 59	00 27	25 43	22 09	23 59
42	04 48	00 06	25 13	21 31	23 20
43	04 37	29♎44	24 41	20 51	22 38
44	04 26	29 22	24 10	20 11	21 54
45	04 15	29 00	23 37	19 28	21 09
46	04 03	28 37	23 04	18 45	20 20
47	03 52	28 15	22 30	18 00	19 29
48	03 40	27 51	21 56	17 14	18 35
49	03 28	27 27	21 20	16 26	17 38
50	03 16	27 03	20 44	15 37	16 37
51	03 03	26 38	20 07	14 45	15 32
52	02 51	26 13	19 29	13 52	14 23
53	02 38	25 48	18 50	12 57	13 10
54	02 25	25 21	18 10	12 00	11 51
55	02 11	24 54	17 29	11 00	10 27
56	01 57	24 27	16 47	09 58	08 56
57	01 43	23 59	16 03	08 54	07 19
58	01 29	23 30	15 18	07 47	05 34
59	01 14	23 00	14 32	06 37	03 41
60	00♎58	22♎30	13♏45	05♐24	01♑38

10h 48m 0s — 162° 0' 0" — 10 ♍ 30

LAT.	11	12	ASC	2	3
0	13♎03	14♏28	13♐24	11♑02	09♒34
5	12 06	12 49	11 30	09 16	08 23
10	11 13	11 14	09 36	07 27	07 07
15	10 22	09 41	07 42	05 33	05 45
20	09 32	08 09	05 45	03 33	04 15
21	09 22	07 50	05 22	03 08	03 56
22	09 12	07 32	04 58	02 43	03 36
23	09 02	07 13	04 34	02 17	03 16
24	08 52	06 55	04 09	01 51	02 55
25	08 42	06 36	03 45	01 24	02 33
26	08 33	06 17	03 20	00 57	02 11
27	08 23	05 58	02 55	00 30	01 49
28	08 13	05 39	02 30	00 02	01 25
29	08 03	05 20	02 05	29♐33	01 01
30	07 53	05 01	01 39	29 04	00 36
31	07 43	04 42	01 13	28 34	00 10
32	07 32	04 23	00 46	28 04	29♑44
33	07 22	04 03	00 20	27 33	29 16
34	07 12	03 43	29♏52	27 01	28 48
35	07 02	03 24	29 25	26 28	28 18
36	06 51	03 03	28 57	25 55	27 47
37	06 41	02 43	28 29	25 21	27 15
38	06 30	02 23	28 00	24 46	26 41
39	06 20	02 02	27 30	24 10	26 06
40	06 09	01 41	27 01	23 33	25 30
41	05 58	01 20	26 30	22 55	24 52
42	05 47	00 58	25 59	22 16	24 12
43	05 36	00 36	25 28	21 36	23 29
44	05 25	00 14	24 56	20 55	22 45
45	05 13	29♎51	24 23	20 12	21 59
46	05 02	29 29	23 49	19 28	21 10
47	04 50	29 05	23 15	18 43	20 18
48	04 38	28 42	22 40	17 56	19 23
49	04 26	28 18	22 04	17 07	18 25
50	04 13	27 53	21 27	16 17	17 23
51	04 01	27 28	20 50	15 25	16 17
52	03 48	27 02	20 11	14 31	15 07
53	03 35	26 36	19 32	13 35	13 52
54	03 21	26 10	18 51	12 36	12 32
55	03 08	25 42	18 09	11 36	11 07
56	02 54	25 15	17 26	10 33	09 34
57	02 39	24 46	16 42	09 27	07 55
58	02 25	24 17	15 57	08 19	06 08
59	02 09	23 47	15 10	07 08	04 12
60	01♎54	23♎16	14♏21	05♐54	02♑07

10h 52m 0s — 163° 0' 0" — 11 ♍ 34

LAT.	11	12	ASC	2	3
0	14♎07	15♏28	14♐20	11♑58	10♒33
5	13 10	13 49	12 25	10 11	09 22
10	12 16	12 13	10 31	08 21	08 06
15	11 25	10 39	08 36	06 27	06 44
20	10 34	09 06	06 38	04 26	05 13
21	10 24	08 47	06 14	04 01	04 54
22	10 14	08 28	05 50	03 35	04 34
23	10 04	08 10	05 26	03 09	04 13
24	09 54	07 51	05 02	02 43	03 52
25	09 44	07 32	04 37	02 16	03 31
26	09 34	07 13	04 12	01 49	03 09
27	09 24	06 54	03 47	01 21	02 46
28	09 14	06 35	03 21	00 53	02 22
29	09 03	06 16	02 56	00 24	01 58
30	08 53	05 57	02 30	29♐54	01 33
31	08 43	05 37	02 03	29 24	01 07
32	08 33	05 17	01 37	28 54	00 40
33	08 22	04 58	01 10	28 22	00 12
34	08 12	04 38	00 42	27 50	29♑43
35	08 02	04 18	00 14	27 17	29 13
36	07 51	03 57	29♏46	26 44	28 42
37	07 40	03 37	29 17	26 09	28 09
38	07 30	03 16	28 48	25 34	27 36
39	07 19	02 55	28 19	24 57	27 00
40	07 08	02 34	27 48	24 20	26 23
41	06 57	02 12	27 18	23 41	25 44
42	06 46	01 50	26 46	23 02	25 04
43	06 34	01 28	26 14	22 21	24 21
44	06 23	01 06	25 42	21 39	23 37
45	06 11	00 43	25 08	20 56	22 49
46	06 00	00 20	24 34	20 11	22 00
47	05 48	29♎56	24 00	19 25	21 07
48	05 36	29 32	23 24	18 38	20 11
49	05 23	29 08	22 48	17 48	19 12
50	05 11	28 43	22 11	16 57	18 09
51	04 58	28 17	21 32	16 04	17 03
52	04 45	27 52	20 53	15 09	15 51
53	04 32	27 25	20 13	14 12	14 35
54	04 18	26 58	19 32	13 13	13 14
55	04 04	26 30	18 49	12 12	11 46
56	03 50	26 02	18 06	11 08	10 12
57	03 35	25 33	17 21	10 01	08 31
58	03 21	25 04	16 35	08 51	06 42
59	03 05	24 33	15 47	07 39	04 44
60	02♎50	24♎02	14♏58	06♐24	02♑37

10h 56m 0s — 164° 0' 0" — 12 ♍ 39

LAT.	11	12	ASC	2	3
0	15♎12	16♏28	15♐16	12♑53	11♒32
5	14 14	14 48	13 20	11 06	10 21
10	13 20	13 11	11 25	09 16	09 05
15	12 27	11 37	09 30	07 21	07 43
20	11 36	10 03	07 31	05 19	06 12
21	11 26	09 44	07 07	04 54	05 52
22	11 16	09 25	06 43	04 28	05 32
23	11 05	09 06	06 19	04 02	05 11
24	10 55	08 47	05 54	03 35	04 50
25	10 45	08 28	05 29	03 08	04 29
26	10 35	08 09	05 04	02 41	04 06
27	10 25	07 50	04 38	02 13	03 43
28	10 14	07 31	04 13	01 44	03 19
29	10 04	07 11	03 47	01 15	02 55
30	09 54	06 52	03 20	00 45	02 30
31	09 43	06 32	02 54	00 15	02 03
32	09 33	06 12	02 27	29♐44	01 36
33	09 23	05 52	02 00	29 12	01 08
34	09 12	05 32	01 32	28 40	00 39
35	09 01	05 12	01 04	28 06	00 09
36	08 51	04 51	00 35	27 32	29♑37
37	08 40	04 30	00 06	26 57	29 04
38	08 29	04 09	29♏37	26 21	28 30
39	08 18	03 48	29 07	25 45	27 54
40	08 07	03 26	28 36	25 07	27 17
41	07 56	03 05	28 05	24 28	26 38
42	07 45	02 43	27 33	23 48	25 57
43	07 33	02 20	27 01	23 07	25 14
44	07 21	01 57	26 28	22 24	24 28
45	07 10	01 34	25 54	21 40	23 40
46	06 58	01 11	25 20	20 55	22 50
47	06 46	00 47	24 45	20 08	21 57
48	06 33	00 23	24 09	19 20	21 00
49	06 21	29♎58	23 32	18 30	20 00
50	06 08	29 33	22 54	17 38	18 56
51	05 55	29 07	22 15	16 44	17 48
52	05 42	28 41	21 35	15 48	16 36
53	05 28	28 14	20 55	14 50	15 19
54	05 15	27 47	20 13	13 50	13 56
55	05 01	27 19	19 30	12 47	12 27
56	04 46	26 50	18 45	11 42	10 51
57	04 32	26 21	18 00	10 34	09 08
58	04 17	25 50	17 13	09 24	07 17
59	04 01	25 20	16 25	08 10	05 17
60	03♎45	24♎48	15♏35	06♐53	03♑07

11h 0m 0s — 165° 0' 0" — 13 ♍ 43

LAT.	11	12	ASC	2	3
0	16♎17	17♏28	16♐11	13♑49	12♒32
5	15 18	15 47	14 16	12 01	11 21
10	14 23	14 10	12 20	10 11	10 05
15	13 30	12 35	10 24	08 15	08 42
20	12 38	11 00	08 25	06 13	07 10
21	12 28	10 41	08 00	05 47	06 51
22	12 17	10 22	07 36	05 21	06 30
23	12 07	10 03	07 11	04 55	06 10
24	11 57	09 44	06 46	04 28	05 48
25	11 46	09 24	06 21	04 00	05 27
26	11 36	09 05	05 56	03 33	05 04
27	11 26	08 46	05 30	03 04	04 41
28	11 15	08 26	05 04	02 36	04 17
29	11 05	08 07	04 38	02 06	03 52
30	10 54	07 47	04 11	01 36	03 27
31	10 44	07 27	03 44	01 05	03 00
32	10 33	07 07	03 17	00 34	02 33
33	10 23	06 47	02 50	00 02	02 05
34	10 12	06 26	02 22	29♐29	01 35
35	10 01	06 06	01 53	28 55	01 05
36	09 50	05 45	01 24	28 21	00 33
37	09 40	05 24	00 55	27 46	00 00
38	09 29	05 03	00 25	27 09	29♑25
39	09 17	04 41	29♏55	26 32	28 49
40	09 06	04 19	29 24	25 54	28 11
41	08 55	03 57	28 52	25 14	27 31
42	08 43	03 35	28 20	24 34	26 50
43	08 32	03 12	27 47	23 52	26 06
44	08 20	02 49	27 14	23 09	25 20
45	08 08	02 26	26 40	22 24	24 32
46	07 56	02 02	26 05	21 38	23 41
47	07 44	01 38	25 29	20 51	22 47
48	07 31	01 13	24 53	20 02	21 49
49	07 19	00 48	24 15	19 11	20 48
50	07 06	00 23	23 37	18 18	19 44
51	06 53	29♎56	22 58	17 24	18 35
52	06 39	29 30	22 18	16 27	17 21
53	06 25	29 03	21 36	15 28	16 02
54	06 12	28 35	20 54	14 27	14 38
55	05 57	28 07	20 10	13 23	13 07
56	05 43	27 38	19 25	12 17	11 30
57	05 28	27 08	18 39	11 08	09 45
58	05 13	26 37	17 51	09 56	07 52
59	04 57	26 06	17 02	08 41	05 49
60	04♎41	25♎34	16♏11	07♐23	03♑37

11h 4m 0s — 166° 0' 0" — 14 ♍ 48

LAT.	11	12	ASC	2	3
0	17♎21	18♏28	17♐07	14♑44	13♒32
5	16 22	16 46	15 11	12 57	12 21
10	15 26	15 08	13 15	11 06	11 04
15	14 32	13 32	11 18	09 09	09 41
20	13 40	11 57	09 18	07 06	08 09
21	13 29	11 38	08 53	06 40	07 49
22	13 19	11 18	08 28	06 14	07 29
23	13 08	10 59	08 04	05 47	07 08
24	12 58	10 40	07 39	05 20	06 47
25	12 48	10 20	07 13	04 53	06 25
26	12 37	10 01	06 48	04 25	06 02
27	12 27	09 41	06 22	03 56	05 39
28	12 16	09 22	05 56	03 27	05 15
29	12 06	09 02	05 29	02 57	04 50
30	11 55	08 42	05 02	02 27	04 24
31	11 44	08 22	04 35	01 56	03 58
32	11 34	08 02	04 08	01 25	03 30
33	11 23	07 41	03 40	00 52	03 02
34	11 12	07 21	03 11	00 19	02 32
35	11 01	07 00	02 43	29♐45	02 01
36	10 50	06 39	02 14	29 10	01 29
37	10 39	06 17	01 44	28 34	00 55
38	10 28	05 56	01 14	27 58	00 20
39	10 17	05 34	00 43	27 20	29♑44
40	10 05	05 12	00 12	26 41	29 06
41	09 54	04 50	29♏40	26 01	28 26
42	09 42	04 27	29 07	25 20	27 44
43	09 30	04 04	28 34	24 38	26 59
44	09 19	03 41	28 00	23 54	26 13
45	09 06	03 17	27 26	23 09	25 24
46	08 54	02 53	26 50	22 22	24 32
47	08 42	02 29	26 14	21 34	23 37
48	08 29	02 04	25 37	20 44	22 39
49	08 16	01 38	24 59	19 53	21 37
50	08 03	01 12	24 21	18 59	20 31
51	07 50	00 46	23 41	18 04	19 21
52	07 36	00 19	23 00	17 06	18 07
53	07 23	29♎52	22 18	16 06	16 47
54	07 08	29 23	21 35	15 04	15 21
55	06 54	28 55	20 50	14 00	13 49
56	06 39	28 25	20 05	12 52	12 09
57	06 24	27 55	19 18	11 42	10 22
58	06 09	27 24	18 30	10 29	08 27
59	05 53	26 52	17 40	09 13	06 22
60	05♎37	26♎20	16♏48	07♐53	04♑07

11h 8m 0s — 167° 0' 0" — 15 ♍ 53

LAT.	11	12	ASC	2	3
0	18♎26	19♏27	18♐02	15♑40	14♒32
5	17 26	17 45	16 06	13 52	13 21
10	16 29	16 07	14 09	12 01	12 04
15	15 35	14 30	12 12	10 04	10 41
20	14 42	12 54	10 11	08 00	09 08
21	14 31	12 34	09 46	07 34	08 49
22	14 20	12 15	09 21	07 07	08 28
23	14 10	11 56	08 56	06 40	08 07
24	13 59	11 36	08 31	06 13	07 46
25	13 49	11 17	08 05	05 45	07 24
26	13 38	10 57	07 40	05 17	07 01
27	13 28	10 37	07 13	04 48	06 37
28	13 17	10 17	06 47	04 19	06 13
29	13 06	09 57	06 20	03 49	05 48
30	12 56	09 37	05 53	03 18	05 22
31	12 45	09 17	05 26	02 47	04 55
32	12 34	08 56	04 58	02 15	04 28
33	12 23	08 36	04 30	01 42	03 59
34	12 12	08 15	04 01	01 09	03 29
35	12 01	07 54	03 32	00 35	02 58
36	11 50	07 32	03 03	29♐59	02 25
37	11 39	07 11	02 33	29 23	01 51
38	11 27	06 49	02 02	28 46	01 16
39	11 16	06 27	01 31	28 08	00 39
40	11 05	06 05	01 00	27 29	00 01
41	10 53	05 42	00 27	26 48	29♑20
42	10 41	05 19	29♏55	26 07	28 38
43	10 29	04 56	29 21	25 24	27 53
44	10 17	04 33	28 47	24 39	27 06
45	10 05	04 09	28 12	23 54	26 16
46	09 52	03 44	27 36	23 06	25 24
47	09 40	03 19	26 59	22 18	24 28
48	09 27	02 54	26 22	21 27	23 29
49	09 14	02 29	25 43	20 35	22 26
50	09 01	02 02	25 04	19 40	21 20
51	08 47	01 36	24 24	18 44	20 09
52	08 34	01 08	23 42	17 45	18 53
53	08 20	00 40	23 00	16 45	17 31
54	08 05	00 12	22 16	15 42	16 04
55	07 51	29♎43	21 31	14 36	14 30
56	07 36	29 13	20 45	13 27	12 49
57	07 21	28 42	19 57	12 16	11 00
58	07 05	28 11	19 08	11 02	09 03
59	06 49	27 39	18 17	09 44	06 56
60	06♎33	27♎06	17♏25	08♐23	04♑38

Koch Table of Houses for Latitudes 0° to 60° North

11h 12m 0s — 16 ♍ 57 — 168° 0' 0"

LAT.	11	12	ASC	2	3
0	19♎30	20♏26	18♐58	16♑36	15♒32
5	18 30	18 44	17 01	14 48	14 21
10	17 33	17 05	15 04	12 56	13 04
15	16 37	15 28	13 05	10 58	11 41
20	15 44	13 51	11 04	08 53	10 08
21	15 33	13 31	10 39	08 27	09 48
22	15 22	13 12	10 14	08 01	09 27
23	15 11	12 52	09 49	07 34	09 06
24	15 01	12 32	09 23	07 06	08 45
25	14 50	12 12	08 58	06 38	08 23
26	14 39	11 53	08 32	06 10	08 00
27	14 29	11 33	08 05	05 41	07 36
28	14 18	11 13	07 39	05 11	07 12
29	14 07	10 52	07 12	04 41	06 46
30	13 56	10 32	06 44	04 10	06 20
31	13 45	10 12	06 17	03 38	05 53
32	13 34	09 51	05 49	03 06	05 25
33	13 23	09 30	05 20	02 33	04 56
34	13 12	09 09	04 51	01 59	04 26
35	13 01	08 48	04 22	01 24	03 55
36	12 50	08 26	03 52	00 49	03 22
37	12 38	08 05	03 22	00 12	02 48
38	12 27	07 43	02 51	29♐35	02 12
39	12 15	07 20	02 20	28 56	01 35
40	12 04	06 58	01 48	28 16	00 56
41	11 52	06 35	01 15	27 35	00 15
42	11 40	06 12	00 42	26 53	29♑32
43	11 28	05 48	00 08	26 10	28 47
44	11 16	05 24	29♏33	25 25	27 59
45	11 03	05 00	28 58	24 39	27 09
46	10 51	04 35	28 21	23 51	26 16
47	10 38	04 10	27 44	23 01	25 19
48	10 25	03 45	27 06	22 10	24 20
49	10 12	03 19	26 27	21 17	23 16
50	09 58	02 52	25 48	20 22	22 08
51	09 45	02 25	25 07	19 24	20 56
52	09 31	01 58	24 25	18 25	19 39
53	09 17	01 29	23 41	17 23	18 16
54	09 02	01 00	22 57	16 19	16 48
55	08 47	00 31	22 11	15 12	15 12
56	08 32	00 01	21 24	14 03	13 29
57	08 17	29♎30	20 36	12 50	11 39
58	08 01	28 58	19 46	11 35	09 39
59	07 45	28 25	18 55	10 16	07 29
60	07♎28	27♎52	18♏02	08♐53	05♑09

11h 16m 0s — 18 ♍ 02 — 169° 0' 0"

LAT.	11	12	ASC	2	3
0	20♎34	21♏26	19♐53	17♑32	16♒33
5	19 33	19 43	17 56	15 43	15 21
10	18 36	18 03	15 58	13 51	14 04
15	17 40	16 25	13 59	11 53	12 41
20	16 45	14 47	11 57	09 47	11 08
21	16 34	14 28	11 32	09 21	10 48
22	16 24	14 08	11 07	08 54	10 27
23	16 13	13 48	10 41	08 27	10 06
24	16 02	13 28	10 16	08 00	09 44
25	15 51	13 08	09 50	07 31	09 22
26	15 40	12 48	09 24	07 03	08 59
27	15 30	12 28	08 57	06 33	08 35
28	15 19	12 08	08 30	06 03	08 11
29	15 08	11 48	08 03	05 33	07 45
30	14 57	11 27	07 35	05 02	07 19
31	14 46	11 06	07 08	04 30	06 52
32	14 35	10 46	06 39	03 57	06 24
33	14 23	10 24	06 11	03 24	05 54
34	14 12	10 03	05 41	02 50	05 24
35	14 01	09 42	05 12	02 15	04 52
36	13 50	09 20	04 42	01 39	04 19
37	13 38	08 58	04 11	01 02	03 45
38	13 26	08 36	03 40	00 24	03 09
39	13 15	08 13	03 08	29♐45	02 31
40	13 03	07 51	02 36	29 04	01 52
41	12 51	07 27	02 03	28 23	01 11
42	12 39	07 04	01 29	27 40	00 27
43	12 27	06 40	00 55	26 56	29♑41
44	12 14	06 16	00 20	26 11	28 53
45	12 02	05 52	29♏44	25 24	28 02
46	11 49	05 27	29 07	24 35	27 08
47	11 36	05 01	28 30	23 45	26 11
48	11 23	04 35	27 51	22 53	25 11
49	11 10	04 09	27 12	21 59	24 06
50	10 56	03 42	26 31	21 03	22 58
51	10 42	03 15	25 50	20 05	21 44
52	10 28	02 47	25 07	19 05	20 26
53	10 14	02 18	24 23	18 02	19 02
54	09 59	01 49	23 38	16 57	17 32
55	09 44	01 19	22 52	15 49	15 55
56	09 29	00 48	22 04	14 38	14 10
57	09 13	00 17	21 15	13 25	12 17
58	08 57	29♎45	20 25	12 08	10 15
59	08 41	29 12	19 32	10 47	08 03
60	08♎24	28♎38	18♏38	09♐24	05♑40

11h 20m 0s — 19 ♍ 07 — 170° 0' 0"

LAT.	11	12	ASC	2	3
0	21♎38	22♏25	20♐49	18♑28	17♒33
5	20 37	20 41	18 51	16 39	16 22
10	19 38	19 01	16 53	14 47	15 05
15	18 42	17 22	14 53	12 48	13 41
20	17 47	15 44	12 50	10 42	12 08
21	17 36	15 24	12 25	10 15	11 48
22	17 25	15 04	12 00	09 48	11 27
23	17 14	14 44	11 34	09 21	11 06
24	17 03	14 24	11 08	08 53	10 44
25	16 52	14 04	10 42	08 25	10 22
26	16 41	13 44	10 16	07 56	09 58
27	16 30	13 24	09 49	07 26	09 35
28	16 19	13 03	09 22	06 56	09 10
29	16 08	12 43	08 54	06 25	08 44
30	15 57	12 22	08 27	05 54	08 18
31	15 46	12 01	07 59	05 22	07 51
32	15 35	11 40	07 30	04 49	07 22
33	15 24	11 19	07 01	04 15	06 53
34	15 12	10 57	06 32	03 40	06 22
35	15 01	10 36	06 02	03 05	05 50
36	14 49	10 14	05 31	02 29	05 17
37	14 38	09 52	05 00	01 51	04 42
38	14 26	09 29	04 29	01 13	04 06
39	14 14	09 06	03 57	00 33	03 28
40	14 02	08 43	03 24	29♐53	02 48
41	13 50	08 20	02 51	29 11	02 07
42	13 38	07 56	02 17	28 28	01 23
43	13 26	07 32	01 42	27 43	00 36
44	13 13	07 08	01 06	26 57	29♑48
45	13 00	06 43	00 30	26 09	28 56
46	12 47	06 18	29♏53	25 20	28 02
47	12 34	05 52	29 15	24 29	27 04
48	12 21	05 26	28 36	23 36	26 03
49	12 08	04 59	27 56	22 42	24 57
50	11 54	04 32	27 15	21 45	23 48
51	11 40	04 04	26 33	20 46	22 33
52	11 26	03 36	25 50	19 45	21 14
53	11 11	03 07	25 05	18 41	19 48
54	10 56	02 37	24 20	17 35	18 17
55	10 41	02 07	23 33	16 26	16 38
56	10 26	01 36	22 44	15 14	14 51
57	10 10	01 04	21 54	13 59	12 57
58	09 54	00 31	21 03	12 41	10 52
59	09 37	29♎58	20 10	11 19	08 38
60	09♎20	29♎23	19♏15	09♐54	06♑12

11h 24m 0s — 20 ♍ 12 — 171° 0' 0"

LAT.	11	12	ASC	2	3
0	22♎42	23♏23	21♐44	19♑24	18♒34
5	21 40	21 40	19 46	17 35	17 23
10	20 41	19 59	17 48	15 42	16 06
15	19 44	18 20	15 47	13 43	14 42
20	18 49	16 41	13 44	11 36	13 08
21	18 38	16 21	13 18	11 09	12 48
22	18 27	16 01	12 53	10 42	12 27
23	18 16	15 41	12 27	10 15	12 06
24	18 05	15 20	12 01	09 47	11 44
25	17 54	15 00	11 34	09 18	11 22
26	17 42	14 40	11 08	08 49	10 58
27	17 31	14 19	10 41	08 19	10 34
28	17 20	13 59	10 14	07 49	10 09
29	17 09	13 38	09 46	07 18	09 44
30	16 58	13 17	09 18	06 46	09 17
31	16 47	12 56	08 50	06 14	08 50
32	16 35	12 35	08 21	05 40	08 21
33	16 24	12 13	07 51	05 06	07 52
34	16 12	11 52	07 22	04 31	07 21
35	16 01	11 30	06 52	03 56	06 49
36	15 49	11 08	06 21	03 19	06 15
37	15 37	10 45	05 50	02 41	05 40
38	15 25	10 22	05 18	02 02	05 04
39	15 14	10 00	04 45	01 22	04 25
40	15 01	09 36	04 12	00 41	03 45
41	14 49	09 13	03 39	29♐59	03 03
42	14 37	08 49	03 04	29 15	02 19
43	14 24	08 24	02 29	28 30	01 32
44	14 12	08 00	01 53	27 43	00 43
45	13 59	07 35	01 16	26 55	29♑51
46	13 46	07 09	00 39	26 05	28 55
47	13 32	06 43	00 00	25 14	27 57
48	13 19	06 17	29♏21	24 20	26 55
49	13 05	05 50	28 40	23 25	25 49
50	12 51	05 22	27 59	22 27	24 38
51	12 37	04 54	27 16	21 27	23 22
52	12 23	04 25	26 32	20 25	22 02
53	12 08	03 56	25 47	19 20	20 35
54	11 53	03 26	25 01	18 13	19 02
55	11 38	02 55	24 13	17 03	17 21
56	11 22	02 24	23 24	15 50	15 33
57	11 06	01 51	22 34	14 34	13 36
58	10 50	01 18	21 41	13 14	11 30
59	10 33	00 44	20 48	11 51	09 13
60	10♎16	00♏09	19♏52	10♐25	06♑44

11h 28m 0s — 21 ♍ 17 — 172° 0' 0"

LAT.	11	12	ASC	2	3
0	23♎46	24♏22	22♐39	20♑20	19♒35
5	22 43	22 38	20 41	18 31	18 24
10	21 44	20 57	18 42	16 38	17 07
15	20 47	19 17	16 41	14 38	15 43
20	19 51	17 37	14 37	12 31	14 09
21	19 39	17 17	14 11	12 04	13 49
22	19 28	16 57	13 46	11 36	13 28
23	19 17	16 37	13 20	11 09	13 06
24	19 06	16 16	12 53	10 41	12 44
25	18 55	15 56	12 27	10 12	12 22
26	18 43	15 35	12 00	09 42	11 58
27	18 32	15 15	11 33	09 12	11 34
28	18 21	14 54	11 05	08 42	11 09
29	18 10	14 33	10 38	08 11	10 44
30	17 58	14 12	10 09	07 39	10 17
31	17 47	13 51	09 41	07 06	09 49
32	17 35	13 29	09 12	06 32	09 21
33	17 24	13 08	08 42	05 58	08 51
34	17 12	12 46	08 12	05 23	08 20
35	17 01	12 24	07 42	04 47	07 47
36	16 49	12 01	07 11	04 09	07 14
37	16 37	11 39	06 39	03 31	06 38
38	16 25	11 16	06 07	02 52	06 02
39	16 13	10 53	05 34	02 12	05 23
40	16 01	10 29	05 01	01 30	04 42
41	15 48	10 05	04 27	00 47	04 00
42	15 36	09 41	03 52	00 03	03 15
43	15 23	09 16	03 16	29♐17	02 28
44	15 10	08 52	02 40	28 30	01 38
45	14 57	08 26	02 03	27 41	00 45
46	14 44	08 00	01 25	26 51	29♑50
47	14 31	07 34	00 46	25 58	28 50
48	14 17	07 07	00 06	25 04	27 47
49	14 03	06 40	29♏25	24 08	26 40
50	13 49	06 12	28 43	23 09	25 29
51	13 35	05 44	27 59	22 09	24 12
52	13 20	05 14	27 15	21 05	22 50
53	13 05	04 45	26 29	20 00	21 22
54	12 50	04 14	25 42	18 51	19 48
55	12 35	03 43	24 54	17 40	18 06
56	12 19	03 11	24 04	16 26	16 15
57	12 03	02 39	23 13	15 08	14 16
58	11 46	02 05	22 20	13 48	12 08
59	11 29	01 31	21 25	12 23	09 48
60	11♎12	00♏55	20♏29	10♐55	07♑17

11h 32m 0s — 22 ♍ 23 — 173° 0' 0"

LAT.	11	12	ASC	2	3
0	24♎50	25♏21	23♐34	21♑17	20♒36
5	23 47	23 36	21 36	19 27	19 25
10	22 47	21 54	19 37	17 34	18 08
15	21 49	20 14	17 35	15 34	16 44
20	20 52	18 34	15 30	13 25	15 10
21	20 41	18 13	15 05	12 58	14 50
22	20 30	17 53	14 39	12 31	14 29
23	20 18	17 33	14 13	12 03	14 07
24	20 07	17 12	13 46	11 35	13 45
25	19 56	16 52	13 19	11 06	13 23
26	19 44	16 31	12 52	10 36	12 59
27	19 33	16 10	12 25	10 06	12 35
28	19 22	15 49	11 57	09 35	12 10
29	19 10	15 28	11 29	09 04	11 44
30	18 59	15 07	11 01	08 31	11 17
31	18 47	14 46	10 32	07 58	10 49
32	18 36	14 24	10 03	07 25	10 20
33	18 24	14 02	09 33	06 50	09 50
34	18 12	13 40	09 02	06 14	09 19
35	18 01	13 18	08 32	05 38	08 47
36	17 49	12 55	08 00	05 00	08 13
37	17 37	12 32	07 29	04 22	07 37
38	17 24	12 09	06 56	03 42	07 00
39	17 12	11 46	06 23	03 01	06 21
40	17 00	11 22	05 49	02 19	05 40
41	16 47	10 58	05 15	01 36	04 57
42	16 35	10 33	04 39	00 51	04 12
43	16 22	10 09	04 04	00 05	03 24
44	16 09	09 43	03 27	29♐17	02 34
45	15 56	09 18	02 49	28 28	01 41
46	15 42	08 52	02 11	27 36	00 44
47	15 29	08 25	01 31	26 43	29♑45
48	15 15	07 58	00 51	25 48	28 41
49	15 01	07 30	00 09	24 51	27 33
50	14 47	07 02	29♏27	23 52	26 20
51	14 32	06 33	28 43	22 50	25 03
52	14 18	06 04	27 58	21 46	23 39
53	14 03	05 34	27 12	20 40	22 10
54	13 47	05 03	26 24	19 30	20 34
55	13 31	04 31	25 35	18 18	18 50
56	13 15	03 59	24 44	17 02	16 58
57	12 59	03 26	23 52	15 44	14 57
58	12 42	02 52	22 59	14 21	12 46
59	12 25	02 17	22 03	12 56	10 24
60	12♎07	01♏41	21♏06	11♐26	07♑50

11h 36m 0s — 23 ♍ 28 — 174° 0' 0"

LAT.	11	12	ASC	2	3
0	25♎53	26♏19	24♐30	22♑13	21♒37
5	24 50	24 34	22 31	20 24	20 26
10	23 49	22 52	20 31	18 30	19 09
15	22 51	21 11	18 29	16 29	17 45
20	21 54	19 30	16 24	14 20	16 11
21	21 42	19 10	15 58	13 53	15 51
22	21 31	18 49	15 32	13 26	15 30
23	21 20	18 29	15 05	12 58	15 08
24	21 08	18 08	14 39	12 29	14 46
25	20 57	17 48	14 12	12 00	14 23
26	20 45	17 27	13 45	11 30	14 00
27	20 34	17 06	13 17	11 00	13 36
28	20 22	16 45	12 49	10 29	13 11
29	20 11	16 23	12 21	09 57	12 45
30	19 59	16 02	11 52	09 24	12 18
31	19 48	15 40	11 23	08 51	11 50
32	19 36	15 18	10 54	08 17	11 21
33	19 24	14 56	10 24	07 42	10 50
34	19 12	14 34	09 53	07 06	10 19
35	19 00	14 12	09 22	06 29	09 46
36	18 48	13 49	08 50	05 51	09 12
37	18 36	13 26	08 18	05 13	08 36
38	18 24	13 02	07 45	04 32	07 59
39	18 12	12 39	07 12	03 51	07 20
40	17 59	12 15	06 38	03 09	06 39
41	17 46	11 50	06 03	02 25	05 55
42	17 34	11 26	05 27	01 40	05 10
43	17 21	11 01	04 51	00 53	04 22
44	17 08	10 35	04 14	00 04	03 31
45	16 54	10 09	03 36	29♐14	02 37
46	16 41	09 43	02 57	28 22	01 40
47	16 27	09 16	02 17	27 29	00 39
48	16 13	08 48	01 36	26 33	29♑35
49	15 59	08 20	00 54	25 35	28 26
50	15 45	07 52	00 11	24 35	27 12
51	15 30	07 23	29♏26	23 32	25 54
52	15 15	06 53	28 41	22 27	24 29
53	15 00	06 23	27 54	21 19	22 59
54	14 44	05 51	27 06	20 09	21 21
55	14 28	05 19	26 16	18 55	19 36
56	14 12	04 47	25 25	17 39	17 42
57	13 55	04 13	24 32	16 19	15 38
58	13 38	03 39	23 37	14 55	13 25
59	13 21	03 03	22 41	13 28	11 00
60	13♎03	02♏27	21♏43	11♐57	08♑23

11h 40m 0s — 24 ♍ 33 — 175° 0' 0"

LAT.	11	12	ASC	2	3
0	26♎57	27♏17	25♐25	23♑10	22♒39
5	25 53	25 32	23 26	21 20	21 28
10	24 52	23 50	21 26	19 26	20 11
15	23 53	22 08	19 24	17 25	18 47
20	22 55	20 27	17 17	15 16	17 13
21	22 44	20 06	16 51	14 48	16 52
22	22 32	19 45	16 25	14 21	16 31
23	22 21	19 25	15 58	13 52	16 10
24	22 09	19 04	15 32	13 24	15 48
25	21 58	18 43	15 05	12 54	15 25
26	21 46	18 22	14 37	12 24	15 01
27	21 35	18 01	14 09	11 54	14 37
28	21 23	17 40	13 41	11 22	14 12
29	21 11	17 18	13 13	10 50	13 46
30	21 00	16 57	12 44	10 18	13 19
31	20 48	16 35	12 15	09 44	12 50
32	20 36	16 13	11 45	09 10	12 21
33	20 24	15 51	11 14	08 34	11 51
34	20 12	15 28	10 44	07 58	11 19
35	20 00	15 06	10 12	07 21	10 46
36	19 48	14 43	09 40	06 43	10 12
37	19 36	14 19	09 08	06 04	09 36
38	19 23	13 56	08 35	05 23	08 58
39	19 11	13 32	08 01	04 41	08 19
40	18 58	13 08	07 27	03 58	07 37
41	18 45	12 43	06 51	03 14	06 54
42	18 33	12 18	06 15	02 28	06 08
43	18 19	11 53	05 39	01 41	05 19
44	18 06	11 27	05 01	00 52	04 28
45	17 53	11 01	04 22	00 01	03 33
46	17 39	10 34	03 43	29♐09	02 36
47	17 25	10 07	03 03	28 14	01 35
48	17 11	09 39	02 21	27 18	00 29
49	16 57	09 11	01 39	26 19	29♑20
50	16 42	08 42	00 55	25 18	28 05
51	16 27	08 12	00 10	24 14	26 45
52	16 12	07 42	29♏24	23 08	25 20
53	15 57	07 12	28 36	22 00	23 48
54	15 41	06 40	27 47	20 48	22 08
55	15 25	06 08	26 57	19 33	20 21
56	15 09	05 34	26 05	18 16	18 26
57	14 52	05 00	25 11	16 54	16 20
58	14 35	04 26	24 16	15 29	14 04
59	14 17	03 50	23 19	14 01	11 37
60	13♎59	03♏13	22♏20	12♐28	08♑57

Koch Table of Houses for Latitudes 0° to 60° North

11h 44m 0s — 176° 0' 0" — 25 ♍ 38

LAT.	11	12	ASC	2	3
0	28♎00	28♏15	26♐20	24♑06	23♒41
5	26 55	26 30	24 21	22 17	22 30
10	25 54	24 47	22 20	20 22	21 13
15	24 55	23 05	20 18	18 21	19 49
20	23 57	21 23	18 11	16 11	18 15
21	23 45	21 02	17 45	15 44	17 54
22	23 33	20 42	17 18	15 16	17 33
23	23 22	20 21	16 52	14 47	17 12
24	23 10	20 00	16 25	14 18	16 49
25	22 59	19 39	15 57	13 49	16 27
26	22 47	19 18	15 30	13 19	16 03
27	22 35	18 56	15 02	12 48	15 38
28	22 24	18 35	14 34	12 16	15 13
29	22 12	18 13	14 05	11 44	14 47
30	22 00	17 52	13 36	11 11	14 20
31	21 48	17 30	13 06	10 37	13 52
32	21 36	17 07	12 36	10 03	13 22
33	21 24	16 45	12 05	09 27	12 52
34	21 12	16 22	11 34	08 51	12 20
35	21 00	16 00	11 03	08 13	11 47
36	20 48	15 36	10 31	07 35	11 12
37	20 35	15 13	09 58	06 55	10 36
38	20 23	14 49	09 24	06 14	09 58
39	20 10	14 25	08 50	05 32	09 18
40	19 57	14 01	08 15	04 48	08 37
41	19 45	13 36	07 40	04 04	07 53
42	19 31	13 10	07 03	03 17	07 06
43	19 18	12 45	06 26	02 29	06 17
44	19 05	12 19	05 48	01 40	05 26
45	18 51	11 52	05 09	00 48	04 31
46	18 37	11 25	04 29	29♐55	03 32
47	18 23	10 58	03 49	29 00	02 30
48	18 09	10 30	03 07	28 03	01 24
49	17 55	10 01	02 23	27 03	00 14
50	17 40	09 32	01 39	26 01	28♑59
51	17 25	09 02	00 54	24 57	27 38
52	17 10	08 32	00 07	23 50	26 11
53	16 54	08 00	29♏19	22 40	24 37
54	16 38	07 28	28 29	21 28	22 57
55	16 22	06 56	27 38	20 12	21 08
56	16 05	06 22	26 45	18 53	19 10
57	15 48	05 48	25 51	17 30	17 03
58	15 31	05 12	24 55	16 04	14 44
59	15 13	04 36	23 57	14 33	12 14
60	14♎55	03♏59	22♏57	12♐59	09♑31

11h 48m 0s — 177° 0' 0" — 26 ♍ 44

LAT.	11	12	ASC	2	3
0	29♎03	29♏13	27♐15	25♑03	24♒42
5	27 58	27 27	25 16	23 14	23 32
10	26 56	25 44	23 15	21 19	22 15
15	25 57	24 02	21 12	19 17	20 51
20	24 58	22 19	19 04	17 07	19 17
21	24 46	21 58	18 38	16 39	18 56
22	24 35	21 38	18 12	16 11	18 35
23	24 23	21 17	17 45	15 43	18 14
24	24 11	20 56	17 18	15 14	17 52
25	24 00	20 35	16 50	14 44	17 29
26	23 48	20 13	16 22	14 14	17 05
27	23 36	19 52	15 54	13 43	16 40
28	23 24	19 30	15 26	13 11	16 15
29	23 12	19 08	14 57	12 38	15 49
30	23 00	18 47	14 27	12 05	15 21
31	22 48	18 24	13 58	11 31	14 53
32	22 36	18 02	13 27	10 56	14 24
33	22 24	17 39	12 57	10 20	13 53
34	22 12	17 17	12 25	09 43	13 21
35	22 00	16 53	11 53	09 06	12 48
36	21 47	16 30	11 21	08 27	12 13
37	21 35	16 06	10 48	07 47	11 37
38	21 22	15 42	10 14	07 05	10 59
39	21 10	15 18	09 40	06 23	10 19
40	20 57	14 53	09 04	05 39	09 36
41	20 44	14 28	08 28	04 54	08 52
42	20 30	14 03	07 52	04 07	08 05
43	20 17	13 37	07 14	03 18	07 16
44	20 03	13 11	06 36	02 28	06 24
45	19 50	12 44	05 56	01 36	05 28
46	19 36	12 17	05 16	00 42	04 30
47	19 22	11 49	04 35	29♐46	03 27
48	19 07	11 20	03 52	28 48	02 20
49	18 53	10 52	03 08	27 48	01 09
50	18 38	10 22	02 24	26 45	29♑53
51	18 22	09 52	01 38	25 40	28 31
52	18 07	09 21	00 50	24 32	27 03
53	17 51	08 49	00 01	23 21	25 28
54	17 35	08 17	29♏11	22 07	23 46
55	17 19	07 44	28 19	20 50	21 55
56	17 02	07 10	27 26	19 30	19 56
57	16 45	06 35	26 31	18 06	17 46
58	16 27	05 59	25 34	16 38	15 25
59	16 09	05 22	24 35	15 06	12 52
60	15♎50	04♏45	23♏34	13♐31	10♑06

11h 52m 0s — 178° 0' 0" — 27 ♍ 49

LAT.	11	12	ASC	2	3
0	00♏06	00♐11	28♐10	26♑00	25♒44
5	29♎01	28♏25	26 10	24 11	24 34
10	27 58	26 41	24 10	22 16	23 18
15	26 58	24 59	22 06	20 14	21 54
20	25 59	23 15	19 58	18 03	20 19
21	25 47	22 54	19 32	17 35	19 59
22	25 36	22 34	19 05	17 07	19 38
23	25 24	22 13	18 38	16 38	19 16
24	25 12	21 51	18 11	16 09	18 54
25	25 00	21 30	17 43	15 39	18 31
26	24 49	21 09	17 15	15 09	18 07
27	24 37	20 47	16 47	14 37	17 43
28	24 25	20 25	16 18	14 05	17 17
29	24 13	20 03	15 49	13 33	16 51
30	24 01	19 41	15 19	12 59	16 24
31	23 49	19 19	14 49	12 25	15 55
32	23 37	18 57	14 19	11 50	15 26
33	23 24	18 34	13 48	11 14	14 55
34	23 12	18 11	13 16	10 37	14 23
35	23 00	17 47	12 44	09 58	13 49
36	22 47	17 24	12 11	09 19	13 15
37	22 34	17 00	11 38	08 39	12 38
38	22 22	16 36	11 04	07 57	12 00
39	22 09	16 11	10 29	07 14	11 19
40	21 56	15 46	09 54	06 30	10 37
41	21 43	15 21	09 17	05 44	09 52
42	21 29	14 55	08 40	04 56	09 05
43	21 16	14 29	08 02	04 07	08 15
44	21 02	14 03	07 23	03 17	07 23
45	20 48	13 36	06 43	02 24	06 27
46	20 34	13 08	06 03	01 29	05 27
47	20 20	12 40	05 21	00 33	04 24
48	20 05	12 11	04 38	29♐34	03 17
49	19 50	11 42	03 54	28 33	02 05
50	19 35	11 12	03 08	27 29	00 47
51	19 20	10 42	02 22	26 23	29♑24
52	19 04	10 10	01 34	25 14	27 55
53	18 48	09 38	00 44	24 02	26 19
54	18 32	09 06	29♏53	22 47	24 35
55	18 15	08 32	29 01	21 29	22 43
56	17 58	07 58	28 06	20 07	20 41
57	17 41	07 22	27 10	18 42	18 30
58	17 23	06 46	26 13	17 13	16 06
59	17 05	06 09	25 13	15 40	13 31
60	16♎46	05♏30	24♏11	14♐02	10♑42

11h 56m 0s — 179° 0' 0" — 28 ♍ 55

LAT.	11	12	ASC	2	3
0	01♏08	01♐08	29♐05	26♑57	26♒47
5	00 03	29♏22	27 05	25 08	25 36
10	29♎00	27 38	25 04	23 13	24 20
15	28 00	25 55	23 00	21 11	22 56
20	27 00	24 12	20 52	18 59	21 22
21	26 49	23 51	20 25	18 31	21 02
22	26 37	23 30	19 58	18 03	20 41
23	26 25	23 08	19 31	17 34	20 19
24	26 13	22 47	19 04	17 05	19 57
25	26 01	22 26	18 36	16 35	19 34
26	25 49	22 04	18 08	16 04	19 10
27	25 37	21 42	17 40	15 33	18 45
28	25 25	21 21	17 11	15 00	18 20
29	25 13	20 58	16 41	14 28	17 53
30	25 01	20 36	16 12	13 54	17 26
31	24 49	20 14	15 41	13 19	16 58
32	24 37	19 51	15 11	12 44	16 28
33	24 24	19 28	14 39	12 07	15 57
34	24 12	19 05	14 07	11 30	15 25
35	23 59	18 41	13 35	10 51	14 51
36	23 47	18 18	13 02	10 12	14 16
37	23 34	17 54	12 28	09 31	13 40
38	23 21	17 29	11 54	08 49	13 01
39	23 08	17 04	11 19	08 06	12 20
40	22 55	16 39	10 43	07 21	11 38
41	22 42	16 14	10 06	06 34	10 53
42	22 28	15 48	09 29	05 47	10 05
43	22 14	15 21	08 50	04 57	09 15
44	22 01	14 54	08 11	04 06	08 22
45	21 47	14 27	07 31	03 12	07 26
46	21 32	13 59	06 49	02 17	06 26
47	21 18	13 31	06 07	01 20	05 22
48	21 03	13 02	05 24	00 20	04 14
49	20 48	12 32	04 39	29♐18	03 01
50	20 33	12 02	03 53	28 14	01 43
51	20 17	11 31	03 06	27 07	00 19
52	20 02	11 00	02 17	25 57	28♑48
53	19 45	10 27	01 27	24 44	27 11
54	19 29	09 54	00 35	23 28	25 26
55	19 12	09 20	29♏42	22 08	23 32
56	18 55	08 45	28 47	20 45	21 28
57	18 37	08 10	27 50	19 18	19 14
58	18 19	07 33	26 52	17 48	16 48
59	18 01	06 55	25 51	16 13	14 10
60	17♎42	06♏16	24♏48	14♐34	11♑18

12h 0m 0s — 180° 0' 0" — 00 ♎ 00

LAT.	11	12	ASC	2	3
0	02♏11	02♐05	00♑00	27♑55	27♒49
5	01 05	00 19	28♐00	26 05	26 39
10	00 02	28♏35	25 59	24 10	25 23
15	29♎01	26 52	23 55	22 08	23 59
20	28 02	25 08	21 46	19 55	22 25
21	27 50	24 47	21 19	19 28	22 05
22	27 38	24 25	20 52	18 59	21 44
23	27 26	24 04	20 25	18 30	21 22
24	27 14	23 43	19 57	18 01	21 00
25	27 02	23 21	19 29	17 30	20 37
26	26 50	23 00	19 01	17 00	20 13
27	26 38	22 38	18 32	16 28	19 48
28	26 26	22 16	18 03	15 56	19 23
29	26 13	21 53	17 34	15 23	18 56
30	26 01	21 31	17 04	14 49	18 29
31	25 49	21 08	16 33	14 14	18 00
32	25 37	20 46	16 02	13 38	17 31
33	25 24	20 22	15 31	13 01	17 00
34	25 12	19 59	14 59	12 24	16 28
35	24 59	19 35	14 26	11 45	15 54
36	24 46	19 11	13 53	11 05	15 19
37	24 33	18 47	13 19	10 24	14 42
38	24 20	18 22	12 44	09 41	14 03
39	24 07	17 57	12 08	08 58	13 22
40	23 54	17 32	11 32	08 12	12 39
41	23 40	17 06	10 55	07 25	11 54
42	23 27	16 40	10 17	06 37	11 06
43	23 13	16 14	09 39	05 47	10 16
44	22 59	15 46	08 59	04 55	09 22
45	22 45	15 19	08 18	04 01	08 25
46	22 31	14 51	07 36	03 05	07 25
47	22 16	14 22	06 54	02 07	06 21
48	22 01	13 53	06 10	01 07	05 12
49	21 46	13 23	05 24	00 04	03 58
50	21 31	12 52	04 38	28♐59	02 39
51	21 15	12 21	03 50	27 51	01 14
52	20 59	11 49	03 01	26 40	29♑42
53	20 43	11 16	02 10	25 26	28 04
54	20 26	10 43	01 18	24 08	26 17
55	20 09	10 08	00 24	22 48	24 21
56	19 51	09 33	29♏28	21 23	22 15
57	19 34	08 57	28 30	19 55	19 59
58	19 15	08 20	27 31	18 23	17 31
59	18 57	07 41	26 29	16 47	14 49
60	18♎37	07♏02	25♏26	15♐06	11♑54

12h 4m 0s — 181° 0' 0" — 01 ♎ 05

LAT.	11	12	ASC	2	3
0	03♏13	03♐03	00♑55	28♑52	28♒52
5	02 07	01 16	28♐55	27 02	27 42
10	01 04	29♏32	26 54	25 07	26 26
15	00 03	27 48	24 49	23 05	25 03
20	29♎03	26 04	22 40	20 52	23 29
21	28 51	25 43	22 13	20 24	23 08
22	28 39	25 21	21 46	19 56	22 47
23	28 27	25 00	21 18	19 27	22 26
24	28 14	24 38	20 51	18 57	22 03
25	28 02	24 17	20 23	18 27	21 40
26	27 50	23 55	19 54	17 56	21 16
27	27 38	23 33	19 25	17 24	20 52
28	27 26	23 11	18 56	16 51	20 26
29	27 14	22 48	18 26	16 18	20 00
30	27 01	22 26	17 56	15 44	19 32
31	26 49	22 03	17 25	15 09	19 04
32	26 36	21 40	16 54	14 33	18 34
33	26 24	21 17	16 22	13 56	18 03
34	26 11	20 53	15 50	13 18	17 31
35	25 59	20 29	15 17	12 39	16 57
36	25 46	20 05	14 43	11 58	16 21
37	25 33	19 41	14 09	11 17	15 44
38	25 20	19 16	13 34	10 34	15 05
39	25 06	18 51	12 58	09 50	14 24
40	24 53	18 25	12 22	09 04	13 41
41	24 39	17 59	11 44	08 17	12 56
42	24 26	17 33	11 06	07 28	12 08
43	24 12	17 06	10 27	06 37	11 17
44	23 58	16 38	09 47	05 45	10 23
45	23 43	16 10	09 06	04 50	09 26
46	23 29	15 42	08 24	03 54	08 25
47	23 14	15 13	07 40	02 55	07 20
48	22 59	14 43	06 56	01 54	06 10
49	22 44	14 13	06 10	00 50	04 56
50	22 28	13 42	05 23	29♐44	03 36
51	22 12	13 11	04 34	28 35	02 10
52	21 56	12 38	03 44	27 23	00 37
53	21 40	12 05	02 53	26 08	28♑57
54	21 23	11 31	02 00	24 49	27 09
55	21 06	10 57	01 05	23 27	25 11
56	20 48	10 21	00 09	22 02	23 04
57	20 30	09 44	29♏10	20 32	20 45
58	20 11	09 07	28 10	18 59	18 14
59	19 52	08 28	27 08	17 21	15 30
60	19♎33	07♏48	26♏03	15♐38	12♑31

12h 8m 0s — 182° 0' 0" — 02 ♎ 11

LAT.	11	12	ASC	2	3
0	04♏16	04♐00	01♑50	29♑49	29♒54
5	03 09	02 13	29♐50	28 00	28 45
10	02 06	00 29	27 49	26 05	27 29
15	01 04	28♏45	25 44	24 02	26 06
20	00 04	27 00	23 34	21 49	24 32
21	29♎51	26 38	23 07	21 21	24 12
22	29 39	26 17	22 40	20 53	23 51
23	29 27	25 56	22 12	20 23	23 29
24	29 15	25 34	21 44	19 53	23 07
25	29 03	25 12	21 16	19 23	22 44
26	28 51	24 50	20 47	18 52	22 20
27	28 38	24 28	20 18	18 20	21 56
28	28 26	24 06	19 49	17 47	21 30
29	28 14	23 43	19 19	17 14	21 04
30	28 01	23 21	18 49	16 39	20 36
31	27 49	22 58	18 18	16 04	20 07
32	27 36	22 35	17 46	15 28	19 38
33	27 24	22 11	17 14	14 51	19 07
34	27 11	21 47	16 42	14 12	18 34
35	26 58	21 23	16 08	13 33	18 00
36	26 45	20 59	15 35	12 52	17 25
37	26 32	20 34	15 00	12 10	16 48
38	26 19	20 09	14 25	11 27	16 08
39	26 05	19 44	13 49	10 43	15 27
40	25 52	19 18	13 12	09 56	14 44
41	25 38	18 52	12 34	09 09	13 58
42	25 24	18 25	11 55	08 19	13 10
43	25 10	17 58	11 16	07 28	12 19
44	24 56	17 30	10 35	06 35	11 24
45	24 42	17 02	09 54	05 40	10 27
46	24 27	16 33	09 11	04 43	09 25
47	24 12	16 04	08 27	03 43	08 20
48	23 57	15 34	07 42	02 41	07 09
49	23 41	15 04	06 56	01 37	05 54
50	23 26	14 33	06 08	00 29	04 33
51	23 10	14 01	05 19	29♐19	03 06
52	22 53	13 28	04 28	28 06	01 33
53	22 37	12 54	03 36	26 50	29♑51
54	22 20	12 20	02 43	25 31	28 01
55	22 02	11 45	01 47	24 07	26 02
56	21 44	11 09	00 50	22 40	23 53
57	21 26	10 32	29♏51	21 09	21 32
58	21 07	09 53	28 49	19 34	18 58
59	20 48	09 14	27 46	17 55	16 11
60	20♎29	08♏34	26♏40	16♐11	13♑09

12h 12m 0s — 183° 0' 0" — 03 ♎ 16

LAT.	11	12	ASC	2	3
0	05♏18	04♐57	02♑45	00♒47	00♓57
5	04 11	03 10	00 45	28♑58	29♒48
10	03 07	01 26	28♐44	27 03	28 33
15	02 05	29♏41	26 39	25 00	27 10
20	01 04	27 56	24 28	22 46	25 36
21	00 52	27 34	24 01	22 18	25 16
22	00 40	27 13	23 34	21 50	24 55
23	00 28	26 51	23 06	21 20	24 33
24	00 16	26 30	22 38	20 50	24 11
25	00 03	26 08	22 10	20 20	23 48
26	29♎51	25 46	21 41	19 48	23 24
27	29 39	25 23	21 12	19 16	23 00
28	29 26	25 01	20 42	18 43	22 34
29	29 14	24 38	20 12	18 10	22 08
30	29 01	24 16	19 41	17 35	21 40
31	28 49	23 52	19 10	17 00	21 12
32	28 36	23 29	18 38	16 23	20 42
33	28 23	23 05	18 06	15 46	20 11
34	28 11	22 42	17 33	15 07	19 38
35	27 58	22 17	17 00	14 28	19 04
36	27 45	21 53	16 26	13 47	18 29
37	27 31	21 28	15 51	13 04	17 51
38	27 18	21 03	15 15	12 21	17 12
39	27 05	20 37	14 39	11 36	16 31
40	26 51	20 11	14 02	10 49	15 47
41	26 37	19 45	13 24	10 01	15 01
42	26 23	19 18	12 45	09 11	14 13
43	26 09	18 50	12 05	08 19	13 21
44	25 55	18 22	11 24	07 25	12 27
45	25 40	17 54	10 42	06 30	11 28
46	25 25	17 25	09 58	05 32	10 26
47	25 10	16 55	09 14	04 32	09 20
48	24 55	16 25	08 28	03 29	08 09
49	24 39	15 54	07 42	02 24	06 54
50	24 23	15 23	06 53	01 16	05 32
51	24 07	14 50	06 04	00 05	04 04
52	23 51	14 17	05 13	28♐50	02 29
53	23 34	13 44	04 20	27 33	00 46
54	23 17	13 09	03 25	26 12	28♑55
55	22 59	12 33	02 29	24 48	26 54
56	22 41	11 57	01 31	23 19	24 42
57	22 22	11 19	00 31	21 47	22 19
58	22 03	10 40	29♏29	20 10	19 43
59	21 44	10 00	28 24	18 29	16 53
60	21♎24	09♏19	27♏18	16♐43	13♑47

Koch Table of Houses for Latitudes 0° to 60° North

12h 16m 0s — 184° 0' 0" — 04 ♎ 22

LAT.	11	12	ASC	2	3
0	06♏19	05♐54	03♑40	01♒45	02♓00
5	05 13	04 07	01 41	29♑56	00 51
10	04 09	02 22	29♐39	28 01	29♒37
15	03 06	00 38	27 33	25 58	28 14
20	02 05	28♏52	25 22	23 44	26 41
21	01 53	28 30	24 55	23 16	26 20
22	01 41	28 09	24 28	22 47	25 59
23	01 28	27 47	24 00	22 18	25 38
24	01 16	27 25	23 32	21 48	25 16
25	01 04	27 03	23 03	21 17	24 53
26	00 51	26 41	22 34	20 45	24 29
27	00 39	26 19	22 05	20 13	24 04
28	00 27	25 56	21 35	19 40	23 39
29	00 14	25 33	21 05	19 06	23 12
30	00 01	25 10	20 34	18 31	22 45
31	29♎49	24 47	20 03	17 56	22 16
32	29 36	24 24	19 31	17 19	21 46
33	29 23	24 00	18 58	16 41	21 15
34	29 10	23 36	18 25	16 03	20 43
35	28 57	23 11	17 52	15 22	20 09
36	28 44	22 47	17 17	14 41	19 33
37	28 31	22 22	16 42	13 59	18 55
38	28 17	21 56	16 06	13 15	18 16
39	28 04	21 30	15 29	12 29	17 35
40	27 50	21 04	14 52	11 42	16 51
41	27 36	20 37	14 13	10 54	16 05
42	27 22	20 10	13 34	10 03	15 16
43	27 07	19 43	12 54	09 11	14 24
44	26 53	19 14	12 12	08 17	13 29
45	26 38	18 46	11 30	07 20	12 31
46	26 23	18 16	10 46	06 22	11 28
47	26 08	17 47	10 01	05 21	10 22
48	25 53	17 16	09 15	04 17	09 10
49	25 37	16 45	08 28	03 11	07 54
50	25 21	16 13	07 39	02 02	06 31
51	25 04	15 40	06 49	00 50	05 02
52	24 48	15 07	05 57	29♐35	03 26
53	24 31	14 33	05 03	28 16	01 42
54	24 13	13 57	04 08	26 54	29♑49
55	23 55	13 21	03 11	25 29	27 47
56	23 37	12 44	02 12	23 59	25 33
57	23 19	12 06	01 11	22 25	23 07
58	22 59	11 27	00 08	20 47	20 28
59	22 40	10 47	29♏03	19 04	17 35
60	22♎20	10♏05	27♏56	17♐16	14♑26

12h 20m 0s — 185° 0' 0" — 05 ♎ 27

LAT.	11	12	ASC	2	3
0	07♏21	06♐50	04♑35	02♒43	03♓03
5	06 14	05 04	02 36	00 54	01 55
10	05 10	03 19	00 34	28♑59	00 41
15	04 07	01 34	28♐28	26 56	29♒18
20	03 06	29♏48	26 17	24 42	27 45
21	02 53	29 26	25 49	24 14	27 25
22	02 41	29 04	25 22	23 45	27 04
23	02 29	28 43	24 54	23 15	26 43
24	02 16	28 21	24 26	22 45	26 21
25	02 04	27 59	23 57	22 14	25 58
26	01 52	27 36	23 28	21 43	25 34
27	01 39	27 14	22 58	21 10	25 09
28	01 27	26 51	22 28	20 37	24 44
29	01 14	26 28	21 58	20 03	24 17
30	01 01	26 05	21 27	19 28	23 50
31	00 49	25 42	20 56	18 52	23 21
32	00 36	25 18	20 23	18 15	22 51
33	00 23	24 54	19 51	17 37	22 20
34	00 10	24 30	19 17	16 58	21 48
35	29♎57	24 05	18 43	16 18	21 13
36	29 43	23 40	18 09	15 36	20 38
37	29 30	23 15	17 33	14 53	20 00
38	29 16	22 50	16 57	14 09	19 21
39	29 03	22 24	16 20	13 23	18 39
40	28 49	21 57	15 42	12 36	17 55
41	28 35	21 30	15 03	11 47	17 09
42	28 20	21 03	14 24	10 56	16 20
43	28 06	20 35	13 43	10 03	15 28
44	27 51	20 07	13 01	09 08	14 33
45	27 36	19 38	12 18	08 11	13 34
46	27 21	19 08	11 34	07 12	12 31
47	27 06	18 38	10 49	06 10	11 24
48	26 50	18 07	10 02	05 06	10 12
49	26 34	17 35	09 14	03 59	08 55
50	26 18	17 03	08 25	02 49	07 31
51	26 02	16 30	07 34	01 36	06 01
52	25 45	15 56	06 41	00 20	04 24
53	25 28	15 22	05 47	29♐00	02 39
54	25 10	14 46	04 51	27 37	00 44
55	24 52	14 10	03 53	26 10	28♑40
56	24 34	13 32	02 54	24 39	26 24
57	24 15	12 54	01 52	23 03	23 56
58	23 55	12 14	00 48	21 23	21 15
59	23 35	11 33	29♏42	19 39	18 19
60	23♎15	10♏51	28♏33	17♐49	15♑06

12h 24m 0s — 186° 0' 0" — 06 ♎ 32

LAT.	11	12	ASC	2	3
0	08♏23	07♐47	05♑30	03♒41	04♓07
5	07 15	06 00	03 31	01 52	02 59
10	06 11	04 15	01 29	29♑57	01 45
15	05 08	02 30	29♐23	27 54	00 23
20	04 06	00 44	27 11	25 40	28♒50
21	03 54	00 22	26 44	25 12	28 30
22	03 42	00 00	26 16	24 43	28 09
23	03 29	29♏38	25 48	24 13	27 48
24	03 17	29 16	25 20	23 43	27 26
25	03 04	28 54	24 51	23 12	27 03
26	02 52	28 32	24 22	22 40	26 39
27	02 39	28 09	23 52	22 08	26 15
28	02 27	27 46	23 22	21 34	25 49
29	02 14	27 23	22 51	21 00	25 23
30	02 01	27 00	22 20	20 25	24 55
31	01 48	26 36	21 48	19 49	24 27
32	01 35	26 13	21 16	19 12	23 57
33	01 22	25 49	20 43	18 34	23 26
34	01 09	25 24	20 10	17 54	22 53
35	00 56	24 59	19 35	17 14	22 19
36	00 43	24 34	19 00	16 32	21 43
37	00 29	24 09	18 25	15 49	21 06
38	00 15	23 43	17 48	15 04	20 26
39	00 02	23 17	17 11	14 18	19 44
40	29♎48	22 50	16 33	13 30	19 00
41	29 33	22 23	15 53	12 40	18 14
42	29 19	21 55	15 13	11 49	17 25
43	29 04	21 27	14 32	10 55	16 32
44	28 50	20 59	13 50	10 00	15 37
45	28 35	20 29	13 07	09 02	14 38
46	28 19	20 00	12 22	08 02	13 35
47	28 04	19 29	11 36	07 00	12 27
48	27 48	18 58	10 49	05 55	11 14
49	27 32	18 26	10 01	04 47	09 56
50	27 16	17 54	09 11	03 36	08 32
51	26 59	17 20	08 19	02 22	07 01
52	26 42	16 46	07 26	01 05	05 23
53	26 25	16 11	06 31	29♐44	03 37
54	26 07	15 35	05 34	28 20	01 41
55	25 49	14 58	04 36	26 51	29♑34
56	25 30	14 20	03 35	25 19	27 17
57	25 11	13 41	02 33	23 42	24 47
58	24 51	13 01	01 28	22 00	22 02
59	24 31	12 19	00 21	20 14	19 03
60	24♎10	11♏37	29♏11	18♐23	15♑47

12h 28m 0s — 187° 0' 0" — 07 ♎ 37

LAT.	11	12	ASC	2	3
0	09♏24	08♐43	06♑26	04♒39	05♓10
5	08 17	06 57	04 26	02 51	04 03
10	07 12	05 12	02 24	00 56	02 49
15	06 09	03 26	00 18	28♑53	01 28
20	05 07	01 39	28♐06	26 39	29♒55
21	04 54	01 18	27 38	26 10	29 35
22	04 42	00 56	27 11	25 41	29 15
23	04 29	00 34	26 43	25 11	28 53
24	04 17	00 12	26 14	24 41	28 31
25	04 04	29♏50	25 45	24 10	28 08
26	03 52	29 27	25 16	23 38	27 45
27	03 39	29 04	24 46	23 05	27 20
28	03 26	28 41	24 16	22 32	26 55
29	03 14	28 18	23 45	21 58	26 28
30	03 01	27 55	23 14	21 22	26 01
31	02 48	27 31	22 42	20 46	25 32
32	02 35	27 07	22 09	20 09	25 03
33	02 22	26 43	21 36	19 30	24 31
34	02 09	26 18	21 02	18 51	23 59
35	01 55	25 54	20 28	18 10	23 25
36	01 42	25 28	19 52	17 28	22 49
37	01 28	25 03	19 16	16 44	22 11
38	01 14	24 37	18 40	15 59	21 32
39	01 00	24 10	18 02	15 12	20 50
40	00 46	23 43	17 23	14 24	20 06
41	00 32	23 16	16 44	13 34	19 19
42	00 18	22 48	16 03	12 42	18 30
43	00 03	22 20	15 22	11 48	17 38
44	29♎48	21 51	14 39	10 52	16 42
45	29 33	21 21	13 55	09 54	15 42
46	29 17	20 51	13 10	08 54	14 39
47	29 02	20 20	12 24	07 50	13 31
48	28 46	19 49	11 36	06 45	12 17
49	28 30	19 17	10 47	05 36	10 59
50	28 13	18 44	09 57	04 24	09 34
51	27 56	18 10	09 04	03 09	08 02
52	27 39	17 36	08 11	01 51	06 23
53	27 21	17 00	07 15	00 29	04 35
54	27 03	16 24	06 18	29♐03	02 38
55	26 45	15 46	05 18	27 33	00 30
56	26 26	15 08	04 17	25 59	28♑10
57	26 07	14 28	03 13	24 21	25 38
58	25 47	13 48	02 08	22 38	22 50
59	25 27	13 06	00 59	20 49	19 48
60	25♎06	12♏22	29♏49	18♐56	16♑28

12h 32m 0s — 188° 0' 0" — 08 ♎ 43

LAT.	11	12	ASC	2	3
0	10♏25	09♐40	07♑21	05♒38	06♓14
5	09 18	07 53	05 21	03 49	05 07
10	08 13	06 08	03 19	01 55	03 54
15	07 10	04 22	01 13	29♑52	02 33
20	06 07	02 35	29♐01	27 37	01 01
21	05 55	02 14	28 33	27 09	00 41
22	05 42	01 52	28 05	26 40	00 20
23	05 30	01 30	27 37	26 10	29♒59
24	05 17	01 07	27 08	25 40	29 37
25	05 04	00 45	26 39	25 08	29 14
26	04 52	00 22	26 10	24 36	28 51
27	04 39	00 00	25 40	24 04	28 26
28	04 26	29♏36	25 10	23 30	28 01
29	04 13	29 13	24 39	22 56	27 35
30	04 01	28 50	24 07	22 20	27 07
31	03 48	28 26	23 35	21 44	26 39
32	03 34	28 02	23 02	21 06	26 09
33	03 21	27 37	22 29	20 27	25 38
34	03 08	27 13	21 55	19 48	25 05
35	02 54	26 48	21 20	19 07	24 31
36	02 41	26 22	20 45	18 24	23 55
37	02 27	25 56	20 08	17 40	23 18
38	02 13	25 30	19 31	16 55	22 38
39	01 59	25 04	18 53	16 08	21 56
40	01 45	24 36	18 14	15 19	21 12
41	01 31	24 09	17 34	14 29	20 26
42	01 16	23 41	16 54	13 36	19 36
43	01 01	23 12	16 12	12 42	18 43
44	00 46	22 43	15 29	11 45	17 47
45	00 31	22 13	14 44	10 46	16 48
46	00 15	21 43	13 59	09 45	15 44
47	00 00	21 12	13 12	08 41	14 35
48	29♎44	20 40	12 24	07 35	13 22
49	29 27	20 08	11 34	06 25	12 02
50	29 10	19 34	10 43	05 12	10 37
51	28 53	19 00	09 50	03 57	09 04
52	28 36	18 25	08 56	02 37	07 24
53	28 18	17 49	07 59	01 14	05 35
54	28 00	17 13	07 01	29♐47	03 36
55	27 41	16 35	06 01	28 16	01 26
56	27 22	15 56	04 59	26 40	29♑05
57	27 03	15 16	03 54	25 00	26 29
58	26 43	14 34	02 48	23 15	23 40
59	26 22	13 52	01 39	21 25	20 34
60	26♎01	13♏08	00♐27	19♐30	17♑10

12h 36m 0s — 189° 0' 0" — 09 ♎ 48

LAT.	11	12	ASC	2	3
0	11♏26	10♐36	08♑16	06♒37	07♓18
5	10 18	08 50	06 17	04 48	06 11
10	09 13	07 04	04 15	02 54	04 59
15	08 10	05 19	02 08	00 51	03 38
20	07 07	03 31	29♐55	28♑36	02 07
21	06 55	03 09	29 28	28 08	01 47
22	06 42	02 47	29 00	27 39	01 26
23	06 30	02 25	28 32	27 09	01 05
24	06 17	02 03	28 03	26 38	00 43
25	06 04	01 40	27 34	26 07	00 21
26	05 52	01 18	27 04	25 35	29♒57
27	05 39	00 55	26 34	25 02	29 33
28	05 26	00 32	26 04	24 29	29 08
29	05 13	00 08	25 32	23 54	28 41
30	05 00	29♏45	25 01	23 18	28 14
31	04 47	29 21	24 28	22 42	27 45
32	04 34	28 56	23 56	22 04	27 16
33	04 21	28 32	23 22	21 25	26 45
34	04 07	28 07	22 48	20 45	26 12
35	03 54	27 42	22 13	20 04	25 38
36	03 40	27 16	21 37	19 21	25 02
37	03 26	26 50	21 00	18 37	24 25
38	03 12	26 24	20 23	17 51	23 45
39	02 58	25 57	19 45	17 04	23 03
40	02 44	25 30	19 06	16 15	22 19
41	02 29	25 02	18 25	15 24	21 32
42	02 14	24 34	17 44	14 31	20 43
43	02 00	24 05	17 02	13 36	19 50
44	01 44	23 35	16 18	12 39	18 54
45	01 29	23 05	15 33	11 39	17 54
46	01 13	22 35	14 48	10 37	16 49
47	00 57	22 03	14 00	09 33	15 40
48	00 41	21 31	13 11	08 25	14 26
49	00 25	20 58	12 21	07 15	13 07
50	00 08	20 25	11 29	06 01	11 40
51	29♎51	19 50	10 36	04 44	10 07
52	29 33	19 15	09 41	03 24	08 26
53	29 15	18 39	08 44	02 00	06 35
54	28 57	18 01	07 45	00 31	04 35
55	28 38	17 23	06 44	28♐59	02 24
56	28 19	16 44	05 41	27 22	00 00
57	27 59	16 03	04 35	25 40	27♑22
58	27 39	15 21	03 28	23 53	24 30
59	27 18	14 38	02 18	22 02	21 20
60	26♎56	13♏54	01♐05	20♐04	17♑53

12h 40m 0s — 190° 0' 0" — 10 ♎ 53

LAT.	11	12	ASC	2	3
0	12♏27	11♐32	09♑11	07♒35	08♓22
5	11 19	09 46	07 12	05 48	07 16
10	10 14	08 00	05 10	03 53	06 04
15	09 11	06 15	03 04	01 50	04 44
20	08 08	04 27	00 51	29♑36	03 13
21	07 55	04 05	00 23	29 07	02 53
22	07 42	03 43	29♐55	28 38	02 33
23	07 30	03 21	29 27	28 08	02 12
24	07 17	02 58	28 58	27 38	01 50
25	07 04	02 36	28 28	27 06	01 27
26	06 51	02 13	27 59	26 34	01 04
27	06 39	01 50	27 29	26 01	00 40
28	06 26	01 27	26 58	25 27	00 14
29	06 13	01 03	26 27	24 53	29♒48
30	06 00	00 39	25 55	24 17	29 21
31	05 46	00 15	25 22	23 40	28 53
32	05 33	29♏51	24 49	23 02	28 23
33	05 20	29 26	24 15	22 23	27 52
34	05 06	29 01	23 41	21 43	27 20
35	04 53	28 36	23 06	21 01	26 46
36	04 39	28 10	22 30	20 18	26 10
37	04 25	27 44	21 53	19 34	25 32
38	04 11	27 17	21 15	18 48	24 53
39	03 57	26 50	20 36	18 00	24 11
40	03 42	26 23	19 57	17 11	23 27
41	03 28	25 55	19 16	16 19	22 40
42	03 13	25 26	18 35	15 26	21 50
43	02 58	24 57	17 52	14 30	20 57
44	02 43	24 28	17 08	13 33	20 01
45	02 27	23 57	16 23	12 33	19 00
46	02 11	23 26	15 36	11 30	17 56
47	01 55	22 55	14 49	10 25	16 47
48	01 39	22 22	13 59	09 16	15 32
49	01 22	21 49	13 09	08 05	14 12
50	01 05	21 15	12 16	06 51	12 45
51	00 48	20 40	11 22	05 33	11 11
52	00 30	20 05	10 26	04 11	09 28
53	00 12	19 28	09 28	02 46	07 37
54	29♎53	18 50	08 29	01 16	05 35
55	29 34	18 12	07 27	29♐42	03 22
56	29 15	17 32	06 23	28 03	00 57
57	28 55	16 51	05 17	26 20	28♑17
58	28 34	16 08	04 08	24 32	25 21
59	28 13	15 25	02 57	22 38	22 08
60	27♎51	14♏40	01♐43	20♐39	18♑37

12h 44m 0s — 191° 0' 0" — 11 ♎ 58

LAT.	11	12	ASC	2	3
0	13♏27	12♐28	10♑07	08♒34	09♓26
5	12 20	10 42	08 08	06 47	08 20
10	11 14	08 57	06 06	04 53	07 09
15	10 11	07 11	03 59	02 50	05 50
20	09 08	05 23	01 46	00 36	04 19
21	08 55	05 01	01 18	00 07	04 00
22	08 42	04 39	00 50	29♑38	03 39
23	08 30	04 16	00 22	29 08	03 18
24	08 17	03 54	29♐53	28 37	02 57
25	08 04	03 31	29 23	28 06	02 34
26	07 51	03 08	28 53	27 34	02 11
27	07 38	02 45	28 23	27 01	01 47
28	07 25	02 22	27 52	26 27	01 22
29	07 12	01 58	27 21	25 52	00 56
30	06 59	01 34	26 49	25 16	00 29
31	06 46	01 10	26 16	24 39	00 00
32	06 32	00 46	25 43	24 01	29♒31
33	06 19	00 21	25 09	23 22	29 00
34	06 05	29♏56	24 34	22 41	28 27
35	05 52	29 30	23 59	21 59	27 53
36	05 38	29 04	23 22	21 16	27 18
37	05 24	28 38	22 45	20 31	26 40
38	05 10	28 11	22 07	19 45	26 01
39	04 55	27 44	21 28	18 57	25 19
40	04 41	27 16	20 49	18 07	24 35
41	04 26	26 48	20 08	17 15	23 48
42	04 11	26 19	19 26	16 21	22 58
43	03 56	25 50	18 43	15 26	22 05
44	03 41	25 20	17 58	14 27	21 09
45	03 25	24 49	17 13	13 27	20 08
46	03 09	24 18	16 26	12 23	19 03
47	02 53	23 46	15 37	11 17	17 54
48	02 36	23 13	14 48	10 08	16 39
49	02 19	22 40	13 56	08 56	15 18
50	02 02	22 06	13 03	07 41	13 51
51	01 45	21 31	12 08	06 22	12 16
52	01 27	20 54	11 12	04 59	10 32
53	01 08	20 17	10 13	03 32	08 40
54	00 50	19 39	09 13	02 01	06 37
55	00 30	19 00	08 10	00 26	04 22
56	00 11	18 20	07 05	28♐46	01 54
57	29♎51	17 38	05 58	27 01	29♑12
58	29 30	16 55	04 49	25 11	26 13
59	29 08	16 11	03 36	23 15	22 57
60	28♎46	15♏25	02♐21	21♐14	19♑22

Koch Table of Houses for Latitudes 0° to 60° North

12h 48m 0s — 13 ♎ 03 — 192° 0' 0"

LAT.	11	12	ASC	2	3
0	14♏28	13♐24	11♑02	09♒34	10♓30
5	13 20	11 38	09 03	07 46	09 25
10	12 15	09 53	07 02	05 53	08 14
15	11 11	08 07	04 55	03 50	06 56
20	10 08	06 19	02 41	01 36	05 26
21	09 55	05 57	02 14	01 07	05 06
22	09 42	05 34	01 45	00 38	04 46
23	09 29	05 12	01 17	00 08	04 25
24	09 17	04 49	00 48	29♑37	04 04
25	09 04	04 27	00 18	29 06	03 42
26	08 51	04 04	29♐48	28 33	03 18
27	08 38	03 41	29 18	28 00	02 54
28	08 25	03 17	28 47	27 26	02 29
29	08 12	02 53	28 15	26 51	02 04
30	07 58	02 29	27 43	26 15	01 36
31	07 45	02 05	27 10	25 38	01 08
32	07 32	01 40	26 37	25 00	00 39
33	07 18	01 16	26 03	24 21	00 08
34	07 05	00 50	25 28	23 40	29♒36
35	06 51	00 25	24 52	22 58	29 02
36	06 37	29♏58	24 16	22 14	28 26
37	06 23	29 32	23 38	21 29	27 49
38	06 08	29 05	23 00	20 43	27 09
39	05 54	28 38	22 21	19 54	26 28
40	05 39	28 10	21 41	19 04	25 43
41	05 25	27 41	20 59	18 12	24 57
42	05 09	27 12	20 17	17 18	24 07
43	04 54	26 43	19 33	16 21	23 14
44	04 39	26 12	18 49	15 22	22 17
45	04 23	25 42	18 03	14 21	21 16
46	04 07	25 10	17 15	13 17	20 12
47	03 50	24 38	16 26	12 10	19 02
48	03 34	24 05	15 36	11 01	17 46
49	03 17	23 31	14 44	09 48	16 25
50	02 59	22 56	13 50	08 31	14 57
51	02 42	22 21	12 55	07 11	13 21
52	02 24	21 44	11 58	05 47	11 37
53	02 05	21 07	10 59	04 19	09 44
54	01 46	20 28	09 57	02 47	07 39
55	01 27	19 49	08 54	01 10	05 23
56	01 07	19 08	07 48	29♐29	02 53
57	00 46	18 26	06 40	27 42	00 08
58	00 25	17 42	05 29	25 50	27♑07
59	00 04	16 57	04 16	23 52	23 47
60	29♎41	16♏11	03♐00	21♐49	20♑08

12h 52m 0s — 14 ♎ 07 — 193° 0' 0"

LAT.	11	12	ASC	2	3
0	15♏28	14♐20	11♑58	10♒33	11♓34
5	14 20	12 34	09 59	08 46	10 30
10	13 15	10 49	07 58	06 53	09 20
15	12 11	09 03	05 51	04 50	08 02
20	11 07	07 14	03 37	02 36	06 33
21	10 55	06 52	03 09	02 07	06 13
22	10 42	06 30	02 41	01 38	05 53
23	10 29	06 08	02 12	01 08	05 33
24	10 16	05 45	01 43	00 38	05 11
25	10 03	05 22	01 14	00 06	04 49
26	09 50	04 59	00 43	29♑34	04 26
27	09 37	04 36	00 13	29 01	04 02
28	09 24	04 12	29♐42	28 26	03 38
29	09 11	03 48	29 10	27 51	03 12
30	08 58	03 24	28 38	27 15	02 45
31	08 44	03 00	28 05	26 38	02 17
32	08 31	02 35	27 31	26 00	01 47
33	08 17	02 10	26 57	25 20	01 17
34	08 04	01 45	26 22	24 39	00 45
35	07 50	01 19	25 46	23 57	00 11
36	07 36	00 53	25 09	23 13	29♒35
37	07 21	00 26	24 31	22 28	28 58
38	07 07	29♏59	23 53	21 41	28 19
39	06 53	29 31	23 13	20 52	27 37
40	06 38	29 03	22 33	20 02	26 53
41	06 23	28 34	21 51	19 09	26 06
42	06 08	28 05	21 08	18 14	25 16
43	05 52	27 35	20 25	17 17	24 23
44	05 37	27 05	19 39	16 18	23 26
45	05 21	26 34	18 53	15 16	22 26
46	05 05	26 02	18 05	14 12	21 21
47	04 48	25 29	17 16	13 04	20 10
48	04 31	24 56	16 25	11 54	18 55
49	04 14	24 22	15 32	10 40	17 33
50	03 57	23 47	14 38	09 22	16 05
51	03 39	23 11	13 42	08 01	14 28
52	03 20	22 34	12 44	06 36	12 43
53	03 02	21 56	11 44	05 07	10 48
54	02 43	21 17	10 42	03 33	08 43
55	02 23	20 37	09 38	01 55	06 25
56	02 03	19 56	08 31	00 12	03 53
57	01 42	19 13	07 22	28♐23	01 06
58	01 21	18 29	06 10	26 30	28♑01
59	00 59	17 44	04 56	24 30	24 38
60	00♏36	16♏57	03♐39	22♐25	20♑55

12h 56m 0s — 15 ♎ 12 — 194° 0' 0"

LAT.	11	12	ASC	2	3
0	16♏28	15♐16	12♑53	11♒32	12♓39
5	15 20	13 30	10 55	09 46	11 35
10	14 15	11 45	08 53	07 53	10 26
15	13 11	09 59	06 47	05 51	09 08
20	12 07	08 10	04 33	03 37	07 40
21	11 54	07 48	04 05	03 08	07 21
22	11 41	07 26	03 37	02 39	07 01
23	11 29	07 03	03 08	02 09	06 40
24	11 16	06 41	02 39	01 38	06 19
25	11 03	06 18	02 09	01 07	05 57
26	10 50	05 55	01 39	00 34	05 34
27	10 37	05 31	01 08	00 01	05 11
28	10 24	05 08	00 37	29♑27	04 46
29	10 10	04 44	00 05	28 52	04 20
30	09 57	04 19	29♐32	28 16	03 54
31	09 43	03 55	28 59	27 38	03 26
32	09 30	03 30	28 26	27 00	02 56
33	09 16	03 05	27 51	26 20	02 26
34	09 02	02 39	27 16	25 39	01 54
35	08 48	02 13	26 40	24 56	01 20
36	08 34	01 47	26 03	24 12	00 45
37	08 20	01 20	25 25	23 27	00 08
38	08 06	00 53	24 46	22 40	29♒28
39	07 51	00 25	24 06	21 51	28 47
40	07 36	29♏57	23 25	21 00	28 03
41	07 21	29 28	22 43	20 07	27 16
42	07 06	28 58	22 00	19 12	26 26
43	06 50	28 28	21 16	18 14	25 33
44	06 35	27 57	20 30	17 14	24 36
45	06 19	27 26	19 43	16 12	23 36
46	06 02	26 54	18 55	15 07	22 30
47	05 46	26 21	18 05	13 58	21 20
48	05 29	25 48	17 14	12 47	20 04
49	05 11	25 13	16 21	11 32	18 42
50	04 54	24 38	15 26	10 14	17 13
51	04 36	24 01	14 29	08 52	15 36
52	04 17	23 24	13 30	07 26	13 50
53	03 58	22 46	12 30	05 55	11 55
54	03 39	22 06	11 27	04 20	09 48
55	03 19	21 26	10 22	02 41	07 28
56	02 59	20 44	09 14	00 56	04 54
57	02 38	20 01	08 04	29♐05	02 04
58	02 16	19 16	06 51	27 10	28♑57
59	01 54	18 30	05 36	25 08	25 30
60	01♏31	17♏43	04♐17	23♐01	21♑43

13h 0m 0s — 16 ♎ 17 — 195° 0' 0"

LAT.	11	12	ASC	2	3
0	17♏28	16♐11	13♑49	12♒32	13♓43
5	16 20	14 26	11 51	10 46	12 40
10	15 15	12 41	09 50	08 54	11 32
15	14 11	10 55	07 43	06 52	10 15
20	13 07	09 06	05 29	04 38	08 48
21	12 54	08 44	05 01	04 09	08 28
22	12 41	08 21	04 32	03 40	08 09
23	12 28	07 59	04 04	03 10	07 48
24	12 15	07 36	03 34	02 39	07 27
25	12 02	07 13	03 05	02 08	07 05
26	11 49	06 50	02 34	01 35	06 43
27	11 36	06 27	02 04	01 02	06 19
28	11 23	06 03	01 32	00 28	05 55
29	11 09	05 39	01 00	29♑53	05 29
30	10 56	05 14	00 28	29 16	05 03
31	10 43	04 50	29♐54	28 39	04 35
32	10 29	04 25	29 20	28 00	04 06
33	10 15	04 00	28 45	27 20	03 36
34	10 01	03 34	28 10	26 39	03 04
35	09 47	03 08	27 34	25 57	02 30
36	09 33	02 41	26 56	25 12	01 55
37	09 19	02 14	26 18	24 27	01 18
38	09 04	01 47	25 39	23 39	00 39
39	08 49	01 19	24 59	22 50	29♒57
40	08 34	00 50	24 18	21 58	29 13
41	08 19	00 21	23 36	21 05	28 27
42	08 04	29♏51	22 52	20 10	27 37
43	07 48	29 21	22 08	19 12	26 44
44	07 32	28 50	21 22	18 11	25 47
45	07 16	28 18	20 34	17 08	24 46
46	07 00	27 46	19 45	16 02	23 41
47	06 43	27 13	18 55	14 53	22 31
48	06 26	26 39	18 03	13 41	21 15
49	06 08	26 04	17 09	12 26	19 52
50	05 51	25 29	16 14	11 06	18 23
51	05 32	24 52	15 16	09 43	16 45
52	05 14	24 14	14 17	08 16	14 59
53	04 55	23 35	13 16	06 44	13 02
54	04 35	22 56	12 12	05 08	10 54
55	04 15	22 14	11 06	03 27	08 32
56	03 55	21 32	09 57	01 40	05 57
57	03 33	20 48	08 46	29♐48	03 04
58	03 12	20 03	07 32	27 50	29♑54
59	02 49	19 17	06 16	25 47	26 24
60	02♏26	18♏29	04♐56	23♐37	22♑32

13h 4m 0s — 17 ♎ 21 — 196° 0' 0"

LAT.	11	12	ASC	2	3
0	18♏28	17♐07	14♑44	13♒32	14♓48
5	17 20	15 22	12 47	11 47	13 46
10	16 14	13 37	10 46	09 55	12 38
15	15 10	11 51	08 39	07 53	11 22
20	14 06	10 02	06 25	05 39	09 55
21	13 53	09 40	05 57	05 11	09 36
22	13 40	09 17	05 28	04 42	09 17
23	13 27	08 55	05 00	04 12	08 57
24	13 15	08 32	04 30	03 41	08 36
25	13 01	08 09	04 00	03 09	08 14
26	12 48	07 45	03 30	02 37	07 52
27	12 35	07 22	02 59	02 04	07 28
28	12 22	06 58	02 28	01 29	07 04
29	12 09	06 34	01 56	00 54	06 39
30	11 55	06 10	01 23	00 18	06 12
31	11 42	05 45	00 49	29♑40	05 45
32	11 28	05 20	00 15	29 01	05 16
33	11 14	04 54	29♐40	28 21	04 46
34	11 00	04 28	29 05	27 40	04 14
35	10 46	04 02	28 28	26 57	03 41
36	10 32	03 35	27 51	26 13	03 06
37	10 17	03 08	27 12	25 27	02 29
38	10 03	02 41	26 33	24 39	01 50
39	09 48	02 12	25 53	23 49	01 08
40	09 33	01 44	25 11	22 58	00 25
41	09 17	01 14	24 28	22 04	29♒38
42	09 02	00 45	23 45	21 08	28 49
43	08 46	00 14	23 00	20 10	27 56
44	08 30	29♏43	22 13	19 09	26 59
45	08 14	29 11	21 25	18 05	25 58
46	07 57	28 38	20 36	16 59	24 53
47	07 40	28 05	19 45	15 49	23 42
48	07 23	27 31	18 53	14 36	22 26
49	07 06	26 55	17 58	13 20	21 03
50	06 48	26 19	17 02	12 00	19 33
51	06 29	25 42	16 04	10 35	17 55
52	06 10	25 04	15 04	09 07	16 08
53	05 51	24 25	14 02	07 34	14 10
54	05 31	23 45	12 57	05 56	12 01
55	05 11	23 03	11 50	04 13	09 38
56	04 50	22 20	10 41	02 25	07 00
57	04 29	21 36	09 29	00 31	04 06
58	04 07	20 51	08 14	28♐32	00 53
59	03 44	20 03	06 56	26 26	27♑19
60	03♏21	19♏15	05♐35	24♐14	23♑23

13h 8m 0s — 18 ♎ 26 — 197° 0' 0"

LAT.	11	12	ASC	2	3
0	19♏27	18♐02	15♑40	14♒32	15♓53
5	18 19	16 17	13 43	12 47	14 51
10	17 14	14 33	11 42	10 56	13 44
15	16 10	12 47	09 36	08 55	12 29
20	15 06	10 58	07 21	06 41	11 03
21	14 53	10 35	06 53	06 13	10 44
22	14 40	10 13	06 25	05 43	10 25
23	14 27	09 50	05 56	05 14	10 05
24	14 14	09 27	05 26	04 43	09 44
25	14 01	09 04	04 57	04 11	09 23
26	13 48	08 41	04 26	03 39	09 01
27	13 34	08 17	03 55	03 05	08 37
28	13 21	07 53	03 23	02 31	08 13
29	13 08	07 29	02 51	01 56	07 48
30	12 54	07 05	02 18	01 19	07 22
31	12 40	06 40	01 45	00 42	06 55
32	12 27	06 15	01 10	00 03	06 26
33	12 13	05 49	00 35	29♑23	05 56
34	11 59	05 23	29♐59	28 41	05 25
35	11 45	04 57	29 23	27 58	04 52
36	11 30	04 30	28 45	27 14	04 17
37	11 16	04 03	28 06	26 28	03 40
38	11 01	03 35	27 27	25 40	03 01
39	10 46	03 06	26 46	24 50	02 20
40	10 31	02 37	26 04	23 58	01 37
41	10 16	02 08	25 22	23 04	00 50
42	10 00	01 38	24 37	22 07	00 01
43	09 44	01 07	23 52	21 09	29♒08
44	09 28	00 36	23 05	20 07	28 11
45	09 12	00 04	22 17	19 03	27 11
46	08 55	29♏31	21 27	17 56	26 05
47	08 38	28 57	20 36	16 46	24 55
48	08 20	28 22	19 42	15 32	23 38
49	08 03	27 47	18 48	14 14	22 15
50	07 45	27 10	17 51	12 53	20 45
51	07 26	26 33	16 52	11 28	19 07
52	07 07	25 54	15 51	09 58	17 19
53	06 48	25 15	14 48	08 24	15 20
54	06 28	24 34	13 43	06 45	13 09
55	06 07	23 52	12 35	05 01	10 45
56	05 46	23 09	11 25	03 11	08 06
57	05 24	22 24	10 11	01 15	05 09
58	05 02	21 38	08 56	29♐13	01 52
59	04 39	20 50	07 37	27 05	28♑15
60	04♏16	20♏00	06♐15	24♐51	24♑14

13h 12m 0s — 19 ♎ 30 — 198° 0' 0"

LAT.	11	12	ASC	2	3
0	20♏26	18♐58	16♑36	15♒32	16♓57
5	19 19	17 13	14 39	13 48	15 57
10	18 13	15 29	12 39	11 57	14 50
15	17 09	13 42	10 32	09 57	13 36
20	16 05	11 53	08 18	07 43	12 11
21	15 52	11 31	07 50	07 15	11 53
22	15 39	11 09	07 21	06 46	11 34
23	15 26	10 46	06 52	06 16	11 14
24	15 13	10 23	06 23	05 45	10 53
25	15 00	10 00	05 53	05 14	10 32
26	14 47	09 37	05 22	04 41	10 10
27	14 33	09 13	04 51	04 08	09 47
28	14 20	08 49	04 20	03 33	09 23
29	14 07	08 25	03 47	02 58	08 58
30	13 53	08 00	03 14	02 22	08 32
31	13 39	07 35	02 40	01 44	08 05
32	13 25	07 10	02 06	01 05	07 37
33	13 11	06 44	01 31	00 25	07 07
34	12 57	06 18	00 55	29♑43	06 36
35	12 43	05 51	00 18	29 00	06 03
36	12 29	05 24	29♐40	28 15	05 29
37	12 14	04 57	29 01	27 29	04 52
38	11 59	04 29	28 21	26 41	04 13
39	11 44	04 00	27 40	25 50	03 32
40	11 29	03 31	26 58	24 58	02 49
41	11 14	03 02	26 15	24 04	02 03
42	10 58	02 31	25 30	23 07	01 14
43	10 42	02 00	24 45	22 08	00 21
44	10 26	01 29	23 57	21 06	29♒24
45	10 09	00 56	23 09	20 01	28 24
46	09 52	00 23	22 18	18 54	27 19
47	09 35	29♏49	21 26	17 43	26 08
48	09 18	29 14	20 33	16 28	24 52
49	09 00	28 38	19 37	15 10	23 28
50	08 41	28 01	18 40	13 48	21 58
51	08 23	27 24	17 40	12 21	20 19
52	08 04	26 45	16 39	10 51	18 30
53	07 44	26 05	15 35	09 15	16 31
54	07 24	25 24	14 29	07 34	14 19
55	07 03	24 41	13 20	05 48	11 54
56	06 42	23 57	12 09	03 57	09 12
57	06 20	23 12	10 54	01 59	06 13
58	05 57	22 25	09 37	29♐56	02 54
59	05 34	21 37	08 17	27 45	29♑13
60	05♏10	20♏46	06♐54	25♐29	25♑07

13h 16m 0s — 20 ♎ 34 — 199° 0' 0"

LAT.	11	12	ASC	2	3
0	21♏26	19♐53	17♑32	16♒33	18♓02
5	20 18	18 09	15 36	14 49	17 02
10	19 13	16 24	13 35	12 59	15 57
15	18 08	14 38	11 29	10 59	14 44
20	17 04	12 49	09 15	08 46	13 20
21	16 51	12 27	08 47	08 18	13 02
22	16 38	12 05	08 18	07 48	12 43
23	16 25	11 42	07 49	07 19	12 23
24	16 12	11 19	07 19	06 48	12 03
25	15 59	10 56	06 49	06 16	11 42
26	15 46	10 32	06 19	05 44	11 20
27	15 32	10 08	05 48	05 11	10 57
28	15 19	09 44	05 16	04 36	10 33
29	15 05	09 20	04 43	04 01	10 09
30	14 52	08 55	04 10	03 24	09 43
31	14 38	08 30	03 36	02 47	09 16
32	14 24	08 05	03 02	02 08	08 48
33	14 10	07 39	02 26	01 27	08 19
34	13 56	07 13	01 50	00 46	07 48
35	13 42	06 46	01 13	00 02	07 15
36	13 27	06 19	00 35	29♑17	06 41
37	13 12	05 51	29♐56	28 31	06 04
38	12 58	05 23	29 16	27 42	05 26
39	12 42	04 54	28 35	26 52	04 45
40	12 27	04 25	27 52	25 59	04 02
41	12 12	03 55	27 09	25 05	03 16
42	11 56	03 25	26 24	24 08	02 27
43	11 40	02 54	25 37	23 08	01 35
44	11 23	02 22	24 50	22 06	00 38
45	11 07	01 49	24 01	21 00	29♒38
46	10 50	01 15	23 10	19 52	28 33
47	10 32	00 41	22 17	18 40	27 22
48	10 15	00 06	21 23	17 25	26 06
49	09 57	29♏30	20 27	16 06	24 43
50	09 38	28 53	19 29	14 43	23 12
51	09 19	28 14	18 29	13 16	21 33
52	09 00	27 35	17 27	11 44	19 44
53	08 40	26 55	16 22	10 07	17 43
54	08 20	26 13	15 15	08 25	15 31
55	07 59	25 30	14 05	06 37	13 04
56	07 37	24 46	12 53	04 44	10 20
57	07 15	24 00	11 38	02 44	07 19
58	06 52	23 12	10 20	00 39	03 57
59	06 29	22 23	08 58	28♐26	00 12
60	06♏05	21♏32	07♐34	26♐07	26♑02

Koch Table of Houses for Latitudes 0° to 60° North

13h 20m 0s — 200° 0' 0" — 21 ♎ 38

LAT.	11	12	ASC	2	3
0	22♏25	20♐49	18♑28	17♒33	19♓07
5	21 17	19 05	16 32	15 51	18 08
10	20 12	17 20	14 32	14 01	17 04
15	19 07	15 34	12 26	12 01	15 51
20	18 03	13 45	10 12	09 49	14 29
21	17 50	13 23	09 44	09 21	14 10
22	17 37	13 00	09 15	08 51	13 52
23	17 24	12 38	08 46	08 22	13 32
24	17 11	12 15	08 16	07 51	13 12
25	16 58	11 51	07 46	07 20	12 51
26	16 45	11 28	07 16	06 47	12 30
27	16 31	11 04	06 44	06 14	12 07
28	16 18	10 40	06 13	05 39	11 44
29	16 04	10 15	05 40	05 04	11 20
30	15 50	09 51	05 07	04 28	10 54
31	15 37	09 26	04 33	03 50	10 28
32	15 23	09 00	03 58	03 11	10 00
33	15 09	08 34	03 22	02 30	09 30
34	14 54	08 08	02 46	01 49	09 00
35	14 40	07 41	02 09	01 05	08 27
36	14 26	07 14	01 30	00 20	07 53
37	14 11	06 46	00 51	29♑33	07 17
38	13 56	06 18	00 11	28 45	06 39
39	13 41	05 49	29♐29	27 54	05 59
40	13 25	05 19	28 47	27 01	05 16
41	13 10	04 49	28 03	26 06	04 30
42	12 54	04 18	27 17	25 09	03 41
43	12 37	03 47	26 31	24 09	02 49
44	12 21	03 15	25 43	23 06	01 53
45	12 04	02 42	24 53	22 00	00 53
46	11 47	02 08	24 02	20 51	29♒48
47	11 30	01 33	23 09	19 39	28 37
48	11 12	00 58	22 14	18 23	27 21
49	10 54	00 21	21 18	17 03	25 58
50	10 35	29♏44	20 19	15 39	24 27
51	10 16	29 05	19 18	14 11	22 47
52	09 56	28 26	18 15	12 37	20 58
53	09 36	27 45	17 09	10 59	18 57
54	09 16	27 03	16 02	09 16	16 30
55	08 55	26 19	14 51	07 27	14 15
56	08 33	25 34	13 38	05 31	11 30
57	08 11	24 48	12 21	03 30	08 26
58	07 48	24 00	11 02	01 22	05 01
59	07 24	23 10	09 39	29♐07	01 12
60	06♏59	22♏18	08♐14	26♐46	26♑58

13h 24m 0s — 201° 0' 0" — 22 ♎ 42

LAT.	11	12	ASC	2	3
0	23♏23	21♐44	19♑24	18♒34	20♓12
5	22 16	20 00	17 29	16 52	19 14
10	21 11	18 16	15 29	15 03	18 10
15	20 07	16 30	13 23	13 04	16 59
20	19 02	14 41	11 09	10 52	15 37
21	18 49	14 19	10 41	10 24	15 20
22	18 36	13 56	10 12	09 55	15 01
23	18 23	13 33	09 43	09 25	14 42
24	18 10	13 10	09 14	08 55	14 22
25	17 57	12 47	08 43	08 23	14 02
26	17 43	12 24	08 13	07 51	13 40
27	17 30	12 00	07 41	07 18	13 18
28	17 16	11 35	07 09	06 43	12 55
29	17 03	11 11	06 37	06 08	12 31
30	16 49	10 46	06 03	05 31	12 06
31	16 35	10 21	05 29	04 54	11 39
32	16 21	09 55	04 54	04 14	11 12
33	16 07	09 29	04 19	03 34	10 43
34	15 53	09 03	03 42	02 52	10 12
35	15 38	08 36	03 05	02 09	09 40
36	15 24	08 08	02 26	01 24	09 06
37	15 09	07 40	01 47	00 37	08 31
38	14 54	07 12	01 06	29♑48	07 53
39	14 39	06 43	00 24	28 57	07 13
40	14 23	06 13	29♐41	28 04	06 30
41	14 07	05 43	28 57	27 09	05 45
42	13 51	05 12	28 12	26 11	04 56
43	13 35	04 40	27 25	25 10	04 04
44	13 19	04 08	26 36	24 07	03 09
45	13 02	03 35	25 46	23 01	02 09
46	12 44	03 01	24 54	21 51	01 04
47	12 27	02 26	24 01	20 38	29♒53
48	12 09	01 50	23 06	19 22	28 37
49	11 51	01 13	22 08	18 01	27 14
50	11 32	00 35	21 09	16 36	25 43
51	11 13	29♏56	20 07	15 06	24 03
52	10 53	29 16	19 03	13 32	22 13
53	10 33	28 35	17 57	11 52	20 12
54	10 12	27 52	16 48	10 07	17 58
55	09 50	27 08	15 37	08 17	15 28
56	09 28	26 23	14 22	06 20	12 41
57	09 06	25 36	13 05	04 16	09 35
58	08 43	24 47	11 45	02 06	06 07
59	08 19	23 57	10 21	29♐49	02 15
60	07♏54	23♏04	08♐54	27♐25	27♑55

13h 28m 0s — 202° 0' 0" — 23 ♎ 46

LAT.	11	12	ASC	2	3
0	24♏22	22♐39	20♑20	19♒35	21♓17
5	23 15	20 56	18 25	17 54	20 20
10	22 10	19 12	16 26	16 05	19 17
15	21 05	17 26	14 21	14 07	18 07
20	20 01	15 37	12 06	11 56	16 47
21	19 48	15 15	11 38	11 28	16 29
22	19 35	14 52	11 10	10 59	16 11
23	19 22	14 29	10 41	10 29	15 52
24	19 09	14 06	10 11	09 59	15 32
25	18 55	13 43	09 41	09 27	15 12
26	18 42	13 19	09 10	08 55	14 51
27	18 29	12 55	08 39	08 22	14 29
28	18 15	12 31	08 07	07 47	14 06
29	18 01	12 07	07 34	07 12	13 42
30	17 48	11 42	07 00	06 36	13 17
31	17 34	11 16	06 26	05 58	12 51
32	17 20	10 51	05 51	05 19	12 24
33	17 06	10 24	05 15	04 38	11 55
34	16 51	09 58	04 39	03 56	11 25
35	16 37	09 31	04 01	03 13	10 53
36	16 22	09 03	03 22	02 27	10 20
37	16 07	08 35	02 42	01 40	09 45
38	15 52	08 07	02 02	00 51	09 07
39	15 37	07 37	01 20	00 00	08 28
40	15 21	07 08	00 36	29♑07	07 45
41	15 05	06 37	29♐52	28 12	07 00
42	14 49	06 06	29 06	27 14	06 12
43	14 33	05 34	28 19	26 13	05 20
44	14 16	05 01	27 30	25 09	04 25
45	13 59	04 28	26 39	24 02	03 25
46	13 42	03 54	25 47	22 52	02 21
47	13 24	03 18	24 53	21 38	01 11
48	13 06	02 42	23 57	20 21	29♒54
49	12 47	02 05	22 59	18 59	28 31
50	12 28	01 27	21 59	17 34	27 00
51	12 09	00 48	20 57	16 03	25 21
52	11 49	00 07	19 52	14 27	23 30
53	11 29	29♏25	18 45	12 47	21 29
54	11 08	28 42	17 36	11 00	19 13
55	10 46	27 58	16 23	09 08	16 43
56	10 24	27 11	15 08	07 09	13 54
57	10 01	26 24	13 49	05 03	10 46
58	09 38	25 35	12 28	02 51	07 15
59	09 13	24 44	11 02	00 32	03 19
60	08♏48	23♏51	09♐34	28♐05	28♑55

13h 32m 0s — 203° 0' 0" — 24 ♎ 50

LAT.	11	12	ASC	2	3
0	25♏21	23♐34	21♑17	20♒36	22♓23
5	24 14	21 51	19 22	18 56	21 26
10	23 09	20 08	17 23	17 08	20 24
15	22 04	18 22	15 18	15 11	19 15
20	21 00	16 33	13 04	13 00	17 56
21	20 47	16 11	12 36	12 32	17 38
22	20 34	15 48	12 07	12 03	17 20
23	20 21	15 25	11 38	11 33	17 02
24	20 07	15 02	11 09	11 03	16 43
25	19 54	14 39	10 38	10 32	16 22
26	19 41	14 15	10 08	10 00	16 02
27	19 27	13 51	09 36	09 26	15 40
28	19 14	13 27	09 04	08 52	15 17
29	19 00	13 02	08 31	08 17	14 54
30	18 46	12 37	07 58	07 40	14 29
31	18 32	12 12	07 23	07 03	14 04
32	18 18	11 46	06 48	06 24	13 37
33	18 04	11 20	06 12	05 43	13 08
34	17 50	10 53	05 35	05 01	12 39
35	17 35	10 26	04 58	04 17	12 07
36	17 20	09 58	04 19	03 32	11 34
37	17 05	09 30	03 39	02 45	10 59
38	16 50	09 01	02 58	01 56	10 22
39	16 35	08 32	02 15	01 05	09 43
40	16 19	08 02	01 32	00 11	09 01
41	16 03	07 31	00 47	29♑15	08 16
42	15 47	07 00	00 01	28 17	07 28
43	15 30	06 28	29♐13	27 16	06 37
44	15 14	05 55	28 24	26 12	05 42
45	14 56	05 21	27 33	25 04	04 42
46	14 39	04 47	26 40	23 54	03 38
47	14 21	04 11	25 46	22 39	02 29
48	14 03	03 35	24 49	21 21	01 13
49	13 44	02 57	23 51	19 59	29♒50
50	13 25	02 18	22 50	18 32	28 19
51	13 05	01 39	21 47	17 00	26 39
52	12 45	00 58	20 42	15 24	24 49
53	12 25	00 16	19 34	13 42	22 46
54	12 04	29♏32	18 23	11 54	20 30
55	11 42	28 47	17 10	09 59	17 59
56	11 19	28 00	15 53	07 59	15 09
57	10 56	27 12	14 34	05 51	11 58
58	10 32	26 22	13 11	03 37	08 25
59	10 08	25 30	11 44	01 15	04 24
60	09♏42	24♏37	10♐14	28♐45	29♑56

13h 36m 0s — 204° 0' 0" — 25 ♎ 53

LAT.	11	12	ASC	2	3
0	26♏19	24♐30	22♑13	21♒37	23♓28
5	25 12	22 47	20 19	19 58	22 32
10	24 07	21 04	18 21	18 11	21 32
15	23 03	19 18	16 16	16 14	20 24
20	21 58	17 29	14 02	14 04	19 05
21	21 45	17 07	13 34	13 36	18 48
22	21 32	16 44	13 05	13 08	18 30
23	21 19	16 21	12 36	12 38	18 12
24	21 06	15 58	12 07	12 08	17 53
25	20 53	15 35	11 36	11 37	17 33
26	20 39	15 11	11 06	11 05	17 13
27	20 26	14 47	10 34	10 32	16 51
28	20 12	14 23	10 02	09 57	16 29
29	19 58	13 58	09 29	09 22	16 06
30	19 45	13 33	08 55	08 46	15 42
31	19 31	13 07	08 21	08 08	15 16
32	19 17	12 42	07 46	07 29	14 50
33	19 02	12 15	07 10	06 48	14 22
34	18 48	11 48	06 33	06 06	13 52
35	18 33	11 21	05 55	05 23	13 21
36	18 18	10 53	05 16	04 37	12 49
37	18 03	10 25	04 35	03 50	12 14
38	17 48	09 56	03 54	03 01	11 37
39	17 33	09 27	03 12	02 09	10 58
40	17 17	08 56	02 28	01 16	10 17
41	17 01	08 26	01 43	00 20	09 33
42	16 44	07 54	00 56	29♑21	08 45
43	16 28	07 22	00 08	28 20	07 54
44	16 11	06 49	29♐18	27 15	07 00
45	15 54	06 15	28 27	26 07	06 01
46	15 36	05 40	27 34	24 56	04 57
47	15 18	05 04	26 39	23 41	03 47
48	15 00	04 27	25 42	22 22	02 32
49	14 41	03 49	24 43	20 59	01 09
50	14 22	03 10	23 41	19 32	29♒39
51	14 02	02 30	22 38	17 59	27 59
52	13 42	01 49	21 32	16 21	26 08
53	13 21	01 06	20 23	14 37	24 06
54	12 59	00 22	19 11	12 48	21 49
55	12 37	29♏36	17 57	10 52	19 16
56	12 15	28 49	16 39	08 49	16 25
57	11 51	28 00	15 18	06 40	13 13
58	11 27	27 10	13 54	04 23	09 36
59	11 02	26 17	12 27	01 58	05 32
60	10♏37	25♏23	10♐55	29♐26	00♒58

13h 40m 0s — 205° 0' 0" — 26 ♎ 57

LAT.	11	12	ASC	2	3
0	27♏17	25♐25	23♑10	22♒39	24♓33
5	26 11	23 43	21 17	21 00	23 39
10	25 06	22 00	19 19	19 14	22 39
15	24 01	20 14	17 14	17 18	21 40
20	22 57	18 25	15 00	15 09	20 15
21	22 44	18 03	14 32	14 41	19 58
22	22 31	17 40	14 04	14 13	19 41
23	22 18	17 17	13 34	13 43	19 23
24	22 04	16 54	13 05	13 13	19 04
25	21 51	16 31	12 35	12 42	18 44
26	21 38	16 07	12 04	12 10	18 24
27	21 24	15 43	11 32	11 37	18 03
28	21 11	15 19	11 00	11 03	17 41
29	20 57	14 54	10 27	10 28	17 18
30	20 43	14 29	09 53	09 52	16 54
31	20 29	14 03	09 19	09 14	16 29
32	20 15	13 37	08 44	08 35	16 03
33	20 00	13 11	08 07	07 54	15 36
34	19 46	12 44	07 30	07 12	15 07
35	19 31	12 17	06 52	06 29	14 36
36	19 16	11 49	06 13	05 43	14 04
37	19 01	11 20	05 32	04 56	13 29
38	18 46	10 51	04 51	04 07	12 53
39	18 30	10 21	04 08	03 15	12 15
40	18 15	09 51	03 24	02 21	11 34
41	17 58	09 20	02 39	01 25	10 50
42	17 42	08 48	01 52	00 26	10 03
43	17 25	08 16	01 03	29♑24	09 12
44	17 08	07 42	00 13	28 19	08 18
45	16 51	07 08	29♐21	27 11	07 20
46	16 33	06 33	28 28	26 00	06 16
47	16 15	05 57	27 32	24 44	05 07
48	15 57	05 20	26 35	23 25	03 52
49	15 38	04 42	25 35	22 01	02 30
50	15 18	04 02	24 33	20 32	00 59
51	14 58	03 22	23 29	18 58	29♒20
52	14 38	02 40	22 22	17 19	27 29
53	14 17	01 57	21 12	15 34	25 26
54	13 55	01 12	20 00	13 43	23 09
55	13 33	00 26	18 44	11 46	20 36
56	13 10	29♏38	17 26	09 41	17 43
57	12 46	28 49	16 04	07 29	14 29
58	12 22	27 58	14 38	05 10	10 49
59	11 57	27 05	13 09	02 43	06 42
60	11♏31	26♏09	11♐36	00♑08	02♒03

13h 44m 0s — 206° 0' 0" — 28 ♎ 00

LAT.	11	12	ASC	2	3
0	28♏15	26♐20	24♑06	23♒41	25♓38
5	27 09	24 38	22 14	22 03	24 45
10	26 04	22 55	20 16	20 18	23 46
15	25 00	21 10	18 12	18 23	22 48
20	23 55	19 22	15 59	16 14	21 25
21	23 42	18 59	15 31	15 47	21 08
22	23 29	18 37	15 02	15 18	20 51
23	23 16	18 14	14 33	14 49	20 33
24	23 03	17 50	14 03	14 19	20 15
25	22 50	17 27	13 33	13 48	19 56
26	22 36	17 03	13 02	13 16	19 36
27	22 23	16 39	12 31	12 43	19 15
28	22 09	16 15	11 58	12 09	18 54
29	21 55	15 50	11 25	11 34	18 31
30	21 41	15 25	10 52	10 58	18 07
31	21 27	14 59	10 17	10 20	17 43
32	21 13	14 33	09 42	09 41	17 17
33	20 59	14 07	09 05	09 01	16 50
34	20 44	13 40	08 28	08 19	16 21
35	20 29	13 12	07 50	07 35	15 51
36	20 14	12 44	07 10	06 50	15 19
37	19 59	12 15	06 30	06 02	14 45
38	19 44	11 46	05 48	05 13	14 10
39	19 28	11 16	05 05	04 21	13 31
40	19 12	10 46	04 21	03 28	12 51
41	18 56	10 15	03 35	02 31	12 08
42	18 40	09 43	02 48	01 32	11 21
43	18 23	09 10	01 59	00 30	10 31
44	18 06	08 36	01 09	29♑25	09 38
45	17 48	08 02	00 16	28 16	08 39
46	17 30	07 26	29♐22	27 04	07 36
47	17 12	06 50	28 26	25 48	06 28
48	16 53	06 12	27 28	24 28	05 13
49	16 34	05 34	26 28	23 03	03 51
50	16 15	04 54	25 25	21 33	02 21
51	15 55	04 13	24 20	19 58	00 42
52	15 34	03 31	23 12	18 18	28♒52
53	15 13	02 47	22 02	16 32	26 49
54	14 51	02 02	20 48	14 39	24 31
55	14 29	01 16	19 32	12 40	21 57
56	14 05	00 27	18 12	10 34	19 03
57	13 41	29♏37	16 49	08 20	15 47
58	13 17	28 46	15 22	05 58	12 05
59	12 51	27 52	13 52	03 28	07 53
60	12♏25	26♏56	12♐18	00♑50	03♒10

13h 48m 0s — 207° 0' 0" — 29 ♎ 03

LAT.	11	12	ASC	2	3
0	29♏13	27♐15	25♑03	24♒42	26♓44
5	28 07	25 34	23 11	23 06	25 51
10	27 02	23 51	21 13	21 22	24 54
15	25 58	22 07	19 11	19 28	23 49
20	24 54	20 18	16 57	17 20	22 35
21	24 41	19 55	16 29	16 52	22 19
22	24 28	19 33	16 01	16 24	22 02
23	24 14	19 10	15 32	15 55	21 44
24	24 01	18 47	15 02	15 25	21 26
25	23 48	18 23	14 32	14 54	21 07
26	23 34	17 59	14 01	14 23	20 48
27	23 21	17 35	13 30	13 50	20 27
28	23 07	17 11	12 57	13 16	20 06
29	22 53	16 46	12 24	12 41	19 44
30	22 39	16 21	11 50	12 05	19 21
31	22 25	15 55	11 16	11 27	18 56
32	22 11	15 29	10 40	10 48	18 31
33	21 57	15 02	10 04	10 08	18 04
34	21 42	14 35	09 26	09 26	17 36
35	21 27	14 08	08 48	08 43	17 06
36	21 12	13 39	08 08	07 57	16 35
37	20 57	13 11	07 28	07 10	16 02
38	20 42	12 41	06 46	06 20	15 26
39	20 26	12 11	06 03	05 29	14 49
40	20 10	11 41	05 18	04 34	14 09
41	19 54	11 09	04 32	03 38	13 26
42	19 37	10 37	03 44	02 38	12 40
43	19 20	10 04	02 55	01 36	11 51
44	19 03	09 30	02 04	00 31	10 57
45	18 45	08 56	01 12	29♑22	10 00
46	18 27	08 20	00 17	28 09	08 58
47	18 09	07 43	29♐21	26 52	07 50
48	17 50	07 05	28 22	25 32	06 35
49	17 31	06 27	27 21	24 06	05 14
50	17 11	05 46	26 18	22 36	03 44
51	16 51	05 05	25 12	21 00	02 05
52	16 30	04 23	24 03	19 18	00 15
53	16 09	03 38	22 52	17 31	28♒12
54	15 47	02 53	21 38	15 37	25 55
55	15 24	02 06	20 20	13 35	23 20
56	15 01	01 17	18 59	11 27	20 25
57	14 36	00 26	17 35	09 11	17 07
58	14 11	29♏34	16 07	06 47	13 22
59	13 46	28 39	14 35	04 14	09 07
60	13♏19	27♏42	12♐59	01♑33	04♒19

Koch Table of Houses for Latitudes 0° to 60° North

13h 52m 0s — 208° 0' 0" — 00 ♏ 06

LAT.	11	12	ASC	2	3
0	00♐11	28♐10	26♑00	25♒44	27♓49
5	29♏05	26 29	24 09	24 09	26 58
10	28 00	24 47	22 13	22 26	26 01
15	26 56	23 03	20 09	20 33	24 58
20	25 52	21 14	17 56	18 26	23 45
21	25 39	20 52	17 29	17 58	23 29
22	25 26	20 29	17 00	17 30	23 12
23	25 13	20 06	16 31	17 02	22 55
24	24 59	19 43	16 01	16 32	22 37
25	24 46	19 20	15 31	16 01	22 19
26	24 33	18 56	15 00	15 30	22 00
27	24 19	18 32	14 29	14 57	21 40
28	24 05	18 07	13 56	14 23	21 19
29	23 52	17 42	13 23	13 48	20 57
30	23 38	17 17	12 49	13 12	20 34
31	23 23	16 51	12 15	12 35	20 10
32	23 09	16 25	11 39	11 56	19 45
33	22 55	15 58	11 03	11 16	19 19
34	22 40	15 31	10 25	10 34	18 51
35	22 25	15 03	09 46	09 50	18 22
36	22 10	14 35	09 07	09 05	17 51
37	21 55	14 06	08 26	08 18	17 18
38	21 39	13 37	07 44	07 28	16 44
39	21 24	13 07	07 00	06 36	16 07
40	21 08	12 36	06 16	05 42	15 27
41	20 51	12 04	05 29	04 46	14 45
42	20 35	11 32	04 41	03 46	13 59
43	20 18	10 59	03 52	02 43	13 11
44	20 00	10 25	03 01	01 38	12 18
45	19 43	09 50	02 08	00 28	11 21
46	19 24	09 14	01 13	29♑15	10 20
47	19 06	08 37	00 16	27 58	09 12
48	18 47	07 59	29♐16	26 36	07 59
49	18 28	07 19	28 15	25 10	06 38
50	18 08	06 39	27 11	23 39	05 09
51	17 47	05 57	26 04	22 02	03 30
52	17 26	05 14	24 55	20 19	01 40
53	17 05	04 30	23 43	18 31	29♒38
54	16 42	03 43	22 27	16 35	27 20
55	16 19	02 56	21 09	14 32	24 45
56	15 56	02 06	19 47	12 22	21 49
57	15 31	01 15	18 21	10 03	18 29
58	15 06	00 22	16 52	07 36	14 42
59	14 40	29♏26	15 19	05 01	10 23
60	14♏13	28♏29	13♐41	02♑17	05♒30

13h 56m 0s — 209° 0' 0" — 01 ♏ 08

LAT.	11	12	ASC	2	3
0	01♐08	29♐05	26♑57	26♒47	28♓55
5	00 03	27 25	25 07	25 12	28 04
10	28♏58	25 43	23 11	23 30	27 09
15	27 55	23 59	21 08	21 38	26 07
20	26 50	22 11	18 56	19 32	24 55
21	26 37	21 48	18 28	19 05	24 40
22	26 24	21 26	17 59	18 37	24 23
23	26 11	21 03	17 30	18 08	24 07
24	25 58	20 39	17 01	17 39	23 49
25	25 44	20 16	16 31	17 08	23 31
26	25 31	19 52	16 00	16 37	23 12
27	25 17	19 28	15 28	16 05	22 52
28	25 04	19 03	14 56	15 31	22 32
29	24 50	18 38	14 23	14 56	22 11
30	24 36	18 13	13 49	14 20	21 48
31	24 22	17 47	13 14	13 43	21 25
32	24 07	17 21	12 38	13 05	21 00
33	23 53	16 54	12 02	12 24	20 34
34	23 38	16 27	11 24	11 43	20 07
35	23 23	15 59	10 45	10 59	19 38
36	23 08	15 31	10 06	10 14	19 08
37	22 53	15 02	09 25	09 26	18 36
38	22 37	14 32	08 42	08 37	18 01
39	22 21	14 02	07 59	07 45	17 25
40	22 05	13 31	07 14	06 51	16 46
41	21 49	12 59	06 27	05 54	16 04
42	21 32	12 27	05 39	04 54	15 20
43	21 15	11 53	04 49	03 52	14 31
44	20 57	11 19	03 58	02 45	13 40
45	20 40	10 44	03 04	01 36	12 43
46	20 21	10 08	02 09	00 22	11 42
47	20 03	09 30	01 11	29♑05	10 36
48	19 44	08 52	00 11	27 43	09 23
49	19 24	08 12	29♐09	26 16	08 03
50	19 04	07 31	28 05	24 43	06 34
51	18 43	06 49	26 57	23 06	04 56
52	18 22	06 06	25 47	21 22	03 07
53	18 01	05 21	24 34	19 31	01 04
54	17 38	04 34	23 18	17 34	28♒47
55	17 15	03 46	21 58	15 30	26 11
56	16 51	02 56	20 35	13 17	23 15
57	16 26	02 04	19 08	10 56	19 54
58	16 01	01 10	17 37	08 27	16 04
59	15 34	00 14	16 02	05 49	11 42
60	15♏07	29♏15	14♐23	03♑02	06♒43

14h 0m 0s — 210° 0' 0" — 02 ♏ 11

LAT.	11	12	ASC	2	3
0	02♐05	00♑00	27♑55	27♒49	00♈00
5	01 00	28♐20	26 05	26 16	29♓11
10	29♏56	26 39	24 10	24 35	28 17
15	28 53	24 55	22 08	22 44	27 16
20	27 48	23 07	19 55	20 39	26 06
21	27 35	22 45	19 28	20 12	25 50
22	27 22	22 22	18 59	19 44	25 34
23	27 09	21 59	18 30	19 16	25 18
24	26 56	21 36	18 01	18 46	25 01
25	26 42	21 13	17 30	18 16	24 43
26	26 29	20 49	17 00	17 45	24 25
27	26 15	20 24	16 28	17 13	24 05
28	26 02	20 00	15 56	16 39	23 45
29	25 48	19 35	15 23	16 05	23 24
30	25 34	19 10	14 49	15 29	23 02
31	25 19	18 44	14 14	14 52	22 39
32	25 05	18 17	13 38	14 13	22 15
33	24 51	17 51	13 01	13 33	21 50
34	24 36	17 23	12 24	12 52	21 23
35	24 21	16 55	11 45	12 08	20 55
36	24 06	16 27	11 05	11 23	20 25
37	23 50	15 58	10 24	10 36	19 53
38	23 35	15 28	09 41	09 46	19 19
39	23 19	14 58	08 58	08 55	18 44
40	23 03	14 26	08 12	08 00	18 05
41	22 46	13 54	07 25	07 03	17 24
42	22 29	13 22	06 37	06 03	16 40
43	22 12	12 48	05 47	05 01	15 53
44	21 55	12 14	04 55	03 54	15 02
45	21 37	11 38	04 01	02 44	14 06
46	21 18	11 02	03 05	01 30	13 06
47	21 00	10 24	02 07	00 12	12 00
48	20 40	09 45	01 07	28♑50	10 48
49	20 21	09 05	00 04	27 22	09 28
50	20 00	08 24	28♐59	25 49	08 01
51	19 40	07 42	27 51	24 10	06 23
52	19 18	06 58	26 40	22 25	04 34
53	18 56	06 12	25 26	20 34	02 32
54	18 34	05 25	24 08	18 35	00 15
55	18 10	04 36	22 48	16 28	27♒39
56	17 46	03 46	21 23	14 14	24 42
57	17 21	02 53	19 55	11 51	21 20
58	16 55	01 58	18 23	09 19	17 28
59	16 28	01 01	16 47	06 38	13 03
60	16♏01	00♐02	15♐06	03♑47	07♒59

14h 4m 0s — 211° 0' 0" — 03 ♏ 13

LAT.	11	12	ASC	2	3
0	03♐03	00♑55	28♑52	28♒52	01♈05
5	01 58	29♐16	27 03	27 19	00 17
10	00 54	27 35	25 09	25 39	29♓24
15	29♏51	25 52	23 07	23 49	28 25
20	28 46	24 04	20 55	21 46	27 16
21	28 33	23 41	20 28	21 19	27 01
22	28 20	23 19	19 59	20 52	26 46
23	28 07	22 56	19 30	20 24	26 29
24	27 54	22 33	19 01	19 54	26 13
25	27 40	22 09	18 31	19 24	25 55
26	27 27	21 45	18 00	18 53	25 37
27	27 13	21 21	17 28	18 21	25 18
28	27 00	20 57	16 56	17 48	24 59
29	26 46	20 31	16 23	17 14	24 38
30	26 32	20 06	15 49	16 38	24 17
31	26 17	19 40	15 14	16 01	23 54
32	26 03	19 14	14 38	15 23	23 30
33	25 48	18 47	14 02	14 43	23 05
34	25 34	18 19	13 24	14 02	22 39
35	25 19	17 52	12 45	13 18	22 11
36	25 04	17 23	12 05	12 33	21 42
37	24 48	16 54	11 23	11 46	21 11
38	24 32	16 24	10 41	10 56	20 38
39	24 16	15 53	09 57	10 05	20 03
40	24 00	15 22	09 11	09 10	19 25
41	23 44	14 50	08 24	08 14	18 45
42	23 27	14 17	07 36	07 14	18 01
43	23 09	13 43	06 45	06 11	17 15
44	22 52	13 08	05 53	05 04	16 24
45	22 34	12 33	04 59	03 54	15 30
46	22 15	11 56	04 02	02 40	14 30
47	21 56	11 18	03 04	01 21	13 25
48	21 37	10 39	02 03	29♑58	12 14
49	21 17	09 59	00 59	28 29	10 55
50	20 57	09 17	29♐53	26 56	09 28
51	20 36	08 34	28 45	25 16	07 52
52	20 14	07 50	27 33	23 30	06 04
53	19 52	07 04	26 18	21 37	04 02
54	19 29	06 16	24 59	19 37	01 45
55	19 06	05 27	23 38	17 28	29♒10
56	18 41	04 36	22 12	15 12	26 12
57	18 16	03 42	20 43	12 46	22 49
58	17 50	02 47	19 09	10 12	18 55
59	17 23	01 49	17 31	07 27	14 26
60	16♏55	00♐49	15♐49	04♑33	09♒17

14h 8m 0s — 212° 0' 0" — 04 ♏ 16

LAT.	11	12	ASC	2	3
0	04♐00	01♑50	29♑49	29♒54	02♈11
5	02 55	00 12	28 01	28 23	01 24
10	01 52	28♐31	26 08	26 45	00 32
15	00 48	26 48	24 07	24 56	29♓34
20	29♏44	25 00	21 56	22 53	28 27
21	29 31	24 38	21 28	22 27	28 12
22	29 18	24 15	21 00	22 00	27 57
23	29 05	23 53	20 31	21 32	27 41
24	28 52	23 29	20 01	21 03	27 25
25	28 38	23 06	19 31	20 33	27 08
26	28 25	22 42	19 00	20 02	26 50
27	28 11	22 18	18 29	19 30	26 32
28	27 57	21 53	17 57	18 58	26 12
29	27 44	21 28	17 23	18 23	25 52
30	27 30	21 03	16 50	17 48	25 31
31	27 15	20 37	16 15	17 11	25 09
32	27 01	20 10	15 39	16 33	24 46
33	26 46	19 43	15 02	15 53	24 21
34	26 32	19 16	14 24	15 12	23 56
35	26 16	18 48	13 45	14 29	23 29
36	26 01	18 19	13 05	13 44	23 00
37	25 46	17 50	12 24	12 57	22 29
38	25 30	17 20	11 41	12 07	21 57
39	25 14	16 49	10 57	11 16	21 22
40	24 58	16 18	10 11	10 22	20 45
41	24 41	15 45	09 24	09 25	20 06
42	24 24	15 12	08 35	08 25	19 23
43	24 07	14 38	07 44	07 21	18 37
44	23 49	14 03	06 51	06 15	17 48
45	23 31	13 27	05 57	05 04	16 54
46	23 12	12 50	05 00	03 50	15 55
47	22 53	12 12	04 01	02 31	14 51
48	22 34	11 33	02 59	01 07	13 41
49	22 14	10 52	01 55	29♑38	12 23
50	21 53	10 10	00 49	28 04	10 57
51	21 32	09 27	29♐39	26 23	09 21
52	21 10	08 42	28 26	24 36	07 34
53	20 48	07 56	27 11	22 41	05 33
54	20 25	07 08	25 51	20 39	03 17
55	20 01	06 18	24 28	18 29	00 42
56	19 36	05 26	23 02	16 11	27♒44
57	19 11	04 32	21 31	13 43	24 20
58	18 44	03 36	19 56	11 06	20 24
59	18 17	02 37	18 16	08 18	15 52
60	17♏48	01♐36	16♐32	05♑21	10♒39

14h 12m 0s — 213° 0' 0" — 05 ♏ 18

LAT.	11	12	ASC	2	3
0	04♐57	02♑45	00♒47	00♓57	03♈16
5	03 52	01 07	29♑00	29♒27	02 30
10	02 49	29♐28	27 07	27 50	01 40
15	01 46	27 45	25 07	26 02	00 43
20	00 42	25 57	22 56	24 01	29♓38
21	00 29	25 35	22 28	23 35	29 23
22	00 16	25 12	22 00	23 08	29 08
23	00 03	24 49	21 31	22 40	28 53
24	29♏50	24 26	21 02	22 12	28 37
25	29 36	24 03	20 32	21 42	28 20
26	29 23	23 39	20 01	21 12	28 03
27	29 09	23 15	19 30	20 40	27 45
28	28 55	22 50	18 58	20 07	27 26
29	28 41	22 25	18 24	19 34	27 07
30	28 27	22 00	17 51	18 58	26 46
31	28 13	21 34	17 16	18 22	26 24
32	27 59	21 07	16 40	17 44	26 02
33	27 44	20 40	16 03	17 04	25 38
34	27 29	20 13	15 25	16 23	25 13
35	27 14	19 44	14 46	15 40	24 46
36	26 59	19 16	14 06	14 55	24 18
37	26 43	18 46	13 24	14 08	23 48
38	26 28	18 16	12 41	13 19	23 16
39	26 11	17 45	11 57	12 28	22 42
40	25 55	17 14	11 11	11 34	22 06
41	25 38	16 41	10 23	10 37	21 27
42	25 21	16 08	09 34	09 37	20 45
43	25 04	15 34	08 43	08 33	20 00
44	24 46	14 59	07 50	07 27	19 12
45	24 28	14 22	06 55	06 16	18 19
46	24 09	13 45	05 58	05 01	17 21
47	23 50	13 07	04 58	03 42	16 18
48	23 30	12 27	03 56	02 18	15 08
49	23 10	11 46	02 52	00 48	13 52
50	22 50	11 04	01 44	29♑13	12 27
51	22 28	10 20	00 34	27 31	10 52
52	22 06	09 35	29♐21	25 43	09 06
53	21 44	08 48	28 04	23 47	07 06
54	21 20	07 59	26 44	21 44	04 50
55	20 56	07 09	25 20	19 32	02 16
56	20 31	06 16	23 52	17 11	29♒18
57	20 06	05 21	22 20	14 41	25 53
58	19 39	04 24	20 43	12 01	21 56
59	19 11	03 25	19 02	09 10	17 21
60	18♏42	02♐23	17♐16	06♑09	12♒03

14h 16m 0s — 214° 0' 0" — 06 ♏ 19

LAT.	11	12	ASC	2	3
0	05♐54	03♑40	01♒45	02♓00	04♈22
5	04 50	02 03	29♑59	00 32	03 37
10	03 47	00 24	28 07	28♒56	02 48
15	02 44	28♐41	26 07	27 09	01 52
20	01 40	26 54	23 57	25 10	00 48
21	01 27	26 32	23 29	24 44	00 34
22	01 14	26 09	23 01	24 17	00 20
23	01 01	25 46	22 33	23 49	00 05
24	00 47	25 23	22 03	23 21	29♓49
25	00 34	25 00	21 33	22 52	29 33
26	00 21	24 36	21 03	22 22	29 16
27	00 07	24 12	20 31	21 50	28 59
28	29♏53	23 47	19 59	21 18	28 40
29	29 39	23 22	19 26	20 44	28 21
30	29 25	22 57	18 52	20 09	28 01
31	29 11	22 31	18 17	19 33	27 40
32	28 56	22 04	17 41	18 55	27 18
33	28 42	21 37	17 04	18 16	26 54
34	28 27	21 09	16 26	17 35	26 30
35	28 12	20 41	15 47	16 52	26 04
36	27 57	20 12	15 07	16 08	25 36
37	27 41	19 43	14 25	15 21	25 07
38	27 25	19 13	13 42	14 32	24 36
39	27 09	18 42	12 58	13 40	24 03
40	26 52	18 10	12 12	12 46	23 27
41	26 36	17 37	11 24	11 49	22 49
42	26 18	17 04	10 34	10 49	22 08
43	26 01	16 29	09 43	09 46	21 24
44	25 43	15 54	08 50	08 39	20 36
45	25 25	15 18	07 54	07 29	19 44
46	25 06	14 40	06 57	06 13	18 47
47	24 47	14 01	05 57	04 54	17 45
48	24 27	13 21	04 54	03 29	16 37
49	24 07	12 40	03 49	01 59	15 22
50	23 46	11 57	02 41	00 23	13 58
51	23 24	11 13	01 30	28♑41	12 24
52	23 02	10 28	00 16	26 51	10 39
53	22 39	09 40	28♐58	24 54	08 40
54	22 16	08 51	27 37	22 49	06 26
55	21 52	08 00	26 11	20 36	03 51
56	21 26	07 07	24 42	18 13	00 54
57	21 00	06 11	23 09	15 40	27♒29
58	20 33	05 14	21 31	12 57	23 31
59	20 05	04 13	19 48	10 03	18 53
60	19♏36	03♐11	18♐00	06♑59	13♒30

14h 20m 0s — 215° 0' 0" — 07 ♏ 21

LAT.	11	12	ASC	2	3
0	06♐50	04♑35	02♒43	03♓03	05♈27
5	05 47	02 59	00 58	01 36	04 43
10	04 44	01 20	29♑06	00 01	03 55
15	03 41	29♐38	27 07	28♒17	03 01
20	02 38	27 51	24 58	26 18	01 59
21	02 25	27 29	24 31	25 53	01 46
22	02 12	27 06	24 03	25 26	01 32
23	01 58	26 44	23 34	24 59	01 17
24	01 45	26 21	23 05	24 31	01 02
25	01 32	25 57	22 35	24 02	00 46
26	01 18	25 33	22 04	23 32	00 29
27	01 05	25 09	21 33	23 01	00 12
28	00 51	24 44	21 01	22 29	29♓54
29	00 37	24 19	20 28	21 55	29 36
30	00 23	23 54	19 54	21 21	29 16
31	00 09	23 28	19 19	20 45	28 55
32	29♏54	23 01	18 43	20 07	28 34
33	29 40	22 34	18 06	19 28	28 11
34	29 25	22 06	17 28	18 48	27 47
35	29 10	21 38	16 49	18 05	27 22
36	28 54	21 09	16 09	17 21	26 55
37	28 38	20 40	15 27	16 34	26 26
38	28 23	20 09	14 44	15 45	25 56
39	28 06	19 38	13 59	14 54	25 23
40	27 50	19 06	13 13	14 00	24 49
41	27 33	18 34	12 25	13 03	24 11
42	27 16	18 00	11 35	12 03	23 31
43	26 58	17 25	10 44	11 00	22 48
44	26 40	16 50	09 50	09 53	22 01
45	26 22	16 13	08 54	08 42	21 10
46	26 03	15 35	07 56	07 27	20 15
47	25 43	14 56	06 56	06 07	19 14
48	25 24	14 16	05 53	04 42	18 07
49	25 03	13 34	04 47	03 11	16 52
50	24 42	12 51	03 38	01 35	15 30
51	24 21	12 07	02 26	29♑52	13 57
52	23 58	11 21	01 11	28 01	12 14
53	23 35	10 33	29♐53	26 03	10 16
54	23 11	09 43	28 30	23 57	08 02
55	22 47	08 51	27 04	21 41	05 29
56	22 21	07 57	25 33	19 16	02 32
57	21 55	07 01	23 58	16 41	29♒07
58	21 28	06 03	22 19	13 55	25 08
59	20 59	05 02	20 35	10 58	20 28
60	20♏29	03♐58	18♐45	07♑49	15♒00

Koch Table of Houses for Latitudes 0° to 60° North

LAT.	14h 24m 0s — 08 ♏ 23 — 216° 0' 0" 11	12	ASC	2	3
0	07♐47	05♑30	03♒41	04♓07	06♈32
5	06 44	03 54	01 57	02 41	05 50
10	05 41	02 16	00 06	01 07	05 03
15	04 39	00 35	28♑08	29♒24	04 11
20	03 35	28♐48	26 00	27 27	03 10
21	03 22	28 26	25 32	27 02	02 57
22	03 09	28 04	25 04	26 36	02 43
23	02 56	27 41	24 36	26 09	02 29
24	02 43	27 18	24 07	25 41	02 14
25	02 30	26 54	23 37	25 12	01 59
26	02 16	26 31	23 06	24 43	01 43
27	02 02	26 06	22 35	24 12	01 26
28	01 49	25 42	22 03	23 40	01 09
29	01 35	25 17	21 30	23 07	00 50
30	01 21	24 51	20 56	22 33	00 31
31	01 06	24 25	20 21	21 57	00 11
32	00 52	23 58	19 46	21 20	29♓50
33	00 37	23 31	19 09	20 41	29 28
34	00 22	23 04	18 31	20 01	29 04
35	00 07	22 35	17 52	19 19	28 40
36	29♏52	22 06	17 11	18 34	28 13
37	29 36	21 37	16 29	17 48	27 46
38	29 20	21 06	15 46	16 59	27 16
39	29 04	20 35	15 01	16 08	26 44
40	28 47	20 03	14 15	15 15	26 10
41	28 30	19 30	13 27	14 18	25 34
42	28 13	18 56	12 37	13 18	24 55
43	27 55	18 22	11 45	12 15	24 13
44	27 37	17 46	10 51	11 08	23 27
45	27 19	17 09	09 55	09 57	22 37
46	27 00	16 31	08 56	08 42	21 42
47	26 40	15 51	07 55	07 22	20 43
48	26 20	15 11	06 52	05 56	19 37
49	26 00	14 29	05 45	04 25	18 24
50	25 38	13 45	04 36	02 48	17 03
51	25 17	13 00	03 23	01 04	15 32
52	24 54	12 14	02 07	29♑12	13 49
53	24 31	11 25	00 48	27 13	11 53
54	24 07	10 35	29♐24	25 05	09 41
55	23 42	09 43	27 57	22 48	07 09
56	23 16	08 48	26 25	20 21	04 13
57	22 50	07 51	24 49	17 43	00 48
58	22 22	06 52	23 08	14 54	26♒48
59	21 53	05 50	21 22	11 53	22 05
60	21♏23	04♐46	19♐30	08♑41	16♒34

LAT.	14h 28m 0s — 09 ♏ 24 — 217° 0' 0" 11	12	ASC	2	3
0	08♐43	06♑26	04♒39	05♓10	07♈37
5	07 41	04 50	02 56	03 46	06 56
10	06 38	03 13	01 07	02 14	06 11
15	05 36	01 32	29♑09	00 32	05 20
20	04 33	29♐45	27 01	28♒37	04 21
21	04 20	29 23	26 34	28 12	04 08
22	04 07	29 01	26 06	27 46	03 55
23	03 54	28 38	25 38	27 19	03 41
24	03 41	28 15	25 09	26 52	03 27
25	03 27	27 52	24 39	26 23	03 12
26	03 14	27 28	24 09	25 54	02 56
27	03 00	27 04	23 38	25 24	02 40
28	02 46	26 39	23 06	24 52	02 23
29	02 32	26 14	22 33	24 19	02 05
30	02 18	25 49	21 59	23 45	01 47
31	02 04	25 23	21 24	23 10	01 27
32	01 50	24 56	20 48	22 33	01 07
33	01 35	24 29	20 12	21 55	00 45
34	01 20	24 01	19 34	21 15	00 22
35	01 05	23 33	18 54	20 33	29♓58
36	00 49	23 04	18 14	19 49	29 33
37	00 34	22 34	17 32	19 03	29 05
38	00 18	22 03	16 49	18 15	28 37
39	00 01	21 32	16 04	17 24	28 06
40	29♏45	21 00	15 17	16 30	27 33
41	29 28	20 27	14 29	15 34	26 57
42	29 10	19 53	13 39	14 34	26 19
43	28 52	19 18	12 47	13 31	25 38
44	28 34	18 42	11 52	12 24	24 53
45	28 16	18 05	10 56	11 13	24 04
46	27 57	17 26	09 57	09 58	23 11
47	27 37	16 47	08 56	08 37	22 12
48	27 17	16 06	07 52	07 12	21 08
49	26 56	15 24	06 45	05 40	19 56
50	26 35	14 40	05 34	04 02	18 37
51	26 13	13 54	04 21	02 18	17 07
52	25 50	13 07	03 04	00 25	15 26
53	25 27	12 18	01 44	28♑25	13 32
54	25 02	11 28	00 19	26 15	11 21
55	24 37	10 35	28♐51	23 56	08 50
56	24 11	09 39	27 18	21 27	05 55
57	23 44	08 42	25 40	18 46	02 31
58	23 16	07 42	23 57	15 54	28♒30
59	22 47	06 39	22 09	12 50	23 46
60	22♏17	05♐34	20♐16	09♑34	18♒11

LAT.	14h 32m 0s — 10 ♏ 25 — 218° 0' 0" 11	12	ASC	2	3
0	09♐40	07♑21	05♒38	06♓14	08♈43
5	08 37	05 46	03 55	04 51	08 03
10	07 36	04 09	02 07	03 20	07 19
15	06 34	02 29	00 11	01 40	06 29
20	05 30	00 43	28♑03	29♒46	05 32
21	05 17	00 21	27 36	29 22	05 20
22	05 04	29♐59	27 09	28 56	05 07
23	04 51	29 36	26 41	28 30	04 53
24	04 38	29 13	26 12	28 03	04 39
25	04 25	28 50	25 42	27 35	04 25
26	04 11	28 26	25 12	27 06	04 10
27	03 58	28 02	24 41	26 36	03 54
28	03 44	27 37	24 09	26 05	03 37
29	03 30	27 12	23 36	25 32	03 20
30	03 16	26 46	23 02	24 59	03 02
31	03 02	26 20	22 28	24 24	02 43
32	02 47	25 54	21 52	23 47	02 23
33	02 32	25 27	21 15	23 09	02 02
34	02 17	24 59	20 37	22 29	01 40
35	02 02	24 30	19 58	21 48	01 17
36	01 47	24 01	19 17	21 04	00 52
37	01 31	23 31	18 35	20 18	00 25
38	01 15	23 01	17 52	19 30	29♓57
39	00 59	22 29	17 07	18 40	29 27
40	00 42	21 57	16 20	17 47	28 55
41	00 25	21 24	15 32	16 50	28 21
42	00 07	20 50	14 41	15 51	27 43
43	29♏50	20 15	13 49	14 48	27 03
44	29 31	19 38	12 55	13 41	26 19
45	29 13	19 01	11 58	12 30	25 32
46	28 53	18 22	10 58	11 15	24 40
47	28 34	17 43	09 57	09 54	23 43
48	28 13	17 01	08 52	08 28	22 40
49	27 53	16 19	07 44	06 57	21 29
50	27 31	15 35	06 34	05 18	20 11
51	27 09	14 49	05 20	03 33	18 44
52	26 46	14 01	04 02	01 40	17 05
53	26 22	13 12	02 41	29♑38	15 12
54	25 58	12 20	01 15	27 27	13 03
55	25 33	11 27	29♐45	25 06	10 33
56	25 06	10 31	28 11	22 35	07 40
57	24 39	09 33	26 31	19 52	04 16
58	24 11	08 32	24 47	16 57	00 16
59	23 41	07 28	22 57	13 49	25♒30
60	23♏10	06♐22	21♐02	10♑29	19♒51

LAT.	14h 36m 0s — 11 ♏ 26 — 219° 0' 0" 11	12	ASC	2	3
0	10♐36	08♑16	06♒37	07♓18	09♈48
5	09 34	06 42	04 55	05 56	09 09
10	08 33	05 06	03 08	04 27	08 26
15	07 31	03 26	01 12	02 48	07 39
20	06 28	01 40	29♑06	00 56	06 43
21	06 15	01 18	28 39	00 32	06 31
22	06 02	00 56	28 12	00 07	06 19
23	05 49	00 34	27 44	29♒41	06 06
24	05 36	00 11	27 15	29 14	05 52
25	05 22	29♐47	26 45	28 47	05 38
26	05 09	29 24	26 15	28 18	05 23
27	04 55	28 59	25 44	27 48	05 08
28	04 42	28 35	25 12	27 18	04 52
29	04 28	28 10	24 40	26 46	04 35
30	04 14	27 44	24 06	26 12	04 18
31	03 59	27 18	23 31	25 38	03 59
32	03 45	26 52	22 56	25 02	03 40
33	03 30	26 24	22 19	24 24	03 20
34	03 15	25 57	21 41	23 45	02 58
35	03 00	25 28	21 02	23 03	02 35
36	02 44	24 59	20 21	22 20	02 11
37	02 29	24 29	19 39	21 35	01 46
38	02 12	23 58	18 56	20 47	01 18
39	01 56	23 27	18 11	19 57	00 49
40	01 39	22 54	17 24	19 04	00 18
41	01 22	22 21	16 35	18 08	29♓44
42	01 05	21 47	15 45	17 09	29 08
43	00 47	21 12	14 52	16 06	28 29
44	00 28	20 35	13 57	14 59	27 46
45	00 10	19 58	13 00	13 49	27 00
46	29♏50	19 19	12 01	12 33	26 09
47	29 30	18 39	10 58	11 13	25 14
48	29 10	17 57	09 53	09 47	24 12
49	28 49	17 14	08 45	08 14	23 03
50	28 27	16 30	07 34	06 36	21 47
51	28 05	15 43	06 19	04 50	20 21
52	27 42	14 55	05 00	02 56	18 44
53	27 18	14 05	03 38	00 53	16 53
54	26 54	13 13	02 11	28♑40	14 46
55	26 28	12 19	00 40	26 18	12 18
56	26 01	11 23	29♐05	23 44	09 26
57	25 34	10 24	27 24	20 58	06 04
58	25 05	09 22	25 38	18 00	02 04
59	24 35	08 18	23 46	14 49	27♒18
60	24♏04	07♐10	21♐49	11♑24	21♒36

LAT.	14h 40m 0s — 12 ♏ 27 — 220° 0' 0" 11	12	ASC	2	3
0	11♐32	09♑11	07♒35	08♓22	10♈53
5	10 31	07 38	05 55	07 01	10 15
10	09 29	06 03	04 09	05 34	09 34
15	08 28	04 23	02 14	03 57	08 48
20	07 25	02 38	00 09	02 07	07 54
21	07 12	02 16	29♑42	01 43	07 43
22	06 59	01 54	29 15	01 18	07 30
23	06 46	01 31	28 47	00 53	07 18
24	06 33	01 09	28 18	00 26	07 05
25	06 20	00 45	27 49	29♒59	06 51
26	06 07	00 22	27 19	29 31	06 37
27	05 53	29♐58	26 48	29 02	06 22
28	05 39	29 33	26 16	28 31	06 07
29	05 25	29 08	25 44	28 00	05 50
30	05 11	28 42	25 10	27 27	05 33
31	04 57	28 16	24 36	26 53	05 16
32	04 42	27 50	24 00	26 17	04 57
33	04 28	27 23	23 23	25 40	04 37
34	04 13	26 55	22 45	25 01	04 16
35	03 57	26 26	22 06	24 20	03 54
36	03 42	25 57	21 26	23 37	03 31
37	03 26	25 27	20 44	22 52	03 06
38	03 10	24 56	20 00	22 05	02 40
39	02 53	24 25	19 15	21 15	02 11
40	02 37	23 52	18 28	20 22	01 41
41	02 19	23 19	17 39	19 27	01 08
42	02 02	22 44	16 49	18 28	00 33
43	01 44	22 09	15 56	17 25	29♓55
44	01 25	21 32	15 01	16 19	29 14
45	01 07	20 54	14 04	15 08	28 29
46	00 47	20 15	13 04	13 53	27 39
47	00 27	19 35	12 01	12 32	26 45
48	00 07	18 53	10 55	11 06	25 45
49	29♏46	18 10	09 47	09 34	24 38
50	29 24	17 25	08 35	07 55	23 23
51	29 01	16 38	07 19	06 08	21 59
52	28 38	15 50	06 00	04 13	20 24
53	28 14	14 59	04 36	02 09	18 36
54	27 49	14 07	03 09	29♑56	16 30
55	27 23	13 12	01 36	27 31	14 05
56	26 56	12 15	29♐59	24 55	11 15
57	26 29	11 15	28 17	22 07	07 55
58	26 00	10 12	26 29	19 06	03 55
59	25 29	09 07	24 36	15 51	29♒09
60	24♏58	07♐59	22♐36	12♑22	23♒24

LAT.	14h 44m 0s — 13 ♏ 27 — 221° 0' 0" 11	12	ASC	2	3
0	12♐28	10♑07	08♒34	09♓26	11♈58
5	11 27	08 34	06 55	08 07	11 22
10	10 26	06 59	05 10	06 41	10 42
15	09 25	05 20	03 17	05 06	09 57
20	08 23	03 36	01 12	03 18	09 05
21	08 10	03 14	00 46	02 54	08 54
22	07 57	02 52	00 18	02 30	08 42
23	07 44	02 30	29♑51	02 05	08 30
24	07 31	02 07	29 22	01 39	08 17
25	07 17	01 44	28 53	01 12	08 04
26	07 04	01 20	28 23	00 44	07 51
27	06 51	00 56	27 52	00 15	07 36
28	06 37	00 31	27 21	29♒45	07 21
29	06 23	00 06	26 48	29 14	07 06
30	06 09	29♐41	26 15	28 42	06 49
31	05 54	29 15	25 41	28 08	06 32
32	05 40	28 48	25 05	27 33	06 14
33	05 25	28 21	24 28	26 56	05 55
34	05 10	27 53	23 50	26 17	05 35
35	04 55	27 24	23 11	25 37	05 13
36	04 39	26 55	22 31	24 54	04 51
37	04 24	26 25	21 49	24 10	04 27
38	04 07	25 54	21 05	23 23	04 01
39	03 51	25 23	20 20	22 34	03 34
40	03 34	24 50	19 33	21 41	03 04
41	03 17	24 16	18 44	20 46	02 33
42	02 59	23 42	17 53	19 48	01 58
43	02 41	23 06	17 01	18 45	01 22
44	02 23	22 30	16 05	17 39	00 41
45	02 04	21 52	15 08	16 29	29♓58
46	01 44	21 12	14 07	15 14	29 10
47	01 24	20 32	13 04	13 53	28 17
48	01 03	19 49	11 58	12 27	27 18
49	00 42	19 06	10 49	10 55	26 13
50	00 20	18 21	09 36	09 15	25 01
51	29♏57	17 33	08 20	07 28	23 39
52	29 34	16 44	07 00	05 32	22 06
53	29 10	15 53	05 35	03 28	20 19
54	28 45	15 00	04 07	01 13	18 16
55	28 19	14 05	02 33	28♑47	15 54
56	27 52	13 07	00 55	26 09	13 06
57	27 23	12 07	29♐11	23 18	09 47
58	26 54	11 03	27 21	20 13	05 50
59	26 23	09 57	25 26	16 54	01 03
60	25♏51	08♐47	23♐24	13♑21	25♒16

LAT.	14h 48m 0s — 14 ♏ 28 — 222° 0' 0" 11	12	ASC	2	3
0	13♐24	11♑02	09♒34	10♓30	13♈03
5	12 23	09 30	07 56	09 13	12 28
10	11 23	07 56	06 11	07 49	11 49
15	10 22	06 18	04 19	06 15	11 06
20	09 20	04 34	02 16	04 29	10 16
21	09 07	04 12	01 49	04 06	10 05
22	08 54	03 50	01 22	03 42	09 54
23	08 41	03 28	00 55	03 17	09 42
24	08 28	03 05	00 27	02 52	09 30
25	08 15	02 42	29♑58	02 25	09 17
26	08 02	02 18	29 28	01 58	09 04
27	07 48	01 54	28 57	01 29	08 50
28	07 34	01 30	28 26	01 00	08 36
29	07 20	01 05	27 53	00 29	08 21
30	07 06	00 39	27 20	29♒57	08 05
31	06 52	00 13	26 46	29 24	07 48
32	06 37	29♐47	26 10	28 49	07 31
33	06 23	29 19	25 34	28 13	07 12
34	06 08	28 52	24 56	27 35	06 53
35	05 52	28 23	24 17	26 55	06 32
36	05 37	27 54	23 37	26 13	06 11
37	05 21	27 24	22 55	25 29	05 47
38	05 05	26 53	22 11	24 42	05 23
39	04 48	26 21	21 26	23 53	04 56
40	04 31	25 48	20 39	23 01	04 28
41	04 14	25 15	19 50	22 07	03 57
42	03 56	24 40	18 59	21 09	03 24
43	03 38	24 04	18 06	20 07	02 48
44	03 20	23 27	17 10	19 01	02 09
45	03 01	22 49	16 12	17 51	01 27
46	02 41	22 09	15 12	16 36	00 41
47	02 21	21 29	14 08	15 16	29♓49
48	02 00	20 46	13 02	13 50	28 53
49	01 39	20 02	11 52	12 17	27 49
50	01 17	19 16	10 39	10 37	26 39
51	00 54	18 29	09 22	08 50	25 19
52	00 30	17 40	08 01	06 53	23 48
53	00 06	16 48	06 36	04 48	22 04
54	29♏40	15 54	05 06	02 32	20 04
55	29 14	14 58	03 31	00 04	17 44
56	28 47	14 00	01 51	27♑24	14 59
57	28 18	12 58	00 06	24 30	11 43
58	27 48	11 54	28♐14	21 23	07 47
59	27 17	10 47	26 17	18 00	03 01
60	26♏45	09♐36	24♐13	14♑22	27♒12

LAT.	14h 52m 0s — 15 ♏ 28 — 223° 0' 0" 11	12	ASC	2	3
0	14♐20	11♑58	10♒33	11♓34	14♈07
5	13 20	10 27	08 56	10 19	13 34
10	12 20	08 53	07 13	08 56	12 57
15	11 19	07 16	05 22	07 25	12 15
20	10 17	05 32	03 20	05 40	11 27
21	10 04	05 10	02 53	05 18	11 17
22	09 52	04 49	02 27	04 54	11 06
23	09 39	04 26	01 59	04 30	10 55
24	09 26	04 04	01 31	04 05	10 43
25	09 12	03 40	01 02	03 39	10 31
26	08 59	03 17	00 33	03 12	10 18
27	08 46	02 53	00 03	02 44	10 05
28	08 32	02 29	29♑31	02 15	09 51
29	08 18	02 04	28 59	01 45	09 36
30	08 04	01 38	28 26	01 13	09 21
31	07 50	01 12	27 52	00 40	09 05
32	07 35	00 46	27 16	00 06	08 48
33	07 20	00 18	26 40	29♒30	08 30
34	07 05	29♐50	26 02	28 53	08 11
35	06 50	29 22	25 23	28 13	07 52
36	06 34	28 53	24 43	27 32	07 31
37	06 18	28 22	24 01	26 48	07 08
38	06 02	27 51	23 17	26 02	06 44
39	05 46	27 20	22 32	25 14	06 19
40	05 29	26 47	21 45	24 23	05 51
41	05 11	26 13	20 56	23 28	05 22
42	04 54	25 38	20 05	22 31	04 50
43	04 35	25 02	19 12	21 29	04 15
44	04 17	24 25	18 16	20 24	03 38
45	03 58	23 47	17 18	19 14	02 57
46	03 38	23 07	16 17	17 59	02 12
47	03 18	22 26	15 13	16 39	01 22
48	02 57	21 43	14 06	15 13	00 27
49	02 35	20 59	12 56	13 41	29♓26
50	02 13	20 13	11 42	12 01	28 17
51	01 50	19 25	10 25	10 13	27 00
52	01 26	18 35	09 03	08 16	25 31
53	01 02	17 43	07 36	06 10	23 50
54	00 36	16 49	06 06	03 52	21 53
55	00 09	15 52	04 30	01 23	19 36
56	29♏42	14 53	02 48	28♑41	16 54
57	29 13	13 51	01 01	25 45	13 40
58	28 43	12 46	29♐08	22 34	09 47
59	28 11	11 37	27 09	19 07	05 02
60	27♏38	10♐25	25♐02	15♑25	29♒13

Koch Table of Houses for Latitudes 0° to 60° North

14h 56m 0s — 224° 0' 0" — 16 ♏ 28

LAT.	11	12	ASC	2	3
0	15♐16	12♑53	11♒32	12♓39	15♈12
5	14 16	11 23	09 57	11 25	14 40
10	13 16	09 50	08 15	10 04	14 04
15	12 16	08 13	06 25	08 34	13 24
20	11 14	06 30	04 24	06 52	12 38
21	11 02	06 09	03 58	06 30	12 28
22	10 49	05 47	03 31	06 07	12 18
23	10 36	05 25	03 04	05 43	12 07
24	10 23	05 02	02 36	05 18	11 56
25	10 10	04 39	02 08	04 53	11 44
26	09 57	04 16	01 38	04 26	11 32
27	09 43	03 52	01 08	03 59	11 19
28	09 29	03 28	00 37	03 30	11 05
29	09 15	03 03	00 05	03 01	10 51
30	09 01	02 37	29♑32	02 30	10 37
31	08 47	02 11	28 58	01 57	10 21
32	08 33	01 45	28 23	01 24	10 05
33	08 18	01 17	27 47	00 48	09 48
34	08 03	00 50	27 09	00 11	09 30
35	07 48	00 21	26 30	29♒32	09 11
36	07 32	29♐52	25 50	28 51	08 51
37	07 16	29 21	25 08	28 08	08 29
38	07 00	28 50	24 25	27 23	08 06
39	06 43	28 19	23 39	26 35	07 41
40	06 26	27 46	22 52	25 45	07 15
41	06 09	27 12	22 03	24 51	06 46
42	05 51	26 37	21 12	23 54	06 16
43	05 33	26 01	20 19	22 53	05 42
44	05 14	25 24	19 23	21 48	05 06
45	04 55	24 45	18 25	20 39	04 27
46	04 35	24 05	17 23	19 24	03 43
47	04 15	23 24	16 19	18 05	02 55
48	03 54	22 41	15 12	16 39	02 02
49	03 32	21 56	14 01	15 06	01 03
50	03 09	21 10	12 47	13 27	29♓56
51	02 46	20 21	11 28	11 38	28 41
52	02 22	19 31	10 06	09 41	27 15
53	01 57	18 38	08 38	07 34	25 37
54	01 32	17 44	07 06	05 15	23 43
55	01 05	16 46	05 29	02 45	21 29
56	00 37	15 46	03 46	00 01	18 50
57	00 08	14 43	01 58	27♑02	15 40
58	29♏37	13 37	00 03	23 48	11 49
59	29 05	12 28	28♐01	20 17	07 07
60	28♏32	11♐15	25♐53	16♑29	01♓17

15h 0m 0s — 225° 0' 0" — 17 ♏ 28

LAT.	11	12	ASC	2	3
0	16♐11	13♑49	12♒32	13♓43	16♈17
5	15 12	12 20	10 58	12 31	15 46
10	14 13	10 48	09 17	11 12	15 12
15	13 13	09 11	07 29	09 44	14 33
20	12 12	07 29	05 28	08 04	13 49
21	11 59	07 08	05 03	07 42	13 40
22	11 46	06 46	04 37	07 20	13 30
23	11 33	06 24	04 10	06 56	13 19
24	11 20	06 01	03 42	06 32	13 08
25	11 07	05 38	03 14	06 07	12 57
26	10 54	05 15	02 44	05 41	12 45
27	10 41	04 51	02 14	05 14	12 33
28	10 27	04 27	01 44	04 46	12 20
29	10 13	04 02	01 12	04 17	12 07
30	09 59	03 37	00 39	03 47	11 53
31	09 45	03 11	00 05	03 15	11 38
32	09 30	02 44	29♑30	02 42	11 22
33	09 15	02 17	28 54	02 07	11 06
34	09 00	01 49	28 17	01 30	10 48
35	08 45	01 20	27 38	00 52	10 30
36	08 29	00 51	26 58	00 12	10 11
37	08 14	00 21	26 16	29♒30	09 50
38	07 57	29♐50	25 32	28 45	09 28
39	07 41	29 18	24 47	27 58	09 04
40	07 24	28 45	24 00	27 07	08 39
41	07 06	28 11	23 11	26 14	08 11
42	06 48	27 36	22 20	25 18	07 42
43	06 30	27 00	21 26	24 17	07 10
44	06 11	26 22	20 31	23 13	06 35
45	05 52	25 44	19 32	22 04	05 57
46	05 32	25 03	18 30	20 51	05 15
47	05 11	24 22	17 26	19 31	04 29
48	04 50	23 38	16 18	18 06	03 38
49	04 29	22 53	15 07	16 34	02 40
50	04 06	22 07	13 52	14 54	01 36
51	03 43	21 18	12 33	13 05	00 23
52	03 19	20 27	11 09	11 08	29♓00
53	02 53	19 34	09 41	09 00	27 25
54	02 27	18 39	08 08	06 41	25 34
55	02 00	17 41	06 30	04 08	23 23
56	01 32	16 40	04 45	01 22	20 48
57	01 03	15 36	02 55	28♑21	17 42
58	00 32	14 29	00 58	25 04	13 55
59	00 00	13 19	28♐55	21 29	09 15
60	29♏26	12♐05	26♐44	17♑36	03♓26

15h 4m 0s — 226° 0' 0" — 18 ♏ 28

LAT.	11	12	ASC	2	3
0	17♐07	14♑44	13♒32	14♓48	17♈21
5	16 08	13 16	11 59	13 38	16 52
10	15 09	11 45	10 20	12 21	16 19
15	14 10	10 09	08 32	10 55	15 42
20	13 09	08 28	06 34	09 17	15 00
21	12 56	08 06	06 08	08 55	14 51
22	12 44	07 45	05 42	08 33	14 41
23	12 31	07 23	05 15	08 10	14 31
24	12 18	07 00	04 48	07 47	14 21
25	12 05	06 37	04 20	07 22	14 10
26	11 51	06 14	03 51	06 57	13 59
27	11 38	05 50	03 21	06 30	13 47
28	11 24	05 26	02 50	06 03	13 35
29	11 11	05 01	02 19	05 34	13 22
30	10 56	04 36	01 46	05 04	13 08
31	10 42	04 10	01 13	04 33	12 54
32	10 28	03 44	00 38	04 00	12 39
33	10 13	03 17	00 02	03 26	12 24
34	09 58	02 49	29♑25	02 50	12 07
35	09 43	02 20	28 46	02 13	11 49
36	09 27	01 51	28 06	01 33	11 31
37	09 11	01 21	27 24	00 51	11 11
38	08 55	00 49	26 41	00 07	10 50
39	08 38	00 17	25 56	29♒21	10 27
40	08 21	29♐44	25 09	28 31	10 03
41	08 04	29 10	24 20	27 39	09 36
42	07 46	28 35	23 29	26 43	09 08
43	07 27	27 59	22 35	25 43	08 37
44	07 08	27 21	21 39	24 40	08 04
45	06 49	26 42	20 40	23 31	07 27
46	06 29	26 02	19 39	22 18	06 47
47	06 08	25 20	18 34	20 59	06 03
48	05 47	24 37	17 26	19 34	05 13
49	05 25	23 51	16 14	18 02	04 18
50	05 03	23 04	14 58	16 23	03 16
51	04 39	22 15	13 39	14 34	02 06
52	04 15	21 24	12 14	12 37	00 46
53	03 49	20 30	10 45	10 28	29♓13
54	03 23	19 34	09 11	08 08	27 26
55	02 56	18 36	07 31	05 34	25 19
56	02 27	17 34	05 46	02 47	22 48
57	01 58	16 30	03 54	29♑43	19 46
58	01 26	15 22	01 55	26 22	16 03
59	00 54	14 10	29♐49	22 43	11 26
60	00♐19	12♐55	27♐36	18♑45	05♓40

15h 8m 0s — 227° 0' 0" — 19 ♏ 27

LAT.	11	12	ASC	2	3
0	18♐02	15♑40	14♒32	15♓53	18♈26
5	17 04	14 13	13 01	14 44	17 57
10	16 06	12 43	11 23	13 29	17 26
15	15 07	11 08	09 36	12 05	16 51
20	14 06	09 27	07 39	10 29	16 11
21	13 53	09 05	07 14	10 09	16 02
22	13 41	08 44	06 48	09 47	15 53
23	13 28	08 22	06 22	09 25	15 43
24	13 15	08 00	05 54	09 01	15 33
25	13 02	07 37	05 27	08 37	15 23
26	12 49	07 14	04 58	08 12	15 12
27	12 35	06 50	04 28	07 47	15 01
28	12 22	06 26	03 58	07 20	14 49
29	12 08	06 01	03 27	06 52	14 37
30	11 54	05 36	02 54	06 22	14 24
31	11 40	05 10	02 21	05 52	14 11
32	11 25	04 44	01 46	05 20	13 56
33	11 11	04 17	01 10	04 46	13 41
34	10 56	03 49	00 33	04 11	13 26
35	10 40	03 20	29♑55	03 34	13 09
36	10 25	02 51	29 15	02 55	12 51
37	10 09	02 21	28 33	02 14	12 32
38	09 52	01 50	27 50	01 31	12 12
39	09 36	01 17	27 05	00 45	11 50
40	09 19	00 44	26 18	29♒56	11 27
41	09 01	00 10	25 29	29 04	11 01
42	08 43	29♐35	24 38	28 09	10 34
43	08 25	28 59	23 44	27 10	10 05
44	08 06	28 21	22 48	26 07	09 33
45	07 46	27 42	21 49	25 00	08 58
46	07 26	27 01	20 47	23 47	08 19
47	07 06	26 19	19 42	22 29	07 36
48	06 44	25 35	18 34	21 04	06 49
49	06 22	24 50	17 22	19 33	05 56
50	05 59	24 02	16 06	17 53	04 57
51	05 36	23 13	14 45	16 05	03 49
52	05 11	22 21	13 20	14 07	02 32
53	04 46	21 27	11 50	11 59	01 02
54	04 19	20 30	10 15	09 38	29♓18
55	03 51	19 31	08 34	07 03	27 16
56	03 23	18 29	06 47	04 13	24 49
57	02 53	17 23	04 53	01 07	21 52
58	02 21	16 14	02 52	27♑43	18 14
59	01 48	15 02	00 44	24 00	13 41
60	01♐13	13♐46	28♐28	19♑57	07♓57

15h 12m 0s — 228° 0' 0" — 20 ♏ 26

LAT.	11	12	ASC	2	3
0	18♐58	16♑36	15♒32	16♓57	19♈30
5	18 00	15 10	14 02	15 51	19 03
10	17 02	13 40	12 26	14 38	18 33
15	16 04	12 06	10 41	13 16	18 00
20	15 03	10 26	08 45	11 42	17 22
21	14 51	10 05	08 20	11 22	17 13
22	14 38	09 43	07 54	11 01	17 04
23	14 25	09 21	07 28	10 39	16 55
24	14 12	08 59	07 01	10 16	16 46
25	13 59	08 37	06 34	09 53	16 36
26	13 46	08 14	06 05	09 29	16 26
27	13 33	07 50	05 36	09 03	16 15
28	13 19	07 26	05 06	08 37	16 04
29	13 06	07 01	04 35	08 10	15 52
30	12 52	06 36	04 03	07 41	15 40
31	12 37	06 10	03 29	07 11	15 27
32	12 23	05 44	02 55	06 40	15 13
33	12 08	05 17	02 19	06 07	14 59
34	11 53	04 49	01 43	05 32	14 44
35	11 38	04 21	01 04	04 56	14 28
36	11 22	03 51	00 25	04 18	14 11
37	11 06	03 21	29♑43	03 37	13 53
38	10 50	02 50	29 00	02 55	13 33
39	10 33	02 18	28 15	02 10	13 13
40	10 16	01 45	27 28	01 22	12 50
41	09 59	01 11	26 39	00 31	12 26
42	09 41	00 35	25 48	29♒36	12 01
43	09 22	29♐59	24 55	28 38	11 32
44	09 03	29 21	23 58	27 36	11 02
45	08 44	28 41	22 59	26 29	10 28
46	08 23	28 01	21 57	25 17	09 51
47	08 03	27 18	20 52	24 00	09 11
48	07 41	26 34	19 43	22 36	08 25
49	07 19	25 48	18 31	21 05	07 34
50	06 56	25 01	17 14	19 26	06 37
51	06 32	24 11	15 53	17 38	05 32
52	06 08	23 18	14 27	15 40	04 18
53	05 42	22 24	12 57	13 31	02 52
54	05 15	21 27	11 20	11 10	01 12
55	04 47	20 27	09 38	08 34	29♓14
56	04 18	19 24	07 49	05 43	26 52
57	03 48	18 17	05 54	02 34	23 59
58	03 16	17 08	03 51	29♑07	20 26
59	02 42	15 54	01 41	25 20	15 59
60	02♐07	14♐37	29♐22	21♑11	10♓19

15h 16m 0s — 229° 0' 0" — 21 ♏ 26

LAT.	11	12	ASC	2	3
0	19♐53	17♑32	16♒33	18♓02	20♈34
5	18 56	16 06	15 04	16 57	20 09
10	17 59	14 38	13 29	15 46	19 40
15	17 00	13 05	11 46	14 27	19 09
20	16 00	11 25	09 51	12 56	18 32
21	15 48	11 04	09 26	12 36	18 24
22	15 35	10 43	09 01	12 15	18 16
23	15 23	10 21	08 35	11 54	18 07
24	15 10	09 59	08 09	11 32	17 58
25	14 57	09 37	07 41	11 09	17 49
26	14 44	09 14	07 13	10 45	17 39
27	14 30	08 50	06 44	10 20	17 29
28	14 17	08 26	06 14	09 55	17 18
29	14 03	08 02	05 43	09 28	17 07
30	13 49	07 37	05 12	09 00	16 56
31	13 35	07 11	04 39	08 31	16 43
32	13 21	06 45	04 05	08 00	16 30
33	13 06	06 17	03 29	07 28	16 17
34	12 51	05 50	02 53	06 54	16 02
35	12 36	05 21	02 14	06 19	15 47
36	12 20	04 52	01 35	05 41	15 31
37	12 04	04 22	00 54	05 02	15 14
38	11 48	03 51	00 11	04 20	14 55
39	11 31	03 19	29♑26	03 35	14 36
40	11 14	02 45	28 39	02 48	14 14
41	10 56	02 11	27 51	01 58	13 52
42	10 38	01 36	26 59	01 05	13 27
43	10 20	00 59	26 06	00 07	13 00
44	10 01	00 21	25 10	29♒06	12 31
45	09 41	29♐42	24 11	28 00	11 59
46	09 21	29 01	23 08	26 49	11 24
47	09 00	28 18	22 03	25 32	10 45
48	08 38	27 34	20 54	24 09	10 01
49	08 16	26 48	19 41	22 39	09 13
50	07 53	25 59	18 24	21 00	08 18
51	07 29	25 09	17 02	19 13	07 16
52	07 04	24 17	15 36	17 15	06 05
53	06 38	23 21	14 04	15 06	04 43
54	06 11	22 24	12 27	12 44	03 06
55	05 43	21 23	10 43	10 08	01 12
56	05 14	20 19	08 53	07 15	28♓55
57	04 43	19 12	06 56	04 04	26 08
58	04 11	18 01	04 51	00 34	22 42
59	03 37	16 47	02 38	26♑42	18 20
60	03♐01	15♐28	00♑17	22♑28	12♓45

15h 20m 0s — 230° 0' 0" — 22 ♏ 25

LAT.	11	12	ASC	2	3
0	20♐49	18♑28	17♒33	19♓07	21♈38
5	19 52	17 04	16 06	18 04	21 14
10	18 55	15 36	14 33	16 55	20 47
15	17 57	14 03	12 51	15 38	20 17
20	16 57	12 24	10 58	14 09	19 43
21	16 45	12 04	10 33	13 50	19 35
22	16 33	11 43	10 08	13 30	19 27
23	16 20	11 21	09 43	13 09	19 19
24	16 07	10 59	09 17	12 48	19 10
25	15 54	10 37	08 49	12 25	19 02
26	15 41	10 14	08 22	12 02	18 52
27	15 28	09 51	07 53	11 38	18 43
28	15 14	09 27	07 23	11 13	18 33
29	15 01	09 02	06 53	10 47	18 22
30	14 47	08 37	06 21	10 19	18 11
31	14 33	08 12	05 48	09 51	17 59
32	14 18	07 45	05 15	09 21	17 47
33	14 04	07 18	04 40	08 49	17 34
34	13 49	06 51	04 03	08 16	17 21
35	13 33	06 22	03 25	07 42	17 06
36	13 18	05 53	02 46	07 05	16 51
37	13 02	05 23	02 05	06 26	16 35
38	12 45	04 52	01 22	05 45	16 17
39	12 29	04 20	00 38	05 02	15 58
40	12 12	03 46	29♑51	04 16	15 38
41	11 54	03 12	29 03	03 26	15 17
42	11 36	02 37	28 12	02 34	14 53
43	11 17	02 00	27 18	01 37	14 28
44	10 58	01 22	26 22	00 37	14 00
45	10 38	00 42	25 23	29♒32	13 29
46	10 18	00 01	24 20	28 22	12 56
47	09 57	29♐18	23 15	27 06	12 19
48	09 35	28 34	22 06	25 44	11 38
49	09 13	27 47	20 52	24 14	10 52
50	08 50	26 59	19 35	22 37	09 59
51	08 26	26 08	18 13	20 50	09 00
52	08 01	25 15	16 45	18 53	07 52
53	07 34	24 19	15 13	16 44	06 34
54	07 07	23 21	13 34	14 21	05 01
55	06 39	22 20	11 49	11 44	03 12
56	06 09	21 15	09 58	08 50	01 00
57	05 38	20 07	07 59	05 37	28♓19
58	05 05	18 56	05 52	02 03	24 59
59	04 31	17 40	03 37	28♑08	20 44
60	03♐55	16♐20	01♑13	23♑48	15♓15

15h 24m 0s — 231° 0' 0" — 23 ♏ 23

LAT.	11	12	ASC	2	3
0	21♐44	19♑24	18♒34	20♓12	22♈42
5	20 48	18 01	17 08	19 11	22 19
10	19 51	16 34	15 36	18 04	21 54
15	18 54	15 02	13 56	16 49	21 26
20	17 54	13 24	12 05	15 23	20 53
21	17 42	13 04	11 41	15 04	20 46
22	17 30	12 43	11 16	14 45	20 38
23	17 17	12 21	10 51	14 25	20 31
24	17 05	11 59	10 25	14 04	20 23
25	16 52	11 37	09 58	13 42	20 14
26	16 39	11 14	09 30	13 19	20 06
27	16 25	10 51	09 02	12 56	19 56
28	16 12	10 27	08 33	12 32	19 47
29	15 58	10 03	08 03	12 06	19 37
30	15 44	09 38	07 31	11 39	19 27
31	15 30	09 13	06 59	11 12	19 16
32	15 16	08 47	06 25	10 42	19 04
33	15 01	08 20	05 51	10 12	18 52
34	14 46	07 52	05 14	09 39	18 39
35	14 31	07 24	04 37	09 06	18 25
36	14 15	06 54	03 58	08 30	18 11
37	13 59	06 24	03 17	07 52	17 55
38	13 43	05 53	02 35	07 12	17 39
39	13 26	05 21	01 50	06 29	17 21
40	13 09	04 48	01 04	05 44	17 02
41	12 52	04 14	00 15	04 56	16 41
42	12 34	03 38	29♑25	04 04	16 19
43	12 15	03 01	28 31	03 09	15 55
44	11 56	02 23	27 35	02 09	15 29
45	11 36	01 43	26 36	01 05	15 00
46	11 16	01 02	25 34	29♒56	14 28
47	10 55	00 19	24 28	28 42	13 53
48	10 33	29♐34	23 18	27 20	13 14
49	10 10	28 48	22 05	25 52	12 30
50	09 47	27 59	20 47	24 15	11 41
51	09 23	27 08	19 24	22 29	10 44
52	08 57	26 14	17 56	20 32	09 40
53	08 31	25 18	16 23	18 23	08 25
54	08 04	24 19	14 43	16 01	06 57
55	07 35	23 17	12 57	13 23	05 12
56	07 05	22 12	11 04	10 28	03 06
57	06 33	21 03	09 03	07 13	00 31
58	06 00	19 50	06 54	03 37	27♓17
59	05 26	18 33	04 37	29♑37	23 11
60	04♐49	17♐12	02♑10	25♑12	17♓49

Koch Table of Houses for Latitudes 0° to 60° North

15h 28m 0s — 24 ♏ 22 — 232° 0' 0"

LAT.	11	12	ASC	2	3
0	22♐39	20♑20	19♒35	21♓17	23♈46
5	21 44	18 58	18 11	20 18	23 24
10	20 48	17 32	16 41	19 13	23 01
15	19 51	16 02	15 02	18 01	22 34
20	18 52	14 24	13 12	16 37	22 03
21	18 39	14 04	12 48	16 19	21 56
22	18 27	13 43	12 24	16 00	21 49
23	18 15	13 22	11 59	15 40	21 42
24	18 02	13 00	11 33	15 20	21 35
25	17 49	12 38	11 07	14 59	21 27
26	17 36	12 15	10 40	14 37	21 19
27	17 23	11 52	10 12	14 14	21 10
28	17 10	11 29	09 43	13 50	21 01
29	16 56	11 04	09 13	13 26	20 52
30	16 42	10 40	08 42	13 00	20 42
31	16 28	10 14	08 10	12 33	20 31
32	16 14	09 48	07 37	12 04	20 21
33	15 59	09 21	07 02	11 34	20 09
34	15 44	08 54	06 26	11 03	19 57
35	15 29	08 25	05 49	10 30	19 44
36	15 13	07 56	05 10	09 55	19 30
37	14 57	07 26	04 30	09 18	19 16
38	14 41	06 55	03 48	08 39	19 00
39	14 24	06 23	03 04	07 57	18 44
40	14 07	05 50	02 18	07 13	18 26
41	13 49	05 16	01 29	06 26	18 06
42	13 31	04 40	00 38	05 35	17 45
43	13 13	04 03	29♑45	04 41	17 23
44	12 53	03 25	28 49	03 43	16 58
45	12 34	02 45	27 50	02 40	16 31
46	12 13	02 04	26 48	01 32	16 01
47	11 52	01 20	25 42	00 18	15 27
48	11 30	00 35	24 32	28♒58	14 50
49	11 07	29♐48	23 18	27 31	14 09
50	10 44	28 59	22 00	25 55	13 22
51	10 20	28 08	20 37	24 10	12 29
52	09 54	27 14	19 08	22 14	11 27
53	09 28	26 17	17 34	20 06	10 16
54	09 00	25 18	15 54	17 43	08 52
55	08 31	24 15	14 06	15 05	07 12
56	08 01	23 09	12 12	12 09	05 12
57	07 29	21 59	10 09	08 52	02 44
58	06 55	20 46	07 58	05 13	29♓38
59	06 20	19 27	05 38	01 09	25 40
60	05♐43	18♐05	03♑09	26♑39	20♓27

15h 32m 0s — 25 ♏ 21 — 233° 0' 0"

LAT.	11	12	ASC	2	3
0	23♐34	21♑17	20♒36	22♓23	24♈50
5	22 39	19 55	19 14	21 25	24 29
10	21 44	18 31	17 45	20 23	24 07
15	20 47	17 01	16 08	19 12	23 42
20	19 49	15 24	14 20	17 51	23 13
21	19 37	15 04	13 56	17 34	23 07
22	19 24	14 43	13 33	17 15	23 00
23	19 12	14 22	13 08	16 56	22 54
24	18 59	14 01	12 43	16 37	22 46
25	18 47	13 39	12 17	16 16	22 39
26	18 34	13 16	11 50	15 55	22 31
27	18 21	12 53	11 22	15 33	22 23
28	18 07	12 30	10 53	15 10	22 15
29	17 54	12 06	10 24	14 46	22 06
30	17 40	11 41	09 53	14 21	21 57
31	17 26	11 16	09 22	13 54	21 47
32	17 12	10 50	08 49	13 27	21 37
33	16 57	10 23	08 15	12 58	21 26
34	16 42	09 56	07 39	12 27	21 15
35	16 27	09 28	07 02	11 55	21 03
36	16 11	08 58	06 24	11 21	20 50
37	15 55	08 28	05 44	10 45	20 36
38	15 39	07 57	05 02	10 07	20 22
39	15 22	07 25	04 18	09 26	20 06
40	15 05	06 52	03 32	08 43	19 49
41	14 47	06 18	02 44	07 57	19 31
42	14 29	05 42	01 53	07 07	19 11
43	14 11	05 05	01 00	06 14	18 50
44	13 51	04 27	00 04	05 17	18 27
45	13 31	03 47	29♑05	04 16	18 01
46	13 11	03 06	28 03	03 09	17 33
47	12 50	02 22	26 57	01 57	17 01
48	12 28	01 37	25 47	00 38	16 26
49	12 05	00 50	24 33	29♒12	15 47
50	11 41	00 00	23 15	27 37	15 03
51	11 17	29♐08	21 51	25 53	14 13
52	10 51	28 14	20 22	23 58	13 15
53	10 24	27 17	18 47	21 50	12 07
54	09 56	26 17	17 06	19 29	10 48
55	09 27	25 14	15 17	16 50	09 13
56	08 57	24 07	13 21	13 53	07 19
57	08 25	22 56	11 17	10 35	04 57
58	07 51	21 41	09 04	06 53	01 59
59	07 15	20 22	06 41	02 46	28♓10
60	06♐37	18♐58	04♑08	28♑09	23♓07

15h 36m 0s — 26 ♏ 19 — 234° 0' 0"

LAT.	11	12	ASC	2	3
0	24♐30	22♑13	21♒37	23♓28	25♈53
5	23 35	20 53	20 17	22 33	25 34
10	22 40	19 29	18 50	21 32	25 13
15	21 44	18 00	17 14	20 24	24 50
20	20 46	16 25	15 28	19 06	24 23
21	20 34	16 05	15 05	18 49	24 17
22	20 22	15 44	14 41	18 31	24 11
23	20 09	15 23	14 17	18 13	24 05
24	19 57	15 02	13 52	17 54	23 58
25	19 44	14 40	13 27	17 34	23 51
26	19 31	14 18	13 00	17 13	23 44
27	19 18	13 55	12 33	16 52	23 37
28	19 05	13 32	12 05	16 30	23 29
29	18 51	13 08	11 35	16 06	23 21
30	18 38	12 43	11 05	15 42	23 12
31	18 24	12 18	10 34	15 16	23 03
32	18 09	11 52	10 01	14 49	22 53
33	17 55	11 26	09 28	14 21	22 43
34	17 40	10 58	08 52	13 52	22 33
35	17 25	10 30	08 16	13 20	22 21
36	17 09	10 01	07 38	12 47	22 09
37	16 53	09 31	06 58	12 12	21 57
38	16 37	09 00	06 16	11 35	21 43
39	16 20	08 28	05 33	10 56	21 28
40	16 03	07 55	04 47	10 14	21 12
41	15 45	07 21	04 00	09 29	20 55
42	15 27	06 45	03 09	08 41	20 37
43	15 08	06 08	02 16	07 49	20 17
44	14 49	05 30	01 21	06 53	19 55
45	14 29	04 50	00 22	05 53	19 31
46	14 09	04 08	29♑20	04 48	19 05
47	13 47	03 25	28 14	03 37	18 35
48	13 25	02 39	27 04	02 19	18 02
49	13 02	01 52	25 50	00 54	17 26
50	12 39	01 02	24 31	29♒21	16 44
51	12 14	00 10	23 07	27 38	15 57
52	11 48	29♐15	21 37	25 44	15 02
53	11 21	28 17	20 01	23 38	13 58
54	10 53	27 17	18 19	21 16	12 43
55	10 24	26 13	16 29	18 38	11 14
56	09 53	25 05	14 32	15 41	09 26
57	09 20	23 54	12 26	12 22	07 11
58	08 46	22 38	10 10	08 38	04 22
59	08 10	21 17	07 45	04 26	00 43
60	07♐32	19♐52	05♑10	29♑44	25♓51

15h 40m 0s — 27 ♏ 17 — 235° 0' 0"

LAT.	11	12	ASC	2	3
0	25♐25	23♑10	22♒39	24♓33	26♈57
5	24 31	21 51	21 20	23 40	26 39
10	23 37	20 28	19 55	22 42	26 20
15	22 41	19 00	18 21	21 36	25 58
20	21 43	17 26	16 36	20 21	25 33
21	21 31	17 06	16 14	20 04	25 28
22	21 19	16 45	15 51	19 47	25 22
23	21 07	16 25	15 27	19 29	25 16
24	20 54	16 03	15 02	19 11	25 10
25	20 42	15 42	14 37	18 52	25 03
26	20 29	15 20	14 11	18 32	24 57
27	20 16	14 57	13 44	18 11	24 50
28	20 03	14 34	13 16	17 50	24 43
29	19 49	14 10	12 47	17 27	24 35
30	19 35	13 46	12 18	17 03	24 27
31	19 22	13 21	11 47	16 39	24 18
32	19 07	12 55	11 15	16 13	24 10
33	18 53	12 28	10 41	15 45	24 00
34	18 38	12 01	10 07	15 17	23 50
35	18 23	11 33	09 30	14 46	23 40
36	18 07	11 04	08 53	14 14	23 29
37	17 51	10 34	08 13	13 40	23 17
38	17 35	10 03	07 32	13 04	23 04
39	17 18	09 31	06 49	12 26	22 50
40	17 01	08 58	06 04	11 45	22 36
41	16 43	08 24	05 16	11 01	22 20
42	16 25	07 48	04 26	10 15	22 03
43	16 07	07 11	03 34	09 24	21 44
44	15 47	06 33	02 38	08 30	21 23
45	15 27	05 53	01 39	07 31	21 01
46	15 07	05 11	00 37	06 27	20 36
47	14 45	04 27	29♑31	05 18	20 09
48	14 23	03 42	28 22	04 02	19 38
49	14 00	02 54	27 07	02 38	19 04
50	13 36	02 04	25 48	01 07	18 25
51	13 11	01 12	24 24	29♒25	17 40
52	12 45	00 16	22 54	27 33	16 49
53	12 18	29♐18	21 17	25 28	15 49
54	11 50	28 17	19 34	23 07	14 39
55	11 20	27 12	17 43	20 30	13 15
56	10 49	26 04	15 44	17 32	11 33
57	10 16	24 52	13 36	14 12	09 26
58	09 42	23 35	11 19	10 26	06 45
59	09 05	22 13	08 51	06 10	03 16
60	08♐26	20♐46	06♑12	01♒23	28♓37

15h 44m 0s — 28 ♏ 15 — 236° 0' 0"

LAT.	11	12	ASC	2	3
0	26♐20	24♑06	23♒41	25♓38	28♈00
5	25 27	22 48	22 23	24 47	27 44
10	24 33	21 27	21 00	23 51	27 26
15	23 38	20 00	19 28	22 48	27 06
20	22 40	18 27	17 45	21 36	26 43
21	22 28	18 07	17 23	21 20	26 38
22	22 16	17 47	17 00	21 03	26 32
23	22 04	17 26	16 37	20 46	26 27
24	21 52	17 05	16 13	20 28	26 21
25	21 39	16 44	15 48	20 10	26 15
26	21 27	16 22	15 22	19 51	26 09
27	21 14	15 59	14 56	19 31	26 03
28	21 00	15 36	14 28	19 10	25 56
29	20 47	15 13	14 00	18 48	25 49
30	20 33	14 48	13 31	18 25	25 42
31	20 19	14 23	13 00	18 01	25 34
32	20 05	13 58	12 29	17 36	25 26
33	19 51	13 32	11 56	17 10	25 17
34	19 36	13 04	11 21	16 42	25 08
35	19 21	12 36	10 46	16 13	24 58
36	19 05	12 08	10 08	15 42	24 48
37	18 50	11 38	09 29	15 09	24 37
38	18 33	11 07	08 48	14 34	24 25
39	18 17	10 35	08 06	13 57	24 12
40	17 59	10 02	07 21	13 17	23 59
41	17 42	09 28	06 34	12 35	23 44
42	17 23	08 52	05 44	11 49	23 28
43	17 05	08 15	04 52	11 00	23 11
44	16 45	07 37	03 57	10 08	22 52
45	16 25	06 57	02 58	09 10	22 31
46	16 05	06 15	01 56	08 08	22 08
47	15 43	05 31	00 51	07 00	21 42
48	15 21	04 45	29♑41	05 46	21 14
49	14 58	03 57	28 26	04 24	20 42
50	14 34	03 07	27 07	02 54	20 05
51	14 09	02 14	25 43	01 15	19 24
52	13 43	01 19	24 12	29♒24	18 36
53	13 15	00 20	22 35	27 20	17 40
54	12 47	29♐18	20 51	25 01	16 34
55	12 17	28 13	18 59	22 24	15 16
56	11 45	27 04	16 59	19 27	13 40
57	11 12	25 50	14 49	16 06	11 40
58	10 37	24 33	12 29	12 18	09 09
59	10 00	23 10	09 59	08 00	05 51
60	09♐21	21♐41	07♑17	03♒07	01♈25

15h 48m 0s — 29 ♏ 13 — 237° 0' 0"

LAT.	11	12	ASC	2	3
0	27♐15	25♑03	24♒42	26♓44	29♈03
5	26 22	23 46	23 27	25 55	28 48
10	25 29	22 26	22 05	25 01	28 32
15	24 35	21 00	20 35	24 00	28 13
20	23 37	19 28	18 55	22 51	27 52
21	23 26	19 08	18 33	22 35	27 47
22	23 14	18 48	18 11	22 19	27 43
23	23 02	18 28	17 48	22 03	27 38
24	22 49	18 07	17 24	21 46	27 32
25	22 37	17 46	17 00	21 28	27 27
26	22 24	17 24	16 34	21 10	27 21
27	22 11	17 02	16 08	20 51	27 15
28	21 58	16 39	15 41	20 31	27 09
29	21 45	16 15	15 13	20 10	27 03
30	21 31	15 51	14 44	19 48	26 56
31	21 18	15 27	14 14	19 25	26 49
32	21 03	15 01	13 43	19 00	26 41
33	20 49	14 35	13 11	18 35	26 33
34	20 34	14 08	12 37	18 08	26 25
35	20 19	13 40	12 02	17 40	26 16
36	20 04	13 12	11 25	17 10	26 06
37	19 48	12 42	10 46	16 38	25 56
38	19 32	12 11	10 06	16 05	25 45
39	19 15	11 39	09 23	15 29	25 34
40	18 58	11 06	08 39	14 50	25 21
41	18 40	10 32	07 52	14 09	25 08
42	18 22	09 57	07 03	13 25	24 53
43	18 03	09 20	06 11	12 38	24 37
44	17 44	08 41	05 16	11 46	24 19
45	17 24	08 01	04 18	10 51	24 00
46	17 03	07 19	03 16	09 50	23 39
47	16 41	06 35	02 11	08 44	23 15
48	16 19	05 49	01 01	07 32	22 49
49	15 56	05 01	29♑47	06 12	22 19
50	15 32	04 11	28 28	04 44	21 46
51	15 07	03 17	27 03	03 06	21 07
52	14 40	02 21	25 32	01 17	20 23
53	14 13	01 22	23 54	29♒15	19 31
54	13 44	00 20	22 09	26 58	18 29
55	13 14	29♐14	20 16	24 22	17 16
56	12 42	28 04	18 15	21 26	15 46
57	12 09	26 50	16 03	18 05	13 55
58	11 33	25 31	13 41	14 15	11 33
59	10 56	24 07	11 08	09 54	08 26
60	10♐16	22♐37	08♑23	04♒56	04♈14

15h 52m 0s — 00 ♐ 11 — 238° 0' 0"

LAT.	11	12	ASC	2	3
0	28♐10	26♑00	25♒44	27♓49	00♉06
5	27 18	24 45	24 31	27 02	29♈52
10	26 25	23 25	23 11	26 11	29 37
15	25 31	22 01	21 43	25 13	29 21
20	24 35	20 29	20 04	24 06	29 01
21	24 23	20 10	19 43	23 51	28 57
22	24 11	19 50	19 21	23 36	28 53
23	23 59	19 30	18 59	23 20	28 48
24	23 47	19 09	18 35	23 04	28 43
25	23 35	18 48	18 11	22 47	28 39
26	23 22	18 27	17 47	22 29	28 33
27	23 09	18 05	17 21	22 11	28 28
28	22 56	17 42	16 55	21 51	28 22
29	22 43	17 19	16 27	21 31	28 16
30	22 29	16 55	15 59	21 10	28 10
31	22 16	16 30	15 29	20 48	28 04
32	22 02	16 05	14 58	20 25	27 57
33	21 47	15 39	14 26	20 00	27 50
34	21 32	15 12	13 53	19 35	27 42
35	21 17	14 44	13 18	19 08	27 34
36	21 02	14 16	12 42	18 39	27 25
37	20 46	13 46	12 04	18 08	27 16
38	20 30	13 16	11 24	17 36	27 06
39	20 13	12 44	10 42	17 01	26 55
40	19 56	12 11	09 58	16 24	26 44
41	19 38	11 37	09 12	15 44	26 31
42	19 20	11 02	08 23	15 02	26 18
43	19 01	10 25	07 32	14 16	26 03
44	18 42	09 46	06 37	13 26	25 47
45	18 22	09 06	05 39	12 32	25 29
46	18 01	08 24	04 38	11 33	25 10
47	17 40	07 40	03 33	10 29	24 48
48	17 17	06 54	02 23	09 19	24 24
49	16 54	06 06	01 09	08 01	23 56
50	16 30	05 15	29♑50	06 35	23 25
51	16 04	04 21	28 25	05 00	22 50
52	15 38	03 25	26 54	03 13	22 09
53	15 10	02 26	25 16	01 13	21 21
54	14 41	01 23	23 30	28♒57	20 24
55	14 11	00 16	21 36	26 23	19 16
56	13 39	29♐05	19 33	23 28	17 52
57	13 05	27 50	17 20	20 07	16 09
58	12 29	26 30	14 56	16 17	13 56
59	11 51	25 05	12 20	11 53	11 02
60	11♐11	23♐34	09♑31	06♒50	07♈04

15h 56m 0s — 01 ♐ 08 — 239° 0' 0"

LAT.	11	12	ASC	2	3
0	29♐05	26♑57	26♒47	28♓55	01♉08
5	28 14	25 43	25 35	28 10	00 56
10	27 22	24 25	24 17	27 20	00 43
15	26 28	23 01	22 51	26 25	00 28
20	25 32	21 31	21 15	25 21	00 10
21	25 20	21 12	20 54	25 07	00 07
22	25 09	20 52	20 32	24 53	00 03
23	24 57	20 32	20 10	24 38	29♈59
24	24 45	20 12	19 47	24 22	29 54
25	24 32	19 51	19 24	24 06	29 50
26	24 20	19 30	19 00	23 49	29 45
27	24 07	19 08	18 34	23 31	29 40
28	23 54	18 45	18 08	23 13	29 35
29	23 41	18 22	17 41	22 53	29 30
30	23 28	17 59	17 14	22 33	29 24
31	23 14	17 34	16 44	22 12	29 18
32	23 00	17 09	16 14	21 50	29 12
33	22 45	16 43	15 43	21 26	29 06
34	22 31	16 17	15 10	21 01	28 59
35	22 16	15 49	14 36	20 35	28 51
36	22 00	15 21	14 00	20 08	28 43
37	21 45	14 51	13 22	19 38	28 35
38	21 28	14 21	12 43	19 07	28 26
39	21 12	13 49	12 02	18 34	28 16
40	20 55	13 17	11 18	17 58	28 06
41	20 37	12 42	10 32	17 20	27 54
42	20 19	12 07	09 44	16 39	27 42
43	20 00	11 30	08 53	15 55	27 29
44	19 41	10 52	07 59	15 07	27 14
45	19 21	10 11	07 02	14 15	26 58
46	19 00	09 29	06 01	13 18	26 40
47	18 38	08 45	04 56	12 16	26 20
48	18 16	07 59	03 47	11 07	25 58
49	17 52	07 11	02 33	09 52	25 33
50	17 28	06 20	01 13	08 28	25 04
51	17 03	05 26	29♑48	06 55	24 32
52	16 36	04 29	28 17	05 11	23 54
53	16 08	03 30	26 39	03 13	23 10
54	15 39	02 26	24 52	01 00	22 18
55	15 08	01 19	22 57	28♒28	21 15
56	14 36	00 07	20 53	25 34	19 58
57	14 02	28♐51	18 38	22 14	18 22
58	13 25	27 30	16 12	18 24	16 19
59	12 47	26 04	13 34	13 57	13 37
60	12♐06	24♐31	10♑42	08♒50	09♈55

Koch Table of Houses for Latitudes 0° to 60° North

16h 0m 0s — 240° 0' 0" — 02 ♐ 05

LAT.	11	12	ASC	2	3
0	00♑00	27♑55	27♒49	00♈00	02♉11
5	29♐09	26 41	26 39	29♓17	02 00
10	28 18	25 24	25 23	28 30	01 48
15	27 25	24 02	23 59	27 38	01 35
20	26 29	22 33	22 25	26 37	01 19
21	26 18	22 14	22 05	26 23	01 16
22	26 06	21 55	21 44	26 09	01 12
23	25 54	21 35	21 22	25 55	01 09
24	25 42	21 15	21 00	25 40	01 05
25	25 30	20 54	20 37	25 25	01 01
26	25 18	20 33	20 13	25 08	00 57
27	25 05	20 11	19 48	24 51	00 52
28	24 52	19 49	19 23	24 34	00 48
29	24 39	19 26	18 56	24 15	00 43
30	24 26	19 03	18 29	23 56	00 38
31	24 12	18 39	18 00	23 36	00 33
32	23 58	18 14	17 31	23 15	00 27
33	23 44	17 48	17 00	22 52	00 21
34	23 29	17 22	16 28	22 29	00 15
35	23 14	16 54	15 54	22 04	00 08
36	22 59	16 26	15 19	21 37	00 01
37	22 43	15 57	14 42	21 09	29♈54
38	22 27	15 26	14 03	20 39	29 46
39	22 11	14 55	13 22	20 07	29 37
40	21 53	14 22	12 39	19 33	29 27
41	21 36	13 48	11 54	18 56	29 17
42	21 18	13 13	11 06	18 17	29 06
43	20 59	12 36	10 16	17 34	28 54
44	20 39	11 58	09 22	16 48	28 41
45	20 19	11 18	08 25	15 58	28 26
46	19 58	10 36	07 25	15 03	28 10
47	19 37	09 52	06 21	14 03	27 52
48	19 14	09 05	05 12	12 57	27 32
49	18 51	08 17	03 58	11 44	27 09
50	18 26	07 26	02 39	10 23	26 43
51	18 01	06 32	01 14	08 52	26 14
52	17 34	05 35	29♑42	07 11	25 39
53	17 06	04 34	28 04	05 16	24 59
54	16 37	03 30	26 17	03 05	24 11
55	16 06	02 23	24 21	00 36	23 13
56	15 33	01 10	22 15	27♒44	22 03
57	14 59	29♐53	19 59	24 26	20 35
58	14 22	28 31	17 31	20 35	18 41
59	13 43	27 03	14 49	16 07	16 11
60	13♐01	25♐29	11♑54	10♒56	12♈45

16h 4m 0s — 241° 0' 0" — 03 ♐ 03

LAT.	11	12	ASC	2	3
0	00♑55	28♑52	28♒52	01♈05	03♉13
5	00 05	27 40	27 43	00 25	03 04
10	29♐14	26 24	26 30	29♓40	02 53
15	28 22	25 03	25 08	28 50	02 42
20	27 27	23 35	23 36	27 52	02 28
21	27 15	23 17	23 16	27 40	02 25
22	27 04	22 58	22 56	27 26	02 22
23	26 52	22 38	22 34	27 13	02 19
24	26 40	22 18	22 13	26 58	02 15
25	26 28	21 58	21 50	26 44	02 12
26	26 16	21 37	21 27	26 28	02 08
27	26 03	21 15	21 03	26 12	02 04
28	25 50	20 53	20 38	25 55	02 00
29	25 37	20 31	20 12	25 38	01 56
30	25 24	20 07	19 45	25 20	01 52
31	25 10	19 43	19 17	25 00	01 47
32	24 57	19 19	18 48	24 40	01 42
33	24 42	18 53	18 18	24 19	01 37
34	24 28	18 27	17 46	23 56	01 31
35	24 13	18 00	17 13	23 32	01 25
36	23 58	17 32	16 38	23 07	01 19
37	23 42	17 03	16 02	22 40	01 12
38	23 26	16 33	15 24	22 12	01 05
39	23 09	16 01	14 44	21 41	00 57
40	22 52	15 29	14 01	21 08	00 49
41	22 35	14 55	13 17	20 33	00 40
42	22 17	14 20	12 30	19 55	00 30
43	21 58	13 43	11 40	19 15	00 19
44	21 38	13 05	10 47	18 30	00 07
45	21 18	12 25	09 51	17 42	29♈54
46	20 57	11 43	08 51	16 50	29 40
47	20 36	10 58	07 47	15 52	29 23
48	20 13	10 12	06 38	14 48	29 05
49	19 50	09 23	05 25	13 38	28 45
50	19 25	08 32	04 06	12 19	28 21
51	18 59	07 38	02 41	10 52	27 54
52	18 33	06 41	01 10	09 13	27 23
53	18 04	05 40	29♑31	07 21	26 47
54	17 35	04 36	27 43	05 13	26 03
55	17 04	03 27	25 47	02 47	25 11
56	16 31	02 14	23 40	29♒58	24 07
57	15 56	00 56	21 22	26 42	22 46
58	15 19	29♐33	18 52	22 52	21 02
59	14 39	28 04	16 08	18 24	18 45
60	13♐57	26♐28	13♑09	13♒09	15♈35

16h 8m 0s — 242° 0' 0" — 04 ♐ 00

LAT.	11	12	ASC	2	3
0	01♑50	29♑49	29♒54	02♈11	04♉16
5	01 01	28 39	28 48	01 32	04 07
10	00 11	27 24	27 36	00 50	03 58
15	29♐19	26 05	26 17	00 03	03 48
20	28 24	24 38	24 47	29♓08	03 37
21	28 13	24 19	24 28	28 56	03 34
22	28 02	24 01	24 08	28 43	03 31
23	27 50	23 41	23 47	28 30	03 28
24	27 38	23 22	23 26	28 17	03 26
25	27 26	23 01	23 04	28 03	03 22
26	27 14	22 41	22 41	27 48	03 19
27	27 01	22 20	22 18	27 33	03 16
28	26 49	21 58	21 53	27 17	03 12
29	26 36	21 35	21 28	27 01	03 09
30	26 22	21 12	21 02	26 43	03 05
31	26 09	20 49	20 34	26 25	03 01
32	25 55	20 24	20 06	26 06	02 57
33	25 41	19 59	19 36	25 45	02 52
34	25 27	19 33	19 05	25 24	02 47
35	25 12	19 06	18 33	25 01	02 42
36	24 57	18 38	17 59	24 37	02 36
37	24 41	18 09	17 23	24 12	02 31
38	24 25	17 39	16 45	23 44	02 24
39	24 08	17 08	16 06	23 15	02 17
40	23 51	16 36	15 24	22 44	02 10
41	23 34	16 02	14 40	22 11	02 02
42	23 16	15 27	13 54	21 35	01 53
43	22 57	14 50	13 05	20 56	01 44
44	22 37	14 12	12 13	20 13	01 33
45	22 17	13 32	11 17	19 27	01 21
46	21 56	12 50	10 18	18 37	01 09
47	21 35	12 06	09 14	17 42	00 54
48	21 12	11 20	08 06	16 40	00 38
49	20 48	10 31	06 53	15 33	00 20
50	20 24	09 39	05 35	14 17	29♈59
51	19 58	08 45	04 10	12 53	29 35
52	19 31	07 47	02 39	11 17	29 07
53	19 03	06 46	01 00	09 29	28 34
54	18 33	05 42	29♑12	07 25	27 55
55	18 02	04 33	27 15	05 02	27 08
56	17 28	03 19	25 07	02 16	26 09
57	16 53	02 00	22 48	29♒02	24 56
58	16 16	00 36	20 16	25 15	23 22
59	15 36	29♐05	17 29	20 46	21 17
60	14♐53	27♐28	14♑26	15♒28	18♈23

16h 12m 0s — 243° 0' 0" — 04 ♐ 57

LAT.	11	12	ASC	2	3
0	02♑45	00♒47	00♓57	03♈16	05♉18
5	01 57	29♑38	29♒53	02 40	05 11
10	01 07	28 25	28 43	02 00	05 03
15	00 16	27 06	27 26	01 15	04 55
20	29♐22	25 41	25 59	00 24	04 45
21	29 11	25 23	25 40	00 12	04 43
22	28 59	25 04	25 21	00 00	04 40
23	28 48	24 45	25 00	29♓48	04 38
24	28 36	24 26	24 40	29 36	04 35
25	28 24	24 06	24 18	29 22	04 33
26	28 12	23 45	23 56	29 08	04 30
27	28 00	23 24	23 33	28 54	04 27
28	27 47	23 03	23 09	28 39	04 24
29	27 34	22 41	22 45	28 23	04 21
30	27 21	22 18	22 19	28 07	04 18
31	27 08	21 54	21 52	27 50	04 14
32	26 54	21 30	21 24	27 31	04 11
33	26 40	21 05	20 55	27 12	04 07
34	26 25	20 39	20 25	26 52	04 03
35	26 11	20 13	19 53	26 30	03 58
36	25 56	19 45	19 20	26 08	03 54
37	25 40	19 16	18 45	25 43	03 48
38	25 24	18 47	18 08	25 18	03 43
39	25 07	18 16	17 29	24 50	03 37
40	24 51	17 43	16 48	24 20	03 31
41	24 33	17 10	16 05	23 49	03 24
42	24 15	16 35	15 20	23 14	03 16
43	23 56	15 59	14 31	22 37	03 08
44	23 37	15 20	13 40	21 57	02 58
45	23 17	14 40	12 45	21 13	02 48
46	22 56	13 58	11 46	20 25	02 37
47	22 34	13 14	10 43	19 32	02 24
48	22 11	12 28	09 36	18 34	02 10
49	21 48	11 39	08 24	17 29	01 54
50	21 23	10 48	07 06	16 17	01 36
51	20 57	09 53	05 41	14 55	01 14
52	20 30	08 55	04 10	13 23	00 49
53	20 02	07 54	02 31	11 38	00 20
54	19 32	06 49	00 43	09 38	29♈45
55	19 00	05 39	28♑46	07 19	29 03
56	18 26	04 25	26 37	04 37	28 11
57	17 51	03 05	24 17	01 27	27 05
58	17 13	01 40	21 42	27♒42	25 40
59	16 33	00 08	18 53	23 15	23 47
60	15♐49	28♐29	15♑47	17♒55	21♈09

16h 16m 0s — 244° 0' 0" — 05 ♐ 54

LAT.	11	12	ASC	2	3
0	03♑40	01♒45	02♓00	04♈22	06♉19
5	02 52	00 37	00 58	03 48	06 14
10	02 04	29♑25	29♒50	03 10	06 08
15	01 13	28 08	28 36	02 28	06 01
20	00 20	26 44	27 11	01 39	05 53
21	00 08	26 26	26 53	01 29	05 51
22	29♐57	26 08	26 34	01 18	05 49
23	29 46	25 49	26 14	01 06	05 47
24	29 34	25 30	25 54	00 54	05 45
25	29 22	25 10	25 33	00 42	05 43
26	29 10	24 50	25 11	00 29	05 41
27	28 58	24 29	24 49	00 15	05 39
28	28 45	24 08	24 26	00 01	05 36
29	28 33	23 46	24 02	29♓46	05 33
30	28 20	23 24	23 37	29 31	05 31
31	28 06	23 00	23 11	29 14	05 28
32	27 53	22 36	22 43	28 57	05 25
33	27 39	22 12	22 15	28 39	05 21
34	27 24	21 46	21 45	28 20	05 18
35	27 10	21 20	21 14	28 00	05 14
36	26 55	20 52	20 42	27 38	05 10
37	26 39	20 24	20 08	27 15	05 06
38	26 23	19 54	19 32	26 51	05 01
39	26 07	19 24	18 54	26 25	04 56
40	25 50	18 52	18 14	25 57	04 51
41	25 32	18 18	17 31	25 27	04 45
42	25 14	17 44	16 46	24 55	04 38
43	24 56	17 07	15 59	24 19	04 31
44	24 36	16 29	15 08	23 41	04 23
45	24 16	15 49	14 14	23 00	04 15
46	23 55	15 08	13 16	22 14	04 05
47	23 33	14 24	12 14	21 24	03 54
48	23 11	13 37	11 07	20 28	03 42
49	22 47	12 48	09 56	19 26	03 28
50	22 22	11 57	08 38	18 17	03 12
51	21 56	11 02	07 14	16 59	02 53
52	21 29	10 04	05 44	15 31	02 31
53	21 01	09 02	04 05	13 51	02 05
54	20 30	07 57	02 17	11 55	01 35
55	19 58	06 47	00 19	09 40	00 57
56	19 25	05 31	28♑10	07 03	00 11
57	18 49	04 11	25 48	03 57	29♈13
58	18 11	02 45	23 12	00 16	27 57
59	17 30	01 11	20 20	25♒50	26 15
60	16♐46	29♐31	17♑10	20♒30	23♈54

16h 20m 0s — 245° 0' 0" — 06 ♐ 50

LAT.	11	12	ASC	2	3
0	04♑35	02♒43	03♓03	05♈27	07♉21
5	03 48	01 36	02 03	04 55	07 17
10	03 00	00 26	00 58	04 20	07 12
15	02 10	29♑10	29♒45	03 41	07 07
20	01 17	27 47	28 23	02 55	07 01
21	01 06	27 30	28 06	02 45	06 59
22	00 55	27 12	27 47	02 35	06 58
23	00 44	26 53	27 28	02 24	06 56
24	00 32	26 34	27 09	02 13	06 55
25	00 21	26 15	26 48	02 01	06 53
26	00 09	25 55	26 27	01 49	06 51
27	29♐56	25 35	26 06	01 36	06 49
28	29 44	25 14	25 43	01 23	06 47
29	29 31	24 52	25 20	01 09	06 45
30	29 18	24 30	24 55	00 55	06 43
31	29 05	24 07	24 30	00 39	06 41
32	28 52	23 43	24 03	00 23	06 38
33	28 38	23 19	23 36	00 06	06 36
34	28 24	22 54	23 07	29♓48	06 33
35	28 09	22 27	22 36	29 29	06 30
36	27 54	22 00	22 05	29 09	06 27
37	27 39	21 32	21 31	28 48	06 23
38	27 23	21 03	20 56	28 25	06 19
39	27 06	20 32	20 19	28 00	06 15
40	26 49	20 01	19 40	27 34	06 11
41	26 32	19 27	18 58	27 06	06 06
42	26 14	18 53	18 14	26 35	06 00
43	25 55	18 17	17 27	26 02	05 55
44	25 36	17 39	16 37	25 26	05 48
45	25 16	16 59	15 44	24 47	05 41
46	24 55	16 18	14 47	24 04	05 32
47	24 33	15 34	13 46	23 16	05 23
48	24 10	14 47	12 40	22 24	05 13
49	23 47	13 59	11 29	21 25	05 01
50	23 22	13 07	10 13	20 19	04 47
51	22 56	12 12	08 50	19 05	04 31
52	22 29	11 14	07 19	17 41	04 12
53	22 00	10 12	05 41	16 05	03 50
54	21 29	09 06	03 53	14 13	03 23
55	20 57	07 55	01 55	12 04	02 50
56	20 23	06 39	29♑45	09 32	02 10
57	19 47	05 18	27 22	06 31	01 18
58	19 09	03 51	24 44	02 54	00 11
59	18 27	02 16	21 50	28♒32	28♈41
60	17♐43	00♑34	18♑37	23♒13	26♈35

16h 24m 0s — 246° 0' 0" — 07 ♐ 47

LAT.	11	12	ASC	2	3
0	05♑30	03♒41	04♓07	06♈32	08♉23
5	04 44	02 36	03 09	06 03	08 20
10	03 57	01 27	02 06	05 30	08 16
15	03 07	00 13	00 55	04 54	08 13
20	02 15	28♑51	29♒36	04 11	08 08
21	02 04	28 34	29 19	04 02	08 07
22	01 53	28 16	29 01	03 52	08 06
23	01 42	27 58	28 43	03 42	08 05
24	01 31	27 39	28 24	03 32	08 04
25	01 19	27 20	28 04	03 21	08 03
26	01 07	27 01	27 44	03 10	08 01
27	00 55	26 41	27 23	02 58	08 00
28	00 43	26 20	27 01	02 45	07 59
29	00 30	25 59	26 38	02 32	07 57
30	00 17	25 37	26 14	02 19	07 55
31	00 04	25 14	25 49	02 05	07 54
32	29♐51	24 51	25 24	01 50	07 52
33	29 37	24 26	24 57	01 34	07 50
34	29 23	24 01	24 29	01 17	07 48
35	29 08	23 35	23 59	00 59	07 45
36	28 53	23 09	23 28	00 40	07 43
37	28 38	22 41	22 56	00 20	07 40
38	28 22	22 12	22 21	29♓59	07 37
39	28 06	21 42	21 45	29 36	07 34
40	27 49	21 10	21 07	29 11	07 30
41	27 32	20 37	20 26	28 45	07 26
42	27 14	20 03	19 43	28 16	07 22
43	26 55	19 27	18 57	27 45	07 17
44	26 36	18 49	18 08	27 11	07 12
45	26 16	18 10	17 16	26 35	07 06
46	25 55	17 28	16 20	25 54	06 59
47	25 33	16 45	15 20	25 09	06 51
48	25 10	15 58	14 15	24 20	06 43
49	24 47	15 10	13 05	23 24	06 33
50	24 22	14 18	11 49	22 22	06 21
51	23 56	13 23	10 27	21 12	06 08
52	23 28	12 25	08 57	19 52	05 52
53	22 59	11 22	07 19	18 21	05 33
54	22 29	10 16	05 32	16 35	05 10
55	21 57	09 05	03 34	14 31	04 42
56	21 22	07 49	01 24	12 04	04 07
57	20 46	06 27	29♑00	09 09	03 22
58	20 07	04 58	26 20	05 38	02 24
59	19 25	03 22	23 23	01 21	01 05
60	18♐40	01♑38	20♑07	26♒05	29♈14

16h 28m 0s — 247° 0' 0" — 08 ♐ 43

LAT.	11	12	ASC	2	3
0	06♑26	04♒39	05♓10	07♈37	09♉24
5	05 40	03 36	04 14	07 10	09 22
10	04 53	02 28	03 13	06 40	09 20
15	04 05	01 15	02 06	06 06	09 18
20	03 13	29♑55	00 49	05 27	09 16
21	03 02	29 38	00 32	05 18	09 15
22	02 51	29 21	00 15	05 10	09 14
23	02 40	29 03	29♒57	05 00	09 14
24	02 29	28 45	29 39	04 51	09 13
25	02 17	28 26	29 20	04 41	09 12
26	02 06	28 07	29 00	04 30	09 11
27	01 54	27 47	28 40	04 19	09 10
28	01 42	27 26	28 19	04 08	09 09
29	01 29	27 05	27 57	03 56	09 08
30	01 16	26 44	27 34	03 43	09 07
31	01 03	26 21	27 10	03 30	09 06
32	00 50	25 58	26 45	03 16	09 05
33	00 36	25 34	26 19	03 01	09 03
34	00 22	25 10	25 51	02 46	09 02
35	00 08	24 44	25 23	02 29	09 00
36	29♐53	24 18	24 52	02 12	08 58
37	29 38	23 50	24 21	01 53	08 56
38	29 22	23 21	23 47	01 33	08 54
39	29 06	22 51	23 12	01 12	08 52
40	28 49	22 20	22 35	00 49	08 49
41	28 32	21 48	21 55	00 24	08 46
42	28 14	21 14	21 13	29♓58	08 43
43	27 55	20 38	20 28	29 29	08 39
44	27 36	20 01	19 40	28 57	08 35
45	27 16	19 21	18 49	28 23	08 31
46	26 55	18 40	17 54	27 45	08 25
47	26 33	17 56	16 55	27 03	08 19
48	26 11	17 10	15 51	26 16	08 12
49	25 47	16 22	14 43	25 25	08 04
50	25 22	15 30	13 28	24 26	07 55
51	24 56	14 35	12 07	23 20	07 44
52	24 28	13 37	10 38	22 05	07 31
53	23 59	12 34	09 00	20 38	07 15
54	23 29	11 27	07 14	18 58	06 56
55	22 56	10 16	05 16	17 00	06 32
56	22 22	08 59	03 05	14 40	06 02
57	21 45	07 36	00 41	11 52	05 24
58	21 05	06 07	28♑00	08 28	04 34
59	20 23	04 30	25 01	04 17	03 26
60	19♐38	02♑44	21♑41	29♒05	01♉49

Koch Table of Houses for Latitudes 0° to 60° North

16h 32m 0s — 248° 0' 0" — 09 ♐ 40

LAT.	11	12	ASC	2	3
0	07♑21	05♒38	06♓14	08♈43	10♉25
5	06 36	04 36	05 20	08 18	10 25
10	05 50	03 29	04 22	07 50	10 24
15	05 02	02 18	03 17	07 19	10 24
20	04 11	01 00	02 03	06 43	10 23
21	04 00	00 43	01 46	06 35	10 22
22	03 50	00 26	01 30	06 27	10 22
23	03 39	00 08	01 13	06 18	10 22
24	03 27	29♑50	00 55	06 09	10 22
25	03 16	29 32	00 37	06 00	10 21
26	03 04	29 13	00 18	05 51	10 21
27	02 53	28 53	29♒58	05 40	10 20
28	02 41	28 33	29 37	05 30	10 20
29	02 28	28 13	29 16	05 19	10 19
30	02 16	27 51	28 54	05 07	10 19
31	02 03	27 29	28 31	04 55	10 18
32	01 49	27 07	28 06	04 42	10 17
33	01 36	26 43	27 41	04 29	10 17
34	01 22	26 19	27 15	04 14	10 16
35	01 08	25 53	26 47	03 59	10 15
36	00 53	25 27	26 18	03 43	10 14
37	00 38	25 00	25 47	03 26	10 12
38	00 22	24 32	25 14	03 08	10 11
39	00 06	24 02	24 40	02 48	10 10
40	29♐49	23 31	24 04	02 27	10 08
41	29 32	22 59	23 25	02 04	10 06
42	29 14	22 25	22 44	01 39	10 04
43	28 56	21 50	22 00	01 12	10 01
44	28 36	21 13	21 14	00 43	09 58
45	28 16	20 34	20 24	00 11	09 55
46	27 56	19 52	19 30	29♓36	09 51
47	27 34	19 09	18 32	28 57	09 46
48	27 11	18 23	17 30	28 14	09 41
49	26 47	17 35	16 22	27 25	09 35
50	26 23	16 43	15 08	26 31	09 27
51	25 56	15 48	13 48	25 29	09 19
52	25 29	14 50	12 21	24 19	09 08
53	25 00	13 47	10 44	22 57	08 56
54	24 29	12 40	08 58	21 23	08 40
55	23 56	11 28	07 01	19 31	08 20
56	23 21	10 11	04 50	17 19	07 56
57	22 44	08 47	02 25	14 38	07 24
58	22 05	07 17	29♑44	11 22	06 41
59	21 22	05 38	26 42	07 19	05 43
60	20♐36	03♑51	23♑19	02♓13	04♉21

16h 36m 0s — 249° 0' 0" — 10 ♐ 36

LAT.	11	12	ASC	2	3
0	08♑16	06♒37	07♓18	09♈48	11♉26
5	07 32	05 36	06 26	09 25	11 27
10	06 47	04 31	05 30	09 00	11 28
15	05 59	03 21	04 27	08 32	11 29
20	05 09	02 04	03 16	07 59	11 30
21	04 59	01 48	03 01	07 52	11 30
22	04 48	01 31	02 45	07 44	11 30
23	04 37	01 14	02 28	07 36	11 30
24	04 26	00 56	02 11	07 28	11 30
25	04 15	00 38	01 54	07 20	11 30
26	04 03	00 20	01 35	07 11	11 30
27	03 52	00 00	01 16	07 02	11 30
28	03 40	29♑41	00 56	06 52	11 30
29	03 27	29 20	00 36	06 42	11 30
30	03 15	28 59	00 14	06 32	11 30
31	03 02	28 38	29♒52	06 20	11 30
32	02 49	28 15	29 29	06 09	11 30
33	02 36	27 52	29 04	05 56	11 30
34	02 22	27 28	28 39	05 43	11 29
35	02 08	27 03	28 12	05 29	11 29
36	01 53	26 37	27 43	05 15	11 29
37	01 38	26 10	27 14	04 59	11 28
38	01 22	25 42	26 42	04 42	11 28
39	01 06	25 13	26 09	04 24	11 27
40	00 50	24 43	25 34	04 05	11 26
41	00 33	24 11	24 56	03 44	11 25
42	00 15	23 37	24 16	03 21	11 24
43	29♐56	23 02	23 34	02 56	11 22
44	29 37	22 25	22 48	02 29	11 20
45	29 17	21 47	22 00	02 00	11 18
46	28 56	21 06	21 07	01 28	11 16
47	28 35	20 23	20 11	00 52	11 13
48	28 12	19 37	19 10	00 12	11 09
49	27 48	18 49	18 03	29♓27	11 05
50	27 23	17 57	16 51	28 37	10 59
51	26 57	17 02	15 32	27 39	10 53
52	26 29	16 04	14 06	26 34	10 45
53	26 00	15 01	12 31	25 18	10 35
54	25 29	13 54	10 45	23 49	10 23
55	24 57	12 42	08 49	22 05	10 08
56	24 22	11 24	06 39	20 00	09 48
57	23 44	10 00	04 14	17 28	09 22
58	23 04	08 28	01 31	14 22	08 47
59	22 21	06 49	28♑28	10 28	07 58
60	21♐34	05♑00	25♑02	05♓31	06♉49

16h 40m 0s — 250° 0' 0" — 11 ♐ 32

LAT.	11	12	ASC	2	3
0	09♑11	07♒35	08♓22	10♈53	12♉27
5	08 28	06 36	07 32	10 32	12 29
10	07 43	05 33	06 39	10 10	12 31
15	06 57	04 25	05 39	09 44	12 34
20	06 07	03 09	04 30	09 15	12 36
21	05 57	02 53	04 16	09 08	12 37
22	05 46	02 37	04 00	09 01	12 37
23	05 36	02 20	03 44	08 54	12 38
24	05 25	02 03	03 28	08 47	12 38
25	05 14	01 45	03 11	08 39	12 39
26	05 02	01 27	02 53	08 31	12 39
27	04 51	01 08	02 35	08 23	12 40
28	04 39	00 49	02 16	08 14	12 40
29	04 27	00 29	01 56	08 05	12 41
30	04 14	00 08	01 36	07 56	12 41
31	04 02	29♑47	01 14	07 46	12 41
32	03 49	29 25	00 52	07 35	12 42
33	03 35	29 02	00 28	07 24	12 42
34	03 22	28 38	00 03	07 12	12 43
35	03 08	28 14	29♒37	06 59	12 43
36	02 53	27 48	29 10	06 46	12 43
37	02 38	27 22	28 41	06 32	12 43
38	02 23	26 54	28 11	06 16	12 43
39	02 07	26 25	27 39	06 00	12 44
40	01 50	25 55	27 05	05 42	12 44
41	01 33	25 23	26 28	05 23	12 43
42	01 16	24 50	25 50	05 03	12 43
43	00 57	24 16	25 09	04 40	12 43
44	00 38	23 39	24 25	04 16	12 42
45	00 18	23 01	23 37	03 49	12 41
46	29♐58	22 20	22 46	03 19	12 40
47	29 36	21 37	21 51	02 46	12 38
48	29 13	20 52	20 51	02 10	12 36
49	28 49	20 04	19 47	01 29	12 34
50	28 25	19 12	18 36	00 43	12 30
51	27 58	18 18	17 19	29♓50	12 26
52	27 31	17 19	15 54	28 49	12 21
53	27 01	16 17	14 20	27 39	12 14
54	26 30	15 09	12 36	26 17	12 05
55	25 57	13 57	10 40	24 40	11 53
56	25 22	12 39	08 31	22 44	11 38
57	24 44	11 14	06 06	20 21	11 17
58	24 04	09 41	03 23	17 25	10 49
59	23 20	08 01	00 18	13 43	10 10
60	22♐33	06♑10	26♑50	08♓56	09♉13

16h 44m 0s — 251° 0' 0" — 12 ♐ 28

LAT.	11	12	ASC	2	3
0	10♑07	08♒34	09♓26	11♈58	13♉27
5	09 24	07 37	08 39	11 39	13 31
10	08 40	06 35	07 47	11 19	13 35
15	07 54	05 28	06 50	10 57	13 38
20	07 06	04 15	05 45	10 30	13 43
21	06 55	03 59	05 31	10 25	13 43
22	06 45	03 43	05 16	10 19	13 44
23	06 34	03 27	05 01	10 12	13 45
24	06 24	03 10	04 45	10 06	13 46
25	06 13	02 52	04 29	09 59	13 47
26	06 01	02 34	04 12	09 52	13 48
27	05 50	02 16	03 54	09 44	13 49
28	05 38	01 57	03 36	09 37	13 50
29	05 26	01 37	03 17	09 29	13 51
30	05 14	01 17	02 57	09 20	13 52
31	05 02	00 56	02 37	09 11	13 53
32	04 49	00 34	02 15	09 01	13 54
33	04 35	00 12	01 52	08 51	13 55
34	04 22	29♑49	01 29	08 41	13 55
35	04 08	29 25	01 04	08 30	13 56
36	03 54	28 59	00 37	08 18	13 57
37	03 39	28 33	00 10	08 05	13 58
38	03 23	28 06	29♒41	07 51	13 59
39	03 08	27 38	29 10	07 36	14 00
40	02 51	27 08	28 37	07 20	14 01
41	02 34	26 37	28 02	07 03	14 01
42	02 17	26 04	27 24	06 45	14 02
43	01 58	25 30	26 45	06 24	14 03
44	01 39	24 54	26 02	06 02	14 03
45	01 20	24 16	25 16	05 38	14 03
46	00 59	23 35	24 26	05 11	14 03
47	00 37	22 53	23 33	04 41	14 03
48	00 15	22 08	22 35	04 08	14 03
49	29♐51	21 20	21 32	03 31	14 02
50	29 26	20 29	20 23	02 49	14 00
51	29 00	19 34	19 07	02 01	13 58
52	28 32	18 36	17 44	01 06	13 55
53	28 03	17 33	16 12	00 02	13 51
54	27 32	16 26	14 29	28♓46	13 45
55	26 58	15 13	12 35	27 17	13 37
56	26 23	13 55	10 27	25 29	13 26
57	25 45	12 29	08 03	23 17	13 11
58	25 04	10 56	05 19	20 32	12 50
59	24 20	09 14	02 14	17 03	12 19
60	23♐33	07♑22	28♑42	12♓30	11♉33

16h 48m 0s — 252° 0' 0" — 13 ♐ 24

LAT.	11	12	ASC	2	3
0	11♑02	09♒34	10♓30	13♈03	14♉28
5	10 20	08 37	09 45	12 47	14 33
10	09 37	07 37	08 56	12 29	14 38
15	08 52	06 32	08 02	12 09	14 43
20	08 04	05 21	07 00	11 46	14 49
21	07 54	05 05	06 46	11 41	14 50
22	07 44	04 49	06 32	11 36	14 51
23	07 33	04 33	06 17	11 30	14 52
24	07 23	04 17	06 02	11 24	14 54
25	07 12	04 00	05 47	11 18	14 55
26	07 01	03 42	05 31	11 12	14 56
27	06 49	03 24	05 14	11 06	14 58
28	06 38	03 05	04 57	10 59	14 59
29	06 26	02 46	04 38	10 52	15 01
30	06 14	02 26	04 20	10 44	15 02
31	06 01	02 06	04 00	10 36	15 03
32	05 49	01 45	03 39	10 28	15 05
33	05 36	01 23	03 17	10 19	15 06
34	05 22	01 00	02 55	10 10	15 08
35	05 08	00 36	02 31	10 00	15 09
36	04 54	00 11	02 06	09 49	15 11
37	04 39	29♑46	01 39	09 38	15 13
38	04 24	29 19	01 11	09 25	15 14
39	04 09	28 51	00 41	09 12	15 16
40	03 52	28 22	00 10	08 58	15 17
41	03 35	27 51	29♒36	08 43	15 19
42	03 18	27 19	29 00	08 26	15 20
43	03 00	26 45	28 22	08 08	15 22
44	02 41	26 09	27 40	07 49	15 23
45	02 21	25 31	26 56	07 27	15 25
46	02 01	24 52	26 08	07 03	15 26
47	01 39	24 09	25 16	06 36	15 27
48	01 17	23 25	24 20	06 07	15 28
49	00 53	22 37	23 19	05 33	15 29
50	00 28	21 46	22 12	04 56	15 29
51	00 02	20 52	20 58	04 12	15 29
52	29♐34	19 54	19 37	03 22	15 28
53	29 05	18 52	18 07	02 24	15 27
54	28 33	17 44	16 26	01 16	15 24
55	28 00	16 32	14 34	29♓55	15 19
56	27 25	15 13	12 27	28 16	15 12
57	26 46	13 47	10 04	26 15	15 02
58	26 05	12 13	07 21	23 43	14 47
59	25 21	10 30	04 15	20 28	14 25
60	24♐33	08♑36	00♒41	16♓11	13♉50

16h 52m 0s — 253° 0' 0" — 14 ♐ 20

LAT.	11	12	ASC	2	3
0	11♑58	10♒33	11♓34	14♈07	15♉28
5	11 17	09 38	10 52	13 54	15 34
10	10 34	08 40	10 05	13 39	15 40
15	09 50	07 37	09 14	13 22	15 47
20	09 03	06 27	08 15	13 02	15 55
21	08 53	06 12	08 02	12 57	15 56
22	08 43	05 56	07 48	12 53	15 58
23	08 32	05 40	07 34	12 48	15 59
24	08 22	05 24	07 20	12 43	16 01
25	08 11	05 08	07 05	12 38	16 03
26	08 00	04 50	06 50	12 32	16 05
27	07 49	04 33	06 34	12 27	16 06
28	07 38	04 15	06 18	12 21	16 08
29	07 26	03 56	06 00	12 15	16 10
30	07 14	03 36	05 42	12 08	16 12
31	07 02	03 16	05 23	12 01	16 14
32	06 49	02 55	05 04	11 54	16 16
33	06 36	02 34	04 43	11 46	16 18
34	06 23	02 12	04 21	11 38	16 20
35	06 09	01 48	03 58	11 29	16 22
36	05 55	01 24	03 34	11 20	16 24
37	05 40	00 59	03 09	11 10	16 27
38	05 25	00 32	02 42	11 00	16 29
39	05 10	00 05	02 14	10 48	16 31
40	04 54	29♑36	01 43	10 36	16 33
41	04 37	29 06	01 11	10 23	16 36
42	04 20	28 34	00 37	10 08	16 38
43	04 02	28 01	00 00	09 52	16 41
44	03 43	27 25	29♒20	09 35	16 43
45	03 23	26 48	28 38	09 16	16 46
46	03 03	26 09	27 52	08 55	16 48
47	02 41	25 27	27 02	08 31	16 51
48	02 19	24 43	26 07	08 05	16 53
49	01 55	23 56	25 08	07 36	16 55
50	01 30	23 05	24 03	07 02	16 57
51	01 04	22 11	22 52	06 24	16 59
52	00 36	21 14	21 32	05 39	17 00
53	00 07	20 11	20 04	04 48	17 01
54	29♐36	19 04	18 26	03 46	17 01
55	29 02	17 51	16 36	02 33	17 00
56	28 27	16 32	14 31	01 05	16 57
57	27 48	15 06	12 09	29♓15	16 51
58	27 07	13 31	09 27	26 56	16 42
59	26 22	11 47	06 21	23 57	16 27
60	25♐33	09♑53	02♒46	19♓58	16♉02

16h 56m 0s — 254° 0' 0" — 15 ♐ 16

LAT.	11	12	ASC	2	3
0	12♑53	11♒32	12♓39	15♈12	16♉28
5	12 13	10 39	11 59	15 01	16 35
10	11 31	09 43	11 15	14 48	16 43
15	10 48	08 41	10 26	14 34	16 51
20	10 01	07 33	09 30	14 17	17 00
21	09 51	07 18	09 18	14 13	17 02
22	09 42	07 03	09 05	14 10	17 04
23	09 31	06 48	08 52	14 06	17 06
24	09 21	06 32	08 38	14 01	17 08
25	09 10	06 16	08 24	13 57	17 10
26	09 00	05 59	08 10	13 53	17 12
27	08 49	05 42	07 55	13 48	17 15
28	08 37	05 24	07 39	13 43	17 17
29	08 26	05 06	07 22	13 38	17 19
30	08 14	04 47	07 05	13 32	17 22
31	08 02	04 27	06 47	13 26	17 24
32	07 50	04 07	06 29	13 20	17 27
33	07 37	03 46	06 09	13 14	17 29
34	07 24	03 24	05 48	13 07	17 32
35	07 10	03 01	05 27	12 59	17 34
36	06 56	02 37	05 04	12 51	17 37
37	06 42	02 12	04 40	12 43	17 40
38	06 27	01 47	04 14	12 34	17 43
39	06 11	01 20	03 47	12 24	17 46
40	05 55	00 51	03 18	12 14	17 49
41	05 39	00 21	02 47	12 02	17 52
42	05 22	29♑50	02 14	11 50	17 56
43	05 04	29 17	01 39	11 36	17 59
44	04 45	28 43	01 01	11 21	18 02
45	04 25	28 06	00 20	11 05	18 06
46	04 05	27 27	29♒36	10 47	18 10
47	03 44	26 46	28 48	10 26	18 13
48	03 21	26 02	27 56	10 04	18 17
49	02 58	25 15	26 59	09 38	18 21
50	02 33	24 25	25 56	09 09	18 24
51	02 07	23 32	24 47	08 35	18 28
52	01 39	22 34	23 31	07 56	18 31
53	01 10	21 33	22 05	07 11	18 34
54	00 38	20 25	20 29	06 17	18 37
55	00 05	19 13	18 42	05 12	18 39
56	29♐29	17 54	16 39	03 53	18 40
57	28 51	16 27	14 19	02 15	18 38
58	28 09	14 52	11 39	00 11	18 35
59	27 24	13 07	08 34	27♓29	18 26
60	26♐34	11♑11	04♒58	23♓51	18♉10

17h 0m 0s — 255° 0' 0" — 16 ♐ 11

LAT.	11	12	ASC	2	3
0	13♑49	12♒32	13♓43	16♈17	17♉28
5	13 09	11 41	13 05	16 08	17 36
10	12 29	10 46	12 24	15 57	17 45
15	11 46	09 46	11 38	15 46	17 55
20	11 00	08 40	10 45	15 32	18 06
21	10 50	08 26	10 34	15 29	18 08
22	10 41	08 11	10 22	15 26	18 10
23	10 31	07 56	10 10	15 23	18 13
24	10 20	07 41	09 57	15 20	18 15
25	10 10	07 25	09 44	15 16	18 18
26	10 00	07 08	09 30	15 13	18 20
27	09 49	06 52	09 16	15 09	18 23
28	09 38	06 34	09 01	15 05	18 25
29	09 26	06 16	08 45	15 00	18 28
30	09 15	05 58	08 29	14 56	18 31
31	09 03	05 39	08 12	14 51	18 34
32	08 50	05 19	07 54	14 46	18 37
33	08 38	04 58	07 36	14 41	18 40
34	08 25	04 37	07 16	14 35	18 43
35	08 11	04 14	06 56	14 29	18 46
36	07 57	03 51	06 34	14 22	18 50
37	07 43	03 27	06 11	14 15	18 53
38	07 28	03 01	05 47	14 08	18 57
39	07 13	02 35	05 21	14 00	19 00
40	06 57	02 07	04 54	13 51	19 04
41	06 41	01 38	04 24	13 41	19 08
42	06 24	01 07	03 53	13 31	19 12
43	06 06	00 35	03 19	13 20	19 17
44	05 47	00 01	02 43	13 07	19 21
45	05 28	29♑25	02 04	12 53	19 26
46	05 08	28 46	01 22	12 38	19 30
47	04 47	28 06	00 37	12 21	19 35
48	04 24	27 23	29♒47	12 02	19 40
49	04 01	26 36	28 52	11 40	19 45
50	03 36	25 47	27 52	11 15	19 50
51	03 10	24 54	26 45	10 46	19 56
52	02 42	23 57	25 31	10 13	20 01
53	02 13	22 55	24 09	09 34	20 06
54	01 42	21 49	22 36	08 47	20 11
55	01 08	20 36	20 51	07 51	20 16
56	00 32	19 17	18 52	06 42	20 20
57	29♐53	17 50	16 35	05 16	20 23
58	29 12	16 15	13 57	03 27	20 24
59	28 26	14 29	10 52	01 03	20 22
60	27♐36	12♑32	07♒17	27♓47	20♉15

Koch Table of Houses for Latitudes 0° to 60° North

17h 4m 0s — 256° 0' 0" — 17 ♐ 07

LAT.	11	12	ASC	2	3
0	14♑44	13♒32	14♓48	17♈21	18♉28
5	14 06	12 42	14 12	17 14	18 37
10	13 26	11 49	13 34	17 07	18 48
15	12 44	10 51	12 51	16 58	18 59
20	11 59	09 47	12 01	16 48	19 11
21	11 50	09 33	11 50	16 45	19 13
22	11 40	09 19	11 39	16 43	19 16
23	11 30	09 04	11 28	16 41	19 19
24	11 20	08 49	11 16	16 38	19 22
25	11 10	08 34	11 03	16 35	19 24
26	10 59	08 18	10 50	16 32	19 27
27	10 49	08 02	10 37	16 29	19 30
28	10 38	07 45	10 23	16 26	19 33
29	10 27	07 27	10 08	16 23	19 37
30	10 15	07 09	09 53	16 19	19 40
31	10 03	06 51	09 37	16 16	19 43
32	09 51	06 31	09 20	16 12	19 47
33	09 39	06 11	09 03	16 07	19 50
34	09 26	05 50	08 44	16 03	19 54
35	09 13	05 28	08 25	15 58	19 58
36	08 59	05 06	08 05	15 53	20 02
37	08 45	04 42	07 43	15 47	20 06
38	08 30	04 17	07 20	15 42	20 10
39	08 15	03 51	06 56	15 35	20 14
40	08 00	03 24	06 30	15 28	20 19
41	07 43	02 55	06 02	15 20	20 24
42	07 26	02 25	05 33	15 12	20 29
43	07 09	01 54	05 01	15 03	20 34
44	06 50	01 20	04 27	14 53	20 39
45	06 31	00 45	03 50	14 42	20 44
46	06 11	00 07	03 10	14 29	20 50
47	05 50	29♑27	02 26	14 15	20 56
48	05 28	28 44	01 39	13 59	21 02
49	05 04	27 59	00 47	13 41	21 09
50	04 40	27 10	29♒49	13 21	21 16
51	04 14	26 17	28 46	12 57	21 23
52	03 46	25 21	27 35	12 29	21 30
53	03 17	24 20	26 16	11 56	21 37
54	02 45	23 13	24 46	11 17	21 45
55	02 12	22 01	23 05	10 29	21 52
56	01 36	20 42	21 09	09 31	21 59
57	00 57	19 15	18 55	08 17	22 06
58	00 15	17 40	16 20	06 43	22 12
59	29♐29	15 53	13 18	04 37	22 15
60	28♐39	13♑55	09♒44	01♈46	22♉15

17h 8m 0s — 257° 0' 0" — 18 ♐ 02

LAT.	11	12	ASC	2	3
0	15♑40	14♒32	15♓53	18♈26	19♉27
5	15 02	13 44	15 20	18 21	19 38
10	14 23	12 53	14 44	18 16	19 50
15	13 42	11 57	14 03	18 10	20 02
20	12 58	10 54	13 17	18 03	20 16
21	12 49	10 41	13 07	18 01	20 19
22	12 39	10 27	12 57	17 59	20 22
23	12 30	10 13	12 46	17 58	20 25
24	12 20	09 58	12 35	17 56	20 28
25	12 10	09 43	12 23	17 54	20 31
26	12 00	09 28	12 11	17 52	20 34
27	11 49	09 12	11 58	17 50	20 38
28	11 38	08 56	11 45	17 48	20 41
29	11 27	08 39	11 32	17 45	20 45
30	11 16	08 21	11 17	17 43	20 49
31	11 04	08 03	11 02	17 40	20 52
32	10 52	07 44	10 47	17 37	20 56
33	10 40	07 25	10 30	17 34	21 00
34	10 27	07 04	10 13	17 31	21 05
35	10 14	06 43	09 55	17 27	21 09
36	10 01	06 21	09 36	17 23	21 13
37	09 47	05 58	09 16	17 19	21 18
38	09 33	05 33	08 54	17 15	21 23
39	09 18	05 08	08 31	17 10	21 28
40	09 02	04 41	08 07	17 05	21 33
41	08 46	04 14	07 41	16 59	21 39
42	08 29	03 44	07 13	16 53	21 44
43	08 12	03 13	06 43	16 46	21 50
44	07 54	02 40	06 11	16 38	21 56
45	07 35	02 05	05 36	16 29	22 03
46	07 15	01 28	04 59	16 20	22 09
47	06 54	00 49	04 18	16 09	22 17
48	06 32	00 07	03 33	15 56	22 24
49	06 08	29♑22	02 43	15 42	22 32
50	05 44	28 34	01 49	15 26	22 40
51	05 18	27 42	00 48	15 07	22 48
52	04 50	26 47	29♒41	14 44	22 57
53	04 21	25 46	28 25	14 18	23 06
54	03 50	24 40	27 00	13 46	23 16
55	03 16	23 28	25 22	13 07	23 26
56	02 40	22 10	23 30	12 19	23 36
57	02 01	20 43	21 21	11 17	23 47
58	01 19	19 07	18 49	09 58	23 57
59	00 33	17 20	15 51	08 12	24 06
60	29♐42	15♑21	12♒19	05♈45	24♉12

17h 12m 0s — 258° 0' 0" — 18 ♐ 58

LAT.	11	12	ASC	2	3
0	16♑36	15♒32	16♓57	19♈30	20♉26
5	15 59	14 46	16 27	19 28	20 38
10	15 21	13 56	15 54	19 25	20 51
15	14 41	13 02	15 16	19 22	21 05
20	13 57	12 02	14 33	19 18	21 20
21	13 48	11 49	14 24	19 17	21 24
22	13 39	11 36	14 14	19 16	21 27
23	13 30	11 22	14 04	19 15	21 30
24	13 20	11 08	13 54	19 14	21 34
25	13 10	10 53	13 43	19 13	21 37
26	13 00	10 39	13 32	19 11	21 41
27	12 50	10 23	13 20	19 10	21 45
28	12 39	10 07	13 08	19 09	21 49
29	12 28	09 51	12 55	19 07	21 53
30	12 17	09 34	12 42	19 06	21 57
31	12 06	09 16	12 28	19 04	22 01
32	11 54	08 58	12 14	19 02	22 06
33	11 42	08 39	11 59	19 00	22 10
34	11 29	08 19	11 43	18 58	22 15
35	11 16	07 58	11 26	18 56	22 20
36	11 03	07 37	11 08	18 54	22 25
37	10 49	07 14	10 49	18 51	22 30
38	10 35	06 50	10 29	18 48	22 35
39	10 20	06 26	10 08	18 45	22 41
40	10 05	06 00	09 45	18 41	22 47
41	09 49	05 33	09 21	18 37	22 53
42	09 32	05 04	08 55	18 33	22 59
43	09 15	04 33	08 27	18 28	23 06
44	08 57	04 01	07 57	18 23	23 13
45	08 38	03 27	07 24	18 17	23 20
46	08 18	02 51	06 49	18 10	23 28
47	07 58	02 13	06 10	18 02	23 36
48	07 36	01 31	05 28	17 53	23 45
49	07 13	00 47	04 42	17 42	23 54
50	06 48	00 00	03 50	17 30	24 03
51	06 23	29♑09	02 53	17 16	24 13
52	05 55	28 14	01 49	16 59	24 24
53	05 26	27 14	00 38	16 38	24 35
54	04 55	26 09	29♒16	16 14	24 46
55	04 21	24 58	27 43	15 43	24 59
56	03 45	23 39	25 56	15 05	25 12
57	03 06	22 13	23 52	14 16	25 25
58	02 24	20 37	21 25	13 12	25 39
59	01 37	18 50	18 31	11 45	25 53
60	00♑46	16♑50	15♒03	09♈44	26♉06

17h 16m 0s — 259° 0' 0" — 19 ♐ 53

LAT.	11	12	ASC	2	3
0	17♑32	16♒33	18♓02	20♈34	21♉26
5	16 56	15 48	17 34	20 34	21 39
10	16 19	15 00	17 04	20 34	21 53
15	15 39	14 08	16 29	20 33	22 08
20	14 57	13 10	15 50	20 32	22 25
21	14 48	12 58	15 41	20 32	22 28
22	14 39	12 45	15 32	20 32	22 32
23	14 30	12 31	15 23	20 32	22 36
24	14 20	12 18	15 13	20 31	22 40
25	14 10	12 04	15 04	20 31	22 43
26	14 00	11 49	14 53	20 31	22 48
27	13 50	11 34	14 42	20 30	22 52
28	13 40	11 19	14 31	20 30	22 56
29	13 29	11 03	14 20	20 29	23 00
30	13 18	10 47	14 07	20 29	23 05
31	13 07	10 30	13 55	20 28	23 10
32	12 55	10 12	13 41	20 27	23 14
33	12 44	09 53	13 27	20 27	23 19
34	12 31	09 34	13 12	20 26	23 25
35	12 19	09 14	12 57	20 25	23 30
36	12 05	08 53	12 40	20 24	23 35
37	11 52	08 31	12 23	20 22	23 41
38	11 38	08 08	12 04	20 21	23 47
39	11 23	07 44	11 45	20 19	23 53
40	11 08	07 19	11 24	20 17	24 00
41	10 52	06 52	11 01	20 15	24 07
42	10 36	06 24	10 37	20 13	24 14
43	10 19	05 55	10 11	20 10	24 21
44	10 01	05 24	09 43	20 07	24 29
45	09 42	04 50	09 13	20 03	24 37
46	09 23	04 15	08 40	19 59	24 46
47	09 02	03 37	08 04	19 54	24 55
48	08 41	02 57	07 25	19 49	25 05
49	08 18	02 14	06 41	19 42	25 15
50	07 53	01 27	05 54	19 34	25 25
51	07 28	00 37	05 00	19 24	25 37
52	07 01	29♑43	04 00	19 12	25 49
53	06 31	28 44	02 53	18 58	26 02
54	06 00	27 40	01 36	18 40	26 15
55	05 27	26 29	00 08	18 18	26 30
56	04 51	25 11	28♒27	17 50	26 45
57	04 12	23 46	26 28	17 13	27 02
58	03 29	22 10	24 08	16 24	27 19
59	02 43	20 23	21 20	15 16	27 37
60	01♑51	18♑22	17♒56	13♈40	27♉56

17h 20m 0s — 260° 0' 0" — 20 ♐ 49

LAT.	11	12	ASC	2	3
0	18♑28	17♒33	19♓07	21♈38	22♉25
5	17 53	16 51	18 42	21 40	22 39
10	17 17	16 05	18 14	21 42	22 54
15	16 38	15 14	17 42	21 45	23 11
20	15 56	14 18	17 06	21 47	23 29
21	15 48	14 06	16 59	21 47	23 33
22	15 39	13 54	16 50	21 48	23 37
23	15 30	13 41	16 42	21 48	23 41
24	15 20	13 28	16 33	21 49	23 45
25	15 11	13 15	16 24	21 49	23 49
26	15 01	13 01	16 15	21 50	23 54
27	14 51	12 46	16 05	21 50	23 58
28	14 41	12 31	15 55	21 50	24 03
29	14 31	12 16	15 44	21 51	24 08
30	14 20	12 00	15 33	21 51	24 13
31	14 09	11 44	15 21	21 52	24 18
32	13 57	11 26	15 09	21 52	24 23
33	13 46	11 08	14 56	21 52	24 28
34	13 34	10 50	14 43	21 53	24 34
35	13 21	10 30	14 28	21 53	24 40
36	13 08	10 10	14 13	21 53	24 46
37	12 55	09 49	13 57	21 53	24 52
38	12 41	09 27	13 40	21 53	24 59
39	12 27	09 04	13 22	21 53	25 05
40	12 12	08 39	13 03	21 53	25 13
41	11 56	08 13	12 42	21 53	25 20
42	11 40	07 46	12 20	21 52	25 28
43	11 23	07 17	11 56	21 52	25 36
44	11 05	06 47	11 31	21 51	25 45
45	10 47	06 14	11 03	21 49	25 54
46	10 28	05 40	10 32	21 48	26 03
47	10 07	05 03	09 59	21 46	26 13
48	09 46	04 24	09 23	21 43	26 24
49	09 23	03 42	08 43	21 40	26 35
50	08 59	02 56	07 59	21 36	26 47
51	08 34	02 07	07 09	21 31	26 59
52	08 06	01 14	06 14	21 24	27 13
53	07 38	00 16	05 11	21 16	27 27
54	07 07	29♑12	03 59	21 05	27 43
55	06 33	28 03	02 37	20 51	27 59
56	05 57	26 46	01 02	20 32	28 17
57	05 18	25 21	29♒09	20 07	28 36
58	04 36	23 46	26 56	19 32	28 57
59	03 49	21 59	24 16	18 44	29 19
60	02♑57	19♑58	20♒59	17♈33	29♉42

17h 24m 0s — 261° 0' 0" — 21 ♐ 44

LAT.	11	12	ASC	2	3
0	19♑24	18♒34	20♓12	22♈42	23♉23
5	18 50	17 53	19 49	22 46	23 39
10	18 14	17 09	19 24	22 51	23 55
15	17 37	16 21	18 56	22 56	24 13
20	16 56	15 27	18 23	23 01	24 33
21	16 48	15 16	18 16	23 02	24 37
22	16 39	15 04	18 09	23 04	24 41
23	16 30	14 51	18 01	23 05	24 46
24	16 21	14 39	17 53	23 06	24 50
25	16 12	14 26	17 45	23 07	24 55
26	16 02	14 12	17 37	23 08	24 59
27	15 52	13 59	17 28	23 10	25 04
28	15 42	13 44	17 18	23 11	25 09
29	15 32	13 29	17 09	23 12	25 15
30	15 21	13 14	16 59	23 14	25 20
31	15 11	12 58	16 48	23 15	25 25
32	14 59	12 42	16 37	23 16	25 31
33	14 48	12 24	16 25	23 18	25 37
34	14 36	12 06	16 13	23 19	25 43
35	14 24	11 48	16 00	23 21	25 49
36	14 11	11 28	15 46	23 22	25 56
37	13 58	11 08	15 32	23 24	26 03
38	13 44	10 46	15 17	23 25	26 10
39	13 30	10 24	15 00	23 27	26 17
40	13 16	10 00	14 43	23 28	26 25
41	13 00	09 35	14 24	23 30	26 33
42	12 44	09 09	14 04	23 31	26 41
43	12 28	08 41	13 42	23 32	26 50
44	12 10	08 11	13 19	23 34	26 59
45	11 52	07 40	12 54	23 35	27 09
46	11 33	07 06	12 26	23 36	27 19
47	11 13	06 30	11 56	23 37	27 30
48	10 51	05 52	11 23	23 37	27 42
49	10 29	05 11	10 46	23 38	27 54
50	10 05	04 26	10 06	23 38	28 07
51	09 40	03 38	09 20	23 37	28 21
52	09 13	02 46	08 29	23 35	28 36
53	08 44	01 49	07 32	23 32	28 52
54	08 13	00 47	06 26	23 28	29 09
55	07 40	29♑39	05 09	23 22	29 27
56	07 04	28 23	03 41	23 12	29 47
57	06 25	26 59	01 56	22 58	00♊09
58	05 43	25 25	29♒51	22 38	00 32
59	04 56	23 38	27 20	22 07	00 58
60	04♑04	21♑38	24♒13	21♈20	01♊26

17h 28m 0s — 262° 0' 0" — 22 ♐ 39

LAT.	11	12	ASC	2	3
0	20♑20	19♒35	21♓17	23♈46	24♉22
5	19 47	18 56	20 57	23 52	24 39
10	19 13	18 14	20 34	23 59	24 56
15	18 36	17 28	20 09	24 07	25 16
20	17 56	16 36	19 40	24 15	25 36
21	17 48	16 25	19 34	24 17	25 41
22	17 39	16 14	19 27	24 19	25 46
23	17 31	16 02	19 21	24 21	25 50
24	17 22	15 50	19 14	24 23	25 55
25	17 13	15 37	19 06	24 25	26 00
26	17 03	15 25	18 59	24 27	26 05
27	16 54	15 11	18 51	24 29	26 10
28	16 44	14 58	18 42	24 31	26 16
29	16 34	14 43	18 34	24 33	26 21
30	16 23	14 29	18 25	24 36	26 27
31	16 13	14 13	18 15	24 38	26 33
32	16 02	13 57	18 05	24 40	26 39
33	15 51	13 41	17 55	24 43	26 45
34	15 39	13 23	17 44	24 45	26 52
35	15 27	13 05	17 32	24 48	26 58
36	15 14	12 47	17 20	24 51	27 05
37	15 02	12 27	17 07	24 54	27 13
38	14 48	12 06	16 53	24 56	27 20
39	14 34	11 44	16 39	24 59	27 28
40	14 20	11 22	16 23	25 03	27 36
41	14 05	10 57	16 06	25 06	27 45
42	13 49	10 32	15 48	25 09	27 54
43	13 33	10 05	15 29	25 12	28 04
44	13 15	09 36	15 08	25 16	28 14
45	12 57	09 06	14 45	25 19	28 24
46	12 39	08 33	14 20	25 23	28 35
47	12 19	07 59	13 53	25 27	28 47
48	11 58	07 22	13 24	25 30	28 59
49	11 35	06 42	12 51	25 34	29 13
50	11 12	05 58	12 14	25 38	29 27
51	10 47	05 12	11 33	25 41	29 42
52	10 20	04 21	10 47	25 44	29 58
53	09 52	03 25	09 55	25 47	00♊15
54	09 21	02 24	08 55	25 49	00 34
55	08 48	01 17	07 45	25 50	00 54
56	08 12	00 03	06 24	25 50	01 16
57	07 33	28♑40	04 48	25 46	01 40
58	06 51	27 07	02 53	25 39	02 06
59	06 04	25 22	00 32	25 25	02 34
60	05♑12	23♑21	27♒36	25♈01	03♊06

17h 32m 0s — 263° 0' 0" — 23 ♐ 34

LAT.	11	12	ASC	2	3
0	21♑17	20♒36	22♓23	24♈50	25♉21
5	20 44	19 59	22 05	24 58	25 38
10	20 11	19 19	21 45	25 08	25 57
15	19 35	18 35	21 23	25 18	26 18
20	18 56	17 46	20 57	25 29	26 40
21	18 48	17 35	20 52	25 32	26 45
22	18 40	17 24	20 46	25 34	26 50
23	18 31	17 13	20 40	25 37	26 55
24	18 23	17 01	20 34	25 39	27 00
25	18 14	16 49	20 28	25 42	27 05
26	18 05	16 37	20 21	25 45	27 10
27	17 55	16 24	20 14	25 48	27 16
28	17 46	16 11	20 07	25 51	27 22
29	17 36	15 58	19 59	25 54	27 27
30	17 26	15 43	19 51	25 57	27 33
31	17 15	15 29	19 43	26 01	27 40
32	17 05	15 14	19 34	26 04	27 46
33	16 53	14 58	19 25	26 08	27 53
34	16 42	14 41	19 15	26 11	28 00
35	16 30	14 24	19 05	26 15	28 07
36	16 18	14 06	18 54	26 19	28 14
37	16 05	13 47	18 43	26 23	28 22
38	15 52	13 27	18 31	26 27	28 30
39	15 39	13 06	18 18	26 32	28 39
40	15 24	12 44	18 04	26 37	28 48
41	15 10	12 21	17 49	26 41	28 57
42	14 54	11 56	17 33	26 46	29 06
43	14 38	11 30	17 16	26 52	29 17
44	14 21	11 03	16 58	26 57	29 27
45	14 03	10 33	16 38	27 03	29 38
46	13 45	10 02	16 16	27 09	29 50
47	13 25	09 29	15 52	27 16	00♊03
48	13 04	08 53	15 26	27 22	00 16
49	12 42	08 14	14 56	27 29	00 30
50	12 19	07 32	14 24	27 37	00 45
51	11 54	06 47	13 48	27 44	01 01
52	11 28	05 57	13 07	27 52	01 19
53	11 00	05 03	12 20	28 00	01 37
54	10 29	04 04	11 26	28 08	01 57
55	09 57	02 59	10 24	28 16	02 19
56	09 21	01 46	09 12	28 24	02 43
57	08 42	00 24	07 45	28 31	03 08
58	08 00	28♑53	06 01	28 36	03 37
59	07 13	27 09	03 52	28 38	04 08
60	06♑21	25♑09	01♓10	28♈34	04♊43

Koch Table of Houses for Latitudes 0° to 60° North

17h 36m 0s	264° 0' 0"	24 ♐ 30			
LAT.	11	12	ASC	2	3
0	22♑13	21♒37	23♓28	25♈53	26♉19
5	21 42	21 02	23 12	26 04	26 38
10	21 09	20 24	22 56	26 16	26 58
15	20 34	19 42	22 37	26 28	27 19
20	19 57	18 56	22 15	26 43	27 43
21	19 49	18 45	22 10	26 46	27 48
22	19 41	18 35	22 05	26 49	27 53
23	19 32	18 24	22 00	26 52	27 59
24	19 24	18 13	21 55	26 56	28 04
25	19 15	18 02	21 49	26 59	28 10
26	19 06	17 50	21 43	27 03	28 15
27	18 57	17 38	21 37	27 07	28 21
28	18 48	17 25	21 31	27 10	28 27
29	18 38	17 12	21 25	27 14	28 33
30	18 28	16 59	21 18	27 19	28 40
31	18 18	16 45	21 11	27 23	28 46
32	18 07	16 30	21 03	27 27	28 53
33	17 57	16 15	20 55	27 32	29 00
34	17 45	15 59	20 47	27 37	29 08
35	17 34	15 43	20 38	27 42	29 15
36	17 22	15 26	20 29	27 47	29 23
37	17 10	15 07	20 19	27 52	29 31
38	16 57	14 48	20 09	27 58	29 40
39	16 43	14 28	19 57	28 04	29 49
40	16 29	14 07	19 46	28 10	29 58
41	16 15	13 45	19 33	28 16	00♊08
42	16 00	13 22	19 19	28 23	00 18
43	15 44	12 57	19 04	28 30	00 29
44	15 27	12 30	18 48	28 38	00 40
45	15 10	12 02	18 31	28 46	00 52
46	14 51	11 32	18 12	28 54	01 05
47	14 32	11 00	17 51	29 03	01 18
48	14 12	10 25	17 28	29 13	01 32
49	13 50	09 48	17 03	29 23	01 47
50	13 27	09 07	16 35	29 34	02 03
51	13 03	08 24	16 04	29 45	02 20
52	12 37	07 36	15 28	29 58	02 38
53	12 09	06 44	14 47	00♉11	02 58
54	11 39	05 46	14 01	00 25	03 19
55	11 06	04 42	13 06	00 39	03 43
56	10 31	03 31	12 03	00 55	04 08
57	09 52	02 12	10 46	01 11	04 36
58	09 10	00 42	09 14	01 28	05 06
59	08 23	29♑00	07 20	01 45	05 40
60	07♑31	27♑02	04♓55	02♉00	06♊18

17h 40m 0s	265° 0' 0"	25 ♐ 25			
LAT.	11	12	ASC	2	3
0	23♑10	22♒39	24♓33	26♈57	27♉17
5	22 39	22 06	24 20	27 09	27 37
10	22 08	21 30	24 06	27 23	27 58
15	21 34	20 50	23 50	27 39	28 21
20	20 57	20 06	23 32	27 56	28 46
21	20 49	19 56	23 28	28 00	28 51
22	20 42	19 46	23 24	28 04	28 57
23	20 33	19 36	23 20	28 08	29 02
24	20 25	19 26	23 15	28 12	29 08
25	20 17	19 15	23 11	28 16	29 14
26	20 08	19 04	23 06	28 20	29 20
27	19 59	18 52	23 01	28 25	29 26
28	19 50	18 40	22 56	28 30	29 33
29	19 41	18 28	22 50	28 34	29 39
30	19 31	18 15	22 44	28 39	29 46
31	19 21	18 02	22 38	28 45	29 53
32	19 11	17 48	22 32	28 50	00♊00
33	19 00	17 33	22 26	28 56	00 07
34	18 49	17 18	22 19	29 01	00 15
35	18 38	17 03	22 11	29 08	00 23
36	18 26	16 46	22 04	29 14	00 32
37	18 14	16 29	21 55	29 21	00 40
38	18 01	16 11	21 47	29 28	00 49
39	17 48	15 52	21 37	29 35	00 59
40	17 35	15 32	21 27	29 43	01 08
41	17 20	15 10	21 17	29 51	01 19
42	17 06	14 48	21 05	29 59	01 29
43	16 50	14 24	20 53	00♉08	01 41
44	16 34	13 59	20 39	00 18	01 53
45	16 17	13 32	20 25	00 28	02 05
46	15 59	13 03	20 09	00 39	02 18
47	15 40	12 32	19 52	00 50	02 32
48	15 20	11 59	19 32	01 02	02 47
49	14 58	11 23	19 11	01 16	03 03
50	14 36	10 44	18 47	01 30	03 20
51	14 12	10 02	18 21	01 45	03 38
52	13 46	09 16	17 51	02 01	03 57
53	13 18	08 26	17 16	02 19	04 18
54	12 48	07 30	16 37	02 38	04 40
55	12 16	06 29	15 51	03 00	05 05
56	11 41	05 20	14 57	03 23	05 32
57	11 03	04 03	13 52	03 48	06 01
58	10 21	02 35	12 33	04 15	06 34
59	09 35	00 55	10 54	04 45	07 10
60	08♑43	29♑00	08♓48	05♉18	07♊50

17h 44m 0s	266° 0' 0"	26 ♐ 20			
LAT.	11	12	ASC	2	3
0	24♑06	23♒41	25♓38	28♈00	28♉15
5	23 37	23 09	25 28	28 15	28 36
10	23 06	22 35	25 17	28 31	28 58
15	22 34	21 58	25 04	28 49	29 22
20	21 58	21 16	24 50	29 09	29 49
21	21 50	21 07	24 46	29 14	29 54
22	21 43	20 58	24 43	29 18	00♊00
23	21 35	20 48	24 40	29 23	00 06
24	21 27	20 38	24 36	29 28	00 12
25	21 19	20 28	24 32	29 33	00 18
26	21 10	20 17	24 28	29 38	00 24
27	21 01	20 07	24 24	29 43	00 31
28	20 52	19 55	24 20	29 48	00 38
29	20 43	19 44	24 16	29 54	00 44
30	20 34	19 31	24 11	00♉00	00 52
31	20 24	19 19	24 07	00 06	00 59
32	20 14	19 06	24 02	00 12	01 06
33	20 04	18 52	23 56	00 19	01 14
34	19 53	18 38	23 51	00 26	01 22
35	19 42	18 23	23 45	00 33	01 31
36	19 31	18 07	23 39	00 41	01 39
37	19 19	17 51	23 32	00 48	01 49
38	19 07	17 34	23 25	00 57	01 58
39	18 54	17 16	23 17	01 05	02 08
40	18 40	16 57	23 09	01 15	02 18
41	18 27	16 36	23 01	01 24	02 29
42	18 12	16 15	22 52	01 34	02 40
43	17 57	15 52	22 42	01 45	02 52
44	17 41	15 28	22 31	01 57	03 04
45	17 24	15 03	22 19	02 09	03 18
46	17 06	14 35	22 06	02 22	03 31
47	16 48	14 06	21 52	02 36	03 46
48	16 28	13 34	21 37	02 51	04 02
49	16 07	13 00	21 20	03 07	04 18
50	15 45	12 23	21 01	03 24	04 36
51	15 21	11 43	20 39	03 43	04 55
52	14 56	10 59	20 15	04 03	05 15
53	14 29	10 11	19 47	04 25	05 37
54	13 59	09 17	19 15	04 50	06 00
55	13 27	08 18	18 38	05 17	06 26
56	12 53	07 12	17 54	05 47	06 54
57	12 15	05 58	17 01	06 20	07 25
58	11 34	04 33	15 56	06 57	07 59
59	10 48	02 56	14 35	07 39	08 37
60	09♑56	01♒03	12♓51	08♉27	09♊20

17h 48m 0s	267° 0' 0"	27 ♐ 15			
LAT.	11	12	ASC	2	3
0	25♑03	24♒42	26♓44	29♈03	29♉13
5	24 35	24 13	26 36	29 20	29 35
10	24 05	23 41	26 28	29 39	29 58
15	23 33	23 06	26 18	29 59	00♊24
20	22 59	22 27	26 07	00♉22	00 51
21	22 52	22 18	26 05	00 27	00 57
22	22 44	22 10	26 02	00 32	01 03
23	22 36	22 00	26 00	00 38	01 09
24	22 29	21 51	25 57	00 43	01 15
25	22 21	21 42	25 54	00 49	01 22
26	22 12	21 32	25 51	00 55	01 28
27	22 04	21 21	25 48	01 01	01 35
28	21 55	21 11	25 45	01 07	01 42
29	21 46	21 00	25 42	01 13	01 49
30	21 37	20 48	25 38	01 20	01 57
31	21 28	20 36	25 35	01 27	02 05
32	21 18	20 24	25 31	01 34	02 12
33	21 08	20 11	25 27	01 42	02 21
34	20 58	19 58	25 23	01 50	02 29
35	20 47	19 44	25 18	01 58	02 38
36	20 36	19 29	25 14	02 07	02 47
37	20 24	19 14	25 09	02 16	02 57
38	20 12	18 57	25 04	02 25	03 06
39	20 00	18 40	24 58	02 35	03 17
40	19 47	18 22	24 52	02 46	03 27
41	19 33	18 03	24 45	02 57	03 39
42	19 19	17 43	24 38	03 09	03 50
43	19 04	17 22	24 31	03 21	04 03
44	18 48	16 59	24 23	03 35	04 16
45	18 32	16 35	24 14	03 49	04 29
46	18 15	16 09	24 04	04 04	04 44
47	17 56	15 41	23 54	04 20	04 59
48	17 37	15 11	23 42	04 37	05 15
49	17 16	14 39	23 29	04 56	05 33
50	16 55	14 04	23 15	05 17	05 51
51	16 31	13 25	22 59	05 39	06 11
52	16 06	12 44	22 40	06 03	06 32
53	15 40	11 58	22 19	06 29	06 54
54	15 11	11 07	21 55	06 59	07 19
55	14 40	10 10	21 27	07 31	07 46
56	14 06	09 07	20 53	08 07	08 15
57	13 28	07 56	20 13	08 48	08 47
58	12 47	06 35	19 24	09 34	09 23
59	12 02	05 01	18 21	10 27	10 03
60	11♑10	03♒12	17♓01	11♉28	10♊47

17h 52m 0s	268° 0' 0"	28 ♐ 10			
LAT.	11	12	ASC	2	3
0	26♑00	25♒44	27♓49	00♉06	00♊11
5	25 33	25 17	27 44	00 25	00 34
10	25 04	24 47	27 38	00 46	00 58
15	24 33	24 15	27 32	01 09	01 25
20	24 00	23 38	27 25	01 35	01 53
21	23 53	23 30	27 23	01 40	01 59
22	23 46	23 22	27 21	01 46	02 06
23	23 38	23 13	27 20	01 52	02 12
24	23 31	23 05	27 18	01 58	02 19
25	23 23	22 56	27 16	02 05	02 25
26	23 15	22 46	27 14	02 11	02 32
27	23 07	22 37	27 12	02 18	02 39
28	22 58	22 27	27 10	02 25	02 47
29	22 50	22 16	27 08	02 32	02 54
30	22 41	22 06	27 06	02 40	03 02
31	22 32	21 55	27 03	02 48	03 10
32	22 22	21 43	27 01	02 56	03 18
33	22 12	21 31	26 58	03 04	03 27
34	22 02	21 18	26 55	03 13	03 36
35	21 52	21 05	26 52	03 23	03 45
36	21 41	20 52	26 49	03 32	03 54
37	21 30	20 37	26 46	03 42	04 04
38	21 18	20 22	26 42	03 53	04 14
39	21 06	20 06	26 38	04 05	04 25
40	20 53	19 49	26 34	04 16	04 36
41	20 40	19 31	26 30	04 29	04 48
42	20 26	19 12	26 26	04 42	05 00
43	20 12	18 52	26 21	04 56	05 13
44	19 56	18 31	26 15	05 12	05 26
45	19 40	18 08	26 09	05 28	05 41
46	19 23	17 44	26 03	05 45	05 56
47	19 06	17 18	25 56	06 03	06 11
48	18 47	16 49	25 48	06 23	06 28
49	18 27	16 19	25 39	06 44	06 46
50	18 05	15 46	25 30	07 08	07 05
51	17 42	15 10	25 19	07 33	07 26
52	17 18	14 30	25 06	08 01	07 48
53	16 52	13 47	24 52	08 31	08 11
54	16 23	12 59	24 36	09 05	08 37
55	15 53	12 06	24 17	09 42	09 04
56	15 19	11 06	23 54	10 24	09 35
57	14 42	09 58	23 27	11 11	10 08
58	14 02	08 41	22 54	12 05	10 45
59	13 17	07 12	22 12	13 08	11 26
60	12♑26	05♒27	21♓17	14♉20	12♊13

17h 56m 0s	269° 0' 0"	29 ♐ 05			
LAT.	11	12	ASC	2	3
0	26♑57	26♒47	28♓55	01♉08	01♊08
5	26 31	26 21	28 52	01 30	01 32
10	26 03	25 54	28 49	01 53	01 58
15	25 34	25 23	28 46	02 18	02 25
20	25 01	24 49	28 42	02 47	02 55
21	24 54	24 42	28 42	02 53	03 02
22	24 47	24 34	28 41	03 00	03 08
23	24 40	24 26	28 40	03 06	03 15
24	24 33	24 18	28 39	03 13	03 22
25	24 25	24 10	28 38	03 20	03 29
26	24 18	24 01	28 37	03 27	03 36
27	24 10	23 52	28 36	03 35	03 43
28	24 02	23 43	28 35	03 43	03 51
29	23 53	23 34	28 34	03 51	03 59
30	23 45	23 24	28 33	03 59	04 07
31	23 36	23 13	28 32	04 08	04 15
32	23 27	23 03	28 30	04 17	04 24
33	23 17	22 51	28 29	04 26	04 32
34	23 07	22 40	28 28	04 36	04 42
35	22 57	22 27	28 26	04 46	04 51
36	22 47	22 15	28 25	04 57	05 01
37	22 36	22 01	28 23	05 09	05 11
38	22 24	21 47	28 21	05 20	05 22
39	22 13	21 32	28 19	05 33	05 33
40	22 00	21 16	28 17	05 46	05 44
41	21 47	21 00	28 15	06 00	05 57
42	21 34	20 42	28 13	06 15	06 09
43	21 20	20 24	28 10	06 31	06 23
44	21 05	20 04	28 07	06 47	06 37
45	20 49	19 43	28 05	07 05	06 51
46	20 33	19 20	28 01	07 24	07 07
47	20 15	18 55	27 58	07 45	07 23
48	19 57	18 29	27 54	08 07	07 41
49	19 37	18 01	27 50	08 31	07 59
50	19 16	17 30	27 45	08 57	08 19
51	18 54	16 56	27 39	09 25	08 40
52	18 30	16 19	27 33	09 56	09 02
53	18 05	15 39	27 26	10 30	09 27
54	17 37	14 54	27 18	11 08	09 53
55	17 07	14 04	27 08	11 50	10 22
56	16 34	13 08	26 57	12 37	10 53
57	15 58	12 05	26 43	13 30	11 27
58	15 18	10 52	26 26	14 31	12 05
59	14 34	09 28	26 05	15 42	12 48
60	13♑44	07♒49	25♓38	17♉05	13♊36

18h 0m 0s	270° 0' 0"	00 ♑ 00			
LAT.	11	12	ASC	2	3
0	27♑55	27♒49	00♈00	02♉11	02♊05
5	27 29	27 26	00 00	02 34	02 31
10	27 03	27 00	00 00	03 00	02 57
15	26 34	26 32	00 00	03 28	03 26
20	26 03	26 01	00 00	03 59	03 57
21	25 56	25 54	00 00	04 06	04 04
22	25 49	25 47	00 00	04 13	04 11
23	25 43	25 40	00 00	04 20	04 17
24	25 35	25 32	00 00	04 28	04 25
25	25 28	25 25	00 00	04 35	04 32
26	25 21	25 17	00 00	04 43	04 39
27	25 13	25 09	00 00	04 51	04 47
28	25 05	25 00	00 00	05 00	04 55
29	24 57	24 51	00 00	05 09	05 03
30	24 49	24 42	00 00	05 18	05 11
31	24 40	24 33	00 00	05 27	05 20
32	24 31	24 23	00 00	05 37	05 29
33	24 22	24 12	00 00	05 48	05 38
34	24 13	24 01	00 00	05 59	05 47
35	24 03	23 50	00 00	06 10	05 57
36	23 53	23 38	00 00	06 22	06 07
37	23 42	23 26	00 00	06 34	06 18
38	23 31	23 13	00 00	06 47	06 29
39	23 20	22 59	00 00	07 01	06 40
40	23 08	22 45	00 00	07 15	06 52
41	22 55	22 29	00 00	07 31	07 05
42	22 42	22 13	00 00	07 47	07 18
43	22 28	21 56	00 00	08 04	07 32
44	22 14	21 38	00 00	08 22	07 46
45	21 59	21 18	00 00	08 42	08 01
46	21 43	20 57	00 00	09 03	08 17
47	21 26	20 35	00 00	09 25	08 34
48	21 08	20 10	00 00	09 50	08 52
49	20 49	19 44	00 00	10 16	09 11
50	20 28	19 16	00 00	10 44	09 32
51	20 07	18 45	00 00	11 15	09 53
52	19 43	18 11	00 00	11 49	10 17
53	19 18	17 33	00 00	12 27	10 42
54	18 51	16 52	00 00	13 08	11 09
55	18 22	16 06	00 00	13 54	11 38
56	17 50	15 14	00 00	14 46	12 10
57	17 15	14 15	00 00	15 45	12 45
58	16 36	13 08	00 00	16 52	13 24
59	15 52	11 50	00 00	18 10	14 08
60	15♑03	10♒19	00♈00	19♉41	14♊57

18h 4m 0s	271° 0' 0"	00 ♑ 55			
LAT.	11	12	ASC	2	3
0	28♑52	28♒52	01♈05	03♉13	03♊03
5	28 28	28 30	01 08	03 39	03 29
10	28 02	28 07	01 11	04 06	03 57
15	27 35	27 42	01 14	04 37	04 26
20	27 05	27 13	01 18	05 11	04 59
21	26 58	27 07	01 18	05 18	05 06
22	26 52	27 00	01 19	05 26	05 13
23	26 45	26 54	01 20	05 34	05 20
24	26 38	26 47	01 21	05 42	05 27
25	26 31	26 40	01 22	05 50	05 35
26	26 24	26 33	01 23	05 59	05 42
27	26 17	26 25	01 24	06 08	05 50
28	26 09	26 17	01 25	06 17	05 58
29	26 01	26 09	01 26	06 26	06 07
30	25 53	26 01	01 27	06 36	06 15
31	25 45	25 52	01 28	06 47	06 24
32	25 36	25 43	01 30	06 57	06 33
33	25 28	25 34	01 31	07 09	06 43
34	25 18	25 24	01 32	07 20	06 53
35	25 09	25 14	01 34	07 33	07 03
36	24 59	25 03	01 35	07 45	07 13
37	24 49	24 51	01 37	07 59	07 24
38	24 38	24 40	01 39	08 13	07 36
39	24 27	24 27	01 41	08 28	07 47
40	24 16	24 14	01 43	08 44	08 00
41	24 03	24 00	01 45	09 00	08 13
42	23 51	23 45	01 47	09 18	08 26
43	23 37	23 29	01 50	09 36	08 40
44	23 23	23 13	01 53	09 56	08 55
45	23 09	22 55	01 55	10 18	09 11
46	22 53	22 36	01 59	10 40	09 27
47	22 37	22 15	02 02	11 05	09 45
48	22 19	21 53	02 06	11 31	10 03
49	22 01	21 29	02 10	11 59	10 23
50	21 41	21 03	02 15	12 30	10 44
51	21 20	20 35	02 21	13 04	11 06
52	20 58	20 04	02 27	13 41	11 30
53	20 33	19 30	02 34	14 21	11 55
54	20 07	18 52	02 42	15 06	12 23
55	19 38	18 10	02 52	15 56	12 53
56	19 07	17 23	03 03	16 52	13 26
57	18 33	16 30	03 17	17 55	14 02
58	17 55	15 29	03 34	19 08	14 42
59	17 12	14 18	03 55	20 32	15 26
60	16♑24	12♒55	04♈22	22♉11	16♊16

Koch Table of Houses for Latitudes 0° to 60° North

18h 8m 0s — 272° 0' 0" — 01 ♑ 50

LAT.	11	12	ASC	2	3
0	29♑49	29♒54	02♈11	04♉16	04♊00
5	29 26	29 35	02 16	04 43	04 27
10	29 02	29 14	02 22	05 13	04 56
15	28 35	28 51	02 28	05 45	05 27
20	28 07	28 25	02 35	06 22	06 00
21	28 01	28 20	02 37	06 30	06 07
22	27 54	28 14	02 39	06 38	06 14
23	27 48	28 08	02 40	06 47	06 22
24	27 41	28 02	02 42	06 55	06 29
25	27 35	27 55	02 44	07 04	06 37
26	27 28	27 49	02 46	07 14	06 45
27	27 21	27 42	02 48	07 23	06 53
28	27 13	27 35	02 50	07 33	07 02
29	27 06	27 28	02 52	07 44	07 10
30	26 58	27 20	02 54	07 54	07 19
31	26 50	27 12	02 57	08 05	07 28
32	26 42	27 04	02 59	08 17	07 38
33	26 33	26 56	03 02	08 29	07 48
34	26 24	26 47	03 05	08 42	07 58
35	26 15	26 37	03 08	08 55	08 08
36	26 06	26 28	03 11	09 08	08 19
37	25 56	26 18	03 14	09 23	08 30
38	25 46	26 07	03 18	09 38	08 42
39	25 35	25 55	03 22	09 54	08 54
40	25 24	25 44	03 26	10 11	09 07
41	25 12	25 31	03 30	10 29	09 20
42	25 00	25 18	03 34	10 48	09 34
43	24 47	25 04	03 39	11 08	09 48
44	24 34	24 48	03 45	11 29	10 04
45	24 19	24 32	03 51	11 52	10 20
46	24 04	24 15	03 57	12 16	10 37
47	23 49	23 57	04 04	12 42	10 54
48	23 32	23 37	04 12	13 11	11 13
49	23 14	23 16	04 21	13 41	11 33
50	22 55	22 52	04 30	14 14	11 55
51	22 34	22 27	04 41	14 50	12 18
52	22 12	21 59	04 54	15 30	12 42
53	21 49	21 29	05 08	16 13	13 08
54	21 23	20 55	05 24	17 01	13 37
55	20 56	20 18	05 43	17 54	14 07
56	20 25	19 36	06 06	18 54	14 41
57	19 52	18 49	06 33	20 02	15 18
58	19 15	17 55	07 06	21 19	15 58
59	18 34	16 52	07 48	22 48	16 43
60	17♑47	15♒40	08♈43	24♉33	17♊34

18h 12m 0s — 273° 0' 0" — 02 ♑ 45

LAT.	11	12	ASC	2	3
0	00♒47	00♓57	03♈16	05♉18	04♊57
5	00 25	00 40	03 24	05 47	05 25
10	00 02	00 21	03 32	06 19	05 55
15	29♑36	00 01	03 42	06 54	06 27
20	29 09	29♒38	03 53	07 33	07 01
21	29 03	29 33	03 55	07 42	07 08
22	28 57	29 28	03 58	07 50	07 16
23	28 51	29 22	04 00	08 00	07 24
24	28 45	29 17	04 03	08 09	07 31
25	28 38	29 11	04 06	08 18	07 39
26	28 32	29 05	04 09	08 28	07 48
27	28 25	28 59	04 12	08 39	07 56
28	28 18	28 53	04 15	08 49	08 05
29	28 11	28 47	04 18	09 00	08 14
30	28 03	28 40	04 22	09 12	08 23
31	27 55	28 33	04 25	09 24	08 32
32	27 48	28 26	04 29	09 36	08 42
33	27 39	28 18	04 33	09 49	08 52
34	27 31	28 10	04 37	10 02	09 02
35	27 22	28 02	04 42	10 16	09 13
36	27 13	27 53	04 46	10 31	09 24
37	27 03	27 44	04 51	10 46	09 36
38	26 54	27 35	04 56	11 03	09 48
39	26 43	27 25	05 02	11 20	10 00
40	26 33	27 14	05 08	11 38	10 13
41	26 21	27 03	05 15	11 57	10 27
42	26 10	26 51	05 22	12 17	10 41
43	25 57	26 39	05 29	12 38	10 56
44	25 44	26 25	05 37	13 01	11 12
45	25 31	26 11	05 46	13 25	11 28
46	25 16	25 56	05 56	13 51	11 45
47	25 01	25 40	06 06	14 19	12 04
48	24 45	25 23	06 18	14 49	12 23
49	24 27	25 04	06 31	15 21	12 44
50	24 09	24 43	06 45	15 56	13 05
51	23 49	24 21	07 01	16 35	13 29
52	23 28	23 57	07 20	17 16	13 54
53	23 06	23 31	07 41	18 02	14 20
54	22 41	23 01	08 05	18 53	14 49
55	22 14	22 29	08 33	19 50	15 20
56	21 45	21 53	09 07	20 53	15 54
57	21 13	21 12	09 47	22 04	16 32
58	20 37	20 26	10 36	23 25	17 13
59	19 57	19 33	11 39	24 59	17 58
60	19♑13	18♒32	12♈59	26♉48	18♊50

18h 16m 0s — 274° 0' 0" — 03 ♑ 40

LAT.	11	12	ASC	2	3
0	01♒45	02♓00	04♈22	06♉19	05♊54
5	01 24	01 45	04 32	06 51	06 23
10	01 02	01 29	04 43	07 25	06 54
15	00 38	01 11	04 56	08 02	07 26
20	00 11	00 51	05 10	08 44	08 02
21	00 06	00 46	05 14	08 53	08 10
22	00 00	00 42	05 17	09 02	08 17
23	29♑54	00 37	05 20	09 12	08 25
24	29 48	00 32	05 24	09 22	08 33
25	29 42	00 27	05 28	09 32	08 41
26	29 36	00 22	05 32	09 43	08 50
27	29 29	00 17	05 36	09 53	08 59
28	29 22	00 12	05 40	10 05	09 08
29	29 16	00 06	05 44	10 16	09 17
30	29 08	00 00	05 49	10 29	09 26
31	29 01	29♒54	05 53	10 41	09 36
32	28 54	29 48	05 58	10 54	09 46
33	28 46	29 41	06 04	11 08	09 56
34	28 38	29 34	06 09	11 22	10 07
35	28 29	29 27	06 15	11 37	10 18
36	28 21	29 19	06 21	11 53	10 29
37	28 11	29 12	06 28	12 09	10 41
38	28 02	29 03	06 35	12 26	10 53
39	27 52	28 55	06 43	12 44	11 06
40	27 42	28 45	06 51	13 03	11 20
41	27 31	28 36	06 59	13 24	11 33
42	27 20	28 26	07 08	13 45	11 48
43	27 08	28 15	07 18	14 08	12 03
44	26 56	28 03	07 29	14 32	12 19
45	26 42	27 51	07 41	14 57	12 36
46	26 29	27 38	07 54	15 25	12 54
47	26 14	27 24	08 08	15 54	13 12
48	25 58	27 09	08 23	16 26	13 32
49	25 42	26 53	08 40	17 00	13 53
50	25 24	26 36	08 59	17 37	14 15
51	25 05	26 17	09 21	18 17	14 39
52	24 45	25 57	09 45	19 01	15 04
53	24 23	25 35	10 13	19 49	15 31
54	24 00	25 10	10 45	20 43	16 01
55	23 34	24 43	11 22	21 42	16 33
56	23 06	24 13	12 06	22 48	17 07
57	22 35	23 40	12 59	24 02	17 45
58	22 01	23 03	14 04	25 27	18 26
59	21 23	22 21	15 25	27 04	19 12
60	20♑40	21♒33	17♈09	28♉57	20♊04

18h 20m 0s — 275° 0' 0" — 04 ♑ 35

LAT.	11	12	ASC	2	3
0	02♒43	03♓03	05♈27	07♉21	06♊50
5	02 23	02 51	05 40	07 54	07 21
10	02 02	02 37	05 54	08 30	07 52
15	01 39	02 21	06 10	09 10	08 26
20	01 14	02 04	06 28	09 54	09 03
21	01 09	02 00	06 32	10 04	09 11
22	01 03	01 56	06 36	10 14	09 18
23	00 58	01 52	06 40	10 24	09 27
24	00 52	01 48	06 45	10 34	09 35
25	00 46	01 44	06 49	10 45	09 43
26	00 40	01 40	06 54	10 56	09 52
27	00 34	01 35	06 59	11 08	10 01
28	00 27	01 30	07 04	11 20	10 10
29	00 21	01 26	07 10	11 32	10 19
30	00 14	01 21	07 16	11 45	10 29
31	00 07	01 15	07 22	11 58	10 39
32	00 00	01 10	07 28	12 12	10 49
33	29♑53	01 04	07 34	12 27	11 00
34	29 45	00 59	07 41	12 42	11 11
35	29 37	00 52	07 49	12 57	11 22
36	29 28	00 46	07 56	13 14	11 34
37	29 20	00 39	08 05	13 31	11 46
38	29 11	00 32	08 13	13 49	11 59
39	29 01	00 25	08 23	14 08	12 12
40	28 52	00 17	08 33	14 28	12 25
41	28 41	00 09	08 43	14 50	12 40
42	28 31	00 01	08 55	15 12	12 54
43	28 19	29♒52	09 07	15 36	13 10
44	28 07	29 42	09 21	16 01	13 26
45	27 55	29 32	09 35	16 28	13 43
46	27 42	29 21	09 51	16 57	14 01
47	27 28	29 10	10 08	17 28	14 20
48	27 13	28 58	10 28	18 01	14 40
49	26 57	28 44	10 49	18 37	15 02
50	26 40	28 30	11 13	19 16	15 24
51	26 22	28 15	11 39	19 58	15 48
52	26 03	27 59	12 09	20 44	16 14
53	25 42	27 41	12 44	21 34	16 42
54	25 20	27 22	13 23	22 30	17 12
55	24 55	27 00	14 09	23 31	17 44
56	24 28	26 37	15 03	24 40	18 19
57	23 59	26 12	16 08	25 57	18 57
58	23 26	25 45	17 27	27 25	19 39
59	22 50	25 15	19 06	29 05	20 25
60	22♑10	24♒42	21♈12	01♊00	21♊17

18h 24m 0s — 276° 0' 0" — 05 ♑ 30

LAT.	11	12	ASC	2	3
0	03♒41	04♓07	06♈32	08♉23	07♊47
5	03 22	03 56	06 48	08 58	08 18
10	03 02	03 44	07 04	09 36	08 51
15	02 41	03 32	07 23	10 18	09 26
20	02 17	03 17	07 45	11 04	10 03
21	02 12	03 14	07 50	11 15	10 11
22	02 07	03 11	07 55	11 25	10 19
23	02 01	03 08	08 00	11 36	10 28
24	01 56	03 04	08 05	11 47	10 36
25	01 50	03 01	08 11	11 58	10 45
26	01 45	02 57	08 17	12 10	10 54
27	01 39	02 53	08 23	12 22	11 03
28	01 33	02 50	08 29	12 35	11 12
29	01 27	02 46	08 35	12 48	11 22
30	01 20	02 41	08 42	13 01	11 32
31	01 14	02 37	08 49	13 15	11 42
32	01 07	02 33	08 57	13 30	11 53
33	01 00	02 28	09 05	13 45	12 03
34	00 52	02 23	09 13	14 01	12 15
35	00 45	02 18	09 22	14 17	12 26
36	00 37	02 13	09 31	14 34	12 38
37	00 29	02 08	09 41	14 53	12 50
38	00 20	02 02	09 51	15 12	13 03
39	00 11	01 56	10 03	15 32	13 17
40	00 02	01 50	10 14	15 53	13 31
41	29♑52	01 44	10 27	16 15	13 45
42	29 42	01 37	10 41	16 38	14 00
43	29 31	01 30	10 56	17 03	14 16
44	29 20	01 22	11 12	17 30	14 33
45	29 08	01 14	11 29	17 58	14 50
46	28 55	01 06	11 48	18 28	15 09
47	28 42	00 57	12 09	19 00	15 28
48	28 28	00 47	12 32	19 35	15 48
49	28 13	00 37	12 57	20 12	16 10
50	27 57	00 26	13 25	20 53	16 33
51	27 40	00 15	13 56	21 36	16 57
52	27 22	00 02	14 32	22 24	17 23
53	27 02	29♒49	15 13	23 16	17 51
54	26 41	29 35	15 59	24 14	18 21
55	26 17	29 21	16 54	25 18	18 54
56	25 52	29 05	17 57	26 29	19 29
57	25 24	28 49	19 14	27 48	20 08
58	24 54	28 32	20 46	29 18	20 50
59	24 20	28 15	22 40	01♊00	21 37
60	23♑42	28♒00	25♈05	02♊58	22♊29

18h 28m 0s — 277° 0' 0" — 06 ♑ 26

LAT.	11	12	ASC	2	3
0	04♒39	05♓10	07♈37	09♉24	08♊43
5	04 22	05 02	07 55	10 01	09 16
10	04 03	04 52	08 15	10 41	09 49
15	03 42	04 42	08 37	11 25	10 25
20	03 20	04 31	09 03	12 14	11 04
21	03 15	04 28	09 08	12 25	11 12
22	03 10	04 26	09 14	12 36	11 20
23	03 05	04 23	09 20	12 47	11 29
24	03 00	04 21	09 26	12 59	11 37
25	02 55	04 18	09 32	13 11	11 46
26	02 50	04 15	09 39	13 23	11 55
27	02 44	04 12	09 46	13 36	12 05
28	02 38	04 09	09 53	13 49	12 14
29	02 33	04 06	10 01	14 02	12 24
30	02 27	04 03	10 09	14 17	12 34
31	02 20	03 59	10 17	14 31	12 45
32	02 14	03 56	10 26	14 46	12 55
33	02 07	03 52	10 35	15 02	13 07
34	02 00	03 49	10 45	15 19	13 18
35	01 53	03 45	10 55	15 36	13 30
36	01 46	03 41	11 06	15 54	13 42
37	01 38	03 37	11 17	16 13	13 55
38	01 30	03 33	11 29	16 33	14 08
39	01 21	03 28	11 42	16 54	14 21
40	01 12	03 23	11 56	17 16	14 36
41	01 03	03 19	12 11	17 39	14 50
42	00 54	03 14	12 27	18 04	15 06
43	00 43	03 08	12 44	18 30	15 22
44	00 33	03 03	13 02	18 57	15 39
45	00 22	02 57	13 22	19 27	15 57
46	00 10	02 51	13 44	19 58	16 15
47	29♑57	02 44	14 08	20 31	16 35
48	29 44	02 38	14 34	21 07	16 56
49	29 30	02 31	15 04	21 46	17 18
50	29 15	02 23	15 36	22 28	17 41
51	28 59	02 16	16 12	23 13	18 06
52	28 41	02 08	16 53	24 03	18 32
53	28 23	02 00	17 40	24 57	19 00
54	28 03	01 52	18 34	25 56	19 31
55	27 41	01 44	19 36	27 01	20 03
56	27 17	01 36	20 48	28 14	20 39
57	26 52	01 29	22 15	29 36	21 18
58	26 23	01 24	23 59	01♊07	22 00
59	25 52	01 22	26 08	02 51	22 47
60	25♑17	01♓26	28♈50	04♊51	23♊39

18h 32m 0s — 278° 0' 0" — 07 ♑ 21

LAT.	11	12	ASC	2	3
0	05♒38	06♓14	08♈43	10♉25	09♊40
5	05 21	06 08	09 03	11 04	10 13
10	05 04	06 01	09 26	11 46	10 47
15	04 44	05 53	09 51	12 32	11 24
20	04 24	05 45	10 20	13 24	12 04
21	04 19	05 43	10 26	13 35	12 12
22	04 14	05 41	10 33	13 46	12 21
23	04 10	05 39	10 39	13 58	12 29
24	04 05	05 37	10 46	14 10	12 38
25	04 00	05 35	10 54	14 23	12 47
26	03 55	05 33	11 01	14 35	12 57
27	03 50	05 31	11 09	14 49	13 06
28	03 44	05 29	11 18	15 02	13 16
29	03 39	05 27	11 26	15 17	13 26
30	03 33	05 24	11 35	15 31	13 37
31	03 27	05 22	11 45	15 47	13 47
32	03 21	05 20	11 55	16 03	13 58
33	03 15	05 17	12 05	16 19	14 09
34	03 08	05 15	12 16	16 37	14 21
35	03 02	05 12	12 28	16 55	14 33
36	02 55	05 09	12 40	17 13	14 46
37	02 47	05 06	12 53	17 33	14 58
38	02 40	05 04	13 07	17 54	15 12
39	02 32	05 01	13 21	18 16	15 26
40	02 24	04 57	13 37	18 38	15 40
41	02 15	04 54	13 54	19 03	15 55
42	02 06	04 51	14 12	19 28	16 11
43	01 56	04 48	14 31	19 55	16 27
44	01 46	04 44	14 52	20 24	16 45
45	01 36	04 41	15 15	20 54	17 03
46	01 25	04 37	15 40	21 27	17 21
47	01 13	04 33	16 07	22 01	17 41
48	01 01	04 30	16 36	22 38	18 02
49	00 47	04 26	17 09	23 18	18 25
50	00 33	04 22	17 46	24 02	18 48
51	00 18	04 19	18 27	24 48	19 13
52	00 02	04 16	19 13	25 39	19 40
53	29♑45	04 13	20 05	26 35	20 08
54	29 26	04 11	21 05	27 36	20 39
55	29 06	04 10	22 15	28 43	21 12
56	28 44	04 10	23 36	29 57	21 48
57	28 20	04 14	25 12	01♊20	22 27
58	27 54	04 21	27 07	02 53	23 09
59	27 26	04 35	29 28	04 38	23 56
60	26♑54	04♓59	02♉24	06♊39	24♊48

18h 36m 0s — 279° 0' 0" — 08 ♑ 16

LAT.	11	12	ASC	2	3
0	06♒37	07♓18	09♈48	11♉26	10♊36
5	06 21	07 14	10 11	12 07	11 10
10	06 05	07 09	10 36	12 51	11 46
15	05 47	07 04	11 04	13 39	12 23
20	05 27	06 59	11 37	14 33	13 04
21	05 23	06 58	11 44	14 44	13 12
22	05 19	06 56	11 51	14 56	13 21
23	05 14	06 55	11 59	15 09	13 30
24	05 10	06 54	12 07	15 21	13 39
25	05 05	06 53	12 15	15 34	13 48
26	05 01	06 52	12 23	15 48	13 58
27	04 56	06 50	12 32	16 01	14 08
28	04 51	06 49	12 42	16 16	14 18
29	04 45	06 48	12 51	16 31	14 28
30	04 40	06 46	13 01	16 46	14 39
31	04 35	06 45	13 12	17 02	14 49
32	04 29	06 44	13 23	17 18	15 01
33	04 23	06 42	13 35	17 36	15 12
34	04 17	06 41	13 47	17 54	15 24
35	04 11	06 39	14 00	18 12	15 36
36	04 04	06 38	14 14	18 32	15 49
37	03 57	06 36	14 28	18 52	16 02
38	03 50	06 35	14 43	19 14	16 16
39	03 43	06 33	15 00	19 36	16 30
40	03 35	06 32	15 17	20 00	16 44
41	03 27	06 30	15 36	20 25	17 00
42	03 19	06 29	15 56	20 51	17 16
43	03 10	06 28	16 18	21 19	17 32
44	03 01	06 26	16 41	21 49	17 50
45	02 51	06 25	17 06	22 20	18 08
46	02 41	06 24	17 34	22 54	18 27
47	02 30	06 23	18 04	23 30	18 47
48	02 18	06 23	18 37	24 08	19 09
49	02 06	06 22	19 14	24 49	19 31
50	01 53	06 22	19 54	25 34	19 55
51	01 39	06 23	20 40	26 22	20 20
52	01 24	06 25	21 31	27 14	20 47
53	01 08	06 28	22 28	28 11	21 16
54	00 51	06 32	23 34	29 13	21 47
55	00 33	06 38	24 51	00♊21	22 20
56	00 13	06 48	26 19	01 37	22 56
57	29♑51	07 02	28 04	03 01	23 35
58	29 28	07 22	00♉09	04 35	24 17
59	29 02	07 53	02 40	06 22	25 04
60	28♑34	08♓40	05♉47	08♊22	25♊56

Koch Table of Houses for Latitudes 0° to 60° North

18h 40m 0s — 280° 0' 0" — 09 ♑ 11

LAT.	11	12	ASC	2	3
0	07♒35	08♓22	10♈53	12♉27	11♊32
5	07 21	08 20	11 18	13 09	12 07
10	07 06	08 18	11 46	13 55	12 43
15	06 49	08 15	12 18	14 46	13 22
20	06 31	08 13	12 54	15 42	14 04
21	06 27	08 13	13 01	15 54	14 12
22	06 23	08 12	13 10	16 06	14 21
23	06 19	08 12	13 18	16 19	14 30
24	06 15	08 11	13 27	16 32	14 40
25	06 11	08 11	13 36	16 45	14 49
26	06 06	08 10	13 45	16 59	14 59
27	06 02	08 10	13 55	17 14	15 09
28	05 57	08 10	14 05	17 29	15 19
29	05 52	08 09	14 16	17 44	15 29
30	05 47	08 09	14 27	18 00	15 40
31	05 42	08 08	14 39	18 16	15 51
32	05 37	08 08	14 51	18 34	16 03
33	05 32	08 08	15 04	18 52	16 14
34	05 26	08 07	15 17	19 10	16 26
35	05 20	08 07	15 32	19 30	16 39
36	05 14	08 07	15 47	19 50	16 52
37	05 08	08 07	16 03	20 11	17 05
38	05 01	08 07	16 20	20 33	17 19
39	04 55	08 07	16 38	20 56	17 33
40	04 47	08 07	16 57	21 21	17 48
41	04 40	08 07	17 18	21 47	18 04
42	04 32	08 08	17 40	22 14	18 20
43	04 24	08 08	18 04	22 43	18 37
44	04 15	08 09	18 29	23 13	18 55
45	04 06	08 11	18 57	23 46	19 13
46	03 57	08 12	19 28	24 20	19 32
47	03 47	08 14	20 01	24 57	19 53
48	03 36	08 17	20 37	25 36	20 14
49	03 25	08 20	21 17	26 18	20 37
50	03 13	08 24	22 01	27 04	21 01
51	03 01	08 29	22 51	27 53	21 26
52	02 47	08 36	23 46	28 46	21 54
53	02 33	08 44	24 49	29 44	22 22
54	02 17	08 55	26 01	00♊48	22 53
55	02 01	09 09	27 23	01 57	23 27
56	01 43	09 28	28 58	03 14	24 03
57	01 24	09 53	00♉51	04 39	24 42
58	01 03	10 28	03 04	06 14	25 24
59	00 41	11 16	05 44	08 01	26 11
60	00♒18	12♓27	09♉01	10♊02	27♊03

18h 44m 0s — 281° 0' 0" — 10 ♑ 07

LAT.	11	12	ASC	2	3
0	08♒34	09♓26	11♈58	13♉27	12♊28
5	08 21	09 26	12 26	14 12	13 04
10	08 07	09 26	12 56	15 00	13 41
15	07 52	09 27	13 31	15 52	14 21
20	07 35	09 28	14 10	16 50	15 03
21	07 32	09 28	14 19	17 02	15 12
22	07 28	09 28	14 28	17 15	15 21
23	07 24	09 28	14 37	17 29	15 30
24	07 20	09 29	14 47	17 42	15 40
25	07 17	09 29	14 56	17 56	15 50
26	07 12	09 29	15 07	18 11	16 00
27	07 08	09 30	15 18	18 26	16 10
28	07 04	09 30	15 29	18 41	16 20
29	07 00	09 31	15 40	18 57	16 31
30	06 55	09 31	15 53	19 13	16 42
31	06 50	09 32	16 05	19 30	16 53
32	06 46	09 33	16 19	19 48	17 05
33	06 41	09 33	16 33	20 07	17 16
34	06 35	09 34	16 48	20 26	17 29
35	06 30	09 35	17 03	20 46	17 41
36	06 25	09 36	17 20	21 07	17 55
37	06 19	09 38	17 37	21 29	18 08
38	06 13	09 39	17 56	21 52	18 22
39	06 07	09 41	18 15	22 16	18 37
40	06 00	09 43	18 36	22 41	18 52
41	05 53	09 45	18 59	23 08	19 08
42	05 46	09 47	19 23	23 36	19 24
43	05 39	09 50	19 49	24 05	19 41
44	05 31	09 53	20 17	24 36	19 59
45	05 23	09 57	20 47	25 10	20 18
46	05 14	10 01	21 20	25 45	20 37
47	05 05	10 06	21 56	26 23	20 58
48	04 55	10 11	22 35	27 03	21 19
49	04 45	10 18	23 19	27 46	21 42
50	04 35	10 26	24 06	28 33	22 07
51	04 23	10 36	25 00	29 23	22 32
52	04 11	10 48	26 00	00♊17	22 59
53	03 58	11 02	27 07	01 16	23 29
54	03 45	11 20	28 24	02 20	24 00
55	03 30	11 42	29 52	03 31	24 33
56	03 15	12 10	01♉33	04 49	25 09
57	02 58	12 47	03 32	06 14	25 48
58	02 41	13 36	05 52	07 50	26 31
59	02 23	14 44	08 40	09 37	27 17
60	02♒04	16♓20	12♉04	11♊38	28♊09

18h 48m 0s — 282° 0' 0" — 11 ♑ 02

LAT.	11	12	ASC	2	3
0	09♒34	10♓30	13♈03	14♉28	13♊24
5	09 22	10 32	13 33	15 14	14 01
10	09 09	10 35	14 06	16 04	14 39
15	08 55	10 38	14 44	16 58	15 19
20	08 40	10 42	15 27	17 58	16 03
21	08 36	10 43	15 36	18 11	16 12
22	08 33	10 44	15 46	18 24	16 21
23	08 30	10 45	15 56	18 38	16 30
24	08 26	10 46	16 06	18 52	16 40
25	08 23	10 47	16 17	19 07	16 50
26	08 19	10 49	16 28	19 21	17 00
27	08 15	10 50	16 40	19 37	17 10
28	08 11	10 51	16 52	19 53	17 21
29	08 07	10 53	17 05	20 09	17 32
30	08 03	10 54	17 18	20 26	17 43
31	07 59	10 56	17 32	20 44	17 54
32	07 54	10 58	17 46	21 02	18 06
33	07 50	11 00	18 01	21 21	18 18
34	07 45	11 02	18 17	21 41	18 31
35	07 40	11 04	18 34	22 02	18 44
36	07 35	11 06	18 52	22 23	18 57
37	07 30	11 09	19 11	22 46	19 11
38	07 25	11 12	19 31	23 10	19 25
39	07 19	11 15	19 52	23 34	19 40
40	07 13	11 19	20 15	24 00	19 55
41	07 07	11 23	20 39	24 27	20 11
42	07 01	11 27	21 05	24 56	20 28
43	06 54	11 32	21 33	25 27	20 45
44	06 47	11 37	22 03	25 59	21 03
45	06 40	11 43	22 36	26 33	21 22
46	06 32	11 50	23 11	27 09	21 42
47	06 24	11 58	23 50	27 47	22 02
48	06 15	12 07	24 32	28 29	22 24
49	06 06	12 18	25 18	29 13	22 47
50	05 57	12 30	26 10	00♊00	23 12
51	05 47	12 44	27 07	00 51	23 37
52	05 36	13 01	28 11	01 46	24 05
53	05 25	13 22	29 22	02 46	24 34
54	05 14	13 46	00♉44	03 51	25 05
55	05 01	14 17	02 17	05 02	25 39
56	04 48	14 55	04 04	06 21	26 15
57	04 35	15 44	06 08	07 47	26 54
58	04 21	16 48	08 35	09 23	27 36
59	04 07	18 15	11 29	11 10	28 23
60	03♒54	20♓16	14♉57	13♊10	29♊14

18h 52m 0s — 283° 0' 0" — 11 ♑ 58

LAT.	11	12	ASC	2	3
0	10♒33	11♓34	14♈07	15♉28	14♊20
5	10 22	11 39	14 40	16 16	14 58
10	10 10	11 44	15 16	17 07	15 37
15	09 58	11 50	15 57	18 03	16 18
20	09 44	11 57	16 43	19 06	17 02
21	09 41	11 59	16 53	19 19	17 11
22	09 38	12 01	17 03	19 33	17 21
23	09 35	12 02	17 14	19 47	17 30
24	09 32	12 04	17 25	20 02	17 40
25	09 29	12 06	17 37	20 17	17 50
26	09 26	12 08	17 49	20 32	18 00
27	09 22	12 10	18 02	20 48	18 11
28	09 19	12 12	18 15	21 04	18 22
29	09 15	12 15	18 28	21 21	18 33
30	09 11	12 17	18 43	21 39	18 44
31	09 08	12 20	18 58	21 57	18 56
32	09 04	12 23	19 13	22 16	19 08
33	09 00	12 26	19 30	22 35	19 20
34	08 55	12 29	19 47	22 56	19 33
35	08 51	12 33	20 05	23 17	19 46
36	08 47	12 37	20 24	23 39	19 59
37	08 42	12 41	20 44	24 02	20 13
38	08 37	12 45	21 06	24 27	20 27
39	08 32	12 50	21 29	24 52	20 42
40	08 27	12 55	21 53	25 19	20 58
41	08 21	13 01	22 19	25 46	21 14
42	08 16	13 07	22 47	26 16	21 31
43	08 10	13 14	23 17	26 47	21 48
44	08 04	13 22	23 49	27 20	22 06
45	07 57	13 31	24 24	27 55	22 25
46	07 51	13 40	25 01	28 32	22 45
47	07 43	13 51	25 42	29 11	23 06
48	07 36	14 04	26 27	29 53	23 28
49	07 28	14 18	27 17	00♊38	23 52
50	07 20	14 34	28 11	01 26	24 16
51	07 12	14 53	29 12	02 18	24 42
52	07 03	15 16	00♉19	03 13	25 10
53	06 54	15 42	01 35	04 14	25 39
54	06 44	16 14	03 00	05 20	26 10
55	06 34	16 53	04 38	06 32	26 44
56	06 24	17 41	06 30	07 50	27 20
57	06 13	18 43	08 39	09 17	27 59
58	06 03	20 02	11 11	10 53	28 41
59	05 54	21 48	14 09	12 40	29 27
60	05♒48	24♓15	17♉41	14♊39	00♋18

18h 56m 0s — 284° 0' 0" — 12 ♑ 53

LAT.	11	12	ASC	2	3
0	11♒32	12♓39	15♈12	16♉28	15♊16
5	11 23	12 46	15 48	17 18	15 54
10	11 12	12 53	16 26	18 11	16 34
15	11 01	13 02	17 09	19 09	17 16
20	10 49	13 12	17 59	20 13	18 01
21	10 47	13 15	18 10	20 27	18 10
22	10 44	13 17	18 21	20 41	18 20
23	10 41	13 19	18 32	20 56	18 30
24	10 38	13 22	18 44	21 11	18 40
25	10 36	13 25	18 57	21 26	18 50
26	10 33	13 28	19 10	21 42	19 01
27	10 30	13 31	19 23	21 58	19 11
28	10 27	13 34	19 37	22 15	19 22
29	10 23	13 37	19 52	22 33	19 33
30	10 20	13 41	20 07	22 51	19 45
31	10 17	13 44	20 23	23 09	19 57
32	10 13	13 48	20 40	23 29	20 09
33	10 10	13 53	20 57	23 49	20 21
34	10 06	13 57	21 16	24 10	20 34
35	10 02	14 02	21 35	24 32	20 47
36	09 58	14 07	21 55	24 54	21 01
37	09 54	14 13	22 17	25 18	21 15
38	09 50	14 18	22 40	25 43	21 30
39	09 46	14 25	23 04	26 09	21 45
40	09 41	14 32	23 30	26 36	22 00
41	09 36	14 40	23 58	27 05	22 17
42	09 31	14 48	24 27	27 35	22 34
43	09 26	14 57	24 59	28 06	22 51
44	09 21	15 07	25 33	28 40	23 10
45	09 16	15 18	26 10	29 15	23 29
46	09 10	15 31	26 50	29 53	23 49
47	09 04	15 45	27 34	00♊33	24 10
48	08 58	16 01	28 21	01 16	24 32
49	08 51	16 19	29 13	02 01	24 56
50	08 44	16 39	00♉11	02 50	25 20
51	08 37	17 03	01 14	03 43	25 46
52	08 30	17 31	02 25	04 39	26 14
53	08 23	18 04	03 44	05 40	26 43
54	08 15	18 43	05 14	06 47	27 15
55	08 08	19 31	06 55	07 59	27 48
56	08 01	20 29	08 51	09 18	28 24
57	07 54	21 43	11 05	10 45	29 03
58	07 48	23 17	13 40	12 20	29 45
59	07 45	25 23	16 42	14 07	00♋31
60	07♒45	28♓14	20♉16	16♊05	01♋21

19h 0m 0s — 285° 0' 0" — 13 ♑ 49

LAT.	11	12	ASC	2	3
0	12♒32	13♓43	16♈17	17♉28	16♊11
5	12 24	13 52	16 55	18 19	16 51
10	12 15	14 03	17 36	19 14	17 31
15	12 05	14 14	18 22	20 14	18 14
20	11 54	14 28	19 15	21 20	19 00
21	11 52	14 31	19 26	21 34	19 10
22	11 50	14 34	19 38	21 49	19 19
23	11 47	14 37	19 50	22 04	19 29
24	11 45	14 40	20 03	22 19	19 40
25	11 42	14 44	20 16	22 35	19 50
26	11 40	14 47	20 30	22 52	20 00
27	11 37	14 51	20 44	23 08	20 11
28	11 35	14 55	20 59	23 26	20 22
29	11 32	15 00	21 15	23 44	20 34
30	11 29	15 04	21 31	24 02	20 45
31	11 26	15 09	21 48	24 21	20 57
32	11 23	15 14	22 06	24 41	21 10
33	11 20	15 19	22 24	25 02	21 22
34	11 17	15 25	22 44	25 23	21 35
35	11 14	15 31	23 04	25 46	21 49
36	11 10	15 38	23 26	26 09	22 03
37	11 07	15 45	23 49	26 33	22 17
38	11 03	15 52	24 13	26 59	22 32
39	11 00	16 00	24 39	27 25	22 47
40	10 56	16 09	25 06	27 53	23 03
41	10 52	16 19	25 36	28 22	23 19
42	10 48	16 29	26 07	28 53	23 36
43	10 43	16 40	26 41	29 25	23 54
44	10 39	16 53	27 17	29 59	24 13
45	10 34	17 07	27 56	00♊35	24 32
46	10 30	17 22	28 38	01 14	24 52
47	10 25	17 39	29 23	01 54	25 13
48	10 20	17 58	00♉13	02 37	25 36
49	10 15	18 20	01 08	03 24	25 59
50	10 10	18 45	02 08	04 13	26 24
51	10 04	19 14	03 15	05 06	26 50
52	09 59	19 47	04 29	06 03	27 18
53	09 54	20 26	05 51	07 05	27 47
54	09 49	21 13	07 24	08 11	28 18
55	09 44	22 09	09 09	09 24	28 52
56	09 40	23 18	11 08	10 43	29 28
57	09 37	24 44	13 25	12 10	00♋07
58	09 36	26 33	16 03	13 45	00 48
59	09 38	28 57	19 08	15 31	01 34
60	09♒45	02♈13	22♉43	17♊28	02♋24

19h 4m 0s — 286° 0' 0" — 14 ♑ 44

LAT.	11	12	ASC	2	3
0	13♒32	14♓48	17♈21	18♉28	17♊07
5	13 25	14 59	18 01	19 21	17 47
10	13 17	15 12	18 45	20 17	18 29
15	13 09	15 26	19 34	21 19	19 12
20	13 00	15 43	20 30	22 27	19 59
21	12 58	15 47	20 42	22 42	20 09
22	12 56	15 50	20 55	22 57	20 18
23	12 54	15 54	21 08	23 12	20 29
24	12 52	15 59	21 22	23 28	20 39
25	12 50	16 03	21 36	23 44	20 50
26	12 48	16 07	21 50	24 01	21 00
27	12 45	16 12	22 05	24 18	21 11
28	12 43	16 17	22 21	24 36	21 23
29	12 41	16 22	22 38	24 54	21 34
30	12 38	16 28	22 55	25 13	21 46
31	12 36	16 34	23 13	25 33	21 58
32	12 33	16 40	23 31	25 53	22 10
33	12 31	16 46	23 51	26 14	22 23
34	12 28	16 53	24 12	26 36	22 36
35	12 26	17 01	24 33	26 59	22 50
36	12 23	17 09	24 56	27 23	23 04
37	12 20	17 17	25 20	27 48	23 18
38	12 17	17 26	25 46	28 13	23 33
39	12 14	17 36	26 13	28 40	23 49
40	12 11	17 46	26 42	29 09	24 05
41	12 08	17 58	27 13	29 39	24 21
42	12 04	18 10	27 46	00♊10	24 38
43	12 01	18 24	28 21	00 43	24 56
44	11 58	18 39	28 59	01 17	25 15
45	11 54	18 55	29 40	01 54	25 35
46	11 50	19 13	00♉24	02 33	25 55
47	11 47	19 34	01 12	03 14	26 16
48	11 43	19 56	02 04	03 58	26 39
49	11 39	20 22	03 01	04 45	27 02
50	11 36	20 51	04 04	05 35	27 27
51	11 32	21 25	05 13	06 28	27 53
52	11 29	22 04	06 29	07 26	28 21
53	11 26	22 49	07 55	08 27	28 50
54	11 23	23 43	09 31	09 35	29 22
55	11 21	24 48	11 18	10 47	29 55
56	11 20	26 07	13 21	12 06	00♋31
57	11 22	27 45	15 41	13 33	01 09
58	11 25	29 49	18 21	15 08	01 51
59	11 34	02♈31	21 26	16 53	02 36
60	11♒50	06♈09	25♉02	18♊49	03♋26

19h 8m 0s — 287° 0' 0" — 15 ♑ 40

LAT.	11	12	ASC	2	3
0	14♒32	15♓53	18♈26	19♉27	18♊02
5	14 26	16 06	19 08	20 22	18 43
10	14 20	16 21	19 55	21 20	19 26
15	14 13	16 38	20 46	22 23	20 10
20	14 05	16 58	21 45	23 33	20 57
21	14 04	17 03	21 58	23 48	21 07
22	14 02	17 07	22 12	24 04	21 17
23	14 01	17 12	22 26	24 20	21 28
24	13 59	17 17	22 40	24 36	21 38
25	13 57	17 22	22 55	24 52	21 49
26	13 55	17 28	23 10	25 10	22 00
27	13 54	17 33	23 26	25 27	22 11
28	13 52	17 39	23 42	25 45	22 22
29	13 50	17 45	24 00	26 04	22 34
30	13 48	17 52	24 18	26 24	22 46
31	13 46	17 59	24 37	26 44	22 58
32	13 44	18 06	24 56	27 05	23 11
33	13 42	18 14	25 17	27 26	23 24
34	13 40	18 22	25 39	27 48	23 37
35	13 38	18 31	26 02	28 12	23 51
36	13 36	18 40	26 26	28 36	24 05
37	13 33	18 50	26 51	29 01	24 20
38	13 31	19 00	27 18	29 28	24 35
39	13 29	19 12	27 46	29 55	24 50
40	13 27	19 24	28 17	00♊24	25 06
41	13 24	19 37	28 49	00 54	25 23
42	13 22	19 52	29 23	01 26	25 40
43	13 19	20 08	00♉00	01 59	25 58
44	13 17	20 25	00 40	02 35	26 17
45	13 14	20 44	01 22	03 12	26 37
46	13 12	21 05	02 08	03 51	26 57
47	13 09	21 29	02 58	04 33	27 19
48	13 07	21 55	03 53	05 17	27 41
49	13 05	22 24	04 52	06 04	28 05
50	13 03	22 58	05 57	06 55	28 30
51	13 01	23 36	07 08	07 49	28 56
52	13 00	24 21	08 28	08 46	29 24
53	12 59	25 12	09 56	09 49	29 53
54	12 59	26 14	11 34	10 56	00♋24
55	13 00	27 27	13 24	12 09	00 58
56	13 03	28 55	15 29	13 28	01 33
57	13 09	00♈45	17 51	14 54	02 12
58	13 18	03 04	20 33	16 29	02 53
59	13 33	06 03	23 39	18 13	03 38
60	13♒58	10♈02	27♉14	20♊07	04♋27

Koch Table of Houses for Latitudes 0° to 60° North

19h 12m 0s — 288° 0' 0" — 16 ♑ 36

LAT.	11	12	ASC	2	3
0	15♒32	16♓57	19♈30	20♉26	18♊58
5	15 27	17 13	20 15	21 23	19 40
10	15 22	17 31	21 04	22 23	20 23
15	15 17	17 51	21 58	23 28	21 08
20	15 11	18 14	23 00	24 39	21 56
21	15 10	18 19	23 14	24 55	22 06
22	15 09	18 24	23 28	25 11	22 16
23	15 08	18 30	23 43	25 27	22 27
24	15 06	18 36	23 58	25 43	22 37
25	15 05	18 42	24 13	26 00	22 48
26	15 04	18 48	24 29	26 18	22 59
27	15 02	18 54	24 46	26 36	23 11
28	15 01	19 01	25 03	26 55	23 22
29	14 59	19 08	25 22	27 14	23 34
30	14 58	19 16	25 40	27 34	23 46
31	14 57	19 24	26 00	27 54	23 59
32	14 55	19 32	26 21	28 15	24 11
33	14 54	19 41	26 43	28 37	24 24
34	14 52	19 50	27 05	29 00	24 38
35	14 51	20 00	27 29	29 24	24 52
36	14 49	20 11	27 54	29 49	25 06
37	14 47	20 22	28 21	00♊14	25 21
38	14 46	20 35	28 49	00 41	25 36
39	14 44	20 48	29 19	01 09	25 51
40	14 43	21 02	29 50	01 38	26 08
41	14 41	21 17	00♉24	02 09	26 25
42	14 40	21 34	01 00	02 41	26 42
43	14 38	21 52	01 38	03 15	27 00
44	14 37	22 11	02 20	03 51	27 19
45	14 35	22 33	03 04	04 29	27 39
46	14 34	22 57	03 52	05 08	27 59
47	14 33	23 24	04 44	05 51	28 21
48	14 32	23 53	05 40	06 35	28 43
49	14 31	24 27	06 41	07 23	29 07
50	14 31	25 04	07 48	08 14	29 32
51	14 31	25 48	09 02	09 08	29 58
52	14 32	26 38	10 23	10 06	00♋26
53	14 33	27 36	11 53	11 08	00 55
54	14 36	28 44	13 34	12 16	01 27
55	14 41	00♈05	15 26	13 28	02 00
56	14 48	01 44	17 33	14 47	02 35
57	14 58	03 45	19 56	16 13	03 14
58	15 13	06 17	22 39	17 47	03 55
59	15 35	09 32	25 45	19 30	04 39
60	16♒10	13♈49	29♉19	21♊24	05♋27

19h 16m 0s — 289° 0' 0" — 17 ♑ 32

LAT.	11	12	ASC	2	3
0	16♒33	18♓02	20♈34	21♉26	19♊53
5	16 29	18 21	21 21	22 23	20 36
10	16 25	18 41	22 13	23 25	21 20
15	16 22	19 03	23 10	24 32	22 06
20	16 17	19 30	24 15	25 45	22 54
21	16 17	19 35	24 29	26 01	23 05
22	16 16	19 41	24 44	26 17	23 15
23	16 15	19 48	24 59	26 33	23 26
24	16 14	19 54	25 15	26 50	23 36
25	16 13	20 01	25 31	27 08	23 47
26	16 12	20 08	25 48	27 26	23 59
27	16 11	20 16	26 06	27 44	24 10
28	16 10	20 23	26 24	28 03	24 22
29	16 09	20 31	26 43	28 23	24 34
30	16 08	20 40	27 03	28 43	24 46
31	16 07	20 49	27 23	29 04	24 58
32	16 06	20 59	27 45	29 26	25 11
33	16 05	21 09	28 08	29 48	25 25
34	16 05	21 19	28 31	00♊11	25 38
35	16 04	21 30	28 56	00 35	25 52
36	16 03	21 42	29 23	01 01	26 06
37	16 02	21 55	29 50	01 27	26 21
38	16 01	22 09	00♉19	01 54	26 37
39	16 00	22 24	00 50	02 22	26 52
40	15 59	22 40	01 23	02 52	27 09
41	15 59	22 57	01 58	03 23	27 26
42	15 58	23 15	02 36	03 56	27 43
43	15 57	23 36	03 15	04 30	28 02
44	15 57	23 58	03 58	05 06	28 21
45	15 57	24 22	04 44	05 44	28 40
46	15 57	24 49	05 34	06 25	29 01
47	15 57	25 19	06 27	07 07	29 23
48	15 57	25 52	07 25	07 52	29 45
49	15 58	26 29	08 28	08 40	00♋09
50	16 00	27 11	09 37	09 31	00 34
51	16 02	27 59	10 53	10 26	01 00
52	16 05	28 54	12 16	11 24	01 28
53	16 09	29 58	13 48	12 27	01 57
54	16 15	01♈14	15 31	13 34	02 28
55	16 23	02 43	17 25	14 47	03 02
56	16 34	04 31	19 33	16 05	03 37
57	16 49	06 43	21 57	17 31	04 15
58	17 10	09 28	24 41	19 04	04 56
59	17 41	12 57	27 46	20 46	05 40
60	18♒27	17♈30	01♊18	22♊38	06♋27

19h 20m 0s — 290° 0' 0" — 18 ♑ 28

LAT.	11	12	ASC	2	3
0	17♒33	19♓07	21♈38	22♉25	20♊49
5	17 31	19 28	22 28	23 24	21 32
10	17 29	19 50	23 21	24 27	22 17
15	17 26	20 16	24 21	25 35	23 03
20	17 24	20 45	25 30	26 51	23 53
21	17 23	20 52	25 44	27 07	24 03
22	17 23	20 59	26 00	27 23	24 14
23	17 22	21 06	26 16	27 40	24 24
24	17 22	21 13	26 32	27 57	24 35
25	17 21	21 21	26 49	28 15	24 46
26	17 21	21 29	27 07	28 33	24 58
27	17 20	21 37	27 25	28 52	25 09
28	17 20	21 46	27 44	29 11	25 21
29	17 19	21 55	28 04	29 31	25 33
30	17 19	22 04	28 24	29 52	25 46
31	17 19	22 14	28 46	00♊13	25 58
32	17 18	22 25	29 08	00 35	26 11
33	17 18	22 36	29 32	00 58	26 25
34	17 17	22 48	29 57	01 22	26 38
35	17 17	23 01	00♉23	01 46	26 52
36	17 17	23 14	00 50	02 12	27 07
37	17 17	23 28	01 19	02 38	27 22
38	17 17	23 44	01 49	03 06	27 37
39	17 16	24 00	02 21	03 35	27 53
40	17 16	24 18	02 55	04 05	28 10
41	17 17	24 37	03 32	04 37	28 27
42	17 17	24 57	04 10	05 10	28 44
43	17 17	25 20	04 51	05 44	29 03
44	17 18	25 44	05 35	06 21	29 22
45	17 19	26 11	06 23	06 59	29 42
46	17 20	26 41	07 14	07 40	00♋02
47	17 22	27 14	08 09	08 23	00 24
48	17 24	27 50	09 09	09 08	00 47
49	17 26	28 31	10 13	09 56	01 11
50	17 30	29 17	11 24	10 48	01 35
51	17 34	00♈10	12 41	11 42	02 02
52	17 39	01 11	14 06	12 41	02 29
53	17 46	02 21	15 40	13 43	02 59
54	17 55	03 43	17 24	14 51	03 30
55	18 07	05 20	19 20	16 03	04 03
56	18 22	07 16	21 29	17 21	04 38
57	18 43	09 39	23 54	18 46	05 16
58	19 11	12 35	26 37	20 19	05 56
59	19 50	16 17	29 42	21 59	06 40
60	20♒47	21♈04	03♊10	23♊50	07♋27

19h 24m 0s — 291° 0' 0" — 19 ♑ 24

LAT.	11	12	ASC	2	3
0	18♒34	20♓12	22♈42	23♉23	21♊44
5	18 33	20 35	23 34	24 24	22 28
10	18 32	21 00	24 30	25 29	23 13
15	18 31	21 28	25 33	26 39	24 01
20	18 30	22 01	26 44	27 56	24 51
21	18 30	22 08	26 59	28 12	25 01
22	18 30	22 16	27 15	28 29	25 12
23	18 30	22 24	27 32	28 46	25 23
24	18 30	22 32	27 49	29 04	25 34
25	18 30	22 40	28 06	29 22	25 45
26	18 30	22 49	28 25	29 40	25 57
27	18 30	22 58	28 44	00♊00	26 08
28	18 30	23 08	29 04	00 19	26 20
29	18 30	23 18	29 24	00 40	26 33
30	18 30	23 28	29 46	01 01	26 45
31	18 30	23 40	00♉08	01 22	26 58
32	18 30	23 51	00 31	01 45	27 11
33	18 30	24 04	00 56	02 08	27 24
34	18 31	24 17	01 21	02 32	27 38
35	18 31	24 31	01 48	02 57	27 52
36	18 31	24 45	02 17	03 23	28 07
37	18 32	25 01	02 46	03 50	28 22
38	18 32	25 18	03 18	04 18	28 38
39	18 33	25 36	03 51	04 47	28 54
40	18 34	25 55	04 26	05 17	29 10
41	18 35	26 16	05 04	05 49	29 27
42	18 36	26 39	05 44	06 23	29 45
43	18 38	27 04	06 26	06 58	00♋04
44	18 40	27 31	07 12	07 35	00 23
45	18 42	28 00	08 00	08 13	00 43
46	18 44	28 32	08 53	08 54	01 04
47	18 47	29 08	09 49	09 37	01 25
48	18 51	29 48	10 50	10 23	01 48
49	18 55	00♈33	11 57	11 11	02 12
50	19 01	01 23	13 09	12 03	02 37
51	19 07	02 21	14 28	12 58	03 03
52	19 15	03 26	15 54	13 56	03 31
53	19 25	04 42	17 29	14 59	04 00
54	19 37	06 11	19 15	16 06	04 31
55	19 52	07 55	21 11	17 18	05 03
56	20 12	10 00	23 21	18 36	05 38
57	20 38	12 32	25 46	20 00	06 16
58	21 13	15 38	28 29	21 32	06 56
59	22 02	19 32	01♊32	23 11	07 39
60	23♒11	24♈29	04♊58	25♊00	08♋26

19h 28m 0s — 292° 0' 0" — 20 ♑ 20

LAT.	11	12	ASC	2	3
0	19♒35	21♓17	23♈46	24♉22	22♊39
5	19 35	21 42	24 40	25 24	23 24
10	19 36	22 10	25 38	26 31	24 10
15	19 36	22 41	26 43	27 42	24 58
20	19 37	23 17	27 57	29 00	25 49
21	19 38	23 25	28 14	29 17	26 00
22	19 38	23 33	28 30	29 34	26 10
23	19 38	23 42	28 47	29 52	26 21
24	19 38	23 51	29 05	00♊10	26 33
25	19 39	24 00	29 23	00 28	26 44
26	19 39	24 09	29 42	00 47	26 56
27	19 40	24 20	00♉02	01 07	27 07
28	19 40	24 30	00 23	01 27	27 19
29	19 41	24 41	00 44	01 47	27 32
30	19 41	24 53	01 06	02 09	27 44
31	19 42	25 05	01 29	02 31	27 57
32	19 43	25 18	01 54	02 53	28 11
33	19 43	25 31	02 19	03 17	28 24
34	19 44	25 46	02 45	03 41	28 38
35	19 45	26 01	03 13	04 07	28 52
36	19 46	26 17	03 42	04 33	29 07
37	19 48	26 34	04 13	05 00	29 22
38	19 49	26 52	04 46	05 28	29 38
39	19 50	27 12	05 20	05 58	29 54
40	19 52	27 33	05 56	06 29	00♋11
41	19 54	27 56	06 35	07 01	00 28
42	19 56	28 21	07 16	07 35	00 46
43	19 59	28 48	08 00	08 10	01 04
44	20 02	29 17	08 46	08 47	01 24
45	20 05	29 49	09 36	09 26	01 44
46	20 09	00♈24	10 30	10 08	02 04
47	20 14	01 03	11 28	10 51	02 26
48	20 19	01 46	12 30	11 37	02 49
49	20 25	02 35	13 38	12 25	03 13
50	20 33	03 29	14 52	13 17	03 37
51	20 41	04 31	16 12	14 12	04 04
52	20 52	05 41	17 39	15 10	04 31
53	21 04	07 03	19 16	16 13	05 00
54	21 20	08 37	21 02	17 20	05 31
55	21 40	10 29	22 59	18 32	06 04
56	22 04	12 41	25 10	19 49	06 39
57	22 36	15 22	27 35	21 13	07 16
58	23 19	18 38	00♊16	22 43	07 55
59	24 17	22 41	03 18	24 22	08 38
60	25♒39	27♈47	06♊41	26♊09	09♋24

19h 32m 0s — 293° 0' 0" — 21 ♑ 17

LAT.	11	12	ASC	2	3
0	20♒36	22♓23	24♈50	25♉21	23♊34
5	20 38	22 50	25 46	26 24	24 20
10	20 40	23 20	26 47	27 32	25 07
15	20 42	23 54	27 54	28 45	25 55
20	20 44	24 33	29 11	00♊05	26 47
21	20 45	24 42	29 28	00 22	26 58
22	20 46	24 50	29 45	00 39	27 09
23	20 46	25 00	00♉03	00 57	27 20
24	20 47	25 09	00 21	01 15	27 31
25	20 48	25 19	00 40	01 34	27 43
26	20 49	25 30	01 00	01 53	27 54
27	20 50	25 41	01 20	02 13	28 06
28	20 51	25 52	01 41	02 34	28 18
29	20 52	26 04	02 03	02 55	28 31
30	20 53	26 17	02 26	03 16	28 44
31	20 54	26 30	02 50	03 39	28 57
32	20 55	26 44	03 15	04 02	29 10
33	20 57	26 59	03 41	04 26	29 24
34	20 58	27 14	04 09	04 50	29 38
35	21 00	27 31	04 37	05 16	29 52
36	21 02	27 48	05 08	05 42	00♋07
37	21 04	28 07	05 39	06 10	00 22
38	21 06	28 27	06 13	06 39	00 38
39	21 08	28 48	06 48	07 09	00 54
40	21 11	29 11	07 25	07 40	01 11
41	21 14	29 36	08 05	08 12	01 28
42	21 17	00♈02	08 47	08 46	01 46
43	21 21	00 31	09 32	09 22	02 05
44	21 25	01 03	10 20	09 59	02 24
45	21 29	01 37	11 11	10 39	02 44
46	21 35	02 15	12 06	11 20	03 05
47	21 41	02 57	13 05	12 04	03 27
48	21 48	03 44	14 09	12 50	03 49
49	21 56	04 35	15 17	13 38	04 13
50	22 05	05 34	16 32	14 30	04 38
51	22 16	06 40	17 53	15 25	05 04
52	22 29	07 55	19 22	16 23	05 32
53	22 45	09 22	21 00	17 26	06 01
54	23 04	11 02	22 46	18 33	06 31
55	23 28	13 00	24 44	19 44	07 04
56	23 58	15 20	26 55	21 01	07 38
57	24 36	18 08	29 19	22 24	08 15
58	25 26	21 32	02♊00	23 53	08 55
59	26 34	25 43	04 59	25 30	09 37
60	28♒11	00♉55	08♊19	27♊16	10♋22

19h 36m 0s — 294° 0' 0" — 22 ♑ 13

LAT.	11	12	ASC	2	3
0	21♒37	23♓28	25♈53	26♉19	24♊30
5	21 40	23 57	26 51	27 24	25 16
10	21 44	24 30	27 54	28 33	26 03
15	21 47	25 06	29 05	29 47	26 53
20	21 52	25 49	00♉24	01♊09	27 45
21	21 53	25 58	00 41	01 26	27 56
22	21 54	26 08	00 59	01 44	28 07
23	21 55	26 18	01 17	02 02	28 18
24	21 56	26 28	01 36	02 21	28 29
25	21 57	26 39	01 56	02 40	28 41
26	21 59	26 50	02 16	02 59	28 53
27	22 00	27 02	02 37	03 19	29 05
28	22 01	27 15	02 59	03 40	29 17
29	22 03	27 28	03 22	04 01	29 30
30	22 05	27 41	03 46	04 23	29 43
31	22 06	27 55	04 11	04 46	29 56
32	22 08	28 10	04 36	05 09	00♋09
33	22 10	28 26	05 03	05 34	00 23
34	22 12	28 43	05 31	05 59	00 37
35	22 15	29 01	06 01	06 25	00 52
36	22 17	29 20	06 32	06 51	01 07
37	22 20	29 40	07 04	07 19	01 22
38	22 23	00♈01	07 39	07 48	01 38
39	22 26	00 24	08 15	08 18	01 54
40	22 30	00 49	08 53	08 50	02 11
41	22 34	01 15	09 34	09 23	02 28
42	22 38	01 44	10 17	09 57	02 46
43	22 43	02 15	11 03	10 33	03 05
44	22 48	02 49	11 52	11 11	03 24
45	22 54	03 25	12 44	11 50	03 44
46	23 01	04 06	13 40	12 32	04 05
47	23 09	04 51	14 40	13 15	04 27
48	23 17	05 40	15 45	14 02	04 50
49	23 27	06 36	16 55	14 50	05 13
50	23 39	07 38	18 11	15 42	05 38
51	23 52	08 48	19 33	16 37	06 04
52	24 08	10 08	21 03	17 35	06 32
53	24 27	11 39	22 41	18 38	07 01
54	24 50	13 25	24 28	19 44	07 31
55	25 18	15 29	26 26	20 55	08 03
56	25 53	17 56	28 36	22 11	08 38
57	26 38	20 51	01♊00	23 33	09 14
58	27 36	24 22	03 40	25 02	09 53
59	28 55	28 39	06 37	26 38	10 35
60	00♓46	03♉55	09♊53	28♊22	11♋20

19h 40m 0s — 295° 0' 0" — 23 ♑ 10

LAT.	11	12	ASC	2	3
0	22♒39	24♓33	26♈57	27♉17	25♊25
5	22 43	25 05	27 57	28 24	26 12
10	22 48	25 40	29 02	29 34	27 00
15	22 53	26 19	00♉15	00♊50	27 50
20	22 59	27 05	01 37	02 13	28 43
21	23 01	27 15	01 54	02 30	28 54
22	23 02	27 25	02 13	02 48	29 05
23	23 04	27 36	02 32	03 07	29 16
24	23 05	27 47	02 51	03 26	29 28
25	23 07	27 59	03 12	03 45	29 39
26	23 09	28 11	03 33	04 05	29 51
27	23 11	28 24	03 54	04 25	00♋04
28	23 13	28 37	04 17	04 46	00 16
29	23 15	28 51	04 40	05 08	00 29
30	23 17	29 05	05 05	05 30	00 42
31	23 19	29 21	05 30	05 53	00 55
32	23 22	29 37	05 57	06 17	01 08
33	23 24	29 54	06 24	06 41	01 22
34	23 27	00♈12	06 53	07 06	01 36
35	23 30	00 31	07 24	07 33	01 51
36	23 33	00 51	07 55	08 00	02 06
37	23 37	01 12	08 29	08 28	02 21
38	23 41	01 35	09 04	08 57	02 37
39	23 45	02 00	09 41	09 28	02 54
40	23 49	02 26	10 20	09 59	03 11
41	23 54	02 54	11 02	10 33	03 28
42	24 00	03 25	11 46	11 07	03 46
43	24 05	03 58	12 33	11 43	04 05
44	24 12	04 34	13 23	12 21	04 24
45	24 19	05 13	14 16	13 01	04 44
46	24 28	05 56	15 13	13 42	05 05
47	24 37	06 44	16 14	14 26	05 27
48	24 47	07 36	17 20	15 13	05 50
49	24 59	08 35	18 31	16 01	06 13
50	25 13	09 41	19 47	16 53	06 38
51	25 29	10 55	21 10	17 48	07 04
52	25 48	12 19	22 41	18 46	07 31
53	26 10	13 55	24 19	19 48	08 00
54	26 37	15 47	26 07	20 54	08 31
55	27 10	17 56	28 05	22 05	09 03
56	27 50	20 28	00♊15	23 21	09 37
57	28 42	23 29	02 38	24 42	10 13
58	29 49	27 06	05 16	26 09	10 51
59	01♓19	01♉28	08 10	27 44	11 33
60	03♓25	06♉47	11♊23	29♊26	12♋17

Koch Table of Houses for Latitudes 0° to 60° North

19h 44m 0s — 296° 0' 0" — 24 ♑ 06

LAT.	11	12	ASC	2	3
0	23♒41	25♓38	28♈00	28♉15	26♊20
5	23 46	26 12	29 02	29 23	27 08
10	23 52	26 50	00♉10	00♊35	27 56
15	23 59	27 32	01 24	01 52	28 47
20	24 07	28 21	02 49	03 16	29 40
21	24 09	28 31	03 07	03 34	29 52
22	24 11	28 42	03 26	03 52	00♋03
23	24 13	28 54	03 46	04 11	00 14
24	24 15	29 06	04 06	04 30	00 26
25	24 17	29 18	04 27	04 50	00 38
26	24 19	29 31	04 49	05 10	00 50
27	24 21	29 45	05 11	05 31	01 02
28	24 24	29 59	05 34	05 52	01 15
29	24 27	00♈14	05 58	06 14	01 27
30	24 29	00 29	06 23	06 36	01 40
31	24 32	00 46	06 49	07 00	01 54
32	24 35	01 03	07 17	07 24	02 07
33	24 39	01 21	07 45	07 48	02 21
34	24 42	01 40	08 15	08 14	02 36
35	24 46	02 00	08 46	08 40	02 50
36	24 50	02 22	09 18	09 08	03 05
37	24 54	02 45	09 52	09 36	03 21
38	24 59	03 09	10 28	10 06	03 37
39	25 04	03 35	11 06	10 36	03 53
40	25 09	04 03	11 46	11 08	04 10
41	25 15	04 33	12 29	11 42	04 28
42	25 22	05 05	13 14	12 16	04 46
43	25 29	05 41	14 01	12 53	05 04
44	25 37	06 19	14 52	13 31	05 24
45	25 45	07 00	15 46	14 11	05 44
46	25 55	07 46	16 44	14 52	06 05
47	26 06	08 36	17 46	15 36	06 27
48	26 18	09 32	18 53	16 23	06 49
49	26 32	10 34	20 04	17 12	07 13
50	26 48	11 43	21 22	18 03	07 38
51	27 07	13 01	22 46	18 58	08 04
52	27 29	14 29	24 16	19 56	08 31
53	27 55	16 09	25 55	20 58	08 59
54	28 25	18 05	27 43	22 03	09 30
55	29 03	20 20	29 41	23 13	10 02
56	29 49	22 57	01♊50	24 29	10 35
57	00♓47	26 03	04 12	25 49	11 11
58	02 03	29 44	06 48	27 15	11 49
59	03 45	04♉10	09 40	28 49	12 30
60	06♓06	09♉30	12♊50	00♋29	13♋14

19h 48m 0s — 297° 0' 0" — 25 ♑ 03

LAT.	11	12	ASC	2	3
0	24♒42	26♓44	29♈03	29♉13	27♊15
5	24 49	27 20	00♉07	00♊22	28 03
10	24 57	28 00	01 17	01 35	28 53
15	25 05	28 45	02 34	02 54	29 44
20	25 15	29 36	04 01	04 19	00♋38
21	25 17	29 48	04 20	04 37	00 49
22	25 20	00♈00	04 39	04 56	01 01
23	25 22	00 12	05 00	05 15	01 12
24	25 25	00 24	05 20	05 34	01 24
25	25 27	00 38	05 42	05 54	01 36
26	25 30	00 52	06 04	06 15	01 48
27	25 33	01 06	06 27	06 36	02 00
28	25 36	01 21	06 51	06 57	02 13
29	25 39	01 37	07 15	07 19	02 26
30	25 42	01 53	07 41	07 42	02 39
31	25 46	02 10	08 08	08 06	02 52
32	25 49	02 29	08 36	08 30	03 06
33	25 53	02 48	09 05	08 55	03 20
34	25 57	03 08	09 35	09 21	03 35
35	26 02	03 30	10 07	09 47	03 49
36	26 06	03 52	10 40	10 15	04 04
37	26 12	04 17	11 15	10 44	04 20
38	26 17	04 42	11 52	11 13	04 36
39	26 23	05 10	12 31	11 44	04 53
40	26 29	05 40	13 12	12 17	05 09
41	26 36	06 11	13 55	12 50	05 27
42	26 44	06 46	14 40	13 25	05 45
43	26 52	07 23	15 29	14 01	06 04
44	27 02	08 03	16 20	14 40	06 23
45	27 12	08 47	17 15	15 20	06 43
46	27 23	09 35	18 14	16 02	07 04
47	27 36	10 28	19 17	16 46	07 26
48	27 50	11 26	20 24	17 32	07 49
49	28 06	12 31	21 36	18 21	08 12
50	28 24	13 43	22 54	19 12	08 37
51	28 46	15 05	24 19	20 07	09 03
52	29 11	16 37	25 50	21 05	09 30
53	29 40	18 22	27 29	22 06	09 58
54	00♓15	20 22	29 17	23 11	10 28
55	00 57	22 41	01♊14	24 21	11 00
56	01 49	25 23	03 23	25 35	11 34
57	02 55	28 33	05 43	26 55	12 09
58	04 20	02♉18	08 18	28 20	12 47
59	06 13	06 45	11 07	29 52	13 27
60	08♓51	12♉05	14♊13	01♋31	14♋11

19h 52m 0s — 298° 0' 0" — 26 ♑ 00

LAT.	11	12	ASC	2	3
0	25♒44	27♓49	00♉06	00♊11	28♊10
5	25 53	28 28	01 12	01 21	28 59
10	26 02	29 10	02 24	02 36	29 49
15	26 12	29 57	03 43	03 55	00♋41
20	26 23	00♈52	05 13	05 22	01 36
21	26 26	01 04	05 32	05 41	01 47
22	26 29	01 17	05 52	05 59	01 58
23	26 32	01 30	06 13	06 19	02 10
24	26 34	01 43	06 34	06 38	02 22
25	26 38	01 57	06 56	06 59	02 34
26	26 41	02 12	07 19	07 19	02 46
27	26 44	02 27	07 42	07 40	02 59
28	26 48	02 43	08 07	08 02	03 11
29	26 51	02 59	08 32	08 25	03 24
30	26 55	03 17	08 58	08 48	03 38
31	26 59	03 35	09 26	09 11	03 51
32	27 03	03 54	09 54	09 36	04 05
33	27 08	04 15	10 24	10 01	04 19
34	27 13	04 36	10 55	10 27	04 33
35	27 18	04 59	11 27	10 54	04 48
36	27 24	05 23	12 01	11 22	05 03
37	27 29	05 48	12 37	11 51	05 19
38	27 36	06 16	13 15	12 21	05 35
39	27 43	06 45	13 54	12 52	05 52
40	27 50	07 16	14 36	13 24	06 09
41	27 58	07 49	15 20	13 58	06 26
42	28 07	08 25	16 06	14 33	06 44
43	28 16	09 04	16 55	15 10	07 03
44	28 27	09 47	17 47	15 48	07 23
45	28 39	10 33	18 43	16 28	07 43
46	28 51	11 23	19 42	17 10	08 04
47	29 06	12 18	20 46	17 54	08 25
48	29 22	13 20	21 54	18 40	08 48
49	29 40	14 27	23 07	19 29	09 12
50	00♓01	15 43	24 25	20 21	09 36
51	00 25	17 07	25 50	21 15	10 02
52	00 53	18 43	27 21	22 13	10 29
53	01 26	20 31	29 00	23 14	10 57
54	02 05	22 35	00♊48	24 18	11 27
55	02 52	24 58	02 45	25 27	11 58
56	03 51	27 44	04 53	26 41	12 32
57	05 04	00♉58	07 12	28 00	13 07
58	06 38	04 45	09 44	29 24	13 44
59	08 43	09 14	12 31	00♋55	14 24
60	11♓37	14♉32	15♊34	02♋32	15♋07

19h 56m 0s — 299° 0' 0" — 26 ♑ 57

LAT.	11	12	ASC	2	3
0	26♒47	28♓55	01♉08	01♊08	29♊05
5	26 56	29 35	02 17	02 20	29 55
10	27 07	00♈20	03 30	03 36	00♋46
15	27 18	01 10	04 52	04 57	01 38
20	27 32	02 08	06 24	06 25	02 33
21	27 35	02 20	06 44	06 43	02 45
22	27 38	02 34	07 04	07 02	02 56
23	27 41	02 47	07 26	07 22	03 08
24	27 45	03 02	07 47	07 42	03 20
25	27 48	03 16	08 10	08 02	03 32
26	27 52	03 32	08 33	08 23	03 44
27	27 56	03 48	08 57	08 45	03 57
28	28 00	04 05	09 22	09 07	04 10
29	28 04	04 22	09 48	09 29	04 23
30	28 08	04 40	10 15	09 53	04 36
31	28 13	05 00	10 43	10 17	04 50
32	28 18	05 20	11 12	10 41	05 03
33	28 23	05 41	11 42	11 07	05 18
34	28 29	06 04	12 14	11 33	05 32
35	28 35	06 28	12 47	12 00	05 47
36	28 41	06 53	13 22	12 28	06 02
37	28 48	07 20	13 58	12 57	06 18
38	28 55	07 48	14 36	13 27	06 34
39	29 03	08 19	15 16	13 59	06 51
40	29 11	08 52	15 59	14 31	07 08
41	29 20	09 27	16 43	15 05	07 25
42	29 30	10 05	17 30	15 40	07 43
43	29 41	10 45	18 20	16 17	08 02
44	29 53	11 30	19 13	16 55	08 22
45	00♓06	12 18	20 09	17 35	08 42
46	00 20	13 10	21 09	18 17	09 03
47	00 37	14 08	22 13	19 02	09 24
48	00 55	15 12	23 22	19 48	09 47
49	01 15	16 22	24 35	20 37	10 10
50	01 39	17 41	25 54	21 28	10 35
51	02 06	19 08	27 19	22 22	11 01
52	02 37	20 47	28 50	23 19	11 27
53	03 13	22 39	00♊29	24 20	11 56
54	03 57	24 47	02 17	25 24	12 25
55	04 49	27 13	04 13	26 33	12 56
56	05 53	00♉02	06 20	27 46	13 29
57	07 14	03 18	08 38	29 04	14 04
58	08 58	07 08	11 08	00♋27	14 41
59	11 15	11 36	13 52	01 56	15 21
60	14♓25	16♉51	16♊51	03♋32	16♋03

20h 0m 0s — 300° 0' 0" — 27 ♑ 55

LAT.	11	12	ASC	2	3
0	27♒49	00♈00	02♉11	02♊05	00♋00
5	28 00	00 43	03 21	03 19	00 51
10	28 12	01 30	04 37	04 36	01 42
15	28 25	02 22	06 01	05 58	02 35
20	28 41	03 23	07 35	07 27	03 31
21	28 44	03 37	07 55	07 46	03 42
22	28 48	03 51	08 16	08 05	03 54
23	28 51	04 05	08 38	08 25	04 06
24	28 55	04 20	09 00	08 45	04 18
25	28 59	04 35	09 23	09 06	04 30
26	29 03	04 52	09 47	09 27	04 42
27	29 08	05 09	10 12	09 49	04 55
28	29 12	05 26	10 37	10 11	05 08
29	29 17	05 45	11 04	10 34	05 21
30	29 22	06 04	11 31	10 57	05 34
31	29 27	06 24	12 00	11 21	05 48
32	29 33	06 45	12 29	11 46	06 02
33	29 39	07 08	13 00	12 12	06 16
34	29 45	07 31	13 32	12 38	06 31
35	29 52	07 56	14 06	13 06	06 46
36	29 59	08 23	14 41	13 34	07 01
37	00♓06	08 51	15 18	14 03	07 17
38	00 14	09 21	15 57	14 34	07 33
39	00 23	09 53	16 38	15 05	07 49
40	00 33	10 27	17 21	15 38	08 07
41	00 43	11 04	18 06	16 12	08 24
42	00 54	11 43	18 54	16 47	08 42
43	01 06	12 26	19 44	17 24	09 01
44	01 19	13 12	20 38	18 02	09 21
45	01 34	14 02	21 35	18 42	09 41
46	01 50	14 57	22 35	19 24	10 02
47	02 08	15 57	23 39	20 08	10 23
48	02 28	17 03	24 48	20 55	10 46
49	02 51	18 16	26 02	21 43	11 09
50	03 17	19 37	27 21	22 34	11 34
51	03 46	21 08	28 46	23 28	11 59
52	04 21	22 49	00♊18	24 25	12 26
53	05 01	24 44	01 56	25 26	12 54
54	05 49	26 55	03 43	26 30	13 23
55	06 47	29 24	05 39	27 37	13 54
56	07 57	02♉16	07 45	28 50	14 27
57	09 25	05 34	10 01	00♋07	15 01
58	11 19	09 25	12 29	01 29	15 38
59	13 49	13 53	15 11	02 57	16 17
60	17♓15	19♉04	18♊06	04♋31	16♋59

20h 4m 0s — 301° 0' 0" — 28 ♑ 52

LAT.	11	12	ASC	2	3
0	28♒52	01♈05	03♉13	03♊03	00♋55
5	29 04	01 50	04 25	04 17	01 46
10	29 17	02 40	05 43	05 35	02 38
15	29 32	03 35	07 09	06 59	03 32
20	29 50	04 39	08 45	08 29	04 28
21	29 53	04 53	09 06	08 48	04 40
22	29 57	05 07	09 28	09 08	04 51
23	00♓01	05 22	09 50	09 28	05 03
24	00 06	05 38	10 13	09 48	05 15
25	00 10	05 54	10 36	10 09	05 28
26	00 15	06 11	11 00	10 30	05 40
27	00 20	06 29	11 26	10 52	05 53
28	00 25	06 47	11 52	11 15	06 06
29	00 30	07 07	12 19	11 38	06 19
30	00 36	07 27	12 46	12 01	06 32
31	00 42	07 48	13 16	12 26	06 46
32	00 48	08 10	13 46	12 51	07 00
33	00 54	08 34	14 17	13 17	07 15
34	01 01	08 59	14 50	13 43	07 29
35	01 09	09 25	15 24	14 11	07 44
36	01 17	09 52	16 00	14 39	08 00
37	01 25	10 22	16 38	15 09	08 15
38	01 34	10 53	17 17	15 39	08 32
39	01 44	11 26	17 58	16 11	08 48
40	01 54	12 02	18 42	16 43	09 05
41	02 06	12 40	19 28	17 18	09 23
42	02 18	13 21	20 16	17 53	09 41
43	02 31	14 05	21 07	18 30	10 00
44	02 46	14 53	22 01	19 08	10 19
45	03 02	15 45	22 58	19 49	10 39
46	03 20	16 42	23 59	20 31	11 00
47	03 40	17 44	25 04	21 15	11 22
48	04 02	18 53	26 13	22 01	11 44
49	04 27	20 08	27 27	22 49	12 08
50	04 56	21 32	28 47	23 40	12 32
51	05 28	23 05	00♊12	24 34	12 57
52	06 06	24 49	01 43	25 31	13 24
53	06 50	26 47	03 21	26 30	13 52
54	07 42	29 00	05 08	27 34	14 21
55	08 45	01♉32	07 03	28 41	14 52
56	10 02	04 26	09 07	29 53	15 24
57	11 38	07 46	11 22	01♋09	15 58
58	13 41	11 36	13 48	02 30	16 35
59	16 23	16 03	16 26	03 56	17 13
60	20♓05	21♉10	19♊18	05♋29	17♋54

20h 8m 0s — 302° 0' 0" — 29 ♑ 49

LAT.	11	12	ASC	2	3
0	29♒54	02♈11	04♉16	04♊00	01♋50
5	00♓08	02 58	05 29	05 15	02 42
10	00 23	03 49	06 49	06 35	03 35
15	00 39	04 47	08 17	07 59	04 29
20	00 59	05 54	09 56	09 31	05 25
21	01 03	06 09	10 17	09 50	05 37
22	01 07	06 24	10 39	10 10	05 49
23	01 12	06 40	11 01	10 30	06 01
24	01 17	06 56	11 25	10 51	06 13
25	01 21	07 13	11 49	11 12	06 25
26	01 27	07 31	12 13	11 33	06 38
27	01 32	07 49	12 39	11 55	06 51
28	01 38	08 09	13 05	12 18	07 04
29	01 44	08 29	13 33	12 41	07 17
30	01 50	08 50	14 01	13 05	07 31
31	01 56	09 12	14 31	13 30	07 44
32	02 03	09 35	15 02	13 55	07 58
33	02 10	10 00	15 34	14 21	08 13
34	02 18	10 25	16 07	14 48	08 28
35	02 26	10 52	16 42	15 16	08 43
36	02 35	11 21	17 18	15 44	08 58
37	02 44	11 52	17 56	16 14	09 14
38	02 54	12 24	18 36	16 44	09 30
39	03 05	12 59	19 18	17 16	09 47
40	03 16	13 36	20 02	17 49	10 04
41	03 29	14 16	20 48	18 23	10 22
42	03 42	14 58	21 37	18 58	10 40
43	03 57	15 44	22 28	19 35	10 59
44	04 13	16 34	23 23	20 14	11 18
45	04 31	17 28	24 21	20 54	11 38
46	04 50	18 27	25 22	21 36	11 59
47	05 12	19 31	26 27	22 20	12 20
48	05 36	20 41	27 37	23 06	12 43
49	06 04	21 59	28 51	23 54	13 06
50	06 35	23 25	00♊10	24 45	13 30
51	07 10	25 00	01 35	25 39	13 56
52	07 51	26 47	03 06	26 35	14 22
53	08 39	28 47	04 44	27 34	14 50
54	09 36	01♉03	06 30	28 37	15 19
55	10 44	03 37	08 24	29 44	15 49
56	12 08	06 32	10 27	00♋55	16 21
57	13 51	09 53	12 40	02 10	16 55
58	16 04	13 43	15 04	03 30	17 31
59	18 58	18 07	17 40	04 55	18 09
60	22♓56	23♉10	20♊29	06♋26	18♋49

20h 12m 0s — 303° 0' 0" — 00 ♒ 47

LAT.	11	12	ASC	2	3
0	00♓57	03♈16	05♉18	04♊57	02♋45
5	01 12	04 05	06 33	06 14	03 38
10	01 28	04 59	07 55	07 34	04 31
15	01 47	06 00	09 25	09 00	05 25
20	02 08	07 09	11 05	10 32	06 23
21	02 13	07 25	11 27	10 52	06 34
22	02 17	07 41	11 49	11 12	06 46
23	02 22	07 57	12 12	11 32	06 58
24	02 28	08 14	12 36	11 53	07 11
25	02 33	08 32	13 00	12 14	07 23
26	02 39	08 50	13 26	12 36	07 36
27	02 45	09 09	13 52	12 58	07 49
28	02 51	09 29	14 19	13 21	08 02
29	02 57	09 50	14 47	13 45	08 15
30	03 04	10 12	15 16	14 09	08 29
31	03 11	10 35	15 46	14 33	08 42
32	03 19	11 00	16 17	14 59	08 57
33	03 27	11 25	16 49	15 25	09 11
34	03 35	11 52	17 23	15 52	09 26
35	03 44	12 20	17 58	16 20	09 41
36	03 54	12 50	18 35	16 48	09 56
37	04 04	13 22	19 14	17 18	10 12
38	04 15	13 55	19 54	17 49	10 28
39	04 26	14 31	20 37	18 21	10 45
40	04 39	15 10	21 21	18 54	11 02
41	04 52	15 51	22 08	19 28	11 20
42	05 07	16 35	22 57	20 03	11 38
43	05 23	17 22	23 49	20 40	11 57
44	05 41	18 14	24 44	21 19	12 16
45	06 00	19 09	25 42	21 59	12 36
46	06 21	20 10	26 44	22 41	12 57
47	06 45	21 16	27 49	23 25	13 19
48	07 11	22 28	28 59	24 11	13 41
49	07 41	23 48	00♊13	24 59	14 04
50	08 14	25 16	01 32	25 49	14 28
51	08 53	26 54	02 57	26 43	14 53
52	09 37	28 43	04 28	27 39	15 20
53	10 29	00♉45	06 06	28 38	15 47
54	11 31	03 02	07 51	29 40	16 16
55	12 44	05 38	09 44	00♋46	16 46
56	14 14	08 34	11 45	01 56	17 18
57	16 05	11 55	13 57	03 10	17 51
58	18 27	15 45	16 19	04 29	18 27
59	21 34	20 06	18 52	05 53	19 04
60	25♓46	25♉04	21♊37	07♋23	19♋44

Koch Table of Houses for Latitudes 0° to 60° North

20h 16m 0s	304° 0' 0"	01 ♒ 45			
LAT.	11	12	ASC	2	3
0	02♓00	04♈22	06♉19	05♊54	03♋40
5	02 16	05 13	07 37	07 12	04 33
10	02 34	06 09	09 00	08 33	05 27
15	02 54	07 12	10 32	10 00	06 22
20	03 17	08 24	12 15	11 33	07 20
21	03 22	08 40	12 37	11 53	07 32
22	03 28	08 57	13 00	12 13	07 44
23	03 33	09 14	13 23	12 34	07 56
24	03 39	09 32	13 47	12 55	08 08
25	03 45	09 50	14 12	13 16	08 21
26	03 51	10 09	14 38	13 38	08 33
27	03 57	10 29	15 04	14 01	08 46
28	04 04	10 50	15 32	14 24	09 00
29	04 11	11 12	16 00	14 47	09 13
30	04 18	11 35	16 29	15 12	09 27
31	04 26	11 59	17 00	15 37	09 41
32	04 34	12 24	17 31	16 02	09 55
33	04 43	12 50	18 04	16 28	10 09
34	04 52	13 18	18 39	16 56	10 24
35	05 02	13 47	19 14	17 24	10 39
36	05 12	14 18	19 52	17 52	10 55
37	05 23	14 51	20 31	18 22	11 10
38	05 35	15 26	21 12	18 53	11 27
39	05 48	16 03	21 54	19 25	11 43
40	06 01	16 43	22 39	19 58	12 01
41	06 16	17 25	23 26	20 32	12 18
42	06 32	18 11	24 16	21 08	12 37
43	06 49	19 00	25 08	21 45	12 55
44	07 08	19 52	26 03	22 23	13 15
45	07 29	20 50	27 02	23 03	13 35
46	07 52	21 52	28 04	23 45	13 55
47	08 18	23 00	29 09	24 29	14 17
48	08 46	24 14	00♊19	25 15	14 39
49	09 18	25 36	01 34	26 03	15 02
50	09 55	27 06	02 53	26 53	15 26
51	10 36	28 45	04 17	27 46	15 51
52	11 24	00♉36	05 48	28 41	16 17
53	12 20	02 40	07 25	29 40	16 45
54	13 26	04 59	09 09	00♋42	17 13
55	14 44	07 36	11 01	01 47	17 43
56	16 20	10 33	13 01	02 56	18 15
57	18 20	13 54	15 11	04 10	18 48
58	20 51	17 42	17 31	05 27	19 23
59	24 09	22 00	20 01	06 50	20 00
60	28♓35	26♉53	22♊43	08♋19	20♋39

20h 20m 0s	305° 0' 0"	02 ♒ 43			
LAT.	11	12	ASC	2	3
0	03♓03	05♈27	07♉21	06♊50	04♋35
5	03 21	06 20	08 40	08 09	05 29
10	03 40	07 18	10 05	09 32	06 23
15	04 02	08 24	11 39	11 00	07 19
20	04 27	09 39	13 24	12 34	08 17
21	04 32	09 56	13 46	12 54	08 29
22	04 38	10 13	14 09	13 15	08 41
23	04 44	10 31	14 33	13 35	08 53
24	04 50	10 49	14 58	13 57	09 06
25	04 57	11 08	15 23	14 18	09 18
26	05 03	11 28	15 49	14 40	09 31
27	05 10	11 49	16 16	15 03	09 44
28	05 17	12 10	16 44	15 26	09 57
29	05 25	12 33	17 13	15 50	10 11
30	05 33	12 57	17 42	16 14	10 25
31	05 42	13 21	18 13	16 39	10 38
32	05 50	13 47	18 45	17 05	10 53
33	06 00	14 15	19 19	17 32	11 07
34	06 10	14 43	19 53	17 59	11 22
35	06 20	15 14	20 30	18 27	11 37
36	06 31	15 46	21 07	18 56	11 53
37	06 43	16 20	21 47	19 26	12 09
38	06 56	16 56	22 28	19 57	12 25
39	07 10	17 34	23 11	20 29	12 42
40	07 24	18 15	23 56	21 02	12 59
41	07 40	18 59	24 44	21 36	13 17
42	07 57	19 45	25 34	22 12	13 35
43	08 16	20 36	26 26	22 49	13 53
44	08 37	21 30	27 22	23 27	14 13
45	08 59	22 29	28 21	24 07	14 33
46	09 24	23 33	29 23	24 49	14 53
47	09 51	24 42	00♊29	25 33	15 15
48	10 22	25 58	01 38	26 18	15 37
49	10 56	27 22	02 53	27 06	16 00
50	11 35	28 53	04 12	27 56	16 24
51	12 20	00♉35	05 36	28 48	16 49
52	13 11	02 27	07 06	29 44	17 15
53	14 11	04 32	08 43	00♋42	17 42
54	15 21	06 53	10 26	01 43	18 10
55	16 45	09 30	12 17	02 48	18 40
56	18 27	12 28	14 16	03 56	19 11
57	20 34	15 48	16 24	05 08	19 44
58	23 15	19 34	18 41	06 25	20 18
59	26 44	23 50	21 09	07 47	20 55
60	01♈23	28♉37	23♊48	09♋14	21♋34

20h 24m 0s	306° 0' 0"	03 ♒ 41			
LAT.	11	12	ASC	2	3
0	04♓07	06♈32	08♉23	07♊47	05♋30
5	04 26	07 27	09 43	09 07	06 25
10	04 47	08 28	11 10	10 31	07 20
15	05 10	09 36	12 46	12 00	08 16
20	05 37	10 54	14 32	13 35	09 14
21	05 43	11 11	14 55	13 55	09 26
22	05 49	11 29	15 19	14 16	09 38
23	05 55	11 47	15 43	14 37	09 51
24	06 02	12 06	16 08	14 58	10 03
25	06 09	12 26	16 33	15 20	10 16
26	06 16	12 47	17 00	15 42	10 29
27	06 23	13 08	17 27	16 05	10 42
28	06 31	13 30	17 55	16 28	10 55
29	06 39	13 54	18 25	16 52	11 09
30	06 48	14 18	18 55	17 17	11 22
31	06 57	14 44	19 26	17 42	11 36
32	07 07	15 11	19 59	18 08	11 51
33	07 17	15 39	20 32	18 34	12 05
34	07 27	16 08	21 08	19 02	12 20
35	07 39	16 40	21 44	19 30	12 35
36	07 51	17 13	22 22	19 59	12 51
37	08 03	17 48	23 02	20 29	13 07
38	08 17	18 25	23 44	21 00	13 23
39	08 32	19 04	24 27	21 32	13 40
40	08 48	19 46	25 13	22 05	13 57
41	09 05	20 31	26 00	22 39	14 15
42	09 23	21 19	26 51	23 15	14 33
43	09 43	22 11	27 44	23 52	14 52
44	10 05	23 07	28 39	24 30	15 11
45	10 29	24 07	29 38	25 10	15 31
46	10 55	25 12	00♊40	25 52	15 51
47	11 25	26 23	01 46	26 35	16 13
48	11 58	27 41	02 56	27 21	16 35
49	12 34	29 06	04 10	28 08	16 58
50	13 16	00♉39	05 29	28 58	17 21
51	14 03	02 22	06 53	29 50	17 46
52	14 58	04 16	08 23	00♋45	18 12
53	16 02	06 22	09 59	01 43	18 39
54	17 17	08 44	11 41	02 43	19 07
55	18 46	11 22	13 31	03 47	19 36
56	20 34	14 19	15 28	04 55	20 07
57	22 49	17 38	17 34	06 06	20 40
58	25 38	21 22	19 50	07 22	21 14
59	29 17	25 34	22 15	08 43	21 50
60	04♈09	00♊16	24♊50	10♋08	22♋28

20h 28m 0s	307° 0' 0"	04 ♒ 39			
LAT.	11	12	ASC	2	3
0	05♓10	07♈37	09♉24	08♊43	06♋26
5	05 31	08 35	10 46	10 05	07 21
10	05 53	09 37	12 15	11 29	08 16
15	06 18	10 48	13 52	12 59	09 13
20	06 47	12 09	15 40	14 36	10 11
21	06 53	12 26	16 04	14 56	10 23
22	07 00	12 45	16 27	15 17	10 36
23	07 06	13 04	16 52	15 38	10 48
24	07 14	13 23	17 17	15 59	11 01
25	07 21	13 44	17 43	16 21	11 13
26	07 29	14 05	18 10	16 44	11 26
27	07 37	14 27	18 38	17 07	11 39
28	07 45	14 50	19 07	17 30	11 53
29	07 54	15 14	19 36	17 54	12 06
30	08 03	15 39	20 07	18 19	12 20
31	08 13	16 06	20 38	18 44	12 34
32	08 23	16 33	21 11	19 10	12 48
33	08 34	17 02	21 45	19 37	13 03
34	08 45	17 33	22 21	20 04	13 18
35	08 57	18 05	22 58	20 32	13 33
36	09 10	18 39	23 36	21 02	13 49
37	09 24	19 15	24 16	21 32	14 05
38	09 38	19 53	24 58	22 03	14 21
39	09 54	20 34	25 42	22 35	14 38
40	10 11	21 17	26 28	23 08	14 55
41	10 29	22 03	27 16	23 42	15 13
42	10 49	22 53	28 07	24 18	15 31
43	11 10	23 46	29 00	24 55	15 49
44	11 33	24 43	29 56	25 33	16 09
45	11 59	25 44	00♊55	26 13	16 29
46	12 27	26 51	01 57	26 54	16 49
47	12 59	28 03	03 03	27 38	17 10
48	13 34	29 22	04 13	28 23	17 32
49	14 13	00♉48	05 27	29 10	17 55
50	14 57	02 23	06 45	00♋00	18 19
51	15 47	04 07	08 09	00 52	18 43
52	16 45	06 02	09 38	01 46	19 09
53	17 53	08 10	11 13	02 43	19 36
54	19 12	10 31	12 54	03 43	20 04
55	20 47	13 10	14 43	04 46	20 33
56	22 41	16 07	16 39	05 53	21 03
57	25 03	19 25	18 43	07 04	21 35
58	28 01	23 07	20 56	08 19	22 09
59	01♈50	27 14	23 19	09 38	22 45
60	06♈53	01♊51	25♊52	11♋02	23♋23

20h 32m 0s	308° 0' 0"	05 ♒ 38			
LAT.	11	12	ASC	2	3
0	06♓14	08♈43	10♉25	09♊40	07♋21
5	06 36	09 42	11 49	11 02	08 16
10	06 59	10 47	13 19	12 28	09 12
15	07 26	11 59	14 58	13 58	10 09
20	07 57	13 23	16 48	15 36	11 08
21	08 04	13 41	17 12	15 56	11 21
22	08 11	14 00	17 36	16 17	11 33
23	08 18	14 20	18 01	16 38	11 45
24	08 25	14 40	18 27	17 00	11 58
25	08 33	15 01	18 53	17 22	12 11
26	08 41	15 23	19 20	17 45	12 24
27	08 50	15 46	19 48	18 08	12 37
28	08 59	16 10	20 17	18 31	12 50
29	09 08	16 34	20 47	18 56	13 04
30	09 18	17 00	21 18	19 20	13 18
31	09 29	17 27	21 50	19 46	13 32
32	09 39	17 56	22 23	20 12	13 46
33	09 51	18 26	22 58	20 39	14 01
34	10 03	18 57	23 34	21 06	14 16
35	10 16	19 30	24 11	21 35	14 31
36	10 30	20 05	24 50	22 04	14 47
37	10 44	20 42	25 30	22 34	15 03
38	11 00	21 21	26 12	23 05	15 19
39	11 16	22 03	26 56	23 37	15 36
40	11 34	22 47	27 42	24 10	15 53
41	11 54	23 34	28 31	24 44	16 11
42	12 15	24 25	29 22	25 20	16 29
43	12 37	25 19	00♊15	25 57	16 47
44	13 02	26 17	01 11	26 35	17 07
45	13 29	27 20	02 10	27 15	17 26
46	13 59	28 28	03 12	27 56	17 47
47	14 33	29 42	04 18	28 40	18 08
48	15 10	01♉02	05 28	29 25	18 30
49	15 51	02 29	06 42	00♋12	18 53
50	16 38	04 05	08 00	01 01	19 16
51	17 31	05 50	09 23	01 52	19 40
52	18 33	07 46	10 52	02 46	20 06
53	19 44	09 54	12 26	03 43	20 32
54	21 08	12 17	14 06	04 42	21 00
55	22 48	14 55	15 54	05 45	21 29
56	24 48	17 51	17 48	06 51	21 59
57	27 16	21 08	19 51	08 01	22 31
58	00♈22	24 47	22 02	09 14	23 05
59	04 20	28 51	24 22	10 33	23 40
60	09♈33	03♊21	26♊51	11♋55	24♋17

20h 36m 0s	309° 0' 0"	06 ♒ 37			
LAT.	11	12	ASC	2	3
0	07♓18	09♈48	11♉26	10♊36	08♋16
5	07 41	10 49	12 52	11 59	09 12
10	08 06	11 56	14 24	13 26	10 09
15	08 34	13 11	16 04	14 58	11 06
20	09 07	14 37	17 55	16 36	12 06
21	09 14	14 56	18 19	16 56	12 18
22	09 22	15 15	18 44	17 17	12 30
23	09 29	15 35	19 09	17 39	12 43
24	09 37	15 56	19 35	18 01	12 55
25	09 46	16 18	20 02	18 23	13 08
26	09 54	16 41	20 30	18 46	13 21
27	10 04	17 04	20 58	19 09	13 35
28	10 13	17 28	21 27	19 33	13 48
29	10 23	17 54	21 57	19 57	14 02
30	10 33	18 21	22 29	20 22	14 16
31	10 44	18 48	23 01	20 47	14 30
32	10 56	19 18	23 35	21 13	14 44
33	11 08	19 48	24 09	21 40	14 59
34	11 21	20 21	24 46	22 08	15 14
35	11 35	20 54	25 23	22 36	15 29
36	11 49	21 30	26 02	23 06	15 45
37	12 05	22 08	26 43	23 36	16 01
38	12 21	22 48	27 25	24 07	16 17
39	12 39	23 31	28 10	24 39	16 34
40	12 58	24 16	28 56	25 12	16 51
41	13 19	25 04	29 45	25 46	17 08
42	13 41	25 56	00♊35	26 22	17 26
43	14 05	26 51	01 29	26 59	17 45
44	14 31	27 51	02 25	27 37	18 04
45	15 00	28 55	03 24	28 17	18 24
46	15 32	00♉04	04 26	28 58	18 44
47	16 07	01 18	05 32	29 41	19 05
48	16 46	02 40	06 42	00♋26	19 27
49	17 30	04 08	07 55	01 12	19 50
50	18 19	05 45	09 13	02 01	20 13
51	19 16	07 31	10 36	02 52	20 37
52	20 20	09 28	12 04	03 46	21 03
53	21 35	11 37	13 37	04 42	21 29
54	23 03	13 59	15 17	05 41	21 57
55	24 48	16 37	17 03	06 43	22 25
56	26 54	19 32	18 56	07 48	22 55
57	29 29	22 47	20 57	08 57	23 27
58	02♈43	26 23	23 06	10 10	24 00
59	06 49	00♊23	25 23	11 27	24 34
60	12♈11	04♊48	27♊50	12♋48	25♋11

20h 40m 0s	310° 0' 0"	07 ♒ 35			
LAT.	11	12	ASC	2	3
0	08♓22	10♈53	12♉27	11♊32	09♋11
5	08 46	11 56	13 54	12 56	10 08
10	09 13	13 05	15 27	14 24	11 05
15	09 43	14 22	17 09	15 57	12 03
20	10 17	15 51	19 02	17 36	13 03
21	10 25	16 10	19 27	17 56	13 15
22	10 33	16 30	19 52	18 17	13 27
23	10 41	16 51	20 17	18 39	13 40
24	10 50	17 12	20 43	19 01	13 53
25	10 58	17 35	21 11	19 23	14 06
26	11 08	17 58	21 38	19 46	14 19
27	11 17	18 22	22 07	20 09	14 32
28	11 27	18 47	22 37	20 33	14 46
29	11 38	19 13	23 07	20 58	14 59
30	11 49	19 41	23 39	21 23	15 13
31	12 01	20 09	24 12	21 48	15 27
32	12 13	20 39	24 45	22 15	15 42
33	12 26	21 11	25 20	22 42	15 56
34	12 39	21 44	25 57	23 09	16 11
35	12 54	22 18	26 35	23 38	16 27
36	13 09	22 55	27 14	24 07	16 42
37	13 25	23 34	27 55	24 37	16 58
38	13 43	24 15	28 38	25 08	17 15
39	14 02	24 58	29 22	25 40	17 31
40	14 22	25 44	00♊09	26 14	17 48
41	14 43	26 34	00 57	26 48	18 06
42	15 07	27 26	01 48	27 23	18 24
43	15 32	28 23	02 42	28 00	18 43
44	16 00	29 23	03 38	28 38	19 02
45	16 31	00♉28	04 37	29 18	19 22
46	17 04	01 38	05 40	29 59	19 42
47	17 41	02 54	06 45	00♋42	20 03
48	18 22	04 16	07 54	01 26	20 25
49	19 08	05 46	09 08	02 13	20 47
50	20 01	07 23	10 25	03 01	21 10
51	21 00	09 10	11 47	03 52	21 34
52	22 08	11 07	13 15	04 45	21 59
53	23 26	13 16	14 47	05 41	22 26
54	24 59	15 39	16 26	06 39	22 53
55	26 48	18 16	18 11	07 40	23 21
56	29 00	21 10	20 02	08 45	23 51
57	01♈41	24 23	22 01	09 53	24 22
58	05 01	27 57	24 08	11 04	24 55
59	09 16	01♊52	26 23	12 20	25 29
60	14♈45	06♊12	28♊47	13♋40	26♋05

20h 44m 0s	311° 0' 0"	08 ♒ 34			
LAT.	11	12	ASC	2	3
0	09♓26	11♈58	13♉27	12♊28	10♋07
5	09 51	13 03	14 56	13 54	11 04
10	10 20	14 14	16 31	15 22	12 01
15	10 51	15 33	18 14	16 55	13 00
20	11 28	17 04	20 09	18 35	14 00
21	11 36	17 24	20 34	18 56	14 12
22	11 44	17 45	20 59	19 17	14 25
23	11 53	18 06	21 25	19 39	14 37
24	12 02	18 28	21 51	20 01	14 50
25	12 11	18 51	22 19	20 23	15 03
26	12 21	19 15	22 47	20 46	15 16
27	12 31	19 40	23 16	21 10	15 30
28	12 42	20 05	23 46	21 34	15 43
29	12 53	20 32	24 17	21 58	15 57
30	13 04	21 00	24 48	22 23	16 11
31	13 17	21 29	25 21	22 49	16 25
32	13 30	22 00	25 55	23 15	16 39
33	13 43	22 32	26 31	23 43	16 54
34	13 58	23 06	27 07	24 10	17 09
35	14 13	23 41	27 46	24 39	17 24
36	14 29	24 19	28 25	25 08	17 40
37	14 46	24 58	29 06	25 38	17 56
38	15 05	25 40	29 49	26 09	18 12
39	15 24	26 25	00♊34	26 41	18 29
40	15 46	27 12	01 21	27 15	18 46
41	16 08	28 02	02 09	27 49	19 04
42	16 33	28 55	03 01	28 24	19 22
43	17 00	29 53	03 54	29 01	19 40
44	17 29	00♉54	04 50	29 39	19 59
45	18 01	02 00	05 49	00♋18	20 19
46	18 36	03 11	06 52	00 59	20 39
47	19 15	04 28	07 57	01 42	21 00
48	19 59	05 51	09 06	02 26	21 22
49	20 47	07 21	10 19	03 12	21 44
50	21 42	09 00	11 36	04 01	22 07
51	22 44	10 47	12 58	04 51	22 31
52	23 55	12 45	14 24	05 43	22 56
53	25 17	14 54	15 56	06 39	23 22
54	26 54	17 16	17 33	07 36	23 49
55	28 48	19 52	19 17	08 37	24 17
56	01♈05	22 45	21 07	09 41	24 46
57	03 52	25 56	23 04	10 48	25 17
58	07 18	29 26	25 09	11 59	25 49
59	11 40	03♊18	27 22	13 13	26 23
60	17♈15	07♊32	29♊43	14♋32	26♋59

Koch Table of Houses for Latitudes 0° to 60° North

20h 48m 0s   312° 0' 0"   09 ♒ 34

LAT.	11	12	ASC	2	3
0	10♓30	13♈03	14♉28	13♊24	11♋02
5	10 57	14 09	15 58	14 50	12 00
10	11 27	15 22	17 34	16 20	12 58
15	12 00	16 44	19 19	17 54	13 56
20	12 38	18 18	21 15	19 34	14 57
21	12 47	18 38	21 40	19 55	15 09
22	12 56	18 59	22 06	20 17	15 22
23	13 05	19 21	22 32	20 39	15 35
24	13 14	19 44	22 59	21 01	15 48
25	13 24	20 07	23 26	21 23	16 01
26	13 34	20 31	23 55	21 46	16 14
27	13 45	20 57	24 24	22 10	16 27
28	13 56	21 23	24 54	22 34	16 41
29	14 08	21 50	25 25	22 59	16 54
30	14 20	22 19	25 57	23 24	17 08
31	14 33	22 49	26 31	23 50	17 23
32	14 47	23 20	27 05	24 16	17 37
33	15 01	23 53	27 41	24 43	17 52
34	15 16	24 28	28 17	25 11	18 07
35	15 32	25 04	28 56	25 39	18 22
36	15 49	25 42	29 35	26 09	18 38
37	16 07	26 23	00♊17	26 39	18 54
38	16 27	27 05	01 00	27 10	19 10
39	16 47	27 50	01 45	27 42	19 27
40	17 10	28 38	02 32	28 15	19 44
41	17 34	29 29	03 21	28 49	20 01
42	17 59	00♉24	04 12	29 25	20 19
43	18 28	01 22	05 05	00♋01	20 38
44	18 58	02 24	06 02	00 39	20 57
45	19 32	03 31	07 01	01 19	21 16
46	20 09	04 43	08 03	01 59	21 37
47	20 49	06 00	09 08	02 42	21 57
48	21 35	07 24	10 17	03 26	22 19
49	22 26	08 55	11 29	04 12	22 41
50	23 23	10 34	12 46	04 59	23 04
51	24 28	12 22	14 07	05 49	23 28
52	25 42	14 20	15 33	06 42	23 52
53	27 08	16 29	17 03	07 36	24 18
54	28 48	18 50	18 40	08 33	24 45
55	00♈46	21 26	20 22	09 33	25 13
56	03 08	24 17	22 11	10 36	25 42
57	06 01	27 26	24 06	11 43	26 12
58	09 34	00♊53	26 09	12 52	26 44
59	14 01	04 40	28 19	14 06	27 18
60	19♈41	08♊49	00♋38	15♋23	27♋53

20h 52m 0s   313° 0' 0"   10 ♒ 33

LAT.	11	12	ASC	2	3
0	11♓34	14♈07	15♉28	14♊20	11♋58
5	12 03	15 16	16 59	15 47	12 56
10	12 34	16 31	18 37	17 17	13 54
15	13 09	17 55	20 24	18 52	14 53
20	13 49	19 31	22 21	20 33	15 54
21	13 58	19 51	22 46	20 55	16 07
22	14 07	20 13	23 12	21 16	16 19
23	14 17	20 35	23 38	21 38	16 32
24	14 27	20 59	24 06	22 00	16 45
25	14 37	21 23	24 33	22 23	16 58
26	14 48	21 48	25 02	22 46	17 11
27	14 59	22 13	25 32	23 10	17 25
28	15 11	22 40	26 02	23 34	17 38
29	15 23	23 08	26 33	23 59	17 52
30	15 36	23 38	27 06	24 24	18 06
31	15 49	24 08	27 39	24 50	18 20
32	16 04	24 40	28 14	25 16	18 35
33	16 19	25 14	28 50	25 43	18 49
34	16 34	25 49	29 27	26 11	19 04
35	16 51	26 26	00♊05	26 40	19 20
36	17 09	27 05	00 45	27 09	19 35
37	17 28	27 46	01 27	27 39	19 51
38	17 48	28 29	02 10	28 10	20 08
39	18 10	29 15	02 55	28 43	20 24
40	18 33	00♉04	03 42	29 16	20 41
41	18 59	00 56	04 31	29 50	20 59
42	19 26	01 51	05 22	00♋25	21 17
43	19 55	02 50	06 16	01 01	21 35
44	20 27	03 53	07 12	01 39	21 54
45	21 02	05 00	08 11	02 18	22 14
46	21 41	06 13	09 13	02 59	22 34
47	22 24	07 31	10 18	03 41	22 54
48	23 11	08 56	11 26	04 25	23 16
49	24 04	10 27	12 38	05 10	23 38
50	25 03	12 07	13 54	05 58	24 01
51	26 11	13 55	15 15	06 47	24 24
52	27 28	15 53	16 40	07 39	24 49
53	28 58	18 01	18 10	08 33	25 14
54	00♈42	20 22	19 45	09 30	25 41
55	02 44	22 57	21 26	10 29	26 09
56	05 11	25 47	23 13	11 31	26 37
57	08 08	28 53	25 07	12 37	27 07
58	11 46	02♊17	27 08	13 46	27 39
59	16 19	06 00	29 16	14 58	28 12
60	22♈03	10♊03	01♋32	16♋14	28♋47

20h 56m 0s   314° 0' 0"   11 ♒ 32

LAT.	11	12	ASC	2	3
0	12♓39	15♈12	16♉28	15♊16	12♋53
5	13 08	16 22	18 01	16 44	13 52
10	13 41	17 39	19 40	18 15	14 51
15	14 18	19 05	21 28	19 51	15 50
20	15 00	20 43	23 26	21 32	16 51
21	15 09	21 05	23 52	21 54	17 04
22	15 19	21 27	24 18	22 15	17 16
23	15 29	21 50	24 45	22 37	17 29
24	15 39	22 13	25 12	23 00	17 42
25	15 50	22 38	25 40	23 23	17 55
26	16 01	23 03	26 09	23 46	18 09
27	16 13	23 30	26 39	24 10	18 22
28	16 25	23 57	27 10	24 34	18 36
29	16 38	24 26	27 41	24 59	18 49
30	16 52	24 56	28 14	25 24	19 04
31	17 06	25 27	28 47	25 50	19 18
32	17 21	26 00	29 22	26 16	19 32
33	17 36	26 34	29 58	26 43	19 47
34	17 53	27 10	00♊35	27 11	20 02
35	18 11	27 47	01 14	27 40	20 17
36	18 29	28 27	01 54	28 09	20 33
37	18 49	29 09	02 36	28 39	20 49
38	19 10	29 53	03 19	29 11	21 05
39	19 33	00♉39	04 04	29 43	21 22
40	19 57	01 29	04 51	00♋16	21 39
41	20 24	02 21	05 40	00 50	21 56
42	20 52	03 17	06 31	01 25	22 14
43	21 23	04 17	07 25	02 01	22 33
44	21 56	05 20	08 21	02 39	22 52
45	22 33	06 29	09 20	03 18	23 11
46	23 13	07 42	10 21	03 58	23 31
47	23 57	09 01	11 26	04 40	23 52
48	24 47	10 26	12 34	05 23	24 13
49	25 42	11 58	13 46	06 09	24 35
50	26 44	13 37	15 02	06 56	24 57
51	27 54	15 26	16 21	07 45	25 21
52	29 14	17 23	17 46	08 36	25 45
53	00♈47	19 32	19 15	09 30	26 11
54	02 34	21 52	20 49	10 26	26 37
55	04 41	24 26	22 29	11 24	27 04
56	07 12	27 13	24 14	12 26	27 33
57	10 14	00♊17	26 06	13 30	28 02
58	13 57	03 38	28 05	14 38	28 34
59	18 34	07 17	00♋11	15 50	29 06
60	24♈20	11♊15	02♋24	17♋05	29♋41

21h 0m 0s   315° 0' 0"   12 ♒ 32

LAT.	11	12	ASC	2	3
0	13♓43	16♈17	17♉28	16♊11	13♋49
5	14 14	17 29	19 02	17 40	14 48
10	14 48	18 48	20 43	19 12	15 47
15	15 27	20 16	22 31	20 49	16 47
20	16 11	21 56	24 32	22 31	17 48
21	16 20	22 18	24 57	22 52	18 01
22	16 30	22 40	25 23	23 14	18 14
23	16 41	23 04	25 50	23 36	18 27
24	16 52	23 28	26 18	23 59	18 40
25	17 03	23 53	26 46	24 22	18 53
26	17 15	24 19	27 16	24 45	19 06
27	17 27	24 46	27 46	25 09	19 19
28	17 40	25 14	28 16	25 33	19 33
29	17 53	25 43	28 48	25 58	19 47
30	18 07	26 13	29 21	26 23	20 01
31	18 22	26 45	29 55	26 49	20 15
32	18 38	27 18	00♊30	27 16	20 30
33	18 54	27 53	01 06	27 43	20 45
34	19 12	28 30	01 43	28 11	21 00
35	19 30	29 08	02 22	28 40	21 15
36	19 49	29 48	03 02	29 09	21 31
37	20 10	00♉30	03 44	29 39	21 46
38	20 32	01 15	04 28	00♋10	22 03
39	20 56	02 02	05 13	00 42	22 19
40	21 21	02 53	06 00	01 15	22 36
41	21 49	03 46	06 49	01 49	22 54
42	22 18	04 42	07 40	02 24	23 12
43	22 50	05 43	08 34	03 00	23 30
44	23 25	06 47	09 29	03 38	23 49
45	24 03	07 56	10 28	04 16	24 08
46	24 45	09 09	11 30	04 57	24 28
47	25 31	10 29	12 34	05 38	24 49
48	26 22	11 54	13 42	06 22	25 10
49	27 20	13 26	14 53	07 07	25 31
50	28 24	15 06	16 08	07 53	25 54
51	29 37	16 55	17 27	08 42	26 17
52	01♈00	18 52	18 51	09 33	26 41
53	02 35	21 00	20 19	10 26	27 07
54	04 26	23 19	21 52	11 21	27 33
55	06 37	25 52	23 30	12 19	28 00
56	09 12	28 38	25 15	13 20	28 28
57	12 18	01♊39	27 05	14 24	28 57
58	16 05	04 56	29 02	15 31	29 28
59	20 45	08 31	01♋05	16 41	00♌00
60	26♈34	12♊24	03♋16	17♋55	00♌34

21h 4m 0s   316° 0' 0"   13 ♒ 32

LAT.	11	12	ASC	2	3
0	14♓48	17♈21	18♉28	17♊07	14♋44
5	15 20	18 35	20 03	18 37	15 44
10	15 56	19 56	21 45	20 10	16 44
15	16 36	21 26	23 35	21 47	17 44
20	17 22	23 08	25 36	23 30	18 46
21	17 32	23 30	26 02	23 51	18 58
22	17 42	23 53	26 29	24 13	19 11
23	17 53	24 17	26 56	24 35	19 24
24	18 04	24 42	27 24	24 58	19 37
25	18 16	25 07	27 52	25 21	19 50
26	18 28	25 34	28 22	25 44	20 03
27	18 41	26 01	28 52	26 08	20 17
28	18 55	26 30	29 23	26 32	20 31
29	19 09	26 59	29 55	26 57	20 45
30	19 23	27 30	00♊28	27 23	20 59
31	19 39	28 03	01 02	27 49	21 13
32	19 55	28 36	01 37	28 15	21 27
33	20 12	29 12	02 13	28 43	21 42
34	20 30	29 49	02 51	29 10	21 57
35	20 49	00♉28	03 30	29 39	22 12
36	21 09	01 09	04 10	00♋08	22 28
37	21 31	01 52	04 52	00 39	22 44
38	21 54	02 37	05 35	01 10	23 00
39	22 19	03 25	06 21	01 41	23 17
40	22 45	04 15	07 08	02 14	23 34
41	23 14	05 09	07 57	02 48	23 51
42	23 44	06 06	08 48	03 23	24 09
43	24 18	07 07	09 41	03 59	24 27
44	24 54	08 12	10 37	04 36	24 46
45	25 33	09 21	11 35	05 15	25 05
46	26 17	10 36	12 37	05 55	25 25
47	27 05	11 55	13 41	06 36	25 45
48	27 58	13 21	14 48	07 19	26 06
49	28 57	14 54	15 59	08 04	26 28
50	00♈04	16 33	17 13	08 50	26 51
51	01 19	18 22	18 32	09 39	27 14
52	02 45	20 19	19 54	10 29	27 38
53	04 23	22 26	21 22	11 22	28 03
54	06 17	24 45	22 54	12 16	28 28
55	08 31	27 15	24 31	13 14	28 55
56	11 10	29 59	26 14	14 14	29 23
57	14 20	02♊58	28 02	15 17	29 52
58	18 11	06 12	29 57	16 23	00♌23
59	22 53	09 43	01♋59	17 32	00 55
60	28♈43	13♊31	04♋07	18♋45	01♌28

21h 8m 0s   317° 0' 0"   14 ♒ 32

LAT.	11	12	ASC	2	3
0	15♓53	18♈26	19♉27	18♊02	15♋40
5	16 26	19 41	21 04	19 33	16 40
10	17 03	21 04	22 47	21 07	17 40
15	17 45	22 35	24 38	22 44	18 41
20	18 33	24 20	26 40	24 28	19 43
21	18 43	24 42	27 07	24 50	19 56
22	18 54	25 06	27 33	25 11	20 08
23	19 05	25 30	28 01	25 34	20 21
24	19 17	25 55	28 29	25 56	20 34
25	19 29	26 21	28 58	26 20	20 48
26	19 42	26 48	29 27	26 43	21 01
27	19 55	27 16	29 57	27 07	21 14
28	20 09	27 45	00♊29	27 31	21 28
29	20 24	28 15	01 01	27 56	21 42
30	20 39	28 47	01 34	28 22	21 56
31	20 55	29 20	02 08	28 48	22 10
32	21 12	29 54	02 44	29 14	22 25
33	21 30	00♉30	03 20	29 42	22 40
34	21 49	01 07	03 58	00♋10	22 55
35	22 08	01 47	04 37	00 38	23 10
36	22 29	02 28	05 17	01 07	23 26
37	22 52	03 12	05 59	01 38	23 42
38	23 16	03 58	06 43	02 09	23 58
39	23 41	04 46	07 28	02 40	24 14
40	24 09	05 37	08 15	03 13	24 31
41	24 38	06 32	09 04	03 47	24 49
42	25 10	07 29	09 55	04 22	25 06
43	25 45	08 31	10 48	04 58	25 25
44	26 22	09 36	11 44	05 35	25 43
45	27 03	10 46	12 42	06 13	26 02
46	27 48	12 01	13 43	06 53	26 22
47	28 38	13 21	14 47	07 34	26 42
48	29 33	14 47	15 54	08 17	27 03
49	00♈34	16 19	17 04	09 01	27 25
50	01 43	17 59	18 18	09 47	27 47
51	03 00	19 47	19 35	10 35	28 10
52	04 29	21 44	20 57	11 25	28 34
53	06 10	23 50	22 24	12 17	28 58
54	08 07	26 08	23 54	13 11	29 24
55	10 24	28 37	25 30	14 08	29 51
56	13 06	01♊19	27 12	15 07	00♌18
57	16 20	04 15	28 59	16 09	00 47
58	20 13	07 26	00♋52	17 14	01 17
59	24 58	10 53	02 51	18 23	01 49
60	00♉47	14♊35	04♋58	19♋35	02♌22

21h 12m 0s   318° 0' 0"   15 ♒ 32

LAT.	11	12	ASC	2	3
0	16♓57	19♈30	20♉26	18♊58	16♋36
5	17 32	20 47	22 04	20 30	17 37
10	18 11	22 11	23 49	22 04	18 37
15	18 54	23 45	25 41	23 42	19 38
20	19 44	25 31	27 44	25 26	20 40
21	19 55	25 54	28 11	25 48	20 53
22	20 06	26 18	28 38	26 10	21 06
23	20 18	26 43	29 05	26 32	21 19
24	20 30	27 08	29 33	26 55	21 32
25	20 43	27 35	00♊02	27 18	21 45
26	20 56	28 02	00 32	27 42	21 58
27	21 10	28 31	01 03	28 06	22 12
28	21 24	29 00	01 34	28 30	22 26
29	21 39	29 31	02 07	28 55	22 40
30	21 55	00♉03	02 40	29 21	22 54
31	22 12	00 36	03 14	29 47	23 08
32	22 29	01 11	03 50	00♋13	23 23
33	22 48	01 47	04 26	00 41	23 37
34	23 07	02 25	05 04	01 08	23 52
35	23 28	03 05	05 43	01 37	24 08
36	23 49	03 47	06 23	02 06	24 23
37	24 13	04 31	07 05	02 36	24 39
38	24 37	05 18	07 49	03 07	24 55
39	25 04	06 07	08 34	03 39	25 12
40	25 32	06 59	09 21	04 12	25 29
41	26 03	07 53	10 10	04 45	25 46
42	26 36	08 51	11 01	05 20	26 04
43	27 12	09 53	11 54	05 56	26 22
44	27 51	10 59	12 50	06 33	26 40
45	28 33	12 09	13 48	07 11	26 59
46	29 19	13 24	14 48	07 51	27 19
47	00♈11	14 44	15 52	08 31	27 39
48	01 07	16 10	16 58	09 14	28 00
49	02 11	17 43	18 08	09 58	28 21
50	03 21	19 23	19 21	10 44	28 43
51	04 41	21 10	20 38	11 31	29 06
52	06 12	23 07	21 59	12 20	29 30
53	07 56	25 12	23 24	13 12	29 54
54	09 56	27 28	24 54	14 06	00♌20
55	12 16	29 56	26 29	15 02	00 46
56	15 01	02♊36	28 09	16 00	01 13
57	18 17	05 30	29 54	17 02	01 42
58	22 13	08 37	01♋46	18 06	02 12
59	26 59	12 00	03 43	19 13	02 43
60	02♉48	15♊38	05♋47	20♋24	03♌15

21h 16m 0s   319° 0' 0"   16 ♒ 33

LAT.	11	12	ASC	2	3
0	18♓02	20♈34	21♉26	19♊53	17♋32
5	18 38	21 53	23 05	21 26	18 33
10	19 18	23 19	24 50	23 01	19 34
15	20 03	24 54	26 43	24 40	20 35
20	20 55	26 42	28 48	26 24	21 37
21	21 06	27 06	29 14	26 46	21 50
22	21 18	27 30	29 42	27 08	22 03
23	21 30	27 55	00♊09	27 30	22 16
24	21 43	28 21	00 38	27 53	22 29
25	21 56	28 48	01 07	28 16	22 43
26	22 09	29 16	01 37	28 40	22 56
27	22 24	29 45	02 08	29 04	23 09
28	22 39	00♉15	02 39	29 29	23 23
29	22 54	00 46	03 12	29 54	23 37
30	23 11	01 18	03 45	00♋19	23 51
31	23 28	01 52	04 19	00 45	24 06
32	23 46	02 27	04 55	01 12	24 20
33	24 05	03 04	05 32	01 39	24 35
34	24 25	03 43	06 10	02 07	24 50
35	24 47	04 23	06 49	02 36	25 05
36	25 09	05 06	07 29	03 05	25 21
37	25 33	05 50	08 11	03 35	25 36
38	25 59	06 37	08 55	04 06	25 53
39	26 26	07 26	09 40	04 37	26 09
40	26 56	08 19	10 27	05 10	26 26
41	27 27	09 14	11 16	05 44	26 43
42	28 02	10 12	12 07	06 18	27 01
43	28 38	11 15	12 59	06 54	27 19
44	29 19	12 21	13 55	07 30	27 37
45	00♈02	13 31	14 52	08 08	27 56
46	00 50	14 46	15 53	08 48	28 16
47	01 43	16 07	16 56	09 28	28 36
48	02 42	17 33	18 02	10 11	28 57
49	03 47	19 05	19 11	10 54	29 18
50	04 59	20 45	20 24	11 39	29 40
51	06 21	22 32	21 40	12 27	00♌03
52	07 54	24 28	23 00	13 16	00 26
53	09 41	26 32	24 25	14 07	00 50
54	11 44	28 47	25 53	15 00	01 15
55	14 06	01♊13	27 27	15 55	01 41
56	16 54	03 51	29 05	16 53	02 08
57	20 13	06 42	00♋49	17 53	02 37
58	24 10	09 47	02 39	18 57	03 06
59	28 57	13 06	04 34	20 03	03 37
60	04♉44	16♊39	06♋36	21♋13	04♌09

Koch Table of Houses for Latitudes 0° to 60° North

21h 20m 0s — 17 ♒ 33 — 320° 0' 0"

LAT.	11	12	ASC	2	3
0	19♓07	21♈38	22♉25	20♊49	18♋28
5	19 45	22 59	24 05	22 22	19 29
10	20 26	24 26	25 51	23 57	20 31
15	21 12	26 03	27 46	25 37	21 32
20	22 06	27 53	29 51	27 22	22 35
21	22 17	28 17	00♊18	27 44	22 48
22	22 30	28 42	00 45	28 06	23 01
23	22 42	29 07	01 13	28 29	23 14
24	22 55	29 34	01 42	28 51	23 27
25	23 09	00♉01	02 11	29 15	23 40
26	23 23	00 29	02 41	29 38	23 53
27	23 38	00 58	03 12	00♋02	24 07
28	23 53	01 29	03 44	00 27	24 21
29	24 10	02 00	04 16	00 52	24 35
30	24 27	02 33	04 50	01 18	24 49
31	24 44	03 07	05 24	01 44	25 03
32	25 03	03 43	06 00	02 10	25 18
33	25 23	04 20	06 37	02 37	25 32
34	25 44	04 59	07 15	03 05	25 47
35	26 06	05 40	07 54	03 34	26 03
36	26 29	06 23	08 34	04 03	26 18
37	26 54	07 08	09 16	04 33	26 34
38	27 20	07 55	10 00	05 04	26 50
39	27 49	08 45	10 45	05 35	27 07
40	28 19	09 38	11 32	06 08	27 23
41	28 52	10 33	12 21	06 41	27 41
42	29 27	11 32	13 11	07 16	27 58
43	00♈05	12 35	14 04	07 51	28 16
44	00 46	13 41	14 59	08 28	28 35
45	01 31	14 52	15 56	09 06	28 53
46	02 21	16 07	16 56	09 45	29 13
47	03 15	17 28	17 59	10 25	29 33
48	04 15	18 54	19 05	11 07	29 53
49	05 22	20 26	20 13	11 50	00♌14
50	06 37	22 05	21 25	12 35	00 36
51	08 01	23 52	22 41	13 22	00 59
52	09 36	25 47	24 00	14 10	01 22
53	11 24	27 51	25 24	15 01	01 46
54	13 30	00♊04	26 51	15 53	02 11
55	15 55	02 29	28 24	16 48	02 37
56	18 45	05 05	00♋01	17 45	03 04
57	22 05	07 53	01 43	18 45	03 31
58	26 05	10 54	03 31	19 48	04 00
59	00♉51	14 09	05 24	20 53	04 31
60	06♉36	17♊38	07♋24	22♋01	05♌02

21h 24m 0s — 18 ♒ 34 — 321° 0' 0"

LAT.	11	12	ASC	2	3
0	20♓12	22♈42	23♉23	21♊44	19♋24
5	20 51	24 04	25 05	23 18	20 26
10	21 34	25 33	26 52	24 54	21 27
15	22 21	27 12	28 48	26 34	22 29
20	23 17	29 04	00♊54	28 20	23 32
21	23 29	29 28	01 21	28 42	23 45
22	23 41	29 53	01 48	29 04	23 58
23	23 54	00♉19	02 16	29 26	24 11
24	24 08	00 46	02 45	29 49	24 24
25	24 22	01 13	03 15	00♋13	24 38
26	24 37	01 42	03 45	00 36	24 51
27	24 52	02 12	04 16	01 01	25 05
28	25 08	02 42	04 48	01 25	25 18
29	25 25	03 14	05 20	01 50	25 32
30	25 42	03 48	05 54	02 16	25 46
31	26 01	04 22	06 29	02 42	26 01
32	26 20	04 58	07 04	03 08	26 15
33	26 40	05 36	07 41	03 36	26 30
34	27 02	06 15	08 19	04 03	26 45
35	27 25	06 57	08 58	04 32	27 00
36	27 49	07 40	09 39	05 01	27 16
37	28 14	08 25	10 21	05 31	27 31
38	28 42	09 13	11 04	06 02	27 48
39	29 11	10 03	11 49	06 33	28 04
40	29 42	10 56	12 36	07 06	28 21
41	00♈16	11 52	13 25	07 39	28 38
42	00 52	12 51	14 15	08 13	28 55
43	01 31	13 54	15 08	08 48	29 13
44	02 14	15 01	16 03	09 25	29 32
45	03 00	16 11	17 00	10 02	29 50
46	03 51	17 27	17 59	10 41	00♌10
47	04 46	18 47	19 02	11 21	00 30
48	05 48	20 13	20 07	12 03	00 50
49	06 57	21 46	21 15	12 46	01 11
50	08 13	23 24	22 26	13 30	01 33
51	09 39	25 10	23 41	14 17	01 55
52	11 16	27 04	25 00	15 05	02 18
53	13 07	29 07	26 22	15 55	02 42
54	15 14	01♊20	27 49	16 47	03 06
55	17 42	03 42	29 20	17 41	03 32
56	20 34	06 16	00♋55	18 37	03 59
57	23 56	09 02	02 36	19 36	04 26
58	27 56	12 00	04 22	20 38	04 55
59	02♉42	15 11	06 14	21 42	05 25
60	08♉24	18♊36	08♋11	22♋50	05♌56

21h 28m 0s — 19 ♒ 35 — 322° 0' 0"

LAT.	11	12	ASC	2	3
0	21♓17	23♈46	24♉22	22♊39	20♋20
5	21 57	25 09	26 05	24 14	21 23
10	22 41	26 40	27 53	25 51	22 24
15	23 31	28 20	29 49	27 31	23 26
20	24 28	00♉14	01♊57	29 17	24 30
21	24 40	00 38	02 24	29 39	24 43
22	24 53	01 04	02 51	00♋01	24 56
23	25 07	01 30	03 19	00 24	25 09
24	25 21	01 57	03 48	00 47	25 22
25	25 35	02 25	04 18	01 10	25 35
26	25 50	02 54	04 48	01 34	25 49
27	26 06	03 24	05 19	01 58	26 02
28	26 23	03 55	05 51	02 23	26 16
29	26 40	04 28	06 24	02 48	26 30
30	26 58	05 01	06 58	03 14	26 44
31	27 17	05 36	07 32	03 40	26 58
32	27 37	06 13	08 08	04 06	27 13
33	27 58	06 51	08 45	04 33	27 28
34	28 20	07 31	09 23	05 01	27 43
35	28 43	08 12	10 02	05 30	27 58
36	29 08	08 56	10 43	05 59	28 13
37	29 35	09 42	11 25	06 29	28 29
38	00♈03	10 30	12 08	06 59	28 45
39	00 33	11 20	12 53	07 31	29 01
40	01 05	12 13	13 40	08 03	29 18
41	01 39	13 10	14 28	08 36	29 35
42	02 17	14 09	15 19	09 10	29 53
43	02 57	15 12	16 11	09 45	00♌10
44	03 41	16 19	17 05	10 22	00 29
45	04 28	17 30	18 02	10 59	00 47
46	05 20	18 45	19 02	11 38	01 07
47	06 17	20 06	20 03	12 17	01 26
48	07 20	21 32	21 08	12 59	01 47
49	08 31	23 03	22 16	13 41	02 07
50	09 49	24 42	23 26	14 25	02 29
51	11 16	26 27	24 40	15 11	02 51
52	12 55	28 20	25 58	15 59	03 14
53	14 48	00♊22	27 19	16 48	03 38
54	16 57	02 33	28 45	17 40	04 02
55	19 27	04 54	00♋15	18 33	04 27
56	22 20	07 25	01 49	19 29	04 54
57	25 44	10 08	03 29	20 27	05 21
58	29 44	13 03	05 13	21 28	05 49
59	04♉30	16 11	07 03	22 32	06 19
60	10♉09	19♊31	08♋58	23♋38	06♌50

21h 32m 0s — 20 ♒ 36 — 323° 0' 0"

LAT.	11	12	ASC	2	3
0	22♓23	24♈50	25♉21	23♊34	21♋17
5	23 04	26 14	27 04	25 10	22 19
10	23 49	27 46	28 53	26 47	23 22
15	24 40	29 28	00♊51	28 28	24 24
20	25 39	01♉23	02 59	00♋15	25 27
21	25 52	01 48	03 26	00 37	25 40
22	26 05	02 14	03 54	00 59	25 53
23	26 19	02 41	04 22	01 22	26 06
24	26 33	03 08	04 51	01 45	26 19
25	26 48	03 37	05 21	02 08	26 33
26	27 04	04 06	05 51	02 32	26 46
27	27 20	04 36	06 22	02 56	27 00
28	27 37	05 08	06 54	03 21	27 14
29	27 55	05 41	07 27	03 46	27 28
30	28 13	06 15	08 01	04 11	27 42
31	28 33	06 50	08 36	04 37	27 56
32	28 53	07 27	09 12	05 04	28 10
33	29 15	08 05	09 48	05 31	28 25
34	29 38	08 45	10 26	05 59	28 40
35	00♈02	09 27	11 06	06 27	28 55
36	00 27	10 11	11 46	06 56	29 11
37	00 55	10 57	12 28	07 26	29 26
38	01 23	11 45	13 11	07 57	29 42
39	01 54	12 36	13 56	08 28	29 59
40	02 27	13 30	14 43	09 00	00♌15
41	03 03	14 26	15 31	09 33	00 32
42	03 41	15 26	16 21	10 07	00 50
43	04 22	16 29	17 13	10 42	01 08
44	05 07	17 36	18 08	11 18	01 26
45	05 56	18 47	19 04	11 55	01 44
46	06 49	20 02	20 03	12 34	02 03
47	07 48	21 23	21 04	13 13	02 23
48	08 52	22 48	22 08	13 54	02 43
49	10 04	24 20	23 15	14 36	03 04
50	11 23	25 58	24 26	15 20	03 25
51	12 53	27 42	25 39	16 06	03 47
52	14 34	29 35	26 56	16 53	04 10
53	16 28	01♊35	28 16	17 42	04 33
54	18 39	03 45	29 41	18 32	04 58
55	21 10	06 04	01♋09	19 25	05 23
56	24 05	08 33	02 42	20 21	05 49
57	27 29	11 14	04 20	21 18	06 16
58	01♉30	14 06	06 03	22 18	06 44
59	06 14	17 10	07 51	23 21	07 13
60	11♉49	20♊26	09♋44	24♋26	07♌43

21h 36m 0s — 21 ♒ 37 — 324° 0' 0"

LAT.	11	12	ASC	2	3
0	23♓28	25♈53	26♉19	24♊30	22♋13
5	24 10	27 19	28 03	26 06	23 16
10	24 57	28 53	29 54	27 44	24 19
15	25 49	00♉36	01♊52	29 25	25 21
20	26 50	02 33	04 00	01♋12	26 25
21	27 03	02 58	04 28	01 34	26 38
22	27 17	03 24	04 56	01 56	26 51
23	27 31	03 51	05 24	02 19	27 04
24	27 46	04 19	05 53	02 42	27 17
25	28 01	04 48	06 23	03 06	27 30
26	28 17	05 17	06 54	03 29	27 44
27	28 34	05 48	07 25	03 54	27 58
28	28 51	06 20	07 57	04 18	28 11
29	29 10	06 53	08 30	04 43	28 25
30	29 29	07 27	09 04	05 09	28 39
31	29 49	08 03	09 39	05 35	28 54
32	00♈10	08 40	10 14	06 02	29 08
33	00 32	09 19	10 51	06 29	29 23
34	00 56	09 59	11 29	06 56	29 38
35	01 20	10 41	12 08	07 25	29 53
36	01 47	11 26	12 49	07 54	00♌08
37	02 14	12 12	13 31	08 23	00 24
38	02 44	13 01	14 14	08 54	00 40
39	03 16	13 52	14 59	09 25	00 56
40	03 50	14 45	15 45	09 57	01 13
41	04 26	15 42	16 33	10 30	01 30
42	05 05	16 42	17 23	11 04	01 47
43	05 47	17 45	18 15	11 38	02 05
44	06 33	18 52	19 09	12 14	02 23
45	07 23	20 03	20 05	12 51	02 41
46	08 18	21 18	21 04	13 29	03 00
47	09 17	22 38	22 05	14 09	03 20
48	10 23	24 04	23 08	14 49	03 40
49	11 36	25 35	24 15	15 31	04 00
50	12 57	27 12	25 24	16 15	04 22
51	14 28	28 56	26 37	17 00	04 43
52	16 11	00♊48	27 53	17 46	05 06
53	18 07	02 47	29 12	18 35	05 29
54	20 19	04 55	00♋36	19 25	05 53
55	22 51	07 12	02 03	20 17	06 18
56	25 47	09 39	03 35	21 12	06 44
57	29 12	12 17	05 11	22 09	07 10
58	03♉12	15 06	06 52	23 08	07 38
59	07 55	18 07	08 38	24 10	08 07
60	13♉26	21♊19	10♋30	25♋14	08♌37

21h 40m 0s — 22 ♒ 39 — 325° 0' 0"

LAT.	11	12	ASC	2	3
0	24♓33	26♈57	27♉17	25♊25	23♋10
5	25 17	28 24	29 02	27 01	24 13
10	26 05	29 59	00♊54	28 40	25 16
15	26 59	01♉43	02 53	00♋22	26 19
20	28 01	03 42	05 02	02 09	27 22
21	28 14	04 07	05 29	02 31	27 35
22	28 28	04 34	05 57	02 54	27 48
23	28 43	05 01	06 26	03 16	28 02
24	28 58	05 29	06 55	03 39	28 15
25	29 14	05 58	07 25	04 03	28 28
26	29 31	06 28	07 56	04 27	28 42
27	29 48	06 59	08 27	04 51	28 55
28	00♈06	07 31	08 59	05 16	29 09
29	00 24	08 05	09 32	05 41	29 23
30	00 44	08 39	10 06	06 06	29 37
31	01 05	09 15	10 41	06 32	29 51
32	01 26	09 53	11 17	06 59	00♌06
33	01 49	10 32	11 54	07 26	00 20
34	02 13	11 12	12 32	07 54	00 35
35	02 38	11 55	13 11	08 22	00 50
36	03 05	12 39	13 51	08 51	01 06
37	03 34	13 26	14 33	09 20	01 22
38	04 04	14 15	15 16	09 51	01 37
39	04 37	15 06	16 01	10 22	01 54
40	05 11	16 00	16 47	10 54	02 10
41	05 49	16 57	17 35	11 26	02 27
42	06 29	17 57	18 25	12 00	02 44
43	07 12	19 00	19 16	12 35	03 02
44	07 59	20 07	20 10	13 10	03 20
45	08 50	21 18	21 06	13 47	03 38
46	09 45	22 33	22 04	14 25	03 57
47	10 46	23 53	23 04	15 04	04 17
48	11 53	25 18	24 07	15 44	04 36
49	13 08	26 49	25 13	16 26	04 57
50	14 30	28 25	26 22	17 09	05 18
51	16 03	00♊08	27 34	17 53	05 39
52	17 46	01 59	28 49	18 39	06 02
53	19 44	03 57	00♋07	19 27	06 25
54	21 58	06 03	01 30	20 17	06 49
55	24 31	08 19	02 56	21 09	07 13
56	27 28	10 44	04 27	22 03	07 39
57	00♉53	13 19	06 02	22 59	08 05
58	04 52	16 05	07 41	23 57	08 32
59	09 32	19 02	09 25	24 58	09 01
60	15♉00	22♊11	11♋15	26♋02	09♌31

21h 44m 0s — 23 ♒ 41 — 326° 0' 0"

LAT.	11	12	ASC	2	3
0	25♓38	28♈00	28♉15	26♊20	24♋06
5	26 23	29 28	00♊01	27 57	25 10
10	27 12	01♉04	01 53	29 36	26 13
15	28 08	02 51	03 53	01♋19	27 16
20	29 12	04 50	06 03	03 06	28 20
21	29 26	05 16	06 31	03 28	28 33
22	29 40	05 43	06 59	03 51	28 46
23	29 55	06 11	07 27	04 14	28 59
24	00♈11	06 39	07 57	04 37	29 13
25	00 27	07 08	08 27	05 00	29 26
26	00 44	07 38	08 57	05 24	29 39
27	01 01	08 10	09 29	05 48	29 53
28	01 20	08 42	10 01	06 13	00♌07
29	01 39	09 16	10 34	06 38	00 21
30	01 59	09 51	11 08	07 03	00 35
31	02 20	10 27	11 43	07 29	00 49
32	02 42	11 05	12 19	07 56	01 04
33	03 06	11 44	12 56	08 23	01 18
34	03 30	12 25	13 34	08 51	01 33
35	03 56	13 08	14 13	09 19	01 48
36	04 24	13 52	14 53	09 48	02 03
37	04 53	14 39	15 35	10 17	02 19
38	05 24	15 28	16 18	10 47	02 35
39	05 57	16 20	17 02	11 18	02 51
40	06 33	17 14	17 48	11 50	03 08
41	07 11	18 11	18 36	12 23	03 24
42	07 52	19 11	19 26	12 56	03 42
43	08 36	20 14	20 17	13 31	03 59
44	09 24	21 21	21 10	14 06	04 17
45	10 16	22 31	22 06	14 42	04 35
46	11 13	23 47	23 03	15 20	04 54
47	12 15	25 06	24 03	15 59	05 13
48	13 23	26 31	25 06	16 39	05 33
49	14 38	28 01	26 11	17 20	05 53
50	16 02	29 37	27 19	18 03	06 14
51	17 36	01♊19	28 30	18 47	06 36
52	19 21	03 09	29 44	19 32	06 58
53	21 20	05 06	01♋02	20 20	07 21
54	23 34	07 11	02 23	21 09	07 44
55	26 09	09 24	03 49	22 00	08 08
56	29 06	11 47	05 18	22 53	08 34
57	02♉31	14 20	06 51	23 49	09 00
58	06 29	17 03	08 29	24 46	09 27
59	11 07	19 57	10 12	25 47	09 55
60	16♉30	23♊01	12♋00	26♋49	10♌24

21h 48m 0s — 24 ♒ 42 — 327° 0' 0"

LAT.	11	12	ASC	2	3
0	26♓44	29♈03	29♉13	27♊15	25♋03
5	27 30	00♉33	01♊00	28 53	26 08
10	28 20	02 10	02 53	00♋32	27 11
15	29 17	03 58	04 53	02 15	28 14
20	00♈22	05 59	07 04	04 03	29 18
21	00 37	06 25	07 32	04 25	29 31
22	00 52	06 52	08 00	04 48	29 44
23	01 07	07 20	08 29	05 11	29 57
24	01 23	07 48	08 58	05 34	00♌10
25	01 40	08 18	09 28	05 57	00 24
26	01 57	08 48	09 59	06 21	00 37
27	02 15	09 20	10 30	06 45	00 51
28	02 34	09 53	11 02	07 10	01 05
29	02 53	10 26	11 36	07 35	01 19
30	03 14	11 02	12 09	08 00	01 33
31	03 36	11 38	12 44	08 26	01 47
32	03 58	12 16	13 20	08 53	02 01
33	04 22	12 56	13 57	09 20	02 16
34	04 47	13 37	14 35	09 47	02 31
35	05 14	14 20	15 14	10 16	02 46
36	05 42	15 05	15 54	10 44	03 01
37	06 12	15 52	16 36	11 14	03 17
38	06 44	16 41	17 19	11 44	03 32
39	07 18	17 32	18 03	12 15	03 49
40	07 54	18 26	18 49	12 46	04 05
41	08 33	19 23	19 37	13 19	04 22
42	09 15	20 23	20 26	13 52	04 39
43	10 00	21 27	21 17	14 26	04 56
44	10 48	22 33	22 10	15 01	05 14
45	11 41	23 44	23 05	15 38	05 32
46	12 39	24 59	24 02	16 15	05 51
47	13 42	26 18	25 02	16 53	06 10
48	14 52	27 42	26 04	17 33	06 30
49	16 08	29 12	27 08	18 14	06 50
50	17 33	00♊47	28 16	18 56	07 10
51	19 08	02 29	29 26	19 40	07 32
52	20 54	04 17	00♋39	20 25	07 54
53	22 54	06 13	01 56	21 12	08 16
54	25 10	08 16	03 16	22 01	08 40
55	27 44	10 28	04 40	22 51	09 04
56	00♉42	12 49	06 08	23 44	09 29
57	04 07	15 19	07 40	24 39	09 54
58	08 04	17 59	09 17	25 36	10 21
59	12 39	20 50	10 58	26 35	10 49
60	17♉57	23♊51	12♋44	27♋37	11♌18

Koch Table of Houses for Latitudes 0° to 60° North

21h 52m 0s — 328° 0' 0" — 25 ♒ 44

LAT.	11	12	ASC	2	3
0	27♓49	00♉06	00♊11	28♊10	26♋00
5	28 36	01 37	01 59	29 48	27 05
10	29 28	03 15	03 52	01♋29	28 08
15	00♈26	05 04	05 53	03 12	29 12
20	01 33	07 07	08 04	05 00	00♌16
21	01 48	07 33	08 32	05 22	00 29
22	02 03	08 00	09 00	05 45	00 42
23	02 19	08 28	09 29	06 07	00 55
24	02 35	08 57	09 59	06 31	01 08
25	02 52	09 27	10 29	06 54	01 22
26	03 10	09 58	11 00	07 18	01 35
27	03 28	10 30	11 31	07 42	01 49
28	03 48	11 02	12 03	08 07	02 03
29	04 08	11 37	12 37	08 32	02 16
30	04 29	12 12	13 10	08 57	02 30
31	04 51	12 49	13 45	09 23	02 45
32	05 14	13 27	14 21	09 50	02 59
33	05 39	14 07	14 58	10 17	03 14
34	06 04	14 48	15 36	10 44	03 28
35	06 31	15 31	16 15	11 12	03 44
36	07 00	16 16	16 55	11 41	03 59
37	07 31	17 03	17 36	12 10	04 14
38	08 03	17 53	18 19	12 40	04 30
39	08 38	18 44	19 03	13 11	04 46
40	09 15	19 38	19 49	13 42	05 02
41	09 54	20 35	20 36	14 15	05 19
42	10 37	21 35	21 25	14 48	05 36
43	11 23	22 39	22 16	15 22	05 53
44	12 12	23 45	23 09	15 57	06 11
45	13 06	24 56	24 03	16 33	06 29
46	14 05	26 10	25 00	17 10	06 48
47	15 09	27 29	25 59	17 48	07 07
48	16 19	28 53	27 01	18 27	07 26
49	17 37	00♊22	28 05	19 08	07 46
50	19 03	01 56	29 11	19 50	08 07
51	20 39	03 37	00♋21	20 33	08 28
52	22 26	05 24	01 34	21 18	08 50
53	24 27	07 19	02 49	22 04	09 12
54	26 43	09 21	04 09	22 52	09 35
55	29 18	11 31	05 32	23 42	09 59
56	02♉16	13 49	06 58	24 34	10 24
57	05 40	16 17	08 29	25 28	10 49
58	09 36	18 54	10 04	26 24	11 16
59	14 08	21 42	11 44	27 23	11 43
60	19♉21	24♊39	13♋28	28♋24	12♌12

21h 56m 0s — 329° 0' 0" — 26 ♒ 47

LAT.	11	12	ASC	2	3
0	28♓55	01♉08	01♊08	29♊05	26♋57
5	29 43	02 41	02 57	00♋44	28 02
10	00♈36	04 21	04 51	02 25	29 06
15	01 35	06 11	06 53	04 08	00♌09
20	02 44	08 14	09 05	05 56	01 14
21	02 59	08 41	09 32	06 19	01 27
22	03 14	09 08	10 01	06 41	01 40
23	03 31	09 36	10 30	07 04	01 53
24	03 47	10 06	10 59	07 27	02 06
25	04 05	10 36	11 29	07 51	02 20
26	04 23	11 07	12 00	08 15	02 33
27	04 42	11 39	12 32	08 39	02 47
28	05 01	12 12	13 04	09 03	03 00
29	05 22	12 46	13 37	09 29	03 14
30	05 43	13 22	14 11	09 54	03 28
31	06 06	13 59	14 46	10 20	03 43
32	06 30	14 37	15 22	10 46	03 57
33	06 55	15 17	15 58	11 13	04 12
34	07 21	15 58	16 36	11 41	04 26
35	07 49	16 42	17 15	12 08	04 41
36	08 18	17 27	17 55	12 37	04 56
37	08 49	18 14	18 37	13 06	05 12
38	09 22	19 04	19 19	13 36	05 28
39	09 57	19 55	20 03	14 07	05 44
40	10 35	20 50	20 49	14 38	06 00
41	11 15	21 46	21 36	15 10	06 16
42	11 59	22 46	22 24	15 43	06 33
43	12 45	23 49	23 15	16 17	06 51
44	13 36	24 56	24 07	16 52	07 08
45	14 30	26 06	25 01	17 27	07 26
46	15 30	27 20	25 58	18 04	07 45
47	16 35	28 39	26 56	18 42	08 04
48	17 46	00♊02	27 57	19 21	08 23
49	19 05	01 31	29 01	20 01	08 43
50	20 32	03 04	00♋07	20 43	09 03
51	22 08	04 44	01 15	21 26	09 24
52	23 56	06 30	02 27	22 10	09 46
53	25 58	08 23	03 42	22 56	10 08
54	28 15	10 23	05 01	23 44	10 31
55	00♉50	12 32	06 22	24 33	10 54
56	03 48	14 48	07 48	25 24	11 19
57	07 11	17 14	09 17	26 18	11 44
58	11 05	19 48	10 51	27 13	12 10
59	15 34	22 33	12 29	28 11	12 37
60	20♉43	25♊27	14♋11	29♋11	13♌05

22h 0m 0s — 330° 0' 0" — 27 ♒ 49

LAT.	11	12	ASC	2	3
0	00♈00	02♉11	02♊05	00♋00	27♋55
5	00 49	03 44	03 55	01 40	29 00
10	01 43	05 25	05 50	03 21	00♌04
15	02 44	07 16	07 52	05 05	01 07
20	03 54	09 21	10 05	06 53	02 12
21	04 10	09 48	10 32	07 15	02 25
22	04 26	10 16	11 01	07 38	02 38
23	04 42	10 44	11 30	08 01	02 51
24	04 59	11 14	11 59	08 24	03 04
25	05 17	11 44	12 30	08 47	03 18
26	05 35	12 15	13 00	09 11	03 31
27	05 55	12 47	13 32	09 36	03 45
28	06 15	13 21	14 04	10 00	03 58
29	06 36	13 55	14 37	10 25	04 12
30	06 58	14 31	15 11	10 50	04 26
31	07 21	15 08	15 46	11 16	04 41
32	07 45	15 47	16 22	11 43	04 55
33	08 10	16 27	16 59	12 09	05 09
34	08 37	17 08	17 36	12 37	05 24
35	09 05	17 52	18 15	13 05	05 39
36	09 35	18 37	18 55	13 33	05 54
37	10 07	19 24	19 36	14 02	06 10
38	10 41	20 14	20 19	14 32	06 25
39	11 16	21 05	21 02	15 02	06 41
40	11 55	22 00	21 48	15 34	06 57
41	12 36	22 57	22 35	16 06	07 14
42	13 20	23 57	23 23	16 38	07 31
43	14 07	24 59	24 13	17 12	07 48
44	14 58	26 06	25 05	17 46	08 05
45	15 54	27 16	25 59	18 22	08 23
46	16 54	28 30	26 55	18 58	08 42
47	18 00	29 48	27 53	19 36	09 00
48	19 12	01♊10	28 53	20 15	09 20
49	20 32	02 38	29 56	20 55	09 39
50	21 59	04 11	01♋01	21 36	10 00
51	23 37	05 50	02 09	22 18	10 20
52	25 26	07 35	03 20	23 02	10 42
53	27 28	09 26	04 34	23 48	11 04
54	29 45	11 25	05 52	24 35	11 26
55	02♉21	13 32	07 12	25 24	11 50
56	05 18	15 46	08 37	26 14	12 14
57	08 40	18 09	10 05	27 07	12 39
58	12 32	20 41	11 37	28 02	13 05
59	16 57	23 22	13 13	28 59	13 32
60	22♉01	26♊13	14♋54	29♋58	13♌59

22h 4m 0s — 331° 0' 0" — 28 ♒ 52

LAT.	11	12	ASC	2	3
0	01♈05	03♉13	03♊03	00♋55	28♋52
5	01 56	04 48	04 53	02 35	29 57
10	02 51	06 30	06 49	04 17	01♌02
15	03 53	08 22	08 52	06 01	02 05
20	05 05	10 28	11 04	07 49	03 10
21	05 20	10 55	11 32	08 12	03 23
22	05 37	11 23	12 01	08 34	03 36
23	05 53	11 52	12 30	08 57	03 49
24	06 11	12 21	12 59	09 21	04 02
25	06 29	12 52	13 29	09 44	04 16
26	06 48	13 23	14 00	10 08	04 29
27	07 08	13 55	14 32	10 32	04 43
28	07 28	14 29	15 04	10 57	04 56
29	07 49	15 04	15 37	11 22	05 10
30	08 12	15 40	16 11	11 47	05 24
31	08 35	16 17	16 46	12 13	05 38
32	09 00	16 55	17 22	12 39	05 53
33	09 26	17 36	17 58	13 06	06 07
34	09 53	18 17	18 36	13 33	06 22
35	10 22	19 01	19 15	14 01	06 37
36	10 52	19 46	19 54	14 29	06 52
37	11 24	20 34	20 35	14 58	07 07
38	11 59	21 23	21 18	15 28	07 23
39	12 35	22 15	22 01	15 58	07 39
40	13 14	23 09	22 46	16 29	07 55
41	13 56	24 06	23 33	17 01	08 11
42	14 40	25 06	24 21	17 33	08 28
43	15 29	26 08	25 11	18 07	08 45
44	16 20	27 15	26 02	18 41	09 03
45	17 17	28 24	26 56	19 16	09 20
46	18 18	29 38	27 51	19 52	09 39
47	19 24	00♊55	28 49	20 30	09 57
48	20 37	02 17	29 49	21 08	10 16
49	21 57	03 44	00♋51	21 48	10 36
50	23 26	05 17	01 55	22 29	10 56
51	25 04	06 54	03 03	23 11	11 17
52	26 53	08 38	04 13	23 54	11 38
53	28 56	10 29	05 26	24 39	11 59
54	01♉13	12 26	06 42	25 26	12 22
55	03 49	14 30	08 02	26 14	12 45
56	06 45	16 43	09 25	27 04	13 09
57	10 06	19 04	10 52	27 56	13 34
58	13 56	21 33	12 23	28 50	13 59
59	18 18	24 11	13 58	29 46	14 26
60	23♉17	26♊58	15♋37	00♌45	14♌53

22h 8m 0s — 332° 0' 0" — 29 ♒ 54

LAT.	11	12	ASC	2	3
0	02♈11	04♉16	04♊00	01♋50	29♋49
5	03 02	05 51	05 51	03 31	00♌55
10	03 59	07 34	07 47	05 13	02 00
15	05 02	09 27	09 51	06 57	03 04
20	06 15	11 34	12 04	08 46	04 08
21	06 31	12 02	12 31	09 08	04 21
22	06 48	12 30	13 00	09 31	04 34
23	07 05	12 58	13 29	09 54	04 47
24	07 23	13 28	13 59	10 17	05 01
25	07 41	13 59	14 29	10 40	05 14
26	08 00	14 30	15 00	11 04	05 27
27	08 20	15 03	15 31	11 28	05 41
28	08 41	15 37	16 04	11 53	05 55
29	09 03	16 12	16 37	12 18	06 08
30	09 26	16 48	17 11	12 43	06 22
31	09 50	17 25	17 45	13 09	06 37
32	10 15	18 04	18 21	13 35	06 51
33	10 41	18 44	18 57	14 02	07 05
34	11 09	19 26	19 35	14 29	07 20
35	11 38	20 10	20 14	14 57	07 35
36	12 09	20 55	20 53	15 25	07 50
37	12 42	21 42	21 34	15 54	08 05
38	13 16	22 32	22 16	16 23	08 21
39	13 53	23 24	23 00	16 53	08 36
40	14 33	24 18	23 44	17 24	08 52
41	15 15	25 14	24 31	17 56	09 09
42	16 01	26 14	25 19	18 28	09 25
43	16 49	27 17	26 08	19 01	09 42
44	17 42	28 22	26 59	19 35	10 00
45	18 39	29 32	27 52	20 10	10 17
46	19 40	00♊45	28 47	20 46	10 36
47	20 48	02 02	29 44	21 23	10 54
48	22 01	03 24	00♋44	22 01	11 13
49	23 22	04 50	01 45	22 41	11 32
50	24 51	06 21	02 49	23 21	11 52
51	26 30	07 58	03 56	24 03	12 13
52	28 20	09 41	05 05	24 46	12 34
53	00♉22	11 29	06 17	25 30	12 55
54	02 40	13 25	07 33	26 17	13 18
55	05 15	15 28	08 51	27 04	13 41
56	08 11	17 38	10 13	27 54	14 04
57	11 31	19 57	11 39	28 45	14 29
58	15 18	22 24	13 08	29 38	14 54
59	19 37	24 59	14 41	00♌34	15 20
60	24♉30	27♊43	16♋19	01♌31	15♌47

22h 12m 0s — 333° 0' 0" — 00 ♓ 57

LAT.	11	12	ASC	2	3
0	03♈16	05♉18	04♊57	02♋45	00♌47
5	04 09	06 54	06 49	04 26	01 53
10	05 06	08 38	08 45	06 09	02 58
15	06 11	10 32	10 49	07 53	04 02
20	07 25	12 40	13 03	09 42	05 06
21	07 41	13 08	13 31	10 05	05 19
22	07 58	13 36	13 59	10 27	05 32
23	08 16	14 05	14 28	10 50	05 46
24	08 34	14 35	14 58	11 13	05 59
25	08 53	15 06	15 28	11 37	06 12
26	09 12	15 37	15 59	12 01	06 26
27	09 33	16 10	16 30	12 25	06 39
28	09 54	16 44	17 03	12 49	06 53
29	10 16	17 19	17 36	13 14	07 07
30	10 39	17 55	18 10	13 39	07 21
31	11 04	18 33	18 44	14 05	07 35
32	11 29	19 12	19 20	14 31	07 49
33	11 56	19 52	19 56	14 58	08 03
34	12 24	20 34	20 34	15 25	08 18
35	12 54	21 17	21 12	15 52	08 33
36	13 25	22 03	21 52	16 21	08 48
37	13 58	22 50	22 32	16 49	09 03
38	14 34	23 40	23 14	17 19	09 18
39	15 11	24 31	23 57	17 49	09 34
40	15 51	25 26	24 42	18 19	09 50
41	16 34	26 22	25 28	18 51	10 06
42	17 20	27 22	26 16	19 23	10 23
43	18 09	28 24	27 05	19 56	10 40
44	19 03	29 29	27 56	20 30	10 57
45	20 00	00♊38	28 48	21 04	11 15
46	21 02	01 51	29 43	21 40	11 33
47	22 10	03 08	00♋39	22 17	11 51
48	23 25	04 28	01 38	22 55	12 10
49	24 46	05 54	02 39	23 33	12 29
50	26 16	07 24	03 42	24 14	12 49
51	27 55	09 00	04 48	24 55	13 09
52	29 45	10 42	05 57	25 37	13 30
53	01♉48	12 29	07 08	26 22	13 51
54	04 05	14 23	08 22	27 07	14 13
55	06 40	16 25	09 40	27 54	14 36
56	09 35	18 33	11 01	28 43	14 59
57	12 53	20 49	12 25	29 34	15 24
58	16 38	23 13	13 53	00♌26	15 49
59	20 53	25 46	15 25	01 21	16 14
60	25♉41	28♊27	17♋01	02♌18	16♌41

22h 16m 0s — 334° 0' 0" — 02 ♓ 00

LAT.	11	12	ASC	2	3
0	04♈22	06♉19	05♊54	03♋40	01♌45
5	05 15	07 57	07 46	05 22	02 51
10	06 14	09 42	09 44	07 05	03 56
15	07 20	11 37	11 48	08 50	05 00
20	08 35	13 46	14 01	10 38	06 05
21	08 52	14 13	14 29	11 01	06 18
22	09 09	14 42	14 58	11 23	06 31
23	09 27	15 11	15 27	11 46	06 44
24	09 45	15 41	15 57	12 10	06 57
25	10 04	16 12	16 27	12 33	07 10
26	10 24	16 44	16 58	12 57	07 24
27	10 45	17 17	17 29	13 21	07 37
28	11 06	17 51	18 02	13 45	07 51
29	11 29	18 26	18 35	14 10	08 05
30	11 53	19 02	19 08	14 35	08 19
31	12 17	19 40	19 43	15 01	08 33
32	12 43	20 19	20 18	15 27	08 47
33	13 10	20 59	20 55	15 53	09 01
34	13 39	21 41	21 32	16 20	09 16
35	14 09	22 25	22 10	16 48	09 31
36	14 41	23 10	22 50	17 16	09 46
37	15 15	23 58	23 30	17 45	10 01
38	15 50	24 47	24 12	18 14	10 16
39	16 29	25 39	24 55	18 44	10 32
40	17 09	26 32	25 39	19 14	10 48
41	17 52	27 29	26 25	19 45	11 04
42	18 39	28 28	27 12	20 17	11 20
43	19 29	29 30	28 01	20 50	11 37
44	20 22	00♊35	28 51	21 24	11 54
45	21 21	01 44	29 44	21 58	12 12
46	22 24	02 56	00♋38	22 34	12 30
47	23 32	04 12	01 34	23 10	12 48
48	24 47	05 32	02 32	23 48	13 07
49	26 09	06 57	03 32	24 26	13 26
50	27 39	08 27	04 35	25 06	13 45
51	29 18	10 02	05 40	25 47	14 05
52	01♉08	11 42	06 48	26 29	14 26
53	03 11	13 28	07 58	27 13	14 47
54	05 29	15 21	09 12	27 58	15 09
55	08 03	17 20	10 28	28 44	15 31
56	10 57	19 26	11 48	29 33	15 55
57	14 13	21 40	13 11	00♌23	16 19
58	17 55	24 02	14 38	01 14	16 43
59	22 07	26 32	16 08	02 08	17 09
60	26♉50	29♊10	17♋42	03♌04	17♌35

22h 20m 0s — 335° 0' 0" — 03 ♓ 03

LAT.	11	12	ASC	2	3
0	05♈27	07♉21	06♊50	04♋35	02♌43
5	06 21	09 00	08 43	06 17	03 49
10	07 21	10 46	10 41	08 00	04 54
15	08 28	12 42	12 46	09 46	05 59
20	09 45	14 51	15 00	11 35	07 03
21	10 02	15 19	15 28	11 57	07 16
22	10 19	15 47	15 56	12 20	07 29
23	10 37	16 17	16 26	12 43	07 42
24	10 56	16 47	16 55	13 06	07 56
25	11 16	17 18	17 25	13 29	08 09
26	11 36	17 50	17 56	13 53	08 22
27	11 57	18 23	18 28	14 17	08 36
28	12 19	18 57	19 00	14 41	08 49
29	12 42	19 32	19 33	15 06	09 03
30	13 06	20 08	20 07	15 31	09 17
31	13 31	20 46	20 41	15 57	09 31
32	13 57	21 25	21 16	16 23	09 45
33	14 24	22 06	21 53	16 49	10 00
34	14 53	22 48	22 30	17 16	10 14
35	15 24	23 31	23 08	17 43	10 29
36	15 56	24 17	23 47	18 11	10 44
37	16 31	25 04	24 28	18 40	10 59
38	17 07	25 53	25 09	19 09	11 14
39	17 45	26 45	25 52	19 39	11 30
40	18 26	27 39	26 36	20 09	11 45
41	19 10	28 35	27 21	20 40	12 02
42	19 57	29 34	28 08	21 12	12 18
43	20 48	00♊36	28 57	21 44	12 35
44	21 42	01 41	29 47	22 18	12 52
45	22 40	02 49	00♋39	22 52	13 09
46	23 44	04 00	01 32	23 27	13 27
47	24 53	05 16	02 28	24 03	13 45
48	26 08	06 35	03 25	24 40	14 03
49	27 30	07 59	04 25	25 18	14 22
50	29 01	09 28	05 27	25 58	14 42
51	00♉40	11 02	06 31	26 38	15 02
52	02 31	12 41	07 38	27 20	15 22
53	04 34	14 26	08 48	28 03	15 43
54	06 51	16 17	10 00	28 48	16 05
55	09 24	18 14	11 16	29 34	16 27
56	12 17	20 19	12 34	00♌22	16 50
57	15 31	22 31	13 56	01 11	17 14
58	19 11	24 50	15 22	02 02	17 38
59	23 18	27 17	16 51	02 55	18 03
60	27♉57	29♊52	18♋24	03♌51	18♌29

Koch Table of Houses for Latitudes 0° to 60° North

22h 24m 0s	04 ♓ 07		336° 0' 0"		
LAT.	11	12	ASC	2	3
0	06♈32	08♉23	07♊47	05♋30	03♌41
5	07 28	10 02	09 41	07 13	04 48
10	08 28	11 49	11 39	08 56	05 53
15	09 36	13 46	13 44	10 42	06 57
20	10 55	15 56	15 58	12 31	08 02
21	11 12	16 24	16 26	12 53	08 15
22	11 30	16 52	16 55	13 16	08 28
23	11 48	17 22	17 24	13 39	08 41
24	12 07	17 52	17 53	14 02	08 54
25	12 27	18 23	18 24	14 25	09 07
26	12 47	18 55	18 54	14 49	09 21
27	13 09	19 28	19 26	15 13	09 34
28	13 31	20 03	19 58	15 37	09 48
29	13 54	20 38	20 31	16 02	10 02
30	14 18	21 14	21 05	16 27	10 15
31	14 44	21 52	21 39	16 53	10 29
32	15 10	22 31	22 14	17 18	10 43
33	15 38	23 12	22 50	17 45	10 58
34	16 08	23 54	23 27	18 12	11 12
35	16 39	24 37	24 05	18 39	11 27
36	17 11	25 23	24 44	19 07	11 42
37	17 46	26 10	25 25	19 35	11 57
38	18 23	26 59	26 06	20 04	12 12
39	19 02	27 51	26 48	20 33	12 27
40	19 43	28 44	27 32	21 04	12 43
41	20 27	29 40	28 17	21 34	12 59
42	21 15	00♊39	29 04	22 06	13 16
43	22 06	01 40	29 52	22 38	13 32
44	23 00	02 45	00♋42	23 11	13 49
45	23 59	03 53	01 33	23 45	14 06
46	25 03	05 04	02 26	24 20	14 24
47	26 13	06 19	03 21	24 56	14 42
48	27 28	07 38	04 18	25 33	15 00
49	28 51	09 01	05 17	26 11	15 19
50	00♉21	10 28	06 19	26 50	15 38
51	02 01	12 01	07 22	27 30	15 58
52	03 52	13 39	08 28	28 11	16 18
53	05 54	15 23	09 37	28 54	16 39
54	08 11	17 12	10 49	29 38	17 01
55	10 44	19 08	12 03	00♌24	17 23
56	13 35	21 11	13 21	01 11	17 45
57	16 47	23 20	14 42	02 00	18 09
58	20 24	25 37	16 06	02 50	18 33
59	24 28	28 02	17 33	03 43	18 58
60	29♉02	00♋34	19♋05	04♌37	19♌23

22h 28m 0s	05 ♓ 10		337° 0' 0"		
LAT.	11	12	ASC	2	3
0	07♈37	09♉24	08♊43	06♋26	04♌39
5	08 34	11 04	10 38	08 09	05 46
10	09 36	12 52	12 37	09 52	06 51
15	10 45	14 49	14 42	11 38	07 56
20	12 04	17 00	16 56	13 27	09 00
21	12 22	17 28	17 24	13 49	09 13
22	12 40	17 57	17 53	14 12	09 26
23	12 58	18 27	18 22	14 35	09 39
24	13 17	18 57	18 51	14 58	09 53
25	13 38	19 28	19 22	15 21	10 06
26	13 58	20 00	19 52	15 45	10 19
27	14 20	20 34	20 24	16 09	10 33
28	14 43	21 08	20 56	16 33	10 46
29	15 06	21 43	21 29	16 58	11 00
30	15 31	22 20	22 02	17 23	11 14
31	15 56	22 57	22 37	17 48	11 28
32	16 23	23 36	23 12	18 14	11 42
33	16 52	24 17	23 48	18 40	11 56
34	17 21	24 59	24 25	19 07	12 10
35	17 53	25 43	25 02	19 34	12 25
36	18 26	26 28	25 41	20 02	12 40
37	19 01	27 15	26 21	20 30	12 55
38	19 38	28 04	27 02	20 59	13 10
39	20 17	28 55	27 45	21 28	13 25
40	20 59	29 49	28 28	21 58	13 41
41	21 44	00♊45	29 13	22 29	13 57
42	22 32	01 43	29 59	23 00	14 13
43	23 23	02 44	00♋47	23 32	14 30
44	24 18	03 48	01 36	24 05	14 46
45	25 18	04 56	02 27	24 39	15 04
46	26 22	06 06	03 20	25 13	15 21
47	27 31	07 21	04 14	25 49	15 39
48	28 47	08 39	05 11	26 25	15 57
49	00♉10	10 01	06 09	27 03	16 16
50	01 41	11 28	07 10	27 42	16 35
51	03 21	13 00	08 13	28 21	16 55
52	05 11	14 36	09 18	29 02	17 15
53	07 14	16 18	10 26	29 44	17 35
54	09 30	18 06	11 37	00♌28	17 56
55	12 01	20 01	12 50	01 13	18 18
56	14 51	22 01	14 07	02 00	18 41
57	18 02	24 09	15 26	02 48	19 04
58	21 35	26 23	16 49	03 38	19 28
59	25 36	28 45	18 16	04 30	19 52
60	00♊04	01♋15	19♋46	05♌23	20♌18

22h 32m 0s	06 ♓ 14		338° 0' 0"		
LAT.	11	12	ASC	2	3
0	08♈43	10♉25	09♊40	07♋21	05♌38
5	09 40	12 06	11 35	09 04	06 45
10	10 43	13 55	13 34	10 48	07 50
15	11 53	15 53	15 39	12 34	08 55
20	13 13	18 04	17 54	14 23	09 59
21	13 31	18 32	18 22	14 45	10 12
22	13 49	19 01	18 50	15 08	10 25
23	14 08	19 31	19 19	15 31	10 38
24	14 28	20 01	19 49	15 54	10 51
25	14 48	20 33	20 19	16 17	11 05
26	15 09	21 05	20 50	16 41	11 18
27	15 31	21 38	21 21	17 05	11 31
28	15 54	22 13	21 53	17 29	11 45
29	16 18	22 48	22 26	17 53	11 59
30	16 43	23 24	23 00	18 18	12 12
31	17 09	24 02	23 34	18 44	12 26
32	17 36	24 41	24 09	19 09	12 40
33	18 05	25 22	24 45	19 36	12 54
34	18 35	26 04	25 21	20 02	13 09
35	19 07	26 47	25 59	20 29	13 23
36	19 40	27 33	26 38	20 57	13 38
37	20 15	28 20	27 18	21 25	13 53
38	20 53	29 09	27 58	21 53	14 08
39	21 32	00♊00	28 40	22 23	14 23
40	22 15	00 53	29 24	22 52	14 39
41	23 00	01 48	00♋08	23 23	14 55
42	23 48	02 46	00 54	23 54	15 11
43	24 40	03 47	01 41	24 26	15 27
44	25 35	04 51	02 30	24 59	15 44
45	26 35	05 58	03 21	25 32	16 01
46	27 39	07 08	04 13	26 06	16 18
47	28 49	08 22	05 07	26 42	16 36
48	00♉06	09 39	06 03	27 18	16 54
49	01 29	11 01	07 01	27 55	17 13
50	03 00	12 26	08 01	28 33	17 32
51	04 39	13 57	09 03	29 12	17 51
52	06 30	15 33	10 08	29 53	18 11
53	08 31	17 13	11 15	00♌35	18 31
54	10 47	19 00	12 24	01 18	18 52
55	13 17	20 52	13 37	02 02	19 14
56	16 06	22 51	14 52	02 49	19 36
57	19 14	24 57	16 11	03 36	19 59
58	22 45	27 09	17 32	04 25	20 22
59	26 41	29 28	18 58	05 16	20 47
60	01♊05	01♋55	20♋26	06♌09	21♌12

22h 36m 0s	07 ♓ 18		339° 0' 0"		
LAT.	11	12	ASC	2	3
0	09♈48	11♉26	10♊36	08♋16	06♌37
5	10 46	13 08	12 31	10 00	07 44
10	11 50	14 57	14 31	11 44	08 49
15	13 01	16 56	16 37	13 30	09 53
20	14 23	19 08	18 51	15 19	10 58
21	14 40	19 36	19 19	15 41	11 11
22	14 59	20 05	19 48	16 04	11 24
23	15 18	20 35	20 17	16 27	11 37
24	15 38	21 05	20 46	16 50	11 50
25	15 58	21 37	21 17	17 13	12 03
26	16 20	22 09	21 47	17 36	12 17
27	16 42	22 42	22 19	18 00	12 30
28	17 05	23 17	22 51	18 25	12 44
29	17 29	23 52	23 23	18 49	12 57
30	17 54	24 29	23 57	19 14	13 11
31	18 21	25 06	24 31	19 39	13 25
32	18 48	25 46	25 06	20 05	13 39
33	19 17	26 26	25 41	20 31	13 53
34	19 48	27 08	26 18	20 57	14 07
35	20 20	27 51	26 55	21 24	14 22
36	20 54	28 36	27 34	21 52	14 36
37	21 29	29 23	28 13	22 20	14 51
38	22 07	00♊12	28 54	22 48	15 06
39	22 47	01 03	29 36	23 17	15 21
40	23 30	01 56	00♋19	23 47	15 37
41	24 15	02 51	01 03	24 17	15 53
42	25 04	03 49	01 48	24 48	16 09
43	25 56	04 50	02 35	25 20	16 25
44	26 51	05 53	03 24	25 52	16 41
45	27 51	06 59	04 14	26 25	16 58
46	28 56	08 09	05 06	26 59	17 16
47	00♉07	09 22	05 59	27 34	17 33
48	01 23	10 38	06 54	28 10	17 51
49	02 46	11 59	07 52	28 47	18 09
50	04 17	13 24	08 51	29 25	18 28
51	05 57	14 54	09 53	00♌04	18 47
52	07 47	16 28	10 57	00 44	19 07
53	09 48	18 08	12 03	01 25	19 27
54	12 02	19 53	13 12	02 08	19 48
55	14 32	21 43	14 23	02 52	20 10
56	17 19	23 40	15 38	03 37	20 32
57	20 25	25 44	16 55	04 24	20 54
58	23 53	27 54	18 15	05 13	21 17
59	27 45	00♋11	19 39	06 03	21 41
60	02♊05	02♋35	21♋06	06♌56	22♌06

22h 40m 0s	08 ♓ 22		340° 0' 0"		
LAT.	11	12	ASC	2	3
0	10♈53	12♉27	11♊32	09♋11	07♌35
5	11 52	14 09	13 28	10 55	08 43
10	12 56	15 59	15 28	12 40	09 48
15	14 09	17 59	17 34	14 26	10 53
20	15 31	20 11	19 48	16 15	11 57
21	15 50	20 39	20 16	16 37	12 10
22	16 08	21 09	20 45	17 00	12 23
23	16 28	21 38	21 14	17 22	12 36
24	16 48	22 09	21 44	17 45	12 49
25	17 09	22 40	22 14	18 09	13 02
26	17 30	23 13	22 44	18 32	13 15
27	17 53	23 46	23 16	18 56	13 29
28	18 16	24 21	23 47	19 20	13 42
29	18 40	24 56	24 20	19 45	13 56
30	19 06	25 32	24 53	20 09	14 10
31	19 32	26 10	25 27	20 34	14 23
32	20 00	26 49	26 02	21 00	14 37
33	20 30	27 30	26 38	21 26	14 51
34	21 00	28 11	27 14	21 52	15 06
35	21 33	28 55	27 51	22 19	15 20
36	22 07	29 40	28 30	22 46	15 34
37	22 43	00♊27	29 09	23 14	15 49
38	23 21	01 15	29 49	23 42	16 04
39	24 01	02 06	00♋31	24 11	16 19
40	24 44	02 59	01 13	24 41	16 35
41	25 30	03 54	01 57	25 11	16 50
42	26 19	04 51	02 43	25 42	17 06
43	27 11	05 51	03 29	26 13	17 23
44	28 07	06 54	04 17	26 45	17 39
45	29 07	08 00	05 07	27 18	17 56
46	00♉12	09 09	05 58	27 52	18 13
47	01 23	10 21	06 51	28 27	18 30
48	02 39	11 37	07 46	29 02	18 48
49	04 02	12 57	08 42	29 39	19 06
50	05 33	14 21	09 41	00♌16	19 25
51	07 13	15 49	10 42	00 55	19 44
52	09 02	17 23	11 45	01 34	20 04
53	11 03	19 01	12 51	02 15	20 24
54	13 17	20 44	13 58	02 57	20 44
55	15 45	22 33	15 09	03 41	21 05
56	18 30	24 29	16 22	04 26	21 27
57	21 34	26 30	17 39	05 12	21 49
58	24 59	28 38	18 58	06 00	22 12
59	28 48	00♋53	20 21	06 50	22 36
60	03♊02	03♋14	21♋46	07♌42	23♌01

22h 44m 0s	09 ♓ 26		341° 0' 0"		
LAT.	11	12	ASC	2	3
0	11♈58	13♉27	12♊28	10♋07	08♌34
5	12 58	15 11	14 24	11 51	09 42
10	14 03	17 01	16 25	13 36	10 47
15	15 16	19 01	18 31	15 22	11 52
20	16 40	21 14	20 45	17 11	12 56
21	16 58	21 42	21 13	17 33	13 09
22	17 17	22 12	21 42	17 55	13 22
23	17 37	22 41	22 11	18 18	13 35
24	17 57	23 12	22 41	18 41	13 48
25	18 18	23 44	23 11	19 04	14 01
26	18 40	24 16	23 41	19 28	14 14
27	19 03	24 49	24 12	19 52	14 28
28	19 27	25 24	24 44	20 16	14 41
29	19 51	25 59	25 17	20 40	14 55
30	20 17	26 36	25 50	21 05	15 08
31	20 44	27 13	26 24	21 30	15 22
32	21 12	27 52	26 58	21 55	15 36
33	21 41	28 33	27 34	22 21	15 50
34	22 12	29 14	28 10	22 47	16 04
35	22 45	29 58	28 47	23 14	16 18
36	23 19	00♊43	29 25	23 41	16 33
37	23 56	01 29	00♋04	24 09	16 48
38	24 34	02 18	00 44	24 37	17 02
39	25 15	03 08	01 25	25 06	17 18
40	25 58	04 01	02 08	25 35	17 33
41	26 44	04 55	02 51	26 05	17 48
42	27 33	05 52	03 36	26 35	18 04
43	28 25	06 52	04 23	27 06	18 20
44	29 22	07 54	05 10	27 38	18 37
45	00♉22	09 00	05 59	28 11	18 53
46	01 27	10 08	06 50	28 45	19 10
47	02 38	11 20	07 43	29 19	19 28
48	03 54	12 35	08 37	29 54	19 45
49	05 17	13 54	09 33	00♌30	20 03
50	06 48	15 17	10 31	01 07	20 22
51	08 27	16 44	11 31	01 46	20 41
52	10 16	18 16	12 33	02 25	21 00
53	12 17	19 53	13 38	03 05	21 20
54	14 29	21 35	14 45	03 47	21 40
55	16 56	23 23	15 55	04 30	22 01
56	19 40	25 16	17 07	05 14	22 23
57	22 41	27 16	18 22	06 00	22 45
58	26 03	29 21	19 40	06 48	23 08
59	29 48	01♋34	21 02	07 37	23 31
60	03♊58	03♋53	22♋26	08♌28	23♌55

22h 48m 0s	10 ♓ 30		342° 0' 0"		
LAT.	11	12	ASC	2	3
0	13♈03	14♉28	13♊24	11♋02	09♌34
5	14 03	16 12	15 21	12 47	10 41
10	15 10	18 03	17 21	14 31	11 47
15	16 24	20 03	19 28	16 18	12 51
20	17 49	22 17	21 42	18 07	13 55
21	18 07	22 45	22 10	18 29	14 08
22	18 26	23 14	22 39	18 51	14 21
23	18 46	23 44	23 08	19 14	14 34
24	19 07	24 15	23 37	19 37	14 47
25	19 28	24 46	24 07	20 00	15 00
26	19 50	25 19	24 38	20 23	15 13
27	20 13	25 52	25 09	20 47	15 27
28	20 37	26 27	25 40	21 11	15 40
29	21 02	27 02	26 13	21 35	15 53
30	21 28	27 38	26 46	22 00	16 07
31	21 55	28 16	27 20	22 25	16 21
32	22 23	28 55	27 54	22 50	16 35
33	22 53	29 35	28 29	23 16	16 49
34	23 24	00♊17	29 05	23 42	17 03
35	23 57	01 00	29 42	24 09	17 17
36	24 31	01 45	00♋20	24 36	17 31
37	25 08	02 31	00 59	25 03	17 46
38	25 47	03 19	01 39	25 31	18 01
39	26 28	04 10	02 20	26 00	18 16
40	27 11	05 02	03 02	26 29	18 31
41	27 57	05 56	03 45	26 58	18 46
42	28 46	06 53	04 30	27 29	19 02
43	29 39	07 52	05 15	28 00	19 18
44	00♉36	08 54	06 03	28 31	19 34
45	01 36	09 59	06 51	29 04	19 51
46	02 41	11 06	07 42	29 37	20 08
47	03 52	12 17	08 34	00♌11	20 25
48	05 08	13 32	09 27	00 46	20 42
49	06 32	14 50	10 23	01 22	21 00
50	08 02	16 12	11 20	01 59	21 19
51	09 41	17 39	12 20	02 36	21 37
52	11 30	19 09	13 21	03 15	21 56
53	13 29	20 45	14 25	03 55	22 16
54	15 41	22 26	15 31	04 36	22 36
55	18 06	24 12	16 40	05 19	22 57
56	20 48	26 03	17 51	06 03	23 18
57	23 47	28 01	19 06	06 48	23 40
58	27 06	00♋04	20 23	07 35	24 03
59	00♊47	02 15	21 43	08 23	24 26
60	04♊53	04♋31	23♋06	09♌14	24♌50

22h 52m 0s	11 ♓ 34		343° 0' 0"		
LAT.	11	12	ASC	2	3
0	14♈07	15♉28	14♊20	11♋58	10♌33
5	15 09	17 13	16 17	13 43	11 41
10	16 16	19 04	18 18	15 27	12 46
15	17 31	21 05	20 24	17 13	13 50
20	18 57	23 19	22 39	19 02	14 54
21	19 16	23 47	23 07	19 25	15 07
22	19 35	24 17	23 35	19 47	15 20
23	19 55	24 46	24 04	20 10	15 33
24	20 16	25 17	24 34	20 33	15 46
25	20 37	25 49	25 03	20 56	15 59
26	20 59	26 21	25 34	21 19	16 12
27	21 23	26 55	26 05	21 43	16 26
28	21 47	27 29	26 37	22 07	16 39
29	22 12	28 04	27 09	22 31	16 52
30	22 38	28 41	27 42	22 55	17 06
31	23 05	29 18	28 15	23 20	17 20
32	23 34	29 57	28 50	23 45	17 33
33	24 04	00♊37	29 25	24 11	17 47
34	24 35	01 19	00♋01	24 37	18 01
35	25 08	02 02	00 37	25 03	18 15
36	25 43	02 46	01 15	25 30	18 30
37	26 20	03 32	01 54	25 57	18 44
38	26 59	04 20	02 33	26 25	18 59
39	27 40	05 10	03 14	26 54	19 14
40	28 23	06 02	03 56	27 23	19 29
41	29 10	06 56	04 38	27 52	19 44
42	29 59	07 53	05 23	28 22	20 00
43	00♉52	08 51	06 08	28 53	20 16
44	01 49	09 53	06 55	29 24	20 32
45	02 49	10 57	07 43	29 56	20 48
46	03 55	12 04	08 33	00♌29	21 05
47	05 05	13 14	09 24	01 03	21 22
48	06 22	14 28	10 18	01 38	21 40
49	07 45	15 46	11 12	02 13	21 57
50	09 15	17 07	12 09	02 50	22 15
51	10 53	18 32	13 08	03 27	22 34
52	12 41	20 02	14 09	04 06	22 53
53	14 40	21 36	15 12	04 45	23 12
54	16 51	23 15	16 17	05 26	23 32
55	19 15	24 59	17 25	06 08	23 53
56	21 54	26 49	18 35	06 51	24 14
57	24 51	28 45	19 49	07 36	24 36
58	28 08	00♋47	21 04	08 22	24 58
59	01♊45	02 55	22 23	09 10	25 21
60	05♊46	05♋09	23♋45	10♌00	25♌44

Koch Table of Houses for Latitudes 0° to 60° North

22h 56m 0s — 344° 0' 0" — 12 ♓ 39

LAT.	11	12	ASC	2	3
0	15♈12	16♉28	15♊16	12♋53	11♌32
5	16 14	18 13	17 13	14 38	12 40
10	17 22	20 05	19 14	16 23	13 46
15	18 38	22 07	21 21	18 09	14 50
20	20 05	24 21	23 35	19 58	15 54
21	20 24	24 49	24 03	20 20	16 07
22	20 43	25 18	24 32	20 43	16 20
23	21 03	25 48	25 00	21 05	16 33
24	21 24	26 19	25 30	21 28	16 45
25	21 46	26 51	26 00	21 51	16 59
26	22 08	27 23	26 30	22 15	17 12
27	22 32	27 56	27 01	22 38	17 25
28	22 56	28 31	27 32	23 02	17 38
29	23 21	29 06	28 04	23 26	17 51
30	23 48	29 42	28 37	23 50	18 05
31	24 15	00♊20	29 11	24 15	18 18
32	24 44	00 59	29 45	24 40	18 32
33	25 14	01 39	00♋20	25 06	18 46
34	25 46	02 20	00 55	25 32	19 00
35	26 19	03 03	01 32	25 58	19 14
36	26 54	03 47	02 09	26 25	19 28
37	27 31	04 33	02 48	26 52	19 43
38	28 10	05 21	03 27	27 19	19 57
39	28 52	06 11	04 07	27 48	20 12
40	29 35	07 02	04 49	28 16	20 27
41	00♉22	07 56	05 32	28 46	20 43
42	01 11	08 52	06 15	29 15	20 58
43	02 04	09 50	07 00	29 46	21 14
44	03 01	10 51	07 47	00♌17	21 30
45	04 02	11 55	08 35	00 49	21 46
46	05 07	13 01	09 24	01 22	22 03
47	06 18	14 11	10 15	01 55	22 20
48	07 34	15 24	11 07	02 29	22 37
49	08 57	16 40	12 02	03 05	22 54
50	10 27	18 00	12 58	03 41	23 12
51	12 05	19 25	13 56	04 18	23 31
52	13 52	20 53	14 56	04 56	23 50
53	15 50	22 26	15 58	05 35	24 09
54	17 59	24 04	17 03	06 15	24 29
55	20 22	25 47	18 10	06 57	24 49
56	23 00	27 35	19 19	07 40	25 10
57	25 54	29 29	20 31	08 24	25 31
58	29 07	01♋28	21 46	09 09	25 53
59	02♊41	03 34	23 04	09 57	26 16
60	06♊37	05♋46	24♋25	10♌45	26♌39

23h 0m 0s — 345° 0' 0" — 13 ♓ 43

LAT.	11	12	ASC	2	3
0	16♈17	17♉28	16♊11	13♋49	12♌32
5	17 20	19 14	18 09	15 34	13 40
10	18 28	21 06	20 10	17 19	14 45
15	19 45	23 08	22 17	19 05	15 49
20	21 12	25 22	24 31	20 54	16 53
21	21 32	25 51	24 59	21 16	17 06
22	21 51	26 20	25 28	21 39	17 19
23	22 12	26 50	25 56	22 01	17 32
24	22 33	27 21	26 26	22 24	17 45
25	22 55	27 52	26 55	22 47	17 58
26	23 17	28 25	27 26	23 10	18 11
27	23 41	28 58	27 56	23 33	18 24
28	24 05	29 32	28 28	23 57	18 37
29	24 31	00♊07	29 00	24 21	18 51
30	24 57	00 44	29 32	24 46	19 04
31	25 25	01 21	00♋06	25 10	19 17
32	25 54	02 00	00 40	25 35	19 31
33	26 24	02 40	01 15	26 00	19 45
34	26 56	03 21	01 50	26 26	19 59
35	27 30	04 03	02 26	26 52	20 13
36	28 05	04 48	03 04	27 19	20 27
37	28 42	05 33	03 42	27 46	20 41
38	29 21	06 21	04 21	28 13	20 56
39	00♉03	07 10	05 01	28 41	21 11
40	00 47	08 02	05 42	29 10	21 26
41	01 33	08 55	06 24	29 39	21 41
42	02 23	09 50	07 08	00♌09	21 56
43	03 16	10 48	07 52	00 39	22 12
44	04 13	11 49	08 38	01 10	22 28
45	05 14	12 52	09 26	01 42	22 44
46	06 19	13 58	10 15	02 14	23 00
47	07 29	15 07	11 05	02 47	23 17
48	08 45	16 19	11 57	03 21	23 34
49	10 08	17 34	12 51	03 56	23 52
50	11 37	18 54	13 46	04 31	24 09
51	13 15	20 17	14 44	05 08	24 28
52	15 01	21 44	15 43	05 46	24 46
53	16 58	23 16	16 44	06 25	25 05
54	19 06	24 52	17 48	07 04	25 25
55	21 28	26 33	18 54	07 46	25 45
56	24 03	28 20	20 03	08 28	26 05
57	26 56	00♋12	21 14	09 12	26 27
58	00♊06	02 10	22 28	09 57	26 48
59	03 36	04 13	23 44	10 43	27 11
60	07♊28	06♋23	25♋04	11♌31	27♌34

23h 4m 0s — 346° 0' 0" — 14 ♓ 48

LAT.	11	12	ASC	2	3
0	17♈21	18♉28	17♊07	14♋44	13♌32
5	18 25	20 14	19 05	16 30	14 40
10	19 34	22 07	21 07	18 15	15 45
15	20 52	24 09	23 13	20 01	16 49
20	22 20	26 23	25 27	21 50	17 53
21	22 39	26 52	25 55	22 12	18 06
22	22 59	27 21	26 23	22 34	18 19
23	23 20	27 51	26 52	22 57	18 31
24	23 41	28 22	27 21	23 19	18 44
25	24 03	28 53	27 51	23 42	18 57
26	24 26	29 26	28 21	24 05	19 10
27	24 49	29 59	28 52	24 29	19 23
28	25 14	00♊33	29 23	24 52	19 36
29	25 40	01 08	29 55	25 16	19 50
30	26 06	01 44	00♋28	25 41	20 03
31	26 34	02 22	01 01	26 05	20 17
32	27 04	03 00	01 34	26 30	20 30
33	27 34	03 40	02 09	26 55	20 44
34	28 06	04 21	02 44	27 21	20 58
35	28 40	05 04	03 20	27 47	21 12
36	29 15	05 48	03 57	28 13	21 26
37	29 52	06 33	04 35	28 40	21 40
38	00♉32	07 20	05 14	29 07	21 54
39	01 13	08 09	05 54	29 35	22 09
40	01 57	09 00	06 35	00♌03	22 24
41	02 44	09 53	07 17	00 32	22 39
42	03 34	10 48	08 00	01 02	22 54
43	04 27	11 46	08 44	01 32	23 10
44	05 24	12 46	09 30	02 03	23 25
45	06 24	13 48	10 17	02 34	23 41
46	07 30	14 53	11 05	03 06	23 58
47	08 40	16 02	11 55	03 39	24 14
48	09 56	17 13	12 46	04 12	24 31
49	11 18	18 28	13 39	04 47	24 49
50	12 47	19 46	14 34	05 22	25 06
51	14 24	21 08	15 31	05 59	25 24
52	16 10	22 34	16 30	06 36	25 43
53	18 05	24 05	17 30	07 14	26 02
54	20 12	25 40	18 33	07 54	26 21
55	22 32	27 19	19 38	08 34	26 41
56	25 06	29 04	20 46	09 16	27 01
57	27 56	00♋55	21 56	09 59	27 22
58	01♊03	02 50	23 09	10 44	27 44
59	04 30	04 52	24 24	11 30	28 06
60	08♊17	06♋59	25♋43	12♌17	28♌29

23h 8m 0s — 347° 0' 0" — 15 ♓ 53

LAT.	11	12	ASC	2	3
0	18♈26	19♉27	18♊02	15♋40	14♌32
5	19 30	21 14	20 01	17 26	15 40
10	20 40	23 07	22 02	19 11	16 45
15	21 58	25 10	24 09	20 57	17 49
20	23 27	27 24	26 23	22 46	18 53
21	23 47	27 53	26 51	23 08	19 05
22	24 07	28 22	27 19	23 30	19 18
23	24 27	28 52	27 48	23 52	19 31
24	24 49	29 22	28 17	24 15	19 44
25	25 11	29 54	28 46	24 38	19 57
26	25 34	00♊26	29 17	25 01	20 10
27	25 58	00 59	29 47	25 24	20 23
28	26 22	01 34	00♋18	25 48	20 36
29	26 48	02 09	00 50	26 12	20 49
30	27 15	02 45	01 22	26 36	21 02
31	27 43	03 22	01 55	27 00	21 16
32	20 13	04 00	02 29	27 25	21 29
33	28 43	04 40	03 03	27 50	21 43
34	29 15	05 21	03 38	28 15	21 56
35	29 49	06 03	04 14	28 41	22 10
36	00♉25	06 47	04 51	29 07	22 24
37	01 02	07 32	05 29	29 34	22 39
38	01 41	08 19	06 07	00♌01	22 53
39	02 23	09 08	06 47	00 29	23 07
40	03 07	09 58	07 27	00 57	23 22
41	03 54	10 51	08 09	01 26	23 37
42	04 44	11 46	08 52	01 55	23 52
43	05 37	12 43	09 35	02 25	24 08
44	06 34	13 42	10 21	02 55	24 23
45	07 34	14 44	11 07	03 26	24 39
46	08 39	15 48	11 55	03 58	24 55
47	09 50	16 56	12 44	04 31	25 12
48	11 05	18 06	13 35	05 04	25 29
49	12 27	19 20	14 28	05 38	25 46
50	13 55	20 38	15 22	06 13	26 03
51	15 32	21 59	16 18	06 49	26 21
52	17 17	23 24	17 16	07 26	26 40
53	19 12	24 53	18 16	08 04	26 58
54	21 17	26 27	19 18	08 43	27 17
55	23 35	28 05	20 22	09 23	27 37
56	26 07	29 48	21 29	10 04	27 57
57	28 54	01♋37	22 38	10 47	28 18
58	01♊59	03 30	23 50	11 31	28 39
59	05 22	05 30	25 04	12 16	29 01
60	09♊05	07♋35	26♋21	13♌03	29♌24

23h 12m 0s — 348° 0' 0" — 16 ♓ 57

LAT.	11	12	ASC	2	3
0	19♈30	20♉26	18♊58	16♋36	15♌32
5	20 35	22 14	20 57	18 22	16 40
10	21 46	24 07	22 58	20 07	17 45
15	23 04	26 10	25 05	21 53	18 49
20	24 34	28 24	27 19	23 41	19 52
21	24 54	28 53	27 46	24 03	20 05
22	25 14	29 22	28 15	24 26	20 18
23	25 35	29 52	28 43	24 48	20 31
24	25 56	00♊23	29 12	25 11	20 43
25	26 18	00 54	29 42	25 33	20 56
26	26 42	01 27	00♋12	25 56	21 09
27	27 06	02 00	00 42	26 19	21 22
28	27 31	02 34	01 13	26 43	21 35
29	27 56	03 09	01 45	27 07	21 48
30	28 24	03 45	02 17	27 31	22 02
31	28 52	04 22	02 50	27 55	22 15
32	29 21	05 00	03 23	28 20	22 28
33	29 52	05 39	03 57	28 44	22 42
34	00♉24	06 20	04 32	29 10	22 55
35	00 58	07 02	05 08	29 35	23 09
36	01 34	07 46	05 44	00♌02	23 23
37	02 11	08 31	06 22	00 28	23 37
38	02 51	09 17	07 00	00 55	23 52
39	03 32	10 06	07 39	01 22	24 06
40	04 17	10 56	08 19	01 50	24 21
41	05 03	11 48	09 01	02 19	24 35
42	05 53	12 42	09 43	02 48	24 51
43	06 46	13 39	10 27	03 17	25 06
44	07 43	14 38	11 11	03 48	25 21
45	08 44	15 39	11 57	04 18	25 37
46	09 48	16 43	12 45	04 50	25 53
47	10 58	17 50	13 34	05 22	26 10
48	12 14	18 59	14 24	05 55	26 26
49	13 35	20 12	15 16	06 29	26 43
50	15 03	21 29	16 10	07 04	27 01
51	16 39	22 49	17 05	07 39	27 18
52	18 23	24 13	18 02	08 16	27 36
53	20 16	25 41	19 01	08 53	27 55
54	22 21	27 13	20 03	09 32	28 14
55	24 37	28 50	21 06	10 11	28 33
56	27 07	00♋31	22 12	10 52	28 53
57	29 52	02 18	23 20	11 34	29 14
58	02♊53	04 10	24 31	12 18	29 35
59	06 13	06 08	25 44	13 03	29 56
60	09♊52	08♋11	27♋00	13♌49	00♍19

23h 16m 0s — 349° 0' 0" — 18 ♓ 02

LAT.	11	12	ASC	2	3
0	20♈34	21♉26	19♊53	17♋32	16♌33
5	21 40	23 13	21 52	19 18	17 40
10	22 51	25 07	23 54	21 03	18 46
15	24 10	27 10	26 01	22 49	19 49
20	25 41	29 24	28 14	24 37	20 52
21	26 00	29 53	28 42	24 59	21 05
22	26 21	00♊22	29 10	25 21	21 18
23	26 42	00 52	29 38	25 44	21 30
24	27 03	01 23	00♋07	26 06	21 43
25	27 26	01 54	00 37	26 29	21 56
26	27 49	02 26	01 07	26 52	22 09
27	28 13	02 59	01 37	27 15	22 22
28	28 38	03 33	02 08	27 38	22 35
29	29 04	04 08	02 39	28 02	22 48
30	29 31	04 44	03 11	28 26	23 01
31	00♉00	05 21	03 44	28 50	23 14
32	00 29	05 59	04 17	29 14	23 28
33	01 00	06 38	04 51	29 39	23 41
34	01 33	07 19	05 26	00♌04	23 55
35	02 07	08 01	06 01	00 30	24 08
36	02 42	08 44	06 38	00 56	24 22
37	03 20	09 29	07 15	01 22	24 36
38	03 59	10 15	07 53	01 49	24 50
39	04 41	11 03	08 32	02 16	25 05
40	05 25	11 53	09 11	02 44	25 19
41	06 12	12 45	09 52	03 12	25 34
42	07 02	13 39	10 34	03 41	25 49
43	07 55	14 34	11 17	04 10	26 04
44	08 51	15 33	12 02	04 40	26 19
45	09 52	16 33	12 47	05 11	26 35
46	10 57	17 37	13 34	05 42	26 51
47	12 06	18 43	14 23	06 14	27 07
48	13 21	19 52	15 12	06 47	27 24
49	14 42	21 04	16 04	07 20	27 41
50	16 09	22 19	16 57	07 54	27 58
51	17 44	23 38	17 52	08 29	28 15
52	19 28	25 01	18 48	09 06	28 33
53	21 20	26 28	19 47	09 43	28 52
54	23 23	27 59	20 47	10 21	29 10
55	25 38	29 34	21 50	11 00	29 30
56	28 06	01♋14	22 55	11 40	29 49
57	00♊48	02 59	24 02	12 22	00♍09
58	03 47	04 49	25 11	13 05	00 30
59	07 03	06 45	26 24	13 49	00 52
60	10♊38	08♋46	27♋39	14♌35	01♍14

23h 20m 0s — 350° 0' 0" — 19 ♓ 07

LAT.	11	12	ASC	2	3
0	21♈38	22♉25	20♊49	18♋28	17♌33
5	22 44	24 12	22 48	20 14	18 41
10	23 56	26 07	24 50	22 00	19 46
15	25 16	28 10	26 56	23 45	20 49
20	26 47	00♊24	29 09	25 33	21 52
21	27 07	00 53	29 37	25 55	22 05
22	27 27	01 22	00♋05	26 17	22 18
23	27 48	01 52	00 33	26 39	22 30
24	28 10	02 22	01 02	27 02	22 43
25	28 33	02 54	01 32	27 24	22 56
26	28 56	03 26	02 01	27 47	23 09
27	29 20	03 59	02 31	28 10	23 21
28	29 46	04 33	03 02	28 33	23 34
29	00♉12	05 07	03 33	28 57	23 47
30	00 39	05 43	04 05	29 21	24 00
31	01 07	06 20	04 38	29 45	24 14
32	01 37	06 58	05 11	00♌09	24 27
33	02 08	07 37	05 45	00 34	24 40
34	02 40	08 17	06 19	00 59	24 54
35	03 14	08 59	06 54	01 24	25 07
36	03 50	09 42	07 30	01 50	25 21
37	04 28	10 26	08 07	02 16	25 35
38	05 07	11 12	08 45	02 43	25 49
39	05 49	12 00	09 24	03 10	26 03
40	06 33	12 49	10 03	03 37	26 18
41	07 20	13 41	10 44	04 05	26 32
42	08 10	14 34	11 25	04 34	26 47
43	09 03	15 30	12 08	05 03	27 02
44	09 59	16 27	12 52	05 32	27 17
45	11 00	17 27	13 37	06 03	27 33
46	12 04	18 30	14 24	06 34	27 49
47	13 13	19 35	15 11	07 05	28 05
48	14 28	20 44	16 01	07 38	28 21
49	15 48	21 55	16 51	08 11	28 38
50	17 15	23 09	17 44	08 45	28 55
51	18 49	24 27	18 38	09 20	29 12
52	20 32	25 49	19 34	09 55	29 30
53	22 23	27 14	20 32	10 32	29 48
54	24 25	28 44	21 31	11 10	00♍07
55	26 38	00♋18	22 33	11 48	00 26
56	29 03	01 57	23 37	12 28	00 45
57	01♊43	03 40	24 43	13 09	01 05
58	04 39	05 28	25 52	13 52	01 26
59	07 52	07 22	27 03	14 35	01 47
60	11♊23	09♋21	28♋17	15♌20	02♍09

23h 24m 0s — 351° 0' 0" — 20 ♓ 12

LAT.	11	12	ASC	2	3
0	22♈42	23♉23	21♊44	19♋24	18♌34
5	23 49	25 12	23 43	21 10	19 42
10	25 01	27 06	25 45	22 56	20 47
15	26 22	29 09	27 52	24 41	21 50
20	27 53	01♊24	00♋05	26 29	22 53
21	28 13	01 52	00 32	26 51	23 05
22	28 34	02 21	01 00	27 13	23 18
23	28 55	02 51	01 28	27 35	23 30
24	29 17	03 22	01 57	27 57	23 43
25	29 39	03 53	02 26	28 20	23 56
26	00♉03	04 25	02 56	28 42	24 08
27	00 27	04 58	03 26	29 05	24 21
28	00 52	05 31	03 56	29 28	24 34
29	01 19	06 06	04 28	29 52	24 47
30	01 46	06 42	04 59	00♌15	25 00
31	02 15	07 18	05 32	00 39	25 13
32	02 44	07 56	06 04	01 04	25 26
33	03 15	08 35	06 38	01 28	25 39
34	03 48	09 15	07 12	01 53	25 53
35	04 22	09 56	07 47	02 18	26 06
36	04 58	10 39	08 23	02 44	26 20
37	05 35	11 23	09 00	03 10	26 34
38	06 15	12 09	09 37	03 36	26 48
39	06 57	12 56	10 15	04 03	27 02
40	07 41	13 45	10 54	04 30	27 16
41	08 28	14 36	11 35	04 58	27 31
42	09 17	15 29	12 16	05 26	27 46
43	10 10	16 24	12 58	05 55	28 00
44	11 06	17 21	13 42	06 25	28 16
45	12 06	18 21	14 27	06 55	28 31
46	13 11	19 23	15 12	07 25	28 47
47	14 20	20 27	16 00	07 57	29 03
48	15 34	21 35	16 49	08 29	29 19
49	16 53	22 45	17 39	09 02	29 35
50	18 20	23 59	18 31	09 35	29 52
51	19 53	25 16	19 24	10 10	00♍09
52	21 34	26 36	20 19	10 45	00 27
53	23 25	28 00	21 16	11 21	00 45
54	25 25	29 29	22 15	11 59	01 03
55	27 36	01♋01	23 16	12 37	01 22
56	00♊00	02 38	24 19	13 16	01 41
57	02 38	04 20	25 25	13 57	02 01
58	05 30	06 07	26 32	14 39	02 21
59	08 40	07 58	27 42	15 22	02 42
60	12♊07	09♋56	28♋55	16♌06	03♍04

Koch Table of Houses for Latitudes 0° to 60° North

23h 28m 0s — 352° 0' 0" — 21 ♓ 17

LAT.	11	12	ASC	2	3
0	23♈46	24♉22	22♊39	20♋20	19♌35
5	24 53	26 11	24 39	22 07	20 42
10	26 06	28 05	26 41	23 52	21 47
15	27 27	00♊08	28 47	25 38	22 50
20	28 59	02 23	00♋59	27 25	23 53
21	29 19	02 51	01 27	27 46	24 05
22	29 40	03 20	01 55	28 08	24 18
23	00♉01	03 50	02 23	28 30	24 30
24	00 23	04 20	02 52	28 53	24 43
25	00 46	04 52	03 21	29 15	24 56
26	01 09	05 24	03 50	29 38	25 08
27	01 34	05 56	04 20	00♌00	25 21
28	01 59	06 30	04 50	00 24	25 34
29	02 25	07 04	05 21	00 47	25 47
30	02 53	07 40	05 53	01 10	25 59
31	03 21	08 16	06 25	01 34	26 12
32	03 51	08 54	06 58	01 58	26 26
33	04 22	09 33	07 31	02 23	26 39
34	04 55	10 12	08 05	02 47	26 52
35	05 29	10 53	08 40	03 12	27 06
36	06 05	11 36	09 15	03 38	27 19
37	06 42	12 20	09 52	04 04	27 33
38	07 22	13 05	10 29	04 30	27 47
39	08 04	13 52	11 07	04 56	28 01
40	08 48	14 41	11 46	05 24	28 15
41	09 34	15 31	12 26	05 51	28 29
42	10 24	16 24	13 06	06 19	28 44
43	11 17	17 18	13 48	06 48	28 59
44	12 13	18 15	14 31	07 17	29 14
45	13 12	19 14	15 16	07 47	29 29
46	14 16	20 15	16 01	08 17	29 45
47	15 25	21 19	16 48	08 48	00♍00
48	16 38	22 25	17 36	09 20	00 16
49	17 58	23 35	18 26	09 52	00 33
50	19 23	24 48	19 17	10 26	00 50
51	20 56	26 03	20 10	11 00	01 07
52	22 36	27 23	21 04	11 35	01 24
53	24 25	28 46	22 01	12 11	01 42
54	26 24	00♋13	22 59	12 47	02 00
55	28 34	01 44	23 59	13 25	02 19
56	00♊55	03 20	25 01	14 04	02 38
57	03 31	05 00	26 06	14 44	02 57
58	06 20	06 45	27 12	15 26	03 17
59	09 26	08 35	28 21	16 08	03 38
60	12♊50	10♋30	29♋33	16♌52	03♍59

23h 32m 0s — 353° 0' 0" — 22 ♓ 23

LAT.	11	12	ASC	2	3
0	24♈50	25♉21	23♊34	21♋17	20♌36
5	25 57	27 09	25 34	23 03	21 43
10	27 11	29 04	27 36	24 48	22 48
15	28 32	01♊07	29 42	26 34	23 51
20	00♉05	03 21	01♋54	28 21	24 53
21	00 25	03 50	02 22	28 42	25 06
22	00 45	04 19	02 49	29 04	25 18
23	01 07	04 49	03 17	29 26	25 31
24	01 29	05 19	03 46	29 48	25 43
25	01 52	05 50	04 15	00♌10	25 56
26	02 15	06 22	04 44	00 33	26 08
27	02 40	06 55	05 14	00 56	26 21
28	03 05	07 28	05 44	01 19	26 34
29	03 32	08 02	06 15	01 42	26 46
30	03 59	08 38	06 46	02 05	26 59
31	04 28	09 14	07 18	02 29	27 12
32	04 57	09 51	07 51	02 53	27 25
33	05 29	10 30	08 24	03 17	27 38
34	06 01	11 09	08 58	03 42	27 51
35	06 35	11 50	09 32	04 06	28 05
36	07 11	12 32	10 08	04 32	28 18
37	07 49	13 16	10 44	04 57	28 32
38	08 28	14 01	11 20	05 23	28 46
39	09 10	14 48	11 58	05 50	29 00
40	09 54	15 36	12 37	06 17	29 14
41	10 41	16 26	13 16	06 44	29 28
42	11 30	17 18	13 57	07 12	29 42
43	12 22	18 12	14 38	07 40	29 57
44	13 18	19 08	15 21	08 09	00♍12
45	14 18	20 06	16 05	08 39	00 27
46	15 21	21 06	16 50	09 09	00 43
47	16 29	22 10	17 36	09 40	00 58
48	17 43	23 15	18 24	10 11	01 14
49	19 01	24 24	19 13	10 43	01 30
50	20 26	25 36	20 03	11 16	01 47
51	21 58	26 51	20 56	11 50	02 04
52	23 37	28 09	21 49	12 24	02 21
53	25 25	29 31	22 45	13 00	02 39
54	27 22	00♋57	23 42	13 36	02 57
55	29 30	02 27	24 42	14 14	03 15
56	01♊50	04 01	25 43	14 52	03 34
57	04 22	05 39	26 47	15 32	03 53
58	07 10	07 22	27 52	16 12	04 13
59	10 12	09 11	29 01	16 54	04 33
60	13♊32	11♋04	00♌11	17♌38	04♍54

23h 36m 0s — 354° 0' 0" — 23 ♓ 28

LAT.	11	12	ASC	2	3
0	25♈53	26♉19	24♊30	22♋13	21♌37
5	27 01	28 08	26 29	24 00	22 45
10	28 15	00♊03	28 31	25 45	23 49
15	29 37	02 06	00♋37	27 30	24 52
20	01♉10	04 20	02 49	29 16	25 54
21	01 30	04 48	03 16	29 38	26 06
22	01 51	05 17	03 44	00♌00	26 18
23	02 12	05 47	04 12	00 22	26 31
24	02 34	06 17	04 40	00 44	26 43
25	02 57	06 48	05 09	01 06	26 56
26	03 21	07 20	05 38	01 28	27 08
27	03 45	07 52	06 08	01 51	27 21
28	04 11	08 26	06 38	02 14	27 33
29	04 37	09 00	07 09	02 37	27 46
30	05 05	09 35	07 40	03 00	27 59
31	05 33	10 11	08 12	03 24	28 12
32	06 03	10 48	08 44	03 47	28 25
33	06 34	11 26	09 17	04 11	28 38
34	07 07	12 06	09 50	04 36	28 51
35	07 41	12 46	10 25	05 01	29 04
36	08 17	13 28	11 00	05 26	29 17
37	08 54	14 11	11 35	05 51	29 31
38	09 34	14 56	12 12	06 17	29 45
39	10 16	15 42	12 49	06 43	29 58
40	11 00	16 30	13 27	07 10	00♍12
41	11 46	17 20	14 07	07 37	00 27
42	12 35	18 11	14 47	08 05	00 41
43	13 28	19 05	15 28	08 33	00 56
44	14 23	20 00	16 10	09 01	01 10
45	15 22	20 58	16 53	09 31	01 25
46	16 25	21 58	17 38	10 00	01 41
47	17 33	23 00	18 24	10 31	01 56
48	18 46	24 05	19 11	11 02	02 12
49	20 04	25 13	19 59	11 34	02 28
50	21 28	26 24	20 49	12 06	02 44
51	22 59	27 38	21 41	12 40	03 01
52	24 37	28 55	22 34	13 14	03 18
53	26 23	00♋16	23 29	13 49	03 35
54	28 19	01 40	24 26	14 25	03 53
55	00♊26	03 09	25 24	15 02	04 11
56	02 43	04 41	26 25	15 40	04 30
57	05 13	06 18	27 27	16 19	04 49
58	07 58	08 00	28 32	16 59	05 09
59	10 57	09 46	29 39	17 41	05 29
60	14♊13	11♋37	00♌49	18♌23	05♍50

23h 40m 0s — 355° 0' 0" — 24 ♓ 33

LAT.	11	12	ASC	2	3
0	26♈57	27♉17	25♊25	23♋10	22♌39
5	28 05	29 06	27 24	24 56	23 46
10	29 19	01♊01	29 26	26 41	24 50
15	00♉42	03 04	01♋32	28 26	25 53
20	02 15	05 18	03 43	00♌12	26 54
21	02 35	05 46	04 11	00 34	27 07
22	02 56	06 15	04 38	00 56	27 19
23	03 17	06 45	05 06	01 17	27 31
24	03 39	07 15	05 34	01 39	27 44
25	04 02	07 46	06 03	02 01	27 56
26	04 26	08 17	06 32	02 24	28 08
27	04 51	08 50	07 02	02 46	28 21
28	05 16	09 23	07 32	03 09	28 33
29	05 43	09 57	08 02	03 32	28 46
30	06 10	10 32	08 33	03 55	28 59
31	06 39	11 08	09 04	04 18	29 11
32	07 09	11 45	09 37	04 42	29 24
33	07 40	12 23	10 09	05 06	29 37
34	08 12	13 02	10 43	05 30	29 50
35	08 47	13 42	11 17	05 55	00♍03
36	09 22	14 24	11 51	06 20	00 17
37	10 00	15 07	12 27	06 45	00 30
38	10 39	15 51	13 03	07 10	00 44
39	11 21	16 37	13 40	07 36	00 57
40	12 05	17 24	14 18	08 03	01 11
41	12 51	18 13	14 57	08 30	01 25
42	13 40	19 04	15 36	08 57	01 40
43	14 32	19 57	16 17	09 25	01 54
44	15 27	20 52	16 59	09 53	02 09
45	16 26	21 49	17 42	10 22	02 24
46	17 29	22 48	18 26	10 52	02 39
47	18 36	23 50	19 11	11 22	02 54
48	19 48	24 54	19 58	11 53	03 10
49	21 05	26 01	20 46	12 25	03 26
50	22 29	27 11	21 35	12 57	03 42
51	23 59	28 24	22 26	13 30	03 58
52	25 36	29 40	23 19	14 04	04 15
53	27 21	01♋00	24 13	14 38	04 32
54	29 16	02 23	25 09	15 14	04 50
55	01♊20	03 50	26 07	15 50	05 08
56	03 36	05 21	27 06	16 28	05 26
57	06 04	06 57	28 08	17 06	05 45
58	08 45	08 37	29 12	17 46	06 05
59	11 41	10 21	00♌18	18 27	06 25
60	14♊54	12♋11	01♌27	19♌09	06♍45

23h 44m 0s — 356° 0' 0" — 25 ♓ 38

LAT.	11	12	ASC	2	3
0	28♈00	28♉15	26♊20	24♋06	23♌41
5	29 09	00♊04	28 19	25 53	24 47
10	00♉23	01 59	00♋21	27 38	25 51
15	01 46	04 02	02 27	29 22	26 54
20	03 19	06 16	04 38	01♌08	27 55
21	03 40	06 44	05 05	01 30	28 07
22	04 01	07 13	05 32	01 51	28 19
23	04 22	07 42	06 00	02 13	28 32
24	04 44	08 12	06 28	02 35	28 44
25	05 07	08 43	06 57	02 57	28 56
26	05 31	09 15	07 26	03 19	29 09
27	05 56	09 47	07 55	03 41	29 21
28	06 21	10 20	08 25	04 04	29 33
29	06 48	10 54	08 55	04 27	29 46
30	07 15	11 29	09 26	04 50	29 59
31	07 44	12 04	09 57	05 13	00♍11
32	08 14	12 41	10 29	05 36	00 24
33	08 45	13 19	11 02	06 00	00 37
34	09 17	13 57	11 35	06 24	00 50
35	09 51	14 38	12 08	06 49	01 03
36	10 27	15 19	12 43	07 13	01 16
37	11 05	16 01	13 18	07 38	01 29
38	11 44	16 45	13 54	08 04	01 43
39	12 25	17 31	14 31	08 30	01 56
40	13 09	18 18	15 08	08 56	02 10
41	13 55	19 06	15 47	09 23	02 24
42	14 44	19 57	16 26	09 50	02 38
43	15 36	20 49	17 06	10 17	02 53
44	16 31	21 43	17 48	10 46	03 07
45	17 29	22 40	18 30	11 14	03 22
46	18 32	23 38	19 14	11 44	03 37
47	19 38	24 39	19 59	12 13	03 52
48	20 50	25 43	20 45	12 44	04 07
49	22 06	26 49	21 32	13 15	04 23
50	23 29	27 58	22 21	13 47	04 39
51	24 58	29 10	23 11	14 20	04 56
52	26 34	00♋25	24 03	14 53	05 12
53	28 18	01 44	24 57	15 27	05 29
54	00♊11	03 06	25 52	16 03	05 47
55	02 13	04 31	26 49	16 39	06 05
56	04 27	06 01	27 48	17 16	06 23
57	06 53	07 35	28 49	17 54	06 41
58	09 32	09 13	29 52	18 33	07 01
59	12 25	10 56	00♌57	19 13	07 20
60	15♊34	12♋44	02♌04	19♌55	07♍40

23h 48m 0s — 357° 0' 0" — 26 ♓ 44

LAT.	11	12	ASC	2	3
0	29♈03	29♉13	27♊15	25♋03	24♌42
5	00♉12	01♊02	29 15	26 50	25 49
10	01 27	02 57	01♋16	28 34	26 53
15	02 50	05 00	03 21	00♌19	27 55
20	04 24	07 14	05 32	02 04	28 56
21	04 44	07 42	05 59	02 26	29 08
22	05 05	08 10	06 26	02 47	29 20
23	05 27	08 40	06 54	03 09	29 32
24	05 49	09 10	07 22	03 30	29 44
25	06 12	09 40	07 50	03 52	29 57
26	06 36	10 12	08 19	04 14	00♍09
27	07 00	10 44	08 48	04 37	00 21
28	07 26	11 17	09 18	04 59	00 34
29	07 52	11 50	09 48	05 22	00 46
30	08 20	12 25	10 19	05 44	00 59
31	08 48	13 00	10 50	06 08	01 11
32	09 18	13 37	11 22	06 31	01 24
33	09 49	14 14	11 54	06 55	01 37
34	10 22	14 53	12 27	07 18	01 49
35	10 56	15 32	13 00	07 43	02 02
36	11 31	16 13	13 34	08 07	02 15
37	12 09	16 56	14 09	08 32	02 29
38	12 48	17 39	14 45	08 57	02 42
39	13 29	18 24	15 21	09 23	02 55
40	14 13	19 11	15 58	09 49	03 09
41	14 59	19 59	16 36	10 15	03 23
42	15 47	20 49	17 15	10 42	03 37
43	16 39	21 41	17 55	11 10	03 51
44	17 33	22 35	18 36	11 38	04 05
45	18 32	23 30	19 18	12 06	04 20
46	19 34	24 28	20 02	12 35	04 35
47	20 40	25 28	20 46	13 05	04 50
48	21 51	26 31	21 32	13 35	05 05
49	23 06	27 36	22 18	14 06	05 21
50	24 28	28 44	23 07	14 37	05 37
51	25 56	29 55	23 56	15 10	05 53
52	27 31	01♋10	24 47	15 43	06 09
53	29 14	02 27	25 40	16 16	06 26
54	01♊05	03 48	26 35	16 51	06 43
55	03 06	05 12	27 31	17 27	07 01
56	05 18	06 41	28 29	18 03	07 19
57	07 41	08 13	29 29	18 41	07 38
58	10 17	09 50	00♌31	19 20	07 57
59	13 07	11 31	01 36	20 00	08 16
60	16♊13	13♋17	02♌42	20♌41	08♍36

23h 52m 0s — 358° 0' 0" — 27 ♓ 49

LAT.	11	12	ASC	2	3
0	00♉06	00♊11	28♊10	26♋00	25♌44
5	01 15	02 00	00♋10	27 47	26 51
10	02 31	03 55	02 11	29 31	27 54
15	03 54	05 58	04 16	01♌15	28 56
20	05 28	08 11	06 26	03 00	29 56
21	05 48	08 39	06 53	03 22	00♍09
22	06 09	09 07	07 20	03 43	00 21
23	06 31	09 37	07 48	04 04	00 33
24	06 53	10 07	08 16	04 26	00 45
25	07 16	10 37	08 44	04 48	00 57
26	07 40	11 08	09 13	05 10	01 09
27	08 04	11 40	09 42	05 32	01 22
28	08 30	12 13	10 11	05 54	01 34
29	08 56	12 46	10 41	06 17	01 46
30	09 24	13 21	11 11	06 39	01 59
31	09 53	13 56	11 42	07 02	02 11
32	10 22	14 32	12 14	07 25	02 24
33	10 53	15 09	12 46	07 49	02 36
34	11 26	15 48	13 18	08 13	02 49
35	12 00	16 27	13 52	08 37	03 02
36	12 35	17 08	14 25	09 01	03 15
37	13 12	17 50	15 00	09 26	03 28
38	13 52	18 33	15 35	09 51	03 41
39	14 33	19 17	16 11	10 16	03 55
40	15 16	20 04	16 48	10 42	04 08
41	16 02	20 51	17 26	11 08	04 22
42	16 50	21 41	18 05	11 35	04 36
43	17 41	22 32	18 44	12 02	04 50
44	18 36	23 25	19 25	12 30	05 04
45	19 33	24 20	20 06	12 58	05 18
46	20 35	25 17	20 49	13 27	05 33
47	21 40	26 17	21 33	13 56	05 48
48	22 51	27 19	22 18	14 26	06 03
49	24 06	28 23	23 04	14 56	06 19
50	25 27	29 31	23 52	15 27	06 34
51	26 54	00♋41	24 41	15 59	06 50
52	28 27	01 54	25 32	16 32	07 07
53	00♊09	03 10	26 24	17 06	07 23
54	01 59	04 29	27 17	17 40	07 40
55	03 58	05 53	28 13	18 15	07 58
56	06 07	07 20	29 10	18 51	08 16
57	08 28	08 51	00♌09	19 28	08 34
58	11 02	10 26	01 11	20 07	08 53
59	13 49	12 05	02 14	20 46	09 12
60	16♊51	13♋49	03♌20	21♌26	09♍31

23h 56m 0s — 359° 0' 0" — 28 ♓ 55

LAT.	11	12	ASC	2	3
0	01♉08	01♊08	29♊05	26♋57	26♌47
5	02 18	02 58	01♋05	28 44	27 53
10	03 34	04 53	03 06	00♌28	28 56
15	04 57	06 55	05 11	02 12	29 57
20	06 31	09 08	07 20	03 56	00♍57
21	06 52	09 36	07 47	04 17	01 09
22	07 13	10 04	08 14	04 39	01 21
23	07 34	10 33	08 42	05 00	01 33
24	07 57	11 03	09 09	05 22	01 46
25	08 20	11 33	09 37	05 43	01 58
26	08 44	12 04	10 06	06 05	02 10
27	09 08	12 36	10 35	06 27	02 22
28	09 34	13 09	11 04	06 49	02 34
29	10 00	13 42	11 34	07 12	02 46
30	10 28	14 16	12 04	07 34	02 59
31	10 56	14 51	12 35	07 57	03 11
32	11 26	15 27	13 06	08 20	03 24
33	11 57	16 04	13 38	08 43	03 36
34	12 29	16 42	14 10	09 07	03 49
35	13 03	17 21	14 43	09 31	04 01
36	13 39	18 02	15 17	09 55	04 14
37	14 16	18 43	15 51	10 19	04 27
38	14 55	19 26	16 26	10 44	04 40
39	15 36	20 10	17 02	11 09	04 54
40	16 19	20 56	17 38	11 35	05 07
41	17 04	21 43	18 16	12 01	05 21
42	17 52	22 32	18 54	12 27	05 34
43	18 43	23 23	19 33	12 54	05 48
44	19 37	24 15	20 13	13 22	06 02
45	20 34	25 10	20 54	13 50	06 17
46	21 35	26 06	21 36	14 18	06 31
47	22 40	27 05	22 20	14 47	06 46
48	23 50	28 06	23 04	15 17	07 01
49	25 04	29 10	23 50	15 47	07 16
50	26 24	00♋16	24 37	16 18	07 32
51	27 50	01 25	25 26	16 49	07 48
52	29 23	02 37	26 16	17 22	08 04
53	01♊03	03 52	27 07	17 55	08 20
54	02 51	05 11	28 00	18 29	08 37
55	04 49	06 33	28 55	19 03	08 54
56	06 56	07 58	29 51	19 39	09 12
57	09 15	09 28	00♌50	20 16	09 30
58	11 46	11 01	01 50	20 53	09 49
59	14 30	12 39	02 52	21 32	10 08
60	17♊29	14♋22	03♌57	22♌12	10♍27

Table I Time Zones of the World

STANDARD TIME NAME	MERIDIAN	h m
GREENWICH (UNIVERSAL TIME)	0	0
AZORES	15°W	1
	30	2
EAST BRAZIL	45	3
NEWFOUNDLAND	52°W 30′	3:30
ATLANTIC	60	4
EASTERN	75	5
CENTRAL	90	6
MOUNTAIN	105	7
PACIFIC	120	8
YUKON, ALASKA	135	9
HAWAII	150	10
SAMOA	165	11
INT'L DATE LINE	180°W	12

STANDARD TIME NAME	MERIDIAN	h m
CENTRAL EUROPEAN	15°E	1
EGYPT, FINLAND	30	2
BAGHDAD, USSR ZONE 1	45	3
USSR ZONE 2	60	4
PAKISTAN, USSR ZONE 3	75	5
INDIA	82°E 30′	5:30
BANGLADESH, USSR ZONE 4	90	6
BURMA	97°E 30′	6:30
JAVA, INDOCHINA	105	7
CHINA, W. AUSTRALIA	120	8
JAPAN	135	9
S. AUSTRALIA	142°E 30′	9:30
GUAM, E. AUSTRALIA	150	10
SOLOMONS	165	11
NEW ZEALAND	180°E	12

Table II Solar-Sidereal Time Correction

	0h	1h	2h	3h	4h	5h	6h	7h	8h	9h	10h	11h	12h	13h	14h	15h	16h	17h	18h	19h	20h	21h	22h	23h	
MIN	m s	m s	m s	m s	m s	m s	m s	m s	m s	m s	m s	m s	m s	m s	m s	m s	m s	m s	m s	m s	m s	m s	m s	m s	MIN
0	0 0	0 10	0 20	0 30	0 39	0 49	0 59	1 9	1 19	1 29	1 39	1 48	1 58	2 8	2 18	2 28	2 38	2 48	2 57	3 7	3 17	3 27	3 37	3 47	0
1	0 0	0 10	0 20	0 30	0 40	0 49	0 59	1 9	1 19	1 29	1 39	1 49	1 58	2 8	2 18	2 28	2 38	2 48	2 58	3 7	3 17	3 27	3 37	3 47	1
2	0 0	0 10	0 20	0 30	0 40	0 50	0 59	1 9	1 19	1 29	1 39	1 49	1 59	2 8	2 18	2 28	2 38	2 48	2 58	3 8	3 17	3 27	3 37	3 47	2
3	0 0	0 10	0 20	0 30	0 40	0 50	0 60	1 9	1 19	1 29	1 39	1 49	1 59	2 9	2 18	2 28	2 38	2 48	2 58	3 8	3 18	3 27	3 37	3 47	3
4	0 1	0 11	0 20	0 30	0 40	0 50	0 60	1 10	1 20	1 29	1 39	1 49	1 59	2 9	2 19	2 29	2 38	2 48	2 58	3 8	3 18	3 28	3 37	3 47	4
5	0 1	0 11	0 21	0 30	0 40	0 50	0 60	1 10	1 20	1 30	1 39	1 49	1 59	2 9	2 19	2 29	2 39	2 48	2 58	3 8	3 18	3 28	3 38	3 48	5
6	0 1	0 11	0 21	0 31	0 40	0 50	1 0	1 10	1 20	1 30	1 40	1 49	1 59	2 9	2 19	2 29	2 39	2 49	2 58	3 8	3 18	3 28	3 38	3 48	6
7	0 1	0 11	0 21	0 31	0 41	0 50	1 0	1 10	1 20	1 30	1 40	1 50	1 59	2 9	2 19	2 29	2 39	2 49	2 59	3 8	3 18	3 28	3 38	3 48	7
8	0 1	0 11	0 21	0 31	0 41	0 51	1 0	1 10	1 20	1 30	1 40	1 50	1 60	2 9	2 19	2 29	2 39	2 49	2 59	3 9	3 18	3 28	3 38	3 48	8
9	0 1	0 11	0 21	0 31	0 41	0 51	1 1	1 10	1 20	1 30	1 40	1 50	1 60	2 10	2 19	2 29	2 39	2 49	2 59	3 9	3 19	3 28	3 38	3 48	9
10	0 2	0 11	0 21	0 31	0 41	0 51	1 1	1 11	1 20	1 30	1 40	1 50	1 60	2 10	2 20	2 29	2 39	2 49	2 59	3 9	3 19	3 29	3 38	3 48	10
11	0 2	0 12	0 22	0 31	0 41	0 51	1 1	1 11	1 21	1 31	1 40	1 50	2 0	2 10	2 20	2 30	2 40	2 49	2 59	3 9	3 19	3 29	3 39	3 49	11
12	0 2	0 12	0 22	0 32	0 41	0 51	1 1	1 11	1 21	1 31	1 41	1 50	2 0	2 10	2 20	2 30	2 40	2 50	2 59	3 9	3 19	3 29	3 39	3 49	12
13	0 2	0 12	0 22	0 32	0 42	0 51	1 1	1 11	1 21	1 31	1 41	1 51	2 0	2 10	2 20	2 30	2 40	2 50	2 60	3 9	3 19	3 29	3 39	3 49	13
14	0 2	0 12	0 22	0 32	0 42	0 52	1 1	1 11	1 21	1 31	1 41	1 51	2 1	2 10	2 20	2 30	2 40	2 50	2 60	3 10	3 19	3 29	3 39	3 49	14
15	0 2	0 12	0 22	0 32	0 42	0 52	1 2	1 11	1 21	1 31	1 41	1 51	2 1	2 11	2 20	2 30	2 40	2 50	2 60	3 10	3 20	3 29	3 39	3 49	15
16	0 3	0 12	0 22	0 32	0 42	0 52	1 2	1 12	1 21	1 31	1 41	1 51	2 1	2 11	2 21	2 30	2 40	2 50	3 0	3 10	3 20	3 30	3 39	3 49	16
17	0 3	0 13	0 23	0 32	0 42	0 52	1 2	1 12	1 22	1 32	1 41	1 51	2 1	2 11	2 21	2 31	2 40	2 50	3 0	3 10	3 20	3 30	3 40	3 49	17
18	0 3	0 13	0 23	0 33	0 42	0 52	1 2	1 12	1 22	1 32	1 42	1 51	2 1	2 11	2 21	2 31	2 41	2 51	3 0	3 10	3 20	3 30	3 40	3 50	18
19	0 3	0 13	0 23	0 33	0 43	0 52	1 2	1 12	1 22	1 32	1 42	1 52	2 1	2 11	2 21	2 31	2 41	2 51	3 1	3 10	3 20	3 30	3 40	3 50	19
20	0 3	0 13	0 23	0 33	0 43	0 53	1 2	1 12	1 22	1 32	1 42	1 52	2 2	2 11	2 21	2 31	2 41	2 51	3 1	3 11	3 20	3 30	3 40	3 50	20
21	0 3	0 13	0 23	0 33	0 43	0 53	1 3	1 12	1 22	1 32	1 42	1 52	2 2	2 12	2 21	2 31	2 41	2 51	3 1	3 11	3 21	3 30	3 40	3 50	21
22	0 4	0 13	0 23	0 33	0 43	0 53	1 3	1 13	1 22	1 32	1 42	1 52	2 2	2 12	2 22	2 31	2 41	2 51	3 1	3 11	3 21	3 31	3 40	3 50	22
23	0 4	0 14	0 23	0 33	0 43	0 53	1 3	1 13	1 23	1 32	1 42	1 52	2 2	2 12	2 22	2 32	2 41	2 51	3 1	3 11	3 21	3 31	3 41	3 50	23
24	0 4	0 14	0 24	0 34	0 43	0 53	1 3	1 13	1 23	1 33	1 43	1 52	2 2	2 12	2 22	2 32	2 42	2 52	3 1	3 11	3 21	3 31	3 41	3 51	24
25	0 4	0 14	0 24	0 34	0 44	0 53	1 3	1 13	1 23	1 33	1 43	1 53	2 2	2 12	2 22	2 32	2 42	2 52	3 2	3 11	3 21	3 31	3 41	3 51	25
26	0 4	0 14	0 24	0 34	0 44	0 54	1 3	1 13	1 23	1 33	1 43	1 53	2 3	2 12	2 22	2 32	2 42	2 52	3 2	3 12	3 21	3 31	3 41	3 51	26
27	0 4	0 14	0 24	0 34	0 44	0 54	1 4	1 13	1 23	1 33	1 43	1 53	2 3	2 13	2 22	2 32	2 42	2 52	3 2	3 12	3 22	3 31	3 41	3 51	27
28	0 5	0 14	0 24	0 34	0 44	0 54	1 4	1 14	1 23	1 33	1 43	1 53	2 3	2 13	2 23	2 32	2 42	2 52	3 2	3 12	3 22	3 32	3 41	3 51	28
29	0 5	0 15	0 24	0 34	0 44	0 54	1 4	1 14	1 24	1 33	1 43	1 53	2 3	2 13	2 23	2 33	2 42	2 52	3 2	3 12	3 22	3 32	3 42	3 51	29
30	0 5	0 15	0 25	0 34	0 44	0 54	1 4	1 14	1 24	1 34	1 43	1 53	2 3	2 13	2 23	2 33	2 43	2 52	3 2	3 12	3 22	3 32	3 42	3 52	30
31	0 5	0 15	0 25	0 35	0 45	0 54	1 4	1 14	1 24	1 34	1 44	1 54	2 3	2 13	2 23	2 33	2 43	2 53	3 3	3 12	3 22	3 32	3 42	3 52	31
32	0 5	0 15	0 25	0 35	0 45	0 55	1 4	1 14	1 24	1 34	1 44	1 54	2 4	2 13	2 23	2 33	2 43	2 53	3 3	3 13	3 22	3 32	3 42	3 52	32
33	0 5	0 15	0 25	0 35	0 45	0 55	1 5	1 14	1 24	1 34	1 44	1 54	2 4	2 14	2 23	2 33	2 43	2 53	3 3	3 13	3 23	3 32	3 42	3 52	33
34	0 6	0 15	0 25	0 35	0 45	0 55	1 5	1 15	1 24	1 34	1 44	1 54	2 4	2 14	2 24	2 33	2 43	2 53	3 3	3 13	3 23	3 33	3 42	3 52	34
35	0 6	0 16	0 25	0 35	0 45	0 55	1 5	1 15	1 25	1 34	1 44	1 54	2 4	2 14	2 24	2 34	2 43	2 53	3 3	3 13	3 23	3 33	3 43	3 52	35
36	0 6	0 16	0 26	0 35	0 45	0 55	1 5	1 15	1 25	1 35	1 44	1 54	2 4	2 14	2 24	2 34	2 44	2 53	3 3	3 13	3 23	3 33	3 43	3 53	36
37	0 6	0 16	0 26	0 36	0 46	0 55	1 5	1 15	1 25	1 35	1 45	1 54	2 4	2 14	2 24	2 34	2 44	2 54	3 3	3 13	3 23	3 33	3 43	3 53	37
38	0 6	0 16	0 26	0 36	0 46	0 56	1 5	1 15	1 25	1 35	1 45	1 55	2 5	2 14	2 24	2 34	2 44	2 54	3 4	3 14	3 23	3 33	3 43	3 53	38
39	0 6	0 16	0 26	0 36	0 46	0 56	1 6	1 15	1 25	1 35	1 45	1 55	2 5	2 15	2 24	2 34	2 44	2 54	3 4	3 14	3 24	3 33	3 43	3 53	39
40	0 7	0 16	0 26	0 36	0 46	0 56	1 6	1 16	1 25	1 35	1 45	1 55	2 5	2 15	2 25	2 34	2 44	2 54	3 4	3 14	3 24	3 34	3 43	3 53	40
41	0 7	0 17	0 26	0 36	0 46	0 56	1 6	1 16	1 26	1 35	1 45	1 55	2 5	2 15	2 25	2 35	2 44	2 54	3 4	3 14	3 24	3 34	3 44	3 53	41
42	0 7	0 17	0 27	0 36	0 46	0 56	1 6	1 16	1 26	1 36	1 45	1 55	2 5	2 15	2 25	2 35	2 45	2 54	3 4	3 14	3 24	3 34	3 44	3 54	42
43	0 7	0 17	0 27	0 37	0 46	0 56	1 6	1 16	1 26	1 36	1 46	1 55	2 5	2 15	2 25	2 35	2 45	2 55	3 4	3 14	3 24	3 34	3 44	3 54	43
44	0 7	0 17	0 27	0 37	0 47	0 57	1 6	1 16	1 26	1 36	1 46	1 56	2 6	2 15	2 25	2 35	2 45	2 55	3 5	3 15	3 24	3 34	3 44	3 54	44
45	0 7	0 17	0 27	0 37	0 47	0 57	1 7	1 16	1 26	1 36	1 46	1 56	2 6	2 16	2 25	2 35	2 45	2 55	3 5	3 15	3 25	3 34	3 44	3 54	45
46	0 8	0 17	0 27	0 37	0 47	0 57	1 7	1 17	1 26	1 36	1 46	1 56	2 6	2 16	2 26	2 35	2 45	2 55	3 5	3 15	3 25	3 35	3 44	3 54	46
47	0 8	0 18	0 27	0 37	0 47	0 57	1 7	1 17	1 27	1 36	1 46	1 56	2 6	2 16	2 26	2 36	2 45	2 55	3 5	3 15	3 25	3 35	3 45	3 54	47
48	0 8	0 18	0 28	0 37	0 47	0 57	1 7	1 17	1 27	1 37	1 46	1 56	2 6	2 16	2 26	2 36	2 46	2 55	3 5	3 15	3 25	3 35	3 45	3 55	48
49	0 8	0 18	0 28	0 38	0 47	0 57	1 7	1 17	1 27	1 37	1 47	1 56	2 6	2 16	2 26	2 36	2 46	2 56	3 5	3 15	3 25	3 35	3 45	3 55	49
50	0 8	0 18	0 28	0 38	0 48	0 57	1 7	1 17	1 27	1 37	1 47	1 57	2 6	2 16	2 26	2 36	2 46	2 56	3 6	3 15	3 25	3 35	3 45	3 55	50
51	0 8	0 18	0 28	0 38	0 48	0 58	1 8	1 17	1 27	1 37	1 47	1 57	2 7	2 17	2 26	2 36	2 46	2 56	3 6	3 16	3 26	3 35	3 45	3 55	51
52	0 9	0 18	0 28	0 38	0 48	0 58	1 8	1 18	1 27	1 37	1 47	1 57	2 7	2 17	2 27	2 36	2 46	2 56	3 6	3 16	3 26	3 36	3 45	3 55	52
53	0 9	0 19	0 28	0 38	0 48	0 58	1 8	1 18	1 28	1 37	1 47	1 57	2 7	2 17	2 27	2 37	2 46	2 56	3 6	3 16	3 26	3 36	3 46	3 55	53
54	0 9	0 19	0 29	0 38	0 48	0 58	1 8	1 18	1 28	1 38	1 47	1 57	2 7	2 17	2 27	2 37	2 47	2 56	3 6	3 16	3 26	3 36	3 46	3 56	54
55	0 9	0 19	0 29	0 39	0 48	0 58	1 8	1 18	1 28	1 38	1 48	1 57	2 7	2 17	2 27	2 37	2 47	2 57	3 6	3 16	3 26	3 36	3 46	3 56	55
56	0 9	0 19	0 29	0 39	0 49	0 58	1 8	1 18	1 28	1 38	1 48	1 58	2 7	2 17	2 27	2 37	2 47	2 57	3 7	3 16	3 26	3 36	3 46	3 56	56
57	0 9	0 19	0 29	0 39	0 49	0 59	1 9	1 18	1 28	1 38	1 48	1 58	2 8	2 17	2 27	2 37	2 47	2 57	3 7	3 17	3 26	3 36	3 46	3 56	57
58	0 10	0 19	0 29	0 39	0 49	0 59	1 9	1 19	1 28	1 38	1 48	1 58	2 8	2 18	2 28	2 37	2 47	2 57	3 7	3 17	3 27	3 37	3 46	3 56	58
59	0 10	0 20	0 29	0 39	0 49	0 59	1 9	1 19	1 29	1 38	1 48	1 58	2 8	2 18	2 28	2 38	2 47	2 57	3 7	3 17	3 27	3 37	3 47	3 56	59
60	0 10	0 20	0 30	0 39	0 49	0 59	1 9	1 19	1 29	1 39	1 48	1 58	2 8	2 18	2 28	2 38	2 48	2 57	3 7	3 17	3 27	3 37	3 47	3 57	60

Table III
Time Correction for Longitude

DEGREES									MINUTES		
°	h	m	°	h	m	°	h	m	′	m	s
1	0	4	61	4	4	121	8	4	1	0	4
2	0	8	62	4	8	122	8	8	2	0	8
3	0	12	63	4	12	123	8	12	3	0	12
4	0	16	64	4	16	124	8	16	4	0	16
5	0	20	65	4	20	125	8	20	5	0	20
6	0	24	66	4	24	126	8	24	6	0	24
7	0	28	67	4	28	127	8	28	7	0	28
8	0	32	68	4	32	128	8	32	8	0	32
9	0	36	69	4	36	129	8	36	9	0	36
10	0	40	70	4	40	130	8	40	10	0	40
11	0	44	71	4	44	131	8	44	11	0	44
12	0	48	72	4	48	132	8	48	12	0	48
13	0	52	73	4	52	133	8	52	13	0	52
14	0	56	74	4	56	134	8	56	14	0	56
15	1	0	75	5	0	135	9	0	15	1	0
16	1	4	76	5	4	136	9	4	16	1	4
17	1	8	77	5	8	137	9	8	17	1	8
18	1	12	78	5	12	138	9	12	18	1	12
19	1	16	79	5	16	139	9	16	19	1	16
20	1	20	80	5	20	140	9	20	20	1	20
21	1	24	81	5	24	141	9	24	21	1	24
22	1	28	82	5	28	142	9	28	22	1	28
23	1	32	83	5	32	143	9	32	23	1	32
24	1	36	84	5	36	144	9	36	24	1	36
25	1	40	85	5	40	145	9	40	25	1	40
26	1	44	86	5	44	146	9	44	26	1	44
27	1	48	87	5	48	147	9	48	27	1	48
28	1	52	88	5	52	148	9	52	28	1	52
29	1	56	89	5	56	149	9	56	29	1	56
30	2	0	90	6	0	150	10	0	30	2	0
31	2	4	91	6	4	151	10	4	31	2	4
32	2	8	92	6	8	152	10	8	32	2	8
33	2	12	93	6	12	153	10	12	33	2	12
34	2	16	94	6	16	154	10	16	34	2	16
35	2	20	95	6	20	155	10	20	35	2	20
36	2	24	96	6	24	156	10	24	36	2	24
37	2	28	97	6	28	157	10	28	37	2	28
38	2	32	98	6	32	158	10	32	38	2	32
39	2	36	99	6	36	159	10	36	39	2	36
40	2	40	100	6	40	160	10	40	40	2	40
41	2	44	101	6	44	161	10	44	41	2	44
42	2	48	102	6	48	162	10	48	42	2	48
43	2	52	103	6	52	163	10	52	43	2	52
44	2	56	104	6	56	164	10	56	44	2	56
45	3	0	105	7	0	165	11	0	45	3	0
46	3	4	106	7	4	166	11	4	46	3	4
47	3	8	107	7	8	167	11	8	47	3	8
48	3	12	108	7	12	168	11	12	48	3	12
49	3	16	109	7	16	169	11	16	49	3	16
50	3	20	110	7	20	170	11	20	50	3	20
51	3	24	111	7	24	171	11	24	51	3	24
52	3	28	112	7	28	172	11	28	52	3	28
53	3	32	113	7	32	173	11	32	53	3	32
54	3	36	114	7	36	174	11	36	54	3	36
55	3	40	115	7	40	175	11	40	55	3	40
56	3	44	116	7	44	176	11	44	56	3	44
57	3	48	117	7	48	177	11	48	57	3	48
58	3	52	118	7	52	178	11	52	58	3	52
59	3	56	119	7	56	179	11	56	59	3	56
60	4	0	120	8	0	180	12	0	60	4	0

Table IV
Universal to Ephemeris Time Correction (△T)

ADD TO UNIVERSAL TIME
ENTRIES FOR JULY 1st

YEAR	SECONDS	YEAR	SECONDS
1860	3	1922	22
1861	3	1923	22
1862	3	1924	22
1863	3	1925	23
1864	2	1926	23
1865	2	1927	23
1866	1	1928	23
1867	1	1929	23
1868	0	1930	23
1869	−1	1931	23
1870	−2	1932	24
1871	−3	1933	24
1872	−5	1934	24
1873	−6	1935	24
1874	−7	1936	24
1875	−7	1937	24
1876	−8	1938	24
1877	−8	1939	24
1878	−8	1940	24
1879	−8	1941	25
1880	−8	1942	25
1881	−8	1943	25
1882	−8	1944	26
1883	−8	1945	27
1884	−8	1946	27
1885	−8	1947	28
1886	−8	1948	28
1887	−8	1949	29
1888	−8	1950	29
1889	−8	1951	30
1890	−8	1952	30
1891	−8	1953	31
1892	−8	1954	31
1893	−8	1955	31
1894	−8	1956	32
1895	−8	1957	32
1896	−7	1958	32
1897	−7	1959	33
1898	−6	1960	33
1899	−5	1961	34
1900	−4	1962	34
1901	−3	1963	35
1902	−1	1964	35
1903	0	1965	36
1904	2	1966	37
1905	3	1967	38
1906	5	1968	39
1907	6	1969	40
1908	8	1970	41
1909	9	1971	42
1910	10	1972	43
1911	12	1973	44
1912	13	1974	45
1913	14	1975	46
1914	15	1976	47
1915	16	1977	48
1916	17	1978	49
1917	18	1979	50
1918	19	1980	51
1919	20	1981	52
1920	21	1982	53
1921	21	1983	53

Table V Diurnal Motion of the Sun

TIME	24 HOUR TRAVEL																				TIME
	57′ 12″	57′ 14″	57′ 16″	57′ 18″	57′ 20″	57′ 22″	57′ 24″	57′ 26″	57′ 28″	57′ 30″	57′ 32″	57′ 34″	57′ 36″	57′ 38″	57′ 40″	57′ 42″	57′ 44″	57′ 46″	57′ 48″	57′ 50″	
MINUTES	′ ″	′ ″	′ ″	′ ″	′ ″	′ ″	′ ″	′ ″	′ ″	′ ″	′ ″	′ ″	′ ″	′ ″	′ ″	′ ″	′ ″	′ ″	′ ″	′ ″	MINUTES
1	2	2	2	2	2	2	2	2	2	2	2	2	2	2	2	2	2	2	2	2	1
2	5	5	5	5	5	5	5	5	5	5	5	5	5	5	5	5	5	5	5	5	2
3	7	7	7	7	7	7	7	7	7	7	7	7	7	7	7	7	7	7	7	7	3
4	10	10	10	10	10	10	10	10	10	10	10	10	10	10	10	10	10	10	10	10	4
5	12	12	12	12	12	12	12	12	12	12	12	12	12	12	12	12	12	12	12	12	5
6	14	14	14	14	14	14	14	14	14	14	14	14	14	14	14	14	14	14	14	14	6
7	17	17	17	17	17	17	17	17	17	17	17	17	17	17	17	17	17	17	17	17	7
8	19	19	19	19	19	19	19	19	19	19	19	19	19	19	19	19	19	19	19	19	8
9	21	21	21	21	22	22	22	22	22	22	22	22	22	22	22	22	22	22	22	22	9
10	24	24	24	24	24	24	24	24	24	24	24	24	24	24	24	24	24	24	24	24	10
11	26	26	26	26	26	26	26	26	26	26	26	26	26	26	26	26	26	26	26	27	11
12	29	29	29	29	29	29	29	29	29	29	29	29	29	29	29	29	29	29	29	29	12
13	31	31	31	31	31	31	31	31	31	31	31	31	31	31	31	31	31	31	31	31	13
14	33	33	33	33	33	33	33	34	34	34	34	34	34	34	34	34	34	34	34	34	14
15	36	36	36	36	36	36	36	36	36	36	36	36	36	36	36	36	36	36	36	36	15
16	38	38	38	38	38	38	38	38	38	38	38	38	38	38	38	38	38	39	39	39	16
17	41	41	41	41	41	41	41	41	41	41	41	41	41	41	41	41	41	41	41	41	17
18	43	43	43	43	43	43	43	43	43	43	43	43	43	43	43	43	43	43	43	43	18
19	45	45	45	45	45	45	45	45	45	46	46	46	46	46	46	46	46	46	46	46	19
20	48	48	48	48	48	48	48	48	48	48	48	48	48	48	48	48	48	48	48	48	20
21	50	50	50	50	50	50	50	50	50	50	50	50	50	50	50	50	51	51	51	51	21
22	52	52	52	53	53	53	53	53	53	53	53	53	53	53	53	53	53	53	53	53	22
23	55	55	55	55	55	55	55	55	55	55	55	55	55	55	55	55	55	55	55	55	23
24	57	57	57	57	57	57	57	57	57	58	58	58	58	58	58	58	58	58	58	58	24
25	1 0	1 0	1 0	1 0	1 0	1 0	1 0	1 0	1 0	1 0	1 0	1 0	1 0	1 0	1 0	1 0	1 0	1 0	1 0	1 0	25
26	1 2	1 2	1 2	1 2	1 2	1 2	1 2	1 2	1 2	1 2	1 2	1 2	1 2	1 2	1 2	1 3	1 3	1 3	1 3	1 3	26
27	1 4	1 4	1 4	1 4	1 5	1 5	1 5	1 5	1 5	1 5	1 5	1 5	1 5	1 5	1 5	1 5	1 5	1 5	1 5	1 5	27
28	1 7	1 7	1 7	1 7	1 7	1 7	1 7	1 7	1 7	1 7	1 7	1 7	1 7	1 7	1 7	1 7	1 7	1 7	1 7	1 7	28
29	1 9	1 9	1 9	1 9	1 9	1 9	1 9	1 9	1 9	1 9	1 10	1 10	1 10	1 10	1 10	1 10	1 10	1 10	1 10	1 10	29
30	1 12	1 12	1 12	1 12	1 12	1 12	1 12	1 12	1 12	1 12	1 12	1 12	1 12	1 12	1 12	1 12	1 12	1 12	1 12	1 12	30
31	1 14	1 14	1 14	1 14	1 14	1 14	1 14	1 14	1 14	1 14	1 14	1 14	1 14	1 14	1 14	1 15	1 15	1 15	1 15	1 15	31
32	1 16	1 16	1 16	1 16	1 16	1 16	1 17	1 17	1 17	1 17	1 17	1 17	1 17	1 17	1 17	1 17	1 17	1 17	1 17	1 17	32
33	1 19	1 19	1 19	1 19	1 19	1 19	1 19	1 19	1 19	1 19	1 19	1 19	1 19	1 19	1 19	1 19	1 19	1 19	1 19	1 20	33
34	1 21	1 21	1 21	1 21	1 21	1 21	1 21	1 21	1 21	1 21	1 22	1 22	1 22	1 22	1 22	1 22	1 22	1 22	1 22	1 22	34
35	1 23	1 23	1 24	1 24	1 24	1 24	1 24	1 24	1 24	1 24	1 24	1 24	1 24	1 24	1 24	1 24	1 24	1 24	1 24	1 24	35
36	1 26	1 26	1 26	1 26	1 26	1 26	1 26	1 26	1 26	1 26	1 26	1 26	1 26	1 26	1 27	1 27	1 27	1 27	1 27	1 27	36
37	1 28	1 28	1 28	1 28	1 28	1 28	1 28	1 29	1 29	1 29	1 29	1 29	1 29	1 29	1 29	1 29	1 29	1 29	1 29	1 29	37
38	1 31	1 31	1 31	1 31	1 31	1 31	1 31	1 31	1 31	1 31	1 31	1 31	1 31	1 31	1 31	1 31	1 31	1 31	1 32	1 32	38
39	1 33	1 33	1 33	1 33	1 33	1 33	1 33	1 33	1 33	1 33	1 33	1 34	1 34	1 34	1 34	1 34	1 34	1 34	1 34	1 34	39
40	1 35	1 35	1 35	1 36	1 36	1 36	1 36	1 36	1 36	1 36	1 36	1 36	1 36	1 36	1 36	1 36	1 36	1 36	1 36	1 36	40
41	1 38	1 38	1 38	1 38	1 38	1 38	1 38	1 38	1 38	1 38	1 38	1 38	1 38	1 38	1 39	1 39	1 39	1 39	1 39	1 39	41
42	1 40	1 40	1 40	1 40	1 40	1 40	1 40	1 41	1 41	1 41	1 41	1 41	1 41	1 41	1 41	1 41	1 41	1 41	1 41	1 41	42
43	1 42	1 43	1 43	1 43	1 43	1 43	1 43	1 43	1 43	1 43	1 43	1 43	1 43	1 43	1 43	1 43	1 43	1 43	1 44	1 44	43
44	1 45	1 45	1 45	1 45	1 45	1 45	1 45	1 45	1 45	1 45	1 45	1 46	1 46	1 46	1 46	1 46	1 46	1 46	1 46	1 46	44
45	1 47	1 47	1 47	1 47	1 48	1 48	1 48	1 48	1 48	1 48	1 48	1 48	1 48	1 48	1 48	1 48	1 48	1 48	1 48	1 48	45
46	1 50	1 50	1 50	1 50	1 50	1 50	1 50	1 50	1 50	1 50	1 50	1 50	1 50	1 50	1 51	1 51	1 51	1 51	1 51	1 51	46
47	1 52	1 52	1 52	1 52	1 52	1 52	1 52	1 52	1 53	1 53	1 53	1 53	1 53	1 53	1 53	1 53	1 53	1 53	1 53	1 53	47
48	1 54	1 54	1 55	1 55	1 55	1 55	1 55	1 55	1 55	1 55	1 55	1 55	1 55	1 55	1 55	1 55	1 55	1 56	1 56	1 56	48
49	1 57	1 57	1 57	1 57	1 57	1 57	1 57	1 57	1 57	1 57	1 57	1 58	1 58	1 58	1 58	1 58	1 58	1 58	1 58	1 58	49
50	1 59	1 59	1 59	1 59	1 59	2 0	2 0	2 0	2 0	2 0	2 0	2 0	2 0	2 0	2 0	2 0	2 0	2 0	2 0	2 0	50
51	2 2	2 2	2 2	2 2	2 2	2 2	2 2	2 2	2 2	2 2	2 2	2 2	2 2	2 2	2 3	2 3	2 3	2 3	2 3	2 3	51
52	2 4	2 4	2 4	2 4	2 4	2 4	2 4	2 4	2 5	2 5	2 5	2 5	2 5	2 5	2 5	2 5	2 5	2 5	2 5	2 5	52
53	2 6	2 6	2 6	2 7	2 7	2 7	2 7	2 7	2 7	2 7	2 7	2 7	2 7	2 7	2 7	2 7	2 7	2 8	2 8	2 8	53
54	2 9	2 9	2 9	2 9	2 9	2 9	2 9	2 9	2 9	2 9	2 9	2 10	2 10	2 10	2 10	2 10	2 10	2 10	2 10	2 10	54
55	2 11	2 11	2 11	2 11	2 11	2 11	2 12	2 12	2 12	2 12	2 12	2 12	2 12	2 12	2 12	2 12	2 12	2 12	2 12	2 13	55
56	2 13	2 14	2 14	2 14	2 14	2 14	2 14	2 14	2 14	2 14	2 14	2 14	2 14	2 14	2 15	2 15	2 15	2 15	2 15	2 15	56
57	2 16	2 16	2 16	2 16	2 16	2 16	2 16	2 16	2 16	2 17	2 17	2 17	2 17	2 17	2 17	2 17	2 17	2 17	2 17	2 17	57
58	2 18	2 18	2 18	2 18	2 19	2 19	2 19	2 19	2 19	2 19	2 19	2 19	2 19	2 19	2 19	2 19	2 20	2 20	2 20	2 20	58
59	2 21	2 21	2 21	2 21	2 21	2 21	2 21	2 21	2 21	2 21	2 21	2 22	2 22	2 22	2 22	2 22	2 22	2 22	2 22	2 22	59
60	2 23	2 23	2 23	2 23	2 23	2 23	2 24	2 24	2 24	2 24	2 24	2 24	2 24	2 24	2 24	2 24	2 24	2 24	2 25	2 25	60
HOURS																					HOURS
1	2 23	2 23	2 23	2 23	2 23	2 23	2 24	2 24	2 24	2 24	2 24	2 24	2 24	2 24	2 24	2 24	2 24	2 24	2 25	2 25	1
2	4 46	4 46	4 46	4 47	4 47	4 47	4 47	4 47	4 47	4 48	4 48	4 48	4 48	4 48	4 48	4 49	4 49	4 49	4 49	4 49	2
3	7 9	7 9	7 10	7 10	7 10	7 10	7 11	7 11	7 11	7 11	7 12	7 12	7 12	7 12	7 13	7 13	7 13	7 13	7 14	7 14	3
4	9 32	9 32	9 33	9 33	9 33	9 34	9 34	9 34	9 35	9 35	9 35	9 36	9 36	9 36	9 37	9 37	9 37	9 38	9 38	9 38	4
5	11 55	11 55	11 56	11 56	11 57	11 57	11 58	11 58	11 58	11 59	11 59	12 0	12 0	12 0	12 1	12 1	12 2	12 2	12 3	12 3	5
6	14 18	14 19	14 19	14 20	14 20	14 21	14 21	14 22	14 22	14 23	14 23	14 24	14 24	14 25	14 25	14 26	14 26	14 27	14 27	14 28	6
7	16 41	16 42	16 42	16 43	16 43	16 44	16 45	16 45	16 46	16 46	16 47	16 47	16 48	16 49	16 49	16 50	16 50	16 51	16 52	16 52	7
8	19 4	19 5	19 5	19 6	19 7	19 7	19 8	19 9	19 9	19 10	19 11	19 11	19 12	19 13	19 13	19 14	19 15	19 15	19 16	19 17	8
9	21 27	21 28	21 29	21 29	21 30	21 31	21 32	21 32	21 33	21 34	21 35	21 35	21 36	21 37	21 38	21 38	21 39	21 40	21 41	21 41	9
10	23 50	23 51	23 52	23 53	23 53	23 54	23 55	23 56	23 57	23 58	23 58	23 59	24 0	24 1	24 2	24 3	24 3	24 4	24 5	24 6	10
11	26 13	26 14	26 15	26 16	26 17	26 18	26 19	26 19	26 20	26 21	26 22	26 23	26 24	26 25	26 26	26 27	26 28	26 29	26 30	26 30	11
12	28 36	28 37	28 38	28 39	28 40	28 41	28 42	28 43	28 44	28 45	28 46	28 47	28 48	28 49	28 50	28 51	28 52	28 53	28 54	28 55	12
13	30 59	31 0	31 1	31 2	31 3	31 4	31 6	31 7	31 8	31 9	31 10	31 11	31 12	31 13	31 14	31 15	31 16	31 17	31 19	31 20	13
14	33 22	33 23	33 24	33 26	33 27	33 28	33 29	33 30	33 31	33 33	33 34	33 35	33 36	33 37	33 38	33 40	33 41	33 42	33 43	33 44	14
15	35 45	35 46	35 48	35 49	35 50	35 51	35 53	35 54	35 55	35 56	35 58	35 59	36 0	36 1	36 3	36 4	36 5	36 6	36 8	36 9	15
16	38 8	38 9	38 11	38 12	38 13	38 15	38 16	38 17	38 19	38 20	38 21	38 23	38 24	38 25	38 27	38 28	38 29	38 31	38 32	38 33	16
17	40 31	40 32	40 34	40 35	40 37	40 38	40 40	40 41	40 42	40 44	40 45	40 47	40 48	40 49	40 51	40 52	40 54	40 55	40 57	40 58	17
18	42 54	42 56	42 57	42 59	43 0	43 2	43 3	43 5	43 6	43 8	43 9	43 11	43 12	43 14	43 15	43 17	43 18	43 20	43 21	43 23	18
19	45 17	45 19	45 20	45 22	45 23	45 25	45 27	45 28	45 30	45 31	45 33	45 34	45 36	45 38	45 39	45 41	45 42	45 44	45 46	45 47	19
20	47 40	47 42	47 43	47 45	47 47	47 48	47 50	47 52	47 53	47 55	47 57	47 58	48 0	48 2	48 3	48 5	48 7	48 8	48 10	48 12	20
21	50 3	50 5	50 7	50 8	50 10	50 12	50 14	50 15	50 17	50 19	50 21	50 22	50 24	50 26	50 28	50 29	50 31	50 33	50 35	50 36	21
22	52 26	52 28	52 30	52 32	52 33	52 35	52 37	52 39	52 41	52 43	52 44	52 46	52 48	52 50	52 52	52 54	52 55	52 57	52 59	53 1	22
23	54 49	54 51	54 53	54 55	54 57	54 59	55 1	55 2	55 4	55 6	55 8	55 10	55 12	55 14	55 16	55 18	55 20	55 22	55 24	55 25	23
24	57 12	57 14	57 16	57 18	57 20	57 22	57 24	57 26	57 28	57 30	57 32	57 34	57 36	57 38	57 40	57 42	57 44	57 46	57 48	57 50	24

Table V Diurnal Motion of the Sun

TIME	24 HOUR TRAVEL																				TIME
	′ ″ 57 52	′ ″ 57 54	′ ″ 57 56	′ ″ 57 58	′ ″ 58 0	′ ″ 58 2	′ ″ 58 4	′ ″ 58 6	′ ″ 58 8	′ ″ 58 10	′ ″ 58 12	′ ″ 58 14	′ ″ 58 16	′ ″ 58 18	′ ″ 58 20	′ ″ 58 22	′ ″ 58 24	′ ″ 58 26	′ ″ 58 28	′ ″ 58 30	
	′ ″	′ ″	′ ″	′ ″	′ ″	′ ″	′ ″	′ ″	′ ″	′ ″	′ ″	′ ″	′ ″	′ ″	′ ″	′ ″	′ ″	′ ″	′ ″	′ ″	
MINUTES 1	2	2	2	2	2	2	2	2	2	2	2	2	2	2	2	2	2	2	2	2	1 MINUTES
2	5	5	5	5	5	5	5	5	5	5	5	5	5	5	5	5	5	5	5	5	2
3	7	7	7	7	7	7	7	7	7	7	7	7	7	7	7	7	7	7	7	7	3
4	10	10	10	10	10	10	10	10	10	10	10	10	10	10	10	10	10	10	10	10	4
5	12	12	12	12	12	12	12	12	12	12	12	12	12	12	12	12	12	12	12	12	5
6	14	14	14	14	15	15	15	15	15	15	15	15	15	15	15	15	15	15	15	15	6
7	17	17	17	17	17	17	17	17	17	17	17	17	17	17	17	17	17	17	17	17	7
8	19	19	19	19	19	19	19	19	19	19	19	19	19	19	19	19	19	19	19	20	8
9	22	22	22	22	22	22	22	22	22	22	22	22	22	22	22	22	22	22	22	22	9
10	24	24	24	24	24	24	24	24	24	24	24	24	24	24	24	24	24	24	24	24	10
11	27	27	27	27	27	27	27	27	27	27	27	27	27	27	27	27	27	27	27	27	11
12	29	29	29	29	29	29	29	29	29	29	29	29	29	29	29	29	29	29	29	29	12
13	31	31	31	31	31	31	31	31	31	32	32	32	32	32	32	32	32	32	32	32	13
14	34	34	34	34	34	34	34	34	34	34	34	34	34	34	34	34	34	34	34	34	14
15	36	36	36	36	36	36	36	36	36	36	36	36	36	36	36	36	37	37	37	37	15
16	39	39	39	39	39	39	39	39	39	39	39	39	39	39	39	39	39	39	39	39	16
17	41	41	41	41	41	41	41	41	41	41	41	41	41	41	41	41	41	41	41	41	17
18	43	43	43	43	44	44	44	44	44	44	44	44	44	44	44	44	44	44	44	44	18
19	46	46	46	46	46	46	46	46	46	46	46	46	46	46	46	46	46	46	46	46	19
20	48	48	48	48	48	48	48	48	48	48	49	49	49	49	49	49	49	49	49	49	20
21	51	51	51	51	51	51	51	51	51	51	51	51	51	51	51	51	51	51	51	51	21
22	53	53	53	53	53	53	53	53	53	53	53	53	53	53	53	54	54	54	54	54	22
23	55	55	56	56	56	56	56	56	56	56	56	56	56	56	56	56	56	56	56	56	23
24	58	58	58	58	58	58	58	58	58	58	58	58	58	58	58	58	58	58	58	59	24
25	1 0	1 0	1 0	1 0	1 0	1 0	1 0	1 1	1 1	1 1	1 1	1 1	1 1	1 1	1 1	1 1	1 1	1 1	1 1	1 1	25
26	1 3	1 3	1 3	1 3	1 3	1 3	1 3	1 3	1 3	1 3	1 3	1 3	1 3	1 3	1 3	1 3	1 3	1 3	1 3	1 3	26
27	1 5	1 5	1 5	1 5	1 5	1 5	1 5	1 5	1 5	1 5	1 5	1 6	1 6	1 6	1 6	1 6	1 6	1 6	1 6	1 6	27
28	1 8	1 8	1 8	1 8	1 8	1 8	1 8	1 8	1 8	1 8	1 8	1 8	1 8	1 8	1 8	1 8	1 8	1 8	1 8	1 8	28
29	1 10	1 10	1 10	1 10	1 10	1 10	1 10	1 10	1 10	1 10	1 10	1 10	1 10	1 10	1 10	1 11	1 11	1 11	1 11	1 11	29
30	1 12	1 12	1 12	1 12	1 13	1 13	1 13	1 13	1 13	1 13	1 13	1 13	1 13	1 13	1 13	1 13	1 13	1 13	1 13	1 13	30
31	1 15	1 15	1 15	1 15	1 15	1 15	1 15	1 15	1 15	1 15	1 15	1 15	1 15	1 15	1 15	1 15	1 15	1 15	1 16	1 16	31
32	1 17	1 17	1 17	1 17	1 17	1 17	1 17	1 17	1 18	1 18	1 18	1 18	1 18	1 18	1 18	1 18	1 18	1 18	1 18	1 18	32
33	1 20	1 20	1 20	1 20	1 20	1 20	1 20	1 20	1 20	1 20	1 20	1 20	1 20	1 20	1 20	1 20	1 20	1 20	1 20	1 20	33
34	1 22	1 22	1 22	1 22	1 22	1 22	1 22	1 22	1 22	1 22	1 22	1 22	1 23	1 23	1 23	1 23	1 23	1 23	1 23	1 23	34
35	1 24	1 24	1 24	1 25	1 25	1 25	1 25	1 25	1 25	1 25	1 25	1 25	1 25	1 25	1 25	1 25	1 25	1 25	1 25	1 25	35
36	1 27	1 27	1 27	1 27	1 27	1 27	1 27	1 27	1 27	1 27	1 27	1 27	1 27	1 27	1 28	1 28	1 28	1 28	1 28	1 28	36
37	1 29	1 29	1 29	1 29	1 29	1 29	1 30	1 30	1 30	1 30	1 30	1 30	1 30	1 30	1 30	1 30	1 30	1 30	1 30	1 30	37
38	1 32	1 32	1 32	1 32	1 32	1 32	1 32	1 32	1 32	1 32	1 32	1 32	1 32	1 32	1 32	1 32	1 32	1 33	1 33	1 33	38
39	1 34	1 34	1 34	1 34	1 34	1 34	1 34	1 34	1 34	1 35	1 35	1 35	1 35	1 35	1 35	1 35	1 35	1 35	1 35	1 35	39
40	1 36	1 37	1 37	1 37	1 37	1 37	1 37	1 37	1 37	1 37	1 37	1 37	1 37	1 37	1 37	1 37	1 37	1 37	1 37	1 38	40
41	1 39	1 39	1 39	1 39	1 39	1 39	1 39	1 39	1 39	1 39	1 39	1 39	1 40	1 40	1 40	1 40	1 40	1 40	1 40	1 40	41
42	1 41	1 41	1 41	1 41	1 42	1 42	1 42	1 42	1 42	1 42	1 42	1 42	1 42	1 42	1 42	1 42	1 42	1 42	1 42	1 42	42
43	1 44	1 44	1 44	1 44	1 44	1 44	1 44	1 44	1 44	1 44	1 44	1 44	1 44	1 44	1 45	1 45	1 45	1 45	1 45	1 45	43
44	1 46	1 46	1 46	1 46	1 46	1 46	1 46	1 47	1 47	1 47	1 47	1 47	1 47	1 47	1 47	1 47	1 47	1 47	1 47	1 47	44
45	1 49	1 49	1 49	1 49	1 49	1 49	1 49	1 49	1 49	1 49	1 49	1 49	1 49	1 49	1 49	1 49	1 50	1 50	1 50	1 50	45
46	1 51	1 51	1 51	1 51	1 51	1 51	1 51	1 51	1 51	1 51	1 52	1 52	1 52	1 52	1 52	1 52	1 52	1 52	1 52	1 52	46
47	1 53	1 53	1 53	1 54	1 54	1 54	1 54	1 54	1 34	1 54	1 54	1 54	1 54	1 54	1 54	1 54	1 54	1 54	1 54	1 55	47
48	1 56	1 56	1 56	1 56	1 56	1 56	1 56	1 56	1 56	1 56	1 56	1 56	1 57	1 57	1 57	1 57	1 57	1 57	1 57	1 57	48
49	1 58	1 58	1 58	1 58	1 58	1 58	1 59	1 59	1 59	1 59	1 59	1 59	1 59	1 59	1 59	1 59	1 59	1 59	1 59	1 59	49
50	2 1	2 1	2 1	2 1	2 1	2 1	2 1	2 1	2 1	2 1	2 1	2 1	2 1	2 1	2 2	2 2	2 2	2 2	2 2	2 2	50
51	2 3	2 3	2 3	2 3	2 3	2 3	2 3	2 3	2 4	2 4	2 4	2 4	2 4	2 4	2 4	2 4	2 4	2 4	2 4	2 4	51
52	2 5	2 5	2 6	2 6	2 6	2 6	2 6	2 6	2 6	2 6	2 6	2 6	2 6	2 6	2 6	2 6	2 7	2 7	2 7	2 7	52
53	2 8	2 8	2 8	2 8	2 8	2 8	2 8	2 8	2 8	2 8	2 9	2 9	2 9	2 9	2 9	2 9	2 9	2 9	2 9	2 9	53
54	2 10	2 10	2 10	2 10	2 11	2 11	2 11	2 11	2 11	2 11	2 11	2 11	2 11	2 11	2 11	2 11	2 11	2 11	2 12	2 12	54
55	2 13	2 13	2 13	2 13	2 13	2 13	2 13	2 13	2 13	2 13	2 13	2 13	2 14	2 14	2 14	2 14	2 14	2 14	2 14	2 14	55
56	2 15	2 15	2 15	2 15	2 15	2 15	2 15	2 16	2 16	2 16	2 16	2 16	2 16	2 16	2 16	2 16	2 16	2 16	2 16	2 17	56
57	2 17	2 18	2 18	2 18	2 18	2 18	2 18	2 18	2 18	2 18	2 18	2 18	2 18	2 18	2 19	2 19	2 19	2 19	2 19	2 19	57
58	2 20	2 20	2 20	2 20	2 20	2 20	2 20	2 20	2 20	2 21	2 21	2 21	2 21	2 21	2 21	2 21	2 21	2 21	2 21	2 21	58
59	2 22	2 22	2 22	2 23	2 23	2 23	2 23	2 23	2 23	2 23	2 23	2 23	2 23	2 23	2 23	2 23	2 24	2 24	2 24	2 24	59
60	2 25	2 25	2 25	2 25	2 25	2 25	2 25	2 25	2 25	2 25	2 26	2 26	2 26	2 26	2 26	2 26	2 26	2 26	2 26	2 26	60
HOURS 1	2 25	2 25	2 25	2 25	2 25	2 25	2 25	2 25	2 25	2 25	2 26	2 26	2 26	2 26	2 26	2 26	2 26	2 26	2 26	2 26	1 HOURS
2	4 49	4 50	4 50	4 50	4 50	4 50	4 50	4 51	4 51	4 51	4 51	4 51	4 51	4 52	4 52	4 52	4 52	4 52	4 52	4 53	2
3	7 14	7 14	7 15	7 15	7 15	7 15	7 16	7 16	7 16	7 16	7 17	7 17	7 17	7 17	7 18	7 18	7 18	7 18	7 19	7 19	3
4	9 39	9 39	9 39	9 40	9 40	9 40	9 41	9 41	9 41	9 42	9 42	9 42	9 43	9 43	9 43	9 44	9 44	9 44	9 45	9 45	4
5	12 3	12 4	12 4	12 5	12 5	12 5	12 6	12 6	12 7	12 7	12 8	12 8	12 8	12 9	12 9	12 10	12 10	12 10	12 11	12 11	5
6	14 28	14 29	14 29	14 30	14 30	14 31	14 31	14 32	14 32	14 33	14 33	14 34	14 34	14 35	14 35	14 36	14 36	14 37	14 37	14 38	6
7	16 53	16 53	16 54	16 54	16 55	16 56	16 56	16 57	16 57	16 58	16 59	16 59	17 0	17 0	17 1	17 1	17 2	17 3	17 3	17 4	7
8	19 17	19 18	19 19	19 19	19 20	19 21	19 21	19 22	19 23	19 23	19 24	19 25	19 25	19 26	19 27	19 27	19 28	19 29	19 29	19 30	8
9	21 42	21 43	21 44	21 44	21 45	21 46	21 47	21 47	21 48	21 49	21 50	21 50	21 51	21 52	21 53	21 53	21 54	21 55	21 56	21 56	9
10	24 7	24 8	24 8	24 9	24 10	24 11	24 12	24 13	24 13	24 14	24 15	24 16	24 17	24 18	24 18	24 19	24 20	24 21	24 22	24 23	10
11	26 31	26 32	26 33	26 34	26 35	26 36	26 37	26 38	26 39	26 40	26 41	26 41	26 42	26 43	26 44	26 45	26 46	26 47	26 48	26 49	11
12	28 56	28 57	28 58	28 59	29 0	29 1	29 2	29 3	29 4	29 5	29 6	29 7	29 8	29 9	29 10	29 11	29 12	29 13	29 14	29 15	12
13	31 21	31 22	31 23	31 24	31 25	31 26	31 27	31 28	31 29	31 30	31 32	31 33	31 34	31 35	31 36	31 37	31 38	31 39	31 40	31 41	13
14	33 45	33 47	33 48	33 49	33 50	33 51	33 52	33 54	33 55	33 56	33 57	33 58	33 59	34 1	34 2	34 3	34 4	34 5	34 6	34 8	14
15	36 10	36 11	36 13	36 14	36 15	36 16	36 18	36 19	36 20	36 21	36 23	36 24	36 25	36 26	36 28	36 29	36 30	36 31	36 33	36 34	15
16	38 35	38 36	38 37	38 39	38 40	38 41	38 43	38 44	38 45	38 47	38 48	38 49	38 51	38 52	38 53	38 55	38 56	38 57	38 59	39 0	16
17	40 59	41 1	41 2	41 4	41 5	41 6	41 8	41 9	41 11	41 12	41 14	41 15	41 16	41 18	41 19	41 21	41 22	41 23	41 25	41 26	17
18	43 24	43 26	43 27	43 29	43 30	43 32	43 33	43 35	43 36	43 38	43 39	43 41	43 42	43 44	43 45	43 47	43 48	43 50	43 51	43 53	18
19	45 49	45 50	45 52	45 53	45 55	45 57	45 58	46 0	46 1	46 3	46 5	46 6	46 8	46 9	46 11	46 12	46 14	46 16	46 17	46 19	19
20	48 13	48 15	48 17	48 18	48 20	48 22	48 23	48 25	48 27	48 28	48 30	48 32	48 33	48 35	48 37	48 38	48 40	48 42	48 43	48 45	20
21	50 38	50 40	50 42	50 43	50 45	50 47	50 49	50 50	50 52	50 54	50 56	50 57	50 59	51 1	51 3	51 4	51 6	51 8	51 10	51 11	21
22	53 3	53 5	53 6	53 8	53 10	53 12	53 14	53 16	53 17	53 19	53 21	53 23	53 25	53 27	53 28	53 30	53 32	53 34	53 36	53 38	22
23	55 27	55 29	55 31	55 33	55 35	55 37	55 39	55 41	55 43	55 45	55 47	55 48	55 50	55 52	55 54	55 56	55 58	56 0	56 2	56 4	23
24	57 52	57 54	57 56	57 58	58 0	58 2	58 4	58 6	58 8	58 10	58 12	58 14	58 16	58 18	58 20	58 22	58 24	58 26	58 28	58 30	24

Table V Diurnal Motion of the Sun

TIME	24 HOUR TRAVEL																				TIME
	58 32	58 34	58 36	58 38	58 40	58 42	58 44	58 46	58 48	58 50	58 52	58 54	58 56	58 58	59 0	59 2	59 4	59 6	59 8	59 10	
	′ ″	′ ″	′ ″	′ ″	′ ″	′ ″	′ ″	′ ″	′ ″	′ ″	′ ″	′ ″	′ ″	′ ″	′ ″	′ ″	′ ″	′ ″	′ ″	′ ″	
MINUTES																					MINUTES
1	2	2	2	2	2	2	2	2	2	2	2	2	2	2	2	2	2	2	2	2	1
2	5	5	5	5	5	5	5	5	5	5	5	5	5	5	5	5	5	5	5	5	2
3	7	7	7	7	7	7	7	7	7	7	7	7	7	7	7	7	7	7	7	7	3
4	10	10	10	10	10	10	10	10	10	10	10	10	10	10	10	10	10	10	10	10	4
5	12	12	12	12	12	12	12	12	12	12	12	12	12	12	12	12	12	12	12	12	5
6	15	15	15	15	15	15	15	15	15	15	15	15	15	15	15	15	15	15	15	15	6
7	17	17	17	17	17	17	17	17	17	17	17	17	17	17	17	17	17	17	17	17	7
8	20	20	20	20	20	20	20	20	20	20	20	20	20	20	20	20	20	20	20	20	8
9	22	22	22	22	22	22	22	22	22	22	22	22	22	22	22	22	22	22	22	22	9
10	24	24	24	24	24	24	24	24	25	25	25	25	25	25	25	25	25	25	25	25	10
11	27	27	27	27	27	27	27	27	27	27	27	27	27	27	27	27	27	27	27	27	11
12	29	29	29	29	29	29	29	29	29	29	29	29	29	29	30	30	30	30	30	30	12
13	32	32	32	32	32	32	32	32	32	32	32	32	32	32	32	32	32	32	32	32	13
14	34	34	34	34	34	34	34	34	34	34	34	34	34	34	34	34	34	34	34	35	14
15	37	37	37	37	37	37	37	37	37	37	37	37	37	37	37	37	37	37	37	37	15
16	39	39	39	39	39	39	39	39	39	39	39	39	39	39	39	39	39	39	39	39	16
17	41	41	42	42	42	42	42	42	42	42	42	42	42	42	42	42	42	42	42	42	17
18	44	44	44	44	44	44	44	44	44	44	44	44	44	44	44	44	44	44	44	44	18
19	46	46	46	46	46	46	46	47	47	47	47	47	47	47	47	47	47	47	47	47	19
20	49	49	49	49	49	49	49	49	49	49	49	49	49	49	49	49	49	49	49	49	20
21	51	51	51	51	51	51	51	51	51	51	52	52	52	52	52	52	52	52	52	52	21
22	54	54	54	54	54	54	54	54	54	54	54	54	54	54	54	54	54	54	54	54	22
23	56	56	56	56	56	56	56	56	56	56	56	56	56	57	57	57	57	57	57	57	23
24	59	59	59	59	59	59	59	59	59	59	59	59	59	59	59	59	59	59	59	59	24
25	1 1	1 1	1 1	1 1	1 1	1 1	1 1	1 1	1 1	1 1	1 1	1 1	1 1	1 1	1 1	1 1	1 2	1 2	1 2	1 2	25
26	1 3	1 3	1 3	1 4	1 4	1 4	1 4	1 4	1 4	1 4	1 4	1 4	1 4	1 4	1 4	1 4	1 4	1 4	1 4	1 4	26
27	1 6	1 6	1 6	1 6	1 6	1 6	1 6	1 6	1 6	1 6	1 6	1 6	1 6	1 6	1 6	1 6	1 6	1 6	1 7	1 7	27
28	1 8	1 8	1 8	1 8	1 8	1 8	1 9	1 9	1 9	1 9	1 9	1 9	1 9	1 9	1 9	1 9	1 9	1 9	1 9	1 9	28
29	1 11	1 11	1 11	1 11	1 11	1 11	1 11	1 11	1 11	1 11	1 11	1 11	1 11	1 11	1 11	1 11	1 11	1 11	1 11	1 11	29
30	1 13	1 13	1 13	1 13	1 13	1 13	1 13	1 13	1 14	1 14	1 14	1 14	1 14	1 14	1 14	1 14	1 14	1 14	1 14	1 14	30
31	1 16	1 16	1 16	1 16	1 16	1 16	1 16	1 16	1 16	1 16	1 16	1 16	1 16	1 16	1 16	1 16	1 16	1 16	1 16	1 16	31
32	1 18	1 18	1 18	1 18	1 18	1 18	1 18	1 18	1 18	1 18	1 18	1 19	1 19	1 19	1 19	1 19	1 19	1 19	1 19	1 19	32
33	1 20	1 21	1 21	1 21	1 21	1 21	1 21	1 21	1 21	1 21	1 21	1 21	1 21	1 21	1 21	1 21	1 21	1 21	1 21	1 21	33
34	1 23	1 23	1 23	1 23	1 23	1 23	1 23	1 23	1 23	1 23	1 23	1 23	1 23	1 24	1 24	1 24	1 24	1 24	1 24	1 24	34
35	1 25	1 25	1 25	1 26	1 26	1 26	1 26	1 26	1 26	1 26	1 26	1 26	1 26	1 26	1 26	1 26	1 26	1 26	1 26	1 26	35
36	1 28	1 28	1 28	1 28	1 28	1 28	1 28	1 28	1 28	1 28	1 28	1 28	1 28	1 28	1 29	1 29	1 29	1 29	1 29	1 29	36
37	1 30	1 30	1 30	1 30	1 30	1 30	1 31	1 31	1 31	1 31	1 31	1 31	1 31	1 31	1 31	1 31	1 31	1 31	1 31	1 31	37
38	1 33	1 33	1 33	1 33	1 33	1 33	1 33	1 33	1 33	1 33	1 33	1 33	1 33	1 33	1 33	1 33	1 34	1 34	1 34	1 34	38
39	1 35	1 35	1 35	1 35	1 35	1 35	1 35	1 35	1 36	1 36	1 36	1 36	1 36	1 36	1 36	1 36	1 36	1 36	1 36	1 36	39
40	1 38	1 38	1 38	1 38	1 38	1 38	1 38	1 38	1 38	1 38	1 38	1 38	1 38	1 38	1 38	1 38	1 38	1 39	1 39	1 39	40
41	1 40	1 40	1 40	1 40	1 40	1 40	1 40	1 40	1 40	1 41	1 41	1 41	1 41	1 41	1 41	1 41	1 41	1 41	1 41	1 41	41
42	1 42	1 42	1 43	1 43	1 43	1 43	1 43	1 43	1 43	1 43	1 43	1 43	1 43	1 43	1 43	1 43	1 43	1 43	1 43	1 44	42
43	1 45	1 45	1 45	1 45	1 45	1 45	1 45	1 45	1 45	1 45	1 45	1 46	1 46	1 46	1 46	1 46	1 46	1 46	1 46	1 46	43
44	1 47	1 47	1 47	1 47	1 48	1 48	1 48	1 48	1 48	1 48	1 48	1 48	1 48	1 48	1 48	1 48	1 48	1 48	1 48	1 48	44
45	1 50	1 50	1 50	1 50	1 50	1 50	1 50	1 50	1 50	1 50	1 50	1 50	1 51	1 51	1 51	1 51	1 51	1 51	1 51	1 51	45
46	1 52	1 52	1 52	1 52	1 52	1 53	1 53	1 53	1 53	1 53	1 53	1 53	1 53	1 53	1 53	1 53	1 53	1 53	1 53	1 53	46
47	1 55	1 55	1 55	1 55	1 55	1 55	1 55	1 55	1 55	1 55	1 55	1 55	1 55	1 55	1 56	1 56	1 56	1 56	1 56	1 56	47
48	1 57	1 57	1 57	1 57	1 57	1 57	1 57	1 58	1 58	1 58	1 58	1 58	1 58	1 58	1 58	1 58	1 58	1 58	1 58	1 58	48
49	2 0	2 0	2 0	2 0	2 0	2 0	2 0	2 0	2 0	2 0	2 0	2 0	2 0	2 0	2 0	2 1	2 1	2 1	2 1	2 1	49
50	2 2	2 2	2 2	2 2	2 2	2 2	2 2	2 2	2 3	2 3	2 3	2 3	2 3	2 3	2 3	2 3	2 3	2 3	2 3	2 3	50
51	2 4	2 4	2 5	2 5	2 5	2 5	2 5	2 5	2 5	2 5	2 5	2 5	2 5	2 5	2 5	2 5	2 6	2 6	2 6	2 6	51
52	2 7	2 7	2 7	2 7	2 7	2 7	2 7	2 7	2 7	2 7	2 8	2 8	2 8	2 8	2 8	2 8	2 8	2 8	2 8	2 8	52
53	2 9	2 9	2 9	2 9	2 10	2 10	2 10	2 10	2 10	2 10	2 10	2 10	2 10	2 10	2 10	2 10	2 10	2 11	2 11	2 11	53
54	2 12	2 12	2 12	2 12	2 12	2 12	2 12	2 12	2 12	2 12	2 12	2 13	2 13	2 13	2 13	2 13	2 13	2 13	2 13	2 13	54
55	2 14	2 14	2 14	2 14	2 14	2 15	2 15	2 15	2 15	2 15	2 15	2 15	2 15	2 15	2 15	2 15	2 15	2 15	2 16	2 16	55
56	2 17	2 17	2 17	2 17	2 17	2 17	2 17	2 17	2 17	2 17	2 17	2 17	2 18	2 18	2 18	2 18	2 18	2 18	2 18	2 18	56
57	2 19	2 19	2 19	2 19	2 19	2 19	2 19	2 20	2 20	2 20	2 20	2 20	2 20	2 20	2 20	2 20	2 20	2 20	2 20	2 21	57
58	2 21	2 22	2 22	2 22	2 22	2 22	2 22	2 22	2 22	2 22	2 22	2 22	2 23	2 23	2 23	2 23	2 23	2 23	2 23	2 23	58
59	2 24	2 24	2 24	2 24	2 24	2 24	2 24	2 24	2 25	2 25	2 25	2 25	2 25	2 25	2 25	2 25	2 25	2 25	2 25	2 25	59
60	2 26	2 26	2 27	2 27	2 27	2 27	2 27	2 27	2 27	2 27	2 27	2 27	2 27	2 27	2 28	2 28	2 28	2 28	2 28	2 28	60
HOURS																					HOURS
1	2 26	2 26	2 27	2 27	2 27	2 27	2 27	2 27	2 27	2 27	2 27	2 27	2 27	2 27	2 28	2 28	2 28	2 28	2 28	2 28	1
2	4 53	4 53	4 53	4 53	4 53	4 54	4 54	4 54	4 54	4 54	4 54	4 55	4 55	4 55	4 55	4 55	4 55	4 56	4 56	4 56	2
3	7 19	7 19	7 20	7 20	7 20	7 20	7 21	7 21	7 21	7 21	7 22	7 22	7 22	7 22	7 23	7 23	7 23	7 23	7 24	7 24	3
4	9 45	9 46	9 46	9 46	9 47	9 47	9 47	9 48	9 48	9 48	9 49	9 49	9 49	9 50	9 50	9 50	9 51	9 51	9 51	9 52	4
5	12 12	12 12	12 13	12 13	12 13	12 14	12 14	12 15	12 15	12 15	12 16	12 16	12 17	12 17	12 18	12 18	12 18	12 19	12 19	12 20	5
6	14 38	14 39	14 39	14 40	14 40	14 41	14 41	14 42	14 42	14 43	14 43	14 44	14 44	14 45	14 45	14 46	14 46	14 47	14 47	14 48	6
7	17 4	17 5	17 6	17 6	17 7	17 7	17 8	17 8	17 9	17 10	17 10	17 11	17 11	17 12	17 13	17 13	17 14	17 14	17 15	17 15	7
8	19 31	19 31	19 32	19 33	19 33	19 34	19 35	19 35	19 36	19 37	19 37	19 38	19 39	19 39	19 40	19 41	19 41	19 42	19 43	19 43	8
9	21 57	21 58	21 59	21 59	22 0	22 1	22 2	22 2	22 3	22 4	22 5	22 5	22 6	22 7	22 8	22 8	22 9	22 10	22 11	22 11	9
10	24 23	24 24	24 25	24 26	24 27	24 28	24 28	24 29	24 30	24 31	24 32	24 33	24 33	24 34	24 35	24 36	24 37	24 38	24 38	24 39	10
11	26 50	26 51	26 52	26 52	26 53	26 54	26 55	26 56	26 57	26 58	26 59	27 0	27 1	27 2	27 3	27 3	27 4	27 5	27 6	27 7	11
12	29 16	29 17	29 18	29 19	29 20	29 21	29 22	29 23	29 24	29 25	29 26	29 27	29 28	29 29	29 30	29 31	29 32	29 33	29 34	29 35	12
13	31 42	31 43	31 45	31 46	31 47	31 48	31 49	31 50	31 51	31 52	31 53	31 54	31 55	31 56	31 58	31 59	32 0	32 1	32 2	32 3	13
14	34 9	34 10	34 11	34 12	34 13	34 15	34 16	34 17	34 18	34 19	34 20	34 22	34 23	34 24	34 25	34 26	34 27	34 29	34 30	34 31	14
15	36 35	36 36	36 38	36 39	36 40	36 41	36 43	36 44	36 45	36 46	36 48	36 49	36 50	36 51	36 53	36 54	36 55	36 56	36 58	36 59	15
16	39 1	39 3	39 4	39 5	39 7	39 8	39 9	39 11	39 12	39 13	39 15	39 16	39 17	39 19	39 20	39 21	39 23	39 24	39 25	39 27	16
17	41 28	41 29	41 31	41 32	41 33	41 35	41 36	41 38	41 39	41 40	41 42	41 43	41 45	41 46	41 48	41 49	41 50	41 52	41 53	41 55	17
18	43 54	43 56	43 57	43 59	44 0	44 2	44 3	44 5	44 6	44 8	44 9	44 11	44 12	44 14	44 15	44 17	44 18	44 20	44 21	44 23	18
19	46 20	46 22	46 24	46 25	46 27	46 28	46 30	46 31	46 33	46 35	46 36	46 38	46 39	46 41	46 43	46 44	46 46	46 47	46 49	46 50	19
20	48 47	48 48	48 50	48 52	48 53	48 55	48 57	48 58	49 0	49 2	49 3	49 5	49 7	49 8	49 10	49 12	49 13	49 15	49 17	49 18	20
21	51 13	51 15	51 17	51 18	51 20	51 22	51 24	51 25	51 27	51 29	51 31	51 32	51 34	51 36	51 38	51 39	51 41	51 43	51 45	51 46	21
22	53 39	53 41	53 43	53 45	53 47	53 49	53 50	53 52	53 54	53 56	53 58	54 0	54 1	54 3	54 5	54 7	54 9	54 11	54 12	54 14	22
23	56 6	56 8	56 10	56 11	56 13	56 15	56 17	56 19	56 21	56 23	56 25	56 27	56 29	56 31	56 33	56 34	56 36	56 38	56 40	56 42	23
24	58 32	58 34	58 36	58 38	58 40	58 42	58 44	58 46	58 48	58 50	58 52	58 54	58 56	58 58	59 0	59 2	59 4	59 6	59 8	59 10	24

Table V Diurnal Motion of the Sun

TIME	24 HOUR TRAVEL																				TIME
	59′ 12″	59′ 14″	59′ 16″	59′ 18″	59′ 20″	59′ 22″	59′ 24″	59′ 26″	59′ 28″	59′ 30″	59′ 32″	59′ 34″	59′ 36″	59′ 38″	59′ 40″	59′ 42″	59′ 44″	59′ 46″	59′ 48″	59′ 50″	
MINUTES	′ ″	′ ″	′ ″	′ ″	′ ″	′ ″	′ ″	′ ″	′ ″	′ ″	′ ″	′ ″	′ ″	′ ″	′ ″	′ ″	′ ″	′ ″	′ ″	′ ″	MINUTES
1	2	2	2	2	2	2	2	2	2	2	2	2	2	2	2	2	2	2	2	2	1
2	5	5	5	5	5	5	5	5	5	5	5	5	5	5	5	5	5	5	5	5	2
3	7	7	7	7	7	7	7	7	7	7	7	7	7	7	7	7	7	7	7	7	3
4	10	10	10	10	10	10	10	10	10	10	10	10	10	10	10	10	10	10	10	10	4
5	12	12	12	12	12	12	12	12	12	12	12	12	12	12	12	12	12	12	12	12	5
6	15	15	15	15	15	15	15	15	15	15	15	15	15	15	15	15	15	15	15	15	6
7	17	17	17	17	17	17	17	17	17	17	17	17	17	17	17	17	17	17	17	17	7
8	20	20	20	20	20	20	20	20	20	20	20	20	20	20	20	20	20	20	20	20	8
9	22	22	22	22	22	22	22	22	22	22	22	22	22	22	22	22	22	22	22	22	9
10	25	25	25	25	25	25	25	25	25	25	25	25	25	25	25	25	25	25	25	25	10
11	27	27	27	27	27	27	27	27	27	27	27	27	27	27	27	27	27	27	27	27	11
12	30	30	30	30	30	30	30	30	30	30	30	30	30	30	30	30	30	30	30	30	12
13	32	32	32	32	32	32	32	32	32	32	32	32	32	32	32	32	32	32	32	32	13
14	35	35	35	35	35	35	35	35	35	35	35	35	35	35	35	35	35	35	35	35	14
15	37	37	37	37	37	37	37	37	37	37	37	37	37	37	37	37	37	37	37	37	15
16	39	39	40	40	40	40	40	40	40	40	40	40	40	40	40	40	40	40	40	40	16
17	42	42	42	42	42	42	42	42	42	42	42	42	42	42	42	42	42	42	42	42	17
18	44	44	44	44	45	45	45	45	45	45	45	45	45	45	45	45	45	45	45	45	18
19	47	47	47	47	47	47	47	47	47	47	47	47	47	47	47	47	47	47	47	47	19
20	49	49	49	49	49	49	50	50	50	50	50	50	50	50	50	50	50	50	50	50	20
21	52	52	52	52	52	52	52	52	52	52	52	52	52	52	52	52	52	52	52	52	21
22	54	54	54	54	54	54	54	54	55	55	55	55	55	55	55	55	55	55	55	55	22
23	57	57	57	57	57	57	57	57	57	57	57	57	57	57	57	57	57	57	57	57	23
24	59	59	59	59	59	59	59	59	59	1 0	1 0	1 0	1 0	1 0	1 0	1 0	1 0	1 0	1 0	1 0	24
25	1 2	1 2	1 2	1 2	1 2	1 2	1 2	1 2	1 2	1 2	1 2	1 2	1 2	1 2	1 2	1 2	1 2	1 2	1 2	1 2	25
26	1 4	1 4	1 4	1 4	1 4	1 4	1 4	1 4	1 4	1 4	1 4	1 5	1 5	1 5	1 5	1 5	1 5	1 5	1 5	1 5	26
27	1 7	1 7	1 7	1 7	1 7	1 7	1 7	1 7	1 7	1 7	1 7	1 7	1 7	1 7	1 7	1 7	1 7	1 7	1 7	1 7	27
28	1 9	1 9	1 9	1 9	1 9	1 9	1 9	1 9	1 9	1 9	1 9	1 9	1 10	1 10	1 10	1 10	1 10	1 10	1 10	1 10	28
29	1 12	1 12	1 12	1 12	1 12	1 12	1 12	1 12	1 12	1 12	1 12	1 12	1 12	1 12	1 12	1 12	1 12	1 12	1 12	1 12	29
30	1 14	1 14	1 14	1 14	1 14	1 14	1 14	1 14	1 14	1 14	1 14	1 14	1 15	1 15	1 15	1 15	1 15	1 15	1 15	1 15	30
31	1 16	1 17	1 17	1 17	1 17	1 17	1 17	1 17	1 17	1 17	1 17	1 17	1 17	1 17	1 17	1 17	1 17	1 17	1 17	1 17	31
32	1 19	1 19	1 19	1 19	1 19	1 19	1 19	1 19	1 19	1 19	1 19	1 19	1 19	1 20	1 20	1 20	1 20	1 20	1 20	1 20	32
33	1 21	1 21	1 21	1 22	1 22	1 22	1 22	1 22	1 22	1 22	1 22	1 22	1 22	1 22	1 22	1 22	1 22	1 22	1 22	1 22	33
34	1 24	1 24	1 24	1 24	1 24	1 24	1 24	1 24	1 24	1 24	1 24	1 24	1 24	1 24	1 25	1 25	1 25	1 25	1 25	1 25	34
35	1 26	1 26	1 26	1 26	1 27	1 27	1 27	1 27	1 27	1 27	1 27	1 27	1 27	1 27	1 27	1 27	1 27	1 27	1 27	1 27	35
36	1 29	1 29	1 29	1 29	1 29	1 29	1 29	1 29	1 29	1 29	1 29	1 29	1 29	1 29	1 30	1 30	1 30	1 30	1 30	1 30	36
37	1 31	1 31	1 31	1 31	1 31	1 32	1 32	1 32	1 32	1 32	1 32	1 32	1 32	1 32	1 32	1 32	1 32	1 32	1 32	1 32	37
38	1 34	1 34	1 34	1 34	1 34	1 34	1 34	1 34	1 34	1 34	1 34	1 34	1 34	1 34	1 34	1 35	1 35	1 35	1 35	1 35	38
39	1 36	1 36	1 36	1 36	1 36	1 36	1 37	1 37	1 37	1 37	1 37	1 37	1 37	1 37	1 37	1 37	1 37	1 37	1 37	1 37	39
40	1 39	1 39	1 39	1 39	1 39	1 39	1 39	1 39	1 39	1 39	1 39	1 39	1 39	1 39	1 39	1 40	1 40	1 40	1 40	1 40	40
41	1 41	1 41	1 41	1 41	1 41	1 41	1 41	1 42	1 42	1 42	1 42	1 42	1 42	1 42	1 42	1 42	1 42	1 42	1 42	1 42	41
42	1 44	1 44	1 44	1 44	1 44	1 44	1 44	1 44	1 44	1 44	1 44	1 44	1 44	1 44	1 44	1 44	1 45	1 45	1 45	1 45	42
43	1 46	1 46	1 46	1 46	1 46	1 46	1 46	1 46	1 47	1 47	1 47	1 47	1 47	1 47	1 47	1 47	1 47	1 47	1 47	1 47	43
44	1 49	1 49	1 49	1 49	1 49	1 49	1 49	1 49	1 49	1 49	1 49	1 49	1 49	1 49	1 49	1 49	1 50	1 50	1 50	1 50	44
45	1 51	1 51	1 51	1 51	1 51	1 51	1 51	1 51	1 52	1 52	1 52	1 52	1 52	1 52	1 52	1 52	1 52	1 52	1 52	1 52	45
46	1 53	1 54	1 54	1 54	1 54	1 54	1 54	1 54	1 54	1 54	1 54	1 54	1 54	1 54	1 54	1 54	1 54	1 55	1 55	1 55	46
47	1 56	1 56	1 56	1 56	1 56	1 56	1 56	1 56	1 56	1 57	1 57	1 57	1 57	1 57	1 57	1 57	1 57	1 57	1 57	1 57	47
48	1 58	1 58	1 59	1 59	1 59	1 59	1 59	1 59	1 59	1 59	1 59	1 59	1 59	1 59	1 59	1 59	1 59	2 0	2 0	2 0	48
49	2 1	2 1	2 1	2 1	2 1	2 1	2 1	2 1	2 1	2 1	2 2	2 2	2 2	2 2	2 2	2 2	2 2	2 2	2 2	2 2	49
50	2 3	2 3	2 3	2 4	2 4	2 4	2 4	2 4	2 4	2 4	2 4	2 4	2 4	2 4	2 4	2 4	2 4	2 5	2 5	2 5	50
51	2 6	2 6	2 6	2 6	2 6	2 6	2 6	2 6	2 6	2 6	2 7	2 7	2 7	2 7	2 7	2 7	2 7	2 7	2 7	2 7	51
52	2 8	2 8	2 8	2 8	2 9	2 9	2 9	2 9	2 9	2 9	2 9	2 9	2 9	2 9	2 9	2 9	2 9	2 9	2 10	2 10	52
53	2 11	2 11	2 11	2 11	2 11	2 11	2 11	2 11	2 11	2 11	2 11	2 12	2 12	2 12	2 12	2 12	2 12	2 12	2 12	2 12	53
54	2 13	2 13	2 13	2 13	2 14	2 14	2 14	2 14	2 14	2 14	2 14	2 14	2 14	2 14	2 14	2 14	2 14	2 14	2 15	2 15	54
55	2 16	2 16	2 16	2 16	2 16	2 16	2 16	2 16	2 16	2 16	2 16	2 17	2 17	2 17	2 17	2 17	2 17	2 17	2 17	2 17	55
56	2 18	2 18	2 18	2 18	2 18	2 19	2 19	2 19	2 19	2 19	2 19	2 19	2 19	2 19	2 19	2 19	2 19	2 19	2 20	2 20	56
57	2 21	2 21	2 21	2 21	2 21	2 21	2 21	2 21	2 21	2 21	2 21	2 21	2 22	2 22	2 22	2 22	2 22	2 22	2 22	2 22	57
58	2 23	2 23	2 23	2 23	2 23	2 23	2 24	2 24	2 24	2 24	2 24	2 24	2 24	2 24	2 24	2 24	2 24	2 24	2 25	2 25	58
59	2 26	2 26	2 26	2 26	2 26	2 26	2 26	2 26	2 26	2 26	2 26	2 26	2 27	2 27	2 27	2 27	2 27	2 27	2 27	2 27	59
60	2 28	2 28	2 28	2 28	2 28	2 28	2 29	2 29	2 29	2 29	2 29	2 29	2 29	2 29	2 29	2 29	2 29	2 29	2 30	2 30	60
HOURS																					HOURS
1	2 28	2 28	2 28	2 28	2 28	2 28	2 29	2 29	2 29	2 29	2 29	2 29	2 29	2 29	2 29	2 29	2 29	2 29	2 30	2 30	1
2	4 56	4 56	4 56	4 57	4 57	4 57	4 57	4 57	4 57	4 58	4 58	4 58	4 58	4 58	4 58	4 59	4 59	4 59	4 59	4 59	2
3	7 24	7 24	7 25	7 25	7 25	7 25	7 26	7 26	7 26	7 26	7 27	7 27	7 27	7 27	7 28	7 28	7 28	7 28	7 29	7 29	3
4	9 52	9 52	9 53	9 53	9 53	9 54	9 54	9 54	9 55	9 55	9 55	9 56	9 56	9 56	9 57	9 57	9 57	9 58	9 58	9 58	4
5	12 20	12 20	12 21	12 21	12 22	12 22	12 23	12 23	12 23	12 24	12 24	12 25	12 25	12 25	12 26	12 26	12 27	12 27	12 28	12 28	5
6	14 48	14 49	14 49	14 50	14 50	14 51	14 51	14 52	14 52	14 53	14 53	14 54	14 54	14 55	14 55	14 56	14 56	14 57	14 57	14 58	6
7	17 16	17 17	17 17	17 18	17 18	17 19	17 20	17 20	17 21	17 21	17 22	17 22	17 23	17 24	17 24	17 25	17 25	17 26	17 27	17 27	7
8	19 44	19 45	19 45	19 46	19 47	19 47	19 48	19 49	19 49	19 50	19 51	19 51	19 52	19 53	19 53	19 54	19 55	19 55	19 56	19 57	8
9	22 12	22 13	22 14	22 14	22 15	22 16	22 17	22 17	22 18	22 19	22 20	22 20	22 21	22 22	22 23	22 23	22 24	22 25	22 26	22 26	9
10	24 40	24 41	24 42	24 43	24 43	24 44	24 45	24 46	24 47	24 48	24 48	24 49	24 50	24 51	24 52	24 53	24 53	24 54	24 55	24 56	10
11	27 8	27 9	27 10	27 11	27 12	27 13	27 14	27 14	27 15	27 16	27 17	27 18	27 19	27 20	27 21	27 22	27 23	27 24	27 25	27 25	11
12	29 36	29 37	29 38	29 39	29 40	29 41	29 42	29 43	29 44	29 45	29 46	29 47	29 48	29 49	29 50	29 51	29 52	29 53	29 54	29 55	12
13	32 4	32 5	32 6	32 7	32 8	32 9	32 11	32 12	32 13	32 14	32 15	32 16	32 17	32 18	32 19	32 20	32 21	32 22	32 24	32 25	13
14	34 32	34 33	34 34	34 36	34 37	34 38	34 39	34 40	34 41	34 43	34 44	34 45	34 46	34 47	34 48	34 50	34 51	34 52	34 53	34 54	14
15	37 0	37 1	37 3	37 4	37 5	37 6	37 8	37 9	37 10	37 11	37 13	37 14	37 15	37 16	37 18	37 19	37 20	37 21	37 23	37 24	15
16	39 28	39 29	39 31	39 32	39 33	39 35	39 36	39 37	39 39	39 40	39 41	39 43	39 44	39 45	39 47	39 48	39 49	39 51	39 52	39 53	16
17	41 56	41 57	41 59	42 0	42 2	42 3	42 5	42 6	42 7	42 9	42 10	42 12	42 13	42 14	42 16	42 17	42 19	42 20	42 22	42 23	17
18	44 24	44 26	44 27	44 29	44 30	44 32	44 33	44 35	44 36	44 38	44 39	44 41	44 42	44 44	44 45	44 47	44 48	44 50	44 51	44 53	18
19	46 52	46 54	46 55	46 57	46 58	47 0	47 2	47 3	47 5	47 6	47 8	47 9	47 11	47 13	47 14	47 16	47 17	47 19	47 21	47 22	19
20	49 20	49 22	49 23	49 25	49 27	49 28	49 30	49 32	49 33	49 35	49 37	49 38	49 40	49 42	49 43	49 45	49 47	49 48	49 50	49 52	20
21	51 48	51 50	51 52	51 53	51 55	51 57	51 59	52 0	52 2	52 4	52 6	52 7	52 9	52 11	52 13	52 14	52 16	52 18	52 20	52 21	21
22	54 16	54 18	54 20	54 22	54 23	54 25	54 27	54 29	54 31	54 33	54 34	54 36	54 38	54 40	54 42	54 44	54 45	54 47	54 49	54 51	22
23	56 44	56 46	56 48	56 50	56 52	56 54	56 56	56 57	56 59	57 1	57 3	57 5	57 7	57 9	57 11	57 13	57 15	57 17	57 19	57 20	23
24	59 12	59 14	59 16	59 18	59 20	59 22	59 24	59 26	59 28	59 30	59 32	59 34	59 36	59 38	59 40	59 42	59 44	59 46	59 48	59 50	24

Table V Diurnal Motion of the Sun

TIME	24 HOUR TRAVEL 59′ 52″	59′ 54″	59′ 56″	59′ 58″	60′ 0″	60′ 2″	60′ 4″	60′ 6″	60′ 8″	60′ 10″	60′ 12″	60′ 14″	60′ 16″	60′ 18″	60′ 20″	60′ 22″	60′ 24″	60′ 26″	60′ 28″	60′ 30″	TIME
MINUTES	′ ″	′ ″	′ ″	′ ″	′ ″	′ ″	′ ″	′ ″	′ ″	′ ″	′ ″	′ ″	′ ″	′ ″	′ ″	′ ″	′ ″	′ ″	′ ″	′ ″	MINUTES
1	2	2	2	2	3	3	3	3	3	3	3	3	3	3	3	3	3	3	3	3	1
2	5	5	5	5	5	5	5	5	5	5	5	5	5	5	5	5	5	5	5	5	2
3	7	7	7	7	8	8	8	8	8	8	8	8	8	8	8	8	8	8	8	8	3
4	10	10	10	10	10	10	10	10	10	10	10	10	10	10	10	10	10	10	10	10	4
5	12	12	12	12	13	13	13	13	13	13	13	13	13	13	13	13	13	13	13	13	5
6	15	15	15	15	15	15	15	15	15	15	15	15	15	15	15	15	15	15	15	15	6
7	17	17	17	17	18	18	18	18	18	18	18	18	18	18	18	18	18	18	18	18	7
8	20	20	20	20	20	20	20	20	20	20	20	20	20	20	20	20	20	20	20	20	8
9	22	22	22	22	23	23	23	23	23	23	23	23	23	23	23	23	23	23	23	23	9
10	25	25	25	25	25	25	25	25	25	25	25	25	25	25	25	25	25	25	25	25	10
11	27	27	27	27	28	28	28	28	28	28	28	28	28	28	28	28	28	28	28	28	11
12	30	30	30	30	30	30	30	30	30	30	30	30	30	30	30	30	30	30	30	30	12
13	32	32	32	32	33	33	33	33	33	33	33	33	33	33	33	33	33	33	33	33	13
14	35	35	35	35	35	35	35	35	35	35	35	35	35	35	35	35	35	35	35	35	14
15	37	37	37	37	38	38	38	38	38	38	38	38	38	38	38	38	38	38	38	38	15
16	40	40	40	40	40	40	40	40	40	40	40	40	40	40	40	40	40	40	40	40	16
17	42	42	42	42	43	43	43	43	43	43	43	43	43	43	43	43	43	43	43	43	17
18	45	45	45	45	45	45	45	45	45	45	45	45	45	45	45	45	45	45	45	45	18
19	47	47	47	47	48	48	48	48	48	48	48	48	48	48	48	48	48	48	48	48	19
20	50	50	50	50	50	50	50	50	50	50	50	50	50	50	50	50	50	50	50	50	20
21	52	52	52	52	53	53	53	53	53	53	53	53	53	53	53	53	53	53	53	53	21
22	55	55	55	55	55	55	55	55	55	55	55	55	55	55	55	55	55	55	55	55	22
23	57	57	57	57	58	58	58	58	58	58	58	58	58	58	58	58	58	58	58	58	23
24	1 0	1 0	1 0	1 0	1 0	1 0	1 0	1 0	1 0	1 0	1 0	1 0	1 0	1 0	1 0	1 0	1 0	1 0	1 0	1 1	24
25	1 2	1 2	1 2	1 2	1 3	1 3	1 3	1 3	1 3	1 3	1 3	1 3	1 3	1 3	1 3	1 3	1 3	1 3	1 3	1 3	25
26	1 5	1 5	1 5	1 5	1 5	1 5	1 5	1 5	1 5	1 5	1 5	1 5	1 5	1 5	1 5	1 5	1 5	1 5	1 6	1 6	26
27	1 7	1 7	1 7	1 7	1 8	1 8	1 8	1 8	1 8	1 8	1 8	1 8	1 8	1 8	1 8	1 8	1 8	1 8	1 8	1 8	27
28	1 10	1 10	1 10	1 10	1 10	1 10	1 10	1 10	1 10	1 10	1 10	1 10	1 10	1 10	1 10	1 10	1 10	1 11	1 11	1 11	28
29	1 12	1 12	1 12	1 12	1 13	1 13	1 13	1 13	1 13	1 13	1 13	1 13	1 13	1 13	1 13	1 13	1 13	1 13	1 13	1 13	29
30	1 15	1 15	1 15	1 15	1 15	1 15	1 15	1 15	1 15	1 15	1 15	1 15	1 15	1 15	1 15	1 15	1 16	1 16	1 16	1 16	30
31	1 17	1 17	1 17	1 17	1 18	1 18	1 18	1 18	1 18	1 18	1 18	1 18	1 18	1 18	1 18	1 18	1 18	1 18	1 18	1 18	31
32	1 20	1 20	1 20	1 20	1 20	1 20	1 20	1 20	1 20	1 20	1 20	1 20	1 20	1 20	1 20	1 20	1 21	1 21	1 21	1 21	32
33	1 22	1 22	1 22	1 22	1 23	1 23	1 23	1 23	1 23	1 23	1 23	1 23	1 23	1 23	1 23	1 23	1 23	1 23	1 23	1 23	33
34	1 25	1 25	1 25	1 25	1 25	1 25	1 25	1 25	1 25	1 25	1 25	1 25	1 25	1 25	1 25	1 26	1 26	1 26	1 26	1 26	34
35	1 27	1 27	1 27	1 27	1 28	1 28	1 28	1 28	1 28	1 28	1 28	1 28	1 28	1 28	1 28	1 28	1 28	1 28	1 28	1 28	35
36	1 30	1 30	1 30	1 30	1 30	1 30	1 30	1 30	1 30	1 30	1 30	1 30	1 30	1 30	1 31	1 31	1 31	1 31	1 31	1 31	36
37	1 32	1 32	1 32	1 32	1 33	1 33	1 33	1 33	1 33	1 33	1 33	1 33	1 33	1 33	1 33	1 33	1 33	1 33	1 33	1 33	37
38	1 35	1 35	1 35	1 35	1 35	1 35	1 35	1 35	1 35	1 35	1 35	1 35	1 35	1 35	1 36	1 36	1 36	1 36	1 36	1 36	38
39	1 37	1 37	1 37	1 37	1 38	1 38	1 38	1 38	1 38	1 38	1 38	1 38	1 38	1 38	1 38	1 38	1 38	1 38	1 38	1 38	39
40	1 40	1 40	1 40	1 40	1 40	1 40	1 40	1 40	1 40	1 40	1 40	1 40	1 40	1 41	1 41	1 41	1 41	1 41	1 41	1 41	40
41	1 42	1 42	1 42	1 42	1 43	1 43	1 43	1 43	1 43	1 43	1 43	1 43	1 43	1 43	1 43	1 43	1 43	1 43	1 43	1 43	41
42	1 45	1 45	1 45	1 45	1 45	1 45	1 45	1 45	1 45	1 45	1 45	1 45	1 45	1 46	1 46	1 46	1 46	1 46	1 46	1 46	42
43	1 47	1 47	1 47	1 47	1 48	1 48	1 48	1 48	1 48	1 48	1 48	1 48	1 48	1 48	1 48	1 48	1 48	1 48	1 48	1 48	43
44	1 50	1 50	1 50	1 50	1 50	1 50	1 50	1 50	1 50	1 50	1 50	1 50	1 50	1 51	1 51	1 51	1 51	1 51	1 51	1 51	44
45	1 52	1 52	1 52	1 52	1 53	1 53	1 53	1 53	1 53	1 53	1 53	1 53	1 53	1 53	1 53	1 53	1 53	1 53	1 53	1 53	45
46	1 55	1 55	1 55	1 55	1 55	1 55	1 55	1 55	1 55	1 55	1 55	1 55	1 56	1 56	1 56	1 56	1 56	1 56	1 56	1 56	46
47	1 57	1 57	1 57	1 57	1 58	1 58	1 58	1 58	1 58	1 58	1 58	1 58	1 58	1 58	1 58	1 58	1 58	1 58	1 58	1 58	47
48	2 0	2 0	2 0	2 0	2 0	2 0	2 0	2 0	2 0	2 0	2 0	2 0	2 1	2 1	2 1	2 1	2 1	2 1	2 1	2 1	48
49	2 2	2 2	2 2	2 2	2 3	2 3	2 3	2 3	2 3	2 3	2 3	2 3	2 3	2 3	2 3	2 3	2 3	2 3	2 3	2 4	49
50	2 5	2 5	2 5	2 5	2 5	2 5	2 5	2 5	2 5	2 5	2 5	2 5	2 6	2 6	2 6	2 6	2 6	2 6	2 6	2 6	50
51	2 7	2 7	2 7	2 7	2 8	2 8	2 8	2 8	2 8	2 8	2 8	2 8	2 8	2 8	2 8	2 8	2 8	2 8	2 8	2 9	51
52	2 10	2 10	2 10	2 10	2 10	2 10	2 10	2 10	2 10	2 10	2 10	2 11	2 11	2 11	2 11	2 11	2 11	2 11	2 11	2 11	52
53	2 12	2 12	2 12	2 12	2 13	2 13	2 13	2 13	2 13	2 13	2 13	2 13	2 13	2 13	2 13	2 13	2 13	2 13	2 14	2 14	53
54	2 15	2 15	2 15	2 15	2 15	2 15	2 15	2 15	2 15	2 15	2 15	2 16	2 16	2 16	2 16	2 16	2 16	2 16	2 16	2 16	54
55	2 17	2 17	2 17	2 17	2 18	2 18	2 18	2 18	2 18	2 18	2 18	2 18	2 18	2 18	2 18	2 18	2 18	2 18	2 19	2 19	55
56	2 20	2 20	2 20	2 20	2 20	2 20	2 20	2 20	2 20	2 20	2 20	2 21	2 21	2 21	2 21	2 21	2 21	2 21	2 21	2 21	56
57	2 22	2 22	2 22	2 22	2 23	2 23	2 23	2 23	2 23	2 23	2 23	2 23	2 23	2 23	2 23	2 23	2 23	2 23	2 24	2 24	57
58	2 25	2 25	2 25	2 25	2 25	2 25	2 25	2 25	2 25	2 25	2 25	2 26	2 26	2 26	2 26	2 26	2 26	2 26	2 26	2 26	58
59	2 27	2 27	2 27	2 27	2 28	2 28	2 28	2 28	2 28	2 28	2 28	2 28	2 28	2 28	2 28	2 28	2 28	2 29	2 29	2 29	59
60	2 30	2 30	2 30	2 30	2 30	2 30	2 30	2 30	2 30	2 30	2 31	2 31	2 31	2 31	2 31	2 31	2 31	2 31	2 31	2 31	60
HOURS																					HOURS
1	2 30	2 30	2 30	2 30	2 30	2 30	2 30	2 30	2 30	2 30	2 31	2 31	2 31	2 31	2 31	2 31	2 31	2 31	2 31	2 31	1
2	4 59	5 0	5 0	5 0	5 0	5 0	5 0	5 1	5 1	5 1	5 1	5 1	5 1	5 2	5 2	5 2	5 2	5 2	5 2	5 3	2
3	7 29	7 29	7 30	7 30	7 30	7 30	7 31	7 31	7 31	7 31	7 32	7 32	7 32	7 32	7 33	7 33	7 33	7 33	7 34	7 34	3
4	9 59	9 59	9 59	10 0	10 0	10 0	10 1	10 1	10 1	10 2	10 2	10 2	10 3	10 3	10 3	10 4	10 4	10 4	10 5	10 5	4
5	12 28	12 29	12 29	12 30	12 30	12 30	12 31	12 31	12 32	12 32	12 33	12 33	12 33	12 34	12 34	12 35	12 35	12 35	12 36	12 36	5
6	14 58	14 59	14 59	15 0	15 0	15 1	15 1	15 2	15 2	15 3	15 3	15 4	15 4	15 5	15 5	15 6	15 6	15 7	15 7	15 8	6
7	17 28	17 28	17 29	17 29	17 30	17 31	17 31	17 32	17 32	17 33	17 34	17 34	17 35	17 35	17 36	17 36	17 37	17 38	17 38	17 39	7
8	19 57	19 58	19 59	19 59	20 0	20 1	20 1	20 2	20 3	20 3	20 4	20 5	20 5	20 6	20 7	20 7	20 8	20 9	20 9	20 10	8
9	22 27	22 28	22 29	22 29	22 30	22 31	22 32	22 32	22 33	22 34	22 35	22 35	22 36	22 37	22 38	22 38	22 39	22 40	22 41	22 41	9
10	24 57	24 58	24 58	24 59	25 0	25 1	25 2	25 3	25 3	25 4	25 5	25 6	25 7	25 8	25 8	25 9	25 10	25 11	25 12	25 13	10
11	27 26	27 27	27 28	27 29	27 30	27 31	27 32	27 33	27 34	27 35	27 36	27 36	27 37	27 38	27 39	27 40	27 41	27 42	27 43	27 44	11
12	29 56	29 57	29 58	29 59	30 0	30 1	30 2	30 3	30 4	30 5	30 6	30 7	30 8	30 9	30 10	30 11	30 12	30 13	30 14	30 15	12
13	32 26	32 27	32 28	32 29	32 30	32 31	32 32	32 33	32 34	32 35	32 37	32 38	32 39	32 40	32 41	32 42	32 43	32 44	32 45	32 46	13
14	34 55	34 57	34 58	34 59	35 0	35 1	35 2	35 4	35 5	35 6	35 7	35 8	35 9	35 11	35 12	35 13	35 14	35 15	35 16	35 18	14
15	37 25	37 26	37 28	37 29	37 30	37 31	37 33	37 34	37 35	37 36	37 38	37 39	37 40	37 41	37 43	37 44	37 45	37 46	37 48	37 49	15
16	39 55	39 56	39 57	39 59	40 0	40 1	40 3	40 4	40 5	40 7	40 8	40 9	40 11	40 12	40 13	40 15	40 16	40 17	40 19	40 20	16
17	42 24	42 26	42 27	42 29	42 30	42 31	42 33	42 34	42 36	42 37	42 39	42 40	42 41	42 43	42 44	42 46	42 47	42 48	42 50	42 51	17
18	44 54	44 56	44 57	44 59	45 0	45 2	45 3	45 5	45 6	45 8	45 9	45 11	45 12	45 14	45 15	45 17	45 18	45 20	45 21	45 23	18
19	47 24	47 25	47 27	47 28	47 30	47 32	47 33	47 35	47 36	47 38	47 40	47 41	47 43	47 44	47 46	47 47	47 49	47 51	47 52	47 54	19
20	49 53	49 55	49 57	49 58	50 0	50 2	50 3	50 5	50 7	50 8	50 10	50 12	50 13	50 15	50 17	50 18	50 20	50 22	50 23	50 25	20
21	52 23	52 25	52 27	52 28	52 30	52 32	52 34	52 35	52 37	52 39	52 41	52 42	52 44	52 46	52 48	52 49	52 51	52 53	52 55	52 56	21
22	54 53	54 55	54 56	54 58	55 0	55 2	55 4	55 6	55 7	55 9	55 11	55 13	55 15	55 17	55 18	55 20	55 22	55 24	55 26	55 28	22
23	57 22	57 24	57 26	57 28	57 30	57 32	57 34	57 36	57 38	57 40	57 42	57 43	57 45	57 47	57 49	57 51	57 53	57 55	57 57	57 59	23
24	59 52	59 54	59 56	59 58	60 0	60 2	60 4	60 6	60 8	60 10	60 12	60 14	60 16	60 18	60 20	60 22	60 24	60 26	60 28	60 30	24

Table V Diurnal Motion of the Sun

TIME	24 HOUR TRAVEL																				TIME
	' "	' "	' "	' "	' "	' "	' "	' "	' "	' "	' "	' "	' "	' "	' "	' "	' "	' "	' "	' "	
	60 32	60 34	60 36	60 38	60 40	60 42	60 44	60 46	60 48	60 50	60 52	60 54	60 56	60 58	61 0	61 2	61 4	61 6	61 8	61 10	
	' "	' "	' "	' "	' "	' "	' "	' "	' "	' "	' "	' "	' "	' "	' "	' "	' "	' "	' "	' "	
MINUTES																					MINUTES
1	3	3	3	3	3	3	3	3	3	3	3	3	3	3	3	3	3	3	3	3	1
2	5	5	5	5	5	5	5	5	5	5	5	5	5	5	5	5	5	5	5	5	2
3	8	8	8	8	8	8	8	8	8	8	8	8	8	8	8	8	8	8	8	8	3
4	10	10	10	10	10	10	10	10	10	10	10	10	10	10	10	10	10	10	10	10	4
5	13	13	13	13	13	13	13	13	13	13	13	13	13	13	13	13	13	13	13	13	5
6	15	15	15	15	15	15	15	15	15	15	15	15	15	15	15	15	15	15	15	15	6
7	18	18	18	18	18	18	18	18	18	18	18	18	18	18	18	18	18	18	18	18	7
8	20	20	20	20	20	20	20	20	20	20	20	20	20	20	20	20	20	20	20	20	8
9	23	23	23	23	23	23	23	23	23	23	23	23	23	23	23	23	23	23	23	23	9
10	25	25	25	25	25	25	25	25	25	25	25	25	25	25	25	25	25	25	25	25	10
11	28	28	28	28	28	28	28	28	28	28	28	28	28	28	28	28	28	28	28	28	11
12	30	30	30	30	30	30	30	30	30	30	30	30	30	30	31	31	31	31	31	31	12
13	33	33	33	33	33	33	33	33	33	33	33	33	33	33	33	33	33	33	33	33	13
14	35	35	35	35	35	35	35	35	35	35	36	36	36	36	36	36	36	36	36	36	14
15	38	38	38	38	38	38	38	38	38	38	38	38	38	38	38	38	38	38	38	38	15
16	40	40	40	40	40	40	40	41	41	41	41	41	41	41	41	41	41	41	41	41	16
17	43	43	43	43	43	43	43	43	43	43	43	43	43	43	43	43	43	43	43	43	17
18	45	45	45	45	46	46	46	46	46	46	46	46	46	46	46	46	46	46	46	46	18
19	48	48	48	48	48	48	48	48	48	48	48	48	48	48	48	48	48	48	48	48	19
20	50	50	51	51	51	51	51	51	51	51	51	51	51	51	51	51	51	51	51	51	20
21	53	53	53	53	53	53	53	53	53	53	53	53	53	53	53	53	53	53	53	54	21
22	55	56	56	56	56	56	56	56	56	56	56	56	56	56	56	56	56	56	56	56	22
23	58	58	58	58	58	58	58	58	58	58	58	58	58	58	58	58	59	59	59	59	23
24	1 1	1 1	1 1	1 1	1 1	1 1	1 1	1 1	1 1	1 1	1 1	1 1	1 1	1 1	1 1	1 1	1 1	1 1	1 1	1 1	24
25	1 3	1 3	1 3	1 3	1 3	1 3	1 3	1 3	1 3	1 3	1 3	1 3	1 3	1 4	1 4	1 4	1 4	1 4	1 4	1 4	25
26	1 6	1 6	1 6	1 6	1 6	1 6	1 6	1 6	1 6	1 6	1 6	1 6	1 6	1 6	1 6	1 6	1 6	1 6	1 6	1 6	26
27	1 8	1 8	1 8	1 8	1 8	1 8	1 8	1 8	1 8	1 8	1 8	1 9	1 9	1 9	1 9	1 9	1 9	1 9	1 9	1 9	27
28	1 11	1 11	1 11	1 11	1 11	1 11	1 11	1 11	1 11	1 11	1 11	1 11	1 11	1 11	1 11	1 11	1 11	1 11	1 11	1 11	28
29	1 13	1 13	1 13	1 13	1 13	1 13	1 13	1 13	1 13	1 14	1 14	1 14	1 14	1 14	1 14	1 14	1 14	1 14	1 14	1 14	29
30	1 16	1 16	1 16	1 16	1 16	1 16	1 16	1 16	1 16	1 16	1 16	1 16	1 16	1 16	1 16	1 16	1 16	1 16	1 16	1 16	30
31	1 18	1 18	1 18	1 18	1 18	1 18	1 18	1 18	1 19	1 19	1 19	1 19	1 19	1 19	1 19	1 19	1 19	1 19	1 19	1 19	31
32	1 21	1 21	1 21	1 21	1 21	1 21	1 21	1 21	1 21	1 21	1 21	1 21	1 21	1 21	1 21	1 21	1 21	1 21	1 22	1 22	32
33	1 23	1 23	1 23	1 23	1 23	1 23	1 24	1 24	1 24	1 24	1 24	1 24	1 24	1 24	1 24	1 24	1 24	1 24	1 24	1 24	33
34	1 26	1 26	1 26	1 26	1 26	1 26	1 26	1 26	1 26	1 26	1 26	1 26	1 26	1 26	1 26	1 26	1 27	1 27	1 27	1 27	34
35	1 28	1 28	1 28	1 28	1 28	1 29	1 29	1 29	1 29	1 29	1 29	1 29	1 29	1 29	1 29	1 29	1 29	1 29	1 29	1 29	35
36	1 31	1 31	1 31	1 31	1 31	1 31	1 31	1 31	1 31	1 31	1 31	1 31	1 31	1 31	1 32	1 32	1 32	1 32	1 32	1 32	36
37	1 33	1 33	1 33	1 33	1 34	1 34	1 34	1 34	1 34	1 34	1 34	1 34	1 34	1 34	1 34	1 34	1 34	1 34	1 34	1 34	37
38	1 36	1 36	1 36	1 36	1 36	1 36	1 36	1 36	1 36	1 36	1 36	1 36	1 36	1 37	1 37	1 37	1 37	1 37	1 37	1 37	38
39	1 38	1 38	1 38	1 39	1 39	1 39	1 39	1 39	1 39	1 39	1 39	1 39	1 39	1 39	1 39	1 39	1 39	1 39	1 39	1 39	39
40	1 41	1 41	1 41	1 41	1 41	1 41	1 41	1 41	1 41	1 41	1 41	1 42	1 42	1 42	1 42	1 42	1 42	1 42	1 42	1 42	40
41	1 43	1 43	1 44	1 44	1 44	1 44	1 44	1 44	1 44	1 44	1 44	1 44	1 44	1 44	1 44	1 44	1 44	1 44	1 44	1 44	41
42	1 46	1 46	1 46	1 46	1 46	1 46	1 46	1 46	1 46	1 46	1 47	1 47	1 47	1 47	1 47	1 47	1 47	1 47	1 47	1 47	42
43	1 48	1 49	1 49	1 49	1 49	1 49	1 49	1 49	1 49	1 49	1 49	1 49	1 49	1 49	1 49	1 49	1 49	1 49	1 50	1 50	43
44	1 51	1 51	1 51	1 51	1 51	1 51	1 51	1 51	1 51	1 52	1 52	1 52	1 52	1 52	1 52	1 52	1 52	1 52	1 52	1 52	44
45	1 54	1 54	1 54	1 54	1 54	1 54	1 54	1 54	1 54	1 54	1 54	1 54	1 54	1 54	1 54	1 54	1 55	1 55	1 55	1 55	45
46	1 56	1 56	1 56	1 56	1 56	1 56	1 56	1 56	1 57	1 57	1 57	1 57	1 57	1 57	1 57	1 57	1 57	1 57	1 57	1 57	46
47	1 59	1 59	1 59	1 59	1 59	1 59	1 59	1 59	1 59	1 59	1 59	1 59	1 59	1 59	1 59	2 0	2 0	2 0	2 0	2 0	47
48	2 1	2 1	2 1	2 1	2 1	2 1	2 1	2 2	2 2	2 2	2 2	2 2	2 2	2 2	2 2	2 2	2 2	2 2	2 2	2 2	48
49	2 4	2 4	2 4	2 4	2 4	2 4	2 4	2 4	2 4	2 4	2 4	2 4	2 4	2 4	2 5	2 5	2 5	2 5	2 5	2 5	49
50	2 6	2 6	2 6	2 6	2 6	2 6	2 7	2 7	2 7	2 7	2 7	2 7	2 7	2 7	2 7	2 7	2 7	2 7	2 7	2 7	50
51	2 9	2 9	2 9	2 9	2 9	2 9	2 9	2 9	2 9	2 9	2 9	2 9	2 9	2 10	2 10	2 10	2 10	2 10	2 10	2 10	51
52	2 11	2 11	2 11	2 11	2 11	2 12	2 12	2 12	2 12	2 12	2 12	2 12	2 12	2 12	2 12	2 12	2 12	2 12	2 12	2 13	52
53	2 14	2 14	2 14	2 14	2 14	2 14	2 14	2 14	2 14	2 14	2 14	2 14	2 15	2 15	2 15	2 15	2 15	2 15	2 15	2 15	53
54	2 16	2 16	2 16	2 16	2 17	2 17	2 17	2 17	2 17	2 17	2 17	2 17	2 17	2 17	2 17	2 17	2 17	2 17	2 18	2 18	54
55	2 19	2 19	2 19	2 19	2 19	2 19	2 19	2 19	2 19	2 19	2 19	2 20	2 20	2 20	2 20	2 20	2 20	2 20	2 20	2 20	55
56	2 21	2 21	2 21	2 21	2 22	2 22	2 22	2 22	2 22	2 22	2 22	2 22	2 22	2 22	2 22	2 22	2 22	2 23	2 23	2 23	56
57	2 24	2 24	2 24	2 24	2 24	2 24	2 24	2 24	2 24	2 24	2 25	2 25	2 25	2 25	2 25	2 25	2 25	2 25	2 25	2 25	57
58	2 26	2 26	2 26	2 27	2 27	2 27	2 27	2 27	2 27	2 27	2 27	2 27	2 27	2 27	2 27	2 27	2 28	2 28	2 28	2 28	58
59	2 29	2 29	2 29	2 29	2 29	2 29	2 29	2 29	2 29	2 30	2 30	2 30	2 30	2 30	2 30	2 30	2 30	2 30	2 30	2 30	59
60	2 31	2 31	2 32	2 32	2 32	2 32	2 32	2 32	2 32	2 32	2 32	2 32	2 32	2 32	2 33	2 33	2 33	2 33	2 33	2 33	60
HOURS																					HOURS
1	2 31	2 31	2 32	2 32	2 32	2 32	2 32	2 32	2 32	2 32	2 32	2 32	2 32	2 32	2 33	2 33	2 33	2 33	2 33	2 33	1
2	5 3	5 3	5 3	5 3	5 3	5 4	5 4	5 4	5 4	5 4	5 4	5 5	5 5	5 5	5 5	5 5	5 5	5 6	5 6	5 6	2
3	7 34	7 34	7 35	7 35	7 35	7 35	7 36	7 36	7 36	7 36	7 37	7 37	7 37	7 37	7 38	7 38	7 38	7 38	7 39	7 39	3
4	10 5	10 6	10 6	10 6	10 7	10 7	10 7	10 8	10 8	10 8	10 9	10 9	10 9	10 10	10 10	10 10	10 11	10 11	10 11	10 12	4
5	12 37	12 37	12 38	12 38	12 38	12 39	12 39	12 40	12 40	12 40	12 41	12 41	12 42	12 42	12 43	12 43	12 43	12 44	12 44	12 45	5
6	15 8	15 9	15 9	15 10	15 10	15 11	15 11	15 12	15 12	15 13	15 13	15 14	15 14	15 15	15 15	15 16	15 16	15 17	15 17	15 18	6
7	17 39	17 40	17 41	17 41	17 42	17 42	17 43	17 43	17 44	17 45	17 45	17 46	17 46	17 47	17 48	17 48	17 49	17 49	17 50	17 50	7
8	20 11	20 11	20 12	20 13	20 13	20 14	20 15	20 15	20 16	20 17	20 17	20 18	20 19	20 19	20 20	20 21	20 21	20 22	20 23	20 23	8
9	22 42	22 43	22 44	22 44	22 45	22 46	22 47	22 47	22 48	22 49	22 50	22 50	22 51	22 52	22 53	22 53	22 54	22 55	22 56	22 56	9
10	25 13	25 14	25 15	25 16	25 17	25 18	25 18	25 19	25 20	25 21	25 22	25 23	25 23	25 24	25 25	25 26	25 27	25 28	25 28	25 29	10
11	27 45	27 46	27 47	27 47	27 48	27 49	27 50	27 51	27 52	27 53	27 54	27 55	27 56	27 57	27 58	27 58	27 59	28 0	28 1	28 2	11
12	30 16	30 17	30 18	30 19	30 20	30 21	30 22	30 23	30 24	30 25	30 26	30 27	30 28	30 29	30 30	30 31	30 32	30 33	30 34	30 35	12
13	32 47	32 48	32 50	32 51	32 52	32 53	32 54	32 55	32 56	32 57	32 58	32 59	33 0	33 1	33 3	33 4	33 5	33 6	33 7	33 8	13
14	35 19	35 20	35 21	35 22	35 23	35 25	35 26	35 27	35 28	35 29	35 30	35 32	35 33	35 34	35 35	35 36	35 37	35 39	35 40	35 41	14
15	37 50	37 51	37 53	37 54	37 55	37 56	37 58	37 59	38 0	38 1	38 3	38 4	38 5	38 6	38 8	38 9	38 10	38 11	38 13	38 14	15
16	40 21	40 23	40 24	40 25	40 27	40 28	40 29	40 31	40 32	40 33	40 35	40 36	40 37	40 39	40 40	40 41	40 43	40 44	40 45	40 47	16
17	42 53	42 54	42 56	42 57	42 58	43 0	43 1	43 3	43 4	43 5	43 7	43 8	43 10	43 11	43 13	43 14	43 15	43 17	43 18	43 20	17
18	45 24	45 26	45 27	45 29	45 30	45 32	45 33	45 35	45 36	45 38	45 39	45 41	45 42	45 44	45 45	45 47	45 48	45 50	45 51	45 53	18
19	47 55	47 57	47 59	48 0	48 2	48 3	48 5	48 6	48 8	48 10	48 11	48 13	48 14	48 16	48 18	48 19	48 21	48 22	48 24	48 25	19
20	50 27	50 28	50 30	50 32	50 33	50 35	50 37	50 38	50 40	50 42	50 43	50 45	50 47	50 48	50 50	50 52	50 53	50 55	50 57	50 58	20
21	52 58	53 0	53 2	53 3	53 5	53 7	53 9	53 10	53 12	53 14	53 16	53 17	53 19	53 21	53 23	53 24	53 26	53 28	53 30	53 31	21
22	55 29	55 31	55 33	55 35	55 37	55 39	55 40	55 42	55 44	55 46	55 48	55 50	55 51	55 53	55 55	55 57	55 59	56 1	56 2	56 4	22
23	58 1	58 3	58 5	58 6	58 8	58 10	58 12	58 14	58 16	58 18	58 20	58 22	58 24	58 26	58 28	58 29	58 31	58 33	58 35	58 37	23
24	60 32	60 34	60 36	60 38	60 40	60 42	60 44	60 46	60 48	60 50	60 52	60 54	60 56	60 58	61 0	61 2	61 4	61 6	61 8	61 10	24

Table VI Semidiurnal Motion of the Moon

12 HOUR TRAVEL

TIME	5° 55'	5° 56'	5° 57'	5° 58'	5° 59'	6° 0'	6° 1'	6° 2'	6° 3'	6° 4'	6° 5'	6° 6'	6° 7'	6° 8'	6° 9'	TIME
MINUTES 1	0 30	0 30	0 30	0 30	0 30	0 30	0 30	0 30	0 30	0 30	0 30	0 31	0 31	0 31	0 31	1
2	0 59	0 59	1 0	1 0	1 0	1 0	1 0	1 0	1 0	1 0	1 1	1 1	1 1	1 1	1 1	2
3	1 29	1 29	1 29	1 30	1 30	1 30	1 30	1 31	1 31	1 31	1 31	1 31	1 31	1 31	1 31	3
4	1 58	1 59	1 59	1 59	2 0	2 0	2 0	2 1	2 1	2 1	2 1	2 2	2 2	2 2	2 2	4
5	2 28	2 28	2 29	2 29	2 29	2 30	2 30	2 30	2 31	2 31	2 32	2 32	2 33	2 33	2 34	5
6	2 57	2 58	2 58	2 59	2 59	3 0	3 0	3 0	3 1	3 1	3 2	3 2	3 3	3 3	3 4	6
7	3 27	3 28	3 28	3 29	3 29	3 30	3 31	3 31	3 32	3 32	3 33	3 34	3 34	3 35	3 35	7
8	3 57	3 57	3 58	3 58	3 59	4 0	4 1	4 1	4 2	4 3	4 3	4 4	4 5	4 5	4 6	8
9	4 26	4 27	4 28	4 28	4 29	4 30	4 30	4 31	4 31	4 32	4 33	4 34	4 35	4 36	4 37	9
10	4 56	4 57	4 57	4 58	4 59	5 0	5 1	5 2	5 2	5 3	5 4	5 5	5 6	5 7	5 8	10
11	5 25	5 26	5 27	5 28	5 29	5 30	5 31	5 32	5 33	5 34	5 35	5 35	5 36	5 37	5 38	11
12	5 55	5 56	5 57	5 58	5 59	6 0	6 1	6 2	6 3	6 4	6 5	6 6	6 7	6 8	6 9	12
13	6 25	6 26	6 27	6 28	6 29	6 30	6 31	6 32	6 33	6 34	6 35	6 36	6 38	6 39	6 40	13
14	6 54	6 55	6 57	6 58	6 59	7 0	7 1	7 2	7 3	7 4	7 5	7 6	7 8	7 9	7 10	14
15	7 24	7 25	7 26	7 27	7 29	7 30	7 31	7 32	7 34	7 35	7 36	7 38	7 39	7 40	7 41	15
16	7 53	7 55	7 56	7 57	7 59	8 0	8 1	8 3	8 4	8 5	8 7	8 8	8 9	8 11	8 12	16
17	8 23	8 24	8 26	8 27	8 29	8 30	8 31	8 33	8 34	8 36	8 37	8 38	8 40	8 41	8 43	17
18	8 52	8 54	8 55	8 57	8 58	9 0	9 1	9 3	9 4	9 6	9 7	9 9	9 10	9 12	9 13	18
19	9 22	9 24	9 25	9 27	9 28	9 30	9 32	9 33	9 35	9 36	9 38	9 39	9 41	9 43	9 44	19
20	9 52	9 53	9 55	9 57	9 58	10 0	10 2	10 3	10 5	10 7	10 8	10 10	10 12	10 13	10 15	20
21	10 21	10 23	10 25	10 26	10 28	10 30	10 32	10 33	10 35	10 37	10 39	10 40	10 42	10 44	10 46	21
22	10 51	10 53	10 54	10 56	10 58	11 0	11 2	11 4	11 5	11 7	11 9	11 11	11 13	11 15	11 16	22
23	11 20	11 22	11 24	11 26	11 28	11 30	11 32	11 34	11 36	11 38	11 40	11 41	11 43	11 45	11 47	23
24	11 50	11 52	11 54	11 56	11 58	12 0	12 2	12 4	12 6	12 8	12 10	12 12	12 14	12 16	12 18	24
25	12 20	12 22	12 24	12 26	12 28	12 30	12 32	12 34	12 36	12 38	12 40	12 42	12 45	12 47	12 49	25
26	12 49	12 51	12 53	12 56	12 58	13 0	13 2	13 4	13 6	13 9	13 11	13 13	13 15	13 17	13 19	26
27	13 19	13 21	13 23	13 25	13 28	13 30	13 32	13 34	13 37	13 39	13 41	13 43	13 46	13 48	13 50	27
28	13 48	13 51	13 53	13 55	13 58	14 0	14 2	14 5	14 7	14 9	14 12	14 14	14 16	14 19	14 21	28
29	14 18	14 20	14 23	14 25	14 28	14 30	14 32	14 35	14 37	14 40	14 42	14 44	14 47	14 49	14 52	29
30	14 47	14 50	14 52	14 55	14 57	15 0	15 2	15 5	15 7	15 10	15 12	15 15	15 17	15 20	15 22	30
31	15 17	15 20	15 22	15 25	15 27	15 30	15 33	15 35	15 38	15 40	15 43	15 45	15 48	15 51	15 53	31
32	15 47	15 49	15 52	15 55	15 57	16 0	16 3	16 5	16 8	16 11	16 13	16 16	16 19	16 21	16 24	32
33	16 16	16 19	16 22	16 24	16 27	16 30	16 33	16 35	16 38	16 41	16 44	16 46	16 49	16 52	16 55	33
34	16 46	16 49	16 52	16 54	16 57	17 0	17 3	17 6	17 8	17 11	17 14	17 17	17 20	17 23	17 26	34
35	17 15	17 18	17 21	17 24	17 27	17 30	17 33	17 36	17 39	17 42	17 45	17 48	17 50	17 53	17 56	35
36	17 45	17 48	17 51	17 54	17 57	18 0	18 3	18 6	18 9	18 12	18 15	18 18	18 21	18 24	18 27	36
37	18 15	18 18	18 21	18 24	18 27	18 30	18 33	18 36	18 39	18 42	18 45	18 49	18 52	18 55	18 58	37
38	18 44	18 47	18 50	18 54	18 57	19 0	19 3	19 6	19 9	19 13	19 16	19 19	19 22	19 25	19 29	38
39	19 14	19 17	19 20	19 23	19 27	19 30	19 33	19 37	19 40	19 43	19 46	19 49	19 53	19 56	19 59	39
40	19 43	19 47	19 50	19 53	19 57	20 0	20 3	20 7	20 10	20 13	20 17	20 20	20 23	20 27	20 30	40
41	20 13	20 16	20 20	20 23	20 27	20 30	20 33	20 37	20 40	20 44	20 47	20 50	20 54	20 57	21 1	41
42	20 42	20 46	20 49	20 53	20 56	21 0	21 4	21 7	21 11	21 14	21 18	21 21	21 24	21 28	21 31	42
43	21 12	21 16	21 19	21 23	21 26	21 30	21 34	21 37	21 41	21 44	21 48	21 52	21 55	21 59	22 2	43
44	21 42	21 45	21 49	21 53	21 56	22 0	22 4	22 7	22 11	22 15	22 18	22 22	22 26	22 29	22 33	44
45	22 11	22 15	22 19	22 23	22 26	22 30	22 34	22 38	22 41	22 45	22 49	22 53	22 56	23 0	23 4	45
46	22 41	22 45	22 49	22 52	22 56	23 0	23 4	23 8	23 12	23 15	23 19	23 23	23 27	23 31	23 35	46
47	23 10	23 14	23 18	23 22	23 26	23 30	23 34	23 38	23 42	23 46	23 50	23 53	23 57	24 1	24 5	47
48	23 40	23 44	23 48	23 52	23 56	24 0	24 4	24 8	24 12	24 16	24 20	24 24	24 28	24 32	24 36	48
49	24 10	24 14	24 18	24 22	24 26	24 30	24 34	24 38	24 42	24 46	24 50	24 55	24 59	25 3	25 7	49
50	24 39	24 43	24 47	24 52	24 56	25 0	25 4	25 8	25 12	25 17	25 21	25 25	25 29	25 33	25 37	50
51	25 9	25 13	25 17	25 22	25 26	25 30	25 34	25 38	25 43	25 47	25 51	25 56	26 0	26 4	26 8	51
52	25 38	25 43	25 47	25 51	25 56	26 0	26 4	26 9	26 13	26 17	26 22	26 26	26 30	26 35	26 39	52
53	26 8	26 12	26 17	26 21	26 26	26 30	26 34	26 39	26 43	26 48	26 52	26 57	27 1	27 5	27 10	53
54	26 38	26 42	26 46	26 51	26 56	27 0	27 4	27 9	27 13	27 18	27 23	27 27	27 31	27 36	27 41	54
55	27 7	27 12	27 16	27 21	27 25	27 30	27 35	27 39	27 44	27 48	27 53	27 57	28 2	28 7	28 11	55
56	27 37	27 41	27 46	27 51	27 55	28 0	28 5	28 9	28 14	28 19	28 23	28 28	28 33	28 37	28 42	56
57	28 6	28 11	28 16	28 20	28 25	28 30	28 35	28 39	28 44	28 49	28 54	28 58	29 3	29 8	29 13	57
58	28 36	28 41	28 45	28 50	28 55	29 0	29 5	29 10	29 15	29 19	29 24	29 29	29 34	29 39	29 44	58
59	29 5	29 10	29 15	29 20	29 25	29 30	29 35	29 40	29 45	29 50	29 55	30 0	30 4	30 9	30 14	59
60	29 35	29 40	29 45	29 50	29 55	30 0	30 5	30 10	30 15	30 20	30 25	30 30	30 35	30 40	30 45	60
HOURS 1	29 35	29 40	29 45	29 50	29 55	30 0	30 5	30 10	30 15	30 20	30 25	30 30	30 35	30 40	30 45	1
2	59 10	59 20	59 30	59 40	59 50	60 0	1 0 10	1 0 20	1 0 30	1 0 40	1 0 50	1 1 0	1 1 10	1 1 20	1 1 30	2
3	1 28 45	1 29 0	1 29 15	1 29 30	1 29 45	1 30 0	1 30 15	1 30 30	1 30 45	1 31 0	1 31 15	1 31 30	1 31 45	1 32 0	1 32 15	3
4	1 58 20	1 58 40	1 59 0	1 59 20	1 59 40	2 0 0	2 0 20	2 0 40	2 1 0	2 1 20	2 1 40	2 2 0	2 2 20	2 2 40	2 3 0	4
5	2 27 55	2 28 20	2 28 45	2 29 10	2 29 35	2 30 0	2 30 25	2 30 50	2 31 15	2 31 40	2 32 5	2 32 30	2 32 55	2 33 20	2 33 45	5
6	2 57 30	2 58 0	2 58 30	2 59 0	2 59 30	3 0 0	3 0 30	3 1 0	3 1 30	3 2 0	3 2 30	3 3 0	3 3 30	3 4 0	3 4 30	6
7	3 27 5	3 27 40	3 28 15	3 28 50	3 29 25	3 30 0	3 30 35	3 31 10	3 31 45	3 32 20	3 32 55	3 33 30	3 34 5	3 34 40	3 35 15	7
8	3 56 40	3 57 20	3 58 0	3 58 40	3 59 20	4 0 0	4 0 40	4 1 20	4 2 0	4 2 40	4 3 20	4 4 0	4 4 40	4 5 20	4 6 0	8
9	4 26 15	4 27 0	4 27 45	4 28 30	4 29 15	4 30 0	4 30 45	4 31 30	4 32 15	4 33 0	4 33 45	4 34 30	4 35 15	4 36 0	4 36 45	9
10	4 55 50	4 56 40	4 57 30	4 58 20	4 59 10	5 0 0	5 0 50	5 1 40	5 2 30	5 3 20	5 4 10	5 5 0	5 5 50	5 6 40	5 7 30	10
11	5 25 25	5 26 20	5 27 15	5 28 10	5 29 5	5 30 0	5 30 55	5 31 50	5 32 45	5 33 40	5 34 35	5 35 30	5 36 25	5 37 20	5 38 15	11
12	5 55 0	5 56 0	5 57 0	5 58 0	5 59 0	6 0 0	6 1 0	6 2 0	6 3 0	6 4 0	6 5 0	6 6 0	6 7 0	6 8 0	6 9 0	12

Table VI Semidiurnal Motion of the Moon

	12 HOUR TRAVEL															
TIME	6° 10'	6° 11'	6° 12'	6° 13'	6° 14'	6° 15'	6° 16'	6° 17'	6° 18'	6° 19'	6° 20'	6° 21'	6° 22'	6° 23'	6° 24'	TIME
MINUTES																**MINUTES**
1	0 31	0 31	0 31	0 31	0 31	0 31	0 31	0 31	0 32	0 32	0 32	0 32	0 32	0 32	0 32	1
2	1 2	1 2	1 2	1 2	1 2	1 3	1 3	1 3	1 3	1 3	1 3	1 4	1 4	1 4	1 4	2
3	1 33	1 33	1 33	1 33	1 34	1 34	1 34	1 34	1 34	1 34	1 35	1 35	1 35	1 36	1 36	3
4	2 3	2 4	2 4	2 4	2 5	2 5	2 5	2 6	2 6	2 6	2 7	2 7	2 7	2 8	2 8	4
5	2 34	2 35	2 35	2 35	2 36	2 36	2 37	2 37	2 38	2 38	2 38	2 39	2 39	2 40	2 40	5
6	3 5	3 5	3 6	3 7	3 7	3 8	3 8	3 8	3 9	3 9	3 10	3 11	3 11	3 11	3 12	6
7	3 36	3 36	3 37	3 38	3 38	3 39	3 39	3 40	3 41	3 41	3 42	3 42	3 43	3 43	3 44	7
8	4 7	4 7	4 8	4 9	4 9	4 10	4 11	4 11	4 12	4 13	4 13	4 14	4 14	4 15	4 16	8
9	4 38	4 38	4 39	4 40	4 41	4 41	4 42	4 43	4 43	4 44	4 45	4 46	4 46	4 47	4 48	9
10	5 8	5 9	5 10	5 11	5 12	5 12	5 13	5 14	5 15	5 15	5 16	5 17	5 17	5 18	5 19	10
11	5 39	5 40	5 41	5 42	5 43	5 44	5 45	5 46	5 46	5 47	5 48	5 49	5 50	5 51	5 52	11
12	6 10	6 11	6 12	6 13	6 14	6 15	6 16	6 17	6 18	6 19	6 20	6 21	6 22	6 23	6 24	12
13	6 41	6 42	6 43	6 44	6 45	6 46	6 47	6 48	6 49	6 51	6 52	6 53	6 54	6 55	6 56	13
14	7 12	7 13	7 14	7 15	7 16	7 17	7 19	7 20	7 21	7 22	7 23	7 24	7 26	7 27	7 28	14
15	7 42	7 44	7 45	7 46	7 47	7 49	7 50	7 51	7 53	7 54	7 55	7 56	7 57	7 59	8 0	15
16	8 13	8 15	8 16	8 17	8 19	8 20	8 21	8 23	8 24	8 25	8 27	8 28	8 29	8 31	8 32	16
17	8 44	8 46	8 47	8 48	8 50	8 51	8 53	8 54	8 55	8 57	8 58	9 0	9 1	9 3	9 4	17
18	9 15	9 16	9 18	9 19	9 21	9 22	9 24	9 25	9 27	9 28	9 30	9 31	9 33	9 34	9 36	18
19	9 46	9 47	9 49	9 51	9 52	9 54	9 55	9 57	9 58	10 0	10 2	10 3	10 5	10 6	10 8	19
20	10 17	10 18	10 20	10 22	10 23	10 25	10 27	10 28	10 30	10 32	10 33	10 35	10 37	10 38	10 40	20
21	10 47	10 49	10 51	10 53	10 54	10 56	10 58	11 0	11 1	11 3	11 5	11 7	11 8	11 10	11 12	21
22	11 18	11 20	11 22	11 24	11 26	11 27	11 29	11 31	11 33	11 35	11 37	11 38	11 40	11 42	11 44	22
23	11 49	11 51	11 53	11 55	11 57	11 59	12 1	12 3	12 4	12 6	12 8	12 10	12 12	12 14	12 16	23
24	12 20	12 22	12 24	12 26	12 28	12 30	12 32	12 34	12 36	12 38	12 40	12 42	12 44	12 46	12 48	24
25	12 51	12 53	12 55	12 57	12 59	13 1	13 3	13 5	13 7	13 10	13 12	13 14	13 16	13 18	13 20	25
26	13 22	13 24	13 26	13 28	13 30	13 32	13 35	13 37	13 39	13 41	13 43	13 45	13 48	13 50	13 52	26
27	13 52	13 55	13 57	13 59	14 1	14 4	14 6	14 8	14 10	14 13	14 15	14 17	14 19	14 22	14 24	27
28	14 23	14 26	14 28	14 30	14 33	14 35	14 37	14 40	14 42	14 44	14 47	14 49	14 51	14 54	14 56	28
29	14 54	14 57	14 59	15 1	15 4	15 6	15 9	15 11	15 13	15 16	15 18	15 21	15 23	15 26	15 28	29
30	15 25	15 27	15 30	15 32	15 35	15 37	15 40	15 42	15 45	15 47	15 50	15 52	15 55	15 57	16 0	30
31	15 56	15 58	16 1	16 4	16 6	16 9	16 11	16 14	16 16	16 19	16 22	16 24	16 27	16 29	16 32	31
32	16 27	16 29	16 32	16 35	16 37	16 40	16 43	16 45	16 48	16 51	16 53	16 56	16 59	17 1	17 4	32
33	16 57	17 0	17 3	17 6	17 8	17 11	17 14	17 16	17 19	17 22	17 25	17 28	17 30	17 33	17 36	33
34	17 28	17 31	17 34	17 37	17 40	17 42	17 45	17 48	17 51	17 54	17 57	18 0	18 2	18 5	18 8	34
35	17 59	18 2	18 5	18 8	18 11	18 14	18 17	18 20	18 23	18 25	18 28	18 31	18 34	18 37	18 40	35
36	18 30	18 33	18 36	18 39	18 42	18 45	18 48	18 51	18 54	18 57	19 0	19 3	19 6	19 9	19 12	36
37	19 1	19 4	19 7	19 10	19 13	19 16	19 19	19 22	19 26	19 29	19 32	19 35	19 38	19 41	19 44	37
38	19 32	19 35	19 38	19 41	19 44	19 48	19 51	19 54	19 57	20 0	20 3	20 7	20 10	20 13	20 16	38
39	20 3	20 6	20 9	20 12	20 15	20 19	20 22	20 25	20 29	20 32	20 35	20 38	20 41	20 45	20 48	39
40	20 33	20 37	20 40	20 43	20 47	20 50	20 53	20 57	21 0	21 3	21 7	21 10	21 13	21 17	21 20	40
41	21 4	21 8	21 11	21 14	21 18	21 21	21 25	21 28	21 31	21 35	21 38	21 42	21 45	21 49	21 52	41
42	21 35	21 38	21 42	21 45	21 49	21 53	21 56	22 0	22 3	22 7	22 10	22 14	22 17	22 20	22 24	42
43	22 6	22 9	22 13	22 17	22 20	22 24	22 27	22 31	22 34	22 38	22 42	22 45	22 49	22 52	22 56	43
44	22 37	22 40	22 44	22 48	22 51	22 55	22 59	23 2	23 6	23 10	23 13	23 17	23 21	23 24	23 28	44
45	23 8	23 11	23 15	23 19	23 23	23 26	23 30	23 34	23 38	23 41	23 45	23 49	23 53	23 56	24 0	45
46	23 38	23 42	23 46	23 50	23 54	23 58	24 1	24 5	24 9	24 13	24 17	24 21	24 24	24 28	24 32	46
47	24 9	24 13	24 17	24 21	24 25	24 29	24 33	24 37	24 41	24 44	24 48	24 52	24 56	25 0	25 4	47
48	24 40	24 44	24 48	24 52	24 56	25 0	25 4	25 8	25 12	25 16	25 20	25 24	25 28	25 32	25 36	48
49	25 11	25 15	25 19	25 23	25 27	25 31	25 35	25 39	25 43	25 48	25 52	25 56	26 0	26 4	26 8	49
50	25 42	25 46	25 50	25 54	25 58	26 2	26 7	26 11	26 15	26 19	26 23	26 27	26 32	26 36	26 40	50
51	26 12	26 17	26 21	26 25	26 30	26 34	26 38	26 42	26 46	26 51	26 55	26 59	27 4	27 8	27 12	51
52	26 43	26 48	26 52	26 56	27 1	27 5	27 9	27 14	27 18	27 22	27 27	27 31	27 35	27 40	27 44	52
53	27 14	27 19	27 23	27 27	27 32	27 36	27 41	27 45	27 50	27 54	27 58	28 3	28 7	28 12	28 16	53
54	27 45	27 49	27 54	27 58	28 3	28 8	28 12	28 16	28 21	28 26	28 30	28 34	28 39	28 43	28 48	54
55	28 16	28 20	28 25	28 30	28 34	28 39	28 43	28 48	28 53	28 57	29 2	29 6	29 11	29 15	29 20	55
56	28 47	28 51	28 56	29 1	29 5	29 10	29 15	29 19	29 24	29 29	29 33	29 38	29 43	29 47	29 52	56
57	29 17	29 22	29 27	29 32	29 36	29 41	29 46	29 51	29 55	30 0	30 5	30 10	30 14	30 19	30 24	57
58	29 48	29 53	29 58	30 3	30 8	30 12	30 17	30 22	30 27	30 32	30 37	30 41	30 46	30 51	30 56	58
59	30 19	30 24	30 29	30 34	30 39	30 44	30 49	30 54	30 59	31 3	31 8	31 13	31 18	31 23	31 28	59
60	30 50	30 55	31 0	31 5	31 10	31 15	31 20	31 25	31 30	31 35	31 40	31 45	31 50	31 55	32 0	60
HOURS																**HOURS**
1	30 50	30 55	31 0	31 5	31 10	31 15	31 20	31 25	31 30	31 35	31 40	31 45	31 50	31 55	32 0	1
2	1 1 40	1 1 50	1 2 0	1 2 10	1 2 20	1 2 30	1 2 40	1 2 50	1 3 0	1 3 10	1 3 20	1 3 30	1 3 40	1 3 50	1 4 0	2
3	1 32 30	1 32 45	1 33 0	1 33 15	1 33 30	1 33 45	1 34 0	1 34 15	1 34 30	1 34 45	1 35 0	1 35 15	1 35 30	1 35 45	1 36 0	3
4	2 3 20	2 3 40	2 4 0	2 4 20	2 4 40	2 5 0	2 5 20	2 5 40	2 6 0	2 6 20	2 6 40	2 7 0	2 7 20	2 7 40	2 8 0	4
5	2 34 10	2 34 35	2 35 0	2 35 25	2 35 50	2 36 15	2 36 40	2 37 5	2 37 30	2 37 55	2 38 20	2 38 45	2 39 10	2 39 35	2 40 0	5
6	3 5 0	3 5 30	3 6 0	3 6 30	3 7 0	3 7 30	3 8 0	3 8 30	3 9 0	3 9 30	3 10 0	3 10 30	3 11 0	3 11 30	3 12 0	6
7	3 35 50	3 36 25	3 37 0	3 37 35	3 38 10	3 38 45	3 39 20	3 39 55	3 40 30	3 41 5	3 41 40	3 42 15	3 42 50	3 43 25	3 44 0	7
8	4 6 40	4 7 20	4 8 0	4 8 40	4 9 20	4 10 0	4 10 40	4 11 20	4 12 0	4 12 40	4 13 20	4 14 0	4 14 40	4 15 20	4 16 0	8
9	4 37 30	4 38 15	4 39 0	4 39 45	4 40 30	4 41 15	4 42 0	4 42 45	4 43 30	4 44 15	4 45 0	4 45 45	4 46 30	4 47 15	4 48 0	9
10	5 8 20	5 9 10	5 10 0	5 10 50	5 11 40	5 12 30	5 13 20	5 14 10	5 15 0	5 15 50	5 16 40	5 17 30	5 18 20	5 19 10	5 20 0	10
11	5 39 10	5 40 5	5 41 0	5 41 55	5 42 50	5 43 45	5 44 40	5 45 35	5 46 30	5 47 25	5 48 20	5 49 15	5 50 10	5 51 5	5 52 0	11
12	6 10 0	6 11 0	6 12 0	6 13 0	6 14 0	6 15 0	6 16 0	6 17 0	6 18 0	6 19 0	6 20 0	6 21 0	6 22 0	6 23 0	6 24 0	12

Table VI Semidiurnal Motion of the Moon

	12 HOUR TRAVEL															
TIME	6° 25'	6° 26'	6° 27'	6° 28'	6° 29'	6° 30'	6° 31'	6° 32'	6° 33'	6° 34'	6° 35'	6° 36'	6° 37'	6° 38'	6° 39'	TIME
MINUTES																
1	0 32	0 32	0 32	0 32	0 32	0 33	0 33	0 33	0 33	0 33	0 33	0 33	0 33	0 33	0 33	1
2	1 4	1 4	1 4	1 5	1 5	1 5	1 5	1 5	1 5	1 6	1 6	1 6	1 6	1 6	1 7	2
3	1 36	1 37	1 37	1 37	1 37	1 38	1 38	1 38	1 38	1 39	1 39	1 39	1 39	1 40	1 40	3
4	2 8	2 9	2 9	2 9	2 10	2 10	2 10	2 11	2 11	2 11	2 12	2 12	2 12	2 13	2 13	4
5	2 40	2 41	2 41	2 42	2 42	2 42	2 43	2 43	2 44	2 44	2 45	2 45	2 45	2 46	2 46	5
6	3 12	3 13	3 13	3 14	3 15	3 15	3 15	3 16	3 16	3 17	3 17	3 18	3 19	3 19	3 19	6
7	3 45	3 45	3 46	3 46	3 47	3 47	3 48	3 49	3 49	3 50	3 50	3 51	3 52	3 52	3 53	7
8	4 17	4 17	4 18	4 19	4 19	4 20	4 21	4 21	4 22	4 23	4 23	4 24	4 25	4 25	4 26	8
9	4 49	4 49	4 50	4 51	4 52	4 53	4 53	4 54	4 55	4 55	4 56	4 57	4 58	4 58	4 59	9
10	5 21	5 22	5 23	5 23	5 24	5 25	5 26	5 27	5 27	5 28	5 29	5 30	5 31	5 32	5 32	10
11	5 53	5 54	5 55	5 56	5 57	5 57	5 58	5 59	6 0	6 1	6 3	6 3	6 4	6 5	6 6	11
12	6 25	6 26	6 27	6 28	6 29	6 30	6 31	6 32	6 33	6 34	6 35	6 36	6 37	6 38	6 39	12
13	6 57	6 58	6 59	7 0	7 1	7 2	7 4	7 5	7 6	7 7	7 7	7 9	7 10	7 11	7 12	13
14	7 29	7 30	7 31	7 33	7 34	7 35	7 36	7 37	7 38	7 40	7 41	7 42	7 43	7 44	7 46	14
15	8 1	8 2	8 4	8 5	8 6	8 7	8 9	8 10	8 11	8 12	8 14	8 15	8 16	8 17	8 19	15
16	8 33	8 35	8 36	8 37	8 39	8 40	8 41	8 43	8 44	8 45	8 47	8 48	8 49	8 51	8 52	16
17	9 5	9 7	9 8	9 10	9 11	9 12	9 14	9 15	9 17	9 18	9 20	9 21	9 22	9 24	9 25	17
18	9 37	9 39	9 40	9 42	9 43	9 45	9 46	9 48	9 49	9 51	9 52	9 54	9 55	9 57	9 58	18
19	10 10	10 11	10 13	10 14	10 16	10 17	10 19	10 21	10 22	10 24	10 25	10 27	10 29	10 30	10 32	19
20	10 42	10 43	10 45	10 47	10 48	10 50	10 52	10 53	10 55	10 57	10 58	11 0	11 2	11 3	11 5	20
21	11 14	11 15	11 17	11 19	11 21	11 22	11 24	11 26	11 28	11 29	11 31	11 33	11 35	11 36	11 38	21
22	11 46	11 48	11 49	11 51	11 53	11 55	11 57	11 59	12 0	12 2	12 4	12 6	12 8	12 10	12 11	22
23	12 18	12 20	12 22	12 24	12 26	12 27	12 29	12 31	12 33	12 35	12 37	12 39	12 41	12 43	12 45	23
24	12 50	12 52	12 54	12 56	12 58	13 0	13 2	13 4	13 6	13 8	13 10	13 12	13 14	13 16	13 18	24
25	13 22	13 24	13 26	13 28	13 30	13 32	13 35	13 37	13 39	13 41	13 43	13 45	13 47	13 49	13 51	25
26	13 54	13 56	13 58	14 1	14 3	14 5	14 7	14 9	14 11	14 14	14 16	14 18	14 20	14 22	14 24	26
27	14 26	14 28	14 31	14 33	14 35	14 37	14 40	14 42	14 44	14 46	14 49	14 51	14 53	14 55	14 58	27
28	14 58	15 1	15 3	15 5	15 8	15 10	15 12	15 15	15 17	15 19	15 22	15 24	15 26	15 29	15 31	28
29	15 30	15 33	15 35	15 38	15 40	15 42	15 45	15 47	15 50	15 52	15 55	15 57	15 59	16 2	16 4	29
30	16 3	16 5	16 8	16 10	16 12	16 15	16 18	16 20	16 23	16 25	16 27	16 30	16 33	16 35	16 38	30
31	16 35	16 37	16 40	16 42	16 45	16 48	16 50	16 53	16 55	16 58	17 0	17 3	17 6	17 8	17 11	31
32	17 7	17 9	17 12	17 15	17 17	17 20	17 23	17 25	17 28	17 31	17 33	17 36	17 39	17 41	17 44	32
33	17 39	17 41	17 44	17 47	17 50	17 53	17 55	17 58	18 1	18 4	18 6	18 9	18 12	18 15	18 17	33
34	18 11	18 14	18 16	18 19	18 22	18 25	18 28	18 31	18 34	18 36	18 39	18 42	18 45	18 48	18 50	34
35	18 43	18 46	18 49	18 52	18 55	18 57	19 0	19 3	19 6	19 9	19 12	19 15	19 18	19 21	19 24	35
36	19 15	19 18	19 21	19 24	19 27	19 30	19 33	19 36	19 39	19 42	19 45	19 48	19 51	19 54	19 57	36
37	19 47	19 50	19 53	19 56	19 59	20 3	20 6	20 9	20 12	20 15	20 18	20 21	20 24	20 27	20 30	37
38	20 19	20 22	20 26	20 29	20 32	20 35	20 38	20 41	20 45	20 48	20 51	20 54	20 57	21 0	21 3	38
39	20 51	20 54	20 58	21 1	21 4	21 8	21 11	21 14	21 17	21 20	21 24	21 27	21 30	21 34	21 37	39
40	21 23	21 27	21 30	21 33	21 37	21 40	21 43	21 47	21 50	21 53	21 57	22 0	22 3	22 7	22 10	40
41	21 55	21 59	22 2	22 6	22 9	22 12	22 16	22 19	22 23	22 26	22 30	22 33	22 36	22 40	22 43	41
42	22 27	22 31	22 34	22 38	22 41	22 45	22 49	22 52	22 56	22 59	23 3	23 6	23 9	23 13	23 16	42
43	23 0	23 3	23 7	23 10	23 14	23 18	23 21	23 25	23 28	23 32	24 1	23 39	23 43	23 46	23 50	43
44	23 32	23 35	23 39	23 43	23 46	23 50	23 54	23 57	24 1	24 5	24 8	24 12	24 16	24 19	24 23	44
45	24 4	24 8	24 11	24 15	24 19	24 23	24 26	24 30	24 34	24 38	24 41	24 45	24 49	24 53	24 56	45
46	24 36	24 40	24 44	24 47	24 51	24 55	24 59	25 3	25 7	25 10	25 14	25 18	25 22	25 26	25 30	46
47	25 8	25 12	25 16	25 20	25 24	25 27	25 31	25 35	25 39	25 43	25 47	25 51	25 55	25 59	26 3	47
48	25 40	25 44	25 48	25 52	25 56	26 0	26 4	26 8	26 12	26 16	26 20	26 24	26 28	26 32	26 36	48
49	26 12	26 16	26 20	26 24	26 28	26 33	26 37	26 41	26 45	26 49	26 53	26 57	27 1	27 5	27 9	49
50	26 44	26 48	26 52	26 57	27 1	27 5	27 9	27 13	27 17	27 22	27 26	27 30	27 34	27 38	27 42	50
51	27 16	27 20	27 25	27 29	27 33	27 38	27 42	27 46	27 50	27 54	27 59	28 3	28 7	28 11	28 16	51
52	27 48	27 53	27 57	28 1	28 6	28 10	28 14	28 19	28 23	28 27	28 32	28 36	28 40	28 45	28 49	52
53	28 20	28 25	28 29	28 34	28 38	28 43	28 47	28 51	28 56	29 0	29 5	29 9	29 13	29 18	29 22	53
54	28 53	28 57	29 1	29 6	29 10	29 15	29 19	29 24	29 28	29 33	29 38	29 42	29 46	29 51	29 55	54
55	29 25	29 29	29 34	29 38	29 43	29 48	29 52	29 57	30 1	30 6	30 10	30 15	30 20	30 24	30 29	55
56	29 57	30 1	30 6	30 11	30 15	30 20	30 25	30 29	30 34	30 39	30 43	30 48	30 53	30 57	31 2	56
57	30 29	30 34	30 38	30 43	30 48	30 53	30 57	31 2	31 7	31 11	31 16	31 21	31 26	31 30	31 35	57
58	31 1	31 6	31 11	31 15	31 20	31 25	31 30	31 34	31 40	31 44	31 49	31 54	31 59	32 4	32 8	58
59	31 33	31 38	31 43	31 48	31 53	31 58	32 2	32 7	32 12	32 17	32 22	32 27	32 32	32 37	32 42	59
60	32 5	32 10	32 15	32 20	32 25	32 30	32 35	32 40	32 45	32 50	32 55	33 0	33 5	33 10	33 15	60
HOURS																
1	32 5	32 10	32 15	32 20	32 25	32 30	32 35	32 40	32 45	32 50	32 55	33 0	33 5	33 10	33 15	1
2	1 4 10	1 4 20	1 4 30	1 4 40	1 4 50	1 5 0	1 5 10	1 5 20	1 5 30	1 5 40	1 5 50	1 6 0	1 6 10	1 6 20	1 6 30	2
3	1 36 15	1 36 30	1 36 45	1 37 0	1 37 15	1 37 30	1 37 45	1 38 0	1 38 15	1 38 30	1 38 45	1 39 0	1 39 15	1 39 30	1 39 45	3
4	2 8 20	2 8 40	2 9 0	2 9 20	2 9 40	2 10 0	2 10 20	2 10 40	2 11 0	2 11 20	2 11 40	2 12 0	2 12 20	2 12 40	2 13 0	4
5	2 40 25	2 40 50	2 41 15	2 41 40	2 42 5	2 42 30	2 42 55	2 43 20	2 43 45	2 44 10	2 44 35	2 45 0	2 45 25	2 45 50	2 46 15	5
6	3 12 30	3 13 0	3 13 30	3 14 0	3 14 30	3 15 0	3 15 30	3 16 0	3 16 30	3 17 0	3 17 30	3 18 0	3 18 30	3 19 0	3 19 30	6
7	3 44 35	3 45 10	3 45 45	3 46 20	3 46 55	3 47 30	3 48 5	3 48 40	3 49 15	3 49 50	3 50 25	3 51 0	3 51 35	3 52 10	3 52 45	7
8	4 16 40	4 17 20	4 18 0	4 18 40	4 19 20	4 20 0	4 20 40	4 21 20	4 22 0	4 22 40	4 23 20	4 24 0	4 24 40	4 25 20	4 26 0	8
9	4 48 45	4 49 30	4 50 15	4 51 0	4 51 45	4 52 30	4 53 15	4 54 0	4 54 45	4 55 30	4 56 15	4 57 0	4 57 45	4 58 30	4 59 15	9
10	5 20 50	5 21 40	5 22 30	5 23 20	5 24 10	5 25 0	5 25 50	5 26 40	5 27 30	5 28 20	5 29 10	5 30 0	5 30 50	5 31 40	5 32 30	10
11	5 52 55	5 53 50	5 54 45	5 55 40	5 56 35	5 57 30	5 58 25	5 59 20	6 0 15	6 1 10	6 2 5	6 3 0	6 3 55	6 4 50	6 5 45	11
12	6 25 0	6 26 0	6 27 0	6 28 0	6 29 0	6 30 0	6 31 0	6 32 0	6 33 0	6 34 0	6 35 0	6 36 0	6 37 0	6 38 0	6 39 0	12

Table VI Semidiurnal Motion of the Moon

TIME	6° 40'	6° 41'	6° 42'	6° 43'	6° 44'	6° 45'	6° 46'	6° 47'	6° 48'	6° 49'	6° 50'	6° 51'	6° 52'	6° 53'	6° 54'	TIME
MINUTES 1	0 33	0 33	0 34	0 34	0 34	0 34	0 34	0 34	0 34	0 34	0 34	0 34	0 34	0 34	0 35	1
2	1 7	1 7	1 7	1 7	1 7	1 8	1 8	1 8	1 8	1 8	1 8	1 8	1 9	1 9	1 9	2
3	1 40	1 40	1 41	1 41	1 41	1 41	1 42	1 42	1 42	1 42	1 42	1 43	1 43	1 43	1 43	3
4	2 13	2 14	2 14	2 14	2 15	2 15	2 16	2 16	2 16	2 16	2 17	2 17	2 17	2 18	2 18	4
5	2 47	2 47	2 47	2 48	2 48	2 49	2 49	2 50	2 50	2 50	2 51	2 51	2 52	2 52	2 53	5
6	3 20	3 20	3 21	3 22	3 22	3 23	3 23	3 23	3 24	3 24	3 25	3 26	3 26	3 27	3 27	6
7	3 53	3 54	3 54	3 55	3 56	3 56	3 57	3 57	3 58	3 59	3 59	4 0	4 0	4 1	4 1	7
8	4 27	4 27	4 28	4 29	4 29	4 30	4 31	4 31	4 32	4 33	4 33	4 34	4 35	4 35	4 36	8
9	5 0	5 1	5 1	5 2	5 3	5 4	5 4	5 5	5 6	5 7	5 8	5 8	5 9	5 10	5 10	9
10	5 33	5 34	5 35	5 36	5 37	5 38	5 38	5 39	5 40	5 41	5 42	5 42	5 43	5 44	5 45	10
11	6 7	6 8	6 8	6 9	6 10	6 11	6 12	6 13	6 14	6 15	6 16	6 17	6 18	6 19	6 19	11
12	6 40	6 41	6 42	6 43	6 44	6 45	6 46	6 47	6 48	6 49	6 50	6 51	6 52	6 53	6 54	12
13	7 13	7 14	7 15	7 17	7 18	7 19	7 20	7 21	7 22	7 23	7 24	7 25	7 26	7 27	7 28	13
14	7 47	7 48	7 49	7 50	7 51	7 53	7 54	7 55	7 56	7 57	7 58	7 59	8 1	8 2	8 3	14
15	8 20	8 21	8 22	8 24	8 25	8 26	8 27	8 29	8 30	8 31	8 32	8 34	8 35	8 36	8 37	15
16	8 53	8 55	8 56	8 57	8 59	9 0	9 1	9 3	9 4	9 5	9 7	9 8	9 9	9 11	9 12	16
17	9 27	9 28	9 29	9 31	9 32	9 34	9 35	9 37	9 38	9 39	9 41	9 42	9 44	9 45	9 46	17
18	10 0	10 1	10 3	10 4	10 6	10 7	10 9	10 10	10 12	10 13	10 15	10 16	10 18	10 19	10 21	18
19	10 33	10 35	10 36	10 38	10 40	10 41	10 43	10 44	10 46	10 48	10 49	10 51	10 52	10 54	10 55	19
20	11 7	11 8	11 10	11 12	11 13	11 15	11 17	11 18	11 20	11 22	11 23	11 25	11 27	11 28	11 30	20
21	11 40	11 42	11 43	11 45	11 47	11 49	11 50	11 52	11 54	11 56	11 57	11 59	12 1	12 3	12 4	21
22	12 13	12 15	12 17	12 19	12 21	12 22	12 24	12 26	12 28	12 30	12 32	12 33	12 35	12 37	12 39	22
23	12 47	12 49	12 50	12 52	12 54	12 56	12 58	13 0	13 2	13 4	13 6	13 8	13 10	13 12	13 13	23
24	13 20	13 22	13 24	13 26	13 28	13 30	13 32	13 34	13 36	13 38	13 40	13 42	13 44	13 46	13 48	24
25	13 53	13 55	13 57	14 0	14 2	14 4	14 6	14 8	14 10	14 12	14 14	14 16	14 18	14 20	14 22	25
26	14 27	14 29	14 31	14 33	14 35	14 37	14 40	14 42	14 44	14 46	14 48	14 50	14 53	14 55	14 57	26
27	15 0	15 2	15 4	15 7	15 9	15 11	15 13	15 15	15 18	15 20	15 22	15 25	15 27	15 29	15 31	27
28	15 33	15 36	15 38	15 40	15 43	15 45	15 47	15 50	15 52	15 54	15 57	15 59	16 1	16 4	16 6	28
29	16 7	16 9	16 11	16 14	16 16	16 19	16 21	16 24	16 26	16 28	16 31	16 33	16 36	16 38	16 41	29
30	16 40	16 42	16 45	16 48	16 50	16 53	16 55	16 57	17 0	17 3	17 5	17 8	17 10	17 12	17 15	30
31	17 13	17 16	17 19	17 21	17 24	17 26	17 29	17 31	17 34	17 37	17 39	17 42	17 44	17 47	17 49	31
32	17 47	17 49	17 52	17 55	17 57	18 0	18 3	18 5	18 8	18 11	18 13	18 16	18 19	18 21	18 24	32
33	18 20	18 23	18 26	18 28	18 31	18 34	18 37	18 39	18 42	18 45	18 48	18 50	18 53	18 56	18 59	33
34	18 53	18 56	18 59	19 2	19 5	19 8	19 10	19 13	19 16	19 19	19 22	19 24	19 27	19 30	19 33	34
35	19 27	19 30	19 33	19 35	19 38	19 41	19 44	19 47	19 50	19 53	19 56	19 59	20 2	20 5	20 8	35
36	20 0	20 3	20 6	20 9	20 12	20 15	20 18	20 21	20 24	20 27	20 30	20 33	20 36	20 39	20 42	36
37	20 33	20 36	20 39	20 43	20 46	20 49	20 52	20 55	20 58	21 1	21 4	21 7	21 10	21 13	21 16	37
38	21 7	21 10	21 13	21 16	21 19	21 23	21 26	21 29	21 32	21 35	21 38	21 41	21 45	21 48	21 51	38
39	21 40	21 43	21 46	21 50	21 53	21 56	22 0	22 3	22 6	22 9	22 12	22 16	22 19	22 22	22 26	39
40	22 13	22 17	22 20	22 23	22 27	22 30	22 33	22 37	22 40	22 43	22 47	22 50	22 53	22 57	23 0	40
41	22 47	22 50	22 53	22 57	23 0	23 4	23 7	23 11	23 14	23 17	23 21	23 24	23 28	23 31	23 34	41
42	23 20	23 23	23 27	23 30	23 34	23 38	23 41	23 45	23 48	23 52	23 55	23 59	24 2	24 5	24 9	42
43	23 53	23 57	24 0	24 4	24 8	24 11	24 15	24 18	24 22	24 26	24 29	24 33	24 36	24 40	24 44	43
44	24 27	24 30	24 34	24 38	24 41	24 45	24 49	24 52	24 56	25 0	25 3	25 7	25 11	25 14	25 18	44
45	25 0	25 4	25 8	25 11	25 15	25 19	25 23	25 26	25 30	25 34	25 38	25 41	25 45	25 49	25 53	45
46	25 33	25 37	25 41	25 45	25 49	25 53	25 56	26 0	26 4	26 8	26 12	26 16	26 19	26 23	26 27	46
47	26 7	26 11	26 14	26 18	26 22	26 26	26 30	26 34	26 38	26 42	26 46	26 50	26 54	26 58	27 1	47
48	26 40	26 44	26 48	26 52	26 56	27 0	27 4	27 8	27 12	27 16	27 20	27 24	27 28	27 32	27 36	48
49	27 13	27 17	27 22	27 26	27 30	27 34	27 38	27 42	27 46	27 50	27 54	27 58	28 2	28 6	28 11	49
50	27 47	27 51	27 55	27 59	28 3	28 7	28 12	28 16	28 20	28 24	28 28	28 32	28 37	28 41	28 45	50
51	28 20	28 24	28 28	28 33	28 37	28 41	28 45	28 50	28 54	28 58	29 2	29 7	29 11	29 15	29 19	51
52	28 53	28 58	29 2	29 6	29 11	29 15	29 19	29 24	29 28	29 32	29 37	29 41	29 45	29 50	29 54	52
53	29 27	29 31	29 36	29 40	29 44	29 49	29 53	29 58	30 2	30 6	30 11	30 15	30 20	30 24	30 29	53
54	30 0	30 4	30 9	30 13	30 18	30 23	30 27	30 31	30 36	30 40	30 45	30 49	30 54	30 58	31 3	54
55	30 33	30 38	30 43	30 47	30 52	30 56	31 1	31 5	31 10	31 15	31 19	31 24	31 28	31 33	31 38	55
56	31 7	31 11	31 16	31 21	31 25	31 30	31 35	31 39	31 44	31 49	31 53	31 58	32 3	32 7	32 12	56
57	31 40	31 45	31 49	31 54	31 59	32 4	32 8	32 13	32 18	32 23	32 27	32 32	32 37	32 42	32 46	57
58	32 13	32 18	32 23	32 28	32 33	32 38	32 42	32 47	32 52	32 57	33 2	33 7	33 11	33 16	33 21	58
59	32 47	32 52	32 57	33 1	33 6	33 11	33 16	33 21	33 26	33 31	33 36	33 41	33 46	33 51	33 56	59
60	33 20	33 25	33 30	33 35	33 40	33 45	33 50	33 55	34 0	34 5	34 10	34 15	34 20	34 25	34 30	60
HOURS 1	33 20	33 25	33 30	33 35	33 40	33 45	33 50	33 55	34 0	34 5	34 10	34 15	34 20	34 25	34 30	1
2	1 6 40	1 6 50	1 7 0	1 7 10	1 7 20	1 7 30	1 7 40	1 7 50	1 8 0	1 8 10	1 8 20	1 8 30	1 8 40	1 8 50	1 9 0	2
3	1 40 0	1 40 15	1 40 30	1 40 45	1 41 0	1 41 15	1 41 30	1 41 45	1 42 0	1 42 15	1 42 30	1 42 45	1 43 0	1 43 15	1 43 30	3
4	2 13 20	2 13 40	2 14 0	2 14 20	2 14 40	2 15 0	2 15 20	2 15 40	2 16 0	2 16 20	2 16 40	2 17 0	2 17 20	2 17 40	2 18 0	4
5	2 46 40	2 47 5	2 47 30	2 47 55	2 48 20	2 48 45	2 49 10	2 49 35	2 50 0	2 50 25	2 50 50	2 51 15	2 51 40	2 52 5	2 52 30	5
6	3 20 0	3 20 30	3 21 0	3 21 30	3 22 0	3 22 30	3 23 0	3 23 30	3 24 0	3 24 30	3 25 0	3 25 30	3 26 0	3 26 30	3 27 0	6
7	3 53 20	3 53 55	3 54 30	3 55 5	3 55 40	3 56 15	3 56 50	3 57 25	3 58 0	3 58 35	3 59 10	3 59 45	4 0 20	4 0 55	4 1 30	7
8	4 26 40	4 27 20	4 28 0	4 28 40	4 29 20	4 30 0	4 30 40	4 31 20	4 32 0	4 32 40	4 33 20	4 34 0	4 34 40	4 35 20	4 36 0	8
9	5 0 0	5 0 45	5 1 30	5 2 15	5 3 0	5 3 45	5 4 30	5 5 15	5 6 0	5 6 45	5 7 30	5 8 15	5 9 0	5 9 45	5 10 30	9
10	5 33 20	5 34 10	5 35 0	5 35 50	5 36 40	5 37 30	5 38 20	5 39 10	5 40 0	5 40 50	5 41 40	5 42 30	5 43 20	5 44 10	5 45 0	10
11	6 6 40	6 7 35	6 8 30	6 9 25	6 10 20	6 11 15	6 12 10	6 13 5	6 14 0	6 14 55	6 15 50	6 16 45	6 17 40	6 18 35	6 19 30	11
12	6 40 0	6 41 0	6 42 0	6 43 0	6 44 0	6 45 0	6 46 0	6 47 0	6 48 0	6 49 0	6 50 0	6 51 0	6 52 0	6 53 0	6 54 0	12

Table VI Semidiurnal Motion of the Moon

12 HOUR TRAVEL

TIME	6° 55'	6° 56'	6° 57'	6° 58'	6° 59'	7° 0'	7° 1'	7° 2'	7° 3'	7° 4'	7° 5'	7° 6'	7° 7'	7° 8'	7° 9'	TIME
1	0 35	0 35	0 35	0 35	0 35	0 35	0 35	0 35	0 35	0 35	0 35	0 36	0 36	0 36	0 36	1
2	1 9	1 9	1 9	1 10	1 10	1 10	1 10	1 10	1 11	1 11	1 11	1 11	1 11	1 11	1 11	2
3	1 44	1 44	1 44	1 45	1 45	1 45	1 45	1 46	1 46	1 46	1 46	1 46	1 47	1 47	1 47	3
4	2 18	2 19	2 19	2 19	2 20	2 20	2 20	2 21	2 21	2 21	2 22	2 22	2 22	2 23	2 23	4
5	2 53	2 53	2 54	2 54	2 55	2 55	2 55	2 56	2 56	2 57	2 57	2 57	2 58	2 58	2 59	5
6	3 27	3 28	3 28	3 29	3 30	3 30	3 31	3 31	3 31	3 32	3 32	3 33	3 34	3 34	3 34	6
7	4 2	4 3	4 3	4 4	4 4	4 5	4 6	4 6	4 7	4 7	4 8	4 8	4 9	4 10	4 10	7
8	4 37	4 37	4 38	4 39	4 39	4 40	4 41	4 41	4 42	4 43	4 43	4 44	4 45	4 45	4 46	8
9	5 11	5 12	5 13	5 13	5 14	5 15	5 16	5 16	5 17	5 18	5 19	5 19	5 20	5 21	5 22	9
10	5 46	5 47	5 47	5 48	5 49	5 50	5 51	5 52	5 53	5 53	5 54	5 55	5 56	5 57	5 57	10
11	6 20	6 21	6 22	6 23	6 24	6 25	6 26	6 27	6 28	6 29	6 30	6 31	6 31	6 32	6 33	11
12	6 55	6 56	6 57	6 58	6 59	7 0	7 1	7 2	7 3	7 4	7 5	7 6	7 7	7 8	7 9	12
13	7 30	7 31	7 32	7 33	7 34	7 35	7 36	7 37	7 38	7 39	7 40	7 42	7 43	7 44	7 45	13
14	8 4	8 5	8 6	8 8	8 9	8 10	8 11	8 12	8 13	8 15	8 16	8 17	8 18	8 19	8 20	14
15	8 39	8 40	8 41	8 42	8 44	8 45	8 46	8 47	8 49	8 50	8 51	8 52	8 54	8 55	8 56	15
16	9 13	9 15	9 16	9 17	9 19	9 20	9 21	9 23	9 24	9 25	9 27	9 28	9 29	9 31	9 32	16
17	9 48	9 49	9 51	9 52	9 54	9 55	9 56	9 58	9 59	10 1	10 2	10 3	10 5	10 6	10 8	17
18	10 22	10 24	10 25	10 27	10 28	10 30	10 31	10 33	10 34	10 36	10 37	10 39	10 40	10 42	10 43	18
19	10 57	10 59	11 0	11 2	11 3	11 5	11 7	11 8	11 10	11 11	11 13	11 14	11 16	11 18	11 19	19
20	11 32	11 33	11 35	11 37	11 38	11 40	11 42	11 43	11 45	11 47	11 48	11 50	11 52	11 53	11 55	20
21	12 6	12 8	12 10	12 11	12 13	12 15	12 17	12 18	12 20	12 22	12 24	12 25	12 27	12 29	12 31	21
22	12 41	12 43	12 44	12 46	12 48	12 50	12 52	12 54	12 55	12 57	12 59	13 1	13 3	13 5	13 6	22
23	13 15	13 17	13 19	13 21	13 23	13 25	13 27	13 29	13 31	13 33	13 35	13 36	13 38	13 40	13 42	23
24	13 50	13 52	13 54	13 56	13 58	14 0	14 2	14 4	14 6	14 8	14 10	14 12	14 14	14 16	14 18	24
25	14 25	14 27	14 29	14 31	14 33	14 35	14 37	14 39	14 41	14 43	14 45	14 47	14 50	14 52	14 54	25
26	14 59	15 1	15 3	15 6	15 8	15 10	15 12	15 14	15 16	15 19	15 21	15 23	15 25	15 27	15 29	26
27	15 34	15 36	15 38	15 40	15 43	15 45	15 47	15 49	15 52	15 54	15 56	15 58	16 1	16 3	16 5	27
28	16 8	16 11	16 13	16 15	16 18	16 20	16 22	16 25	16 27	16 29	16 32	16 34	16 36	16 39	16 41	28
29	16 43	16 45	16 48	16 50	16 53	16 55	16 57	17 0	17 2	17 4	17 7	17 9	17 12	17 14	17 17	29
30	17 18	17 20	17 23	17 25	17 27	17 30	17 33	17 35	17 38	17 40	17 42	17 45	17 48	17 50	17 53	30
31	17 52	17 55	17 57	18 0	18 2	18 5	18 8	18 10	18 13	18 15	18 18	18 20	18 23	18 26	18 28	31
32	18 27	18 29	18 32	18 35	18 37	18 40	18 43	18 45	18 48	18 51	18 53	18 56	18 59	19 1	19 4	32
33	19 1	19 4	19 7	19 9	19 12	19 15	19 18	19 20	19 23	19 26	19 29	19 31	19 34	19 37	19 40	33
34	19 36	19 39	19 41	19 44	19 47	19 50	19 53	19 56	19 59	20 1	20 4	20 7	20 10	20 13	20 15	34
35	20 10	20 13	20 16	20 19	20 22	20 25	20 28	20 31	20 34	20 37	20 40	20 42	20 45	20 48	20 51	35
36	20 45	20 48	20 51	20 54	20 57	21 0	21 3	21 6	21 9	21 12	21 15	21 18	21 21	21 24	21 27	36
37	21 20	21 23	21 26	21 29	21 32	21 35	21 38	21 41	21 44	21 47	21 50	21 53	21 57	22 0	22 3	37
38	21 54	21 57	22 0	22 4	22 7	22 10	22 13	22 16	22 19	22 23	22 26	22 29	22 32	22 35	22 38	38
39	22 29	22 32	22 35	22 38	22 42	22 45	22 48	22 52	22 55	22 58	23 1	23 4	23 8	23 11	23 14	39
40	23 3	23 7	23 10	23 13	23 17	23 20	23 23	23 27	23 30	23 33	23 37	23 40	23 43	23 47	23 50	40
41	23 38	23 41	23 45	23 48	23 52	23 55	23 58	24 2	24 5	24 9	24 12	24 15	24 19	24 22	24 26	41
42	24 12	24 16	24 19	24 23	24 26	24 30	24 34	24 37	24 41	24 44	24 48	24 51	24 54	24 58	25 1	42
43	24 47	24 51	24 54	24 58	25 1	25 5	25 9	25 12	25 16	25 19	25 23	25 26	25 30	25 34	25 37	43
44	25 22	25 25	25 29	25 33	25 36	25 40	25 44	25 47	25 51	25 55	25 58	26 2	26 6	26 9	26 13	44
45	25 56	26 0	26 4	26 8	26 11	26 15	26 19	26 23	26 26	26 30	26 34	26 38	26 41	26 45	26 49	45
46	26 31	26 35	26 39	26 42	26 46	26 50	26 54	26 58	27 2	27 5	27 9	27 13	27 17	27 21	27 25	46
47	27 5	27 9	27 13	27 17	27 21	27 25	27 29	27 33	27 37	27 41	27 45	27 48	27 52	27 56	28 0	47
48	27 40	27 44	27 48	27 52	27 56	28 0	28 4	28 8	28 12	28 16	28 20	28 24	28 28	28 32	28 36	48
49	28 15	28 19	28 23	28 27	28 31	28 35	28 39	28 43	28 47	28 51	28 55	29 0	29 4	29 8	29 12	49
50	28 49	28 53	28 57	29 2	29 6	29 10	29 14	29 18	29 22	29 27	29 31	29 35	29 39	29 43	29 47	50
51	29 24	29 28	29 32	29 37	29 41	29 45	29 49	29 53	29 58	30 2	30 6	30 11	30 15	30 19	30 23	51
52	29 58	30 3	30 7	30 11	30 16	30 20	30 24	30 29	30 33	30 37	30 42	30 46	30 50	30 55	30 59	52
53	30 33	30 37	30 42	30 46	30 51	30 55	30 59	31 4	31 8	31 13	31 17	31 22	31 26	31 30	31 35	53
54	31 8	31 12	31 16	31 21	31 25	31 30	31 34	31 39	31 44	31 48	31 53	31 57	32 1	32 6	32 10	54
55	31 42	31 47	31 51	31 56	32 0	32 5	32 10	32 14	32 19	32 23	32 28	32 33	32 37	32 42	32 46	55
56	32 17	32 21	32 26	32 31	32 35	32 40	32 45	32 49	32 54	32 59	33 3	33 8	33 13	33 17	33 22	56
57	32 51	32 56	33 1	33 5	33 10	33 15	33 20	33 24	33 29	33 34	33 39	33 43	33 48	33 53	33 58	57
58	33 26	33 31	33 36	33 40	33 45	33 50	33 55	34 0	34 4	34 9	34 14	34 19	34 24	34 29	34 34	58
59	34 0	34 5	34 10	34 15	34 20	34 25	34 30	34 35	34 40	34 45	34 50	34 55	34 59	35 4	35 9	59
60	34 35	34 40	34 45	34 50	34 55	35 0	35 5	35 10	35 15	35 20	35 25	35 30	35 35	35 40	35 45	60

HOURS	6° 55'	6° 56'	6° 57'	6° 58'	6° 59'	7° 0'	7° 1'	7° 2'	7° 3'	7° 4'	7° 5'	7° 6'	7° 7'	7° 8'	7° 9'	HOURS
1	34 35	34 40	34 45	34 50	34 55	35 0	35 5	35 10	35 15	35 20	35 25	35 30	35 35	35 40	35 45	1
2	1 9 10	1 9 20	1 9 30	1 9 40	1 9 50	1 10 0	1 10 10	1 10 20	1 10 30	1 10 40	1 10 50	1 11 0	1 11 10	1 11 20	1 11 30	2
3	1 43 45	1 44 0	1 44 15	1 44 30	1 44 45	1 45 0	1 45 15	1 45 30	1 45 45	1 46 0	1 46 15	1 46 30	1 46 45	1 47 0	1 47 15	3
4	2 18 20	2 18 40	2 19 0	2 19 20	2 19 40	2 20 0	2 20 20	2 20 40	2 21 0	2 21 20	2 21 40	2 22 0	2 22 20	2 22 40	2 23 0	4
5	2 52 55	2 53 20	2 53 45	2 54 10	2 54 35	2 55 0	2 55 25	2 55 50	2 56 15	2 56 40	2 57 5	2 57 30	2 57 55	2 58 20	2 58 45	5
6	3 27 30	3 28 0	3 28 30	3 29 0	3 29 30	3 30 0	3 30 30	3 31 0	3 31 30	3 32 0	3 32 30	3 33 0	3 33 30	3 34 0	3 34 30	6
7	4 2 5	4 2 40	4 3 15	4 3 50	4 4 25	4 5 0	4 5 35	4 6 10	4 6 45	4 7 20	4 7 55	4 8 30	4 9 5	4 9 40	4 10 15	7
8	4 36 40	4 37 20	4 38 0	4 38 40	4 39 20	4 40 0	4 40 40	4 41 20	4 42 0	4 42 40	4 43 20	4 44 0	4 44 40	4 45 20	4 46 0	8
9	5 11 15	5 12 0	5 12 45	5 13 30	5 14 15	5 15 0	5 15 45	5 16 30	5 17 15	5 18 0	5 18 45	5 19 30	5 20 15	5 21 0	5 21 45	9
10	5 45 50	5 46 40	5 47 30	5 48 20	5 49 10	5 50 0	5 50 50	5 51 40	5 52 30	5 53 20	5 54 10	5 55 0	5 55 50	5 56 40	5 57 30	10
11	6 20 25	6 21 20	6 22 15	6 23 10	6 24 5	6 25 0	6 25 55	6 26 50	6 27 45	6 28 40	6 29 35	6 30 30	6 31 25	6 32 20	6 33 15	11
12	6 55 0	6 56 0	6 57 0	6 58 0	6 59 0	7 0 0	7 1 0	7 2 0	7 3 0	7 4 0	7 5 0	7 6 0	7 7 0	7 8 0	7 9 0	12

Table VI Semidiurnal Motion of the Moon

12 HOUR TRAVEL

TIME	7° 10'	7° 11'	7° 12'	7° 13'	7° 14'	7° 15'	7° 16'	7° 17'	7° 18'	7° 19'	7° 20'	7° 21'	7° 22'	7° 23'	7° 24'	TIME
MINUTES 1	0 36	0 36	0 36	0 36	0 36	0 36	0 36	0 36	0 37	0 37	0 37	0 37	0 37	0 37	0 37	1 **MINUTES**
2	1 12	1 12	1 12	1 12	1 12	1 13	1 13	1 13	1 13	1 13	1 13	1 14	1 14	1 14	1 14	2
3	1 48	1 48	1 48	1 48	1 49	1 49	1 49	1 49	1 50	1 50	1 50	1 50	1 51	1 51	1 51	3
4	2 23	2 24	2 24	2 24	2 25	2 25	2 25	2 26	2 26	2 26	2 27	2 27	2 27	2 28	2 28	4
5	2 59	3 0	3 0	3 0	3 1	3 1	3 2	3 2	3 3	3 3	3 3	3 4	3 4	3 5	3 5	5
6	3 35	3 36	3 36	3 37	3 37	3 38	3 38	3 39	3 39	3 40	3 40	3 41	3 41	3 42	3 42	6
7	4 11	4 11	4 12	4 13	4 13	4 14	4 14	4 15	4 16	4 16	4 17	4 17	4 18	4 18	4 19	7
8	4 47	4 47	4 48	4 49	4 49	4 50	4 51	4 51	4 52	4 53	4 53	4 54	4 55	4 55	4 56	8
9	5 23	5 23	5 24	5 25	5 26	5 26	5 27	5 28	5 29	5 29	5 30	5 31	5 32	5 32	5 33	9
10	5 58	5 59	6 0	6 1	6 2	6 3	6 3	6 4	6 5	6 6	6 7	6 8	6 8	6 9	6 10	10
11	6 34	6 35	6 36	6 37	6 38	6 39	6 40	6 41	6 42	6 42	6 43	6 44	6 45	6 46	6 47	11
12	7 10	7 11	7 12	7 13	7 14	7 15	7 16	7 17	7 18	7 19	7 20	7 21	7 22	7 23	7 24	12
13	7 46	7 47	7 48	7 49	7 50	7 51	7 52	7 53	7 55	7 56	7 57	7 58	7 59	8 0	8 1	13
14	8 22	8 23	8 24	8 25	8 26	8 28	8 29	8 30	8 31	8 32	8 33	8 35	8 36	8 37	8 38	14
15	8 58	8 59	9 0	9 1	9 3	9 4	9 5	9 6	9 8	9 9	9 10	9 11	9 13	9 14	9 15	15
16	9 33	9 35	9 36	9 37	9 39	9 40	9 41	9 43	9 44	9 45	9 47	9 48	9 49	9 51	9 52	16
17	10 9	10 11	10 12	10 13	10 15	10 16	10 18	10 19	10 21	10 22	10 23	10 25	10 26	10 28	10 29	17
18	10 45	10 47	10 48	10 50	10 51	10 53	10 54	10 56	10 57	10 59	11 0	11 2	11 3	11 5	11 6	18
19	11 21	11 22	11 24	11 26	11 27	11 29	11 30	11 32	11 34	11 35	11 37	11 38	11 40	11 41	11 43	19
20	11 57	11 58	12 0	12 2	12 3	12 5	12 7	12 8	12 10	12 12	12 13	12 15	12 17	12 18	12 20	20
21	12 33	12 34	12 36	12 38	12 40	12 41	12 43	12 45	12 47	12 48	12 50	12 52	12 54	12 55	12 57	21
22	13 8	13 10	13 12	13 14	13 16	13 18	13 19	13 21	13 23	13 25	13 27	13 29	13 30	13 32	13 34	22
23	13 44	13 46	13 48	13 50	13 52	13 54	13 56	13 58	14 0	14 1	14 3	14 5	14 7	14 9	14 11	23
24	14 20	14 22	14 24	14 26	14 28	14 30	14 32	14 34	14 36	14 38	14 40	14 42	14 44	14 46	14 48	24
25	14 56	14 58	15 0	15 2	15 4	15 6	15 8	15 10	15 13	15 15	15 17	15 19	15 21	15 23	15 25	25
26	15 32	15 34	15 36	15 38	15 40	15 43	15 45	15 47	15 49	15 51	15 53	15 56	15 58	16 0	16 2	26
27	16 8	16 10	16 12	16 14	16 17	16 19	16 21	16 23	16 26	16 28	16 30	16 32	16 35	16 37	16 39	27
28	16 43	16 46	16 48	16 50	16 53	16 55	16 57	17 0	17 2	17 4	17 7	17 9	17 11	17 14	17 16	28
29	17 19	17 22	17 24	17 26	17 29	17 31	17 34	17 36	17 39	17 41	17 43	17 46	17 48	17 51	17 53	29
30	17 55	17 58	18 0	18 3	18 5	18 8	18 10	18 13	18 15	18 18	18 20	18 23	18 25	18 28	18 30	30
31	18 31	18 33	18 36	18 39	18 41	18 44	18 46	18 49	18 52	18 54	18 57	18 59	19 2	19 4	19 7	31
32	19 7	19 9	19 12	19 15	19 17	19 20	19 23	19 25	19 28	19 31	19 33	19 36	19 39	19 41	19 44	32
33	19 43	19 45	19 48	19 51	19 54	19 56	19 59	20 2	20 5	20 7	20 10	20 13	20 16	20 18	20 21	33
34	20 18	20 21	20 24	20 27	20 30	20 33	20 35	20 38	20 41	20 44	20 47	20 50	20 52	20 55	20 58	34
35	20 54	20 57	21 0	21 3	21 6	21 9	21 12	21 15	21 18	21 20	21 23	21 26	21 29	21 32	21 35	35
36	21 30	21 33	21 36	21 39	21 42	21 45	21 48	21 51	21 54	21 57	22 0	22 3	22 6	22 9	22 12	36
37	22 6	22 9	22 12	22 15	22 18	22 21	22 24	22 27	22 31	22 34	22 37	22 40	22 43	22 46	22 49	37
38	22 42	22 45	22 48	22 51	22 54	22 58	23 1	23 4	23 7	23 10	23 13	23 17	23 20	23 23	23 26	38
39	23 18	23 21	23 24	23 27	23 31	23 34	23 37	23 40	23 44	23 47	23 50	23 53	23 57	24 0	24 3	39
40	23 53	23 57	24 0	24 3	24 7	24 10	24 13	24 17	24 20	24 23	24 27	24 30	24 33	24 37	24 40	40
41	24 29	24 33	24 36	24 39	24 43	24 46	24 50	24 53	24 57	25 0	25 3	25 7	25 10	25 14	25 17	41
42	25 5	25 9	25 12	25 16	25 19	25 23	25 26	25 30	25 33	25 37	25 40	25 44	25 47	25 51	25 54	42
43	25 41	25 44	25 48	25 52	25 55	25 59	26 2	26 6	26 10	26 13	26 17	26 20	26 24	26 27	26 31	43
44	26 17	26 20	26 24	26 28	26 31	26 35	26 39	26 42	26 46	26 50	26 53	26 57	27 1	27 4	27 8	44
45	26 53	26 56	27 0	27 4	27 8	27 11	27 15	27 19	27 23	27 26	27 30	27 34	27 38	27 41	27 45	45
46	27 28	27 32	27 36	27 40	27 44	27 48	27 51	27 55	27 59	28 3	28 7	28 11	28 14	28 18	28 22	46
47	28 4	28 8	28 12	28 16	28 20	28 24	28 28	28 32	28 36	28 39	28 43	28 47	28 51	28 55	28 59	47
48	28 40	28 44	28 48	28 52	28 56	29 0	29 4	29 8	29 12	29 16	29 20	29 24	29 28	29 32	29 36	48
49	29 16	29 20	29 24	29 28	29 32	29 36	29 40	29 44	29 49	29 53	29 57	30 1	30 5	30 9	30 13	49
50	29 52	29 56	30 0	30 4	30 8	30 13	30 17	30 21	30 25	30 29	30 33	30 38	30 42	30 46	30 50	50
51	30 28	30 32	30 36	30 40	30 45	30 49	30 53	30 57	31 2	31 6	31 10	31 14	31 19	31 23	31 27	51
52	31 3	31 8	31 12	31 16	31 21	31 25	31 29	31 34	31 38	31 42	31 47	31 51	31 55	32 0	32 4	52
53	31 39	31 44	31 48	31 52	31 57	32 1	32 6	32 10	32 15	32 19	32 23	32 28	32 32	32 37	32 41	53
54	32 15	32 20	32 24	32 29	32 33	32 38	32 42	32 47	32 51	32 56	33 0	33 5	33 9	33 14	33 18	54
55	32 51	32 55	33 0	33 5	33 9	33 14	33 18	33 23	33 28	33 32	33 37	33 41	33 46	33 50	33 55	55
56	33 27	33 31	33 36	33 41	33 45	33 50	33 55	33 59	34 4	34 9	34 13	34 18	34 23	34 27	34 32	56
57	34 3	34 7	34 12	34 17	34 22	34 26	34 31	34 36	34 41	34 45	34 50	34 55	35 0	35 4	35 9	57
58	34 38	34 43	34 48	34 53	34 58	35 3	35 7	35 12	35 17	35 22	35 27	35 32	35 36	35 41	35 46	58
59	35 14	35 19	35 24	35 29	35 34	35 39	35 44	35 49	35 54	35 58	36 3	36 8	36 13	36 18	36 23	59
60	35 50	35 55	36 0	36 5	36 10	36 15	36 20	36 25	36 30	36 35	36 40	36 45	36 50	36 55	37 0	60
HOURS 1	35 50	35 55	36 0	36 5	36 10	36 15	36 20	36 25	36 30	36 35	36 40	36 45	36 50	36 55	37 0	1 **HOURS**
2	1 11 40	1 11 50	1 12 0	1 12 10	1 12 20	1 12 30	1 12 40	1 12 50	1 13 0	1 13 10	1 13 20	1 13 30	1 13 40	1 13 50	1 14 0	2
3	1 47 30	1 47 45	1 48 0	1 48 15	1 48 30	1 48 45	1 49 0	1 49 15	1 49 30	1 49 45	1 50 0	1 50 15	1 50 30	1 50 45	1 51 0	3
4	2 23 20	2 23 40	2 24 0	2 24 20	2 24 40	2 25 0	2 25 20	2 25 40	2 26 0	2 26 20	2 26 40	2 27 0	2 27 20	2 27 40	2 28 0	4
5	2 59 10	2 59 35	3 0 0	3 0 25	3 0 50	3 1 15	3 1 40	3 2 5	3 2 30	3 2 55	3 3 20	3 3 45	3 4 10	3 4 35	3 5 0	5
6	3 35 0	3 35 30	3 36 0	3 36 30	3 37 0	3 37 30	3 38 0	3 38 30	3 39 0	3 39 30	3 40 0	3 40 30	3 41 0	3 41 30	3 42 0	6
7	4 10 50	4 11 25	4 12 0	4 12 35	4 13 10	4 13 45	4 14 20	4 14 55	4 15 30	4 16 5	4 16 40	4 17 15	4 17 50	4 18 25	4 19 0	7
8	4 46 40	4 47 20	4 48 0	4 48 40	4 49 20	4 50 0	4 50 40	4 51 20	4 52 0	4 52 40	4 53 20	4 54 0	4 54 40	4 55 20	4 56 0	8
9	5 22 30	5 23 15	5 24 0	5 24 45	5 25 30	5 26 15	5 27 0	5 27 45	5 28 30	5 29 15	5 30 0	5 30 45	5 31 30	5 32 15	5 33 0	9
10	5 58 20	5 59 10	6 0 0	6 0 50	6 1 40	6 2 30	6 3 20	6 4 10	6 5 0	6 5 50	6 6 40	6 7 30	6 8 20	6 9 10	6 10 0	10
11	6 34 10	6 35 5	6 36 0	6 36 55	6 37 50	6 38 45	6 39 40	6 40 35	6 41 30	6 42 25	6 43 20	6 44 15	6 45 10	6 46 5	6 47 0	11
12	7 10 0	7 11 0	7 12 0	7 13 0	7 14 0	7 15 0	7 16 0	7 17 0	7 18 0	7 19 0	7 20 0	7 21 0	7 22 0	7 23 0	7 24 0	12

Table VI Semidiurnal Motion of the Moon

TIME	7° 25'	7° 26'	7° 27'	7° 28'	7° 29'	7° 30'	7° 31'	7° 32'	7° 33'	7° 34'	7° 35'	7° 36'	7° 37'	7° 38'	7° 39'	TIME
MINUTES 1	0 37	0 37	0 37	0 37	0 37	0 38	0 38	0 38	0 38	0 38	0 38	0 38	0 38	0 38	0 38	1
2	1 14	1 14	1 15	1 15	1 15	1 15	1 15	1 15	1 15	1 16	1 16	1 16	1 16	1 16	1 16	2
3	1 51	1 51	1 52	1 52	1 52	1 53	1 53	1 53	1 53	1 53	1 54	1 54	1 54	1 54	1 55	3
4	2 28	2 29	2 29	2 29	2 30	2 30	2 30	2 31	2 31	2 31	2 32	2 32	2 32	2 33	2 33	4
5	3 5	3 6	3 6	3 7	3 7	3 8	3 8	3 8	3 9	3 9	3 10	3 10	3 10	3 11	3 11	5
6	3 42	3 43	3 43	3 44	3 45	3 45	3 46	3 46	3 46	3 47	3 47	3 48	3 49	3 49	3 49	6
7	4 20	4 20	4 21	4 21	4 22	4 23	4 23	4 24	4 24	4 25	4 25	4 26	4 27	4 27	4 28	7
8	4 57	4 57	4 58	4 59	4 59	5 0	5 1	5 1	5 2	5 3	5 3	5 4	5 5	5 5	5 6	8
9	5 34	5 34	5 35	5 36	5 37	5 38	5 38	5 39	5 40	5 40	5 41	5 42	5 43	5 43	5 44	9
10	6 11	6 12	6 12	6 13	6 14	6 15	6 16	6 17	6 17	6 18	6 19	6 20	6 21	6 22	6 23	10
11	6 48	6 49	6 50	6 51	6 52	6 53	6 53	6 54	6 55	6 56	6 57	6 58	6 59	7 0	7 1	11
12	7 25	7 26	7 27	7 28	7 29	7 30	7 31	7 32	7 33	7 34	7 35	7 36	7 37	7 38	7 39	12
13	8 2	8 3	8 4	8 5	8 6	8 7	8 9	8 10	8 11	8 12	8 13	8 14	8 15	8 16	8 17	13
14	8 39	8 40	8 42	8 43	8 44	8 45	8 46	8 47	8 48	8 50	8 51	8 52	8 53	8 54	8 55	14
15	9 16	9 17	9 19	9 20	9 21	9 22	9 24	9 25	9 26	9 27	9 29	9 30	9 31	9 32	9 34	15
16	9 53	9 55	9 56	9 57	9 59	10 0	10 1	10 3	10 4	10 5	10 7	10 8	10 9	10 11	10 12	16
17	10 30	10 32	10 33	10 35	10 36	10 37	10 39	10 40	10 42	10 43	10 45	10 46	10 47	10 49	10 50	17
18	11 7	11 9	11 10	11 12	11 13	11 15	11 16	11 18	11 19	11 21	11 22	11 24	11 25	11 27	11 28	18
19	11 45	11 46	11 48	11 49	11 51	11 52	11 54	11 56	11 57	11 59	12 0	12 2	12 4	12 5	12 7	19
20	12 22	12 23	12 25	12 27	12 28	12 30	12 32	12 33	12 35	12 37	12 38	12 40	12 42	12 43	12 45	20
21	12 59	13 0	13 2	13 4	13 6	13 7	13 9	13 11	13 13	13 14	13 16	13 18	13 20	13 21	13 23	21
22	13 36	13 38	13 39	13 41	13 43	13 45	13 47	13 49	13 50	13 52	13 54	13 56	13 58	14 0	14 1	22
23	14 13	14 15	14 17	14 19	14 21	14 22	14 24	14 26	14 28	14 30	14 32	14 34	14 36	14 38	14 40	23
24	14 50	14 52	14 54	14 56	14 58	15 0	15 2	15 4	15 6	15 8	15 10	15 12	15 14	15 16	15 18	24
25	15 27	15 29	15 31	15 33	15 35	15 37	15 40	15 42	15 44	15 46	15 48	15 50	15 52	15 54	15 56	25
26	16 4	16 6	16 8	16 11	16 13	16 15	16 17	16 19	16 22	16 24	16 26	16 28	16 30	16 32	16 34	26
27	16 41	16 44	16 46	16 48	16 50	16 53	16 55	16 57	16 59	17 1	17 4	17 6	17 8	17 11	17 13	27
28	17 18	17 21	17 23	17 25	17 28	17 30	17 32	17 35	17 37	17 39	17 42	17 44	17 46	17 49	17 51	28
29	17 55	17 58	18 0	18 3	18 5	18 8	18 10	18 12	18 15	18 17	18 20	18 22	18 24	18 27	18 29	29
30	18 33	18 35	18 38	18 40	18 42	18 45	18 48	18 50	18 53	18 55	18 57	19 0	19 3	19 5	19 8	30
31	19 10	19 12	19 15	19 17	19 20	19 23	19 25	19 28	19 30	19 33	19 35	19 38	19 41	19 43	19 46	31
32	19 47	19 49	19 52	19 55	19 57	20 0	20 3	20 5	20 8	20 11	20 13	20 16	20 19	20 21	20 24	32
33	20 24	20 26	20 29	20 32	20 35	20 38	20 40	20 43	20 46	20 49	20 51	20 54	20 57	21 0	21 2	33
34	21 1	21 4	21 7	21 9	21 12	21 15	21 18	21 21	21 23	21 26	21 29	21 32	21 35	21 38	21 41	34
35	21 38	21 41	21 44	21 47	21 50	21 53	21 55	21 58	22 1	22 4	22 7	22 10	22 13	22 16	22 19	35
36	22 15	22 18	22 21	22 24	22 27	22 30	22 33	22 36	22 39	22 42	22 45	22 48	22 51	22 54	22 57	36
37	22 52	22 55	22 58	23 1	23 4	23 8	23 11	23 14	23 17	23 20	23 23	23 26	23 29	23 32	23 35	37
38	23 29	23 32	23 35	23 39	23 42	23 45	23 48	23 51	23 54	23 58	24 1	24 4	24 7	24 10	24 14	38
39	24 6	24 9	24 13	24 16	24 19	24 23	24 26	24 29	24 32	24 35	24 39	24 42	24 45	24 49	24 52	39
40	24 43	24 47	24 50	24 53	24 57	25 0	25 3	25 7	25 10	25 13	25 17	25 20	25 23	25 27	25 30	40
41	25 20	25 24	25 27	25 31	25 34	25 38	25 41	25 44	25 48	25 51	25 55	25 58	26 1	26 5	26 8	41
42	25 57	26 1	26 4	26 8	26 11	26 15	26 19	26 22	26 26	26 29	26 33	26 36	26 39	26 43	26 46	42
43	26 35	26 38	26 42	26 45	26 49	26 53	26 56	27 0	27 3	27 7	27 10	27 14	27 18	27 21	27 25	43
44	27 12	27 15	27 19	27 23	27 26	27 30	27 34	27 37	27 41	27 45	27 48	27 52	27 56	27 59	28 3	44
45	27 49	27 53	27 56	28 0	28 4	28 8	28 11	28 15	28 19	28 23	28 26	28 30	28 34	28 38	28 41	45
46	28 26	28 30	28 34	28 37	28 41	28 45	28 49	28 53	28 57	29 0	29 4	29 8	29 12	29 16	29 20	46
47	29 3	29 7	29 11	29 15	29 19	29 22	29 26	29 30	29 34	29 38	29 42	29 46	29 50	29 54	29 58	47
48	29 40	29 44	29 48	29 52	29 56	30 0	30 4	30 8	30 12	30 16	30 20	30 24	30 28	30 32	30 36	48
49	30 17	30 21	30 25	30 29	30 33	30 38	30 42	30 46	30 50	30 54	30 58	31 2	31 6	31 10	31 14	49
50	30 54	30 58	31 2	31 7	31 11	31 15	31 19	31 23	31 27	31 32	31 36	31 40	31 44	31 48	31 52	50
51	31 31	31 35	31 40	31 44	31 48	31 53	31 57	32 1	32 5	32 9	32 14	32 18	32 22	32 26	32 31	51
52	32 8	32 13	32 17	32 21	32 26	32 30	32 34	32 39	32 43	32 47	32 52	32 56	33 0	33 5	33 9	52
53	32 45	32 50	32 54	32 59	33 3	33 8	33 12	33 16	33 21	33 25	33 30	33 34	33 38	33 43	33 47	53
54	33 23	33 27	33 31	33 36	33 40	33 45	33 49	33 54	33 58	34 3	34 8	34 12	34 16	34 21	34 25	54
55	34 0	34 4	34 9	34 13	34 18	34 23	34 27	34 32	34 36	34 41	34 45	34 50	34 55	34 59	35 4	55
56	34 37	34 41	34 46	34 51	34 55	35 0	35 5	35 9	35 14	35 19	35 23	35 28	35 33	35 37	35 42	56
57	35 14	35 18	35 23	35 28	35 33	35 38	35 42	35 47	35 52	35 56	36 1	36 6	36 11	36 15	36 20	57
58	35 51	35 56	36 0	36 5	36 10	36 15	36 20	36 25	36 30	36 34	36 39	36 44	36 49	36 54	36 59	58
59	36 28	36 33	36 38	36 43	36 48	36 53	36 57	37 2	37 7	37 12	37 17	37 22	37 27	37 32	37 37	59
60	37 5	37 10	37 15	37 20	37 25	37 30	37 35	37 40	37 45	37 50	37 55	38 0	38 5	38 10	38 15	60
HOURS 1	37 5	37 10	37 15	37 20	37 25	37 30	37 35	37 40	37 45	37 50	37 55	38 0	38 5	38 10	38 15	1
2	1 14 10	1 14 20	1 14 30	1 14 40	1 14 50	1 15 0	1 15 10	1 15 20	1 15 30	1 15 40	1 15 50	1 16 0	1 16 10	1 16 20	1 16 30	2
3	1 51 15	1 51 30	1 51 45	1 52 0	1 52 15	1 52 30	1 52 45	1 53 0	1 53 15	1 53 30	1 53 45	1 54 0	1 54 15	1 54 30	1 54 45	3
4	2 28 20	2 28 40	2 29 0	2 29 20	2 29 40	2 30 0	2 30 20	2 30 40	2 31 0	2 31 20	2 31 40	2 32 0	2 32 20	2 32 40	2 33 0	4
5	3 5 25	3 5 50	3 6 15	3 6 40	3 7 5	3 7 30	3 7 55	3 8 20	3 8 45	3 9 10	3 9 35	3 10 0	3 10 25	3 10 50	3 11 15	5
6	3 42 30	3 43 0	3 43 30	3 44 0	3 44 30	3 45 0	3 45 30	3 46 0	3 46 30	3 47 0	3 47 30	3 48 0	3 48 30	3 49 0	3 49 30	6
7	4 19 35	4 20 10	4 20 45	4 21 20	4 21 55	4 22 30	4 23 5	4 23 40	4 24 15	4 24 50	4 25 25	4 26 0	4 26 35	4 27 10	4 27 45	7
8	4 56 40	4 57 20	4 58 0	4 58 40	4 59 20	5 0 0	5 0 40	5 1 20	5 2 0	5 2 40	5 3 20	5 4 0	5 4 40	5 5 20	5 6 0	8
9	5 33 45	5 34 30	5 35 15	5 36 0	5 36 45	5 37 30	5 38 15	5 39 0	5 39 45	5 40 30	5 41 15	5 42 0	5 42 45	5 43 30	5 44 15	9
10	6 10 50	6 11 40	6 12 30	6 13 20	6 14 10	6 15 0	6 15 50	6 16 40	6 17 30	6 18 20	6 19 10	6 20 0	6 20 50	6 21 40	6 22 30	10
11	6 47 55	6 48 50	6 49 45	6 50 40	6 51 35	6 52 30	6 53 25	6 54 20	6 55 15	6 56 10	6 57 5	6 58 0	6 58 55	6 59 50	7 0 45	11
12	7 25 0	7 26 0	7 27 0	7 28 0	7 29 0	7 30 0	7 31 0	7 32 0	7 33 0	7 34 0	7 35 0	7 36 0	7 37 0	7 38 0	7 39 0	12

Table VII Diurnal Motion of the Planets

	24 HOUR TRAVEL															
TIME	0° 1'	0° 2'	0° 3'	0° 4'	0° 5'	0° 6'	0° 7'	0° 8'	0° 9'	0° 10'	0° 11'	0° 12'	0° 13'	0° 14'	0° 15'	TIME
MINUTES																**MINUTES**
1	0 0	0 0	0 0	0 0	0 0	0 0	0 0	0 1	0 1	0 1	0 1	0 1	0 1	0 1	0 1	1
2	0 0	0 0	0 0	0 0	0 1	0 1	0 1	0 1	0 1	0 1	0 1	0 2	0 2	0 2	0 2	2
3	0 0	0 0	0 0	0 1	0 1	0 1	0 1	0 1	0 1	0 1	0 1	0 2	0 2	0 2	0 2	3
4	0 0	0 0	0 1	0 1	0 1	0 1	0 1	0 1	0 2	0 2	0 2	0 2	0 2	0 2	0 3	4
5	0 0	0 0	0 1	0 1	0 1	0 1	0 1	0 2	0 2	0 2	0 2	0 3	0 3	0 3	0 3	5
6	0 0	0 1	0 1	0 1	0 1	0 2	0 2	0 2	0 2	0 3	0 3	0 3	0 3	0 4	0 4	6
7	0 0	0 1	0 1	0 1	0 1	0 2	0 2	0 2	0 3	0 3	0 3	0 4	0 4	0 4	0 4	7
8	0 0	0 1	0 1	0 1	0 2	0 2	0 2	0 3	0 3	0 3	0 4	0 4	0 4	0 5	0 5	8
9	0 0	0 1	0 1	0 1	0 2	0 2	0 3	0 3	0 3	0 4	0 4	0 4	0 5	0 5	0 5	9
10	0 0	0 1	0 1	0 2	0 2	0 3	0 3	0 3	0 4	0 4	0 5	0 5	0 5	0 6	0 6	10
11	0 0	0 1	0 1	0 2	0 2	0 3	0 3	0 4	0 4	0 5	0 5	0 6	0 6	0 6	0 7	11
12	0 1	0 1	0 2	0 2	0 3	0 3	0 4	0 4	0 4	0 5	0 5	0 6	0 7	0 7	0 8	12
13	0 1	0 1	0 2	0 2	0 3	0 3	0 4	0 4	0 5	0 5	0 6	0 7	0 7	0 8	0 8	13
14	0 1	0 1	0 2	0 2	0 3	0 4	0 4	0 5	0 5	0 6	0 6	0 7	0 8	0 8	0 9	14
15	0 1	0 1	0 2	0 3	0 3	0 4	0 4	0 5	0 6	0 6	0 7	0 8	0 8	0 9	0 9	15
16	0 1	0 1	0 2	0 3	0 3	0 4	0 5	0 5	0 6	0 7	0 7	0 8	0 9	0 9	0 10	16
17	0 1	0 1	0 2	0 3	0 4	0 4	0 5	0 6	0 6	0 7	0 8	0 8	0 9	0 10	0 11	17
18	0 1	0 2	0 2	0 3	0 4	0 4	0 5	0 6	0 7	0 8	0 8	0 9	0 10	0 11	0 11	18
19	0 1	0 2	0 2	0 3	0 4	0 5	0 6	0 6	0 7	0 8	0 8	0 9	0 10	0 11	0 12	19
20	0 1	0 2	0 3	0 3	0 4	0 5	0 6	0 7	0 8	0 8	0 9	0 10	0 11	0 12	0 12	20
21	0 1	0 2	0 3	0 4	0 5	0 5	0 6	0 7	0 8	0 9	0 10	0 10	0 11	0 12	0 13	21
22	0 1	0 2	0 3	0 4	0 5	0 5	0 6	0 7	0 8	0 9	0 10	0 11	0 12	0 13	0 14	22
23	0 1	0 2	0 3	0 4	0 5	0 6	0 7	0 8	0 9	0 10	0 11	0 12	0 12	0 13	0 14	23
24	0 1	0 2	0 3	0 4	0 5	0 6	0 7	0 8	0 9	0 10	0 11	0 12	0 13	0 14	0 15	24
25	0 1	0 2	0 3	0 4	0 5	0 6	0 7	0 8	0 9	0 10	0 11	0 12	0 14	0 15	0 16	25
26	0 1	0 2	0 3	0 4	0 5	0 7	0 8	0 9	0 10	0 11	0 12	0 13	0 14	0 15	0 16	26
27	0 1	0 2	0 3	0 4	0 6	0 7	0 8	0 9	0 10	0 11	0 12	0 13	0 15	0 16	0 17	27
28	0 1	0 2	0 4	0 5	0 6	0 7	0 8	0 9	0 11	0 12	0 13	0 14	0 15	0 16	0 18	28
29	0 1	0 2	0 4	0 5	0 6	0 7	0 8	0 10	0 11	0 12	0 13	0 14	0 16	0 17	0 18	29
30	0 1	0 3	0 4	0 5	0 6	0 8	0 9	0 10	0 11	0 12	0 14	0 15	0 16	0 18	0 19	30
31	0 1	0 3	0 4	0 5	0 6	0 8	0 9	0 10	0 12	0 13	0 14	0 16	0 17	0 18	0 19	31
32	0 1	0 3	0 4	0 5	0 7	0 8	0 9	0 11	0 12	0 13	0 15	0 16	0 17	0 19	0 20	32
33	0 1	0 3	0 4	0 5	0 7	0 8	0 10	0 11	0 12	0 14	0 15	0 17	0 18	0 19	0 21	33
34	0 1	0 3	0 4	0 6	0 7	0 8	0 10	0 11	0 13	0 14	0 16	0 17	0 18	0 20	0 21	34
35	0 1	0 3	0 4	0 6	0 7	0 9	0 10	0 12	0 13	0 15	0 16	0 18	0 19	0 20	0 22	35
36	0 2	0 3	0 4	0 6	0 8	0 9	0 11	0 12	0 13	0 15	0 17	0 18	0 20	0 21	0 23	36
37	0 2	0 3	0 5	0 6	0 8	0 9	0 11	0 12	0 14	0 15	0 17	0 19	0 20	0 22	0 23	37
38	0 2	0 3	0 5	0 6	0 8	0 9	0 11	0 13	0 14	0 16	0 18	0 19	0 21	0 22	0 24	38
39	0 2	0 3	0 5	0 7	0 8	0 10	0 11	0 13	0 15	0 16	0 18	0 20	0 21	0 23	0 24	39
40	0 2	0 3	0 5	0 7	0 8	0 10	0 12	0 13	0 15	0 17	0 18	0 20	0 22	0 23	0 25	40
41	0 2	0 3	0 5	0 7	0 9	0 10	0 12	0 14	0 15	0 17	0 19	0 21	0 22	0 24	0 26	41
42	0 2	0 4	0 5	0 7	0 9	0 11	0 12	0 14	0 16	0 18	0 19	0 21	0 23	0 25	0 26	42
43	0 2	0 4	0 5	0 7	0 9	0 11	0 13	0 14	0 16	0 18	0 20	0 22	0 23	0 25	0 27	43
44	0 2	0 4	0 5	0 7	0 9	0 11	0 13	0 15	0 17	0 18	0 20	0 22	0 24	0 26	0 28	44
45	0 2	0 4	0 6	0 8	0 9	0 11	0 13	0 15	0 17	0 19	0 21	0 23	0 24	0 26	0 28	45
46	0 2	0 4	0 6	0 8	0 10	0 12	0 13	0 15	0 17	0 19	0 21	0 23	0 25	0 27	0 29	46
47	0 2	0 4	0 6	0 8	0 10	0 12	0 14	0 16	0 18	0 20	0 22	0 24	0 25	0 27	0 29	47
48	0 2	0 4	0 6	0 8	0 10	0 12	0 14	0 16	0 18	0 20	0 22	0 24	0 26	0 28	0 30	48
49	0 2	0 4	0 6	0 8	0 10	0 12	0 14	0 16	0 18	0 20	0 22	0 25	0 27	0 29	0 31	49
50	0 2	0 4	0 6	0 8	0 10	0 12	0 15	0 17	0 19	0 21	0 23	0 25	0 27	0 29	0 31	50
51	0 2	0 4	0 6	0 8	0 11	0 13	0 15	0 17	0 19	0 21	0 23	0 26	0 28	0 30	0 32	51
52	0 2	0 4	0 7	0 9	0 11	0 13	0 15	0 17	0 20	0 22	0 24	0 26	0 28	0 30	0 33	52
53	0 2	0 4	0 7	0 9	0 11	0 13	0 15	0 18	0 20	0 22	0 24	0 27	0 29	0 31	0 33	53
54	0 2	0 4	0 7	0 9	0 11	0 13	0 16	0 18	0 20	0 23	0 25	0 27	0 29	0 32	0 34	54
55	0 2	0 5	0 7	0 9	0 11	0 14	0 16	0 18	0 21	0 23	0 25	0 28	0 30	0 32	0 34	55
56	0 2	0 5	0 7	0 9	0 12	0 14	0 16	0 19	0 21	0 23	0 26	0 28	0 30	0 33	0 35	56
57	0 2	0 5	0 7	0 10	0 12	0 14	0 17	0 19	0 21	0 24	0 26	0 29	0 31	0 33	0 36	57
58	0 2	0 5	0 7	0 10	0 12	0 15	0 17	0 19	0 22	0 24	0 27	0 29	0 31	0 34	0 36	58
59	0 2	0 5	0 7	0 10	0 12	0 15	0 17	0 20	0 22	0 25	0 27	0 30	0 32	0 34	0 37	59
60	0 3	0 5	0 8	0 10	0 12	0 15	0 18	0 20	0 23	0 25	0 28	0 30	0 33	0 35	0 38	60
HOURS																**HOURS**
1	0 3	0 5	0 8	0 10	0 12	0 15	0 18	0 20	0 23	0 25	0 28	0 30	0 33	0 35	0 38	1
2	0 5	0 10	0 15	0 20	0 25	0 30	0 35	0 40	0 45	0 50	0 55	1 0	1 5	1 10	1 15	2
3	0 8	0 15	0 23	0 30	0 38	0 45	0 53	1 0	1 8	1 15	1 23	1 30	1 38	1 45	1 53	3
4	0 10	0 20	0 30	0 40	0 50	1 0	1 10	1 20	1 30	1 40	1 50	2 0	2 10	2 20	2 30	4
5	0 12	0 25	0 38	0 50	1 3	1 15	1 27	1 40	1 53	2 5	2 17	2 30	2 42	2 55	3 8	5
6	0 15	0 30	0 45	1 0	1 15	1 30	1 45	2 0	2 15	2 30	2 45	3 0	3 15	3 30	3 45	6
7	0 18	0 35	0 53	1 10	1 27	1 45	2 3	2 20	2 38	2 55	3 13	3 30	3 48	4 5	4 23	7
8	0 20	0 40	1 0	1 20	1 40	2 0	2 20	2 40	3 0	3 20	3 40	4 0	4 20	4 40	5 0	8
9	0 23	0 45	1 8	1 30	1 53	2 15	2 38	3 0	3 23	3 45	4 8	4 30	4 53	5 15	5 38	9
10	0 25	0 50	1 15	1 40	2 5	2 30	2 55	3 20	3 45	4 10	4 35	5 0	5 25	5 50	6 15	10
11	0 28	0 55	1 23	1 50	2 18	2 45	3 12	3 40	4 8	4 35	5 2	5 30	5 57	6 25	6 53	11
12	0 30	1 0	1 30	2 0	2 30	3 0	3 30	4 0	4 30	5 0	5 30	6 0	6 30	7 0	7 30	12
13	0 33	1 5	1 38	2 10	2 42	3 15	3 48	4 20	4 53	5 25	5 58	6 30	7 3	7 35	8 8	13
14	0 35	1 10	1 45	2 20	2 55	3 30	4 5	4 40	5 15	5 50	6 25	7 0	7 35	8 10	8 45	14
15	0 38	1 15	1 53	2 30	3 8	3 45	4 23	5 0	5 38	6 15	6 53	7 30	8 8	8 45	9 23	15
16	0 40	1 20	2 0	2 40	3 20	4 0	4 40	5 20	6 0	6 40	7 20	8 0	8 40	9 20	10 0	16
17	0 43	1 25	2 8	2 50	3 33	4 15	4 57	5 40	6 23	7 5	7 47	8 30	9 12	9 55	10 38	17
18	0 45	1 30	2 15	3 0	3 45	4 30	5 15	6 0	6 45	7 30	8 15	9 0	9 45	10 30	11 15	18
19	0 48	1 35	2 23	3 10	3 57	4 45	5 32	6 20	7 8	7 55	8 42	9 30	10 17	11 5	11 52	19
20	0 50	1 40	2 30	3 20	4 10	5 0	5 50	6 40	7 30	8 20	9 10	10 0	10 50	11 40	12 30	20
21	0 53	1 45	2 38	3 30	4 23	5 15	6 8	7 0	7 53	8 45	9 38	10 30	11 23	12 15	13 8	21
22	0 55	1 50	2 45	3 40	4 35	5 30	6 25	7 20	8 15	9 10	10 5	11 0	11 55	12 50	13 45	22
23	0 58	1 55	2 53	3 50	4 48	5 45	6 42	7 40	8 38	9 35	10 32	11 30	12 27	13 25	14 23	23
24	1 0	2 0	3 0	4 0	5 0	6 0	7 0	8 0	9 0	10 0	11 0	12 0	13 0	14 0	15 0	24

Table VII Diurnal Motion of the Planets

24 HOUR TRAVEL

TIME	0° 16'	0° 17'	0° 18'	0° 19'	0° 20'	0° 21'	0° 22'	0° 23'	0° 24'	0° 25'	0° 26'	0° 27'	0° 28'	0° 29'	0° 30'	TIME
MINUTES																
1	0 1	0 1	0 1	0 1	0 1	0 1	0 1	0 1	0 1	0 1	0 1	0 1	0 1	0 1	0 1	1
2	0 1	0 1	0 2	0 2	0 2	0 2	0 2	0 2	0 2	0 2	0 2	0 2	0 2	0 2	0 3	2
3	0 2	0 2	0 2	0 2	0 3	0 3	0 3	0 3	0 3	0 3	0 3	0 3	0 4	0 4	0 4	3
4	0 3	0 3	0 3	0 3	0 3	0 4	0 4	0 4	0 4	0 4	0 4	0 5	0 5	0 5	0 5	4
5	0 3	0 4	0 4	0 4	0 4	0 4	0 5	0 5	0 5	0 5	0 5	0 6	0 6	0 6	0 6	5
6	0 4	0 4	0 5	0 5	0 5	0 5	0 6	0 6	0 6	0 6	0 7	0 7	0 7	0 7	0 8	6
7	0 5	0 5	0 5	0 6	0 6	0 6	0 6	0 7	0 7	0 7	0 8	0 8	0 8	0 8	0 9	7
8	0 5	0 6	0 6	0 6	0 7	0 7	0 7	0 8	0 8	0 8	0 9	0 9	0 9	0 10	0 10	8
9	0 6	0 6	0 7	0 7	0 8	0 8	0 8	0 9	0 9	0 9	0 10	0 10	0 11	0 11	0 11	9
10	0 7	0 7	0 8	0 8	0 8	0 9	0 9	0 10	0 10	0 10	0 11	0 11	0 12	0 12	0 13	10
11	0 7	0 8	0 8	0 9	0 9	0 10	0 10	0 11	0 11	0 11	0 12	0 12	0 13	0 13	0 14	11
12	0 8	0 9	0 9	0 10	0 10	0 11	0 11	0 12	0 12	0 13	0 13	0 14	0 14	0 15	0 15	12
13	0 9	0 9	0 10	0 10	0 11	0 11	0 12	0 12	0 13	0 14	0 14	0 15	0 15	0 16	0 16	13
14	0 9	0 10	0 11	0 11	0 12	0 12	0 13	0 13	0 14	0 15	0 15	0 16	0 16	0 17	0 18	14
15	0 10	0 11	0 11	0 12	0 13	0 13	0 14	0 14	0 15	0 16	0 16	0 17	0 18	0 18	0 19	15
16	0 11	0 11	0 12	0 13	0 13	0 14	0 15	0 15	0 16	0 17	0 17	0 18	0 19	0 19	0 20	16
17	0 11	0 12	0 13	0 13	0 14	0 15	0 16	0 16	0 17	0 18	0 18	0 19	0 20	0 21	0 21	17
18	0 12	0 13	0 14	0 14	0 15	0 16	0 17	0 17	0 18	0 19	0 20	0 20	0 21	0 22	0 23	18
19	0 13	0 13	0 14	0 15	0 16	0 17	0 17	0 18	0 19	0 20	0 21	0 21	0 22	0 23	0 24	19
20	0 13	0 14	0 15	0 16	0 17	0 18	0 18	0 19	0 20	0 21	0 22	0 23	0 23	0 24	0 25	20
21	0 14	0 15	0 16	0 17	0 18	0 18	0 19	0 20	0 21	0 22	0 23	0 24	0 25	0 25	0 26	21
22	0 15	0 16	0 17	0 17	0 18	0 19	0 20	0 21	0 22	0 23	0 24	0 25	0 26	0 27	0 28	22
23	0 15	0 16	0 17	0 18	0 19	0 20	0 21	0 22	0 23	0 24	0 25	0 26	0 27	0 28	0 29	23
24	0 16	0 17	0 18	0 19	0 20	0 21	0 22	0 23	0 24	0 25	0 26	0 27	0 28	0 29	0 30	24
25	0 17	0 18	0 19	0 20	0 21	0 22	0 23	0 24	0 25	0 26	0 27	0 28	0 29	0 30	0 31	25
26	0 17	0 18	0 20	0 21	0 22	0 23	0 24	0 25	0 26	0 27	0 28	0 29	0 30	0 31	0 33	26
27	0 18	0 19	0 20	0 21	0 23	0 24	0 25	0 26	0 27	0 28	0 29	0 30	0 32	0 33	0 34	27
28	0 19	0 20	0 21	0 22	0 23	0 25	0 26	0 27	0 28	0 29	0 30	0 32	0 33	0 34	0 35	28
29	0 19	0 21	0 22	0 23	0 24	0 25	0 27	0 28	0 29	0 30	0 31	0 33	0 34	0 35	0 36	29
30	0 20	0 21	0 23	0 24	0 25	0 26	0 28	0 29	0 30	0 31	0 33	0 34	0 35	0 36	0 38	30
31	0 21	0 22	0 23	0 25	0 26	0 27	0 28	0 30	0 31	0 32	0 34	0 35	0 36	0 37	0 39	31
32	0 21	0 23	0 24	0 25	0 27	0 28	0 29	0 31	0 32	0 33	0 35	0 36	0 37	0 39	0 40	32
33	0 22	0 23	0 25	0 26	0 28	0 29	0 30	0 32	0 33	0 34	0 36	0 37	0 39	0 40	0 41	33
34	0 23	0 24	0 26	0 27	0 28	0 30	0 31	0 33	0 34	0 35	0 37	0 38	0 40	0 41	0 43	34
35	0 23	0 25	0 26	0 28	0 29	0 31	0 32	0 34	0 35	0 36	0 38	0 39	0 41	0 42	0 44	35
36	0 24	0 26	0 27	0 29	0 30	0 32	0 33	0 35	0 36	0 38	0 39	0 41	0 42	0 44	0 45	36
37	0 25	0 26	0 28	0 29	0 31	0 32	0 34	0 35	0 37	0 39	0 40	0 42	0 43	0 45	0 46	37
38	0 25	0 27	0 29	0 30	0 32	0 33	0 35	0 36	0 38	0 40	0 41	0 43	0 44	0 46	0 48	38
39	0 26	0 28	0 29	0 31	0 33	0 34	0 36	0 37	0 39	0 41	0 42	0 44	0 46	0 47	0 49	39
40	0 27	0 28	0 30	0 32	0 33	0 35	0 37	0 38	0 40	0 42	0 43	0 45	0 47	0 48	0 50	40
41	0 27	0 29	0 31	0 32	0 34	0 36	0 38	0 39	0 41	0 43	0 44	0 46	0 48	0 50	0 51	41
42	0 28	0 30	0 32	0 33	0 35	0 37	0 39	0 40	0 42	0 44	0 46	0 47	0 49	0 51	0 53	42
43	0 29	0 30	0 32	0 34	0 36	0 38	0 39	0 41	0 43	0 45	0 47	0 48	0 50	0 52	0 54	43
44	0 29	0 31	0 33	0 35	0 37	0 39	0 40	0 42	0 44	0 46	0 48	0 50	0 51	0 53	0 55	44
45	0 30	0 32	0 34	0 36	0 38	0 39	0 41	0 43	0 45	0 47	0 49	0 51	0 53	0 54	0 56	45
46	0 31	0 33	0 35	0 36	0 38	0 40	0 42	0 44	0 46	0 48	0 50	0 52	0 54	0 56	0 58	46
47	0 31	0 33	0 35	0 37	0 39	0 41	0 43	0 45	0 47	0 49	0 51	0 53	0 55	0 57	0 59	47
48	0 32	0 34	0 36	0 38	0 40	0 42	0 44	0 46	0 48	0 50	0 52	0 54	0 56	0 58	1 0	48
49	0 33	0 35	0 37	0 39	0 41	0 43	0 45	0 47	0 49	0 51	0 53	0 55	0 57	0 59	1 1	49
50	0 33	0 35	0 38	0 40	0 42	0 44	0 46	0 48	0 50	0 52	0 54	0 56	0 58	1 0	1 3	50
51	0 34	0 36	0 38	0 40	0 43	0 45	0 47	0 49	0 51	0 53	0 55	0 57	1 0	1 2	1 4	51
52	0 35	0 37	0 39	0 41	0 43	0 46	0 48	0 50	0 52	0 54	0 56	0 59	1 1	1 3	1 5	52
53	0 35	0 38	0 40	0 42	0 44	0 46	0 49	0 51	0 53	0 55	0 57	1 0	1 2	1 4	1 6	53
54	0 36	0 38	0 41	0 43	0 45	0 47	0 50	0 52	0 54	0 56	0 59	1 1	1 3	1 5	1 8	54
55	0 37	0 39	0 41	0 44	0 46	0 48	0 50	0 53	0 55	0 57	1 0	1 2	1 4	1 6	1 9	55
56	0 37	0 40	0 42	0 44	0 47	0 49	0 51	0 54	0 56	0 58	1 1	1 3	1 5	1 8	1 10	56
57	0 38	0 40	0 43	0 45	0 48	0 50	0 52	0 55	0 57	0 59	1 2	1 4	1 7	1 9	1 11	57
58	0 39	0 41	0 44	0 46	0 48	0 51	0 53	0 56	0 58	1 0	1 3	1 5	1 8	1 10	1 13	58
59	0 39	0 42	0 44	0 47	0 49	0 52	0 54	0 57	0 59	1 1	1 4	1 6	1 9	1 11	1 14	59
60	0 40	0 43	0 45	0 48	0 50	0 53	0 55	0 58	1 0	1 3	1 5	1 8	1 10	1 13	1 15	60
HOURS																
1	0 40	0 43	0 45	0 48	0 50	0 53	0 55	0 58	1 0	1 3	1 5	1 8	1 10	1 12	1 15	1
2	1 20	1 25	1 30	1 35	1 40	1 45	1 50	1 55	2 0	2 5	2 10	2 15	2 20	2 25	2 30	2
3	2 0	2 8	2 15	2 23	2 30	2 38	2 45	2 53	3 0	3 8	3 15	3 23	3 30	3 38	3 45	3
4	2 40	2 50	3 0	3 10	3 20	3 30	3 40	3 50	4 0	4 10	4 20	4 30	4 40	4 50	5 0	4
5	3 20	3 32	3 45	3 57	4 10	4 23	4 35	4 47	5 0	5 12	5 25	5 37	5 50	6 2	6 15	5
6	4 0	4 15	4 30	4 45	5 0	5 15	5 30	5 45	6 0	6 15	6 30	6 45	7 0	7 15	7 30	6
7	4 40	4 58	5 15	5 33	5 50	6 8	6 25	6 43	7 0	7 18	7 35	7 53	8 10	8 28	8 45	7
8	5 20	5 40	6 0	6 20	6 40	7 0	7 20	7 40	8 0	8 20	8 40	9 0	9 20	9 40	10 0	8
9	6 0	6 23	6 45	7 8	7 30	7 53	8 15	8 38	9 0	9 23	9 45	10 8	10 30	10 53	11 15	9
10	6 40	7 5	7 30	7 55	8 20	8 45	9 10	9 35	10 0	10 25	10 50	11 15	11 40	12 5	12 30	10
11	7 20	7 47	8 15	8 42	9 10	9 38	10 5	10 32	11 0	11 27	11 55	12 22	12 50	13 17	13 45	11
12	8 0	8 30	9 0	9 30	10 0	10 30	11 0	11 30	12 0	12 30	13 0	13 30	14 0	14 30	15 0	12
13	8 40	9 13	9 45	10 18	10 50	11 23	11 55	12 28	13 0	13 33	14 5	14 38	15 10	15 43	16 15	13
14	9 20	9 55	10 30	11 5	11 40	12 15	12 50	13 25	14 0	14 35	15 10	15 45	16 20	16 55	17 30	14
15	10 0	10 38	11 15	11 53	12 30	13 8	13 45	14 23	15 0	15 38	16 15	16 53	17 30	18 8	18 45	15
16	10 40	11 20	12 0	12 40	13 20	14 0	14 40	15 20	16 0	16 40	17 20	18 0	18 40	19 20	20 0	16
17	11 20	12 2	12 45	13 27	14 10	14 53	15 35	16 18	17 0	17 42	18 25	19 8	19 50	20 33	21 15	17
18	12 0	12 45	13 30	14 15	15 0	15 45	16 30	17 15	18 0	18 45	19 30	20 15	21 0	21 45	22 30	18
19	12 40	13 27	14 15	15 2	15 50	16 38	17 25	18 12	19 0	19 48	20 35	21 23	22 10	22 57	23 45	19
20	13 20	14 10	15 0	15 50	16 40	17 30	18 20	19 10	20 0	20 50	21 40	22 30	23 20	24 10	25 0	20
21	14 0	14 53	15 45	16 38	17 30	18 23	19 15	20 8	21 0	21 53	22 45	23 38	24 30	25 23	26 15	21
22	14 40	15 35	16 30	17 25	18 20	19 15	20 10	21 5	22 0	22 55	23 50	24 45	25 40	26 35	27 30	22
23	15 20	16 18	17 15	18 12	19 10	20 8	21 5	22 3	23 0	23 57	24 55	25 53	26 50	27 48	28 45	23
24	16 0	17 0	18 0	19 0	20 0	21 0	22 0	23 0	24 0	25 0	26 0	27 0	28 0	29 0	30 0	24

Table VII Diurnal Motion of the Planets

24 HOUR TRAVEL

Each planet column gives the travel in ° ′ ″ (the values below are ′ ″).

TIME	0° 31′	0° 32′	0° 33′	0° 34′	0° 35′	0° 36′	0° 37′	0° 38′	0° 39′	0° 40′	0° 41′	0° 42′	0° 43′	0° 44′	0° 45′	TIME
MINUTES																
1	0 1	0 1	0 1	0 1	0 1	0 2	0 2	0 2	0 2	0 2	0 2	0 2	0 2	0 2	0 2	1
2	0 3	0 3	0 3	0 3	0 3	0 3	0 3	0 3	0 3	0 3	0 3	0 4	0 4	0 4	0 4	2
3	0 4	0 4	0 4	0 4	0 4	0 4	0 5	0 5	0 5	0 5	0 5	0 5	0 5	0 5	0 6	3
4	0 5	0 5	0 5	0 6	0 6	0 6	0 6	0 6	0 7	0 7	0 7	0 7	0 7	0 7	0 8	4
5	0 6	0 7	0 7	0 7	0 7	0 8	0 8	0 8	0 8	0 8	0 9	0 9	0 9	0 9	0 9	5
6	0 8	0 8	0 8	0 8	0 9	0 9	0 9	0 9	0 9	0 10	0 10	0 10	0 11	0 11	0 11	6
7	0 9	0 9	0 10	0 10	0 10	0 11	0 11	0 11	0 11	0 11	0 12	0 12	0 12	0 13	0 13	7
8	0 10	0 11	0 11	0 11	0 12	0 12	0 12	0 13	0 13	0 13	0 14	0 14	0 14	0 15	0 15	8
9	0 12	0 12	0 12	0 13	0 13	0 14	0 14	0 14	0 15	0 15	0 15	0 16	0 16	0 17	0 17	9
10	0 13	0 13	0 14	0 14	0 15	0 15	0 15	0 16	0 16	0 17	0 17	0 18	0 18	0 18	0 19	10
11	0 14	0 15	0 15	0 16	0 16	0 17	0 17	0 17	0 18	0 18	0 19	0 19	0 20	0 20	0 21	11
12	0 16	0 16	0 17	0 17	0 18	0 18	0 19	0 19	0 19	0 20	0 20	0 21	0 22	0 22	0 23	12
13	0 17	0 17	0 18	0 18	0 19	0 20	0 20	0 21	0 21	0 22	0 22	0 23	0 23	0 24	0 24	13
14	0 18	0 19	0 19	0 20	0 20	0 21	0 22	0 22	0 23	0 23	0 24	0 25	0 25	0 26	0 26	14
15	0 19	0 20	0 21	0 21	0 22	0 23	0 23	0 24	0 24	0 25	0 26	0 26	0 27	0 28	0 28	15
16	0 21	0 21	0 22	0 23	0 23	0 24	0 25	0 25	0 26	0 27	0 27	0 28	0 29	0 29	0 30	16
17	0 22	0 23	0 23	0 24	0 25	0 26	0 26	0 27	0 28	0 28	0 29	0 30	0 30	0 31	0 32	17
18	0 23	0 24	0 25	0 26	0 26	0 27	0 28	0 29	0 29	0 30	0 31	0 32	0 32	0 33	0 34	18
19	0 25	0 25	0 26	0 27	0 28	0 29	0 29	0 30	0 31	0 32	0 32	0 33	0 34	0 35	0 36	19
20	0 26	0 27	0 28	0 28	0 29	0 30	0 31	0 32	0 32	0 33	0 33	0 34	0 35	0 36	0 38	20
21	0 27	0 28	0 29	0 30	0 31	0 32	0 32	0 33	0 34	0 35	0 36	0 37	0 38	0 38	0 39	21
22	0 28	0 29	0 30	0 31	0 32	0 33	0 34	0 35	0 36	0 37	0 38	0 39	0 39	0 40	0 41	22
23	0 30	0 31	0 32	0 33	0 34	0 35	0 35	0 36	0 37	0 38	0 39	0 40	0 41	0 42	0 43	23
24	0 31	0 32	0 33	0 34	0 35	0 36	0 37	0 38	0 39	0 40	0 41	0 42	0 43	0 44	0 45	24
25	0 32	0 33	0 34	0 35	0 36	0 38	0 39	0 40	0 40	0 41	0 42	0 43	0 44	0 45	0 47	25
26	0 34	0 35	0 36	0 37	0 38	0 39	0 40	0 41	0 42	0 43	0 44	0 46	0 47	0 48	0 49	26
27	0 35	0 36	0 37	0 38	0 39	0 41	0 42	0 43	0 44	0 45	0 46	0 47	0 48	0 49	0 51	27
28	0 36	0 37	0 39	0 40	0 41	0 42	0 43	0 44	0 46	0 47	0 48	0 49	0 50	0 51	0 53	28
29	0 37	0 39	0 40	0 41	0 42	0 44	0 45	0 46	0 47	0 48	0 50	0 51	0 52	0 53	0 54	29
30	0 39	0 40	0 41	0 43	0 44	0 45	0 46	0 48	0 49	0 50	0 51	0 53	0 54	0 55	0 56	30
31	0 40	0 41	0 43	0 44	0 45	0 47	0 48	0 49	0 50	0 52	0 53	0 54	0 56	0 57	0 58	31
32	0 41	0 43	0 44	0 45	0 47	0 48	0 49	0 51	0 52	0 53	0 55	0 56	0 57	0 59	1 0	32
33	0 43	0 44	0 45	0 47	0 48	0 49	0 51	0 52	0 54	0 55	0 56	0 58	0 59	1 0	1 2	33
34	0 44	0 45	0 47	0 48	0 50	0 51	0 52	0 54	0 55	0 57	0 58	1 0	1 1	1 2	1 4	34
35	0 45	0 47	0 48	0 50	0 51	0 53	0 54	0 55	0 57	0 58	1 0	1 1	1 3	1 4	1 6	35
36	0 47	0 48	0 50	0 51	0 53	0 54	0 56	0 57	0 59	1 0	1 1	1 3	1 4	1 6	1 8	36
37	0 48	0 49	0 51	0 52	0 54	0 56	0 57	0 59	1 0	1 2	1 3	1 5	1 6	1 8	1 9	37
38	0 49	0 51	0 52	0 54	0 55	0 57	0 59	1 0	1 2	1 3	1 5	1 7	1 8	1 10	1 11	38
39	0 50	0 52	0 54	0 55	0 57	0 59	1 0	1 2	1 3	1 5	1 7	1 8	1 10	1 11	1 13	39
40	0 52	0 53	0 55	0 57	0 58	1 0	1 2	1 3	1 5	1 7	1 8	1 10	1 12	1 13	1 15	40
41	0 53	0 55	0 56	0 58	1 0	1 1	1 3	1 5	1 7	1 8	1 10	1 12	1 13	1 15	1 17	41
42	0 54	0 56	0 58	1 0	1 1	1 3	1 5	1 7	1 8	1 10	1 12	1 14	1 15	1 17	1 19	42
43	0 56	0 57	0 59	1 1	1 3	1 4	1 6	1 8	1 10	1 11	1 13	1 15	1 17	1 19	1 21	43
44	0 57	0 59	1 0	1 2	1 4	1 6	1 8	1 10	1 11	1 13	1 15	1 17	1 19	1 21	1 23	44
45	0 58	1 0	1 2	1 4	1 6	1 8	1 9	1 11	1 13	1 15	1 17	1 19	1 21	1 23	1 24	45
46	0 59	1 1	1 3	1 5	1 7	1 9	1 11	1 13	1 15	1 17	1 19	1 20	1 22	1 24	1 26	46
47	1 1	1 3	1 5	1 7	1 9	1 11	1 12	1 14	1 16	1 18	1 20	1 22	1 24	1 26	1 28	47
48	1 2	1 4	1 6	1 8	1 10	1 12	1 14	1 16	1 18	1 20	1 22	1 24	1 26	1 28	1 30	48
49	1 3	1 5	1 7	1 9	1 11	1 14	1 16	1 18	1 20	1 21	1 23	1 25	1 27	1 30	1 32	49
50	1 5	1 7	1 9	1 11	1 13	1 15	1 17	1 19	1 21	1 23	1 25	1 27	1 30	1 32	1 34	50
51	1 6	1 8	1 10	1 12	1 14	1 16	1 19	1 21	1 23	1 25	1 27	1 29	1 31	1 34	1 36	51
52	1 7	1 9	1 11	1 14	1 16	1 18	1 20	1 22	1 24	1 27	1 29	1 31	1 33	1 35	1 38	52
53	1 8	1 11	1 13	1 15	1 17	1 19	1 22	1 24	1 26	1 28	1 30	1 33	1 35	1 37	1 39	53
54	1 10	1 12	1 14	1 16	1 19	1 21	1 23	1 26	1 28	1 30	1 32	1 34	1 37	1 39	1 41	54
55	1 11	1 13	1 16	1 18	1 20	1 23	1 25	1 27	1 29	1 32	1 34	1 36	1 39	1 41	1 43	55
56	1 12	1 15	1 17	1 19	1 22	1 24	1 26	1 29	1 31	1 33	1 36	1 38	1 40	1 43	1 45	56
57	1 14	1 16	1 18	1 21	1 23	1 26	1 28	1 30	1 32	1 35	1 37	1 40	1 42	1 45	1 47	57
58	1 15	1 17	1 20	1 22	1 25	1 27	1 29	1 32	1 34	1 36	1 38	1 41	1 43	1 46	1 49	58
59	1 16	1 19	1 21	1 24	1 26	1 29	1 31	1 33	1 36	1 38	1 41	1 43	1 46	1 48	1 51	59
60	1 18	1 20	1 23	1 25	1 27	1 30	1 33	1 35	1 38	1 40	1 42	1 45	1 48	1 50	1 53	60
HOURS																
1	1 18	1 20	1 23	1 25	1 27	1 30	1 33	1 35	1 38	1 40	1 42	1 45	1 48	1 50	1 53	1
2	2 35	2 40	2 45	2 50	2 55	3 0	3 5	3 10	3 15	3 20	3 25	3 30	3 35	3 40	3 45	2
3	3 53	4 0	4 8	4 15	4 23	4 30	4 38	4 45	4 53	5 0	5 8	5 15	5 23	5 30	5 38	3
4	5 10	5 20	5 30	5 40	5 50	6 0	6 10	6 20	6 30	6 40	6 50	7 0	7 10	7 20	7 30	4
5	6 27	6 40	6 52	7 5	7 17	7 30	7 42	7 55	8 7	8 20	8 32	8 45	8 57	9 10	9 22	5
6	7 45	8 0	8 15	8 30	8 45	9 0	9 15	9 30	9 45	10 0	10 15	10 30	10 45	11 0	11 15	6
7	9 3	9 20	9 38	9 55	10 13	10 30	10 48	11 5	11 23	11 40	11 58	12 15	12 33	12 50	13 8	7
8	10 20	10 40	11 0	11 20	11 40	12 0	12 20	12 40	13 0	13 20	13 40	14 0	14 20	14 40	15 0	8
9	11 38	12 0	12 23	12 45	13 8	13 30	13 53	14 15	14 38	15 0	15 23	15 45	16 8	16 30	16 53	9
10	12 55	13 20	13 45	14 10	14 35	15 0	15 25	15 50	16 15	16 40	17 5	17 30	17 55	18 20	18 45	10
11	14 12	14 40	15 7	15 35	16 3	16 30	16 57	17 25	17 53	18 20	18 48	19 15	19 42	20 10	20 38	11
12	15 30	16 0	16 30	17 0	17 30	18 0	18 30	19 0	19 30	20 0	20 30	21 0	21 30	22 0	22 30	12
13	16 48	17 20	17 53	18 25	18 57	19 30	20 3	20 35	21 8	21 40	22 12	22 45	23 18	23 50	24 23	13
14	18 5	18 40	19 15	19 50	20 25	21 0	21 35	22 10	22 45	23 20	23 55	24 30	25 5	25 40	26 15	14
15	19 23	20 0	20 38	21 15	21 53	22 30	23 8	23 45	24 23	25 0	25 38	26 15	26 53	27 30	28 8	15
16	20 40	21 20	22 0	22 40	23 20	24 0	24 40	25 20	26 0	26 40	27 20	28 0	28 40	29 20	30 0	16
17	21 57	22 40	23 23	24 5	24 48	25 30	26 12	26 55	27 38	28 20	29 3	29 45	30 27	31 10	31 53	17
18	23 15	24 0	24 45	25 30	26 15	27 0	27 45	28 30	29 15	30 0	30 45	31 30	32 15	33 0	33 45	18
19	24 33	25 20	26 8	26 55	27 42	28 30	29 18	30 5	30 53	31 40	32 27	33 15	34 3	34 50	35 38	19
20	25 50	26 40	27 30	28 20	29 10	30 0	30 50	31 40	32 30	33 20	34 10	35 0	35 50	36 40	37 30	20
21	27 8	28 0	28 53	29 45	30 38	31 30	32 23	33 15	34 8	35 0	35 53	36 45	37 38	38 30	39 23	21
22	28 25	29 20	30 15	31 10	32 5	33 0	33 55	34 50	35 45	36 40	37 35	38 30	39 25	40 20	41 15	22
23	29 42	30 40	31 38	32 35	33 33	34 30	35 27	36 25	37 23	38 20	39 18	40 15	41 12	42 10	43 8	23
24	31 0	32 0	33 0	34 0	35 0	36 0	37 0	38 0	39 0	40 0	41 0	42 0	43 0	44 0	45 0	24

Table VII Diurnal Motion of the Planets

24 HOUR TRAVEL

TIME	0° 46'	0° 47'	0° 48'	0° 49'	0° 50'	0° 51'	0° 52'	0° 53'	0° 54'	0° 55'	0° 56'	0° 57'	0° 58'	0° 59'	1° 0'	TIME
MINUTES	° ' "	° ' "	° ' "	° ' "	° ' "	° ' "	° ' "	° ' "	° ' "	° ' "	° ' "	° ' "	° ' "	° ' "	° ' "	**MINUTES**
1	0 2	0 2	0 2	0 2	0 2	0 2	0 2	0 2	0 2	0 2	0 2	0 2	0 2	0 2	0 3	1
2	0 4	0 4	0 4	0 4	0 4	0 4	0 4	0 4	0 4	0 4	0 5	0 5	0 5	0 5	0 5	2
3	0 6	0 6	0 6	0 6	0 6	0 6	0 7	0 7	0 7	0 7	0 7	0 7	0 7	0 7	0 8	3
4	0 8	0 8	0 8	0 8	0 8	0 8	0 9	0 9	0 9	0 9	0 9	0 9	0 9	0 10	0 10	4
5	0 10	0 10	0 10	0 10	0 10	0 11	0 11	0 11	0 11	0 11	0 12	0 12	0 12	0 12	0 12	5
6	0 12	0 12	0 12	0 12	0 12	0 13	0 13	0 13	0 13	0 14	0 14	0 14	0 15	0 15	0 15	6
7	0 13	0 14	0 14	0 14	0 15	0 15	0 15	0 15	0 16	0 16	0 16	0 17	0 17	0 17	0 18	7
8	0 15	0 16	0 16	0 16	0 17	0 17	0 17	0 18	0 18	0 18	0 19	0 19	0 19	0 20	0 20	8
9	0 17	0 18	0 18	0 18	0 19	0 19	0 20	0 20	0 20	0 21	0 21	0 21	0 22	0 22	0 23	9
10	0 19	0 20	0 20	0 20	0 21	0 21	0 22	0 22	0 23	0 23	0 23	0 24	0 24	0 25	0 25	10
11	0 21	0 22	0 22	0 22	0 23	0 23	0 24	0 24	0 25	0 25	0 26	0 26	0 27	0 27	0 28	11
12	0 23	0 24	0 24	0 25	0 25	0 26	0 26	0 27	0 27	0 28	0 28	0 29	0 29	0 30	0 30	12
13	0 25	0 25	0 26	0 27	0 27	0 28	0 28	0 29	0 29	0 30	0 30	0 31	0 31	0 32	0 33	13
14	0 27	0 27	0 28	0 29	0 29	0 30	0 30	0 31	0 32	0 32	0 33	0 33	0 34	0 34	0 35	14
15	0 29	0 29	0 30	0 31	0 31	0 32	0 33	0 33	0 34	0 34	0 35	0 36	0 36	0 37	0 38	15
16	0 31	0 31	0 32	0 33	0 33	0 34	0 35	0 35	0 36	0 37	0 37	0 38	0 39	0 39	0 40	16
17	0 33	0 33	0 34	0 35	0 35	0 36	0 37	0 38	0 38	0 39	0 40	0 40	0 41	0 42	0 42	17
18	0 35	0 35	0 36	0 37	0 38	0 38	0 39	0 40	0 41	0 41	0 42	0 43	0 44	0 44	0 45	18
19	0 36	0 37	0 38	0 39	0 40	0 40	0 41	0 42	0 43	0 44	0 44	0 45	0 46	0 47	0 47	19
20	0 38	0 39	0 40	0 41	0 42	0 43	0 43	0 44	0 45	0 46	0 47	0 48	0 48	0 49	0 50	20
21	0 40	0 41	0 42	0 43	0 44	0 45	0 46	0 46	0 47	0 48	0 49	0 50	0 51	0 52	0 52	21
22	0 42	0 43	0 44	0 45	0 46	0 47	0 48	0 49	0 50	0 50	0 51	0 52	0 53	0 54	0 55	22
23	0 44	0 45	0 46	0 47	0 48	0 49	0 50	0 51	0 52	0 53	0 54	0 55	0 56	0 57	0 57	23
24	0 46	0 47	0 48	0 49	0 50	0 51	0 52	0 53	0 54	0 55	0 56	0 57	0 58	0 59	1 0	24
25	0 48	0 49	0 50	0 51	0 52	0 53	0 54	0 55	0 56	0 57	0 58	0 59	1 0	1 1	1 2	25
26	0 50	0 51	0 52	0 53	0 54	0 55	0 56	0 57	0 59	1 0	1 1	1 2	1 3	1 4	1 5	26
27	0 52	0 53	0 54	0 55	0 56	0 57	0 58	1 0	1 1	1 2	1 3	1 4	1 5	1 6	1 8	27
28	0 54	0 55	0 56	0 57	0 58	1 0	1 1	1 2	1 3	1 4	1 5	1 7	1 8	1 9	1 10	28
29	0 56	0 57	0 58	0 59	1 0	1 2	1 3	1 4	1 5	1 6	1 8	1 9	1 10	1 11	1 12	29
30	0 58	0 59	1 0	1 1	1 3	1 4	1 5	1 6	1 8	1 9	1 10	1 11	1 12	1 14	1 15	30
31	0 59	1 1	1 2	1 3	1 5	1 6	1 7	1 8	1 10	1 11	1 12	1 14	1 15	1 16	1 17	31
32	1 1	1 3	1 4	1 5	1 7	1 8	1 9	1 11	1 12	1 13	1 15	1 16	1 17	1 19	1 20	32
33	1 3	1 5	1 6	1 7	1 9	1 10	1 11	1 13	1 14	1 16	1 17	1 18	1 20	1 21	1 23	33
34	1 5	1 7	1 8	1 9	1 11	1 12	1 14	1 15	1 16	1 18	1 19	1 21	1 22	1 24	1 25	34
35	1 7	1 9	1 10	1 11	1 13	1 14	1 16	1 17	1 19	1 20	1 22	1 23	1 25	1 26	1 27	35
36	1 9	1 11	1 12	1 14	1 15	1 16	1 18	1 19	1 21	1 23	1 24	1 26	1 27	1 29	1 30	36
37	1 11	1 12	1 14	1 16	1 17	1 19	1 20	1 22	1 23	1 25	1 26	1 28	1 29	1 31	1 32	37
38	1 13	1 14	1 16	1 18	1 19	1 21	1 22	1 24	1 26	1 27	1 29	1 30	1 32	1 33	1 35	38
39	1 15	1 16	1 18	1 20	1 21	1 23	1 24	1 26	1 28	1 29	1 31	1 33	1 34	1 36	1 38	39
40	1 17	1 18	1 20	1 22	1 23	1 25	1 27	1 28	1 30	1 32	1 33	1 35	1 36	1 38	1 40	40
41	1 19	1 20	1 22	1 24	1 25	1 27	1 29	1 31	1 32	1 34	1 36	1 37	1 39	1 41	1 42	41
42	1 20	1 22	1 24	1 26	1 27	1 29	1 31	1 33	1 34	1 36	1 38	1 40	1 42	1 43	1 45	42
43	1 22	1 24	1 26	1 28	1 30	1 31	1 33	1 35	1 37	1 39	1 40	1 42	1 44	1 46	1 47	43
44	1 24	1 26	1 28	1 30	1 32	1 34	1 35	1 37	1 39	1 41	1 43	1 45	1 46	1 48	1 50	44
45	1 26	1 28	1 30	1 32	1 34	1 36	1 38	1 39	1 41	1 43	1 45	1 47	1 49	1 51	1 53	45
46	1 28	1 30	1 32	1 34	1 36	1 38	1 40	1 42	1 43	1 45	1 47	1 49	1 51	1 53	1 55	46
47	1 30	1 32	1 34	1 36	1 38	1 40	1 42	1 44	1 46	1 48	1 50	1 52	1 54	1 56	1 57	47
48	1 32	1 34	1 36	1 38	1 40	1 42	1 44	1 46	1 48	1 50	1 52	1 54	1 56	1 58	2 0	48
49	1 34	1 36	1 38	1 40	1 42	1 44	1 46	1 48	1 50	1 52	1 54	1 56	1 58	2 0	2 3	49
50	1 36	1 38	1 40	1 42	1 44	1 46	1 48	1 50	1 52	1 53	1 55	1 57	1 59	2 1	2 5	50
51	1 38	1 40	1 42	1 44	1 46	1 48	1 50	1 53	1 55	1 57	1 59	2 1	2 3	2 5	2 8	51
52	1 40	1 42	1 44	1 46	1 48	1 50	1 53	1 55	1 57	1 59	2 1	2 4	2 6	2 8	2 10	52
53	1 42	1 44	1 46	1 48	1 50	1 53	1 55	1 57	1 59	2 1	2 4	2 6	2 8	2 10	2 12	53
54	1 43	1 46	1 48	1 50	1 53	1 55	1 57	1 59	2 1	2 4	2 6	2 8	2 11	2 13	2 15	54
55	1 45	1 48	1 50	1 52	1 55	1 57	1 59	2 1	2 4	2 6	2 8	2 11	2 13	2 15	2 18	55
56	1 47	1 50	1 52	1 54	1 57	1 59	2 1	2 4	2 6	2 8	2 11	2 13	2 15	2 18	2 20	56
57	1 49	1 52	1 54	1 56	1 59	2 1	2 4	2 6	2 8	2 11	2 13	2 15	2 18	2 20	2 23	57
58	1 51	1 54	1 56	1 58	2 1	2 3	2 6	2 8	2 11	2 13	2 15	2 18	2 20	2 23	2 25	58
59	1 53	1 56	1 58	2 0	2 3	2 5	2 8	2 10	2 13	2 15	2 18	2 20	2 23	2 25	2 27	59
60	1 55	1 57	2 0	2 3	2 5	2 8	2 10	2 12	2 15	2 18	2 20	2 23	2 25	2 27	2 30	60
HOURS 1	1 55	1 57	2 0	2 3	2 5	2 8	2 10	2 12	2 15	2 18	2 20	2 23	2 25	2 27	2 30	1 **HOURS**
2	3 50	3 55	4 0	4 5	4 10	4 15	4 20	4 25	4 30	4 35	4 40	4 45	4 50	4 55	5 0	2
3	5 45	5 53	6 0	6 8	6 15	6 23	6 30	6 38	6 45	6 53	7 0	7 8	7 15	7 23	7 30	3
4	7 40	7 50	8 0	8 10	8 20	8 30	8 40	8 50	9 0	9 10	9 20	9 30	9 40	9 50	10 0	4
5	9 35	9 47	10 0	10 12	10 25	10 37	10 50	11 2	11 15	11 27	11 40	11 52	12 5	12 17	12 30	5
6	11 30	11 45	12 0	12 15	12 30	12 45	13 0	13 15	13 30	13 45	14 0	14 15	14 30	14 45	15 0	6
7	13 25	13 43	14 0	14 18	14 35	14 53	15 10	15 28	15 45	16 3	16 20	16 38	16 55	17 12	17 30	7
8	15 20	15 40	16 0	16 20	16 40	17 0	17 20	17 40	18 0	18 20	18 40	19 0	19 20	19 40	20 0	8
9	17 15	17 38	18 0	18 23	18 45	19 8	19 30	19 53	20 15	20 38	21 0	21 23	21 45	22 8	22 30	9
10	19 10	19 35	20 0	20 25	20 50	21 15	21 40	22 5	22 30	22 55	23 20	23 45	24 10	24 35	25 0	10
11	21 5	21 33	22 0	22 27	22 55	23 23	23 50	24 18	24 45	25 12	25 40	26 8	26 35	27 3	27 30	11
12	23 0	23 30	24 0	24 30	25 0	25 30	26 0	26 30	27 0	27 30	28 0	28 30	29 0	29 30	30 0	12
13	24 55	25 27	26 0	26 33	27 5	27 38	28 10	28 42	29 15	29 48	30 20	30 53	31 25	31 57	32 30	13
14	26 50	27 25	28 0	28 35	29 10	29 45	30 20	30 55	31 30	32 5	32 40	33 15	33 50	34 25	35 0	14
15	28 45	29 23	30 0	30 38	31 15	31 53	32 30	33 8	33 45	34 23	35 0	35 38	36 15	36 53	37 30	15
16	30 40	31 20	32 0	32 40	33 20	34 0	34 40	35 20	36 0	36 40	37 20	38 0	38 40	39 20	40 0	16
17	32 35	33 18	34 0	34 42	35 25	36 8	36 50	37 33	38 15	38 57	39 40	40 23	41 5	41 48	42 30	17
18	34 30	35 15	36 0	36 45	37 30	38 15	39 0	39 45	40 30	41 15	42 0	42 45	43 30	44 15	45 0	18
19	36 25	37 12	38 0	38 48	39 35	40 23	41 10	41 57	42 45	43 33	44 20	45 8	45 55	46 42	47 30	19
20	38 20	39 10	40 0	40 50	41 40	42 30	43 20	44 10	45 0	45 50	46 40	47 30	48 20	49 10	50 0	20
21	40 15	41 8	42 0	42 53	43 45	44 38	45 30	46 23	47 15	48 8	49 0	49 53	50 45	51 38	52 30	21
22	42 10	43 5	44 0	44 55	45 50	46 45	47 40	48 35	49 30	50 25	51 20	52 15	53 10	54 5	55 0	22
23	44 5	45 3	46 0	46 57	47 55	48 53	49 50	50 48	51 45	52 42	53 40	54 38	55 35	56 33	57 30	23
24	46 0	47 0	48 0	49 0	50 0	51 0	52 0	53 0	54 0	55 0	56 0	57 0	58 0	59 0	1 0 0	24

Table VII Diurnal Motion of the Planets

	24 HOUR TRAVEL															
TIME	1° 1'	1° 2'	1° 3'	1° 4'	1° 5'	1° 6'	1° 7'	1° 8'	1° 9'	1° 10'	1° 11'	1° 12'	1° 13'	1° 14'	1° 15'	TIME
MINUTES																
1	0 3	0 3	0 3	0 3	0 3	0 3	0 3	0 3	0 6	0 6	0 6	0 6	0 6	0 6	0 6	1
2	0 5	0 5	0 5	0 5	0 5	0 5	0 5	0 6	0 6	0 6	0 6	0 6	0 6	0 6	0 6	2
3	0 8	0 8	0 8	0 8	0 8	0 8	0 8	0 8	0 9	0 9	0 9	0 9	0 9	0 9	0 9	3
4	0 10	0 10	0 11	0 11	0 11	0 11	0 11	0 11	0 12	0 12	0 12	0 12	0 12	0 12	0 12	4
5	0 13	0 13	0 13	0 13	0 14	0 14	0 14	0 14	0 14	0 15	0 15	0 15	0 15	0 15	0 16	5
6	0 15	0 16	0 16	0 16	0 16	0 17	0 17	0 17	0 17	0 18	0 18	0 18	0 18	0 19	0 19	6
7	0 18	0 18	0 18	0 19	0 19	0 19	0 20	0 20	0 20	0 20	0 21	0 21	0 21	0 22	0 22	7
8	0 20	0 21	0 21	0 21	0 22	0 22	0 22	0 23	0 23	0 23	0 24	0 24	0 24	0 25	0 25	8
9	0 23	0 23	0 24	0 24	0 24	0 25	0 25	0 26	0 26	0 26	0 27	0 27	0 27	0 28	0 28	9
10	0 25	0 26	0 26	0 27	0 27	0 28	0 28	0 28	0 29	0 29	0 30	0 30	0 30	0 31	0 31	10
11	0 28	0 28	0 29	0 29	0 30	0 30	0 31	0 31	0 32	0 32	0 33	0 33	0 33	0 34	0 34	11
12	0 31	0 31	0 32	0 32	0 33	0 33	0 34	0 34	0 34	0 35	0 35	0 36	0 36	0 37	0 37	12
13	0 33	0 34	0 34	0 34	0 35	0 36	0 36	0 37	0 37	0 38	0 38	0 39	0 40	0 40	0 41	13
14	0 36	0 36	0 37	0 37	0 38	0 39	0 39	0 40	0 40	0 41	0 41	0 42	0 43	0 43	0 44	14
15	0 38	0 39	0 39	0 40	0 41	0 41	0 42	0 43	0 43	0 44	0 44	0 45	0 46	0 46	0 47	15
16	0 41	0 41	0 42	0 43	0 43	0 44	0 45	0 45	0 46	0 47	0 47	0 48	0 49	0 49	0 50	16
17	0 43	0 44	0 45	0 45	0 46	0 47	0 47	0 48	0 49	0 50	0 50	0 51	0 52	0 52	0 53	17
18	0 46	0 47	0 47	0 48	0 49	0 50	0 50	0 51	0 52	0 53	0 53	0 54	0 55	0 56	0 56	18
19	0 48	0 49	0 50	0 51	0 51	0 52	0 53	0 54	0 55	0 55	0 56	0 57	0 58	0 59	0 59	19
20	0 51	0 52	0 53	0 53	0 54	0 55	0 56	0 57	0 58	0 58	0 59	1 0	1 1	1 2	1 3	20
21	0 53	0 54	0 55	0 56	0 57	0 58	0 59	1 0	1 1	1 1	1 2	1 3	1 4	1 5	1 6	21
22	0 56	0 57	0 58	0 59	1 0	1 1	1 1	1 2	1 3	1 4	1 5	1 6	1 7	1 8	1 9	22
23	0 58	0 59	1 0	1 1	1 2	1 3	1 4	1 4	1 6	1 7	1 8	1 9	1 10	1 11	1 12	23
24	1 1	1 2	1 3	1 4	1 5	1 6	1 7	1 8	1 9	1 10	1 11	1 12	1 13	1 14	1 15	24
25	1 4	1 5	1 6	1 7	1 8	1 9	1 10	1 11	1 12	1 13	1 14	1 15	1 16	1 17	1 18	25
26	1 6	1 7	1 8	1 9	1 10	1 11	1 13	1 14	1 15	1 16	1 17	1 18	1 19	1 20	1 21	26
27	1 9	1 10	1 11	1 12	1 13	1 14	1 15	1 16	1 18	1 19	1 20	1 21	1 22	1 23	1 24	27
28	1 11	1 12	1 14	1 15	1 16	1 17	1 18	1 19	1 20	1 22	1 23	1 24	1 25	1 26	1 27	28
29	1 14	1 15	1 16	1 17	1 19	1 20	1 21	1 22	1 23	1 25	1 26	1 27	1 28	1 29	1 31	29
30	1 16	1 18	1 19	1 20	1 21	1 23	1 24	1 25	1 26	1 27	1 29	1 30	1 31	1 33	1 34	30
31	1 19	1 20	1 21	1 23	1 24	1 25	1 27	1 28	1 29	1 30	1 32	1 33	1 34	1 36	1 37	31
32	1 21	1 23	1 24	1 25	1 27	1 28	1 29	1 31	1 32	1 33	1 35	1 36	1 37	1 39	1 40	32
33	1 24	1 25	1 27	1 28	1 29	1 31	1 32	1 34	1 35	1 36	1 38	1 39	1 40	1 42	1 43	33
34	1 26	1 28	1 29	1 31	1 32	1 34	1 35	1 36	1 38	1 39	1 41	1 42	1 43	1 45	1 46	34
35	1 29	1 30	1 32	1 33	1 35	1 36	1 38	1 39	1 41	1 42	1 44	1 45	1 46	1 48	1 49	35
36	1 31	1 33	1 34	1 36	1 38	1 39	1 41	1 42	1 43	1 45	1 46	1 48	1 49	1 51	1 53	36
37	1 34	1 36	1 37	1 39	1 40	1 42	1 43	1 45	1 46	1 48	1 49	1 51	1 53	1 54	1 56	37
38	1 37	1 38	1 40	1 41	1 43	1 45	1 46	1 48	1 49	1 51	1 52	1 54	1 56	1 57	1 59	38
39	1 39	1 41	1 42	1 44	1 46	1 47	1 49	1 50	1 52	1 54	1 55	1 57	1 59	2 0	2 2	39
40	1 42	1 43	1 45	1 47	1 48	1 50	1 52	1 53	1 55	1 57	1 58	2 0	2 2	2 3	2 5	40
41	1 44	1 46	1 48	1 49	1 51	1 53	1 54	1 56	1 58	2 0	2 1	2 3	2 5	2 6	2 8	41
42	1 47	1 49	1 50	1 52	1 54	1 56	1 57	1 59	2 1	2 3	2 4	2 6	2 8	2 9	2 11	42
43	1 49	1 51	1 53	1 55	1 56	1 58	2 0	2 2	2 4	2 5	2 7	2 9	2 11	2 13	2 14	43
44	1 52	1 54	1 56	1 57	1 59	2 1	2 3	2 5	2 7	2 8	2 10	2 12	2 14	2 16	2 18	44
45	1 54	1 56	1 58	2 0	2 2	2 4	2 6	2 8	2 9	2 11	2 13	2 15	2 17	2 19	2 21	45
46	1 57	1 59	2 1	2 3	2 5	2 7	2 8	2 10	2 12	2 14	2 16	2 18	2 20	2 22	2 24	46
47	1 59	2 1	2 3	2 5	2 7	2 9	2 11	2 13	2 15	2 17	2 19	2 21	2 23	2 25	2 27	47
48	2 2	2 4	2 6	2 8	2 10	2 12	2 14	2 16	2 18	2 20	2 22	2 24	2 26	2 28	2 30	48
49	2 5	2 7	2 9	2 11	2 13	2 15	2 17	2 19	2 21	2 23	2 25	2 27	2 29	2 31	2 33	49
50	2 7	2 9	2 11	2 13	2 15	2 18	2 20	2 22	2 24	2 26	2 28	2 30	2 32	2 34	2 36	50
51	2 10	2 12	2 14	2 16	2 18	2 20	2 22	2 25	2 27	2 29	2 31	2 33	2 35	2 37	2 39	51
52	2 12	2 14	2 16	2 19	2 21	2 23	2 25	2 27	2 30	2 32	2 34	2 36	2 38	2 40	2 42	52
53	2 15	2 17	2 19	2 21	2 24	2 26	2 28	2 30	2 32	2 35	2 37	2 39	2 41	2 43	2 46	53
54	2 17	2 19	2 22	2 24	2 26	2 28	2 31	2 33	2 35	2 38	2 40	2 42	2 44	2 46	2 49	54
55	2 20	2 22	2 24	2 27	2 29	2 31	2 34	2 36	2 38	2 40	2 43	2 45	2 47	2 50	2 52	55
56	2 22	2 25	2 27	2 29	2 32	2 34	2 36	2 39	2 41	2 43	2 46	2 48	2 50	2 53	2 55	56
57	2 25	2 27	2 30	2 32	2 34	2 37	2 39	2 42	2 44	2 46	2 49	2 51	2 53	2 56	2 58	57
58	2 27	2 30	2 32	2 35	2 37	2 39	2 42	2 44	2 47	2 49	2 52	2 54	2 56	2 59	3 1	58
59	2 30	2 32	2 35	2 37	2 40	2 42	2 45	2 47	2 50	2 52	2 55	2 57	2 59	3 2	3 4	59
60	2 33	2 35	2 38	2 40	2 42	2 45	2 47	2 50	2 53	2 55	2 57	3 0	3 2	3 5	3 8	60
HOURS																
1	2 33	2 35	2 38	2 40	2 42	2 45	2 47	2 50	2 53	2 55	2 57	3 0	3 2	3 5	3 8	1
2	5 5	5 10	5 15	5 20	5 25	5 30	5 35	5 40	5 45	5 50	5 55	6 0	6 5	6 10	6 15	2
3	7 38	7 45	7 53	8 0	8 8	8 15	8 23	8 30	8 38	8 45	8 53	9 0	9 8	9 15	9 23	3
4	10 10	10 20	10 30	10 40	10 50	11 0	11 10	11 20	11 30	11 40	11 50	12 0	12 10	12 20	12 30	4
5	12 42	12 55	13 7	13 20	13 32	13 45	13 57	14 10	14 22	14 35	14 47	15 0	15 12	15 25	15 37	5
6	15 15	15 30	15 45	16 0	16 15	16 30	16 45	17 0	17 15	17 30	17 45	18 0	18 15	18 30	18 45	6
7	17 48	18 5	18 23	18 40	18 57	19 15	19 33	19 50	20 8	20 25	20 42	21 0	21 18	21 35	21 53	7
8	20 20	20 40	21 0	21 20	21 40	22 0	22 20	22 40	23 0	23 20	23 40	24 0	24 20	24 40	25 0	8
9	22 53	23 15	23 38	24 0	24 23	24 45	25 8	25 30	25 53	26 15	26 38	27 0	27 23	27 45	28 8	9
10	25 25	25 50	26 15	26 40	27 5	27 30	27 55	28 20	28 45	29 10	29 35	30 0	30 25	30 50	31 15	10
11	27 57	28 25	28 53	29 20	29 48	30 15	30 42	31 10	31 38	32 5	32 33	33 0	33 27	33 55	34 23	11
12	30 30	31 0	31 30	32 0	32 30	33 0	33 30	34 0	34 30	35 0	35 30	36 0	36 30	37 0	37 30	12
13	33 3	33 35	34 8	34 40	35 12	35 45	36 18	36 50	37 23	37 55	38 27	39 0	39 33	40 5	40 38	13
14	35 35	36 10	36 45	37 20	37 55	38 30	39 5	39 40	40 15	40 50	41 25	42 0	42 35	43 10	43 45	14
15	38 8	38 45	39 23	40 0	40 38	41 15	41 53	42 30	43 8	43 45	44 23	45 0	45 38	46 15	46 53	15
16	40 40	41 20	42 0	42 40	43 20	44 0	44 40	45 20	46 0	46 40	47 20	48 0	48 40	49 20	50 0	16
17	43 12	43 55	44 38	45 20	46 3	46 45	47 27	48 10	48 53	49 35	50 18	51 0	51 42	52 25	53 8	17
18	45 45	46 30	47 15	48 0	48 45	49 30	50 15	51 0	51 45	52 30	53 15	54 0	54 45	55 30	56 15	18
19	48 18	49 5	49 53	50 40	51 27	52 15	53 2	53 50	54 38	55 25	56 12	57 0	57 47	58 35	59 23	19
20	50 50	51 40	52 30	53 20	54 10	55 0	55 50	56 40	57 30	58 20	59 10	1 0 0	1 0 50	1 1 40	1 2 30	20
21	53 23	54 15	55 8	56 0	56 53	57 45	58 38	59 30	1 0 23	1 1 15	1 2 8	1 3 0	1 3 53	1 4 45	1 5 38	21
22	55 55	56 50	57 45	58 40	59 35	1 0 30	1 1 25	1 2 20	1 3 15	1 4 10	1 5 5	1 6 0	1 6 55	1 7 50	1 8 45	22
23	58 27	59 25	1 0 23	1 1 20	1 2 18	1 3 15	1 4 12	1 5 10	1 6 8	1 7 5	1 8 3	1 9 0	1 9 57	1 10 55	1 11 53	23
24	1 1 0	1 2 0	1 3 0	1 4 0	1 5 0	1 6 0	1 7 0	1 8 0	1 9 0	1 10 0	1 11 0	1 12 0	1 13 0	1 14 0	1 15 0	24

Table VII Diurnal Motion of the Planets

24 HOUR TRAVEL

MINUTES

TIME	1° 16'	1° 17'	1° 18'	1° 19'	1° 20'	1° 21'	1° 22'	1° 23'	1° 24'	1° 25'	1° 26'	1° 27'	1° 28'	1° 29'	1° 30'	TIME
1	0 3	0 3	0 3	0 3	0 3	0 3	0 3	0 3	0 4	0 4	0 4	0 4	0 4	0 4	0 4	1
2	0 6	0 6	0 7	0 7	0 7	0 7	0 7	0 7	0 7	0 7	0 7	0 7	0 7	0 7	0 8	2
3	0 9	0 10	0 10	0 10	0 10	0 10	0 10	0 10	0 11	0 11	0 11	0 11	0 11	0 11	0 11	3
4	0 13	0 13	0 13	0 13	0 13	0 13	0 14	0 14	0 14	0 14	0 14	0 14	0 15	0 15	0 15	4
5	0 16	0 16	0 16	0 16	0 17	0 17	0 17	0 17	0 18	0 18	0 18	0 18	0 18	0 19	0 19	5
6	0 19	0 19	0 20	0 20	0 20	0 20	0 21	0 21	0 21	0 21	0 22	0 22	0 22	0 22	0 23	6
7	0 22	0 22	0 23	0 23	0 23	0 24	0 24	0 24	0 25	0 25	0 25	0 25	0 26	0 26	0 26	7
8	0 25	0 26	0 26	0 26	0 27	0 27	0 27	0 28	0 28	0 28	0 29	0 29	0 29	0 30	0 30	8
9	0 29	0 29	0 29	0 30	0 30	0 30	0 30	0 31	0 31	0 32	0 32	0 32	0 33	0 33	0 34	9
10	0 32	0 32	0 33	0 33	0 33	0 33	0 34	0 34	0 35	0 35	0 35	0 36	0 36	0 37	0 37	10
11	0 35	0 35	0 36	0 36	0 37	0 37	0 38	0 38	0 39	0 39	0 39	0 40	0 40	0 41	0 41	11
12	0 38	0 39	0 39	0 40	0 40	0 41	0 41	0 42	0 42	0 43	0 43	0 44	0 44	0 45	0 45	12
13	0 41	0 42	0 42	0 43	0 43	0 44	0 44	0 45	0 46	0 46	0 47	0 47	0 48	0 48	0 49	13
14	0 44	0 45	0 46	0 46	0 47	0 47	0 48	0 48	0 49	0 50	0 50	0 51	0 51	0 52	0 53	14
15	0 48	0 48	0 49	0 49	0 50	0 51	0 51	0 52	0 53	0 53	0 54	0 54	0 55	0 56	0 56	15
16	0 51	0 51	0 52	0 53	0 53	0 54	0 55	0 55	0 56	0 57	0 57	0 58	0 59	0 59	1 0	16
17	0 54	0 55	0 55	0 56	0 57	0 57	0 58	0 59	0 59	1 0	1 1	1 2	1 2	1 3	1 4	17
18	0 57	0 58	0 59	0 59	1 0	1 1	1 1	1 2	1 3	1 4	1 4	1 5	1 6	1 7	1 8	18
19	1 0	1 1	1 2	1 3	1 3	1 4	1 5	1 6	1 7	1 7	1 8	1 9	1 10	1 10	1 11	19
20	1 3	1 4	1 5	1 6	1 7	1 7	1 8	1 8	1 9	1 10	1 11	1 12	1 13	1 14	1 15	20
21	1 7	1 7	1 8	1 9	1 10	1 11	1 12	1 13	1 13	1 14	1 16	1 17	1 18	1 19	1 19	21
22	1 10	1 11	1 11	1 12	1 13	1 14	1 15	1 16	1 17	1 19	1 20	1 21	1 22	1 23	1 23	22
23	1 13	1 14	1 15	1 16	1 17	1 18	1 19	1 20	1 21	1 22	1 23	1 24	1 25	1 26	1 26	23
24	1 16	1 17	1 18	1 19	1 20	1 21	1 22	1 23	1 24	1 25	1 26	1 27	1 28	1 29	1 30	24
25	1 19	1 20	1 21	1 22	1 23	1 24	1 25	1 26	1 27	1 29	1 30	1 31	1 32	1 33	1 34	25
26	1 22	1 23	1 24	1 26	1 27	1 28	1 29	1 30	1 31	1 32	1 34	1 35	1 36	1 36	1 38	26
27	1 26	1 27	1 28	1 29	1 30	1 31	1 32	1 33	1 34	1 36	1 37	1 38	1 39	1 40	1 41	27
28	1 29	1 30	1 31	1 32	1 33	1 34	1 36	1 37	1 38	1 39	1 40	1 42	1 43	1 44	1 45	28
29	1 32	1 33	1 34	1 35	1 37	1 38	1 39	1 40	1 42	1 43	1 44	1 45	1 46	1 48	1 49	29
30	1 35	1 36	1 38	1 39	1 40	1 41	1 42	1 44	1 45	1 46	1 48	1 49	1 50	1 51	1 53	30
31	1 38	1 39	1 41	1 42	1 43	1 45	1 46	1 47	1 49	1 50	1 51	1 52	1 54	1 55	1 56	31
32	1 41	1 43	1 44	1 45	1 47	1 48	1 49	1 51	1 52	1 53	1 55	1 56	1 57	1 59	2 0	32
33	1 45	1 46	1 47	1 49	1 50	1 51	1 53	1 54	1 56	1 57	1 58	2 0	2 1	2 2	2 4	33
34	1 48	1 49	1 50	1 52	1 53	1 55	1 56	1 58	1 58	1 59	2 2	2 3	2 5	2 6	2 8	34
35	1 51	1 52	1 54	1 55	1 57	1 58	2 0	2 1	2 2	2 4	2 5	2 7	2 8	2 10	2 11	35
36	1 54	1 56	1 57	1 58	2 0	2 1	2 3	2 4	2 6	2 8	2 9	2 11	2 12	2 13	2 15	36
37	1 57	1 59	2 0	2 2	2 3	2 5	2 6	2 8	2 9	2 11	2 13	2 14	2 16	2 17	2 19	37
38	2 0	2 2	2 4	2 5	2 7	2 8	2 10	2 11	2 13	2 15	2 16	2 18	2 19	2 21	2 23	38
39	2 4	2 5	2 7	2 8	2 10	2 12	2 13	2 15	2 16	2 18	2 20	2 21	2 23	2 25	2 26	39
40	2 7	2 8	2 10	2 12	2 13	2 15	2 17	2 18	2 20	2 22	2 23	2 25	2 27	2 28	2 30	40
41	2 10	2 12	2 13	2 15	2 17	2 18	2 20	2 22	2 23	2 25	2 27	2 29	2 30	2 32	2 34	41
42	2 13	2 15	2 16	2 18	2 20	2 22	2 23	2 25	2 27	2 29	2 31	2 32	2 34	2 36	2 38	42
43	2 16	2 18	2 20	2 22	2 23	2 25	2 27	2 29	2 31	2 32	2 34	2 36	2 38	2 39	2 41	43
44	2 19	2 21	2 23	2 25	2 27	2 28	2 30	2 32	2 34	2 36	2 38	2 39	2 41	2 43	2 45	44
45	2 23	2 24	2 26	2 28	2 30	2 32	2 34	2 36	2 38	2 39	2 41	2 43	2 45	2 47	2 49	45
46	2 26	2 28	2 30	2 31	2 33	2 35	2 37	2 39	2 41	2 43	2 45	2 47	2 49	2 51	2 53	46
47	2 29	2 31	2 33	2 35	2 37	2 39	2 41	2 43	2 45	2 46	2 48	2 50	2 52	2 54	2 56	47
48	2 32	2 34	2 36	2 38	2 40	2 42	2 44	2 46	2 48	2 50	2 52	2 54	2 56	2 58	3 0	48
49	2 35	2 37	2 39	2 41	2 43	2 45	2 47	2 49	2 52	2 54	2 56	2 58	3 0	3 2	3 4	49
50	2 38	2 40	2 42	2 45	2 47	2 49	2 51	2 53	2 55	2 57	2 59	3 1	3 3	3 5	3 8	50
51	2 42	2 44	2 46	2 48	2 50	2 52	2 54	2 56	2 59	3 1	3 3	3 5	3 7	3 9	3 11	51
52	2 45	2 47	2 49	2 51	2 53	2 56	2 58	3 0	3 2	3 4	3 6	3 8	3 11	3 13	3 15	52
53	2 48	2 50	2 52	2 54	2 57	2 59	3 1	3 3	3 5	3 8	3 10	3 12	3 14	3 17	3 19	53
54	2 51	2 53	2 56	2 58	3 0	3 2	3 4	3 7	3 9	3 11	3 13	3 16	3 18	3 20	3 23	54
55	2 54	2 56	2 59	3 1	3 3	3 6	3 8	3 10	3 12	3 15	3 17	3 19	3 22	3 24	3 26	55
56	2 57	3 0	3 2	3 4	3 7	3 9	3 11	3 14	3 16	3 18	3 21	3 23	3 25	3 28	3 30	56
57	3 0	3 3	3 5	3 8	3 10	3 12	3 15	3 17	3 19	3 22	3 24	3 27	3 29	3 31	3 34	57
58	3 4	3 6	3 8	3 11	3 13	3 16	3 18	3 21	3 23	3 25	3 28	3 30	3 33	3 35	3 38	58
59	3 7	3 9	3 12	3 14	3 17	3 19	3 22	3 24	3 27	3 29	3 31	3 34	3 36	3 39	3 41	59
60	3 10	3 12	3 15	3 17	3 20	3 23	3 25	3 27	3 30	3 32	3 35	3 38	3 40	3 42	3 45	60

HOURS

TIME	1° 16'	1° 17'	1° 18'	1° 19'	1° 20'	1° 21'	1° 22'	1° 23'	1° 24'	1° 25'	1° 26'	1° 27'	1° 28'	1° 29'	1° 30'	TIME
1	3 10	3 12	3 15	3 17	3 20	3 23	3 25	3 27	3 30	3 32	3 35	3 38	3 40	3 42	3 45	1
2	6 20	6 25	6 30	6 35	6 40	6 45	6 50	6 55	7 0	7 5	7 10	7 15	7 20	7 25	7 30	2
3	9 30	9 38	9 45	9 53	10 0	10 8	10 15	10 23	10 30	10 38	10 45	10 53	11 0	11 8	11 15	3
4	12 40	12 50	13 0	13 10	13 20	13 30	13 40	13 50	14 0	14 10	14 20	14 30	14 40	14 50	15 0	4
5	15 50	16 3	16 15	16 27	16 40	16 53	17 5	17 18	17 30	17 42	17 55	18 8	18 20	18 33	18 45	5
6	19 0	19 15	19 30	19 45	20 0	20 15	20 30	20 45	21 0	21 15	21 30	21 45	22 0	22 15	22 30	6
7	22 10	22 27	22 45	23 3	23 20	23 38	23 55	24 12	24 30	24 48	25 5	25 23	25 40	25 57	26 15	7
8	25 20	25 40	26 0	26 20	26 40	27 0	27 20	27 40	28 0	28 20	28 40	29 0	29 20	29 40	30 0	8
9	28 30	28 53	29 15	29 38	30 0	30 23	30 45	31 8	31 30	31 53	32 15	32 38	33 0	33 23	33 45	9
10	31 40	32 5	32 30	32 55	33 20	33 45	34 10	34 35	35 0	35 25	35 50	36 15	36 40	37 5	37 30	10
11	34 50	35 18	35 45	36 12	36 40	37 8	37 35	38 3	38 30	38 57	39 25	39 53	40 20	40 48	41 15	11
12	38 0	38 30	39 0	39 30	40 0	40 30	41 0	41 30	42 0	42 30	43 0	43 30	44 0	44 30	45 0	12
13	41 10	41 42	42 15	42 48	43 20	43 53	44 25	44 57	45 30	46 3	46 35	47 8	47 40	48 12	48 45	13
14	44 20	44 55	45 30	46 5	46 40	47 15	47 50	48 25	49 0	49 35	50 10	50 45	51 20	51 55	52 30	14
15	47 30	48 8	48 45	49 23	50 0	50 38	51 15	51 53	52 30	53 8	53 45	54 23	55 0	55 38	56 15	15
16	50 40	51 20	52 0	52 40	53 20	54 0	54 40	55 20	56 0	56 40	57 20	58 0	58 40	59 20	1 0 0	16
17	53 50	54 33	55 15	55 57	56 40	57 23	58 5	58 48	59 30	1 0 12	1 0 55	1 1 38	1 2 20	1 3 3	1 3 45	17
18	57 0	57 45	58 30	59 15	1 0 0	1 0 45	1 1 30	1 2 15	1 3 0	1 3 45	1 4 30	1 5 15	1 6 0	1 6 45	1 7 30	18
19	1 0 10	1 0 57	1 1 45	1 2 32	1 3 20	1 4 8	1 4 55	1 5 42	1 6 30	1 7 17	1 8 5	1 8 53	1 9 40	1 10 27	1 11 15	19
20	1 3 20	1 4 10	1 5 0	1 5 50	1 6 40	1 7 30	1 8 20	1 9 10	1 10 0	1 10 50	1 11 40	1 12 30	1 13 20	1 14 10	1 15 0	20
21	1 6 30	1 7 23	1 8 15	1 9 8	1 10 0	1 10 53	1 11 45	1 12 38	1 13 30	1 14 23	1 15 15	1 16 8	1 17 0	1 17 53	1 18 45	21
22	1 9 40	1 10 35	1 11 30	1 12 25	1 13 20	1 14 15	1 15 10	1 16 5	1 17 0	1 17 55	1 18 50	1 19 45	1 20 40	1 21 35	1 22 30	22
23	1 12 50	1 13 48	1 14 45	1 15 42	1 16 40	1 17 38	1 18 35	1 19 33	1 20 30	1 21 27	1 22 25	1 23 23	1 24 20	1 25 18	1 26 15	23
24	1 16 0	1 17 0	1 18 0	1 19 0	1 20 0	1 21 0	1 22 0	1 23 0	1 24 0	1 25 0	1 26 0	1 27 0	1 28 0	1 29 0	1 30 0	24

Table VII Diurnal Motion of the Planets

TIME	1° 31'	1° 32'	1° 33'	1° 34'	1° 35'	1° 36'	1° 37'	1° 38'	1° 39'	1° 40'	1° 41'	1° 42'	1° 43'	1° 44'	1° 45'	TIME
MINUTES							**24 HOUR TRAVEL**									**MINUTES**
1	0 4	0 4	0 4	0 4	0 4	0 4	0 4	0 4	0 4	0 4	0 4	0 4	0 4	0 4	0 4	1
2	0 8	0 8	0 8	0 8	0 8	0 8	0 8	0 8	0 8	0 8	0 8	0 8	0 9	0 9	0 9	2
3	0 11	0 12	0 12	0 12	0 12	0 12	0 12	0 12	0 12	0 12	0 12	0 13	0 13	0 13	0 13	3
4	0 15	0 15	0 16	0 16	0 16	0 16	0 16	0 16	0 16	0 17	0 17	0 17	0 17	0 17	0 18	4
5	0 19	0 19	0 19	0 20	0 20	0 20	0 20	0 20	0 20	0 21	0 21	0 21	0 21	0 22	0 22	5
6	0 23	0 23	0 23	0 24	0 24	0 24	0 24	0 25	0 25	0 25	0 25	0 26	0 26	0 26	0 26	6
7	0 27	0 27	0 27	0 27	0 28	0 28	0 28	0 29	0 29	0 29	0 29	0 30	0 30	0 30	0 31	7
8	0 30	0 31	0 31	0 31	0 32	0 32	0 32	0 33	0 33	0 33	0 34	0 34	0 34	0 35	0 35	8
9	0 34	0 35	0 35	0 35	0 36	0 36	0 36	0 37	0 37	0 37	0 38	0 38	0 38	0 39	0 39	9
10	0 38	0 38	0 39	0 39	0 40	0 40	0 40	0 40	0 41	0 41	0 42	0 42	0 43	0 43	0 44	10
11	0 42	0 42	0 43	0 43	0 44	0 44	0 44	0 45	0 45	0 46	0 46	0 47	0 47	0 48	0 48	11
12	0 46	0 46	0 47	0 47	0 48	0 48	0 49	0 49	0 50	0 50	0 50	0 51	0 51	0 52	0 53	12
13	0 49	0 50	0 50	0 51	0 51	0 52	0 53	0 53	0 54	0 54	0 55	0 55	0 56	0 56	0 57	13
14	0 53	0 54	0 54	0 55	0 55	0 56	0 57	0 57	0 58	0 58	0 58	0 59	1 0	1 0	1 1	14
15	0 57	0 58	0 58	0 59	0 59	1 0	1 1	1 1	1 1	1 2	1 3	1 3	1 4	1 4	1 6	15
16	1 1	1 1	1 2	1 3	1 3	1 4	1 5	1 5	1 6	1 7	1 7	1 8	1 9	1 9	1 10	16
17	1 4	1 5	1 6	1 7	1 7	1 8	1 9	1 9	1 10	1 11	1 12	1 12	1 13	1 14	1 14	17
18	1 8	1 9	1 10	1 11	1 11	1 12	1 13	1 14	1 14	1 15	1 16	1 16	1 17	1 18	1 19	18
19	1 12	1 13	1 14	1 14	1 15	1 16	1 17	1 18	1 18	1 19	1 20	1 21	1 22	1 22	1 23	19
20	1 16	1 17	1 18	1 18	1 19	1 20	1 21	1 22	1 23	1 23	1 24	1 25	1 26	1 27	1 27	20
21	1 20	1 20	1 21	1 22	1 23	1 24	1 25	1 26	1 27	1 27	1 28	1 29	1 30	1 31	1 32	21
22	1 23	1 24	1 25	1 26	1 27	1 28	1 29	1 30	1 31	1 32	1 33	1 34	1 34	1 35	1 36	22
23	1 27	1 28	1 29	1 30	1 31	1 32	1 33	1 34	1 35	1 36	1 37	1 38	1 39	1 40	1 41	23
24	1 31	1 32	1 33	1 34	1 35	1 36	1 37	1 38	1 39	1 40	1 41	1 42	1 43	1 44	1 45	24
25	1 35	1 36	1 37	1 38	1 39	1 40	1 41	1 42	1 43	1 44	1 45	1 46	1 47	1 48	1 49	25
26	1 39	1 40	1 41	1 42	1 43	1 44	1 45	1 46	1 47	1 48	1 49	1 50	1 52	1 53	1 54	26
27	1 42	1 43	1 45	1 46	1 47	1 48	1 49	1 50	1 51	1 53	1 54	1 55	1 56	1 57	1 58	27
28	1 46	1 47	1 49	1 50	1 51	1 52	1 53	1 54	1 56	1 57	1 58	1 59	2 0	2 1	2 3	28
29	1 50	1 51	1 52	1 54	1 55	1 56	1 57	1 58	2 0	2 1	2 2	2 3	2 4	2 6	2 7	29
30	1 54	1 55	1 56	1 57	1 59	2 0	2 1	2 3	2 4	2 5	2 6	2 8	2 9	2 10	2 11	30
31	1 58	1 59	2 0	2 1	2 3	2 4	2 5	2 7	2 8	2 9	2 10	2 12	2 13	2 14	2 16	31
32	2 1	2 3	2 4	2 5	2 7	2 8	2 9	2 11	2 12	2 13	2 15	2 16	2 17	2 19	2 20	32
33	2 5	2 6	2 8	2 9	2 11	2 12	2 13	2 15	2 16	2 17	2 19	2 20	2 22	2 23	2 24	33
34	2 9	2 10	2 12	2 13	2 15	2 16	2 17	2 19	2 20	2 22	2 23	2 24	2 26	2 27	2 29	34
35	2 13	2 14	2 16	2 17	2 19	2 20	2 21	2 23	2 24	2 26	2 27	2 29	2 30	2 32	2 33	35
36	2 16	2 18	2 19	2 21	2 23	2 24	2 26	2 27	2 28	2 30	2 31	2 33	2 34	2 36	2 38	36
37	2 20	2 22	2 23	2 25	2 26	2 28	2 30	2 31	2 33	2 34	2 36	2 37	2 39	2 40	2 42	37
38	2 24	2 26	2 27	2 29	2 30	2 32	2 34	2 35	2 37	2 38	2 40	2 42	2 43	2 45	2 46	38
39	2 28	2 30	2 31	2 33	2 34	2 36	2 38	2 39	2 41	2 42	2 44	2 46	2 47	2 49	2 51	39
40	2 32	2 33	2 35	2 37	2 38	2 40	2 42	2 43	2 45	2 47	2 48	2 50	2 52	2 53	2 55	40
41	2 35	2 37	2 39	2 41	2 42	2 44	2 46	2 47	2 49	2 51	2 53	2 54	2 56	2 58	2 59	41
42	2 39	2 41	2 43	2 45	2 46	2 48	2 50	2 52	2 53	2 55	2 57	2 58	3 0	3 2	3 4	42
43	2 43	2 45	2 47	2 48	2 50	2 52	2 54	2 56	2 57	2 59	3 1	3 3	3 5	3 6	3 8	43
44	2 47	2 49	2 50	2 52	2 54	2 56	2 58	3 0	3 1	3 3	3 5	3 7	3 9	3 11	3 12	44
45	2 51	2 53	2 54	2 56	2 58	3 0	3 2	3 4	3 6	3 8	3 9	3 11	3 13	3 15	3 17	45
46	2 54	2 56	2 58	3 0	3 2	3 4	3 6	3 8	3 10	3 12	3 14	3 15	3 17	3 19	3 21	46
47	2 58	3 0	3 2	3 4	3 6	3 8	3 10	3 12	3 14	3 16	3 18	3 20	3 22	3 24	3 26	47
48	3 2	3 4	3 6	3 8	3 10	3 12	3 14	3 16	3 18	3 20	3 22	3 24	3 26	3 28	3 30	48
49	3 6	3 8	3 10	3 12	3 14	3 16	3 18	3 20	3 22	3 24	3 26	3 28	3 30	3 32	3 34	49
50	3 10	3 12	3 14	3 16	3 18	3 20	3 22	3 24	3 26	3 28	3 30	3 32	3 35	3 37	3 39	50
51	3 13	3 15	3 18	3 20	3 22	3 24	3 26	3 28	3 30	3 33	3 35	3 37	3 39	3 41	3 43	51
52	3 17	3 19	3 22	3 24	3 26	3 28	3 30	3 32	3 34	3 37	3 39	3 41	3 43	3 45	3 47	52
53	3 21	3 23	3 25	3 28	3 30	3 32	3 34	3 36	3 39	3 41	3 43	3 45	3 47	3 50	3 52	53
54	3 25	3 27	3 29	3 31	3 34	3 36	3 38	3 41	3 43	3 45	3 47	3 49	3 52	3 54	3 56	54
55	3 29	3 31	3 33	3 35	3 38	3 40	3 42	3 45	3 47	3 49	3 51	3 54	3 56	3 58	4 1	55
56	3 32	3 35	3 37	3 39	3 42	3 44	3 46	3 49	3 51	3 53	3 56	3 58	4 0	4 3	4 5	56
57	3 36	3 38	3 41	3 43	3 46	3 48	3 50	3 53	3 55	3 57	4 0	4 2	4 5	4 7	4 9	57
58	3 40	3 42	3 45	3 47	3 50	3 52	3 54	3 57	3 59	4 2	4 4	4 6	4 9	4 11	4 14	58
59	3 44	3 46	3 49	3 51	3 54	3 56	3 58	4 1	4 3	4 6	4 8	4 11	4 13	4 16	4 18	59
60	3 47	3 50	3 53	3 55	3 57	4 0	4 2	4 5	4 8	4 10	4 12	4 15	4 17	4 20	4 23	60
HOURS																**HOURS**
1	3 47	3 50	3 53	3 55	3 57	4 0	4 2	4 5	4 8	4 10	4 12	4 15	4 17	4 20	4 23	1
2	7 35	7 40	7 45	7 50	7 55	8 0	8 5	8 10	8 15	8 20	8 25	8 30	8 35	8 40	8 45	2
3	11 23	11 30	11 38	11 45	11 53	12 0	12 8	12 15	12 23	12 30	12 38	12 45	12 53	13 0	13 8	3
4	15 10	15 20	15 30	15 40	15 50	16 0	16 10	16 20	16 30	16 40	16 50	17 0	17 10	17 20	17 30	4
5	18 57	19 10	19 23	19 35	19 48	20 0	20 12	20 25	20 38	20 50	21 3	21 15	21 27	21 40	21 53	5
6	22 45	23 0	23 15	23 30	23 45	24 0	24 15	24 30	24 45	25 0	25 15	25 30	25 45	26 0	26 15	6
7	26 33	26 50	27 8	27 25	27 42	28 0	28 18	28 35	28 53	29 10	29 27	29 45	30 3	30 20	30 38	7
8	30 20	30 40	31 0	31 20	31 40	32 0	32 20	32 40	33 0	33 20	33 40	34 0	34 20	34 40	35 0	8
9	34 8	34 30	34 53	35 15	35 38	36 0	36 23	36 45	37 8	37 30	37 53	38 15	38 38	39 0	39 23	9
10	37 55	38 20	38 45	39 10	39 35	40 0	40 25	40 50	41 15	41 40	42 5	42 30	42 55	43 20	43 45	10
11	41 42	42 10	42 38	43 5	43 33	44 0	44 27	44 55	45 23	45 50	46 18	46 45	47 12	47 40	48 8	11
12	45 30	46 0	46 30	47 0	47 30	48 0	48 30	49 0	49 30	50 0	50 30	51 0	51 30	52 0	52 30	12
13	49 18	49 50	50 23	50 55	51 27	52 0	52 33	53 5	53 38	54 10	54 42	55 15	55 48	56 20	56 53	13
14	53 5	53 40	54 15	54 50	55 25	56 0	56 35	57 10	57 45	58 20	58 55	59 30	1 0 5	1 0 40	1 1 15	14
15	56 53	57 30	58 8	58 45	59 23	1 0 0	1 0 38	1 1 15	1 1 53	1 2 30	1 3 8	1 3 45	1 4 23	1 5 0	1 5 38	15
16	1 0 40	1 1 20	1 2 0	1 2 40	1 3 20	1 4 0	1 4 40	1 5 20	1 6 0	1 6 40	1 7 20	1 8 0	1 8 40	1 9 20	1 10 0	16
17	1 4 27	1 5 10	1 5 53	1 6 35	1 7 18	1 8 0	1 8 42	1 9 25	1 10 8	1 10 50	1 11 33	1 12 15	1 12 57	1 13 40	1 14 23	17
18	1 8 15	1 9 0	1 9 45	1 10 30	1 11 15	1 12 0	1 12 45	1 13 30	1 14 15	1 15 0	1 15 45	1 16 30	1 17 15	1 18 0	1 18 45	18
19	1 12 2	1 12 50	1 13 38	1 14 25	1 15 12	1 16 0	1 16 47	1 17 35	1 18 23	1 19 10	1 19 57	1 20 45	1 21 32	1 22 20	1 23 8	19
20	1 15 50	1 16 40	1 17 30	1 18 20	1 19 10	1 20 0	1 20 50	1 21 40	1 22 30	1 23 20	1 24 10	1 25 0	1 25 50	1 26 40	1 27 30	20
21	1 19 38	1 20 30	1 21 23	1 22 15	1 23 8	1 24 0	1 24 53	1 25 45	1 26 38	1 27 30	1 28 23	1 29 15	1 30 8	1 31 0	1 31 53	21
22	1 23 25	1 24 20	1 25 15	1 26 10	1 27 5	1 28 0	1 28 55	1 29 50	1 30 45	1 31 40	1 32 35	1 33 30	1 34 25	1 35 20	1 36 15	22
23	1 27 12	1 28 10	1 29 8	1 30 5	1 31 3	1 32 0	1 32 57	1 33 55	1 34 53	1 35 50	1 36 48	1 37 45	1 38 42	1 39 40	1 40 38	23
24	1 31 0	1 32 0	1 33 0	1 34 0	1 35 0	1 36 0	1 37 0	1 38 0	1 39 0	1 40 0	1 41 0	1 42 0	1 43 0	1 44 0	1 45 0	24

Table VII Diurnal Motion of the Planets

| | 24 HOUR TRAVEL | | | | | | | | | | | | | | | |
TIME	1° 46'	1° 47'	1° 48'	1° 49'	1° 50'	1° 51'	1° 52'	1° 53'	1° 54'	1° 55'	1° 56'	1° 57'	1° 58'	1° 59'	2° 0'	TIME
MINUTES 1	0 4	0 4	0 4	0 5	0 5	0 5	0 5	0 5	0 5	0 5	0 5	0 5	0 5	0 5	0 5	1 **MINUTES**
2	0 9	0 9	0 9	0 9	0 9	0 9	0 9	0 9	0 9	0 9	0 10	0 10	0 10	0 10	0 10	2
3	0 13	0 13	0 13	0 14	0 14	0 14	0 14	0 14	0 14	0 14	0 14	0 14	0 15	0 15	0 15	3
4	0 18	0 18	0 18	0 18	0 18	0 18	0 19	0 19	0 19	0 19	0 19	0 19	0 20	0 20	0 20	4
5	0 22	0 22	0 23	0 23	0 23	0 23	0 23	0 23	0 24	0 24	0 24	0 24	0 24	0 25	0 25	5
6	0 27	0 27	0 27	0 27	0 28	0 28	0 28	0 28	0 29	0 29	0 29	0 29	0 30	0 30	0 30	6
7	0 31	0 31	0 32	0 32	0 32	0 32	0 33	0 33	0 33	0 34	0 34	0 34	0 34	0 35	0 35	7
8	0 35	0 36	0 36	0 36	0 37	0 37	0 37	0 38	0 38	0 38	0 39	0 39	0 39	0 40	0 40	8
9	0 40	0 40	0 41	0 41	0 41	0 42	0 42	0 42	0 43	0 43	0 43	0 44	0 44	0 44	0 45	9
10	0 44	0 45	0 45	0 45	0 46	0 46	0 47	0 47	0 48	0 48	0 48	0 48	0 49	0 50	0 50	10
11	0 49	0 49	0 50	0 50	0 50	0 51	0 51	0 52	0 52	0 53	0 53	0 54	0 54	0 55	0 55	11
12	0 53	0 54	0 54	0 55	0 55	0 56	0 56	0 57	0 57	0 58	0 58	0 59	0 59	1 0	1 0	12
13	0 57	0 58	0 59	0 59	1 0	1 0	1 1	1 1	1 2	1 2	1 3	1 3	1 4	1 4	1 5	13
14	1 2	1 2	1 3	1 4	1 4	1 5	1 5	1 6	1 7	1 7	1 8	1 8	1 9	1 9	1 10	14
15	1 6	1 7	1 8	1 8	1 9	1 9	1 10	1 11	1 11	1 12	1 12	1 13	1 14	1 14	1 15	15
16	1 11	1 11	1 12	1 13	1 13	1 14	1 15	1 15	1 16	1 17	1 17	1 18	1 19	1 19	1 20	16
17	1 15	1 16	1 16	1 17	1 18	1 19	1 19	1 20	1 21	1 21	1 22	1 23	1 24	1 24	1 25	17
18	1 19	1 20	1 21	1 22	1 23	1 23	1 24	1 25	1 26	1 26	1 27	1 28	1 29	1 29	1 30	18
19	1 24	1 25	1 26	1 26	1 27	1 28	1 29	1 29	1 30	1 31	1 32	1 33	1 33	1 34	1 35	19
20	1 28	1 29	1 30	1 31	1 32	1 33	1 33	1 34	1 35	1 36	1 37	1 38	1 38	1 39	1 40	20
21	1 33	1 34	1 34	1 35	1 36	1 37	1 38	1 39	1 40	1 41	1 42	1 42	1 43	1 44	1 45	21
22	1 37	1 38	1 39	1 40	1 41	1 42	1 43	1 44	1 45	1 45	1 46	1 47	1 48	1 49	1 50	22
23	1 42	1 43	1 43	1 44	1 45	1 46	1 47	1 48	1 49	1 50	1 51	1 52	1 53	1 54	1 55	23
24	1 46	1 47	1 48	1 49	1 50	1 51	1 52	1 53	1 54	1 55	1 56	1 57	1 58	1 59	2 0	24
25	1 50	1 51	1 53	1 54	1 55	1 56	1 57	1 58	1 59	2 0	2 1	2 2	2 3	2 4	2 5	25
26	1 55	1 56	1 57	1 58	1 59	2 0	2 1	2 2	2 4	2 5	2 6	2 7	2 8	2 9	2 10	26
27	1 59	2 0	2 1	2 3	2 4	2 5	2 6	2 7	2 8	2 9	2 10	2 12	2 13	2 14	2 15	27
28	2 4	2 5	2 6	2 7	2 8	2 9	2 11	2 12	2 13	2 14	2 15	2 16	2 18	2 19	2 20	28
29	2 8	2 9	2 10	2 12	2 13	2 14	2 15	2 17	2 18	2 19	2 20	2 21	2 23	2 24	2 25	29
30	2 12	2 14	2 15	2 16	2 18	2 19	2 20	2 21	2 23	2 24	2 25	2 26	2 27	2 29	2 30	30
31	2 17	2 18	2 19	2 21	2 22	2 23	2 25	2 26	2 27	2 29	2 30	2 31	2 32	2 34	2 35	31
32	2 21	2 23	2 24	2 25	2 27	2 28	2 29	2 31	2 32	2 33	2 35	2 36	2 37	2 39	2 40	32
33	2 26	2 27	2 28	2 30	2 31	2 33	2 34	2 35	2 37	2 38	2 39	2 41	2 42	2 44	2 45	33
34	2 30	2 32	2 33	2 34	2 36	2 37	2 39	2 40	2 42	2 43	2 44	2 46	2 47	2 49	2 50	34
35	2 35	2 36	2 38	2 39	2 40	2 42	2 43	2 45	2 46	2 48	2 49	2 51	2 52	2 54	2 55	35
36	2 39	2 41	2 42	2 43	2 45	2 46	2 48	2 49	2 51	2 53	2 54	2 56	2 57	2 58	3 0	36
37	2 43	2 45	2 46	2 48	2 50	2 51	2 53	2 54	2 56	2 57	2 59	3 0	3 2	3 3	3 5	37
38	2 48	2 49	2 51	2 53	2 54	2 56	2 57	2 59	3 0	3 2	3 4	3 5	3 7	3 8	3 10	38
39	2 52	2 54	2 55	2 57	2 59	3 0	3 2	3 4	3 5	3 7	3 8	3 10	3 12	3 13	3 15	39
40	2 57	2 58	3 0	3 2	3 3	3 5	3 7	3 8	3 10	3 12	3 13	3 15	3 17	3 18	3 20	40
41	3 1	3 3	3 4	3 6	3 8	3 10	3 11	3 13	3 15	3 16	3 18	3 20	3 22	3 23	3 25	41
42	3 5	3 7	3 9	3 11	3 12	3 14	3 16	3 18	3 19	3 21	3 23	3 25	3 27	3 28	3 30	42
43	3 10	3 12	3 13	3 15	3 17	3 19	3 21	3 22	3 24	3 26	3 28	3 30	3 31	3 33	3 35	43
44	3 14	3 16	3 18	3 20	3 22	3 23	3 25	3 27	3 29	3 31	3 33	3 34	3 36	3 38	3 40	44
45	3 19	3 21	3 23	3 24	3 26	3 28	3 30	3 32	3 34	3 36	3 38	3 39	3 41	3 43	3 45	45
46	3 23	3 25	3 27	3 29	3 31	3 33	3 35	3 37	3 38	3 40	3 42	3 44	3 46	3 48	3 50	46
47	3 28	3 30	3 31	3 33	3 35	3 37	3 39	3 41	3 43	3 45	3 47	3 49	3 51	3 53	3 55	47
48	3 32	3 34	3 36	3 38	3 40	3 42	3 44	3 46	3 48	3 50	3 52	3 54	3 56	3 58	4 0	48
49	3 36	3 38	3 41	3 43	3 45	3 47	3 49	3 51	3 53	3 55	3 57	3 59	4 1	4 3	4 5	49
50	3 41	3 43	3 45	3 47	3 49	3 51	3 53	3 55	3 57	4 0	4 2	4 4	4 6	4 8	4 10	50
51	3 45	3 47	3 49	3 52	3 54	3 56	3 58	4 0	4 2	4 4	4 7	4 9	4 11	4 13	4 15	51
52	3 50	3 52	3 54	3 56	3 58	4 0	4 3	4 5	4 7	4 9	4 11	4 13	4 16	4 18	4 20	52
53	3 54	3 56	3 59	4 1	4 3	4 5	4 7	4 10	4 12	4 14	4 16	4 18	4 21	4 23	4 25	53
54	3 58	4 1	4 3	4 5	4 8	4 10	4 12	4 14	4 16	4 19	4 21	4 23	4 26	4 28	4 30	54
55	4 3	4 5	4 8	4 10	4 12	4 14	4 17	4 19	4 21	4 24	4 26	4 28	4 30	4 33	4 35	55
56	4 7	4 10	4 12	4 14	4 17	4 19	4 21	4 24	4 26	4 28	4 31	4 33	4 35	4 38	4 40	56
57	4 12	4 14	4 16	4 19	4 21	4 24	4 26	4 28	4 31	4 33	4 35	4 38	4 40	4 43	4 45	57
58	4 16	4 19	4 21	4 23	4 26	4 28	4 31	4 33	4 35	4 38	4 40	4 43	4 45	4 48	4 50	58
59	4 21	4 23	4 26	4 28	4 30	4 33	4 35	4 38	4 40	4 43	4 45	4 48	4 50	4 53	4 55	59
60	4 25	4 27	4 30	4 32	4 35	4 38	4 40	4 42	4 45	4 47	4 50	4 53	4 55	4 57	5 0	60
HOURS 1	4 25	4 27	4 30	4 32	4 35	4 38	4 40	4 42	4 45	4 47	4 50	4 53	4 55	4 57	5 0	1 **HOURS**
2	8 50	8 55	9 0	9 5	9 10	9 15	9 20	9 25	9 30	9 35	9 40	9 45	9 50	9 55	10 0	2
3	13 15	13 23	13 30	13 38	13 45	13 53	14 0	14 8	14 15	14 23	14 30	14 38	14 45	14 53	15 0	3
4	17 40	17 50	18 0	18 10	18 20	18 30	18 40	18 50	19 0	19 10	19 20	19 30	19 40	19 50	20 0	4
5	22 5	22 18	22 30	22 42	22 55	23 8	23 20	23 33	23 45	23 57	24 10	24 23	24 35	24 48	25 0	5
6	26 30	26 45	27 0	27 15	27 30	27 45	28 0	28 15	28 30	28 45	29 0	29 15	29 30	29 45	30 0	6
7	30 55	31 12	31 30	31 48	32 5	32 23	32 40	32 57	33 15	33 33	33 50	34 8	34 25	34 42	35 0	7
8	35 20	35 40	36 0	36 20	36 40	37 0	37 20	37 40	38 0	38 20	38 40	39 0	39 20	39 40	40 0	8
9	39 45	40 8	40 30	40 53	41 15	41 38	42 0	42 23	42 45	43 8	43 30	43 53	44 15	44 38	45 0	9
10	44 10	44 35	45 0	45 25	45 50	46 15	46 40	47 5	47 30	47 55	48 20	48 45	49 10	49 35	50 0	10
11	48 35	49 3	49 30	49 57	50 25	50 53	51 20	51 48	52 15	52 42	53 10	53 38	54 5	54 33	55 0	11
12	53 0	53 30	54 0	54 30	55 0	55 30	56 0	56 30	57 0	57 30	58 0	58 30	59 0	59 30	1 0 0	12
13	57 25	57 57	58 30	59 3	59 35	1 0 8	1 0 40	1 1 12	1 1 45	1 2 18	1 2 50	1 3 23	1 3 55	1 4 27	1 5 0	13
14	1 1 50	1 2 25	1 3 0	1 3 35	1 4 10	1 4 45	1 5 20	1 5 55	1 6 30	1 7 5	1 7 40	1 8 15	1 8 50	1 9 25	1 10 0	14
15	1 6 15	1 6 53	1 7 30	1 8 8	1 8 45	1 9 23	1 10 0	1 10 38	1 11 15	1 11 53	1 12 30	1 13 8	1 13 45	1 14 23	1 15 0	15
16	1 10 40	1 11 20	1 12 0	1 12 40	1 13 20	1 14 0	1 14 40	1 15 20	1 16 0	1 16 40	1 17 20	1 18 0	1 18 40	1 19 20	1 20 0	16
17	1 15 5	1 15 48	1 16 30	1 17 12	1 17 55	1 18 38	1 19 20	1 20 3	1 20 45	1 21 27	1 22 10	1 22 53	1 23 35	1 24 18	1 25 0	17
18	1 19 30	1 20 15	1 21 0	1 21 45	1 22 30	1 23 15	1 24 0	1 24 45	1 25 30	1 26 15	1 27 0	1 27 45	1 28 30	1 29 15	1 30 0	18
19	1 23 55	1 24 42	1 25 30	1 26 17	1 27 5	1 27 53	1 28 40	1 29 27	1 30 15	1 31 2	1 31 50	1 32 38	1 33 25	1 34 12	1 35 0	19
20	1 28 20	1 29 10	1 30 0	1 30 50	1 31 40	1 32 30	1 33 20	1 34 10	1 35 0	1 35 50	1 36 40	1 37 30	1 38 20	1 39 10	1 40 0	20
21	1 32 45	1 33 38	1 34 30	1 35 23	1 36 15	1 37 8	1 38 0	1 38 53	1 39 45	1 40 38	1 41 30	1 42 23	1 43 15	1 44 8	1 45 0	21
22	1 37 10	1 38 5	1 39 0	1 39 55	1 40 50	1 41 45	1 42 40	1 43 35	1 44 30	1 45 25	1 46 20	1 47 15	1 48 10	1 49 5	1 50 0	22
23	1 41 35	1 42 33	1 43 30	1 44 27	1 45 25	1 46 23	1 47 20	1 48 18	1 49 15	1 50 12	1 51 10	1 52 8	1 53 5	1 54 3	1 55 0	23
24	1 46 0	1 47 0	1 48 0	1 49 0	1 50 0	1 51 0	1 52 0	1 53 0	1 54 0	1 55 0	1 56 0	1 57 0	1 58 0	1 59 0	2 0 0	24

Table VII Diurnal Motion of the Planets

	24 HOUR TRAVEL															
TIME	**2° 1'**	**2° 2'**	**2° 3'**	**2° 4'**	**2° 5'**	**2° 6'**	**2° 7'**	**2° 8'**	**2° 9'**	**2° 10'**	**2° 11'**	**2° 12'**	**2° 13'**	**2° 14'**	**2° 15'**	**TIME**
	° ' "	° ' "	° ' "	° ' "	° ' "	° ' "	° ' "	° ' "	° ' "	° ' "	° ' "	° ' "	° ' "	° ' "	° ' "	
MINUTES																**MINUTES**
1	0 5	0 5	0 5	0 5	0 5	0 5	0 5	0 5	0 5	0 5	0 5	0 5	0 6	0 6	0 6	1
2	0 10	0 10	0 10	0 10	0 10	0 10	0 11	0 11	0 11	0 11	0 11	0 11	0 11	0 11	0 11	2
3	0 15	0 15	0 15	0 15	0 16	0 16	0 16	0 16	0 16	0 16	0 16	0 16	0 17	0 17	0 17	3
4	0 20	0 20	0 20	0 21	0 21	0 21	0 21	0 21	0 21	0 22	0 22	0 22	0 22	0 22	0 22	4
5	0 25	0 25	0 26	0 26	0 26	0 26	0 26	0 27	0 27	0 27	0 27	0 28	0 28	0 28	0 28	5
6	0 30	0 31	0 31	0 31	0 31	0 32	0 32	0 32	0 33	0 33	0 33	0 33	0 33	0 34	0 34	6
7	0 35	0 36	0 36	0 36	0 36	0 37	0 37	0 37	0 38	0 38	0 38	0 39	0 39	0 39	0 39	7
8	0 40	0 41	0 41	0 41	0 42	0 42	0 42	0 43	0 43	0 43	0 44	0 44	0 44	0 45	0 45	8
9	0 45	0 46	0 46	0 47	0 47	0 47	0 48	0 48	0 48	0 49	0 49	0 50	0 50	0 50	0 51	9
10	0 50	0 51	0 51	0 52	0 52	0 53	0 53	0 53	0 54	0 54	0 55	0 55	0 55	0 56	0 56	10
11	0 55	0 56	0 56	0 57	0 57	0 58	0 58	0 59	0 59	1 0	1 0	1 0	1 1	1 1	1 2	11
12	1 0	1 1	1 1	1 2	1 2	1 3	1 3	1 4	1 4	1 5	1 5	1 6	1 6	1 7	1 7	12
13	1 6	1 6	1 7	1 7	1 8	1 8	1 9	1 9	1 10	1 10	1 11	1 11	1 12	1 13	1 13	13
14	1 11	1 11	1 12	1 12	1 13	1 13	1 14	1 15	1 15	1 16	1 16	1 17	1 18	1 18	1 19	14
15	1 16	1 16	1 17	1 17	1 18	1 19	1 19	1 20	1 21	1 21	1 22	1 22	1 23	1 24	1 24	15
16	1 21	1 21	1 22	1 23	1 23	1 24	1 25	1 25	1 26	1 27	1 27	1 28	1 29	1 29	1 30	16
17	1 26	1 26	1 27	1 28	1 29	1 29	1 30	1 31	1 31	1 32	1 33	1 33	1 34	1 35	1 36	17
18	1 31	1 31	1 32	1 33	1 34	1 34	1 35	1 36	1 37	1 37	1 38	1 39	1 40	1 40	1 41	18
19	1 36	1 37	1 37	1 38	1 39	1 40	1 41	1 41	1 42	1 43	1 44	1 44	1 45	1 46	1 47	19
20	1 41	1 42	1 42	1 43	1 44	1 45	1 46	1 47	1 47	1 48	1 49	1 50	1 51	1 52	1 53	20
21	1 46	1 47	1 48	1 49	1 49	1 50	1 51	1 52	1 53	1 54	1 55	1 55	1 56	1 57	1 58	21
22	1 51	1 52	1 53	1 54	1 55	1 56	1 56	1 57	1 58	1 59	2 0	2 1	2 2	2 3	2 4	22
23	1 56	1 57	1 58	1 59	2 0	2 1	2 2	2 3	2 4	2 5	2 6	2 6	2 7	2 8	2 9	23
24	2 1	2 2	2 3	2 4	2 5	2 6	2 7	2 8	2 9	2 10	2 11	2 12	2 13	2 14	2 15	24
25	2 6	2 7	2 8	2 9	2 10	2 11	2 12	2 13	2 14	2 15	2 16	2 17	2 19	2 20	2 21	25
26	2 11	2 12	2 13	2 14	2 15	2 16	2 18	2 19	2 20	2 21	2 22	2 23	2 24	2 25	2 26	26
27	2 16	2 17	2 18	2 19	2 21	2 22	2 23	2 24	2 25	2 26	2 27	2 28	2 30	2 31	2 32	27
28	2 21	2 22	2 23	2 25	2 26	2 27	2 28	2 29	2 30	2 32	2 33	2 34	2 35	2 36	2 38	28
29	2 26	2 27	2 29	2 30	2 31	2 32	2 33	2 35	2 36	2 37	2 38	2 39	2 41	2 42	2 43	29
30	2 31	2 33	2 34	2 35	2 36	2 38	2 39	2 40	2 41	2 42	2 44	2 45	2 46	2 47	2 49	30
31	2 36	2 38	2 39	2 40	2 41	2 43	2 44	2 45	2 47	2 48	2 49	2 50	2 52	2 53	2 54	31
32	2 41	2 43	2 44	2 45	2 47	2 48	2 49	2 51	2 52	2 53	2 55	2 56	2 57	2 59	3 0	32
33	2 46	2 48	2 49	2 50	2 52	2 53	2 55	2 56	2 57	2 59	3 0	3 1	3 3	3 4	3 6	33
34	2 51	2 53	2 54	2 56	2 57	2 58	3 0	3 1	3 3	3 4	3 6	3 7	3 8	3 10	3 11	34
35	2 56	2 58	2 59	3 1	3 2	3 4	3 5	3 7	3 8	3 10	3 11	3 12	3 14	3 15	3 17	35
36	3 1	3 3	3 4	3 6	3 8	3 9	3 11	3 12	3 13	3 15	3 16	3 18	3 19	3 21	3 23	36
37	3 7	3 8	3 10	3 11	3 13	3 14	3 16	3 17	3 19	3 20	3 22	3 23	3 25	3 27	3 28	37
38	3 12	3 13	3 15	3 16	3 18	3 19	3 21	3 23	3 24	3 26	3 27	3 29	3 31	3 32	3 34	38
39	3 17	3 18	3 20	3 21	3 23	3 25	3 26	3 28	3 30	3 31	3 33	3 34	3 36	3 38	3 39	39
40	3 22	3 23	3 25	3 27	3 28	3 30	3 32	3 33	3 35	3 37	3 38	3 40	3 42	3 43	3 45	40
41	3 27	3 28	3 30	3 32	3 34	3 35	3 37	3 39	3 40	3 42	3 44	3 46	3 47	3 49	3 51	41
42	3 32	3 34	3 35	3 37	3 39	3 41	3 42	3 44	3 46	3 47	3 49	3 51	3 53	3 54	3 56	42
43	3 37	3 39	3 40	3 42	3 44	3 46	3 48	3 49	3 51	3 53	3 55	3 57	3 58	4 0	4 2	43
44	3 42	3 44	3 46	3 47	3 49	3 51	3 53	3 55	3 56	3 58	4 0	4 2	4 4	4 6	4 8	44
45	3 47	3 49	3 51	3 53	3 54	3 56	3 58	4 0	4 2	4 4	4 6	4 8	4 9	4 11	4 13	45
46	3 52	3 54	3 56	3 58	4 0	4 1	4 3	4 5	4 7	4 9	4 11	4 13	4 15	4 17	4 19	46
47	3 57	3 59	4 1	4 3	4 5	4 7	4 9	4 11	4 13	4 15	4 17	4 19	4 20	4 22	4 24	47
48	4 2	4 4	4 6	4 8	4 10	4 12	4 14	4 16	4 18	4 20	4 22	4 24	4 26	4 28	4 30	48
49	4 7	4 9	4 11	4 13	4 15	4 17	4 19	4 21	4 23	4 25	4 27	4 29	4 32	4 34	4 36	49
50	4 12	4 14	4 16	4 18	4 20	4 23	4 25	4 27	4 29	4 31	4 33	4 35	4 37	4 39	4 41	50
51	4 17	4 19	4 21	4 23	4 26	4 28	4 30	4 32	4 34	4 36	4 38	4 41	4 43	4 45	4 47	51
52	4 22	4 24	4 27	4 29	4 31	4 33	4 35	4 37	4 40	4 42	4 44	4 46	4 48	4 50	4 53	52
53	4 27	4 29	4 32	4 34	4 36	4 38	4 40	4 43	4 45	4 47	4 49	4 52	4 54	4 56	4 58	53
54	4 32	4 34	4 37	4 39	4 41	4 43	4 46	4 48	4 50	4 52	4 55	4 57	4 59	5 1	5 4	54
55	4 37	4 40	4 42	4 44	4 46	4 49	4 51	4 53	4 56	4 58	5 0	5 3	5 5	5 7	5 9	55
56	4 42	4 45	4 47	4 49	4 52	4 54	4 56	4 59	5 1	5 3	5 6	5 8	5 10	5 13	5 15	56
57	4 47	4 50	4 52	4 54	4 57	4 59	5 2	5 4	5 6	5 9	5 11	5 13	5 16	5 18	5 21	57
58	4 52	4 55	4 57	5 0	5 2	5 4	5 7	5 9	5 12	5 14	5 17	5 19	5 21	5 24	5 26	58
59	4 57	5 0	5 2	5 5	5 7	5 10	5 12	5 15	5 17	5 20	5 22	5 24	5 27	5 29	5 32	59
60	5 2	5 5	5 8	5 10	5 12	5 15	5 17	5 20	5 23	5 25	5 27	5 30	5 32	5 35	5 38	60
HOURS																**HOURS**
1	5 2	5 5	5 8	5 10	5 12	5 15	5 17	5 20	5 23	5 25	5 27	5 30	5 32	5 35	5 38	1
2	10 5	10 10	10 15	10 20	10 25	10 30	10 35	10 40	10 45	10 50	10 55	11 0	11 5	11 10	11 15	2
3	15 8	15 15	15 23	15 30	15 38	15 45	15 53	16 0	16 8	16 15	16 23	16 30	16 38	16 45	16 53	3
4	20 10	20 20	20 30	20 40	20 50	21 0	21 10	21 20	21 30	21 40	21 50	22 0	22 10	22 20	22 30	4
5	25 12	25 25	25 38	25 50	26 3	26 15	26 27	26 40	26 53	27 5	27 17	27 30	27 42	27 55	28 8	5
6	30 15	30 30	30 45	31 0	31 15	31 30	31 45	32 0	32 15	32 30	32 45	33 0	33 15	33 30	33 45	6
7	35 18	35 35	35 53	36 10	36 27	36 45	37 3	37 20	37 38	37 55	38 13	38 30	38 48	39 5	39 23	7
8	40 20	40 40	41 0	41 20	41 40	42 0	42 20	42 40	43 0	43 20	43 40	44 0	44 20	44 40	45 0	8
9	45 23	45 45	46 8	46 30	46 53	47 15	47 38	48 0	48 23	48 45	49 8	49 30	49 53	50 15	50 38	9
10	50 25	50 50	51 15	51 40	52 5	52 30	52 55	53 20	53 45	54 10	54 35	55 0	55 25	55 50	56 15	10
11	55 27	55 55	56 23	56 50	57 18	57 45	58 12	58 40	59 8	59 35	1 0 2	1 0 30	1 0 57	1 1 25	1 1 53	11
12	1 0 30	1 1 0	1 1 30	1 2 0	1 2 30	1 3 0	1 3 30	1 4 0	1 4 30	1 5 0	1 5 30	1 6 0	1 6 30	1 7 0	1 7 30	12
13	1 5 33	1 6 5	1 6 38	1 7 10	1 7 42	1 8 15	1 8 48	1 9 20	1 9 53	1 10 25	1 10 58	1 11 30	1 12 3	1 12 35	1 13 8	13
14	1 10 35	1 11 10	1 11 45	1 12 20	1 12 55	1 13 30	1 14 5	1 14 40	1 15 15	1 15 50	1 16 25	1 17 0	1 17 35	1 18 10	1 18 45	14
15	1 15 38	1 16 15	1 16 53	1 17 30	1 18 8	1 18 45	1 19 23	1 20 0	1 20 38	1 21 15	1 21 53	1 22 30	1 23 8	1 23 45	1 24 23	15
16	1 20 40	1 21 20	1 22 0	1 22 40	1 23 20	1 24 0	1 24 40	1 25 20	1 26 0	1 26 40	1 27 20	1 28 0	1 28 40	1 29 20	1 30 0	16
17	1 25 42	1 26 25	1 27 8	1 27 50	1 28 33	1 29 15	1 29 57	1 30 40	1 31 23	1 32 5	1 32 47	1 33 30	1 34 12	1 34 55	1 35 38	17
18	1 30 45	1 31 30	1 32 15	1 33 0	1 33 45	1 34 30	1 35 15	1 36 0	1 36 45	1 37 30	1 38 15	1 39 0	1 39 45	1 40 30	1 41 15	18
19	1 35 47	1 36 35	1 37 23	1 38 10	1 38 57	1 39 45	1 40 32	1 41 20	1 42 8	1 42 55	1 43 42	1 44 30	1 45 17	1 46 5	1 46 53	19
20	1 40 50	1 41 40	1 42 30	1 43 20	1 44 10	1 45 0	1 45 50	1 46 40	1 47 30	1 48 20	1 49 10	1 50 0	1 50 50	1 51 40	1 52 30	20
21	1 45 53	1 46 45	1 47 38	1 48 30	1 49 23	1 50 15	1 51 8	1 52 0	1 52 53	1 53 45	1 54 38	1 55 30	1 56 23	1 57 15	1 58 8	21
22	1 50 55	1 51 50	1 52 45	1 53 40	1 54 35	1 55 30	1 56 25	1 57 20	1 58 15	1 59 10	2 0 5	2 1 0	2 1 55	2 2 50	2 3 45	22
23	1 55 57	1 56 55	1 57 53	1 58 50	1 59 48	2 0 45	2 1 42	2 2 40	2 3 38	2 4 35	2 5 32	2 6 30	2 7 27	2 8 25	2 9 23	23
24	2 1 0	2 2 0	2 3 0	2 4 0	2 5 0	2 6 0	2 7 0	2 8 0	2 9 0	2 10 0	2 11 0	2 12 0	2 13 0	2 14 0	2 15 0	24

Table VIII Second Difference Interpolation for the Moon

12 HOUR INTERVAL

MEAN SECOND DIFFERENCE

TIME INTVL	1'	2'	3'	4'	5'	6'	7'	8'	9'	10'	TIME INTVL
0–1	0 1	0 2	0 4	0 5	0 6	0 7	0 8	0 10	0 11	0 12	11–12
1–2	0 3	0 7	0 10	0 13	0 16	0 20	0 23	0 26	0 30	0 33	10–11
2–3	0 5	0 10	0 15	0 20	0 25	0 30	0 35	0 40	0 45	0 49	9–10
3–4	0 6	0 12	0 19	0 25	0 31	0 37	0 43	0 50	0 56	1 2	8–9
4–5	0 7	0 14	0 21	0 28	0 35	0 42	0 49	0 56	1 3	1 10	7–8
5–6	0 7	0 15	0 22	0 30	0 37	0 45	0 52	0 60	1 7	1 14	6–7

MEAN SECOND DIFFERENCE

TIME INTVL	11'	12'	13'	14'	15'	16'	17'	18'	19'	20'	TIME INTVL
0–1	0 13	0 14	0 16	0 17	0 18	0 19	0 20	0 22	0 23	0 24	11–12
1–2	0 36	0 39	0 43	0 46	0 49	0 52	0 56	0 59	1 2	1 6	10–11
2–3	0 54	0 59	1 4	1 9	1 14	1 19	1 24	1 29	1 34	1 39	9–10
3–4	1 8	1 14	1 21	1 27	1 33	1 39	1 45	1 52	1 58	2 4	8–9
4–5	1 17	1 24	1 31	1 38	1 45	1 52	1 60	2 7	2 14	2 21	7–8
5–6	1 22	1 29	1 37	1 44	1 52	1 59	2 7	2 14	2 22	2 29	6–7

24 HOUR INTERVAL

MEAN SECOND DIFFERENCE

TIME INTVL	1'	2'	3'	4'	5'	6'	7'	8'	9'	10'	11'	12'	13'	14'	15'	TIME INTVL
0–1	0 1	0 1	0 2	0 2	0 3	0 4	0 4	0 5	0 6	0 6	0 7	0 7	0 8	0 9	0 9	23–24
1–2	0 2	0 4	0 5	0 7	0 9	0 11	0 12	0 14	0 16	0 18	0 19	0 21	0 23	0 25	0 26	22–23
2–3	0 3	0 6	0 8	0 11	0 14	0 17	0 20	0 22	0 25	0 28	0 31	0 34	0 36	0 39	0 42	21–22
3–4	0 4	0 7	0 11	0 15	0 19	0 22	0 26	0 30	0 34	0 37	0 41	0 45	0 49	0 52	0 56	20–21
4–5	0 5	0 9	0 14	0 18	0 23	0 27	0 32	0 37	0 41	0 46	0 50	0 55	0 59	1 4	1 9	19–20
5–6	0 5	0 11	0 16	0 21	0 26	0 32	0 37	0 42	0 48	0 53	0 58	1 4	1 9	1 14	1 19	18–19
6–7	0 6	0 12	0 18	0 24	0 30	0 36	0 41	0 47	0 53	0 59	1 5	1 11	1 17	1 23	1 29	17–18
7–8	0 6	0 13	0 19	0 26	0 32	0 39	0 45	0 52	0 58	1 4	1 11	1 17	1 24	1 30	1 37	16–17
8–9	0 7	0 14	0 21	0 27	0 34	0 41	0 48	0 55	1 2	1 9	1 15	1 22	1 29	1 36	1 43	15–16
9–10	0 7	0 14	0 22	0 29	0 36	0 43	0 50	0 57	1 5	1 12	1 19	1 26	1 33	1 40	1 48	14–15
10–11	0 7	0 15	0 22	0 30	0 37	0 44	0 52	0 59	1 6	1 14	1 21	1 29	1 36	1 43	1 51	13–14
11–12	0 7	0 15	0 22	0 30	0 37	0 45	0 52	0 60	1 7	1 15	1 22	1 30	1 37	1 45	1 52	12–13

MEAN SECOND DIFFERENCE

TIME INTVL	16'	17'	18'	19'	20'	21'	22'	23'	24'	25'	26'	27'	28'	29'	30'	TIME INTVL
0–1	0 10	0 10	0 11	0 12	0 12	0 13	0 13	0 14	0 15	0 15	0 16	0 17	0 17	0 18	0 18	23–24
1–2	0 28	0 30	0 32	0 33	0 35	0 37	0 39	0 40	0 42	0 44	0 46	0 47	0 49	0 51	0 53	22–23
2–3	0 45	0 48	0 50	0 53	0 56	0 59	1 2	1 4	1 7	1 10	1 13	1 16	1 18	1 21	1 24	21–22
3–4	0 60	1 4	1 7	1 11	1 15	1 18	1 22	1 26	1 30	1 33	1 37	1 41	1 45	1 48	1 52	20–21
4–5	1 13	1 18	1 22	1 27	1 31	1 36	1 41	1 45	1 50	1 54	1 59	2 3	2 8	2 13	2 17	19–20
5–6	1 25	1 30	1 35	1 41	1 46	1 51	1 57	2 2	2 7	2 12	2 18	2 23	2 28	2 34	2 39	18–19
6–7	1 35	1 41	1 47	1 53	1 58	2 4	2 10	2 16	2 22	2 28	2 34	2 40	2 46	2 52	2 58	17–18
7–8	1 43	1 50	1 56	2 2	2 9	2 15	2 22	2 28	2 35	2 41	2 48	2 54	3 0	3 7	3 13	16–17
8–9	1 50	1 57	2 4	2 10	2 17	2 24	2 31	2 38	2 45	2 52	2 58	3 5	3 12	3 19	3 26	15–16
9–10	1 55	2 2	2 9	2 16	2 23	2 31	2 38	2 45	2 52	2 59	3 7	3 14	3 21	3 28	3 35	14–15
10–11	1 58	2 6	2 13	2 20	2 28	2 35	2 42	2 50	2 57	3 5	3 12	3 19	3 27	3 34	3 41	13–14
11–12	1 60	2 7	2 15	2 22	2 30	2 37	2 45	2 52	2 60	3 7	3 15	3 22	3 30	3 37	3 45	12–13

Table IX Diurnal Motion Logarithms, 0 to 24 Hours/Degrees

Minutes of Time or Arc	0	1	2	3	4	5	6	7	8	9	10	11	12	13	14	15	16	17	18	19	20	21	22	23	Minutes of Time or Arc
0	INFINITE	1.38021	1.07918	.90309	.77815	.68124	.60206	.53511	.47712	.42597	.38021	.33882	.30103	.26627	.23408	.20412	.17609	.14976	.12494	.10146	.07918	.05799	.03779	.01848	0
1	3.15836	1.37303	1.07558	.90068	.77635	.67980	.60086	.53408	.47622	.42517	.37949	.33816	.30043	.26571	.23357	.20364	.17564	.14934	.12454	.10108	.07882	.05765	.03746	.01817	1
2	2.85733	1.36597	1.07200	.89829	.77455	.67836	.59965	.53305	.47532	.42436	.37877	.33750	.29983	.26516	.23305	.20316	.17519	.14891	.12414	.10070	.07846	.05730	.03713	.01785	2
3	2.68124	1.35902	1.06846	.89591	.77276	.67692	.59846	.53202	.47442	.42356	.37805	.33685	.29922	.26460	.23253	.20267	.17474	.14849	.12373	.10032	.07810	.05696	.03680	.01754	3
4	2.55630	1.35218	1.06494	.89354	.77097	.67549	.59726	.53100	.47352	.42276	.37733	.33619	.29862	.26405	.23202	.20219	.17429	.14806	.12333	.09994	.07774	.05662	.03647	.01723	4
5	2.45939	1.34545	1.06145	.89119	.76920	.67406	.59607	.52997	.47262	.42197	.37661	.33554	.29802	.26349	.23151	.20171	.17384	.14764	.12293	.09956	.07738	.05627	.03615	.01691	5
6	2.38021	1.33882	1.05799	.88885	.76743	.67264	.59488	.52895	.47173	.42117	.37589	.33489	.29743	.26294	.23099	.20123	.17339	.14722	.12253	.09918	.07702	.05593	.03582	.01660	6
7	2.31326	1.33229	1.05456	.88652	.76567	.67122	.59370	.52793	.47083	.42038	.37517	.33424	.29683	.26239	.23048	.20076	.17294	.14679	.12213	.09880	.07666	.05559	.03549	.01629	7
8	2.25527	1.32585	1.05115	.88420	.76391	.66981	.59251	.52692	.46994	.41958	.37446	.33359	.29623	.26184	.22997	.20028	.17249	.14637	.12173	.09842	.07630	.05524	.03516	.01597	8
9	2.20412	1.31951	1.04777	.88190	.76216	.66840	.59134	.52591	.46905	.41879	.37375	.33294	.29563	.26129	.22945	.19980	.17204	.14595	.12133	.09804	.07594	.05490	.03484	.01566	9
10	2.15836	1.31326	1.04442	.87961	.76042	.66700	.59016	.52489	.46817	.41800	.37303	.33229	.29504	.26074	.22894	.19932	.17159	.14553	.12094	.09766	.07558	.05456	.03451	.01535	10
11	2.11697	1.30710	1.04109	.87733	.75869	.66560	.58899	.52389	.46728	.41721	.37232	.33164	.29445	.26019	.22843	.19884	.17114	.14510	.12054	.09729	.07522	.05422	.03418	.01504	11
12	2.07918	1.30103	1.03779	.87506	.75696	.66421	.58782	.52288	.46640	.41642	.37161	.33099	.29385	.25964	.22792	.19837	.17070	.14468	.12014	.09691	.07486	.05388	.03386	.01472	12
13	2.04442	1.29504	1.03451	.87281	.75524	.66282	.58665	.52187	.46552	.41564	.37090	.33035	.29326	.25909	.22741	.19789	.17025	.14426	.11974	.09653	.07450	.05353	.03353	.01441	13
14	2.01223	1.28913	1.03126	.87056	.75353	.66143	.58549	.52087	.46464	.41485	.37019	.32970	.29267	.25854	.22690	.19742	.16980	.14384	.11935	.09616	.07414	.05319	.03321	.01410	14
15	1.98227	1.28330	1.02803	.86833	.75182	.66005	.58433	.51987	.46376	.41407	.36949	.32906	.29208	.25800	.22640	.19694	.16936	.14342	.11895	.09578	.07379	.05285	.03288	.01379	15
16	1.95424	1.27755	1.02482	.86611	.75012	.65868	.58317	.51888	.46288	.41329	.36878	.32842	.29148	.25745	.22589	.19647	.16891	.14300	.11855	.09540	.07343	.05251	.03256	.01348	16
17	1.92791	1.27187	1.02164	.86390	.74843	.65730	.58202	.51788	.46201	.41251	.36808	.32777	.29090	.25690	.22538	.19599	.16847	.14258	.11816	.09503	.07307	.05217	.03223	.01317	17
18	1.90309	1.26627	1.01848	.86170	.74674	.65594	.58087	.51689	.46113	.41173	.36737	.32713	.29031	.25636	.22488	.19552	.16802	.14217	.11776	.09465	.07272	.05183	.03191	.01286	18
19	1.87961	1.26074	1.01535	.85951	.74506	.65457	.57972	.51590	.46026	.41095	.36667	.32649	.28972	.25582	.22437	.19505	.16758	.14175	.11736	.09428	.07236	.05149	.03158	.01254	19
20	1.85733	1.25527	1.01223	.85733	.74339	.65321	.57858	.51491	.45939	.41017	.36597	.32585	.28913	.25527	.22386	.19457	.16714	.14133	.11697	.09390	.07200	.05115	.03126	.01223	20
21	1.83614	1.24988	1.00914	.85517	.74172	.65186	.57744	.51392	.45852	.40940	.36527	.32522	.28854	.25473	.22336	.19410	.16669	.14091	.11658	.09353	.07165	.05081	.03093	.01192	21
22	1.81594	1.24455	1.00607	.85301	.74006	.65051	.57630	.51294	.45766	.40863	.36457	.32458	.28796	.25419	.22286	.19363	.16625	.14049	.11618	.09316	.07129	.05047	.03061	.01161	22
23	1.79663	1.23928	1.00303	.85087	.73841	.64916	.57516	.51196	.45679	.40785	.36387	.32394	.28737	.25365	.22235	.19316	.16581	.14008	.11579	.09278	.07094	.05014	.03029	.01130	23
24	1.77815	1.23408	1.00000	.84873	.73676	.64782	.57403	.51098	.45593	.40708	.36318	.32331	.28679	.25311	.22185	.19269	.16537	.13966	.11539	.09241	.07058	.04980	.02996	.01100	24
25	1.76042	1.22894	0.99699	.84661	.73512	.64648	.57290	.51000	.45507	.40631	.36248	.32267	.28621	.25257	.22135	.19222	.16493	.13925	.11500	.09204	.07023	.04946	.02964	.01069	25
26	1.74339	1.22386	0.99401	.84450	.73348	.64514	.57178	.50903	.45421	.40555	.36179	.32204	.28562	.25203	.22084	.19175	.16449	.13883	.11461	.09166	.06987	.04912	.02932	.01038	26
27	1.72700	1.21884	0.99105	.84239	.73185	.64381	.57065	.50805	.45335	.40478	.36109	.32141	.28504	.25149	.22034	.19128	.16405	.13842	.11421	.09129	.06952	.04878	.02899	.01007	27
28	1.71120	1.21388	0.98810	.84030	.73023	.64249	.56953	.50708	.45250	.40401	.36040	.32077	.28446	.25095	.21984	.19081	.16361	.13800	.11382	.09092	.06916	.04845	.02867	.00976	28
29	1.69596	1.20897	0.98518	.83822	.72861	.64117	.56841	.50612	.45164	.40325	.35971	.32014	.28388	.25041	.21934	.19035	.16317	.13759	.11343	.09055	.06881	.04811	.02835	.00945	29
30	1.68124	1.20412	0.98227	.83614	.72700	.63985	.56730	.50515	.45079	.40249	.35902	.31951	.28330	.24988	.21884	.18988	.16273	.13717	.11304	.09018	.06846	.04777	.02803	.00914	30
31	1.66700	1.19932	0.97939	.83408	.72539	.63853	.56619	.50419	.44994	.40173	.35833	.31888	.28272	.24934	.21834	.18941	.16229	.13676	.11265	.08981	.06810	.04744	.02771	.00884	31
32	1.65321	1.19457	0.97652	.83203	.72379	.63722	.56508	.50322	.44909	.40097	.35765	.31826	.28214	.24881	.21785	.18895	.16185	.13635	.11226	.08943	.06775	.04710	.02739	.00853	32
33	1.63985	1.18988	0.97367	.82998	.72220	.63592	.56397	.50226	.44825	.40021	.35696	.31763	.28157	.24827	.21735	.18848	.16141	.13593	.11187	.08906	.06740	.04676	.02706	.00822	33
34	1.62688	1.18523	0.97084	.82795	.72061	.63462	.56287	.50131	.44740	.39945	.35627	.31700	.28099	.24774	.21685	.18802	.16098	.13552	.11148	.08869	.06705	.04643	.02674	.00791	34
35	1.61429	1.18064	0.96803	.82592	.71903	.63332	.56177	.50035	.44656	.39869	.35559	.31638	.28042	.24720	.21635	.18755	.16054	.13511	.11109	.08832	.06670	.04609	.02642	.00761	35
36	1.60206	1.17609	0.96524	.82391	.71745	.63202	.56067	.49940	.44571	.39794	.35491	.31575	.27984	.24667	.21586	.18709	.16010	.13470	.11070	.08796	.06634	.04576	.02610	.00730	36
37	1.59016	1.17159	0.96246	.82190	.71588	.63073	.55957	.49845	.44487	.39719	.35422	.31513	.27927	.24614	.21536	.18662	.15967	.13429	.11031	.08759	.06599	.04542	.02578	.00699	37
38	1.57858	1.16714	0.95971	.81991	.71432	.62945	.55848	.49750	.44403	.39643	.35354	.31451	.27869	.24561	.21487	.18616	.15923	.13388	.10992	.08722	.06564	.04509	.02546	.00669	38
39	1.56730	1.16273	0.95697	.81792	.71276	.62816	.55739	.49655	.44320	.39568	.35286	.31389	.27812	.24508	.21437	.18570	.15880	.13347	.10953	.08685	.06529	.04475	.02514	.00638	39
40	1.55630	1.15836	0.95424	.81594	.71120	.62688	.55630	.49560	.44236	.39493	.35218	.31326	.27755	.24455	.21388	.18523	.15836	.13306	.10914	.08648	.06494	.04442	.02482	.00607	40
41	1.54558	1.15404	0.95154	.81397	.70966	.62561	.55522	.49466	.44152	.39419	.35150	.31264	.27698	.24402	.21339	.18477	.15793	.13265	.10876	.08611	.06459	.04409	.02450	.00577	41
42	1.53511	1.14976	0.94885	.81201	.70811	.62434	.55414	.49372	.44069	.39344	.35083	.31203	.27641	.24349	.21289	.18431	.15749	.13224	.10837	.08575	.06424	.04375	.02419	.00546	42
43	1.52489	1.14553	0.94617	.81006	.70658	.62307	.55306	.49278	.43986	.39269	.35015	.31141	.27584	.24296	.21240	.18385	.15706	.13183	.10798	.08538	.06389	.04342	.02387	.00516	43
44	1.51491	1.14133	0.94352	.80811	.70504	.62180	.55198	.49184	.43903	.39195	.34948	.31079	.27527	.24244	.21191	.18339	.15663	.13142	.10760	.08501	.06354	.04308	.02355	.00485	44
45	1.50515	1.13717	0.94088	.80618	.70352	.62054	.55091	.49091	.43820	.39121	.34880	.31017	.27470	.24191	.21142	.18293	.15620	.13101	.10721	.08464	.06319	.04275	.02323	.00455	45
46	1.49560	1.13306	0.93825	.80425	.70200	.61929	.54984	.48998	.43738	.39046	.34813	.30956	.27413	.24138	.21093	.18247	.15576	.13061	.10682	.08428	.06284	.04242	.02291	.00424	46
47	1.48626	1.12898	0.93565	.80234	.70048	.61803	.54877	.48905	.43655	.38972	.34746	.30894	.27357	.24086	.21044	.18201	.15533	.13020	.10644	.08391	.06250	.04209	.02259	.00394	47
48	1.47712	1.12494	0.93305	.80043	.69897	.61678	.54770	.48812	.43573	.38899	.34679	.30833	.27300	.24033	.20995	.18155	.15490	.12979	.10605	.08355	.06215	.04175	.02228	.00363	48
49	1.46817	1.12094	0.93048	.79853	.69746	.61554	.54664	.48719	.43491	.38825	.34612	.30772	.27244	.23981	.20946	.18110	.15447	.12938	.10567	.08318	.06180	.04142	.02196	.00333	49
50	1.45939	1.11697	0.92791	.79663	.69596	.61429	.54558	.48626	.43409	.38751	.34545	.30710	.27187	.23928	.20897	.18064	.15404	.12898	.10528	.08282	.06145	.04109	.02164	.00303	50
51	1.45079	1.11304	0.92537	.79475	.69447	.61306	.54452	.48534	.43327	.38678	.34478	.30649	.27131	.23876	.20848	.18018	.15361	.12857	.10490	.08245	.06111	.04076	.02133	.00272	51
52	1.44236	1.10914	0.92283	.79287	.69298	.61182	.54347	.48442	.43245	.38604	.34411	.30588	.27075	.23824	.20800	.17973	.15318	.12817	.10452	.08209	.06076	.04043	.02101	.00242	52
53	1.43409	1.10528	0.92032	.79101	.69149	.61059	.54241	.48350	.43164	.38531	.34345	.30527	.27018	.23772	.20751	.17927	.15275	.12776	.10413	.08172	.06041	.04010	.02069	.00212	53
54	1.42597	1.10146	0.91781	.78915	.69002	.60936	.54136	.48258	.43082	.38458	.34278	.30466	.26962	.23720	.20702	.17881	.15232	.12736	.10375	.08136	.06006	.03977	.02038	.00181	54
55	1.41800	1.09766	0.91532	.78729	.68854	.60813	.54031	.48167	.43001	.38385	.34212	.30406	.26906	.23668	.20654	.17836	.15190	.12695	.10337	.08099	.05972	.03944	.02006	.00151	55
56	1.41017	1.09390	0.91285	.78545	.68707	.60691	.53927	.48076	.42920	.38312	.34146	.30345	.26850	.23616	.20605	.17790	.15147	.12655	.10298	.08063	.05937	.03911	.01974	.00121	56
57	1.40249	1.09018	0.91039	.78361	.68561	.60569	.53823	.47984	.42839	.38239	.34080	.30284	.26794	.23564	.20557	.17745	.15104	.12615	.10260	.08027	.05903	.03878	.01943	.00091	57
58	1.39493	1.08648	0.90794	.78179	.68415	.60448	.53719	.47893	.42758	.38166	.34014	.30224	.26738	.23512	.20509	.17700	.15061	.12574	.10222	.07991	.05868	.03845	.01911	.00060	58
59	1.38751	1.08282	0.90551	.77996	.68269	.60327	.53615	.47803	.42677	.38094	.33948	.30163	.26683	.23460	.20460	.17654	.15019	.12534	.10184	.07954	.05834	.03812	.01880	.00030	59
60	1.38021	1.07918	0.90309	.77815	.68124	.60206	.53511	.47712	.42597	.38021	.33882	.30103	.26627	.23408	.20412	.17609	.14976	.12494	.10146	.07918	.05799	.03779	.01848	.00000	60

Table X Diurnal Motion Logarithms, 0 to 2 Hours/Degrees

	0° 0'	0° 1'	0° 2'	0° 3'	0° 4'	0° 5'	0° 6'	0° 7'	0° 8'	0° 9'	0° 10'	0° 11'	0° 12'	0° 13'	0° 14'	0° 15'	0° 16'	0° 17'	0° 18'	0° 19'	
0"	INFINITE	3.15836	2.85733	2.68124	2.55630	2.45939	2.38021	2.31326	2.25527	2.20412	2.15836	2.11697	2.07918	2.04442	2.01223	1.98227	1.95424	1.92791	1.90309	1.87961	0"
1	4.93651	3.15118	2.85373	2.67884	2.55450	2.45795	2.37901	2.31223	2.25437	2.20332	2.15764	2.11631	2.07858	2.04386	2.01172	1.98179	1.95379	1.92749	1.90269	1.87923	1
2	4.63548	3.14412	2.85015	2.67644	2.55270	2.45651	2.37781	2.31120	2.25347	2.20251	2.15692	2.11566	2.07798	2.04331	2.01120	1.98131	1.95334	1.92706	1.90229	1.87885	2
3	4.45939	3.13717	2.84661	2.67406	2.55091	2.45507	2.37661	2.31017	2.25257	2.20171	2.15620	2.11500	2.07738	2.04275	2.01069	1.98083	1.95289	1.92664	1.90189	1.87847	3
4	4.33445	3.13033	2.84309	2.67170	2.54912	2.45364	2.37541	2.30915	2.25167	2.20091	2.15548	2.11435	2.07678	2.04220	2.01017	1.98035	1.95244	1.92621	1.90148	1.87809	4
5	4.23754	3.12360	2.83960	2.66934	2.54735	2.45221	2.37422	2.30812	2.25077	2.20012	2.15476	2.11369	2.07618	2.04164	2.00966	1.97987	1.95199	1.92579	1.90108	1.87771	5
6"	4.15836	3.11697	2.83614	2.66700	2.54558	2.45079	2.37303	2.30710	2.24988	2.19932	2.15404	2.11304	2.07558	2.04109	2.00914	1.97939	1.95154	1.92537	1.90068	1.87733	6"
7	4.09142	3.11044	2.83271	2.66467	2.54382	2.44938	2.37185	2.30609	2.24898	2.19853	2.15333	2.11239	2.07498	2.04054	2.00863	1.97891	1.95109	1.92494	1.90028	1.87695	7
8	4.03342	3.10400	2.82930	2.66236	2.54206	2.44796	2.37067	2.30507	2.24809	2.19773	2.15261	2.11174	2.07438	2.03999	2.00812	1.97843	1.95064	1.92452	1.89988	1.87657	8
9	3.98227	3.09766	2.82592	2.66005	2.54031	2.44656	2.36949	2.30406	2.24720	2.19694	2.15190	2.11109	2.07379	2.03944	2.00761	1.97795	1.95019	1.92410	1.89949	1.87619	9
10	3.93651	3.09142	2.82257	2.65776	2.53857	2.44515	2.36831	2.30305	2.24632	2.19615	2.15118	2.11044	2.07319	2.03889	2.00709	1.97747	1.94974	1.92368	1.89909	1.87582	10
11"	3.89512	3.08526	2.81924	2.65548	2.53684	2.44375	2.36714	2.30204	2.24543	2.19536	2.15047	2.10979	2.07260	2.03834	2.00658	1.97700	1.94929	1.92326	1.89869	1.87544	11"
12	3.85733	3.07918	2.81594	2.65321	2.53511	2.44236	2.36597	2.30103	2.24455	2.19457	2.14976	2.10914	2.07200	2.03779	2.00607	1.97652	1.94885	1.92283	1.89829	1.87506	12
13	3.82257	3.07319	2.81266	2.65096	2.53339	2.44097	2.36480	2.30003	2.24367	2.19379	2.14905	2.10850	2.07141	2.03724	2.00556	1.97604	1.94840	1.92241	1.89789	1.87468	13
14	3.79039	3.06728	2.80941	2.64871	2.53168	2.43958	2.36364	2.29902	2.24279	2.19300	2.14835	2.10785	2.07082	2.03669	2.00506	1.97557	1.94795	1.92199	1.89750	1.87431	14
15	3.76042	3.06145	2.80618	2.64648	2.52997	2.43820	2.36248	2.29802	2.24191	2.19222	2.14764	2.10721	2.07023	2.03615	2.00455	1.97509	1.94751	1.92157	1.89710	1.87393	15
16"	3.73239	3.05570	2.80297	2.64426	2.52827	2.43683	2.36133	2.29703	2.24103	2.19144	2.14693	2.10657	2.06964	2.03560	2.00404	1.97462	1.94706	1.92115	1.89670	1.87356	16"
17	3.70606	3.05002	2.79979	2.64205	2.52658	2.43545	2.36017	2.29603	2.24016	2.19066	2.14623	2.10593	2.06905	2.03506	2.00353	1.97414	1.94662	1.92073	1.89631	1.87318	17
18	3.68124	3.04442	2.79663	2.63985	2.52489	2.43409	2.35902	2.29504	2.23928	2.18988	2.14553	2.10528	2.06846	2.03451	2.00303	1.97367	1.94617	1.92032	1.89591	1.87281	18
19	3.65776	3.03889	2.79350	2.63766	2.52321	2.43272	2.35787	2.29405	2.23841	2.18910	2.14482	2.10464	2.06787	2.03397	2.00252	1.97320	1.94573	1.91990	1.89552	1.87243	19
20	3.63548	3.03342	2.79039	2.63548	2.52154	2.43136	2.35673	2.29306	2.23754	2.18833	2.14412	2.10400	2.06728	2.03342	2.00202	1.97273	1.94529	1.91948	1.89512	1.87206	20
21"	3.61429	3.02803	2.78729	2.63332	2.51987	2.43001	2.35559	2.29208	2.23668	2.18755	2.14342	2.10337	2.06670	2.03288	2.00151	1.97225	1.94484	1.91906	1.89473	1.87168	21"
22	3.59409	3.02270	2.78423	2.63116	2.51821	2.42866	2.35445	2.29109	2.23581	2.18678	2.14272	2.10273	2.06611	2.03234	2.00101	1.97178	1.94440	1.91865	1.89433	1.87131	22
23	3.57479	3.01744	2.78118	2.62902	2.51656	2.42731	2.35331	2.29011	2.23495	2.18601	2.14203	2.10209	2.06552	2.03180	2.00050	1.97131	1.94396	1.91823	1.89394	1.87093	23
24	3.55630	3.01223	2.77815	2.62688	2.51491	2.42597	2.35218	2.28913	2.23408	2.18523	2.14133	2.10146	2.06494	2.03126	2.00000	1.97084	1.94352	1.91781	1.89354	1.87056	24
25	3.53857	3.00709	2.77515	2.62476	2.51327	2.42463	2.35105	2.28815	2.23322	2.18447	2.14063	2.10082	2.06436	2.03072	1.99950	1.97037	1.94308	1.91740	1.89315	1.87019	25
26"	3.52154	3.00202	2.77216	2.62265	2.51163	2.42330	2.34993	2.28718	2.23236	2.18370	2.13994	2.10019	2.06377	2.03018	1.99900	1.96990	1.94264	1.91698	1.89276	1.86982	26"
27	3.50515	2.99699	2.76920	2.62054	2.51000	2.42197	2.34880	2.28621	2.23151	2.18293	2.13925	2.09956	2.06319	2.02964	1.99849	1.96943	1.94220	1.91657	1.89237	1.86944	27
28	3.48936	2.99203	2.76625	2.61845	2.50838	2.42064	2.34768	2.28524	2.23065	2.18217	2.13855	2.09893	2.06261	2.02910	1.99799	1.96897	1.94176	1.91615	1.89197	1.86907	28
29	3.47412	2.98712	2.76333	2.61637	2.50676	2.41932	2.34656	2.28427	2.22980	2.18140	2.13786	2.09829	2.06203	2.02857	1.99749	1.96850	1.94132	1.91574	1.89158	1.86870	29
30	3.45939	2.98227	2.76042	2.61429	2.50515	2.41800	2.34545	2.28330	2.22894	2.18064	2.13717	2.09766	2.06145	2.02803	1.99699	1.96803	1.94088	1.91532	1.89119	1.86833	30
31"	3.44515	2.97747	2.75754	2.61223	2.50354	2.41669	2.34434	2.28234	2.22809	2.17988	2.13648	2.09704	2.06087	2.02749	1.99650	1.96756	1.94044	1.91491	1.89080	1.86796	31"
32	3.43136	2.97273	2.75467	2.61018	2.50194	2.41538	2.34323	2.28138	2.22724	2.17912	2.13580	2.09641	2.06030	2.02696	1.99600	1.96710	1.94000	1.91450	1.89041	1.86759	32
33	3.41800	2.96803	2.75182	2.60813	2.50035	2.41407	2.34212	2.28042	2.22640	2.17836	2.13511	2.09578	2.05972	2.02642	1.99550	1.96663	1.93956	1.91409	1.89002	1.86722	33
34	3.40503	2.96339	2.74899	2.60610	2.49876	2.41277	2.34102	2.27946	2.22555	2.17760	2.13442	2.09515	2.05914	2.02589	1.99500	1.96617	1.93913	1.91367	1.88963	1.86685	34
35	3.39245	2.95879	2.74618	2.60408	2.49718	2.41147	2.33992	2.27850	2.22471	2.17685	2.13374	2.09453	2.05857	2.02536	1.99451	1.96570	1.93869	1.91326	1.88924	1.86648	35
36"	3.38021	2.95424	2.74339	2.60206	2.49560	2.41017	2.33882	2.27755	2.22386	2.17609	2.13306	2.09390	2.05799	2.02482	1.99401	1.96524	1.93825	1.91285	1.88885	1.86611	36"
37	3.36831	2.94974	2.74061	2.60005	2.49403	2.40888	2.33772	2.27660	2.22302	2.17534	2.13237	2.09328	2.05742	2.02429	1.99351	1.96477	1.93782	1.91244	1.88846	1.86574	37
38	3.35673	2.94529	2.73786	2.59806	2.49247	2.40760	2.33663	2.27565	2.22218	2.17459	2.13169	2.09266	2.05684	2.02376	1.99302	1.96431	1.93738	1.91203	1.88807	1.86537	38
39	3.34545	2.94088	2.73512	2.59607	2.49091	2.40631	2.33554	2.27470	2.22135	2.17384	2.13101	2.09204	2.05627	2.02323	1.99252	1.96385	1.93695	1.91162	1.88768	1.86500	39
40	3.33445	2.93651	2.73239	2.59409	2.48936	2.40503	2.33445	2.27376	2.22051	2.17309	2.13033	2.09142	2.05570	2.02270	1.99203	1.96339	1.93651	1.91121	1.88730	1.86463	40
41"	3.32373	2.93219	2.72969	2.59212	2.48781	2.40376	2.33337	2.27281	2.21968	2.17234	2.12966	2.09080	2.05513	2.02217	1.99154	1.96292	1.93608	1.91080	1.88691	1.86426	41"
42	3.31326	2.92791	2.72700	2.59016	2.48626	2.40249	2.33229	2.27187	2.21884	2.17159	2.12898	2.09018	2.05456	2.02164	1.99105	1.96246	1.93565	1.91039	1.88652	1.86390	42
43	3.30305	2.92368	2.72433	2.58821	2.48473	2.40122	2.33121	2.27093	2.21801	2.17085	2.12830	2.08956	2.05399	2.02111	1.99055	1.96200	1.93521	1.90998	1.88613	1.86353	43
44	3.29306	2.91948	2.72167	2.58627	2.48320	2.39996	2.33013	2.27000	2.21718	2.17010	2.12763	2.08894	2.05342	2.02059	1.99006	1.96154	1.93478	1.90957	1.88575	1.86316	44
45	3.28330	2.91532	2.71903	2.58433	2.48167	2.39869	2.32906	2.26906	2.21635	2.16936	2.12695	2.08832	2.05285	2.02006	1.98957	1.96108	1.93435	1.90916	1.88536	1.86280	45
46"	3.27376	2.91121	2.71641	2.58241	2.48015	2.39744	2.32799	2.26813	2.21553	2.16862	2.12628	2.08771	2.05228	2.01953	1.98908	1.96062	1.93392	1.90876	1.88498	1.86243	46"
47	3.26442	2.90713	2.71380	2.58049	2.47863	2.39618	2.32692	2.26720	2.21470	2.16788	2.12561	2.08709	2.05172	2.01901	1.98859	1.96016	1.93348	1.90835	1.88459	1.86206	47
48	3.25527	2.90309	2.71120	2.57858	2.47712	2.39493	2.32585	2.26627	2.21388	2.16714	2.12494	2.08648	2.05115	2.01848	1.98810	1.95971	1.93305	1.90794	1.88420	1.86170	48
49	3.24632	2.89909	2.70863	2.57668	2.47562	2.39369	2.32479	2.26534	2.21306	2.16640	2.12427	2.08587	2.05059	2.01796	1.98761	1.95925	1.93262	1.90754	1.88382	1.86133	49
50	3.23754	2.89512	2.70606	2.57479	2.47412	2.39245	2.32373	2.26442	2.21224	2.16566	2.12360	2.08526	2.05002	2.01744	1.98712	1.95879	1.93219	1.90713	1.88344	1.86097	50
51"	3.22894	2.89119	2.70352	2.57290	2.47262	2.39121	2.32267	2.26349	2.21142	2.16493	2.12293	2.08464	2.04946	2.01691	1.98664	1.95833	1.93176	1.90672	1.88305	1.86060	51"
52	3.22051	2.88730	2.70099	2.57103	2.47113	2.38997	2.32162	2.26257	2.21060	2.16419	2.12227	2.08403	2.04890	2.01639	1.98615	1.95788	1.93133	1.90632	1.88267	1.86024	52
53	3.21224	2.88344	2.69847	2.56916	2.46965	2.38874	2.32056	2.26165	2.20979	2.16346	2.12160	2.08342	2.04833	2.01587	1.98566	1.95742	1.93090	1.90591	1.88228	1.85987	53
54	3.20412	2.87961	2.69596	2.56730	2.46817	2.38751	2.31951	2.26074	2.20897	2.16273	2.12094	2.08282	2.04777	2.01535	1.98518	1.95697	1.93048	1.90551	1.88190	1.85951	54
55	3.19615	2.87582	2.69348	2.56545	2.46669	2.38629	2.31847	2.25982	2.20816	2.16200	2.12027	2.08221	2.04721	2.01483	1.98469	1.95651	1.93005	1.90511	1.88152	1.85915	55
56"	3.18833	2.87206	2.69100	2.56360	2.46522	2.38506	2.31742	2.25891	2.20735	2.16127	2.11961	2.08160	2.04665	2.01431	1.98421	1.95606	1.92962	1.90470	1.88114	1.85878	56"
57	3.18064	2.86833	2.68854	2.56177	2.46376	2.38385	2.31638	2.25800	2.20654	2.16054	2.11895	2.08099	2.04609	2.01379	1.98372	1.95560	1.92919	1.90430	1.88075	1.85842	57
58	3.17309	2.86463	2.68609	2.55994	2.46230	2.38263	2.31534	2.25709	2.20573	2.15981	2.11829	2.08039	2.04553	2.01327	1.98324	1.95515	1.92877	1.90389	1.88037	1.85806	58
59	3.16566	2.86097	2.68366	2.55812	2.46084	2.38142	2.31430	2.25618	2.20492	2.15909	2.11763	2.07978	2.04498	2.01275	1.98275	1.95470	1.92834	1.90349	1.87999	1.85769	59
60	3.15836	2.85733	2.68124	2.55630	2.45939	2.38021	2.31326	2.25527	2.20412	2.15836	2.11697	2.07918	2.04442	2.01223	1.98227	1.95424	1.92791	1.90309	1.87961	1.85733	60

Table X Diurnal Motion Logarithms, 0 to 2 Hours/Degrees

	0° 20'	0° 21'	0° 22'	0° 23'	0° 24'	0° 25'	0° 26'	0° 27'	0° 28'	0° 29'	0° 30'	0° 31'	0° 32'	0° 33'	0° 34'	0° 35'	0° 36'	0° 37'	0° 38'	0° 39'	
0"	1.85733	1.83614	1.81594	1.79663	1.77815	1.76042	1.74339	1.72700	1.71120	1.69596	1.68124	1.66700	1.65321	1.63985	1.62688	1.61429	1.60206	1.59016	1.57858	1.56730	0"
1	1.85697	1.83580	1.81561	1.79632	1.77785	1.76013	1.74311	1.72673	1.71095	1.69571	1.68100	1.66677	1.65299	1.63963	1.62667	1.61409	1.60186	1.58997	1.57839	1.56711	1
2	1.85661	1.83545	1.81528	1.79601	1.77755	1.75984	1.74283	1.72646	1.71069	1.69547	1.68076	1.66653	1.65276	1.63941	1.62646	1.61388	1.60166	1.58977	1.57820	1.56693	2
3	1.85625	1.83511	1.81495	1.79569	1.77725	1.75955	1.74255	1.72620	1.71043	1.69522	1.68052	1.66630	1.65253	1.63919	1.62625	1.61367	1.60146	1.58957	1.57801	1.56674	3
4	1.85589	1.83477	1.81463	1.79538	1.77695	1.75927	1.74228	1.72593	1.71017	1.69497	1.68028	1.66607	1.65231	1.63897	1.62603	1.61347	1.60126	1.58938	1.57782	1.56656	4
5	1.85553	1.83442	1.81430	1.79506	1.77665	1.75898	1.74200	1.72566	1.70991	1.69472	1.68004	1.66583	1.65208	1.63875	1.62582	1.61326	1.60106	1.58918	1.57763	1.56637	5
6"	1.85517	1.83408	1.81397	1.79475	1.77635	1.75869	1.74172	1.72539	1.70966	1.69447	1.67980	1.66560	1.65186	1.63853	1.62561	1.61306	1.60086	1.58899	1.57744	1.56619	6"
7	1.85481	1.83374	1.81364	1.79444	1.77605	1.75840	1.74144	1.72513	1.70940	1.69422	1.67956	1.66537	1.65163	1.63832	1.62540	1.61285	1.60065	1.58879	1.57725	1.56600	7
8	1.85445	1.83339	1.81332	1.79412	1.77575	1.75811	1.74117	1.72486	1.70914	1.69397	1.67932	1.66514	1.65141	1.63810	1.62518	1.61264	1.60045	1.58860	1.57706	1.56582	8
9	1.85409	1.83305	1.81299	1.79381	1.77545	1.75782	1.74089	1.72459	1.70888	1.69372	1.67908	1.66490	1.65118	1.63788	1.62497	1.61244	1.60025	1.58840	1.57687	1.56563	9
10	1.85373	1.83271	1.81266	1.79350	1.77515	1.75754	1.74061	1.72433	1.70863	1.69348	1.67884	1.66467	1.65096	1.63766	1.62476	1.61223	1.60005	1.58821	1.57668	1.56545	10
11"	1.85337	1.83237	1.81234	1.79319	1.77485	1.75725	1.74034	1.72406	1.70837	1.69323	1.67860	1.66444	1.65073	1.63744	1.62455	1.61203	1.59985	1.58801	1.57649	1.56526	11"
12	1.85301	1.83203	1.81201	1.79287	1.77455	1.75696	1.74006	1.72379	1.70811	1.69298	1.67836	1.66421	1.65051	1.63722	1.62434	1.61182	1.59965	1.58782	1.57630	1.56508	12
13	1.85265	1.83169	1.81168	1.79256	1.77425	1.75667	1.73979	1.72353	1.70786	1.69273	1.67812	1.66398	1.65028	1.63701	1.62412	1.61161	1.59945	1.58763	1.57611	1.56489	13
14	1.85230	1.83134	1.81136	1.79225	1.77395	1.75639	1.73951	1.72326	1.70760	1.69248	1.67788	1.66374	1.65006	1.63679	1.62391	1.61141	1.59925	1.58743	1.57592	1.56471	14
15	1.85194	1.83100	1.81103	1.79194	1.77365	1.75610	1.73923	1.72300	1.70734	1.69224	1.67764	1.66351	1.64983	1.63657	1.62370	1.61120	1.59905	1.58724	1.57573	1.56452	15
16"	1.85158	1.83066	1.81071	1.79163	1.77335	1.75581	1.73896	1.72273	1.70709	1.69199	1.67740	1.66328	1.64961	1.63635	1.62349	1.61100	1.59885	1.58704	1.57554	1.56434	16"
17	1.85122	1.83032	1.81038	1.79132	1.77305	1.75553	1.73868	1.72247	1.70683	1.69174	1.67716	1.66305	1.64938	1.63614	1.62328	1.61079	1.59866	1.58685	1.57535	1.56415	17
18	1.85087	1.82998	1.81006	1.79101	1.77276	1.75524	1.73841	1.72220	1.70658	1.69149	1.67692	1.66282	1.64916	1.63592	1.62307	1.61059	1.59846	1.58665	1.57516	1.56397	18
19	1.85051	1.82964	1.80973	1.79070	1.77246	1.75496	1.73813	1.72193	1.70632	1.69125	1.67668	1.66259	1.64894	1.63570	1.62286	1.61038	1.59826	1.58646	1.57497	1.56379	19
20	1.85015	1.82930	1.80941	1.79039	1.77216	1.75467	1.73786	1.72167	1.70606	1.69100	1.67644	1.66236	1.64871	1.63548	1.62265	1.61018	1.59806	1.58627	1.57479	1.56360	20
21"	1.84980	1.82896	1.80908	1.79008	1.77186	1.75438	1.73758	1.72141	1.70581	1.69075	1.67620	1.66212	1.64849	1.63527	1.62244	1.60997	1.59786	1.58607	1.57460	1.56342	21"
22	1.84944	1.82863	1.80876	1.78977	1.77157	1.75410	1.73731	1.72114	1.70555	1.69051	1.67597	1.66189	1.64826	1.63505	1.62223	1.60977	1.59766	1.58588	1.57441	1.56323	22
23	1.84909	1.82829	1.80844	1.78946	1.77127	1.75381	1.73703	1.72088	1.70530	1.69026	1.67573	1.66166	1.64804	1.63483	1.62201	1.60956	1.59746	1.58568	1.57422	1.56305	23
24	1.84873	1.82795	1.80811	1.78915	1.77097	1.75353	1.73676	1.72061	1.70504	1.69002	1.67549	1.66143	1.64782	1.63462	1.62180	1.60936	1.59726	1.58549	1.57403	1.56287	24
25	1.84838	1.82761	1.80779	1.78884	1.77068	1.75324	1.73648	1.72035	1.70479	1.68977	1.67525	1.66120	1.64759	1.63440	1.62159	1.60915	1.59706	1.58530	1.57384	1.56268	25
26"	1.84802	1.82727	1.80747	1.78853	1.77038	1.75296	1.73621	1.72008	1.70453	1.68952	1.67501	1.66097	1.64737	1.63418	1.62138	1.60895	1.59686	1.58510	1.57365	1.56250	26"
27	1.84767	1.82694	1.80715	1.78822	1.77008	1.75267	1.73594	1.71982	1.70428	1.68928	1.67478	1.66074	1.64715	1.63397	1.62117	1.60875	1.59666	1.58491	1.57347	1.56232	27
28	1.84732	1.82660	1.80682	1.78791	1.76979	1.75239	1.73566	1.71956	1.70403	1.68903	1.67454	1.66051	1.64692	1.63375	1.62096	1.60854	1.59647	1.58472	1.57328	1.56213	28
29	1.84696	1.82626	1.80650	1.78760	1.76949	1.75211	1.73539	1.71929	1.70377	1.68879	1.67430	1.66028	1.64670	1.63353	1.62075	1.60834	1.59627	1.58452	1.57309	1.56195	29
30	1.84661	1.82592	1.80618	1.78729	1.76920	1.75182	1.73512	1.71903	1.70352	1.68854	1.67406	1.66005	1.64648	1.63332	1.62054	1.60813	1.59607	1.58433	1.57290	1.56177	30
31"	1.84626	1.82559	1.80586	1.78699	1.76890	1.75154	1.73484	1.71877	1.70326	1.68830	1.67383	1.65982	1.64626	1.63310	1.62033	1.60793	1.59587	1.58414	1.57271	1.56158	31"
32	1.84590	1.82525	1.80554	1.78668	1.76861	1.75125	1.73457	1.71850	1.70301	1.68805	1.67359	1.65959	1.64603	1.63289	1.62012	1.60773	1.59567	1.58395	1.57253	1.56140	32
33	1.84555	1.82492	1.80522	1.78637	1.76831	1.75097	1.73430	1.71824	1.70276	1.68781	1.67335	1.65936	1.64581	1.63267	1.61991	1.60752	1.59548	1.58375	1.57234	1.56122	33
34	1.84520	1.82458	1.80490	1.78606	1.76802	1.75069	1.73403	1.71798	1.70250	1.68756	1.67311	1.65913	1.64559	1.63245	1.61970	1.60732	1.59528	1.58356	1.57215	1.56103	34
35	1.84485	1.82424	1.80457	1.78576	1.76772	1.75041	1.73375	1.71772	1.70225	1.68732	1.67288	1.65890	1.64537	1.63224	1.61950	1.60712	1.59508	1.58337	1.57196	1.56085	35
36"	1.84450	1.82391	1.80425	1.78545	1.76743	1.75012	1.73348	1.71745	1.70200	1.68707	1.67264	1.65868	1.64514	1.63202	1.61929	1.60691	1.59488	1.58317	1.57178	1.56067	36"
37	1.84414	1.82357	1.80393	1.78514	1.76713	1.74984	1.73321	1.71719	1.70174	1.68683	1.67240	1.65845	1.64492	1.63181	1.61908	1.60671	1.59468	1.58298	1.57159	1.56048	37
38	1.84379	1.82324	1.80361	1.78484	1.76684	1.74956	1.73294	1.71693	1.70149	1.68658	1.67217	1.65822	1.64470	1.63159	1.61887	1.60651	1.59449	1.58279	1.57140	1.56030	38
39	1.84344	1.82290	1.80329	1.78453	1.76655	1.74928	1.73267	1.71667	1.70124	1.68634	1.67193	1.65799	1.64448	1.63138	1.61866	1.60630	1.59429	1.58260	1.57121	1.56012	39
40	1.84309	1.82257	1.80297	1.78423	1.76625	1.74899	1.73239	1.71641	1.70099	1.68609	1.67170	1.65776	1.64426	1.63116	1.61845	1.60610	1.59409	1.58241	1.57103	1.55994	40
41"	1.84274	1.82224	1.80266	1.78392	1.76596	1.74871	1.73212	1.71614	1.70073	1.68585	1.67146	1.65753	1.64404	1.63095	1.61824	1.60590	1.59389	1.58221	1.57084	1.55975	41"
42	1.84239	1.82190	1.80234	1.78361	1.76567	1.74843	1.73185	1.71588	1.70048	1.68561	1.67122	1.65730	1.64381	1.63073	1.61803	1.60569	1.59370	1.58202	1.57065	1.55957	42
43	1.84204	1.82157	1.80202	1.78331	1.76537	1.74815	1.73158	1.71562	1.70023	1.68536	1.67099	1.65707	1.64359	1.63052	1.61782	1.60549	1.59350	1.58183	1.57046	1.55939	43
44	1.84169	1.82124	1.80170	1.78300	1.76508	1.74787	1.73131	1.71536	1.69998	1.68512	1.67075	1.65685	1.64337	1.63030	1.61762	1.60529	1.59330	1.58164	1.57028	1.55921	44
45	1.84134	1.82090	1.80138	1.78270	1.76479	1.74759	1.73104	1.71510	1.69972	1.68488	1.67052	1.65662	1.64315	1.63009	1.61741	1.60509	1.59311	1.58145	1.57009	1.55903	45
46"	1.84100	1.82057	1.80106	1.78239	1.76449	1.74730	1.73077	1.71484	1.69947	1.68463	1.67028	1.65639	1.64293	1.62987	1.61720	1.60488	1.59291	1.58125	1.56990	1.55884	46"
47	1.84065	1.82024	1.80075	1.78209	1.76420	1.74702	1.73050	1.71458	1.69922	1.68439	1.67005	1.65616	1.64271	1.62966	1.61699	1.60468	1.59271	1.58106	1.56972	1.55866	47
48	1.84030	1.81991	1.80043	1.78179	1.76391	1.74674	1.73023	1.71432	1.69897	1.68415	1.66981	1.65594	1.64249	1.62945	1.61678	1.60448	1.59251	1.58087	1.56953	1.55848	48
49	1.83995	1.81957	1.80011	1.78148	1.76362	1.74646	1.72996	1.71406	1.69872	1.68390	1.66958	1.65571	1.64227	1.62923	1.61658	1.60428	1.59232	1.58068	1.56934	1.55830	49
50	1.83960	1.81924	1.79979	1.78118	1.76333	1.74618	1.72969	1.71380	1.69847	1.68366	1.66934	1.65548	1.64205	1.62902	1.61637	1.60408	1.59212	1.58049	1.56916	1.55812	50
51"	1.83926	1.81891	1.79948	1.78087	1.76304	1.74590	1.72942	1.71354	1.69822	1.68342	1.66911	1.65525	1.64183	1.62880	1.61616	1.60387	1.59192	1.58030	1.56897	1.55793	51"
52	1.83891	1.81858	1.79916	1.78057	1.76274	1.74562	1.72915	1.71328	1.69797	1.68318	1.66887	1.65503	1.64161	1.62859	1.61595	1.60367	1.59173	1.58011	1.56879	1.55775	52
53	1.83856	1.81825	1.79884	1.78027	1.76245	1.74534	1.72888	1.71302	1.69772	1.68293	1.66864	1.65480	1.64139	1.62838	1.61574	1.60347	1.59153	1.57991	1.56860	1.55757	53
54	1.83822	1.81792	1.79853	1.77996	1.76216	1.74506	1.72861	1.71276	1.69746	1.68269	1.66840	1.65457	1.64117	1.62816	1.61554	1.60327	1.59134	1.57972	1.56841	1.55739	54
55	1.83787	1.81759	1.79821	1.77966	1.76187	1.74478	1.72834	1.71250	1.69721	1.68245	1.66817	1.65434	1.64095	1.62795	1.61533	1.60307	1.59114	1.57953	1.56823	1.55721	55
56"	1.83752	1.81726	1.79790	1.77936	1.76158	1.74450	1.72807	1.71224	1.69696	1.68221	1.66794	1.65412	1.64073	1.62774	1.61512	1.60286	1.59094	1.57934	1.56804	1.55703	56"
57	1.83718	1.81693	1.79758	1.77906	1.76129	1.74423	1.72780	1.71198	1.69671	1.68197	1.66770	1.65389	1.64051	1.62752	1.61492	1.60266	1.59075	1.57915	1.56786	1.55685	57
58	1.83683	1.81660	1.79726	1.77875	1.76100	1.74395	1.72754	1.71172	1.69646	1.68172	1.66747	1.65367	1.64029	1.62731	1.61471	1.60246	1.59055	1.57896	1.56767	1.55666	58
59	1.83649	1.81627	1.79695	1.77845	1.76071	1.74367	1.72727	1.71146	1.69621	1.68148	1.66723	1.65344	1.64007	1.62710	1.61450	1.60226	1.59036	1.57877	1.56748	1.55648	59
60	1.83614	1.81594	1.79663	1.77815	1.76042	1.74339	1.72700	1.71120	1.69596	1.68124	1.66700	1.65321	1.63985	1.62688	1.61429	1.60206	1.59016	1.57858	1.56730	1.55630	60

Table X Diurnal Motion Logarithms, 0 to 2 Hours/Degrees

	0° 40'	0° 41'	0° 42'	0° 43'	0° 44'	0° 45'	0° 46'	0° 47'	0° 48'	0° 49'	0° 50'	0° 51'	0° 52'	0° 53'	0° 54'	0° 55'	0° 56'	0° 57'	0° 58'	0° 59'	
0"	1.55630	1.54558	1.53511	1.52489	1.51491	1.50515	1.49560	1.48626	1.47712	1.46817	1.45939	1.45079	1.44236	1.43409	1.42597	1.41800	1.41017	1.40249	1.39493	1.38751	0"
1	1.55612	1.54540	1.53494	1.52473	1.51475	1.50499	1.49545	1.48611	1.47697	1.46802	1.45925	1.45065	1.44222	1.43395	1.42583	1.41787	1.41005	1.40236	1.39481	1.38739	1
2	1.55594	1.54523	1.53477	1.52456	1.51458	1.50483	1.49529	1.48596	1.47682	1.46787	1.45910	1.45051	1.44208	1.43381	1.42570	1.41774	1.40992	1.40223	1.39468	1.38727	2
3	1.55576	1.54505	1.53460	1.52439	1.51442	1.50467	1.49513	1.48580	1.47667	1.46772	1.45896	1.45037	1.44194	1.43368	1.42557	1.41761	1.40979	1.40211	1.39456	1.38714	3
4	1.55558	1.54487	1.53442	1.52422	1.51425	1.50451	1.49498	1.48565	1.47652	1.46758	1.45881	1.45022	1.44180	1.43354	1.42543	1.41747	1.40966	1.40198	1.39444	1.38702	4
5	1.55540	1.54470	1.53425	1.52405	1.51409	1.50435	1.49482	1.48550	1.47637	1.46743	1.45867	1.45008	1.44166	1.43340	1.42530	1.41734	1.40953	1.40185	1.39431	1.38690	5
6"	1.55522	1.54452	1.53408	1.52389	1.51392	1.50419	1.49466	1.48534	1.47622	1.46728	1.45852	1.44994	1.44152	1.43327	1.42517	1.41721	1.40940	1.40173	1.39419	1.38678	6"
7	1.55504	1.54434	1.53391	1.52372	1.51376	1.50403	1.49450	1.48519	1.47607	1.46713	1.45838	1.44980	1.44139	1.43313	1.42503	1.41708	1.40927	1.40160	1.39406	1.38665	7
8	1.55486	1.54417	1.53374	1.52355	1.51360	1.50387	1.49435	1.48503	1.47592	1.46699	1.45824	1.44966	1.44125	1.43300	1.42490	1.41695	1.40914	1.40147	1.39394	1.38653	8
9	1.55468	1.54399	1.53356	1.52338	1.51343	1.50370	1.49419	1.48488	1.47577	1.46684	1.45809	1.44952	1.44111	1.43286	1.42476	1.41682	1.40901	1.40135	1.39381	1.38641	9
10	1.55450	1.54382	1.53339	1.52321	1.51327	1.50354	1.49403	1.48473	1.47562	1.46669	1.45795	1.44938	1.44097	1.43272	1.42463	1.41669	1.40888	1.40122	1.39369	1.38629	10
11"	1.55432	1.54364	1.53322	1.52305	1.51310	1.50338	1.49388	1.48457	1.47547	1.46654	1.45780	1.44923	1.44083	1.43259	1.42450	1.41655	1.40875	1.40109	1.39356	1.38616	11"
12	1.55414	1.54347	1.53305	1.52288	1.51294	1.50322	1.49372	1.48442	1.47532	1.46640	1.45766	1.44909	1.44069	1.43245	1.42436	1.41642	1.40863	1.40097	1.39344	1.38604	12
13	1.55396	1.54329	1.53288	1.52271	1.51278	1.50306	1.49356	1.48427	1.47517	1.46625	1.45751	1.44895	1.44055	1.43231	1.42423	1.41629	1.40850	1.40084	1.39332	1.38592	13
14	1.55378	1.54311	1.53271	1.52254	1.51261	1.50290	1.49341	1.48411	1.47502	1.46610	1.45737	1.44881	1.44041	1.43218	1.42410	1.41616	1.40837	1.40071	1.39319	1.38580	14
15	1.55360	1.54294	1.53254	1.52238	1.51245	1.50274	1.49325	1.48396	1.47487	1.46596	1.45723	1.44867	1.44028	1.43204	1.42396	1.41603	1.40824	1.40059	1.39307	1.38567	15
16"	1.55342	1.54276	1.53236	1.52221	1.51229	1.50258	1.49309	1.48381	1.47472	1.46581	1.45708	1.44853	1.44014	1.43191	1.42383	1.41590	1.40811	1.40046	1.39294	1.38555	16"
17	1.55324	1.54259	1.53219	1.52204	1.51212	1.50242	1.49294	1.48365	1.47457	1.46566	1.45694	1.44839	1.44000	1.43177	1.42370	1.41577	1.40798	1.40033	1.39282	1.38543	17
18	1.55306	1.54241	1.53202	1.52187	1.51196	1.50226	1.49278	1.48350	1.47442	1.46552	1.45679	1.44825	1.43986	1.43164	1.42356	1.41564	1.40785	1.40021	1.39269	1.38531	18
19	1.55288	1.54224	1.53185	1.52171	1.51180	1.50210	1.49263	1.48335	1.47427	1.46537	1.45665	1.44810	1.43972	1.43150	1.42343	1.41551	1.40773	1.40008	1.39257	1.38519	19
20	1.55270	1.54206	1.53168	1.52154	1.51163	1.50194	1.49247	1.48320	1.47412	1.46522	1.45651	1.44796	1.43958	1.43136	1.42330	1.41538	1.40760	1.39996	1.39245	1.38506	20
21"	1.55252	1.54189	1.53151	1.52137	1.51147	1.50179	1.49231	1.48304	1.47397	1.46508	1.45636	1.44782	1.43945	1.43123	1.42316	1.41524	1.40747	1.39983	1.39232	1.38494	21"
22	1.55234	1.54171	1.53134	1.52121	1.51131	1.50163	1.49216	1.48289	1.47382	1.46493	1.45622	1.44768	1.43931	1.43109	1.42303	1.41511	1.40734	1.39970	1.39220	1.38482	22
23	1.55216	1.54154	1.53117	1.52104	1.51114	1.50147	1.49200	1.48274	1.47367	1.46478	1.45608	1.44754	1.43917	1.43096	1.42290	1.41498	1.40721	1.39958	1.39207	1.38470	23
24	1.55198	1.54136	1.53100	1.52087	1.51098	1.50131	1.49184	1.48258	1.47352	1.46464	1.45593	1.44740	1.43903	1.43082	1.42276	1.41485	1.40708	1.39945	1.39195	1.38458	24
25	1.55180	1.54119	1.53083	1.52071	1.51082	1.50115	1.49169	1.48243	1.47337	1.46449	1.45579	1.44726	1.43889	1.43069	1.42263	1.41472	1.40696	1.39932	1.39183	1.38445	25
26"	1.55162	1.54101	1.53066	1.52054	1.51065	1.50099	1.49153	1.48228	1.47322	1.46434	1.45564	1.44712	1.43876	1.43055	1.42250	1.41459	1.40683	1.39920	1.39170	1.38433	26"
27	1.55144	1.54084	1.53048	1.52037	1.51049	1.50083	1.49138	1.48213	1.47307	1.46420	1.45550	1.44698	1.43862	1.43041	1.42236	1.41446	1.40670	1.39907	1.39158	1.38421	27
28	1.55127	1.54066	1.53031	1.52021	1.51033	1.50067	1.49122	1.48197	1.47292	1.46405	1.45536	1.44684	1.43848	1.43028	1.42223	1.41433	1.40657	1.39895	1.39145	1.38409	28
29	1.55109	1.54049	1.53014	1.52004	1.51017	1.50051	1.49107	1.48182	1.47277	1.46390	1.45521	1.44670	1.43834	1.43014	1.42210	1.41420	1.40644	1.39882	1.39133	1.38397	29
30	1.55091	1.54031	1.52997	1.51987	1.51000	1.50035	1.49091	1.48167	1.47262	1.46376	1.45507	1.44656	1.43820	1.43001	1.42197	1.41407	1.40631	1.39869	1.39121	1.38385	30
31"	1.55073	1.54014	1.52980	1.51971	1.50984	1.50019	1.49075	1.48152	1.47247	1.46361	1.45493	1.44641	1.43807	1.42987	1.42183	1.41394	1.40619	1.39857	1.39108	1.38372	31"
32	1.55055	1.53997	1.52963	1.51954	1.50968	1.50003	1.49060	1.48136	1.47232	1.46346	1.45478	1.44627	1.43793	1.42974	1.42170	1.41381	1.40606	1.39844	1.39096	1.38360	32
33	1.55037	1.53979	1.52946	1.51937	1.50951	1.49987	1.49044	1.48121	1.47217	1.46332	1.45464	1.44613	1.43779	1.42960	1.42157	1.41368	1.40593	1.39832	1.39084	1.38348	33
34	1.55019	1.53962	1.52929	1.51921	1.50935	1.49972	1.49029	1.48106	1.47202	1.46317	1.45450	1.44599	1.43765	1.42947	1.42144	1.41355	1.40580	1.39819	1.39071	1.38336	34
35	1.55001	1.53944	1.52912	1.51904	1.50919	1.49956	1.49013	1.48091	1.47188	1.46303	1.45436	1.44585	1.43751	1.42933	1.42130	1.41342	1.40567	1.39807	1.39059	1.38324	35
36"	1.54984	1.53927	1.52895	1.51888	1.50903	1.49940	1.48998	1.48076	1.47173	1.46288	1.45421	1.44571	1.43738	1.42920	1.42117	1.41329	1.40555	1.39794	1.39046	1.38312	36"
37	1.54966	1.53910	1.52878	1.51871	1.50887	1.49924	1.48982	1.48060	1.47158	1.46273	1.45407	1.44557	1.43724	1.42906	1.42104	1.41316	1.40542	1.39781	1.39034	1.38299	37
38	1.54948	1.53892	1.52861	1.51854	1.50870	1.49908	1.48967	1.48045	1.47143	1.46259	1.45393	1.44543	1.43710	1.42893	1.42090	1.41303	1.40529	1.39769	1.39022	1.38287	38
39	1.54930	1.53875	1.52844	1.51838	1.50854	1.49892	1.48951	1.48030	1.47128	1.46244	1.45378	1.44529	1.43696	1.42879	1.42077	1.41290	1.40516	1.39756	1.39009	1.38275	39
40	1.54912	1.53857	1.52827	1.51821	1.50838	1.49876	1.48936	1.48015	1.47113	1.46230	1.45364	1.44515	1.43683	1.42866	1.42064	1.41277	1.40503	1.39744	1.38997	1.38263	40
41"	1.54895	1.53840	1.52810	1.51805	1.50822	1.49860	1.48920	1.48000	1.47098	1.46215	1.45350	1.44501	1.43669	1.42852	1.42051	1.41264	1.40491	1.39731	1.38985	1.38251	41"
42	1.54877	1.53823	1.52793	1.51788	1.50805	1.49845	1.48905	1.47984	1.47083	1.46201	1.45335	1.44487	1.43655	1.42839	1.42038	1.41251	1.40478	1.39719	1.38972	1.38239	42
43	1.54859	1.53805	1.52777	1.51772	1.50789	1.49829	1.48889	1.47969	1.47068	1.46186	1.45321	1.44473	1.43641	1.42825	1.42024	1.41238	1.40465	1.39706	1.38960	1.38227	43
44	1.54841	1.53788	1.52760	1.51755	1.50773	1.49813	1.48874	1.47954	1.47054	1.46171	1.45307	1.44459	1.43628	1.42812	1.42011	1.41225	1.40452	1.39694	1.38948	1.38215	44
45	1.54823	1.53771	1.52743	1.51738	1.50757	1.49797	1.48858	1.47939	1.47039	1.46157	1.45293	1.44445	1.43614	1.42798	1.41998	1.41212	1.40440	1.39681	1.38935	1.38202	45
46"	1.54806	1.53753	1.52726	1.51722	1.50741	1.49781	1.48843	1.47924	1.47024	1.46142	1.45278	1.44431	1.43600	1.42785	1.41985	1.41199	1.40427	1.39669	1.38923	1.38190	46"
47	1.54788	1.53736	1.52709	1.51705	1.50725	1.49766	1.48827	1.47909	1.47009	1.46128	1.45264	1.44417	1.43587	1.42771	1.41971	1.41186	1.40414	1.39656	1.38911	1.38178	47
48	1.54770	1.53719	1.52692	1.51689	1.50708	1.49750	1.48812	1.47893	1.46994	1.46113	1.45250	1.44403	1.43573	1.42758	1.41958	1.41173	1.40401	1.39643	1.38899	1.38166	48
49	1.54752	1.53701	1.52675	1.51672	1.50692	1.49734	1.48796	1.47878	1.46979	1.46099	1.45236	1.44389	1.43559	1.42745	1.41945	1.41160	1.40389	1.39631	1.38886	1.38154	49
50	1.54735	1.53684	1.52658	1.51656	1.50676	1.49718	1.48781	1.47863	1.46965	1.46084	1.45221	1.44375	1.43545	1.42731	1.41932	1.41147	1.40376	1.39618	1.38874	1.38142	50
51"	1.54717	1.53667	1.52641	1.51639	1.50660	1.49702	1.48765	1.47848	1.46950	1.46070	1.45207	1.44361	1.43532	1.42718	1.41919	1.41134	1.40363	1.39606	1.38862	1.38130	51"
52	1.54699	1.53649	1.52624	1.51623	1.50644	1.49687	1.48750	1.47833	1.46935	1.46055	1.45193	1.44347	1.43518	1.42704	1.41905	1.41121	1.40350	1.39593	1.38849	1.38118	52
53	1.54682	1.53632	1.52607	1.51606	1.50628	1.49671	1.48734	1.47818	1.46920	1.46041	1.45179	1.44333	1.43504	1.42691	1.41892	1.41108	1.40338	1.39581	1.38837	1.38106	53
54	1.54664	1.53615	1.52591	1.51590	1.50612	1.49655	1.48719	1.47803	1.46905	1.46026	1.45164	1.44320	1.43491	1.42677	1.41879	1.41095	1.40325	1.39568	1.38825	1.38094	54
55	1.54646	1.53598	1.52574	1.51573	1.50595	1.49639	1.48704	1.47788	1.46891	1.46012	1.45150	1.44306	1.43477	1.42664	1.41866	1.41082	1.40312	1.39556	1.38812	1.38081	55
56"	1.54629	1.53580	1.52557	1.51557	1.50579	1.49623	1.48688	1.47772	1.46876	1.45997	1.45136	1.44292	1.43463	1.42651	1.41853	1.41069	1.40300	1.39543	1.38800	1.38069	56"
57	1.54611	1.53563	1.52540	1.51540	1.50563	1.49608	1.48673	1.47757	1.46861	1.45983	1.45122	1.44278	1.43450	1.42637	1.41839	1.41056	1.40287	1.39531	1.38788	1.38057	57
58	1.54593	1.53546	1.52523	1.51524	1.50547	1.49592	1.48657	1.47742	1.46846	1.45968	1.45108	1.44264	1.43436	1.42624	1.41826	1.41043	1.40274	1.39518	1.38776	1.38045	58
59	1.54576	1.53529	1.52506	1.51507	1.50531	1.49576	1.48642	1.47727	1.46831	1.45954	1.45093	1.44250	1.43422	1.42610	1.41813	1.41030	1.40261	1.39506	1.38763	1.38033	59
60	1.54558	1.53511	1.52489	1.51491	1.50515	1.49560	1.48626	1.47712	1.46817	1.45939	1.45079	1.44236	1.43409	1.42597	1.41800	1.41017	1.40249	1.39493	1.38751	1.38021	60

Table X Diurnal Motion Logarithms, 0 to 2 Hours/Degrees

	1° 19'	1° 18'	1° 17'	1° 16'	1° 15'	1° 14'	1° 13'	1° 12'	1° 11'	1° 10'	1° 9'	1° 8'	1° 7'	1° 6'	1° 5'	1° 4'	1° 3'	1° 2'	1° 1'	1° 0'	
0°	1.26074	1.26627	1.27187	1.27755	1.28330	1.28913	1.29504	1.30103	1.30710	1.31326	1.31951	1.32585	1.33229	1.33882	1.34545	1.35218	1.35902	1.36597	1.37303	1.38021	0°
1	1.26064	1.26618	1.27178	1.27745	1.28320	1.28903	1.29494	1.30093	1.30700	1.31316	1.31941	1.32575	1.33218	1.33871	1.34534	1.35207	1.35891	1.36585	1.37291	1.38009	1
2	1.26055	1.26608	1.27168	1.27736	1.28311	1.28894	1.29484	1.30083	1.30690	1.31306	1.31930	1.32564	1.33207	1.33860	1.34523	1.35196	1.35879	1.36574	1.37280	1.37997	2
3	1.26046	1.26599	1.27159	1.27726	1.28301	1.28884	1.29474	1.30073	1.30680	1.31295	1.31920	1.32553	1.33196	1.33849	1.34512	1.35184	1.35868	1.36562	1.37268	1.37985	3
4	1.26037	1.26590	1.27150	1.27717	1.28292	1.28874	1.29464	1.30063	1.30670	1.31285	1.31909	1.32543	1.33186	1.33838	1.34500	1.35173	1.35856	1.36550	1.37256	1.37973	4
5	1.26028	1.26580	1.27140	1.27707	1.28282	1.28864	1.29454	1.30053	1.30659	1.31275	1.31899	1.32532	1.33175	1.33827	1.34489	1.35162	1.35845	1.36539	1.37244	1.37961	5
6°	1.26019	1.26571	1.27131	1.27698	1.28272	1.28854	1.29445	1.30043	1.30649	1.31264	1.31888	1.32522	1.33164	1.33816	1.34478	1.35150	1.35833	1.36527	1.37232	1.37949	6°
7	1.26009	1.26562	1.27121	1.27688	1.28263	1.28845	1.29435	1.30033	1.30639	1.31254	1.31878	1.32511	1.33153	1.33805	1.34467	1.35139	1.35822	1.36515	1.37220	1.37937	7
8	1.26000	1.26553	1.27112	1.27679	1.28253	1.28835	1.29425	1.30023	1.30629	1.31244	1.31867	1.32500	1.33142	1.33794	1.34456	1.35128	1.35810	1.36504	1.37208	1.37925	8
9	1.25991	1.26543	1.27103	1.27669	1.28243	1.28825	1.29415	1.30013	1.30619	1.31233	1.31857	1.32490	1.33132	1.33783	1.34445	1.35117	1.35799	1.36492	1.37197	1.37913	9
10	1.25982	1.26534	1.27093	1.27660	1.28234	1.28815	1.29405	1.30003	1.30609	1.31223	1.31847	1.32479	1.33121	1.33772	1.34434	1.35105	1.35787	1.36480	1.37185	1.37901	10
11°	1.25973	1.26525	1.27084	1.27650	1.28224	1.28806	1.29395	1.29993	1.30598	1.31213	1.31836	1.32468	1.33110	1.33761	1.34423	1.35094	1.35776	1.36469	1.37173	1.37889	11°
12	1.25964	1.26516	1.27075	1.27641	1.28214	1.28796	1.29385	1.29983	1.30588	1.31203	1.31826	1.32458	1.33099	1.33750	1.34411	1.35083	1.35765	1.36457	1.37161	1.37877	12
13	1.25955	1.26506	1.27065	1.27631	1.28205	1.28786	1.29375	1.29973	1.30578	1.31192	1.31815	1.32447	1.33089	1.33740	1.34400	1.35071	1.35753	1.36446	1.37149	1.37865	13
14	1.25945	1.26497	1.27056	1.27622	1.28195	1.28776	1.29365	1.29963	1.30568	1.31182	1.31805	1.32437	1.33078	1.33729	1.34389	1.35060	1.35742	1.36434	1.37137	1.37853	14
15	1.25936	1.26488	1.27046	1.27612	1.28186	1.28767	1.29355	1.29952	1.30558	1.31172	1.31794	1.32426	1.33067	1.33718	1.34378	1.35049	1.35730	1.36422	1.37126	1.37841	15
16°	1.25927	1.26479	1.27037	1.27603	1.28176	1.28757	1.29346	1.29942	1.30548	1.31161	1.31784	1.32415	1.33056	1.33707	1.34367	1.35038	1.35719	1.36411	1.37114	1.37829	16°
17	1.25918	1.26469	1.27028	1.27593	1.28166	1.28747	1.29336	1.29932	1.30537	1.31151	1.31773	1.32405	1.33045	1.33696	1.34356	1.35026	1.35707	1.36399	1.37102	1.37817	17
18	1.25909	1.26460	1.27018	1.27584	1.28157	1.28737	1.29326	1.29922	1.30527	1.31141	1.31763	1.32394	1.33035	1.33685	1.34345	1.35015	1.35696	1.36387	1.37090	1.37805	18
19	1.25900	1.26451	1.27009	1.27574	1.28147	1.28728	1.29316	1.29912	1.30517	1.31130	1.31752	1.32383	1.33024	1.33674	1.34334	1.35004	1.35685	1.36376	1.37078	1.37793	19
20	1.25891	1.26442	1.27000	1.27565	1.28138	1.28718	1.29306	1.29902	1.30507	1.31120	1.31742	1.32373	1.33013	1.33663	1.34323	1.34993	1.35673	1.36364	1.37067	1.37781	20
21°	1.25882	1.26432	1.26990	1.27555	1.28128	1.28708	1.29296	1.29892	1.30497	1.31110	1.31732	1.32362	1.33002	1.33652	1.34312	1.34981	1.35662	1.36353	1.37055	1.37769	21°
22	1.25872	1.26423	1.26981	1.27546	1.28118	1.28698	1.29286	1.29882	1.30487	1.31100	1.31721	1.32352	1.32992	1.33641	1.34301	1.34970	1.35650	1.36341	1.37043	1.37757	22
23	1.25863	1.26414	1.26972	1.27536	1.28109	1.28689	1.29277	1.29872	1.30477	1.31089	1.31711	1.32341	1.32981	1.33630	1.34290	1.34959	1.35639	1.36329	1.37031	1.37745	23
24	1.25854	1.26405	1.26962	1.27527	1.28099	1.28679	1.29267	1.29862	1.30467	1.31079	1.31700	1.32331	1.32970	1.33619	1.34278	1.34948	1.35627	1.36318	1.37019	1.37733	24
25	1.25845	1.26395	1.26953	1.27517	1.28090	1.28669	1.29257	1.29852	1.30456	1.31069	1.31690	1.32320	1.32960	1.33609	1.34267	1.34936	1.35616	1.36306	1.37008	1.37721	25
26°	1.25836	1.26386	1.26943	1.27508	1.28080	1.28660	1.29247	1.29842	1.30446	1.31058	1.31679	1.32309	1.32949	1.33598	1.34256	1.34925	1.35604	1.36295	1.36996	1.37709	26°
27	1.25827	1.26377	1.26934	1.27498	1.28070	1.28650	1.29237	1.29832	1.30436	1.31048	1.31669	1.32299	1.32938	1.33587	1.34245	1.34914	1.35593	1.36283	1.36984	1.37697	27
28	1.25818	1.26368	1.26925	1.27489	1.28061	1.28640	1.29227	1.29822	1.30426	1.31038	1.31659	1.32288	1.32927	1.33576	1.34234	1.34903	1.35582	1.36271	1.36972	1.37685	28
29	1.25809	1.26359	1.26915	1.27479	1.28051	1.28631	1.29218	1.29812	1.30416	1.31028	1.31648	1.32278	1.32917	1.33565	1.34223	1.34892	1.35570	1.36260	1.36961	1.37673	29
30	1.25800	1.26349	1.26906	1.27470	1.28042	1.28621	1.29208	1.29802	1.30406	1.31017	1.31638	1.32267	1.32906	1.33554	1.34212	1.34880	1.35559	1.36248	1.36949	1.37661	30
31°	1.25790	1.26340	1.26897	1.27461	1.28032	1.28611	1.29198	1.29792	1.30396	1.31007	1.31627	1.32257	1.32895	1.33543	1.34201	1.34869	1.35547	1.36237	1.36937	1.37649	31°
32	1.25781	1.26331	1.26887	1.27451	1.28022	1.28601	1.29188	1.29782	1.30385	1.30997	1.31617	1.32246	1.32884	1.33532	1.34190	1.34858	1.35536	1.36225	1.36925	1.37637	32
33	1.25772	1.26321	1.26878	1.27442	1.28013	1.28591	1.29178	1.29772	1.30375	1.30987	1.31607	1.32235	1.32874	1.33521	1.34179	1.34847	1.35525	1.36214	1.36913	1.37625	33
34	1.25763	1.26312	1.26868	1.27432	1.28003	1.28582	1.29168	1.29763	1.30365	1.30976	1.31596	1.32225	1.32863	1.33511	1.34168	1.34835	1.35513	1.36202	1.36901	1.37613	34
35	1.25754	1.26303	1.26859	1.27423	1.27994	1.28572	1.29158	1.29753	1.30355	1.30966	1.31586	1.32214	1.32852	1.33500	1.34157	1.34824	1.35502	1.36190	1.36890	1.37601	35
36°	1.25745	1.26294	1.26850	1.27413	1.27984	1.28562	1.29148	1.29743	1.30345	1.30956	1.31575	1.32204	1.32842	1.33489	1.34146	1.34813	1.35491	1.36179	1.36878	1.37589	36°
37	1.25736	1.26285	1.26841	1.27404	1.27974	1.28553	1.29139	1.29733	1.30335	1.30946	1.31565	1.32193	1.32831	1.33478	1.34135	1.34802	1.35479	1.36167	1.36866	1.37577	37
38	1.25727	1.26276	1.26831	1.27394	1.27965	1.28543	1.29129	1.29723	1.30325	1.30935	1.31555	1.32183	1.32820	1.33467	1.34124	1.34791	1.35468	1.36156	1.36855	1.37565	38
39	1.25718	1.26266	1.26822	1.27385	1.27955	1.28533	1.29119	1.29713	1.30315	1.30925	1.31544	1.32172	1.32809	1.33456	1.34113	1.34779	1.35456	1.36144	1.36843	1.37553	39
40	1.25709	1.26257	1.26813	1.27376	1.27946	1.28524	1.29109	1.29703	1.30304	1.30915	1.31534	1.32162	1.32799	1.33445	1.34102	1.34768	1.35445	1.36133	1.36831	1.37541	40
41°	1.25699	1.26248	1.26803	1.27366	1.27936	1.28514	1.29099	1.29693	1.30294	1.30905	1.31523	1.32151	1.32788	1.33435	1.34091	1.34757	1.35434	1.36121	1.36819	1.37529	41°
42	1.25690	1.26239	1.26794	1.27357	1.27927	1.28504	1.29090	1.29683	1.30284	1.30894	1.31513	1.32141	1.32777	1.33424	1.34080	1.34746	1.35422	1.36109	1.36808	1.37517	42
43	1.25681	1.26230	1.26785	1.27347	1.27917	1.28494	1.29080	1.29673	1.30274	1.30884	1.31503	1.32130	1.32767	1.33413	1.34069	1.34735	1.35411	1.36098	1.36796	1.37505	43
44	1.25672	1.26220	1.26776	1.27338	1.27908	1.28485	1.29070	1.29663	1.30264	1.30874	1.31492	1.32120	1.32756	1.33402	1.34058	1.34723	1.35400	1.36086	1.36784	1.37494	44
45	1.25663	1.26211	1.26766	1.27328	1.27898	1.28475	1.29060	1.29653	1.30254	1.30864	1.31482	1.32109	1.32745	1.33391	1.34047	1.34712	1.35388	1.36075	1.36773	1.37482	45
46°	1.25654	1.26202	1.26757	1.27319	1.27888	1.28465	1.29050	1.29643	1.30244	1.30853	1.31471	1.32098	1.32735	1.33380	1.34036	1.34701	1.35377	1.36063	1.36761	1.37470	46°
47	1.25645	1.26193	1.26748	1.27310	1.27879	1.28456	1.29040	1.29633	1.30234	1.30843	1.31461	1.32088	1.32724	1.33369	1.34025	1.34690	1.35366	1.36052	1.36749	1.37458	47
48	1.25636	1.26184	1.26738	1.27300	1.27869	1.28446	1.29031	1.29623	1.30224	1.30833	1.31451	1.32077	1.32713	1.33359	1.34014	1.34679	1.35354	1.36040	1.36737	1.37446	48
49	1.25627	1.26174	1.26729	1.27291	1.27860	1.28436	1.29021	1.29613	1.30214	1.30823	1.31440	1.32067	1.32703	1.33348	1.34003	1.34668	1.35343	1.36029	1.36726	1.37434	49
50	1.25618	1.26165	1.26720	1.27281	1.27850	1.28427	1.29011	1.29603	1.30204	1.30813	1.31430	1.32056	1.32692	1.33337	1.33992	1.34656	1.35331	1.36017	1.36714	1.37422	50
51°	1.25609	1.26156	1.26710	1.27272	1.27841	1.28417	1.29001	1.29593	1.30194	1.30802	1.31420	1.32046	1.32681	1.33326	1.33981	1.34645	1.35320	1.36006	1.36702	1.37410	51°
52	1.25600	1.26147	1.26701	1.27263	1.27831	1.28407	1.28991	1.29583	1.30184	1.30792	1.31409	1.32035	1.32671	1.33315	1.33970	1.34634	1.35309	1.35994	1.36691	1.37398	52
53	1.25591	1.26138	1.26692	1.27253	1.27822	1.28398	1.28982	1.29573	1.30173	1.30782	1.31399	1.32025	1.32660	1.33304	1.33959	1.34623	1.35297	1.35983	1.36679	1.37386	53
54	1.25582	1.26129	1.26683	1.27244	1.27812	1.28388	1.28972	1.29563	1.30163	1.30772	1.31389	1.32014	1.32649	1.33294	1.33948	1.34612	1.35286	1.35971	1.36667	1.37375	54
55	1.25573	1.26119	1.26673	1.27234	1.27803	1.28378	1.28962	1.29554	1.30153	1.30761	1.31378	1.32004	1.32639	1.33283	1.33937	1.34601	1.35275	1.35960	1.36655	1.37363	55
56°	1.25563	1.26110	1.26664	1.27225	1.27793	1.28369	1.28952	1.29544	1.30143	1.30751	1.31368	1.31993	1.32628	1.33272	1.33926	1.34589	1.35264	1.35948	1.36644	1.37351	56°
57	1.25554	1.26101	1.26655	1.27215	1.27783	1.28359	1.28943	1.29534	1.30133	1.30741	1.31357	1.31983	1.32617	1.33261	1.33915	1.34578	1.35252	1.35937	1.36632	1.37339	57
58	1.25545	1.26092	1.26645	1.27206	1.27774	1.28349	1.28933	1.29524	1.30123	1.30731	1.31347	1.31972	1.32607	1.33250	1.33904	1.34567	1.35241	1.35925	1.36620	1.37327	58
59	1.25536	1.26083	1.26636	1.27197	1.27764	1.28340	1.28923	1.29514	1.30113	1.30721	1.31337	1.31962	1.32596	1.33240	1.33893	1.34556	1.35230	1.35914	1.36609	1.37315	59
60	1.25527	1.26074	1.26627	1.27187	1.27755	1.28330	1.28913	1.29504	1.30103	1.30710	1.31326	1.31951	1.32585	1.33229	1.33882	1.34545	1.35218	1.35902	1.36597	1.37303	60

Table X Diurnal Motion Logarithms, 0 to 2 Hours/Degrees

	1° 20'	1° 21'	1° 22'	1° 23'	1° 24'	1° 25'	1° 26'	1° 27'	1° 28'	1° 29'
0"	1.25527	1.24988	1.24455	1.23928	1.23408	1.22894	1.22386	1.21884	1.21388	1.20897
1	1.25518	1.24979	1.24446	1.23920	1.23400	1.22886	1.22378	1.21876	1.21380	1.20889
2	1.25509	1.24970	1.24437	1.23911	1.23391	1.22877	1.22370	1.21868	1.21372	1.20881
3	1.25500	1.24961	1.24428	1.23902	1.23382	1.22869	1.22361	1.21859	1.21363	1.20873
4	1.25491	1.24952	1.24420	1.23894	1.23374	1.22860	1.22353	1.21851	1.21355	1.20865
5	1.25482	1.24943	1.24411	1.23885	1.23365	1.22852	1.22344	1.21843	1.21347	1.20857
6"	1.25473	1.24934	1.24402	1.23876	1.23357	1.22843	1.22336	1.21834	1.21339	1.20848
7	1.25464	1.24925	1.24393	1.23867	1.23348	1.22835	1.22328	1.21826	1.21330	1.20840
8	1.25455	1.24916	1.24384	1.23859	1.23339	1.22826	1.22319	1.21818	1.21322	1.20832
9	1.25446	1.24907	1.24375	1.23850	1.23331	1.22818	1.22311	1.21810	1.21314	1.20824
10	1.25437	1.24898	1.24367	1.23841	1.23322	1.22809	1.22302	1.21801	1.21306	1.20816
11"	1.25428	1.24890	1.24358	1.23833	1.23314	1.22801	1.22294	1.21793	1.21298	1.20808
12	1.25419	1.24881	1.24349	1.23824	1.23305	1.22792	1.22286	1.21785	1.21289	1.20800
13	1.25410	1.24872	1.24340	1.23815	1.23296	1.22784	1.22277	1.21776	1.21281	1.20792
14	1.25401	1.24863	1.24331	1.23807	1.23288	1.22775	1.22269	1.21768	1.21273	1.20784
15	1.25392	1.24854	1.24323	1.23798	1.23279	1.22767	1.22260	1.21760	1.21265	1.20775
16"	1.25383	1.24845	1.24314	1.23789	1.23271	1.22758	1.22252	1.21751	1.21257	1.20767
17	1.25374	1.24836	1.24305	1.23780	1.23262	1.22750	1.22244	1.21743	1.21248	1.20759
18	1.25365	1.24827	1.24296	1.23772	1.23253	1.22741	1.22235	1.21735	1.21240	1.20751
19	1.25356	1.24818	1.24287	1.23763	1.23245	1.22733	1.22227	1.21727	1.21232	1.20743
20	1.25347	1.24809	1.24279	1.23754	1.23236	1.22724	1.22218	1.21718	1.21224	1.20735
21"	1.25338	1.24800	1.24270	1.23746	1.23228	1.22716	1.22210	1.21710	1.21216	1.20727
22	1.25329	1.24792	1.24261	1.23737	1.23219	1.22707	1.22202	1.21702	1.21207	1.20719
23	1.25320	1.24783	1.24252	1.23728	1.23211	1.22699	1.22193	1.21693	1.21199	1.20711
24	1.25311	1.24774	1.24244	1.23720	1.23202	1.22690	1.22185	1.21685	1.21191	1.20702
25	1.25302	1.24765	1.24235	1.23711	1.23193	1.22682	1.22176	1.21677	1.21183	1.20694
26"	1.25293	1.24756	1.24226	1.23702	1.23185	1.22674	1.22168	1.21669	1.21175	1.20686
27	1.25284	1.24747	1.24217	1.23694	1.23176	1.22665	1.22160	1.21660	1.21166	1.20678
28	1.25275	1.24738	1.24208	1.23685	1.23168	1.22657	1.22151	1.21652	1.21158	1.20670
29	1.25266	1.24729	1.24200	1.23676	1.23159	1.22648	1.22143	1.21644	1.21150	1.20662
30	1.25257	1.24720	1.24191	1.23668	1.23151	1.22640	1.22135	1.21635	1.21142	1.20654
31"	1.25248	1.24712	1.24182	1.23659	1.23142	1.22631	1.22126	1.21627	1.21134	1.20646
32	1.25239	1.24703	1.24173	1.23650	1.23133	1.22623	1.22118	1.21619	1.21126	1.20638
33	1.25230	1.24694	1.24165	1.23642	1.23125	1.22614	1.22110	1.21611	1.21117	1.20630
34	1.25221	1.24685	1.24156	1.23633	1.23116	1.22606	1.22101	1.21602	1.21109	1.20622
35	1.25212	1.24676	1.24147	1.23624	1.23108	1.22597	1.22093	1.21594	1.21101	1.20614
36"	1.25203	1.24667	1.24138	1.23616	1.23099	1.22589	1.22084	1.21586	1.21093	1.20605
37	1.25194	1.24658	1.24129	1.23607	1.23091	1.22580	1.22076	1.21578	1.21085	1.20597
38	1.25185	1.24649	1.24121	1.23598	1.23082	1.22572	1.22068	1.21569	1.21077	1.20589
39	1.25176	1.24641	1.24112	1.23590	1.23074	1.22564	1.22059	1.21561	1.21068	1.20581
40	1.25167	1.24632	1.24103	1.23581	1.23065	1.22555	1.22051	1.21553	1.21060	1.20573
41"	1.25158	1.24623	1.24094	1.23572	1.23056	1.22547	1.22043	1.21545	1.21052	1.20565
42	1.25149	1.24614	1.24086	1.23564	1.23048	1.22538	1.22034	1.21536	1.21044	1.20557
43	1.25140	1.24605	1.24077	1.23555	1.23039	1.22530	1.22026	1.21528	1.21036	1.20549
44	1.25131	1.24596	1.24068	1.23546	1.23031	1.22521	1.22018	1.21520	1.21028	1.20541
45	1.25122	1.24587	1.24059	1.23538	1.23022	1.22513	1.22009	1.21512	1.21019	1.20533
46"	1.25113	1.24579	1.24051	1.23529	1.23014	1.22504	1.22001	1.21503	1.21011	1.20525
47	1.25104	1.24570	1.24042	1.23520	1.23005	1.22496	1.21993	1.21495	1.21003	1.20517
48	1.25095	1.24561	1.24033	1.23512	1.22997	1.22488	1.21984	1.21487	1.20995	1.20509
49	1.25086	1.24552	1.24024	1.23503	1.22988	1.22479	1.21976	1.21479	1.20987	1.20501
50	1.25077	1.24543	1.24016	1.23495	1.22980	1.22471	1.21968	1.21470	1.20979	1.20492
51"	1.25068	1.24534	1.24007	1.23486	1.22971	1.22462	1.21959	1.21462	1.20971	1.20484
52	1.25059	1.24526	1.23998	1.23477	1.22963	1.22454	1.21951	1.21454	1.20962	1.20476
53	1.25050	1.24517	1.23990	1.23469	1.22954	1.22445	1.21943	1.21446	1.20954	1.20468
54	1.25041	1.24508	1.23981	1.23460	1.22945	1.22437	1.21934	1.21437	1.20946	1.20460
55	1.25032	1.24499	1.23972	1.23451	1.22937	1.22429	1.21926	1.21429	1.20938	1.20452
56"	1.25024	1.24490	1.23963	1.23443	1.22928	1.22420	1.21918	1.21421	1.20930	1.20444
57	1.25015	1.24481	1.23955	1.23434	1.22920	1.22412	1.21909	1.21413	1.20922	1.20436
58	1.25006	1.24473	1.23946	1.23426	1.22911	1.22403	1.21901	1.21404	1.20914	1.20428
59	1.24997	1.24464	1.23937	1.23417	1.22903	1.22395	1.21893	1.21396	1.20905	1.20420
60	1.24988	1.24455	1.23928	1.23408	1.22894	1.22386	1.21884	1.21388	1.20897	1.20412

	1° 30'	1° 31'	1° 32'	1° 33'	1° 34'	1° 35'	1° 36'	1° 37'	1° 38'	1° 39'
0"	1.20412	1.19932	1.19457	1.18988	1.18523	1.18064	1.17609	1.17159	1.16714	1.16273
1	1.20404	1.19924	1.19450	1.18980	1.18516	1.18056	1.17602	1.17152	1.16706	1.16265
2	1.20396	1.19916	1.19442	1.18972	1.18508	1.18049	1.17594	1.17144	1.16699	1.16258
3	1.20388	1.19908	1.19434	1.18965	1.18500	1.18041	1.17587	1.17137	1.16691	1.16251
4	1.20380	1.19900	1.19426	1.18957	1.18493	1.18033	1.17579	1.17129	1.16684	1.16243
5	1.20372	1.19892	1.19418	1.18949	1.18485	1.18026	1.17571	1.17122	1.16677	1.16236
6"	1.20364	1.19884	1.19410	1.18941	1.18477	1.18018	1.17564	1.17114	1.16669	1.16229
7	1.20356	1.19876	1.19402	1.18934	1.18470	1.18011	1.17556	1.17107	1.16662	1.16222
8	1.20348	1.19869	1.19395	1.18926	1.18462	1.18003	1.17549	1.17099	1.16655	1.16214
9	1.20340	1.19861	1.19387	1.18918	1.18454	1.17995	1.17541	1.17092	1.16647	1.16207
10	1.20332	1.19853	1.19379	1.18910	1.18447	1.17988	1.17534	1.17085	1.16640	1.16200
11"	1.20324	1.19845	1.19371	1.18902	1.18439	1.17980	1.17526	1.17077	1.16632	1.16192
12	1.20316	1.19837	1.19363	1.18895	1.18431	1.17973	1.17519	1.17070	1.16625	1.16185
13	1.20308	1.19829	1.19355	1.18887	1.18423	1.17965	1.17511	1.17062	1.16618	1.16178
14	1.20300	1.19821	1.19347	1.18879	1.18416	1.17957	1.17504	1.17055	1.16610	1.16170
15	1.20292	1.19813	1.19340	1.18871	1.18408	1.17950	1.17496	1.17047	1.16603	1.16163
16"	1.20284	1.19805	1.19332	1.18864	1.18400	1.17942	1.17489	1.17040	1.16596	1.16156
17	1.20275	1.19797	1.19324	1.18856	1.18393	1.17935	1.17481	1.17032	1.16588	1.16149
18	1.20267	1.19789	1.19316	1.18848	1.18385	1.17927	1.17474	1.17025	1.16581	1.16141
19	1.20259	1.19781	1.19308	1.18840	1.18377	1.17919	1.17466	1.17018	1.16574	1.16134
20	1.20251	1.19773	1.19300	1.18833	1.18370	1.17912	1.17459	1.17010	1.16566	1.16127
21"	1.20243	1.19765	1.19293	1.18825	1.18362	1.17904	1.17451	1.17003	1.16559	1.16119
22	1.20235	1.19757	1.19285	1.18817	1.18354	1.17897	1.17444	1.16995	1.16551	1.16112
23	1.20227	1.19750	1.19277	1.18809	1.18347	1.17889	1.17436	1.16988	1.16544	1.16105
24	1.20219	1.19742	1.19269	1.18802	1.18339	1.17881	1.17429	1.16980	1.16537	1.16098
25	1.20211	1.19734	1.19261	1.18794	1.18331	1.17874	1.17421	1.16973	1.16529	1.16090
26"	1.20203	1.19726	1.19253	1.18786	1.18324	1.17866	1.17414	1.16965	1.16522	1.16083
27	1.20195	1.19718	1.19246	1.18778	1.18316	1.17859	1.17406	1.16958	1.16515	1.16076
28	1.20187	1.19710	1.19238	1.18771	1.18308	1.17851	1.17399	1.16951	1.16507	1.16068
29	1.20179	1.19702	1.19230	1.18763	1.18301	1.17843	1.17391	1.16943	1.16500	1.16061
30	1.20171	1.19694	1.19222	1.18755	1.18293	1.17836	1.17384	1.16936	1.16493	1.16054
31"	1.20163	1.19686	1.19214	1.18747	1.18285	1.17828	1.17376	1.16928	1.16485	1.16047
32	1.20155	1.19678	1.19206	1.18740	1.18278	1.17821	1.17369	1.16921	1.16478	1.16039
33	1.20147	1.19670	1.19199	1.18732	1.18270	1.17813	1.17361	1.16914	1.16471	1.16032
34	1.20139	1.19663	1.19191	1.18724	1.18262	1.17806	1.17354	1.16906	1.16463	1.16025
35	1.20131	1.19655	1.19183	1.18716	1.18255	1.17798	1.17346	1.16899	1.16456	1.16018
36"	1.20123	1.19647	1.19175	1.18709	1.18247	1.17790	1.17339	1.16891	1.16449	1.16010
37	1.20115	1.19639	1.19167	1.18701	1.18239	1.17783	1.17331	1.16884	1.16441	1.16003
38	1.20107	1.19631	1.19160	1.18693	1.18232	1.17775	1.17324	1.16876	1.16434	1.15996
39	1.20099	1.19623	1.19152	1.18685	1.18224	1.17768	1.17316	1.16869	1.16427	1.15989
40	1.20091	1.19615	1.19144	1.18678	1.18217	1.17760	1.17309	1.16862	1.16419	1.15981
41"	1.20084	1.19607	1.19136	1.18670	1.18209	1.17753	1.17301	1.16854	1.16412	1.15974
42	1.20076	1.19599	1.19128	1.18662	1.18201	1.17745	1.17294	1.16847	1.16405	1.15967
43	1.20068	1.19591	1.19120	1.18655	1.18194	1.17737	1.17286	1.16839	1.16397	1.15959
44	1.20060	1.19584	1.19113	1.18647	1.18186	1.17730	1.17279	1.16832	1.16390	1.15952
45	1.20052	1.19576	1.19105	1.18639	1.18178	1.17722	1.17271	1.16825	1.16383	1.15945
46"	1.20044	1.19568	1.19097	1.18631	1.18171	1.17715	1.17264	1.16817	1.16375	1.15938
47	1.20036	1.19560	1.19089	1.18624	1.18163	1.17707	1.17256	1.16810	1.16368	1.15930
48	1.20028	1.19552	1.19081	1.18616	1.18155	1.17700	1.17249	1.16802	1.16361	1.15923
49	1.20020	1.19544	1.19074	1.18608	1.18148	1.17692	1.17241	1.16795	1.16353	1.15916
50	1.20012	1.19536	1.19066	1.18601	1.18140	1.17685	1.17234	1.16788	1.16346	1.15909
51"	1.20004	1.19528	1.19058	1.18593	1.18133	1.17677	1.17226	1.16780	1.16339	1.15901
52	1.19996	1.19520	1.19050	1.18585	1.18125	1.17669	1.17219	1.16773	1.16331	1.15894
53	1.19988	1.19513	1.19042	1.18577	1.18117	1.17662	1.17211	1.16765	1.16324	1.15887
54	1.19980	1.19505	1.19035	1.18570	1.18110	1.17654	1.17204	1.16758	1.16317	1.15880
55	1.19972	1.19497	1.19027	1.18562	1.18102	1.17647	1.17196	1.16751	1.16309	1.15872
56"	1.19964	1.19489	1.19019	1.18554	1.18094	1.17639	1.17189	1.16743	1.16302	1.15865
57	1.19956	1.19481	1.19011	1.18547	1.18087	1.17632	1.17181	1.16736	1.16295	1.15858
58	1.19948	1.19473	1.19004	1.18539	1.18079	1.17624	1.17174	1.16728	1.16287	1.15851
59	1.19940	1.19465	1.18996	1.18531	1.18072	1.17617	1.17167	1.16721	1.16280	1.15843
60	1.19932	1.19457	1.18988	1.18523	1.18064	1.17609	1.17159	1.16714	1.16273	1.15836

Table X Diurnal Motion Logarithms, 0 to 2 Hours/Degrees

	1° 40'	1° 41'	1° 42'	1° 43'	1° 44'	1° 45'	1° 46'	1° 47'	1° 48'	1° 49'	1° 50'	1° 51'	1° 52'	1° 53'	1° 54'	1° 55'	1° 56'	1° 57'	1° 58'	1° 59'	
0"	1.15836	1.15404	1.14976	1.14553	1.14133	1.13717	1.13306	1.12898	1.12494	1.12094	1.11697	1.11304	1.10914	1.10528	1.10146	1.09766	1.09390	1.09018	1.08648	1.08282	0"
1	1.15829	1.15397	1.14969	1.14545	1.14126	1.13710	1.13299	1.12891	1.12487	1.12087	1.11690	1.11297	1.10908	1.10522	1.10139	1.09760	1.09384	1.09011	1.08642	1.08275	1
2	1.15822	1.15390	1.14962	1.14538	1.14119	1.13704	1.13292	1.12884	1.12480	1.12080	1.11684	1.11291	1.10902	1.10516	1.10133	1.09754	1.09378	1.09005	1.08636	1.08269	2
3	1.15815	1.15383	1.14955	1.14531	1.14112	1.13697	1.13285	1.12878	1.12474	1.12074	1.11677	1.11284	1.10895	1.10509	1.10127	1.09748	1.09372	1.08999	1.08630	1.08263	3
4	1.15807	1.15375	1.14948	1.14524	1.14105	1.13690	1.13278	1.12871	1.12467	1.12067	1.11671	1.11278	1.10889	1.10503	1.10120	1.09741	1.09365	1.08993	1.08624	1.08257	4
5	1.15800	1.15368	1.14941	1.14517	1.14098	1.13683	1.13272	1.12864	1.12460	1.12060	1.11664	1.11271	1.10882	1.10496	1.10114	1.09735	1.09359	1.08987	1.08617	1.08251	5
6"	1.15793	1.15361	1.14934	1.14510	1.14091	1.13676	1.13265	1.12857	1.12454	1.12054	1.11658	1.11265	1.10876	1.10490	1.10108	1.09729	1.09353	1.08981	1.08611	1.08245	6"
7	1.15786	1.15354	1.14927	1.14503	1.14084	1.13669	1.13258	1.12851	1.12447	1.12047	1.11651	1.11258	1.10869	1.10484	1.10101	1.09722	1.09347	1.08974	1.08605	1.08239	7
8	1.15778	1.15347	1.14919	1.14496	1.14077	1.13662	1.13251	1.12844	1.12440	1.12041	1.11644	1.11252	1.10863	1.10477	1.10095	1.09716	1.09341	1.08968	1.08599	1.08233	8
9	1.15771	1.15340	1.14912	1.14489	1.14070	1.13655	1.13244	1.12837	1.12434	1.12034	1.11638	1.11245	1.10856	1.10471	1.10089	1.09710	1.09334	1.08962	1.08593	1.08227	9
10	1.15764	1.15333	1.14905	1.14482	1.14063	1.13648	1.13237	1.12830	1.12427	1.12027	1.11631	1.11239	1.10850	1.10464	1.10082	1.09704	1.09328	1.08956	1.08587	1.08221	10
11"	1.15757	1.15325	1.14898	1.14475	1.14056	1.13642	1.13231	1.12824	1.12420	1.12021	1.11625	1.11232	1.10843	1.10458	1.10076	1.09697	1.09322	1.08950	1.08581	1.08215	11"
12	1.15749	1.15318	1.14891	1.14468	1.14049	1.13635	1.13224	1.12817	1.12414	1.12014	1.11618	1.11226	1.10837	1.10452	1.10070	1.09691	1.09316	1.08943	1.08575	1.08209	12
13	1.15742	1.15311	1.14884	1.14461	1.14043	1.13628	1.13217	1.12810	1.12407	1.12007	1.11612	1.11219	1.10831	1.10445	1.10063	1.09685	1.09309	1.08937	1.08568	1.08203	13
14	1.15735	1.15304	1.14877	1.14454	1.14036	1.13621	1.13210	1.12803	1.12400	1.12001	1.11605	1.11213	1.10824	1.10439	1.10057	1.09678	1.09303	1.08931	1.08562	1.08196	14
15	1.15728	1.15297	1.14870	1.14447	1.14029	1.13614	1.13203	1.12797	1.12393	1.11994	1.11598	1.11206	1.10818	1.10432	1.10051	1.09672	1.09297	1.08925	1.08556	1.08190	15
16"	1.15721	1.15290	1.14863	1.14440	1.14022	1.13607	1.13197	1.12790	1.12387	1.11987	1.11592	1.11200	1.10811	1.10426	1.10044	1.09666	1.09291	1.08919	1.08550	1.08184	16"
17	1.15713	1.15282	1.14856	1.14433	1.14015	1.13600	1.13190	1.12783	1.12380	1.11981	1.11585	1.11193	1.10805	1.10420	1.10038	1.09660	1.09285	1.08913	1.08544	1.08178	17
18	1.15706	1.15275	1.14849	1.14426	1.14008	1.13593	1.13183	1.12776	1.12373	1.11974	1.11579	1.11187	1.10798	1.10413	1.10032	1.09653	1.09278	1.08906	1.08538	1.08172	18
19	1.15699	1.15268	1.14842	1.14419	1.14001	1.13587	1.13176	1.12770	1.12367	1.11968	1.11572	1.11180	1.10792	1.10407	1.10025	1.09647	1.09272	1.08900	1.08532	1.08166	19
20	1.15692	1.15261	1.14835	1.14412	1.13994	1.13580	1.13169	1.12763	1.12360	1.11961	1.11566	1.11174	1.10785	1.10400	1.10019	1.09641	1.09266	1.08894	1.08526	1.08160	20
21"	1.15685	1.15254	1.14827	1.14405	1.13987	1.13573	1.13162	1.12756	1.12353	1.11954	1.11559	1.11167	1.10779	1.10394	1.10013	1.09634	1.09260	1.08888	1.08519	1.08154	21"
22	1.15677	1.15247	1.14820	1.14398	1.13980	1.13566	1.13156	1.12749	1.12347	1.11948	1.11552	1.11161	1.10772	1.10388	1.10006	1.09628	1.09253	1.08882	1.08513	1.08148	22
23	1.15670	1.15240	1.14813	1.14391	1.13973	1.13559	1.13149	1.12743	1.12340	1.11941	1.11546	1.11154	1.10766	1.10381	1.10000	1.09622	1.09247	1.08876	1.08507	1.08142	23
24	1.15663	1.15232	1.14806	1.14384	1.13966	1.13552	1.13142	1.12736	1.12333	1.11935	1.11539	1.11148	1.10760	1.10375	1.09994	1.09616	1.09241	1.08869	1.08501	1.08136	24
25	1.15656	1.15225	1.14799	1.14377	1.13959	1.13545	1.13135	1.12729	1.12327	1.11928	1.11533	1.11141	1.10753	1.10369	1.09987	1.09609	1.09235	1.08863	1.08495	1.08130	25
26"	1.15648	1.15218	1.14792	1.14370	1.13952	1.13538	1.13128	1.12722	1.12320	1.11921	1.11526	1.11135	1.10747	1.10362	1.09981	1.09603	1.09229	1.08857	1.08489	1.08124	26"
27	1.15641	1.15211	1.14785	1.14363	1.13945	1.13532	1.13122	1.12716	1.12313	1.11915	1.11520	1.11128	1.10740	1.10356	1.09975	1.09597	1.09222	1.08851	1.08483	1.08118	27
28	1.15634	1.15204	1.14778	1.14356	1.13938	1.13525	1.13115	1.12709	1.12307	1.11908	1.11513	1.11122	1.10734	1.10349	1.09968	1.09591	1.09216	1.08845	1.08477	1.08112	28
29	1.15627	1.15197	1.14771	1.14349	1.13932	1.13518	1.13108	1.12702	1.12300	1.11901	1.11507	1.11115	1.10727	1.10343	1.09962	1.09584	1.09210	1.08839	1.08471	1.08106	29
30	1.15620	1.15190	1.14764	1.14342	1.13925	1.13511	1.13101	1.12695	1.12293	1.11895	1.11500	1.11109	1.10721	1.10337	1.09956	1.09578	1.09204	1.08832	1.08464	1.08099	30
31"	1.15612	1.15183	1.14757	1.14335	1.13918	1.13504	1.13094	1.12689	1.12287	1.11888	1.11493	1.11102	1.10715	1.10330	1.09949	1.09572	1.09197	1.08826	1.08458	1.08093	31"
32	1.15605	1.15175	1.14750	1.14328	1.13911	1.13497	1.13088	1.12682	1.12280	1.11882	1.11487	1.11096	1.10708	1.10324	1.09943	1.09566	1.09191	1.08820	1.08452	1.08087	32
33	1.15598	1.15168	1.14743	1.14321	1.13904	1.13490	1.13081	1.12675	1.12273	1.11875	1.11480	1.11089	1.10702	1.10318	1.09937	1.09559	1.09185	1.08814	1.08446	1.08081	33
34	1.15591	1.15161	1.14736	1.14314	1.13897	1.13484	1.13074	1.12668	1.12267	1.11868	1.11474	1.11083	1.10695	1.10311	1.09930	1.09553	1.09179	1.08808	1.08440	1.08075	34
35	1.15584	1.15154	1.14729	1.14307	1.13890	1.13477	1.13067	1.12662	1.12260	1.11862	1.11467	1.11076	1.10689	1.10305	1.09924	1.09547	1.09173	1.08802	1.08434	1.08069	35
36"	1.15576	1.15147	1.14722	1.14300	1.13883	1.13470	1.13061	1.12655	1.12253	1.11855	1.11461	1.11070	1.10682	1.10298	1.09918	1.09540	1.09166	1.08796	1.08428	1.08063	36"
37	1.15569	1.15140	1.14714	1.14293	1.13876	1.13463	1.13054	1.12648	1.12247	1.11849	1.11454	1.11063	1.10676	1.10292	1.09911	1.09534	1.09160	1.08789	1.08422	1.08057	37
38	1.15562	1.15133	1.14707	1.14286	1.13869	1.13456	1.13047	1.12642	1.12240	1.11842	1.11448	1.11057	1.10670	1.10286	1.09905	1.09528	1.09154	1.08783	1.08416	1.08051	38
39	1.15555	1.15126	1.14700	1.14279	1.13862	1.13449	1.13040	1.12635	1.12233	1.11835	1.11441	1.11050	1.10663	1.10279	1.09899	1.09522	1.09148	1.08777	1.08409	1.08045	39
40	1.15548	1.15118	1.14693	1.14272	1.13855	1.13442	1.13033	1.12628	1.12227	1.11829	1.11435	1.11044	1.10657	1.10273	1.09893	1.09515	1.09142	1.08771	1.08403	1.08039	40
41"	1.15540	1.15111	1.14686	1.14265	1.13848	1.13436	1.13027	1.12621	1.12220	1.11822	1.11428	1.11037	1.10650	1.10267	1.09886	1.09509	1.09135	1.08765	1.08397	1.08033	41"
42	1.15533	1.15104	1.14679	1.14258	1.13842	1.13429	1.13020	1.12615	1.12213	1.11816	1.11421	1.11031	1.10644	1.10260	1.09880	1.09503	1.09129	1.08759	1.08391	1.08027	42
43	1.15526	1.15097	1.14672	1.14251	1.13835	1.13422	1.13013	1.12608	1.12207	1.11809	1.11415	1.11024	1.10637	1.10254	1.09874	1.09497	1.09123	1.08752	1.08385	1.08021	43
44	1.15519	1.15090	1.14665	1.14244	1.13828	1.13415	1.13006	1.12601	1.12200	1.11802	1.11408	1.11018	1.10631	1.10247	1.09867	1.09490	1.09117	1.08746	1.08379	1.08015	44
45	1.15512	1.15083	1.14658	1.14237	1.13821	1.13408	1.12999	1.12595	1.12193	1.11796	1.11402	1.11011	1.10625	1.10241	1.09861	1.09484	1.09111	1.08740	1.08373	1.08009	45
46"	1.15505	1.15076	1.14651	1.14230	1.13814	1.13401	1.12993	1.12588	1.12187	1.11789	1.11395	1.11005	1.10618	1.10235	1.09855	1.09478	1.09104	1.08734	1.08367	1.08003	46"
47	1.15497	1.15069	1.14644	1.14223	1.13807	1.13395	1.12986	1.12581	1.12180	1.11783	1.11389	1.10999	1.10612	1.10228	1.09848	1.09472	1.09098	1.08728	1.08361	1.07997	47
48	1.15490	1.15061	1.14637	1.14217	1.13800	1.13388	1.12979	1.12574	1.12173	1.11776	1.11382	1.10992	1.10605	1.10222	1.09842	1.09465	1.09092	1.08722	1.08355	1.07991	48
49	1.15483	1.15054	1.14630	1.14210	1.13793	1.13381	1.12972	1.12568	1.12167	1.11769	1.11376	1.10986	1.10599	1.10216	1.09836	1.09459	1.09086	1.08716	1.08349	1.07985	49
50	1.15476	1.15047	1.14623	1.14203	1.13786	1.13374	1.12966	1.12561	1.12160	1.11763	1.11369	1.10979	1.10593	1.10209	1.09829	1.09453	1.09080	1.08709	1.08342	1.07978	50
51"	1.15469	1.15040	1.14616	1.14196	1.13779	1.13367	1.12959	1.12554	1.12153	1.11756	1.11363	1.10973	1.10586	1.10203	1.09823	1.09447	1.09073	1.08703	1.08336	1.07972	51"
52	1.15461	1.15033	1.14609	1.14189	1.13773	1.13360	1.12952	1.12548	1.12147	1.11750	1.11356	1.10966	1.10580	1.10197	1.09817	1.09440	1.09067	1.08697	1.08330	1.07966	52
53	1.15454	1.15026	1.14602	1.14182	1.13766	1.13353	1.12945	1.12541	1.12140	1.11743	1.11350	1.10960	1.10573	1.10190	1.09811	1.09434	1.09061	1.08691	1.08324	1.07960	53
54	1.15447	1.15019	1.14595	1.14175	1.13759	1.13347	1.12938	1.12534	1.12133	1.11736	1.11343	1.10953	1.10567	1.10184	1.09804	1.09428	1.09055	1.08685	1.08318	1.07954	54
55	1.15440	1.15012	1.14588	1.14168	1.13752	1.13340	1.12932	1.12527	1.12127	1.11730	1.11337	1.10947	1.10560	1.10178	1.09798	1.09422	1.09049	1.08679	1.08312	1.07948	55
56"	1.15433	1.15005	1.14581	1.14161	1.13745	1.13333	1.12925	1.12521	1.12120	1.11723	1.11330	1.10940	1.10554	1.10171	1.09792	1.09415	1.09042	1.08673	1.08306	1.07942	56"
57	1.15426	1.14998	1.14574	1.14154	1.13738	1.13326	1.12918	1.12514	1.12114	1.11717	1.11324	1.10934	1.10548	1.10165	1.09785	1.09409	1.09036	1.08666	1.08300	1.07936	57
58	1.15418	1.14990	1.14567	1.14147	1.13731	1.13319	1.12911	1.12507	1.12107	1.11710	1.11317	1.10927	1.10541	1.10158	1.09779	1.09403	1.09030	1.08660	1.08294	1.07930	58
59	1.15411	1.14983	1.14560	1.14140	1.13724	1.13312	1.12905	1.12501	1.12100	1.11704	1.11310	1.10921	1.10535	1.10152	1.09773	1.09397	1.09024	1.08654	1.08288	1.07924	59
60	1.15404	1.14976	1.14553	1.14133	1.13717	1.13306	1.12898	1.12494	1.12094	1.11697	1.11304	1.10914	1.10528	1.10146	1.09766	1.09390	1.09018	1.08648	1.08282	1.07918	60

Table XI House Cusp Interpolation Between Sidereal Times

LOCAL SIDEREAL TIME INCREMENT

CUSP INTVL	0 4	0 8	0 12	0 16	0 20	0 24	0 28	0 32	0 36	0 40	0 44	0 48	0 52	0 56	1 0	1 4	1 8	1 12	1 16	1 20	CUSP INTVL
0 31	1	1	2	2	3	3	4	4	5	5	6	6	7	7	8	8	9	9	10	10	0 31
0 32	1	1	2	2	3	3	4	4	5	5	6	6	7	7	8	9	9	10	10	11	0 32
0 33	1	1	2	2	3	3	4	4	5	5	6	7	7	8	8	9	9	10	10	11	0 33
0 34	1	1	2	2	3	3	4	5	5	6	6	7	7	8	9	9	10	10	11	11	0 34
0 35	1	1	2	2	3	3	4	5	5	6	6	7	8	8	9	9	10	10	11	12	0 35
0 36	1	1	2	2	3	4	4	5	5	6	7	7	8	8	9	10	10	11	11	12	0 36
0 37	1	1	2	2	3	4	4	5	6	6	7	7	8	9	9	10	10	11	12	12	0 37
0 38	1	1	2	3	3	4	4	5	6	6	7	8	8	9	10	10	11	11	12	13	0 38
0 39	1	1	2	3	3	4	5	5	6	6	7	8	8	9	10	10	11	12	13	13	0 39
0 40	1	1	2	3	3	4	5	5	6	7	7	8	9	9	10	11	11	12	13	13	0 40
0 41	1	1	2	3	3	4	5	5	6	7	8	8	9	10	10	11	12	12	13	14	0 41
0 42	1	1	2	3	3	4	5	5	6	7	8	8	9	10	11	11	12	13	13	14	0 42
0 43	1	1	2	3	4	4	5	6	6	7	8	9	9	10	11	11	12	13	14	14	0 43
0 44	1	1	2	3	4	4	5	6	7	7	8	9	9	10	11	11	12	13	14	15	0 44
0 45	1	2	2	3	4	4	5	6	7	7	8	9	10	10	11	12	12	13	14	15	0 45
0 46	1	2	2	3	4	5	5	6	7	8	8	9	10	11	12	12	13	14	15	15	0 46
0 47	1	2	2	3	4	5	5	6	7	8	9	9	10	11	12	13	13	14	15	16	0 47
0 48	1	2	2	3	4	5	6	6	7	8	9	10	10	11	12	13	14	14	15	16	0 48
0 49	1	2	2	3	4	5	6	7	7	8	9	10	11	11	12	13	14	15	16	16	0 49
0 50	1	2	3	3	4	5	6	7	7	8	9	10	11	12	13	13	14	15	16	17	0 50
0 51	1	2	3	3	4	5	6	7	8	8	9	10	11	12	13	14	14	15	16	17	0 51
0 52	1	2	3	4	4	5	6	7	8	9	10	10	11	12	13	14	15	16	16	17	0 52
0 53	1	2	3	4	4	5	6	7	8	9	10	11	11	12	13	14	15	16	17	18	0 53
0 54	1	2	3	4	4	5	6	7	8	9	10	11	12	13	14	14	15	16	17	18	0 54
0 55	1	2	3	4	5	5	6	7	8	9	10	11	12	13	14	15	16	17	17	18	0 55
0 56	1	2	3	4	5	6	7	7	8	9	10	11	12	13	14	15	16	17	18	19	0 56
0 57	1	2	3	4	5	6	7	8	9	9	10	11	12	13	14	15	16	17	18	19	0 57
0 58	1	2	3	4	5	6	7	8	9	10	11	12	13	14	15	15	16	17	18	19	0 58
0 59	1	2	3	4	5	6	7	8	9	10	11	12	13	14	15	16	17	18	19	20	0 59
1 0	1	2	3	4	5	6	7	8	9	10	11	12	13	14	15	16	17	18	19	20	1 0
1 1	1	2	3	4	5	6	7	8	9	10	11	12	13	14	15	16	17	18	19	20	1 1
1 2	1	2	3	4	5	6	7	8	9	10	11	12	13	14	16	17	18	19	20	21	1 2
1 3	1	2	3	4	5	6	7	8	9	10	12	13	14	15	16	17	18	19	20	21	1 3
1 4	1	2	3	4	5	6	7	9	10	11	12	13	14	15	16	17	18	19	20	21	1 4
1 5	1	2	3	4	5	6	8	9	10	11	12	13	14	15	16	17	13	20	21	22	1 5
1 6	1	2	3	4	6	7	8	9	10	11	12	13	14	15	17	18	19	20	21	22	1 6
1 7	1	2	3	4	6	7	8	9	10	11	12	13	15	16	17	18	19	20	21	22	1 7
1 8	1	2	3	5	6	7	8	9	10	11	12	14	15	16	17	18	19	20	22	23	1 8
1 9	1	2	3	5	6	7	8	9	10	11	13	14	15	16	17	18	20	21	22	23	1 9
1 10	1	2	4	5	6	7	8	9	10	12	13	14	15	16	18	19	20	21	22	23	1 10
1 11	1	2	4	5	6	7	8	9	11	12	13	14	15	17	18	19	20	21	22	24	1 11
1 12	1	2	4	5	6	7	8	10	11	12	13	14	16	17	18	19	20	22	23	24	1 12
1 13	1	2	4	5	6	7	9	10	11	12	13	15	16	17	18	19	21	22	23	24	1 13
1 14	1	2	4	5	6	7	9	10	11	12	14	15	16	17	19	20	21	22	23	25	1 14
1 15	1	3	4	5	6	7	9	10	11	12	14	15	16	18	19	20	21	23	24	25	1 15
1 16	1	3	4	5	6	8	9	10	11	13	14	15	16	18	19	20	22	23	24	25	1 16
1 17	1	3	4	5	6	8	9	10	12	13	14	15	17	18	19	21	22	23	24	26	1 17
1 18	1	3	4	5	6	8	9	10	12	13	14	16	17	18	20	21	22	23	25	26	1 18
1 19	1	3	4	5	7	8	9	11	12	13	14	16	17	18	20	21	22	24	25	26	1 19
1 20	1	3	4	5	7	8	9	11	12	13	15	16	17	19	20	21	23	24	25	27	1 20
1 21	1	3	4	5	7	8	9	11	12	13	15	16	18	19	20	22	23	24	26	27	1 21
1 22	1	3	4	5	7	8	10	11	12	14	15	16	18	19	21	22	23	25	26	27	1 22
1 23	1	3	4	6	7	8	10	11	12	14	15	17	18	19	21	22	24	25	26	28	1 23
1 24	1	3	4	6	7	8	10	11	13	14	15	17	18	20	21	22	24	25	27	28	1 24
1 25	1	3	4	6	7	8	10	11	13	14	16	17	18	20	21	23	24	26	27	28	1 25
1 26	1	3	4	6	7	9	10	11	13	14	16	17	19	20	22	23	24	26	27	29	1 26
1 27	1	3	4	6	7	9	10	12	13	14	16	17	19	20	22	23	25	26	28	29	1 27
1 28	1	3	4	6	7	9	10	12	13	15	16	18	19	21	22	23	25	26	28	29	1 28
1 29	1	3	4	6	7	9	10	12	13	15	16	18	19	21	22	24	25	27	28	30	1 29
1 30	2	3	5	6	7	9	10	12	13	15	17	18	20	21	23	24	26	27	29	30	1 30
1 31	2	3	5	6	8	9	11	12	14	15	17	18	20	21	23	24	26	27	29	30	1 31
1 32	2	3	5	6	8	9	11	12	14	15	17	18	20	21	23	25	26	28	29	31	1 32
1 33	2	3	5	6	8	9	11	12	14	15	17	19	20	22	23	25	26	28	29	31	1 33
1 34	2	3	5	6	8	9	11	13	14	16	17	19	20	22	24	25	27	28	30	31	1 34
1 35	2	3	5	6	8	9	11	13	14	16	17	19	21	22	24	25	27	29	30	32	1 35
1 36	2	3	5	6	8	10	11	13	14	16	18	19	21	22	24	26	27	29	30	32	1 36
1 37	2	3	5	6	8	10	11	13	15	16	18	19	21	23	24	26	27	29	31	32	1 37
1 38	2	3	5	7	8	10	11	13	15	16	18	20	21	23	25	26	28	29	31	33	1 38
1 39	2	3	5	7	8	10	12	13	15	17	18	20	21	23	25	26	28	30	31	33	1 39
1 40	2	3	5	7	8	10	12	13	15	17	18	20	22	24	25	27	28	30	32	33	1 40
1 41	2	3	5	7	8	10	12	13	15	17	19	20	22	24	25	27	29	30	32	34	1 41
1 42	2	3	5	7	8	10	12	14	15	17	19	20	22	24	26	27	29	31	32	34	1 42
1 43	2	3	5	7	9	10	12	14	15	17	19	21	22	24	26	27	29	31	33	34	1 43
1 44	2	3	5	7	9	10	12	14	16	17	19	21	23	24	26	28	29	31	33	35	1 44
1 45	2	4	5	7	9	10	12	14	16	18	19	21	23	25	26	28	30	31	33	35	1 45
1 46	2	4	5	7	9	11	12	14	16	18	19	21	23	25	27	28	30	32	34	35	1 46
1 47	2	4	5	7	9	11	12	14	16	18	20	21	23	25	27	29	30	32	34	36	1 47
1 48	2	4	5	7	9	11	13	14	16	18	20	22	23	25	27	29	31	32	34	36	1 48
1 49	2	4	5	7	9	11	13	15	16	18	20	22	24	25	27	29	31	33	35	36	1 49
1 50	2	4	6	7	9	11	13	15	17	18	20	22	24	26	28	29	31	33	35	37	1 50
1 51	2	4	6	7	9	11	13	15	17	19	20	22	24	26	28	30	31	33	35	37	1 51
1 52	2	4	6	7	9	11	13	15	17	19	21	22	24	26	28	30	32	34	35	37	1 52
1 53	2	4	6	8	9	11	13	15	17	19	21	23	24	26	28	30	32	34	36	38	1 53
1 54	2	4	6	8	9	11	13	15	17	19	21	23	25	27	29	30	32	34	36	38	1 54
1 55	2	4	6	8	10	11	13	15	17	19	21	23	25	27	29	31	33	35	36	38	1 55
1 56	2	4	6	8	10	12	14	15	17	19	21	23	25	27	29	31	33	35	37	39	1 56
1 57	2	4	6	8	10	12	14	16	18	20	21	23	25	27	29	31	33	35	37	39	1 57
1 58	2	4	6	8	10	12	14	16	18	20	22	24	26	28	30	31	33	35	37	39	1 58
1 59	2	4	6	8	10	12	14	16	18	20	22	24	26	28	30	32	34	36	38	40	1 59
2 0	2	4	6	8	10	12	14	16	18	20	22	24	26	28	30	32	34	36	38	40	2 0

Table XI House Cusp Interpolation Between Sidereal Times

LOCAL SIDEREAL TIME INCREMENT (m s), values given in ° '

CUSP INTVL	1 24	1 28	1 32	1 36	1 40	1 44	1 48	1 52	1 56	2 0	2 4	2 8	2 12	2 16	2 20	2 24	2 28	2 32	2 36	2 40	CUSP INTVL
0 31	11	11	12	12	13	13	14	14	15	16	16	17	17	18	18	19	19	20	20	21	0 31
0 32	11	12	12	13	13	14	14	15	15	16	17	17	18	18	19	19	20	20	21	22	0 32
0 33	12	12	13	13	14	14	15	15	16	17	17	18	18	19	19	20	20	21	22	23	0 33
0 34	12	12	13	14	14	15	15	16	16	17	18	18	19	19	20	20	21	22	22	23	0 34
0 35	12	13	13	14	15	15	16	16	17	18	18	19	19	20	20	21	22	22	23	23	0 35
0 36	13	13	14	14	15	16	16	17	17	18	19	19	20	20	21	22	22	23	23	24	0 36
0 37	13	14	14	15	15	16	17	17	18	19	19	20	20	21	22	22	23	23	24	25	0 37
0 38	13	14	15	15	16	16	17	18	18	19	20	20	21	21	22	22	23	23	24	25	0 38
0 39	14	14	15	16	16	17	18	18	19	19	20	20	21	22	22	23	23	24	25	26	0 39
0 40	14	15	15	16	17	17	18	18	19	19	20	21	21	22	23	23	24	25	25	27	0 40
0 41	14	15	16	16	17	18	18	19	20	21	21	22	23	23	24	25	25	26	27	27	0 41
0 42	15	15	16	17	18	18	19	20	20	21	22	22	23	24	25	25	26	27	27	28	0 42
0 43	15	16	16	17	18	19	19	20	21	22	22	23	24	24	25	26	27	27	28	29	0 43
0 44	15	16	17	18	18	19	20	21	21	22	22	23	24	25	26	26	27	28	29	29	0 44
0 45	16	17	17	18	19	20	20	21	22	23	23	24	25	26	26	27	28	29	29	30	0 45
0 46	16	17	18	19	19	20	21	21	22	23	24	25	25	26	27	27	28	29	30	31	0 46
0 47	16	17	18	19	20	20	21	22	23	24	24	25	26	27	27	28	29	30	31	31	0 47
0 48	17	18	18	19	20	21	22	22	23	24	25	25	26	26	27	28	29	30	31	32	0 48
0 49	17	18	19	20	20	21	22	22	23	24	25	25	26	27	28	29	30	31	32	33	0 49
0 50	18	18	19	20	21	22	23	23	24	25	26	27	28	28	29	30	31	32	33	33	0 50
0 51	18	19	20	20	21	22	23	24	25	26	26	27	28	29	30	31	31	32	33	34	0 51
0 52	18	19	20	21	22	23	23	24	25	26	27	28	29	29	30	31	32	33	34	35	0 52
0 53	19	19	20	21	22	23	24	25	26	27	27	28	29	30	31	32	33	34	34	35	0 53
0 54	19	20	21	22	23	23	24	25	26	27	28	29	30	31	32	32	33	34	35	36	0 54
0 55	19	20	21	22	23	24	25	26	27	28	28	29	30	31	32	33	34	35	36	37	0 55
0 56	20	21	21	22	23	24	25	26	27	28	29	30	31	32	33	34	35	35	36	37	0 56
0 57	20	21	22	23	24	25	26	27	28	29	29	30	31	32	33	34	35	36	37	38	0 57
0 58	20	21	22	23	24	25	26	27	28	29	30	31	32	33	34	35	36	37	38	39	0 58
0 59	21	22	23	24	25	26	27	28	29	30	30	31	32	33	34	35	36	37	38	39	0 59
1 0	21	22	23	24	25	26	27	28	29	30	31	32	33	34	35	36	37	38	39	40	1 0
1 1	21	22	23	24	25	26	27	28	29	31	32	33	34	35	36	37	38	39	40	41	1 1
1 2	22	23	24	25	26	27	28	29	30	31	32	33	34	35	36	37	38	39	40	41	1 2
1 3	22	23	24	25	26	27	28	29	30	32	33	34	35	36	37	38	39	40	41	42	1 3
1 4	22	23	25	26	27	28	29	30	31	32	33	34	35	36	37	38	39	41	42	43	1 4
1 5	23	24	25	26	27	28	29	30	31	33	34	35	36	37	38	39	40	41	42	43	1 5
1 6	23	24	25	26	28	29	30	31	32	33	34	35	36	37	39	40	41	42	44	45	1 6
1 7	23	25	26	27	28	29	30	31	33	34	35	36	37	38	39	40	41	43	44	45	1 7
1 8	24	25	26	27	28	29	31	32	33	34	35	36	37	39	40	41	42	43	44	46	1 8
1 9	24	25	26	28	29	30	31	32	33	35	36	37	38	39	40	41	43	44	45	46	1 9
1 10	25	26	27	28	29	30	32	33	34	35	36	37	39	40	41	42	43	44	46	47	1 10
1 11	25	26	27	28	30	31	32	33	34	36	37	38	39	40	41	43	44	45	46	47	1 11
1 12	25	26	28	29	30	31	32	34	35	36	37	38	40	41	42	43	44	46	47	48	1 12
1 13	26	27	28	29	30	32	33	34	35	37	38	39	40	41	43	44	45	46	47	49	1 13
1 14	26	27	28	30	31	32	33	35	36	37	38	39	41	42	43	44	46	47	48	49	1 14
1 15	26	28	29	30	31	33	34	35	36	38	39	40	41	43	44	45	46	48	49	50	1 15
1 16	27	28	29	30	32	33	34	35	37	38	39	41	42	43	44	46	47	48	49	51	1 16
1 17	27	28	30	31	32	33	35	36	37	39	40	41	42	44	45	46	47	49	50	51	1 17
1 18	27	29	30	31	33	34	35	36	38	39	40	42	43	44	46	47	48	49	51	52	1 18
1 19	28	29	30	32	33	34	36	37	38	40	41	42	43	45	46	47	49	50	51	53	1 19
1 20	28	29	31	32	33	35	36	37	39	40	41	43	44	45	47	48	49	51	52	53	1 20
1 21	28	30	31	32	34	35	36	38	39	41	42	43	45	46	47	49	50	51	53	54	1 21
1 22	29	30	31	33	34	36	37	38	40	41	42	44	45	46	48	49	51	52	53	55	1 22
1 23	29	30	32	33	35	36	37	39	40	42	43	44	46	47	48	50	51	53	54	55	1 23
1 24	29	31	32	33	35	36	38	39	41	42	43	45	46	48	49	50	52	53	55	56	1 24
1 25	30	31	33	34	35	37	38	40	41	43	44	45	47	48	50	51	52	54	55	57	1 25
1 26	30	32	33	34	36	37	39	40	42	43	44	46	47	49	50	52	53	54	56	57	1 26
1 27	30	32	33	35	36	38	39	41	42	44	45	46	48	49	51	52	54	55	57	58	1 27
1 28	31	32	34	35	37	38	40	41	43	44	45	47	48	50	51	53	54	56	57	59	1 28
1 29	31	33	34	36	37	39	40	42	43	45	46	47	49	50	52	53	55	56	58	59	1 29
1 30	32	33	35	36	38	39	41	42	44	45	47	48	50	51	53	54	56	57	59	1 0	1 30
1 31	32	33	35	36	38	39	41	42	44	46	47	49	50	52	53	55	56	58	59	1 1	1 31
1 32	32	34	35	37	38	40	41	43	44	46	48	49	51	52	54	55	57	58	1 0	1 1	1 32
1 33	33	34	36	37	39	40	42	43	45	47	48	50	51	53	54	56	57	59	1 0	1 2	1 33
1 34	33	34	36	38	39	41	42	44	45	47	49	50	52	53	55	56	58	1 0	1 1	1 3	1 34
1 35	33	35	36	38	40	41	43	44	46	48	49	51	52	54	55	57	59	1 0	1 2	1 3	1 35
1 36	34	35	37	38	40	42	43	45	46	48	50	51	53	54	56	58	59	1 1	1 2	1 4	1 36
1 37	34	36	37	39	40	42	44	45	47	49	50	52	53	55	57	58	1 0	1 1	1 3	1 5	1 37
1 38	34	36	38	39	41	42	44	46	47	49	51	52	54	56	57	59	1 1	1 2	1 4	1 5	1 38
1 39	35	36	38	40	41	43	45	46	48	50	51	53	54	56	58	59	1 1	1 3	1 4	1 6	1 39
1 40	35	37	38	40	42	43	45	47	48	50	52	53	55	57	58	1 0	1 2	1 3	1 5	1 7	1 40
1 41	35	37	39	40	42	44	45	47	49	51	52	54	56	57	59	1 1	1 2	1 4	1 6	1 7	1 41
1 42	36	37	39	41	43	44	46	48	49	51	53	54	56	58	1 0	1 1	1 3	1 5	1 7	1 9	1 42
1 43	36	38	39	41	43	45	46	48	50	52	53	55	57	58	1 0	1 2	1 4	1 5	1 7	1 9	1 43
1 44	36	38	40	42	43	45	47	49	50	52	54	55	57	59	1 1	1 3	1 4	1 6	1 8	1 9	1 44
1 45	37	39	40	42	44	46	47	49	51	53	54	56	58	1 0	1 1	1 3	1 5	1 7	1 8	1 10	1 45
1 46	37	39	41	42	44	46	48	49	51	53	55	57	58	1 0	1 2	1 4	1 5	1 7	1 9	1 11	1 46
1 47	37	39	41	43	45	46	48	50	52	54	55	57	59	1 1	1 3	1 5	1 6	1 8	1 10	1 11	1 47
1 48	38	40	41	43	45	47	49	50	52	54	56	58	1 0	1 1	1 3	1 5	1 7	1 8	1 10	1 12	1 48
1 49	38	40	42	44	45	47	49	51	53	55	56	58	1 0	1 2	1 4	1 6	1 7	1 9	1 11	1 13	1 49
1 50	39	40	42	44	46	48	50	51	53	55	57	59	1 1	1 2	1 4	1 6	1 8	1 10	1 12	1 13	1 50
1 51	39	41	43	44	46	48	50	52	54	56	57	59	1 1	1 3	1 5	1 7	1 8	1 10	1 12	1 14	1 51
1 52	39	41	43	45	47	49	50	52	54	56	58	1 0	1 2	1 3	1 5	1 7	1 9	1 11	1 13	1 15	1 52
1 53	40	41	43	45	47	49	51	53	55	57	58	1 0	1 2	1 4	1 6	1 8	1 10	1 12	1 13	1 15	1 53
1 54	40	42	44	46	48	49	51	53	55	57	59	1 1	1 3	1 5	1 7	1 9	1 10	1 12	1 14	1 16	1 54
1 55	40	42	44	46	48	50	52	54	56	58	59	1 1	1 3	1 5	1 7	1 9	1 11	1 13	1 15	1 17	1 55
1 56	41	43	44	46	48	50	52	54	56	58	1 0	1 2	1 4	1 6	1 8	1 10	1 12	1 13	1 15	1 17	1 56
1 57	41	43	45	47	49	51	53	55	57	59	1 0	1 2	1 4	1 6	1 8	1 10	1 12	1 14	1 16	1 18	1 57
1 58	41	43	45	47	49	51	53	55	57	59	1 1	1 3	1 5	1 7	1 9	1 11	1 13	1 15	1 17	1 19	1 58
1 59	42	44	46	48	50	52	54	56	58	1 0	1 1	1 3	1 5	1 7	1 9	1 11	1 13	1 15	1 17	1 19	1 59
2 0	42	44	46	48	50	52	54	56	58	1 0	1 2	1 4	1 6	1 8	1 10	1 12	1 14	1 16	1 18	1 20	2 0

Table XI House Cusp Interpolation Between Sidereal Times

	LOCAL SIDEREAL TIME INCREMENT																				
CUSP INTVL	m s 2 44	m s 2 48	m s 2 52	m s 2 56	m s 3 0	m s 3 4	m s 3 8	m s 3 12	m s 3 16	m s 3 20	m s 3 24	m s 3 28	m s 3 32	m s 3 36	m s 3 40	m s 3 44	m s 3 48	m s 3 52	m s 3 56	m s 4 0	CUSP INTVL
° '	° '	° '	° '	° '	° '	° '	° '	° '	° '	° '	° '	° '	° '	° '	° '	° '	° '	° '	° '	° '	° '
0 31	21	22	22	23	23	24	24	25	25	26	26	27	27	28	28	29	29	30	30	31	0 31
0 32	22	22	23	23	24	25	25	26	26	27	27	28	28	29	29	30	30	31	31	32	0 32
0 33	23	23	24	24	25	25	26	26	27	28	28	29	29	30	30	31	31	32	32	33	0 33
0 34	23	24	24	25	26	26	27	27	28	28	29	29	30	31	31	32	32	33	33	34	0 34
0 35	24	25	25	26	26	27	27	28	29	29	30	30	31	32	32	33	33	34	34	35	0 35
0 36	25	25	26	26	27	28	28	29	29	30	31	31	32	32	33	34	34	35	35	36	0 36
0 37	25	26	27	27	28	28	29	30	30	31	31	32	33	33	34	35	35	36	36	37	0 37
0 38	26	27	27	28	29	29	30	30	31	32	32	33	34	34	35	35	36	37	37	38	0 38
0 39	27	27	28	29	29	30	31	31	32	33	33	34	34	35	36	36	37	38	38	39	0 39
0 40	27	28	29	29	30	31	31	32	33	33	34	35	35	36	37	37	38	39	39	40	0 40
0 41	28	29	29	30	31	31	32	33	33	34	35	36	36	37	38	38	39	40	40	41	0 41
0 42	29	29	30	31	32	32	33	34	34	35	36	36	37	38	39	39	40	41	41	42	0 42
0 43	29	30	31	32	32	33	34	34	35	36	37	37	38	39	39	40	41	42	42	43	0 43
0 44	30	31	32	32	33	34	34	35	36	37	37	38	39	40	40	41	42	43	43	44	0 44
0 45	31	32	32	33	34	35	35	36	37	38	38	39	40	41	41	42	43	44	44	45	0 45
0 46	31	32	33	34	35	35	36	37	38	38	39	40	41	41	42	43	44	44	45	46	0 46
0 47	32	33	34	34	35	36	37	38	38	39	40	41	42	42	43	44	45	45	46	47	0 47
0 48	33	34	34	35	36	37	38	38	39	40	41	42	42	43	44	45	46	46	47	48	0 48
0 49	33	34	35	36	37	38	38	39	40	41	42	42	43	44	45	46	47	47	48	49	0 49
0 50	34	35	36	37	38	38	39	40	41	42	43	43	44	45	46	47	48	48	49	50	0 50
0 51	35	36	37	37	38	39	40	41	42	43	43	44	45	46	47	48	48	49	50	51	0 51
0 52	36	36	37	38	39	40	41	42	42	43	44	45	46	47	48	49	49	50	51	52	0 52
0 53	36	37	38	39	40	41	42	42	43	44	45	46	47	48	49	49	50	51	52	53	0 53
0 54	37	38	39	40	41	41	42	43	44	45	46	47	48	49	50	50	51	52	53	54	0 54
0 55	38	39	39	40	41	42	43	44	45	46	47	48	49	50	50	51	52	53	54	55	0 55
0 56	38	39	40	41	42	43	44	45	46	47	48	49	49	50	51	52	53	54	55	56	0 56
0 57	39	40	41	42	43	44	45	46	47	48	48	49	50	51	52	53	54	55	56	57	0 57
0 58	40	41	42	43	44	44	45	46	47	48	49	50	51	52	53	54	55	56	57	58	0 58
0 59	40	41	42	43	44	45	46	47	48	49	50	51	52	53	54	55	56	57	58	59	0 59
1 0	41	42	43	44	45	46	47	48	49	50	51	52	53	54	55	56	57	58	59	1 0	1 0
1 1	42	43	44	45	46	47	48	49	50	51	52	53	54	55	56	57	58	59	1 0	1 1	1 1
1 2	42	43	44	45	47	48	49	50	51	52	53	54	55	56	57	58	59	1 0	1 1	1 2	1 2
1 3	43	44	45	46	47	48	49	50	51	53	54	55	56	57	58	59	1 0	1 1	1 2	1 3	1 3
1 4	44	45	46	47	48	49	50	51	52	53	54	55	57	58	59	1 0	1 1	1 2	1 3	1 4	1 4
1 5	44	46	47	48	49	50	51	52	53	54	55	56	57	59	1 0	1 1	1 2	1 3	1 4	1 5	1 5
1 6	45	46	47	48	50	51	52	53	54	55	56	57	58	59	1 1	1 2	1 3	1 4	1 5	1 6	1 6
1 7	46	47	48	49	50	51	52	54	55	56	57	58	59	1 0	1 1	1 3	1 4	1 5	1 6	1 7	1 7
1 8	46	48	49	50	51	52	53	54	56	57	58	59	1 0	1 1	1 2	1 3	1 5	1 6	1 7	1 8	1 8
1 9	47	48	49	51	52	53	54	55	56	58	59	1 0	1 1	1 2	1 3	1 4	1 6	1 7	1 8	1 9	1 9
1 10	48	49	50	51	53	54	55	56	57	58	1 0	1 1	1 2	1 3	1 4	1 5	1 7	1 8	1 9	1 10	1 10
1 11	49	50	51	52	53	54	56	57	58	59	1 0	1 2	1 3	1 4	1 5	1 6	1 7	1 9	1 10	1 11	1 11
1 12	49	50	52	53	54	55	56	58	59	1 0	1 1	1 2	1 4	1 5	1 6	1 7	1 8	1 10	1 11	1 12	1 12
1 13	50	51	52	54	55	56	57	58	1 0	1 1	1 2	1 3	1 4	1 6	1 7	1 8	1 9	1 11	1 12	1 13	1 13
1 14	51	52	53	54	56	57	58	59	1 0	1 2	1 3	1 4	1 5	1 7	1 8	1 9	1 10	1 12	1 13	1 14	1 14
1 15	51	53	54	55	56	58	59	1 0	1 1	1 3	1 4	1 5	1 6	1 8	1 9	1 10	1 11	1 13	1 14	1 15	1 15
1 16	52	53	54	56	57	58	1 0	1 1	1 2	1 3	1 5	1 6	1 7	1 8	1 10	1 11	1 12	1 13	1 15	1 16	1 16
1 17	53	54	55	56	58	59	1 0	1 2	1 3	1 4	1 5	1 7	1 8	1 9	1 11	1 12	1 13	1 14	1 16	1 17	1 17
1 18	53	55	56	57	59	1 0	1 1	1 2	1 4	1 5	1 6	1 8	1 9	1 10	1 12	1 13	1 14	1 15	1 17	1 18	1 18
1 19	54	55	57	58	59	1 1	1 2	1 3	1 5	1 6	1 7	1 8	1 10	1 11	1 12	1 14	1 15	1 16	1 18	1 19	1 19
1 20	55	56	57	59	1 0	1 1	1 3	1 4	1 5	1 7	1 8	1 9	1 11	1 12	1 13	1 15	1 16	1 17	1 19	1 20	1 20
1 21	55	57	58	59	1 1	1 2	1 3	1 5	1 6	1 8	1 9	1 10	1 12	1 13	1 14	1 16	1 17	1 18	1 20	1 21	1 21
1 22	56	57	59	1 0	1 2	1 3	1 4	1 6	1 7	1 8	1 10	1 11	1 12	1 14	1 15	1 17	1 18	1 19	1 21	1 22	1 22
1 23	57	58	59	1 1	1 2	1 4	1 5	1 6	1 8	1 9	1 11	1 12	1 13	1 15	1 16	1 17	1 19	1 20	1 22	1 23	1 23
1 24	57	59	1 0	1 2	1 3	1 4	1 6	1 7	1 9	1 10	1 11	1 13	1 14	1 16	1 17	1 18	1 20	1 21	1 23	1 24	1 24
1 25	58	1 0	1 1	1 2	1 4	1 5	1 7	1 8	1 9	1 11	1 12	1 14	1 15	1 17	1 18	1 19	1 21	1 22	1 24	1 25	1 25
1 26	59	1 0	1 2	1 3	1 5	1 6	1 7	1 9	1 10	1 12	1 13	1 15	1 16	1 17	1 19	1 20	1 22	1 23	1 25	1 26	1 26
1 27	59	1 1	1 2	1 4	1 5	1 7	1 8	1 10	1 11	1 13	1 14	1 15	1 17	1 18	1 20	1 21	1 23	1 24	1 26	1 27	1 27
1 28	1 0	1 2	1 3	1 5	1 6	1 7	1 9	1 10	1 12	1 13	1 15	1 16	1 18	1 19	1 21	1 22	1 24	1 25	1 27	1 28	1 28
1 29	1 1	1 2	1 4	1 5	1 7	1 8	1 10	1 11	1 13	1 14	1 16	1 17	1 19	1 20	1 22	1 23	1 25	1 26	1 28	1 29	1 29
1 30	1 2	1 3	1 5	1 6	1 8	1 9	1 11	1 12	1 14	1 15	1 17	1 18	1 20	1 21	1 23	1 24	1 26	1 27	1 29	1 30	1 30
1 31	1 2	1 4	1 5	1 7	1 8	1 10	1 11	1 13	1 14	1 16	1 17	1 19	1 20	1 22	1 23	1 25	1 26	1 28	1 29	1 31	1 31
1 32	1 3	1 4	1 6	1 7	1 9	1 11	1 12	1 14	1 15	1 17	1 18	1 20	1 21	1 23	1 24	1 26	1 27	1 29	1 30	1 32	1 32
1 33	1 4	1 5	1 7	1 8	1 10	1 11	1 13	1 14	1 16	1 18	1 19	1 21	1 22	1 24	1 25	1 27	1 28	1 30	1 31	1 33	1 33
1 34	1 4	1 6	1 7	1 9	1 11	1 12	1 14	1 15	1 17	1 18	1 20	1 21	1 23	1 25	1 26	1 28	1 29	1 31	1 32	1 34	1 34
1 35	1 5	1 7	1 8	1 10	1 11	1 13	1 14	1 16	1 18	1 19	1 21	1 22	1 24	1 26	1 27	1 29	1 30	1 32	1 33	1 35	1 35
1 36	1 6	1 7	1 9	1 10	1 12	1 14	1 15	1 17	1 18	1 20	1 22	1 23	1 25	1 26	1 28	1 30	1 31	1 33	1 34	1 36	1 36
1 37	1 6	1 8	1 10	1 11	1 13	1 14	1 16	1 18	1 19	1 21	1 22	1 24	1 26	1 27	1 29	1 31	1 32	1 34	1 35	1 37	1 37
1 38	1 7	1 9	1 10	1 12	1 14	1 15	1 17	1 18	1 20	1 22	1 23	1 25	1 27	1 28	1 30	1 31	1 33	1 35	1 36	1 38	1 38
1 39	1 8	1 9	1 11	1 13	1 14	1 16	1 18	1 19	1 21	1 23	1 24	1 26	1 27	1 29	1 31	1 32	1 34	1 36	1 37	1 39	1 39
1 40	1 8	1 10	1 12	1 13	1 15	1 17	1 18	1 20	1 22	1 23	1 25	1 27	1 28	1 30	1 32	1 33	1 35	1 37	1 38	1 40	1 40
1 41	1 9	1 11	1 12	1 14	1 16	1 17	1 19	1 21	1 22	1 24	1 26	1 28	1 29	1 31	1 33	1 34	1 36	1 38	1 39	1 41	1 41
1 42	1 10	1 11	1 13	1 15	1 17	1 18	1 20	1 22	1 23	1 25	1 27	1 28	1 30	1 32	1 34	1 35	1 37	1 39	1 40	1 42	1 42
1 43	1 10	1 12	1 14	1 16	1 17	1 19	1 21	1 22	1 24	1 26	1 28	1 29	1 31	1 33	1 34	1 36	1 38	1 40	1 41	1 43	1 43
1 44	1 11	1 13	1 15	1 16	1 18	1 20	1 21	1 23	1 25	1 27	1 28	1 30	1 32	1 34	1 35	1 37	1 39	1 41	1 42	1 44	1 44
1 45	1 12	1 14	1 15	1 17	1 19	1 21	1 22	1 24	1 26	1 28	1 29	1 31	1 33	1 35	1 36	1 38	1 40	1 42	1 43	1 45	1 45
1 46	1 12	1 14	1 16	1 18	1 20	1 21	1 23	1 25	1 27	1 28	1 30	1 32	1 34	1 35	1 37	1 39	1 41	1 42	1 44	1 46	1 46
1 47	1 13	1 15	1 17	1 18	1 20	1 22	1 24	1 26	1 27	1 29	1 31	1 33	1 35	1 36	1 38	1 40	1 42	1 43	1 45	1 47	1 47
1 48	1 14	1 16	1 17	1 19	1 21	1 23	1 25	1 26	1 28	1 30	1 32	1 34	1 35	1 37	1 39	1 41	1 43	1 44	1 46	1 48	1 48
1 49	1 14	1 16	1 18	1 20	1 22	1 24	1 25	1 27	1 29	1 31	1 33	1 34	1 36	1 38	1 40	1 42	1 44	1 45	1 47	1 49	1 49
1 50	1 15	1 17	1 19	1 21	1 23	1 24	1 26	1 28	1 30	1 32	1 34	1 35	1 37	1 39	1 41	1 43	1 45	1 46	1 48	1 50	1 50
1 51	1 16	1 18	1 20	1 21	1 23	1 25	1 27	1 29	1 31	1 33	1 34	1 36	1 38	1 40	1 42	1 44	1 45	1 47	1 49	1 51	1 51
1 52	1 17	1 18	1 20	1 22	1 24	1 26	1 28	1 30	1 31	1 33	1 35	1 37	1 39	1 41	1 43	1 45	1 46	1 48	1 50	1 52	1 52
1 53	1 17	1 19	1 21	1 23	1 25	1 27	1 29	1 30	1 32	1 34	1 36	1 38	1 40	1 42	1 44	1 45	1 47	1 49	1 51	1 53	1 53
1 54	1 18	1 20	1 22	1 24	1 26	1 27	1 29	1 31	1 33	1 35	1 37	1 39	1 41	1 43	1 45	1 46	1 48	1 50	1 52	1 54	1 54
1 55	1 19	1 21	1 22	1 24	1 26	1 28	1 30	1 32	1 34	1 36	1 38	1 40	1 42	1 44	1 45	1 47	1 49	1 51	1 53	1 55	1 55
1 56	1 19	1 21	1 23	1 25	1 27	1 29	1 31	1 33	1 35	1 37	1 39	1 41	1 42	1 44	1 46	1 48	1 50	1 52	1 54	1 56	1 56
1 57	1 20	1 22	1 24	1 26	1 28	1 30	1 32	1 34	1 36	1 38	1 39	1 41	1 43	1 45	1 47	1 49	1 51	1 53	1 55	1 57	1 57
1 58	1 21	1 23	1 25	1 27	1 29	1 30	1 32	1 34	1 36	1 38	1 40	1 42	1 44	1 46	1 48	1 50	1 52	1 54	1 56	1 58	1 58
1 59	1 21	1 23	1 25	1 27	1 29	1 31	1 33	1 35	1 37	1 39	1 41	1 43	1 45	1 47	1 49	1 51	1 53	1 55	1 57	1 59	1 59
2 0	1 22	1 24	1 26	1 28	1 30	1 32	1 34	1 36	1 38	1 40	1 42	1 44	1 46	1 48	1 50	1 52	1 54	1 56	1 58	2 0	2 0

Table XII House Cusp Interpolation Between Latitudes

LAT INCR	1	2	3	4	5	6	7	8	9	10	11	12	13	14	15	16	17	18	19	20	21	22	23	24	25	26	27	28	29	30	LAT INCR
															HOUSE CUSP INTERVAL																
1	0	0	0	0	0	0	0	0	0	0	0	0	0	0	0	0	0	0	0	0	0	0	0	0	0	0	0	0	0	1	1
2	0	0	0	0	0	0	0	0	0	0	0	0	0	0	1	1	1	1	1	1	1	1	1	1	1	1	1	1	1	1	2
3	0	0	0	0	0	0	0	0	0	1	1	1	1	1	1	1	1	1	1	1	1	1	1	1	1	1	1	1	1	2	3
4	0	0	0	0	0	0	0	1	1	1	1	1	1	1	1	1	1	1	1	1	1	1	2	2	2	2	2	2	2	2	4
5	0	0	0	0	0	1	1	1	1	1	1	1	1	1	1	1	1	2	2	2	2	2	2	2	2	2	2	2	2	3	5
6	0	0	0	0	1	1	1	1	1	1	1	1	1	1	2	2	2	2	2	2	2	2	2	2	3	3	3	3	3	3	6
7	0	0	0	0	1	1	1	1	1	1	1	1	2	2	2	2	2	2	2	2	2	3	3	3	3	3	3	3	3	4	7
8	0	0	0	1	1	1	1	1	1	1	1	2	2	2	2	2	2	2	3	3	3	3	3	3	3	3	4	4	4	4	8
9	0	0	0	1	1	1	1	1	1	2	2	2	2	2	2	2	3	3	3	3	3	3	3	4	4	4	4	4	4	5	9
10	0	0	1	1	1	1	1	1	2	2	2	2	2	2	3	3	3	3	3	3	4	4	4	4	4	4	5	5	5	5	10
11	0	0	1	1	1	1	1	1	2	2	2	2	2	3	3	3	3	3	3	4	4	4	4	4	5	5	5	5	5	6	11
12	0	0	1	1	1	1	1	2	2	2	2	2	3	3	3	3	3	4	4	4	4	4	5	5	5	5	5	6	6	6	12
13	0	0	1	1	1	1	2	2	2	2	2	3	3	3	3	3	4	4	4	4	5	5	5	5	5	6	6	6	6	7	13
14	0	0	1	1	1	1	2	2	2	2	3	3	3	3	4	4	4	4	4	5	5	5	5	6	6	6	6	7	7	7	14
15	0	1	1	1	1	2	2	2	2	3	3	3	3	4	4	4	4	5	5	5	5	6	6	6	6	7	7	7	7	8	15
16	0	1	1	1	1	2	2	2	2	3	3	3	3	4	4	4	5	5	5	5	6	6	6	6	7	7	7	7	8	8	16
17	0	1	1	1	1	2	2	2	3	3	3	3	4	4	4	5	5	5	5	6	6	6	7	7	7	7	8	8	8	9	17
18	0	1	1	1	2	2	2	2	3	3	3	4	4	4	5	5	5	5	6	6	6	7	7	7	8	8	8	8	9	9	18
19	0	1	1	1	2	2	2	3	3	3	3	4	4	4	5	5	5	6	6	6	7	7	7	8	8	8	9	9	9	10	19
20	0	1	1	1	2	2	2	3	3	3	4	4	4	5	5	5	6	6	6	7	7	7	8	8	8	9	9	9	10	10	20
21	0	1	1	1	2	2	2	3	3	4	4	4	5	5	5	6	6	6	7	7	7	8	8	8	9	9	9	10	10	11	21
22	0	1	1	1	2	2	3	3	3	4	4	4	5	5	6	6	6	7	7	7	8	8	8	9	9	10	10	10	11	11	22
23	0	1	1	2	2	2	3	3	3	4	4	5	5	5	6	6	7	7	7	8	8	8	9	9	10	10	10	11	11	12	23
24	0	1	1	2	2	2	3	3	4	4	4	5	5	6	6	6	7	7	8	8	8	9	9	10	10	10	11	11	12	12	24
25	0	1	1	2	2	3	3	3	4	4	5	5	5	6	6	7	7	8	8	8	9	9	10	10	10	11	11	12	12	13	25
26	0	1	1	2	2	3	3	3	4	4	5	5	6	6	7	7	7	8	8	9	9	10	10	10	11	11	12	12	13	13	26
27	0	1	1	2	2	3	3	4	4	5	5	5	6	6	7	7	8	8	9	9	9	10	10	11	11	12	12	13	13	14	27
28	0	1	1	2	2	3	3	4	4	5	5	6	6	7	7	7	8	8	9	9	10	10	11	11	12	12	13	13	14	14	28
29	0	1	1	2	2	3	3	4	4	5	5	6	6	7	7	8	8	9	9	10	10	11	11	12	12	13	13	14	14	15	29
30	1	1	2	2	3	3	4	4	5	5	6	6	7	7	8	8	9	9	10	10	11	11	12	12	13	13	14	14	15	15	30
31	1	1	2	2	3	3	4	4	5	5	6	6	7	7	8	8	9	9	10	10	11	11	12	12	13	13	14	14	15	16	31
32	1	1	2	2	3	3	4	4	5	5	6	6	7	7	8	9	9	10	10	11	11	12	12	13	13	14	14	15	15	16	32
33	1	1	2	2	3	3	4	4	5	6	6	7	7	8	8	9	9	10	10	11	12	12	13	13	14	14	15	15	16	16	33
34	1	1	2	2	3	3	4	5	5	6	6	7	7	8	9	9	10	10	11	11	12	12	13	14	14	15	15	16	16	17	34
35	1	1	2	2	3	4	4	5	5	6	6	7	8	8	9	9	10	11	11	12	12	13	13	14	15	15	16	16	17	17	35
36	1	1	2	2	3	4	4	5	5	6	7	7	8	8	9	10	10	11	11	12	13	13	14	14	15	16	16	17	17	18	36
37	1	1	2	2	3	4	4	5	6	6	7	7	8	9	9	10	10	11	12	12	13	14	14	15	15	16	17	17	18	19	37
38	1	1	2	3	3	4	4	5	6	6	7	8	8	9	10	10	11	11	12	13	13	14	15	15	16	16	17	18	18	19	38
39	1	1	2	3	3	4	5	5	6	7	7	8	8	9	10	10	11	12	12	13	14	14	15	16	16	17	18	18	19	20	39
40	1	1	2	3	3	4	5	5	6	7	7	8	9	9	10	11	11	12	13	13	14	15	15	16	17	17	18	19	19	20	40
41	1	1	2	3	3	4	5	5	6	7	8	8	9	10	10	11	12	12	13	14	14	15	16	16	17	18	18	19	20	21	41
42	1	1	2	3	4	4	5	6	6	7	8	8	9	10	11	11	12	13	13	14	15	15	16	17	18	18	19	20	20	21	42
43	1	1	2	3	4	4	5	6	6	7	8	9	9	10	11	11	12	13	14	14	15	16	16	17	18	19	19	20	21	22	43
44	1	1	2	3	4	4	5	6	7	7	8	9	10	10	11	12	12	13	14	15	15	16	17	18	18	19	20	21	21	22	44
45	1	2	2	3	4	5	5	6	7	8	8	9	10	11	11	12	13	14	14	15	16	17	17	18	19	20	20	21	22	23	45
46	1	2	2	3	4	5	5	6	7	8	8	9	10	11	12	12	13	14	15	15	16	17	18	18	19	20	21	21	22	23	46
47	1	2	2	3	4	5	5	6	7	8	9	9	10	11	12	13	13	14	15	16	16	17	18	19	20	20	21	22	23	24	47
48	1	2	2	3	4	5	6	6	7	8	9	10	10	11	12	13	14	14	15	16	17	18	18	19	20	21	22	22	23	24	48
49	1	2	2	3	4	5	6	7	7	8	9	10	11	11	12	13	14	15	16	16	17	18	19	20	20	21	22	23	24	25	49
50	1	2	3	3	4	5	6	7	8	8	9	10	11	12	13	13	14	15	16	17	18	18	19	20	21	22	23	23	24	25	50
51	1	2	3	3	4	5	6	7	8	9	9	10	11	12	13	14	14	15	16	17	18	19	20	20	21	22	23	24	25	26	51
52	1	2	3	3	4	5	6	7	8	9	10	10	11	12	13	14	15	16	16	17	18	19	20	21	22	23	23	24	25	26	52
53	1	2	3	4	4	5	6	7	8	9	10	11	11	12	13	14	15	16	17	18	19	19	20	21	22	23	24	25	26	27	53
54	1	2	3	4	5	5	6	7	8	9	10	11	12	13	14	14	15	16	17	18	19	20	21	22	23	23	24	25	26	27	54
55	1	2	3	4	5	6	6	7	8	9	10	11	12	13	14	15	16	17	17	18	19	20	21	22	23	24	25	26	27	28	55
56	1	2	3	4	5	6	7	7	8	9	10	11	12	13	14	15	16	17	18	19	20	21	21	22	23	24	25	26	27	28	56
57	1	2	3	4	5	6	7	8	9	10	10	11	12	13	14	15	16	17	18	19	20	21	22	23	24	25	26	27	28	29	57
58	1	2	3	4	5	6	7	8	9	10	11	12	13	14	15	15	16	17	18	19	20	21	22	23	24	25	26	27	28	29	58
59	1	2	3	4	5	6	7	8	9	10	11	12	13	14	15	16	17	18	19	20	21	22	23	24	25	26	27	28	29	30	59

Table XII House Cusp Interpolation Between Latitudes

LAT INCR	HOUSE CUSP INTERVAL																														LAT INCR
	31′	32′	33′	34′	35′	36′	37′	38′	39′	40′	41′	42′	43′	44′	45′	46′	47′	48′	49′	50′	51′	52′	53′	54′	55′	56′	57′	58′	59′	60′	
1	1	1	1	1	1	1	1	1	1	1	1	1	1	1	1	1	1	1	1	1	1	1	1	1	1	1	1	1	1	1	1
2	1	1	1	1	1	1	1	1	1	1	1	1	1	1	2	2	2	2	2	2	2	2	2	2	2	2	2	2	2	2	2
3	2	2	2	2	2	2	2	2	2	2	2	2	2	2	2	2	2	2	2	3	3	3	3	3	3	3	3	3	3	3	3
4	2	2	2	2	2	2	2	3	3	3	3	3	3	3	3	3	3	3	3	3	3	3	4	4	4	4	4	4	4	4	4
5	3	3	3	3	3	3	3	3	3	3	3	4	4	4	4	4	4	4	4	4	4	4	4	5	5	5	5	5	5	5	5
6	3	3	3	3	4	4	4	4	4	4	4	4	4	4	5	5	5	5	5	5	5	5	5	5	6	6	6	6	6	6	6
7	4	4	4	4	4	4	4	4	5	5	5	5	5	5	5	5	5	6	6	6	6	6	6	6	6	7	7	7	7	7	7
8	4	4	4	5	5	5	5	5	5	5	5	6	6	6	6	6	6	6	7	7	7	7	7	7	7	7	8	8	8	8	8
9	5	5	5	5	5	5	6	6	6	6	6	6	6	7	7	7	7	7	7	8	8	8	8	8	8	8	9	9	9	9	9
10	5	5	6	6	6	6	6	6	7	7	7	7	7	7	8	8	8	8	8	8	9	9	9	9	9	9	10	10	10	10	10
11	6	6	6	6	6	7	7	7	7	7	8	8	8	8	8	8	9	9	9	9	9	10	10	10	10	10	10	11	11	11	11
12	6	6	7	7	7	7	7	8	8	8	8	8	9	9	9	9	9	10	10	10	10	10	11	11	11	11	11	12	12	12	12
13	7	7	7	7	8	8	8	8	8	9	9	9	9	10	10	10	10	10	11	11	11	11	11	12	12	12	12	13	13	13	13
14	7	7	8	8	8	8	9	9	9	9	10	10	10	10	11	11	11	11	11	12	12	12	12	13	13	13	13	14	14	14	14
15	8	8	8	9	9	9	9	10	10	10	10	11	11	11	11	12	12	12	12	13	13	13	13	14	14	14	14	15	15	15	15
16	8	9	9	9	9	10	10	10	10	11	11	11	11	12	12	12	13	13	13	13	14	14	14	14	15	15	15	15	16	16	16
17	9	9	9	10	10	10	10	11	11	11	12	12	12	12	13	13	13	14	14	14	14	15	15	15	16	16	16	16	17	17	17
18	9	10	10	10	11	11	11	11	12	12	12	13	13	13	14	14	14	15	15	15	16	16	16	16	17	17	17	17	18	18	18
19	10	10	10	11	11	11	12	12	12	13	13	13	14	14	14	15	15	15	16	16	16	16	17	17	17	18	18	18	19	19	19
20	10	11	11	11	12	12	12	13	13	13	14	14	14	15	15	15	16	16	16	17	17	17	18	18	18	19	19	19	20	20	20
21	11	11	12	12	12	13	13	13	14	14	14	15	15	15	16	16	16	17	17	18	18	18	19	19	19	20	20	20	21	21	21
22	11	12	12	12	13	13	14	14	14	15	15	15	16	16	17	17	17	18	18	18	19	19	19	20	20	21	21	21	22	22	22
23	12	12	13	13	13	14	14	15	15	15	16	16	16	17	17	18	18	18	19	19	20	20	20	21	21	21	22	22	23	23	23
24	12	13	13	14	14	14	15	15	16	16	16	17	17	18	18	18	19	19	20	20	20	21	21	22	22	22	23	23	24	24	24
25	13	13	14	14	15	15	15	16	16	17	17	18	18	18	19	19	20	20	20	21	21	22	22	23	23	23	24	24	25	25	25
26	13	14	14	15	15	16	16	16	17	17	18	18	19	19	20	20	20	21	21	22	22	23	23	23	24	24	25	25	26	26	26
27	14	14	15	15	16	16	17	17	18	18	19	19	20	20	21	21	22	22	23	23	23	24	24	25	25	26	26	27	27	27	27
28	14	15	15	16	16	17	17	18	18	19	19	20	20	21	21	21	22	22	23	23	24	24	25	25	26	26	27	27	28	28	28
29	15	15	16	16	17	17	18	18	19	19	20	20	21	21	22	22	23	23	24	24	25	25	26	26	27	27	28	28	29	29	29
30	16	16	17	17	18	18	19	19	20	20	21	21	22	22	23	23	24	24	25	25	26	26	27	27	28	28	29	29	30	30	30
31	16	17	17	18	18	19	19	20	20	21	21	22	22	23	23	24	24	25	25	26	26	27	27	28	28	29	29	30	30	31	31
32	17	17	18	18	19	19	20	20	21	21	22	22	23	23	24	25	25	26	26	27	27	28	28	29	29	30	30	31	31	32	32
33	17	18	18	19	19	20	20	21	21	22	23	23	24	24	25	25	26	26	27	28	28	29	29	30	30	31	31	32	32	33	33
34	18	18	19	19	20	20	21	22	22	23	23	24	24	25	26	26	27	27	28	28	29	29	30	31	31	32	32	33	33	34	34
35	18	19	19	20	20	21	22	22	23	23	24	25	25	26	26	27	27	28	29	29	30	30	31	32	32	33	33	34	34	35	35
36	19	19	20	20	21	22	22	23	23	24	25	25	26	26	27	28	28	29	29	30	31	31	32	32	33	34	34	35	35	36	36
37	19	20	20	21	22	22	23	23	24	25	25	26	27	27	28	28	29	30	30	31	31	32	33	33	34	35	35	36	36	37	37
38	20	20	21	22	22	23	23	24	25	25	26	27	27	28	29	29	30	30	31	32	32	33	34	34	35	35	36	37	37	38	38
39	20	21	21	22	23	23	24	25	25	26	27	27	28	29	29	30	31	31	32	33	33	34	34	35	36	36	37	38	38	39	39
40	21	21	22	23	23	24	25	25	26	27	27	28	29	29	30	31	31	32	33	33	34	35	35	36	37	37	38	39	39	40	40
41	21	22	23	23	24	25	25	26	27	27	28	29	29	30	31	31	32	33	33	34	35	36	36	37	38	38	39	40	40	41	41
42	22	22	23	24	25	25	26	27	27	28	29	29	30	31	32	32	33	34	34	35	36	36	37	38	39	39	40	41	41	42	42
43	22	23	24	24	25	26	27	27	28	29	29	30	31	32	32	33	34	34	35	36	37	37	38	39	39	40	41	42	42	43	43
44	23	23	24	25	26	26	27	28	29	29	30	31	32	32	33	34	34	35	36	37	37	38	39	40	40	41	42	43	43	44	44
45	23	24	25	26	26	27	28	29	29	30	31	32	32	33	34	35	35	36	37	38	38	39	40	41	41	42	43	44	44	45	45
46	24	25	25	26	27	28	28	29	30	31	31	32	33	34	35	35	36	37	38	38	39	40	41	41	42	43	44	44	45	46	46
47	24	25	26	27	27	28	29	30	31	31	32	33	34	34	35	36	37	38	38	39	40	41	42	42	43	44	45	45	46	47	47
48	25	26	26	27	28	29	30	30	31	32	33	34	34	35	36	37	38	38	39	40	41	42	42	43	44	45	46	46	47	48	48
49	25	26	27	28	29	29	30	31	32	33	33	34	35	36	37	38	38	39	40	41	42	42	43	44	45	46	47	47	48	49	49
50	26	27	28	28	29	30	31	32	33	33	34	35	36	37	38	38	39	40	41	42	43	43	44	45	46	47	48	48	49	50	50
51	26	27	28	29	30	31	31	32	33	34	35	36	37	37	38	39	40	41	42	43	43	44	45	46	47	48	48	49	50	51	51
52	27	28	29	29	30	31	32	33	34	35	36	36	37	38	39	40	41	42	42	43	44	45	46	47	48	49	49	50	51	52	52
53	27	28	29	30	31	32	33	34	34	35	36	37	38	39	40	41	42	42	43	44	45	46	47	48	49	49	50	51	52	53	53
54	28	29	30	31	32	32	33	34	35	36	37	38	39	40	41	41	42	43	44	45	46	47	48	49	50	50	51	52	53	54	54
55	28	29	30	31	32	33	34	35	36	37	38	39	39	40	41	42	43	44	45	46	47	48	49	50	50	51	52	53	54	55	55
56	29	30	31	32	33	34	35	35	36	37	38	39	40	41	42	43	44	45	46	47	48	49	49	50	51	52	53	54	55	56	56
57	29	30	31	32	33	34	35	36	37	38	39	40	41	42	43	44	45	46	47	48	48	49	50	51	52	53	54	55	56	57	57
58	30	31	32	33	34	35	36	37	38	39	40	41	42	43	44	44	45	46	47	48	49	50	51	52	53	54	55	56	57	58	58
59	30	31	32	33	34	35	36	37	38	39	40	41	42	43	44	45	46	47	48	49	50	51	52	53	54	55	56	57	58	59	59

Table XII House Cusp Interpolation Between Latitudes

LAT INCR	HOUSE CUSP INTERVAL																								LAT INCR
	1°1'	1°2'	1°3'	1°4'	1°5'	1°6'	1°7'	1°8'	1°9'	1°10'	1°11'	1°12'	1°13'	1°14'	1°15'	1°16'	1°17'	1°18'	1°19'	1°20'	1°21'	1°22'	1°23'	1°24'	
1	1	1	1	1	1	1	1	1	1	1	1	1	1	1	1	1	1	1	1	1	1	1	1	1	1
2	2	2	2	2	2	2	2	2	2	2	2	2	2	2	3	3	3	3	3	3	3	3	3	3	2
3	3	3	3	3	3	3	3	3	3	4	4	4	4	4	4	4	4	4	4	4	4	4	4	4	3
4	4	4	4	4	4	4	4	5	5	5	5	5	5	5	5	5	5	5	5	5	5	5	6	6	4
5	5	5	5	5	5	6	6	6	6	6	6	6	6	6	6	6	6	6	7	7	7	7	7	7	5
6	6	6	6	6	7	7	7	7	7	7	7	7	7	7	8	8	8	8	8	8	8	8	8	8	6
7	7	7	7	7	8	8	8	8	8	8	8	8	9	9	9	9	9	9	9	9	9	10	10	10	7
8	8	8	8	9	9	9	9	9	9	9	9	10	10	10	10	10	10	10	11	11	11	11	11	11	8
9	9	9	9	10	10	10	10	10	10	11	11	11	11	11	11	11	12	12	12	12	12	12	12	13	9
10	10	10	11	11	11	11	11	11	12	12	12	12	12	12	13	13	13	13	13	13	14	14	14	14	10
11	11	11	12	12	12	12	12	12	13	13	13	13	13	14	14	14	14	14	14	15	15	15	15	15	11
12	12	12	13	13	13	13	13	14	14	14	14	14	15	15	15	15	15	16	16	16	16	16	17	17	12
13	13	13	14	14	14	14	15	15	15	15	15	16	16	16	16	16	17	17	17	17	18	18	18	18	13
14	14	14	15	15	15	15	16	16	16	16	17	17	17	17	18	18	18	18	18	19	19	19	19	20	14
15	15	16	16	16	16	17	17	17	17	18	18	18	18	19	19	19	19	20	20	20	20	21	21	21	15
16	16	17	17	17	17	18	18	18	18	19	19	19	19	20	20	20	21	21	21	21	22	22	22	22	16
17	17	18	18	18	18	19	19	19	20	20	20	20	21	21	21	22	22	22	22	23	23	23	24	24	17
18	18	19	19	19	20	20	20	20	21	21	21	22	22	22	23	23	23	23	24	24	24	25	25	25	18
19	19	20	20	20	21	21	21	22	22	22	22	23	23	23	24	24	24	25	25	25	26	26	26	27	19
20	20	21	21	21	22	22	22	23	23	23	24	24	24	25	25	25	26	26	26	27	27	27	28	28	20
21	21	22	22	22	23	23	23	24	24	25	25	25	26	26	26	27	27	27	28	28	28	29	29	29	21
22	22	23	23	23	24	24	24	25	25	26	26	26	27	27	28	28	28	29	29	29	30	30	30	31	22
23	23	24	24	25	25	25	26	26	26	27	27	28	28	28	29	29	30	30	30	31	31	31	32	32	23
24	24	25	25	26	26	26	27	27	28	28	28	29	29	30	30	30	31	31	32	32	32	33	33	34	24
25	25	26	26	27	27	28	28	28	29	29	30	30	30	31	31	32	32	33	33	33	34	34	35	35	25
26	26	27	27	28	28	29	29	29	30	30	31	31	32	32	33	33	33	34	34	35	35	36	36	36	26
27	27	28	28	29	29	30	30	31	31	32	32	32	33	33	34	34	35	35	36	36	36	37	37	38	27
28	28	29	29	30	30	31	31	32	32	33	33	34	34	35	35	35	36	36	37	37	38	38	39	39	28
29	29	30	30	31	31	32	32	33	33	34	34	35	35	36	36	37	37	38	38	39	39	40	40	41	29
30	31	31	32	32	33	33	34	34	35	35	36	36	37	37	38	38	39	39	40	40	41	41	42	42	30
31	32	32	33	33	34	34	35	35	36	36	37	37	38	38	39	39	40	40	41	41	42	42	43	43	31
32	33	33	34	34	35	35	36	36	37	37	38	38	39	39	40	41	41	42	42	43	43	44	44	45	32
33	34	34	35	35	36	36	37	37	38	39	39	40	40	41	41	42	42	43	43	44	45	45	46	46	33
34	35	35	36	36	37	37	38	39	39	40	40	41	41	42	43	43	44	44	45	45	46	46	47	48	34
35	36	36	37	37	38	39	39	40	40	41	41	42	43	43	44	44	45	46	46	47	47	48	48	49	35
36	37	37	38	38	39	40	40	41	41	42	43	43	44	44	45	46	46	47	47	48	49	49	50	50	36
37	38	38	39	39	40	41	41	42	43	43	44	44	45	46	46	47	47	48	49	49	50	51	51	52	37
38	39	39	40	41	41	42	42	43	44	44	45	46	46	47	48	48	49	49	50	51	51	52	53	53	38
39	40	40	41	42	42	43	44	44	45	46	46	47	47	48	49	49	50	51	51	52	53	53	54	55	39
40	41	41	42	43	43	44	45	45	46	47	47	48	49	49	50	51	51	52	53	53	54	55	55	56	40
41	42	42	43	44	44	45	46	46	47	48	49	49	50	51	51	52	53	53	54	55	55	56	57	57	41
42	43	43	44	45	46	46	47	48	48	49	50	50	51	52	53	53	54	55	55	56	57	57	58	59	42
43	44	44	45	46	47	47	48	49	49	50	51	52	52	53	54	54	55	56	57	57	58	59	59	1°0'	43
44	45	45	46	47	48	48	49	50	51	51	52	53	54	54	55	56	56	57	58	59	59	1°0'	1°1'	1°2'	44
45	46	47	47	48	49	50	50	51	52	53	53	54	55	56	56	57	58	59	59	1°0'	1°1'	1°2'	1°2'	1°3'	45
46	47	48	48	49	50	51	51	52	53	54	54	55	56	57	58	58	59	1°0'	1°1'	1°1'	1°2'	1°3'	1°4'	1°4'	46
47	48	49	49	50	51	52	52	53	54	55	56	56	57	58	59	1°0'	1°0'	1°1'	1°2'	1°3'	1°3'	1°4'	1°5'	1°6'	47
48	49	50	50	51	52	53	54	54	55	56	57	58	58	59	1°0'	1°1'	1°2'	1°2'	1°3'	1°4'	1°5'	1°6'	1°6'	1°7'	48
49	50	51	51	52	53	54	55	56	56	57	58	59	1°0'	1°0'	1°1'	1°2'	1°3'	1°4'	1°5'	1°5'	1°6'	1°7'	1°8'	1°9'	49
50	51	52	53	53	54	55	56	57	58	58	59	1°0'	1°1'	1°2'	1°3'	1°3'	1°4'	1°5'	1°6'	1°7'	1°8'	1°8'	1°9'	1°10'	50
51	52	53	54	54	55	56	57	58	59	1°0'	1°0'	1°1'	1°2'	1°3'	1°4'	1°5'	1°5'	1°6'	1°7'	1°8'	1°9'	1°10'	1°11'	1°11'	51
52	53	54	55	55	56	57	58	59	1°0'	1°1'	1°2'	1°2'	1°3'	1°4'	1°5'	1°6'	1°7'	1°8'	1°8'	1°9'	1°10'	1°11'	1°12'	1°13'	52
53	54	55	56	57	57	58	59	1°0'	1°1'	1°2'	1°3'	1°4'	1°4'	1°5'	1°6'	1°7'	1°8'	1°9'	1°10'	1°11'	1°12'	1°12'	1°13'	1°14'	53
54	55	56	57	58	59	59	1°0'	1°1'	1°2'	1°3'	1°4'	1°5'	1°6'	1°7'	1°8'	1°8'	1°9'	1°10'	1°11'	1°12'	1°13'	1°14'	1°15'	1°16'	54
55	56	57	58	59	1°0'	1°1'	1°1'	1°2'	1°3'	1°4'	1°5'	1°6'	1°7'	1°8'	1°9'	1°10'	1°11'	1°12'	1°12'	1°13'	1°14'	1°15'	1°16'	1°17'	55
56	57	58	59	1°0'	1°1'	1°2'	1°3'	1°3'	1°4'	1°5'	1°6'	1°7'	1°8'	1°9'	1°10'	1°11'	1°12'	1°13'	1°14'	1°15'	1°16'	1°17'	1°17'	1°18'	56
57	58	59	1°0'	1°1'	1°2'	1°3'	1°4'	1°5'	1°6'	1°7'	1°7'	1°8'	1°9'	1°10'	1°11'	1°12'	1°13'	1°14'	1°15'	1°16'	1°17'	1°18'	1°19'	1°20'	57
58	59	1°0'	1°1'	1°2'	1°3'	1°4'	1°5'	1°6'	1°7'	1°8'	1°9'	1°10'	1°11'	1°12'	1°13'	1°13'	1°14'	1°15'	1°16'	1°17'	1°18'	1°19'	1°20'	1°21'	58
59	1°0'	1°1'	1°2'	1°3'	1°4'	1°5'	1°6'	1°7'	1°8'	1°9'	1°10'	1°11'	1°12'	1°13'	1°14'	1°15'	1°16'	1°17'	1°18'	1°19'	1°20'	1°21'	1°22'	1°23'	59

Table XII House Cusp Interpolation Between Latitudes

LAT INCR	HOUSE CUSP INTERVAL																								LAT INCR
	1°25'	1°26'	1°27'	1°28'	1°29'	1°30'	1°31'	1°32'	1°33'	1°34'	1°35'	1°36'	1°37'	1°38'	1°39'	1°40'	1°41'	1°42'	1°43'	1°44'	1°45'	1°46'	1°47'	1°48'	
1	1	1	1	1	1	2	2	2	2	2	2	2	2	2	2	2	2	2	2	2	2	2	2	2	1
2	3	3	3	3	3	3	3	3	3	3	3	3	3	3	3	3	3	3	3	3	4	4	4	4	2
3	4	4	4	4	4	5	5	5	5	5	5	5	5	5	5	5	5	5	5	5	5	5	5	5	3
4	6	6	6	6	6	6	6	6	6	6	6	6	6	7	7	7	7	7	7	7	7	7	7	7	4
5	7	7	7	7	7	8	8	8	8	8	8	8	8	8	8	8	8	9	9	9	9	9	9	9	5
6	9	9	9	9	9	9	9	9	9	9	10	10	10	10	10	10	10	10	10	10	11	11	11	11	6
7	10	10	10	10	10	11	11	11	11	11	11	11	11	11	12	12	12	12	12	12	12	12	12	13	7
8	11	11	12	12	12	12	12	12	12	13	13	13	13	13	13	13	13	14	14	14	14	14	14	14	8
9	13	13	13	13	13	14	14	14	14	14	14	14	15	15	15	15	15	15	15	16	16	16	16	16	9
10	14	14	15	15	15	15	15	15	16	16	16	16	16	16	17	17	17	17	17	17	18	18	18	18	10
11	16	16	16	16	16	17	17	17	17	17	17	18	18	18	18	18	19	19	19	19	19	19	20	20	11
12	17	17	17	18	18	18	18	18	19	19	19	19	19	20	20	20	20	20	21	21	21	21	21	22	12
13	18	19	19	19	19	20	20	20	20	20	21	21	21	21	21	22	22	22	22	23	23	23	23	23	13
14	20	20	20	21	21	21	21	21	22	22	22	22	23	23	23	23	24	24	24	24	25	25	25	25	14
15	21	22	22	22	22	23	23	23	23	24	24	24	24	25	25	25	25	26	26	26	26	27	27	27	15
16	23	23	23	23	24	24	24	25	25	25	25	26	26	26	26	27	27	27	27	28	28	28	29	29	16
17	24	24	25	25	25	26	26	26	26	27	27	27	27	28	28	28	29	29	29	29	30	30	30	31	17
18	26	26	26	26	27	27	27	28	28	28	29	29	29	29	30	30	30	31	31	31	32	32	32	32	18
19	27	27	28	28	28	29	29	29	29	30	30	30	31	31	31	32	32	32	33	33	33	34	34	34	19
20	28	29	29	29	30	30	30	31	31	31	32	32	32	33	33	33	34	34	34	35	35	35	36	36	20
21	30	30	30	31	31	32	32	32	33	33	33	34	34	34	35	35	35	36	36	36	37	37	37	38	21
22	31	32	32	32	33	33	33	34	34	34	35	35	36	36	36	37	37	37	38	38	39	39	39	40	22
23	33	33	33	34	34	35	35	35	36	36	36	37	37	38	38	38	39	39	39	40	40	41	41	41	23
24	34	34	35	35	36	36	36	37	37	38	38	38	39	39	40	40	40	41	41	42	42	42	43	43	24
25	35	36	36	37	37	38	38	38	39	39	40	40	40	41	41	42	42	43	43	43	44	44	45	45	25
26	37	37	38	38	39	39	39	40	40	41	41	42	42	42	43	43	44	44	45	45	46	46	46	47	26
27	38	39	39	40	40	41	41	41	42	42	43	43	44	44	45	45	45	46	46	47	47	48	48	49	27
28	40	40	41	41	42	42	42	43	43	44	44	45	45	46	46	47	47	48	48	49	49	49	50	50	28
29	41	42	42	43	43	44	44	44	45	45	46	46	47	47	48	48	49	49	50	50	51	51	52	52	29
30	43	43	44	44	45	45	46	46	47	47	48	48	49	49	50	50	51	51	52	52	53	53	54	54	30
31	44	44	45	45	46	47	47	48	48	49	49	50	50	51	51	52	52	53	53	54	54	55	55	56	31
32	45	46	46	47	47	48	49	49	50	50	51	51	52	52	53	53	54	54	55	55	56	57	57	58	32
33	47	47	48	48	49	50	50	51	51	52	52	53	53	54	54	55	56	56	57	57	58	58	59	59	33
34	48	49	49	50	50	51	52	52	53	53	54	54	55	56	56	57	57	58	58	59	1 0	1 0	1 1	1 1	34
35	50	50	51	51	52	53	53	54	54	55	55	56	57	57	58	58	59	1 0	1 0	1 1	1 1	1 2	1 2	1 3	35
36	51	52	52	53	53	54	55	55	56	56	57	58	58	59	59	1 0	1 1	1 1	1 2	1 2	1 3	1 4	1 4	1 5	36
37	52	53	54	54	55	56	56	57	57	58	59	59	1 0	1 0	1 1	1 2	1 2	1 3	1 4	1 4	1 5	1 5	1 6	1 7	37
38	54	54	55	56	56	57	58	58	59	1 0	1 0	1 1	1 1	1 2	1 3	1 3	1 4	1 5	1 5	1 6	1 7	1 7	1 8	1 8	38
39	55	56	57	57	58	59	59	1 0	1 0	1 1	1 2	1 2	1 3	1 4	1 4	1 5	1 6	1 6	1 7	1 8	1 8	1 9	1 10	1 10	39
40	57	57	58	59	59	1 0	1 1	1 1	1 2	1 3	1 3	1 4	1 5	1 5	1 6	1 7	1 7	1 8	1 9	1 9	1 10	1 11	1 11	1 12	40
41	58	59	59	1 0	1 1	1 2	1 2	1 3	1 4	1 4	1 5	1 6	1 6	1 7	1 8	1 8	1 9	1 10	1 10	1 11	1 12	1 12	1 13	1 14	41
42	1 0	1 0	1 1	1 2	1 2	1 3	1 4	1 4	1 5	1 6	1 7	1 7	1 8	1 9	1 9	1 10	1 11	1 11	1 12	1 13	1 14	1 14	1 15	1 16	42
43	1 1	1 2	1 2	1 3	1 4	1 5	1 5	1 6	1 7	1 7	1 8	1 9	1 10	1 10	1 11	1 12	1 12	1 13	1 14	1 15	1 15	1 16	1 17	1 17	43
44	1 2	1 3	1 4	1 5	1 5	1 6	1 7	1 7	1 8	1 9	1 10	1 10	1 11	1 12	1 13	1 13	1 14	1 15	1 16	1 16	1 17	1 18	1 18	1 19	44
45	1 4	1 5	1 5	1 6	1 7	1 8	1 8	1 9	1 10	1 11	1 11	1 12	1 13	1 14	1 14	1 15	1 16	1 17	1 17	1 18	1 19	1 20	1 20	1 21	45
46	1 5	1 6	1 7	1 7	1 8	1 9	1 10	1 11	1 11	1 12	1 13	1 14	1 14	1 15	1 16	1 17	1 17	1 18	1 19	1 20	1 21	1 21	1 22	1 23	46
47	1 7	1 7	1 8	1 9	1 10	1 11	1 11	1 12	1 13	1 14	1 14	1 15	1 16	1 17	1 18	1 18	1 19	1 20	1 21	1 21	1 22	1 23	1 24	1 25	47
48	1 8	1 9	1 10	1 10	1 11	1 12	1 13	1 14	1 14	1 15	1 16	1 17	1 18	1 18	1 19	1 20	1 21	1 22	1 22	1 23	1 24	1 25	1 26	1 26	48
49	1 9	1 10	1 11	1 12	1 13	1 14	1 14	1 15	1 16	1 17	1 18	1 18	1 19	1 20	1 21	1 22	1 22	1 23	1 24	1 25	1 26	1 27	1 27	1 28	49
50	1 11	1 12	1 13	1 13	1 14	1 15	1 16	1 17	1 18	1 18	1 19	1 20	1 21	1 22	1 23	1 23	1 24	1 25	1 26	1 27	1 28	1 28	1 29	1 30	50
51	1 12	1 13	1 14	1 15	1 16	1 17	1 17	1 18	1 19	1 20	1 21	1 22	1 22	1 23	1 24	1 25	1 26	1 27	1 28	1 28	1 29	1 30	1 31	1 32	51
52	1 14	1 15	1 15	1 16	1 17	1 18	1 19	1 20	1 21	1 21	1 22	1 23	1 24	1 25	1 26	1 27	1 28	1 28	1 29	1 30	1 31	1 32	1 33	1 34	52
53	1 15	1 16	1 17	1 18	1 19	1 20	1 20	1 21	1 22	1 23	1 24	1 25	1 26	1 27	1 27	1 28	1 29	1 30	1 31	1 32	1 33	1 34	1 35	1 35	53
54	1 17	1 17	1 18	1 19	1 20	1 21	1 22	1 23	1 24	1 25	1 26	1 26	1 27	1 28	1 29	1 30	1 31	1 32	1 33	1 34	1 35	1 35	1 36	1 37	54
55	1 18	1 19	1 20	1 21	1 22	1 23	1 23	1 24	1 25	1 26	1 27	1 28	1 29	1 30	1 31	1 32	1 33	1 34	1 34	1 35	1 36	1 37	1 38	1 39	55
56	1 19	1 20	1 21	1 22	1 23	1 24	1 25	1 26	1 27	1 28	1 29	1 30	1 31	1 31	1 32	1 33	1 34	1 35	1 36	1 37	1 38	1 39	1 40	1 41	56
57	1 21	1 22	1 23	1 24	1 25	1 26	1 26	1 27	1 28	1 29	1 30	1 31	1 32	1 33	1 34	1 35	1 36	1 37	1 38	1 39	1 40	1 41	1 42	1 43	57
58	1 22	1 23	1 24	1 25	1 26	1 27	1 28	1 29	1 30	1 31	1 32	1 33	1 34	1 35	1 36	1 37	1 38	1 39	1 40	1 41	1 42	1 42	1 43	1 44	58
59	1 24	1 25	1 26	1 27	1 28	1 29	1 29	1 30	1 31	1 32	1 33	1 34	1 35	1 36	1 37	1 38	1 39	1 40	1 41	1 42	1 43	1 44	1 45	1 46	59

Table XII House Cusp Interpolation Between Latitudes

HOUSE CUSP INTERVAL

Each column heading is given as degrees (°) and minutes ('). Cell values are minutes unless a degree figure is shown (e.g. "1 0" = 1°00').

LAT INCR	1°49'	1°50'	1°51'	1°52'	1°53'	1°54'	1°55'	1°56'	1°57'	1°58'	1°59'	2°0'	2°1'	2°2'	2°3'	2°4'	2°5'	2°6'	2°7'	2°8'	2°9'	2°10'	2°11'	2°12'	LAT INCR
1	2	2	2	2	2	2	2	2	2	2	2	2	2	2	2	2	2	2	2	2	2	2	2	2	1
2	4	4	4	4	4	4	4	4	4	4	4	4	4	4	4	4	4	4	4	4	4	4	4	4	2
3	5	6	6	6	6	6	6	6	6	6	6	6	6	6	6	6	6	6	6	7	7	7	7	7	3
4	7	7	7	7	8	8	8	8	8	8	8	8	8	8	8	8	8	8	9	9	9	9	9	9	4
5	9	9	9	9	9	9	10	10	10	10	10	10	10	10	10	10	10	10	11	11	11	11	11	11	5
6	11	11	11	11	11	11	12	12	12	12	12	12	12	12	12	12	13	13	13	13	13	13	13	13	6
7	13	13	13	13	13	13	13	14	14	14	14	14	14	14	14	14	15	15	15	15	15	15	15	15	7
8	15	15	15	15	15	15	15	15	16	16	16	16	16	16	16	16	17	17	17	17	17	17	17	17	8
9	16	17	17	17	17	17	17	17	18	18	18	18	18	18	19	19	19	19	19	19	20	20	20	20	9
10	18	18	19	19	19	19	19	19	20	20	20	20	20	20	21	21	21	21	21	21	22	22	22	22	10
11	20	20	20	21	21	21	21	21	21	22	22	22	22	22	22	23	23	23	23	23	24	24	24	24	11
12	22	22	22	22	23	23	23	23	24	24	24	24	24	25	25	25	25	25	26	26	26	26	26	26	12
13	24	24	24	24	24	25	25	25	26	26	26	26	26	27	27	27	27	27	28	28	28	28	28	29	13
14	25	26	26	26	26	27	27	27	27	28	28	28	28	29	29	29	29	30	30	30	30	30	31	31	14
15	27	28	28	28	28	29	29	29	29	30	30	30	30	31	31	31	31	32	32	32	32	33	33	33	15
16	29	29	30	30	30	30	31	31	31	31	32	32	32	33	33	33	33	34	34	34	34	35	35	35	16
17	31	31	31	32	32	32	33	33	33	33	34	34	34	35	35	35	36	36	36	37	37	37	37	37	17
18	33	33	33	34	34	34	35	35	35	35	36	36	36	37	37	37	38	38	38	39	39	39	40	42	18
19	35	35	35	35	36	36	36	37	37	37	38	38	38	39	39	39	40	40	40	41	41	41	42	42	19
20	36	37	37	37	38	38	38	39	39	39	40	40	40	41	41	41	42	42	42	43	43	43	44	44	20
21	38	39	39	39	40	40	40	41	41	41	42	42	42	43	43	43	44	44	44	45	45	46	46	46	21
22	40	40	41	41	41	42	42	43	43	43	44	44	44	45	45	45	46	46	47	47	47	48	48	48	22
23	42	42	43	43	43	44	44	44	45	45	46	46	46	47	47	48	48	48	49	49	49	50	50	51	23
24	44	44	44	45	45	46	46	46	47	47	48	48	48	49	49	50	50	50	51	51	52	52	52	53	24
25	45	46	46	47	47	48	48	48	49	49	50	50	50	51	51	51	52	52	53	53	53	54	54	55	25
26	47	48	48	49	49	50	50	50	51	51	52	52	52	53	53	54	54	55	55	55	56	56	57	57	26
27	49	50	50	50	51	51	52	52	53	53	54	54	54	55	55	56	56	57	57	58	58	59	59	59	27
28	51	51	52	52	53	53	54	54	55	55	56	56	56	57	57	58	58	59	59	1 0	1 0	1 1	1 3	1 4	28
29	53	53	54	54	55	55	56	56	57	57	58	58	58	59	59	1 0	1 0	1 1	1 1	1 2	1 3	1 5	1 5	1 6	29
30	55	55	56	56	57	57	58	58	59	59	1 0	1 0	1 1	1 1	1 2	1 3	1 3	1 4	1 4	1 5	1 5	1 6	1 6	1 6	30
31	56	57	57	58	58	59	59	1 0	1 0	1 1	1 1	1 2	1 3	1 3	1 4	1 4	1 5	1 5	1 6	1 6	1 7	1 7	1 8	1 8	31
32	58	59	59	1 0	1 0	1 1	1 1	1 2	1 2	1 3	1 3	1 4	1 5	1 5	1 6	1 6	1 7	1 8	1 8	1 9	1 9	1 10	1 10	1 10	32
33	1 0	1 1	1 1	1 2	1 2	1 3	1 3	1 4	1 4	1 5	1 5	1 6	1 7	1 7	1 8	1 8	1 9	1 10	1 10	1 11	1 11	1 12	1 12	1 13	33
34	1 2	1 2	1 3	1 3	1 4	1 4	1 5	1 5	1 6	1 7	1 7	1 8	1 9	1 9	1 10	1 10	1 11	1 12	1 12	1 13	1 13	1 14	1 14	1 15	34
35	1 4	1 4	1 5	1 5	1 6	1 7	1 7	1 8	1 8	1 9	1 9	1 10	1 11	1 11	1 12	1 12	1 13	1 14	1 14	1 15	1 15	1 16	1 16	1 17	35
36	1 5	1 6	1 7	1 7	1 8	1 8	1 9	1 10	1 10	1 11	1 11	1 12	1 13	1 13	1 14	1 14	1 15	1 16	1 16	1 17	1 17	1 18	1 19	1 19	36
37	1 7	1 8	1 8	1 9	1 10	1 10	1 11	1 12	1 12	1 13	1 13	1 14	1 15	1 15	1 16	1 17	1 17	1 18	1 19	1 20	1 20	1 21	1 21	1 21	37
38	1 9	1 9	1 10	1 10	1 11	1 12	1 12	1 13	1 13	1 14	1 15	1 15	1 16	1 17	1 17	1 18	1 19	1 19	1 20	1 21	1 22	1 23	1 23	1 24	38
39	1 11	1 11	1 12	1 12	1 13	1 13	1 14	1 15	1 15	1 16	1 17	1 17	1 18	1 19	1 19	1 20	1 21	1 22	1 23	1 23	1 24	1 25	1 25	1 26	39
40	1 13	1 13	1 13	1 14	1 15	1 15	1 16	1 17	1 17	1 18	1 19	1 19	1 20	1 21	1 21	1 22	1 23	1 23	1 24	1 25	1 25	1 26	1 27	1 28	40
41	1 14	1 15	1 16	1 17	1 17	1 18	1 19	1 19	1 20	1 21	1 21	1 22	1 23	1 23	1 24	1 25	1 25	1 26	1 27	1 27	1 28	1 29	1 30	1 30	41
42	1 16	1 17	1 18	1 18	1 19	1 20	1 21	1 21	1 22	1 23	1 23	1 24	1 25	1 25	1 26	1 27	1 27	1 28	1 29	1 30	1 30	1 31	1 32	1 32	42
43	1 18	1 19	1 20	1 20	1 21	1 22	1 22	1 23	1 24	1 25	1 25	1 26	1 27	1 27	1 28	1 29	1 29	1 30	1 31	1 32	1 33	1 34	1 34	1 35	43
44	1 20	1 21	1 21	1 22	1 23	1 24	1 24	1 25	1 26	1 27	1 27	1 28	1 29	1 29	1 30	1 31	1 32	1 33	1 34	1 35	1 35	1 36	1 37	1 37	44
45	1 22	1 23	1 23	1 24	1 25	1 26	1 26	1 27	1 28	1 29	1 29	1 30	1 31	1 32	1 32	1 33	1 34	1 35	1 35	1 36	1 37	1 38	1 38	1 39	45
46	1 24	1 24	1 25	1 26	1 27	1 27	1 28	1 29	1 30	1 30	1 31	1 32	1 33	1 34	1 34	1 35	1 36	1 37	1 37	1 38	1 39	1 40	1 40	1 41	46
47	1 25	1 26	1 27	1 28	1 29	1 29	1 30	1 31	1 32	1 32	1 33	1 34	1 35	1 36	1 36	1 37	1 38	1 39	1 40	1 41	1 42	1 43	1 44	1 45	47
48	1 27	1 28	1 29	1 30	1 30	1 31	1 32	1 33	1 34	1 34	1 35	1 36	1 37	1 38	1 38	1 39	1 40	1 41	1 42	1 42	1 43	1 44	1 45	1 46	48
49	1 29	1 30	1 31	1 31	1 32	1 33	1 34	1 35	1 36	1 36	1 37	1 38	1 39	1 40	1 40	1 41	1 42	1 43	1 44	1 45	1 45	1 46	1 47	1 48	49
50	1 31	1 32	1 33	1 33	1 34	1 35	1 36	1 37	1 38	1 38	1 39	1 40	1 41	1 42	1 42	1 43	1 43	1 44	1 45	1 46	1 47	1 48	1 49	1 50	50
51	1 33	1 34	1 34	1 35	1 36	1 37	1 38	1 39	1 39	1 40	1 41	1 42	1 43	1 44	1 44	1 45	1 45	1 46	1 47	1 48	1 49	1 50	1 51	1 52	51
52	1 34	1 35	1 36	1 36	1 37	1 38	1 39	1 40	1 41	1 42	1 43	1 44	1 45	1 45	1 46	1 47	1 48	1 49	1 50	1 51	1 52	1 53	1 54	1 54	52
53	1 36	1 37	1 37	1 38	1 39	1 40	1 41	1 42	1 43	1 44	1 44	1 45	1 46	1 47	1 48	1 49	1 50	1 51	1 52	1 53	1 54	1 55	1 56	1 57	53
54	1 38	1 39	1 40	1 41	1 42	1 43	1 44	1 45	1 46	1 47	1 48	1 49	1 50	1 51	1 52	1 53	1 54	1 55	1 56	1 56	1 57	1 58	1 59	2 0	54
55	1 40	1 41	1 42	1 43	1 44	1 45	1 45	1 46	1 47	1 48	1 49	1 50	1 51	1 52	1 53	1 54	1 55	1 56	1 56	1 57	1 58	1 59	2 0	2 1	55
56	1 42	1 43	1 44	1 45	1 45	1 46	1 47	1 48	1 49	1 50	1 51	1 52	1 53	1 54	1 55	1 56	1 57	1 58	1 59	1 59	2 0	2 1	2 2	2 3	56
57	1 44	1 45	1 45	1 46	1 47	1 48	1 49	1 50	1 51	1 52	1 53	1 54	1 55	1 56	1 57	1 58	1 59	2 0	2 1	2 2	2 4	2 5	2 6	2 8	57
58	1 45	1 46	1 47	1 48	1 49	1 50	1 51	1 52	1 53	1 54	1 55	1 56	1 57	1 58	1 59	2 0	2 2	2 3	2 4	2 5	2 6	2 7	2 8	2 10	58
59	1 47	1 48	1 49	1 50	1 51	1 52	1 53	1 54	1 55	1 56	1 57	1 58	1 59	2 0	2 1	2 2	2 3	2 4	2 5	2 6	2 7	2 8	2 9	2 10	59

Longitudes and Latitudes of Major Cities

Aberdeen, SD	98W29	45N28	6:33:56
Abilene, TX	99W43	32N28	6:38:52
Akron, OH	81W31	41N05	5:26:04
Alameda, CA	122W15	37N46	8:09:00
Albany, GA	84W10	31N35	5:36:40
Albany, NY	73W45	42N39	4:55:00
Albuquerque, NM	106W39	35N05	7:06:36
Alexandria, LA	92W27	31N18	6:09:48
Alexandria, VA	77W03	38N48	5:08:12
Alhambra, CA	118W06	34N08	7:52:24
Allen Park, MI	83W13	42N16	5:32:52
Allentown, PA	75W29	40N37	5:01:56
Alliance, OH	81W06	40N55	5:24:24
Altadena, CA	118W08	34N11	7:52:32
Alton, IL	90W10	38N53	6:00:40
Altoona, PA	78W24	40N31	5:13:36
Amarillo, TX	101W50	35N13	6:47:20
Ames, IA	93W37	42N02	6:14:28
Amherst, NY	78W48	42N59	5:15:12
Amsterdam, NY	74W11	42N56	4:56:44
Anaheim, CA	117W55	33N50	7:51:40
Anchorage, AK	149W54	61N13	9:59:36
Anderson, IN	85W41	40N10	5:42:44
Anderson, SC	82W39	34N31	5:30:36
Annandale, VA	77W12	38N50	5:08:48
Annapolis, MD	76W30	38N59	5:06:00
Ann Arbor, MI	83W45	42N17	5:35:00
Anniston, AL	85W50	33N39	5:43:20
Antioch, CA	121W48	38N01	8:07:12
Appleton, WI	88W25	44N16	5:53:40
Arcade, CA	121W26	38N37	8:05:44
Arcadia, CA	118W02	34N08	7:52:08
Arden, CA	121W23	38N36	8:05:32
Arlington, MA	71W09	42N25	4:44:36
Arlington, TX	97W07	32N44	6:28:28
Arlington, VA	77W07	38N53	5:08:28
Arlington Heights, IL	87W59	42N05	5:51:56
Arvada, CO	105W05	39N50	7:00:20
Asheville, NC	82W33	35N36	5:30:12
Ashland, KY	82W38	38N28	5:30:32
Astoria, NY	73W55	40N46	4:55:40
Athens, GA	83W23	33N57	5:33:32
Atlanta, GA	84W23	33N45	5:37:32
Atlantic City, NJ	74W27	39N21	4:57:48
Attleboro, MA	71W17	41N57	4:45:08
Auburn, NY	76W34	42N56	5:06:16
Augusta, GA	81W58	33N28	5:27:52
Augusta, ME	69W47	44N19	4:39:08
Aurora, CO	104W51	39N44	6:59:24
Aurora, IL	88W19	41N45	5:53:16
Austin, MN	92W58	43N40	6:11:52
Austin, TX	97W45	30N17	6:31:00
Azusa, CA	117W52	34N08	7:51:28
Bakersfield, CA	119W01	35N23	7:56:04
Baldwin, NY	73W36	40N39	4:54:24
Baldwin, PA	79W59	40N23	5:19:56
Baldwin Park, CA	117W58	34N04	7:51:52
Baltimore, MD	76W37	39N17	5:06:28
Bangor, ME	68W46	44N48	4:35:04
Barberton, OH	81W39	41N00	5:26:36
Bartlesville, OK	95W59	36N45	6:23:56
Baton Rouge, LA	91W11	30N27	6:04:44
Battle Creek, MI	85W11	42N19	5:40:44
Bay City, MI	83W54	43N36	5:35:36
Bayonne, NJ	74W07	40N40	4:56:28
Bay Shore, NY	73W15	40N43	4:53:00
Bayside, NY	73W46	40N46	4:55:04
Baytown, TX	94W59	29N43	6:19:56
Beaumont, TX	94W06	30N05	6:16:24
Bell, CA	118W11	33N59	7:52:44
Belleville, IL	89W59	38N31	5:59:56
Belleville, NJ	74W09	40N47	4:56:36
Bellevue, WA	122W12	47N37	8:08:48
Bellflower, CA	118W09	33N53	7:52:36
Bell Gardens, CA	118W10	33N58	7:52:40
Bellingham, WA	122W29	48N46	8:09:56
Belmont, CA	122W17	37N31	8:09:08
Belmont, MA	71W11	42N24	4:44:44
Beloit, WI	89W02	42N31	5:56:08
Bergenfield, NJ	74W00	40N56	4:56:00
Berkeley, CA	122W16	37N52	8:09:04
Berwyn, IL	87W47	41N51	5:51:08
Bessemer, AL	86W58	33N24	5:47:52
Bethel Park, PA	80W01	40N20	5:20:04
Bethesda, MD	77W06	38N59	5:08:24
Bethlehem, PA	75W23	40N37	5:01:32
Bethpage, NY	73W30	40N44	4:54:00
Beverly, MA	70W53	42N33	4:43:32
Beverly Hills, CA	118W25	34N04	7:53:40
Big Spring, TX	101W28	32N15	6:45:52
Billings, MT	108W30	45N47	7:14:00
Biloxi, MS	88W53	30N24	5:55:32
Binghamton, NY	75W55	42N06	5:03:40
Birmingham, AL	86W48	33N31	5:47:12
Birmingham, MI	83W13	42N33	5:32:52
Bismarck, ND	100W47	46N48	6:43:08
Bloomfield, NJ	74W12	40N48	4:56:48
Bloomington, IL	89W00	40N29	5:56:00
Bloomington, IN	86W32	39N10	5:46:08
Bloomington, MN	93W17	44N50	6:13:08
Boardman, OH	80W39	41N02	5:22:36
Boca Raton, FL	80W05	26N21	5:20:20
Boise, ID	116W13	43N37	7:44:52
Bossier City, LA	93W44	32N31	6:14:56
Boston, MA	71W04	42N22	4:44:16
Boulder, CO	105W17	40N01	7:01:08
Bountiful, UT	111W53	40N53	7:27:32
Bowie, MD	76W47	39N00	5:07:08
Bowling Green, KY	86W27	36N59	5:45:48
Braintree, MA	71W00	42N13	4:44:00
Bremerton, WA	122W38	47N34	8:10:32
Brentwood, NY	73W15	40N47	4:53:00
Bridgeport, CT	73W12	41N11	4:52:48
Brighton, NY	77W34	43N08	5:10:16
Bristol, CT	72W57	41N40	4:51:48
Brockton, MA	71W01	42N05	4:44:04
Bronx, NY	73W54	40N51	4:55:36
Brookfield, WI	88W09	43N04	5:52:36
Brookline, MA	71W07	42N20	4:44:28
Brooklyn, NY	73W56	40N38	4:55:44
Brooklyn Center, MN	93W20	45N05	6:13:20
Brooklyn Park, MN	93W23	45N06	6:13:32
Brook Park, OH	80W51	41N24	5:23:24
Broomall, PA	75W22	39N59	5:01:28
Brownsville, TX	97W30	25N54	6:30:00
Bryan, TX	96W22	30N40	6:25:28
Buena Park, CA	118W00	33N52	7:52:00
Buffalo, NY	78W53	42N53	5:15:32
Burbank, CA	118W19	34N11	7:53:16
Burbank, IL	87W45	41N44	5:51:00
Burlingame, CA	122W21	37N35	8:09:24
Burlington, IA	91W14	40N49	6:04:56
Burlington, NC	79W26	36N06	5:17:44
Burlington, VT	73W12	44N29	4:52:48
Calumet City, IL	87W32	41N37	5:50:08
Cambridge, MA	71W06	42N22	4:44:24
Camden, NJ	75W07	39N56	5:00:28
Campbell, CA	121W57	37N17	8:07:48
Canton, OH	81W23	40N48	5:25:32
Cape Girardeau, MO	89W32	37N19	5:58:08
Carmichael, CA	121W19	38N38	8:05:16
Carol City, FL	80W16	25N56	5:21:04
Carson, CA	118W17	33N48	7:53:08
Carson City, NV	119W46	39N10	7:59:04
Casper, WY	106W19	42N51	7:05:16
Castro Valley, CA	122W04	37N42	8:08:16
Catonsville, MD	76W44	39N17	5:06:56
Cedar Falls, IA	92W27	42N32	6:09:48
Cedar Rapids, IA	91W40	41N59	6:06:40
Central Islip, NY	73W12	40N47	4:52:48
Champaign, IL	88W15	40N07	5:53:00
Chapel Hill, NC	79W04	35N55	5:16:16
Charleston, SC	79W56	32N46	5:19:44
Charleston, WV	81W38	38N21	5:26:32
Charleston Heights, SC	80W00	32N51	5:20:00
Charlotte, NC	80W51	35N13	5:23:24
Charlottesville, VA	78W30	38N02	5:14:00
Chattanooga, TN	85W19	35N03	5:41:16
Cheektowaga, NY	78W45	42N54	5:15:00
Chelsea, MA	71W02	42N23	4:44:08
Cherry Hill, NJ	75W02	39N56	5:00:08
Chesapeake, VA	76W17	36N50	5:05:08
Chester, PA	75W22	39N51	5:01:28
Cheyenne, WY	104W49	41N08	6:59:16
Chicago, IL	87W39	41N52	5:50:36
Chicago Heights, IL	87W38	41N31	5:50:32
Chicopee, MA	72W37	42N09	4:50:28
Chino, CA	117W41	34N01	7:50:44
Chula Vista, CA	117W05	32N39	7:48:20
Cicero, IL	87W45	41N51	5:51:00
Cincinnati, OH	84W31	39N06	5:38:04
Citrus Heights, CA	121W17	38N42	8:05:08
Claremont, CA	117W43	34N06	7:50:52
Clarksville, TN	87W21	36N32	5:49:24
Clearwater, FL	82W48	27N58	5:31:12
Cleveland, OH	81W42	41N30	5:26:48
Cleveland Heights, OH	81W34	41N30	5:26:16
Clifton, NJ	74W09	40N52	4:56:36
Clinton, IA	90W12	41N51	6:00:48
Clinton Township, MI	83W58	42N04	5:35:52
Clovis, NM	103W12	34N24	6:52:48
College Park, MD	76W56	38N59	5:07:44
Colorado Springs, CO	104W49	38N50	6:59:16
Colton, CA	117W20	34N04	7:49:20
Columbia, MO	92W20	38N57	6:09:20
Columbia, SC	81W03	34N00	5:24:12
Columbus, GA	84W59	32N28	5:39:56
Columbus, IN	85W55	39N13	5:43:40
Columbus, MS	88W25	33N30	5:53:40
Columbus, OH	83W00	39N58	5:32:00
Compton, CA	118W13	33N54	7:52:52
Concord, CA	122W02	37N59	8:08:08
Concord, NH	71W32	43N12	4:46:08
Coon Rapids, MN	93W19	45N09	6:13:16
Coral Gables, FL	80W16	25N45	5:21:04
Corona, CA	117W34	33N53	7:50:16
Corona, NY	73W52	40N45	4:55:28
Coronado, CA	117W11	32N41	7:48:44
Corpus Christi, TX	97W24	27N47	6:29:36
Corvallis, OR	123W16	44N34	8:13:04
Costa Mesa, CA	117W55	33N38	7:51:40
Council Bluffs, IA	95W52	41N16	6:23:28
Covina, CA	117W52	34N05	7:51:28
Covington, KY	84W31	39N05	5:38:04
Cranford, NJ	74W18	40N40	4:57:12
Cranston, RI	71W26	41N47	4:45:44
Crystal, MN	93W22	45N03	6:13:28
Culver City, CA	118W25	34N01	7:53:40
Cumberland, MD	78W46	39N39	5:15:04
Cuyahoga Falls, OH	81W29	41N08	5:25:56
Cypress, CA	118W02	33N50	7:52:08
Dallas, TX	96W49	32N47	6:27:16
Daly City, CA	122W28	37N42	8:09:52
Danbury, CT	73W28	41N24	4:53:52
Danvers, MA	70W56	42N34	4:43:44
Danville, IL	87W37	40N08	5:50:28
Danville, VA	79W23	36N36	5:17:32
Davenport, IA	90W35	41N32	6:02:20
Davis, CA	121W44	38N33	8:06:56
Dayton, OH	84W12	39N45	5:36:48
Daytona Beach, FL	81W01	29N13	5:24:04
Dearborn, MI	83W11	42N19	5:32:44
Dearborn Heights, MI	83W18	42N20	5:33:12
Decatur, AL	86W59	34N36	5:47:56
Decatur, IL	88W57	39N51	5:55:48
Dedham, MA	71W10	42N15	4:44:40
Deer Park, NY	73W20	40N46	4:53:20
De Kalb, IL	88W46	41N56	5:55:04
Del City, OK	97W26	35N26	6:29:44
Denton, TX	97W08	33N13	6:28:32
Denver, CO	104W59	39N44	6:59:56
Des Moines, IA	93W37	41N35	6:14:28
Des Plaines, IL	87W52	42N03	5:51:28
Detroit, MI	83W03	42N20	5:32:12
Dolton, IL	87W36	41N38	5:50:24
Dothan, AL	85W24	31N13	5:41:36
Dover, DE	75W32	39N10	5:02:08
Downers Grove, IL	88W01	41N49	5:52:04
Downey, CA	118W08	33N56	7:52:32
Drexel Hill, PA	75W18	39N57	5:01:12
Dubuque, IA	90W41	42N30	6:02:44
Duluth, MN	92W07	46N47	6:08:28
Dundalk, MD	76W32	39N16	5:06:08
Durham, NC	78W54	36N00	5:15:36
East Brunswick, NJ	74W25	40N26	4:57:40
East Chicago, IN	87W29	41N38	5:49:56
East Cleveland, OH	81W33	41N33	5:26:12
East Detroit, MI	82W57	42N28	5:31:48
East Hartford, CT	72W37	41N46	4:50:28
East Haven, CT	72W52	41N17	4:51:28
East Lansing, MI	84W29	42N44	5:37:56
East Los Angeles, CA	118W09	34N01	7:52:36
East Meadow, NY	73W34	40N43	4:54:16
Easton, PA	75W13	40N41	5:00:52
East Orange, NJ	74W13	40N46	4:56:52
Eastpoint, GA	84W27	33N41	5:37:48
East Providence, RI	71W22	41N48	4:45:28
East Saint Louis, IL	90W09	38N37	6:00:36
Eau Claire, WI	91W30	44N49	6:06:00
Edina, MN	93W21	44N53	6:13:24
Edison, NJ	74W25	40N31	4:57:40
El Cajon, CA	116W58	32N48	7:47:52
El Cerrito, CA	122W19	37N55	8:09:16
El Dorado, AR	92W40	33N12	6:10:40
Elgin, IL	88W17	42N02	5:53:08
Elizabeth, NJ	74W13	40N40	4:56:52
Elkhart, IN	85W58	41N41	5:43:52
Elmhurst, IL	87W56	41N53	5:51:44
Elmira, NY	76W48	42N06	5:07:12
Elmont, NY	73W43	40N43	4:54:52
El Monte, CA	118W02	34N04	7:52:08
Elmwood Park, IL	87W49	41N56	5:51:16
El Paso, TX	106W29	31N45	7:05:56
Elyria, OH	82W07	41N22	5:28:28
Englewood, CO	104W59	39N39	6:59:56
Enid, OK	97W53	36N24	6:31:32
Erie, PA	80W05	42N08	5:20:20
Escondido, CA	117W05	33N07	7:48:20
Essex, MD	76W29	39N19	5:05:56
Euclid, OH	81W32	41N34	5:26:08
Eugene, OR	123W04	44N05	8:12:16
Eureka, CA	124W09	40N47	8:16:36
Evanston, IL	87W41	42N03	5:50:44
Evansville, IN	87W35	37N58	5:50:20
Everett, MA	71W04	42N24	4:44:16
Everett, WA	122W12	47N59	8:08:48
Evergreen Park, IL	87W41	41N43	5:50:44
Fairborn, OH	84W02	39N49	5:36:08
Fairfield, CA	122W03	38N15	8:08:12
Fairfield, CT	73W16	41N09	4:53:04
Fair Lawn, NJ	74W08	40N56	4:56:32
Fairmont, WV	80W09	39N29	5:20:36
Fall River, MA	71W10	41N43	4:44:40
Fargo, ND	96W48	46N53	6:27:12
Farmers Branch, TX	96W54	32N56	6:27:36
Fayetteville, AR	96W94	36N04	6:30:16
Fayetteville, NC	78W53	35N03	5:15:32
Ferguson, MO	90W18	38N45	6:01:12
Ferndale, MI	83W08	42N28	5:32:32
Findlay, OH	83W39	41N02	5:34:36
Fitchburg, MA	71W48	42N35	4:47:12
Flagstaff, AZ	111W39	35N12	7:26:36
Flint, MI	83W41	43N01	5:34:44
Florence, AL	87W41	34N48	5:50:44
Florence, CA	118W15	33N58	7:53:00
Florence, SC	79W46	34N12	5:19:04
Florissant, MO	90W20	38N48	6:01:20
Flushing, NY	73W49	40N45	4:55:16
Fond Du Lac, WI	88W27	43N47	5:53:48
Fontana, CA	117W26	34N06	7:49:44
Forest Hills, NY	73W51	40N42	4:55:24
Fort Collins, CO	105W05	40N35	7:00:20
Fort Dodge, IA	94W11	42N30	6:16:44
Fort Lauderdale, FL	80W08	26N07	5:20:32
Fort Lee, NJ	73W58	40N51	4:55:52
Fort Myers, FL	81W52	26N39	5:27:28
Fort Pierce, FL	80W20	27N27	5:21:20
Fort Smith, AR	94W25	35N23	6:17:40
Fort Wayne, IN	85W09	41N04	5:40:36
Fort Worth, TX	97W18	32N45	6:29:12
Fountain Valley, CA	117W58	33N42	7:51:52
Framingham, MA	71W25	42N17	4:45:40
Frankfort, KY	84W52	38N12	5:39:28
Franklin Square, NY	73W41	40N43	4:54:44

Longitudes and Latitudes of Major Cities

Freeport, IL	89W36	42N17	5:58:24
Freeport, NY	73W35	40N39	4:54:20
Fremont, CA	121W57	37N32	8:07:48
Fresno, CA	119W47	36N44	7:59:08
Fridley, MN	93W16	45N05	6:13:04
Fullerton, CA	117W56	33N53	7:51:44
Gadsden, AL	86W01	34N01	5:44:04
Gainesville, FL	82W20	29N40	5:29:20
Galesburg, IL	90W22	40N57	6:01:28
Galveston, TX	94W48	29N18	6:19:12
Gardena, CA	118W18	33N53	7:53:12
Garden City, MI	83W21	42N20	5:33:24
Garden City, NY	73W38	40N44	4:54:32
Garden Grove, CA	117W55	33N47	7:51:40
Garfield, NJ	74W06	40N52	4:56:24
Garfield Heights, OH	81W37	41N26	5:26:28
Garland, TX	96W38	32N55	6:26:32
Gary, IN	87W20	41N36	5:49:20
Gastonia, NC	81W11	35N16	5:24:44
Gates, NY	77W41	43N09	5:10:44
Glen Burnie, MD	76W37	39N10	5:06:28
Glen Cove, NY	73W38	40N52	4:54:32
Glendale, AZ	112W11	33N32	7:28:44
Glendale, CA	118W15	34N09	7:53:00
Glendora, CA	117W52	34N08	7:51:28
Gloucester, MA	70W40	42N37	4:42:40
Goldsboro, NC	77W59	35N23	5:11:56
Grand Forks, ND	97W03	47N55	6:28:12
Grand Island, NE	98W21	40N55	6:33:24
Grand Prairie, TX	97W00	32N45	6:28:00
Grand Rapids, MI	85W40	42N58	5:42:40
Granite City, IL	90W09	38N42	6:00:36
Great Falls, MT	111W17	47N30	7:25:08
Greece, NY	77W40	43N14	5:10:40
Greeley, CO	104W42	40N25	6:58:48
Green Bay, WI	88W00	44N31	5:52:00
Greensboro, NC	79W48	36N04	5:19:12
Greenville, MS	91W04	33N24	6:04:16
Greenville, NC	77W23	35N37	5:09:32
Greenville, SC	82W24	34N51	5:29:36
Greenwich, CT	73W38	41N02	4:54:32
Gulfport, MS	89W06	30N22	5:56:24
Hacienda Heights, CA	117W58	34N00	7:51:52
Hackensack, NJ	74W03	40N53	4:56:12
Hagerstown, MD	77W43	39N39	5:10:52
Haltom City, TX	97W16	32N48	6:29:04
Hamden, CT	72W54	41N23	4:51:36
Hamilton, OH	84W34	39N24	5:38:16
Hammond, IN	87W30	41N38	5:50:00
Hampton, VA	76W21	37N02	5:05:24
Hamtramck, MI	83W03	42N24	5:32:12
Harlingen, TX	97W42	26N12	6:30:48
Harrisburg, PA	76W53	40N16	5:07:32
Hartford, CT	72W41	41N46	4:50:44
Harvey, IL	87W50	41N36	5:51:20
Hattiesburg, MS	89W17	31N20	5:57:08
Haverhill, MA	71W05	42N47	4:44:20
Havertown, PA	75W18	39N58	5:01:12
Hawthorne, CA	118W21	33N55	7:53:24
Hayward, CA	122W05	37N40	8:08:20
Hazleton, PA	75W59	40N57	5:03:56
Helena, MT	112W02	46N36	7:28:08
Hempstead, NY	73W38	40N43	4:54:32
Hialeah, FL	80W17	25N50	5:21:08
Hicksville, NY	73W32	40N46	4:54:08
Highland Park, IL	87W48	42N11	5:51:12
Highland Park, MI	83W06	42N24	5:32:24
High Point, NC	80W00	35N57	5:20:00
Hillcrest Center, CA	118W57	35N23	7:55:48
Hilo, HI	155W05	19N44	10:20:20
Hobbs, NM	103W08	32N42	6:52:32
Hoboken, NJ	74W02	40N44	4:56:08
Holland, MI	86W07	42N47	5:44:28
Hollywood, FL	80W09	26N01	5:20:36
Holyoke, MA	72W37	42N12	4:50:28
Honolulu, HI	157W52	21N19	10:31:28
Hot Springs Nat Park, AR	93W03	34N30	6:12:12
Houma, LA	90W43	29N36	6:02:52
Houston, TX	95W22	29N46	6:21:28
Huntington, WV	82W27	38N25	5:29:48
Huntington Beach, CA	118W05	33N40	7:52:20
Huntington Park, CA	118W14	33N58	7:52:56
Huntington Station, NY	73W25	40N51	4:53:40
Huntsville, AL	86W35	34N44	5:46:20
Hurst, TX	97W09	32N49	6:28:36
Hutchinson, KS	97W56	38N05	6:31:44
Idaho Falls, ID	112W02	43N30	7:28:08
Imperial Beach, CA	117W08	32N35	7:48:32
Independence, MO	94W25	39N06	6:17:40
Indianapolis, IN	86W09	39N46	5:44:36
Inglewood, CA	118W21	33N58	7:53:24
Inkster, MI	83W19	42N18	5:33:16
Iowa City, IA	91W32	41N40	6:06:08
Irondequoit, NY	77W35	43N13	5:10:20
Irving, TX	96W56	32N49	6:27:44
Irvington, NJ	74W14	40N44	4:56:56
Ithaca, NY	76W30	42N27	5:06:00
Jackson, MI	84W24	42N15	5:37:36
Jackson, MS	90W12	32N18	6:00:48
Jackson, TN	88W49	35N37	5:55:16
Jacksonville, FL	81W39	30N20	5:26:36
Jamaica, NY	73W47	40N43	4:55:08
Jamestown, NY	79W14	42N06	5:16:56
Janesville, WI	89W01	42N41	5:56:04
Jefferson City, MO	92W10	38N34	6:08:40
Jersey City, NJ	74W04	40N44	4:56:16
Johnson City, TN	82W21	36N19	5:29:24
Joliet, IL	88W05	41N32	5:52:20
Johnstown, PA	78W55	40N19	5:15:40
Jonesboro, AR	90W42	35N50	6:02:48
Joplin, MO	94W31	37N06	6:18:04
Juneau, AK	134W25	58N18	8:57:40
Kailua, HI	157W47	21N24	10:31:08
Kalamazoo, MI	85W35	42N17	5:42:20
Kaneohe, HI	157W48	21N25	10:31:12
Kankakee, IL	87W52	41N07	5:51:28
Kannapolis, NC	80W37	35N30	5:22:28
Kansas City, KS	94W38	39N07	6:18:32
Kansas City, MO	94W35	39N06	6:18:20
Kearny, NJ	74W09	40N46	4:56:36
Kendall, FL	80W19	25N41	5:21:16
Kenner, LA	90W15	29N59	6:01:00
Kenosha, WI	87W49	42N35	5:51:16
Kent, OH	81W22	41N09	5:25:28
Kettering, OH	84W10	39N41	5:36:40
Kew Gardens, NY	73W50	40N42	4:55:20
Key West, FL	81W47	24N33	5:27:08
Killeen, TX	97W44	31N07	6:30:56
Kingsport, TN	82W33	36N33	5:30:12
Kingston, NY	73W59	41N56	4:55:56
Kingsville, TX	97W52	27N31	6:31:28
Kirkwood, MO	90W24	38N35	6:01:36
Knoxville, TN	83W55	35N58	5:35:40
Kokomo, IN	86W08	40N29	5:44:32
Lackawanna, NY	78W50	42N50	5:15:20
La Crosse, WI	91W15	43N48	6:05:00
Lafayette, CA	122W07	37N53	8:08:28
Lafayette, IN	86W54	40N25	5:47:36
Lafayette, LA	92W01	30N14	6:08:04
La Habra, CA	117W57	33N56	7:51:48
Lake Charles, LA	93W13	30N14	6:12:52
Lakeland, FL	81W57	28N03	5:27:48
Lakewood, CA	118W08	33N51	7:52:32
Lakewood, CO	105W05	39N44	7:00:20
Lakewood, NJ	74W13	40N06	4:56:52
Lakewood, OH	81W48	41N29	5:27:12
Lakewood Center, WA	122W32	47N11	8:10:08
La Mesa, CA	117W03	32N46	7:48:12
La Mirada, CA	118W02	33N51	7:52:08
Lancaster, CA	118W08	34N42	7:52:32
Lancaster, OH	82W36	39N43	5:30:24
Lancaster, PA	76W19	40N02	5:05:16
Lansing, IL	87W32	41N33	5:50:08
Lansing, MI	84W33	42N44	5:38:12
La Puente, CA	117W57	34N02	7:51:48
Laredo, TX	99W30	27N30	6:38:00
Las Cruces, NM	106W47	32N19	7:07:08
Las Vegas, NV	115W09	36N10	7:40:36
Lawndale, CA	118W21	33N54	7:53:24
Lawrence, KS	95W14	38N58	6:20:56
Lawrence, MA	71W10	42N43	4:44:40
Lawton, OK	98W25	34N37	6:33:40
Leavenworth, KS	94W55	39N19	6:19:40
Lebanon, PA	76W26	40N20	5:05:44
Lemay, MO	90W16	38N32	6:01:04
Lemon Grove, CA	117W02	32N45	7:48:08
Leominster, MA	71W46	42N32	4:47:04
Levittown, NY	73W31	40N44	4:54:04
Levittown, PA	74W51	40N09	4:59:24
Lewiston, ID	117W01	46N25	7:48:04
Lewiston, ME	70W13	44N06	4:40:52
Lexington, KY	84W30	38N03	5:38:00
Lexington, MA	71W14	42N27	4:44:56
Lima, OH	84W06	40N44	5:36:24
Lincoln, NE	96W41	40N49	6:26:44
Lincoln Park, MI	83W11	42N15	5:32:44
Linden, NJ	74W15	40N38	4:57:00
Lindenhurst, NY	73W23	40N41	4:53:32
Little Rock, AR	92W17	34N45	6:09:08
Littleton, CO	105W01	39N37	7:00:04
Livermore, CA	121W47	37N41	8:07:08
Livingston, NJ	74W19	40N48	4:57:16
Livonia, MI	83W23	42N23	5:33:32
Lockport, NY	78W42	43N10	5:14:48
Lodi, CA	121W16	38N08	8:05:04
Lodi, NJ	74W05	40N53	4:56:20
Lombard, IL	88W01	41N53	5:52:04
Lompoc, CA	120W28	34N38	8:01:52
Long Beach, CA	118W11	33N47	7:52:44
Long Beach, NY	73W39	40N35	4:54:36
Long Branch, NJ	74W00	40N18	4:56:00
Longview, TX	94W44	32N30	6:18:56
Longview, WA	122W57	46N08	8:11:48
Lorain, OH	82W11	41N28	5:28:44
Los Altos, CA	122W07	37N23	8:08:28
Los Angeles, CA	118W15	34N04	7:53:00
Los Gatos, CA	121W59	37N14	8:07:56
Louisville, KY	85W46	38N15	5:43:04
Lowell, MA	71W19	42N38	4:45:16
Lubbock, TX	101W51	33N35	6:47:24
Lynchburg, VA	79W09	37N25	5:16:36
Lynn, MA	70W57	42N28	4:43:48
Lynwood, CA	118W13	33N56	7:52:52
Mcallen, TX	98W14	26N12	6:32:56
Mckeesport, PA	79W51	40N21	5:19:24
Macon, GA	83W38	32N51	5:34:32
Madison, WI	89W24	43N04	5:57:36
Madison Heights, MI	83W06	42N30	5:32:24
Malden, MA	71W04	42N26	4:44:16
Manchester, CT	72W31	41N47	4:50:04
Manchester, NH	71W28	43N00	4:45:52
Manhattan, KS	96W35	39N11	6:26:20
Manhattan Beach, CA	118W25	33N54	7:53:40
Manitowoc, WI	87W41	44N05	5:50:44
Mankato, MN	94W00	44N10	6:16:00
Mansfield, OH	82W31	40N45	5:30:04
Maple Heights, OH	81W34	41N25	5:26:16
Maplewood, MN	93W03	45N00	6:12:12
Marietta, GA	84W33	33N57	5:38:12
Marion, IN	85W40	40N32	5:42:40
Marion, OH	83W08	40N35	5:32:32
Marlboro, MA	71W05	42N47	4:44:20
Marrero, LA	90W06	29N54	6:00:24
Marshalltown, IA	92W55	42N03	6:11:40
Mason City, IA	93W12	43N09	6:12:48
Massapequa, NY	73W29	40N41	4:53:56
Massillon, OH	81W32	40N48	5:26:08
Maywood, IL	87W51	41N53	5:51:24
Mckeesport, PA	79W51	40N21	5:19:24
Medford, MA	71W07	42N25	4:44:28
Medford, OR	122W52	42N19	8:11:28
Melbourne, FL	80W37	28N05	5:22:28
Melrose, MA	71W04	42N27	4:44:16
Memphis, TN	90W03	35N08	6:00:12
Menlo Park, CA	122W12	37N27	8:08:48
Menomonee Falls, WI	88W07	43N11	5:52:28
Mentor, OH	81W21	41N40	5:25:24
Merced, CA	120W29	37N18	8:01:56
Meriden, CT	72W48	41N32	4:51:12
Meridian, MS	88W42	32N22	5:54:48
Merrick, NY	73W33	40N40	4:54:12
Merritt Island, FL	80W42	28N21	5:22:48
Mesa, AZ	111W50	33N25	7:27:20
Mesquite, TX	96W36	32N46	6:26:24
Metairie, LA	90W10	29N58	6:00:40
Methuen, MA	71W11	42N44	4:44:44
Miami, FL	80W11	25N47	5:20:44
Miami Beach, FL	80W08	25N47	5:20:32
Michigan City, IN	86W54	41N43	5:47:36
Middletown, CT	72W39	41N34	4:50:36
Middletown, OH	84W24	39N31	5:37:36
Middletown, RI	71W18	41N32	4:45:12
Midland, MI	84W14	43N37	5:36:56
Midland, TX	102W05	32N00	6:48:20
Midwest City, OK	97W24	35N27	6:29:36
Milford, CT	73W04	41N14	4:52:16
Millbrae, CA	122W24	37N36	8:09:36
Millcreek, UT	111W51	40N43	7:27:24
Milpitas, CA	121W55	37N26	8:07:40
Milton, MA	71W05	42N15	4:44:20
Milwaukee, WI	87W55	43N02	5:51:40
Minneapolis, MN	93W16	44N59	6:13:04
Minnetonka, MN	93W27	44N56	6:13:48
Minot, ND	101W18	48N14	6:45:12
Mishawaka, IN	86W11	41N40	5:44:44
Missoula, MT	114W01	46N52	7:36:04
Mobile, AL	88W03	30N41	5:52:12
Modesto, CA	121W00	37N39	8:04:00
Moline, IL	90W31	41N30	6:02:04
Monroe, LA	92W07	32N30	6:08:28
Monroeville, PA	79W45	40N26	5:19:00
Monrovia, CA	118W00	34N09	7:52:00
Montclair, CA	117W42	34N03	7:50:48
Montclair, NJ	74W13	40N49	4:56:52
Montebello, CA	118W07	34N00	7:52:28
Monterey, CA	121W55	36N37	8:07:40
Monterey Park, CA	118W08	34N04	7:52:32
Montgomery, AL	86W19	32N23	5:45:16
Montpelier, VT	72W35	44N16	4:50:20
Moorhead, MN	96W45	46N53	6:27:00
Morgantown, WV	79W57	39N38	5:19:48
Morton Grove, IL	87W46	42N02	5:51:04
Mountain View, CA	122W05	37N23	8:08:20
Mount Lebanon, PA	80W03	40N23	5:20:12
Mount Prospect, IL	87W56	42N04	5:51:44
Mount Vernon, NY	73W50	40N55	4:55:20
Muncie, IN	85W23	40N12	5:41:32
Murfreesboro, TN	86W24	35N51	5:45:36
Muskegon, MI	86W16	43N14	5:45:04
Muskogee, OK	95W22	35N45	6:21:28
Nansemond, VA	76W35	36N44	5:06:20
Napa, CA	122W17	38N18	8:09:08
Nashua, NH	71W28	42N45	4:45:52
Nashville, TN	86W47	36N10	5:47:08
Natick, MA	71W21	42N17	4:45:24
National City, CA	117W06	32N41	7:48:24
Needham, MA	71W14	42N17	4:44:56
New Albany, IN	85W49	38N18	5:43:16
Newark, CA	122W02	37N32	8:08:08
Newark, NJ	74W10	40N44	4:56:40
Newark, OH	82W24	40N03	5:29:36
New Bedford, MA	70W56	41N38	4:43:44
New Berlin, WI	88W06	42N59	5:52:24
New Britain, CT	72W47	41N40	4:51:08
New Brunswick, NJ	74W27	40N30	4:57:48
Newburgh, NY	74W01	41N30	4:56:04
New Castle, PA	80W21	41N00	5:21:24
New City, NY	73W59	41N09	4:55:56
New Haven, CT	72W55	41N18	4:51:40
New Iberia, LA	91W49	30N01	6:07:16
New London, CT	72W06	41N22	4:48:24
New Orleans, LA	90W04	29N58	6:00:16
Newington, CT	72W44	41N41	4:50:56
Newport, KY	84W30	39N05	5:38:00
Newport, RI	71W19	41N29	4:45:16
Newport Beach, CA	117W56	33N37	7:51:44
Newport News, VA	76W25	36N59	5:05:40
New Rochelle, NY	73W47	40N55	4:55:08
Newton, MA	71W12	42N21	4:44:48
New York, NY	73W57	40N45	4:55:48
Niagara Falls, NY	79W03	43N06	5:16:12
Niles, IL	87W48	42N02	5:51:12
Norfolk, VA	76W17	36N51	5:05:08
Normal, IL	88W59	40N31	5:55:56

Longitudes and Latitudes of Major Cities

Norman, OK	97W26	35N13	6:29:44
Norristown, PA	75W21	40N07	5:01:24
Northampton, MA	72W38	42N19	4:50:32
North Babylon, NY	73W19	40N44	4:53:16
North Bergen, NJ	74W01	40N48	4:56:04
Northbrook, IL	87W50	42N08	5:51:20
North Chicago, IL	87W51	42N19	5:51:24
Northglenn, CO	104W58	39N53	6:59:52
North Highlands, CA	121W22	38N42	8:05:28
North Las Vegas, NV	115W07	36N12	7:40:28
North Little Rock, AR	92W16	34N45	6:09:04
North Miami, FL	80W11	25N54	5:20:44
North Miami Beach, FL	80W10	25N56	5:20:40
North Olmsted, OH	81W56	41N25	5:27:44
North Tonawanda, NY	78W53	43N02	5:15:32
Norwalk, CA	118W05	33N54	7:52:20
Norwalk, CT	73W22	41N07	4:53:28
Norwich, CT	72W05	41N31	4:48:20
Norwood, MA	71W12	42N12	4:44:48
Norwood, OH	84W27	39N10	5:37:48
Novato, CA	122W35	38N06	8:10:20
Nutley, NJ	74W09	40N49	4:56:36
Oakland, CA	122W16	37N49	8:09:04
Oak Lawn, IL	87W44	41N43	5:50:56
Oak Park, IL	87W47	41N53	5:51:08
Oak Park, MI	83W11	42N28	5:32:44
Oak Ridge, TN	84W16	36N01	5:37:04
Oceanside, CA	117W23	33N12	7:49:32
Oceanside, NY	73W38	40N38	4:54:32
Odessa, TX	102W23	31N52	6:49:32
Ogden, UT	111W58	41N13	7:27:52
Oildale, CA	119W01	35N25	7:56:04
Oklahoma City, OK	97W30	35N30	6:30:00
Olympia, WA	122W53	47N03	8:11:32
Omaha, NE	96W01	41N17	6:24:04
Ontario, CA	117W39	34N04	7:50:36
Orange, CA	117W51	33N47	7:51:24
Orange, NJ	74W14	40N46	4:56:56
Orem, UT	111W42	40N19	7:26:48
Orlando, FL	81W23	28N33	5:25:32
Oshkosh, WI	88W33	44N01	5:54:12
Ottumwa, IA	92W25	41N01	6:09:40
Overland Park, KS	94W40	38N58	6:18:40
Owensboro, KY	87W07	37N46	5:48:28
Oxnard, CA	119W10	34N12	7:56:40
Pacifica, CA	122W30	37N36	8:10:00
Paducah, KY	88W37	37N05	5:54:28
Palatine, IL	88W03	42N07	5:52:12
Palm Springs, CA	116W32	33N49	7:46:08
Palo Alto, CA	122W10	37N27	8:08:40
Panama City, FL	85W40	30N10	5:42:40
Paramount, CA	118W10	33N53	7:52:40
Paramus, NJ	74W04	40N55	4:56:16
Parkersburg, WV	81W34	39N16	5:26:16
Park Forest, IL	87W40	41N29	5:50:40
Park Ridge, IL	87W51	42N02	5:51:24
Parkville, MD	76W33	39N23	5:06:12
Parma, OH	81W43	41N23	5:26:52
Parma Heights, OH	81W46	41N23	5:27:04
Pasadena, CA	118W09	34N09	7:52:36
Pasadena, TX	95W13	29N43	6:20:52
Pascagoula, MS	88W33	30N21	5:54:12
Passaic, NJ	74W07	40N51	4:56:28
Paterson, NJ	74W11	40N55	4:56:44
Pawtucket, RI	71W23	41N53	4:45:32
Peabody, MA	70W56	42N31	4:43:44
Pekin, IL	89W40	40N35	5:58:40
Penn Hills, PA	79W52	40N28	5:19:28
Pennsauken, NJ	75W03	39N57	5:00:12
Pensacola, FL	87W13	30N25	5:48:52
Peoria, IL	89W36	40N42	5:58:24
Perth Amboy, NJ	74W16	40N31	4:57:04
Petaluma, CA	122W39	38N14	8:10:36
Petersburg, VA	77W24	37N14	5:09:36
Phenix City, AL	85W00	32N28	5:40:00
Philadelphia, PA	75W10	39N57	5:00:40
Phoenix, AZ	112W04	33N27	7:28:16
Pico Rivera, CA	118W05	33N59	7:52:20
Pierre, SD	100W21	44N22	6:41:24
Pine Bluff, AR	92W01	34N13	6:08:04
Piscataway, NJ	74W28	40N34	4:57:52
Pittsburg, CA	121W53	38N02	8:07:32
Pittsburgh, PA	80W01	40N26	5:20:04
Pittsfield, MA	73W15	42N27	4:53:00
Placentia, CA	117W52	33N53	7:51:28
Plainfield, NJ	74W25	40N37	4:57:40
Plainview, NY	73W29	40N46	4:53:56
Pleasant Hill, CA	122W04	37N57	8:08:16
Pocatello, ID	112W27	42N52	7:29:48
Pomona, CA	117W45	34N04	7:51:00
Pompano Beach, FL	80W08	26N14	5:20:32
Ponca City, OK	97W05	36N42	6:28:20
Pontiac, MI	83W18	42N38	5:33:12
Portage, MI	85W35	42N12	5:42:20
Port Arthur, TX	93W56	29N54	6:15:44
Port Chester, NY	73W40	41N00	4:54:40
Port Huron, MI	82W26	42N58	5:29:44
Portland, ME	70W16	43N39	4:41:04
Portland, OR	122W37	45N32	8:10:28
Portsmouth, NH	70W45	43N05	4:43:00
Portsmouth, OH	83W00	38N44	5:32:00
Portsmouth, VA	76W18	36N50	5:05:12
Pottstown, PA	75W39	40N15	5:02:36
Poughkeepsie, NY	73W56	41N42	4:55:44
Prairie Village, KS	94W38	39N00	6:18:32
Prichard, AL	88W05	30N44	5:52:20
Providence, RI	71W24	41N49	4:45:36
Provo, UT	111W39	40N14	7:26:36
Pueblo, CO	104W36	38N14	6:58:24
Queens, NY	73W52	40N43	4:55:28
Quincy, IL	91W23	39N56	6:05:32
Quincy, MA	71W00	42N15	4:44:00
Racine, WI	87W48	42N44	5:51:12
Rahway, NJ	74W16	40N37	4:57:04
Raleigh, NC	78W38	35N46	5:14:32
Rancho Cordova, CA	121W18	38N36	8:05:12
Randolph, MA	71W02	42N10	4:44:08
Rantoul, IL	88W09	40N19	5:52:36
Rapid City, SD	103W14	44N05	6:52:56
Raytown, MO	94W28	39N01	6:17:52
Reading, PA	75W56	40N20	5:03:44
Redford, MI	83W18	42N23	5:33:12
Redlands, CA	117W11	34N04	7:48:44
Redondo Beach, CA	118W23	33N50	7:53:32
Redwood City, CA	122W15	37N30	8:09:00
Rego Park, NY	73W52	40N44	4:55:28
Reno, NV	119W48	39N31	7:59:12
Renton, WA	122W12	47N29	8:08:48
Revere, MA	71W01	42N25	4:44:04
Rialto, CA	117W22	34N06	7:49:28
Richardson, TX	96W44	32N57	6:26:56
Richfield, MN	93W17	44N53	6:13:08
Richland, WA	119W18	46N17	7:57:12
Richmond, CA	122W21	37N56	8:09:24
Richmond, IN	84W54	39N50	5:39:36
Richmond, VA	77W27	37N33	5:09:48
Ridgewood, NJ	74W07	40N59	4:56:28
Riverside, CA	117W22	33N59	7:49:28
Riverton Heights, WA	122W17	47N28	8:09:08
Roanoke, VA	79W56	37N16	5:19:44
Rochester, MN	92W28	44N01	6:09:52
Rochester, NY	77W37	43N10	5:10:28
Rockford, IL	89W06	42N16	5:56:24
Rock Hill, SC	81W01	34N56	5:24:04
Rock Island, IL	90W34	41N30	6:02:16
Rockville, MD	77W09	39N05	5:08:36
Rockville Centre, NY	73W39	40N40	4:54:36
Rocky Mount, NC	77W46	35N55	5:11:04
Rome, GA	85W10	34N15	5:40:40
Rome, NY	75W27	43N13	5:01:48
Rosemead, CA	118W04	34N05	7:52:16
Roseville, MI	82W56	42N30	5:31:44
Roseville, MN	93W10	45N01	6:12:40
Roswell, NM	104W32	33N24	6:58:08
Rotterdam, NY	74W01	42N49	4:56:04
Royal Oak, MI	83W09	42N30	5:32:36
Sacramento, CA	121W29	38N35	8:05:56
Saginaw, MI	83W57	43N25	5:35:48
Saint Charles, MO	90W29	38N47	6:01:56
Saint Clair Shores, MI	82W54	42N30	5:31:36
Saint Cloud, MN	94W10	45N34	6:16:40
Saint Joseph, MO	94W50	39N46	6:19:20
Saint Louis, MO	90W12	38N37	6:00:48
Saint Louis Park, MN	93W21	44N57	6:13:24
Saint Paul, MN	93W06	44N57	6:12:24
Saint Petersburg, FL	82W39	27N46	5:30:36
Salem, MA	70W53	42N31	4:43:32
Salem, OR	123W02	44N56	8:12:08
Salina, KS	97W37	38N50	6:30:28
Salinas, CA	121W39	36N40	8:06:36
Salt Lake City, UT	111W53	40N45	7:27:32
San Angelo, TX	100W26	31N28	6:41:44
San Antonio, TX	98W30	29N25	6:34:00
San Bernardino, CA	117W19	34N07	7:49:16
San Bruno, CA	122W25	37N38	8:09:40
San Carlos, CA	122W16	37N31	8:09:04
San Diego, CA	117W09	32N43	7:48:36
Sandusky, OH	82W42	41N27	5:30:48
San Francisco, CA	122W25	37N47	8:09:40
San Gabriel, CA	118W06	34N06	7:52:24
San Jose, CA	121W53	37N20	8:07:32
San Leandro, CA	122W09	37N44	8:08:36
San Lorenzo, CA	122W08	37N41	8:08:32
San Luis Obispo, CA	120W40	35N17	8:02:40
San Mateo, CA	122W19	37N34	8:09:16
San Rafael, CA	122W32	37N58	8:10:08
Santa Ana, CA	117W52	33N46	7:51:28
Santa Barbara, CA	119W42	34N25	7:58:48
Santa Clara, CA	121W57	37N21	8:07:48
Santa Cruz, CA	122W01	36N58	8:08:04
Santa Fe, NM	105W57	35N41	7:03:48
Santa Maria, CA	120W26	34N57	8:01:44
Santa Monica, CA	118W29	34N01	7:53:56
Santa Rosa, CA	122W43	38N26	8:10:52
Sarasota, FL	82W32	27N20	5:30:08
Saratoga, CA	122W02	37N16	8:08:08
Saugus, MA	71W01	42N28	4:44:04
Savannah, GA	81W06	32N05	5:24:24
Sayreville, NJ	74W22	40N28	4:57:28
Schenectady, NY	73W57	42N49	4:55:48
Scottsdale, AZ	111W56	33N29	7:27:44
Scranton, PA	75W40	41N25	5:02:40
Seal Beach, CA	118W06	33N44	7:52:24
Seaside, CA	121W50	36N37	8:07:20
Seattle, WA	122W20	47N36	8:09:20
Selma, AL	87W01	32N25	5:48:04
Shaker Heights, OH	81W32	41N29	5:26:08
Shawnee, OK	96W55	35N20	6:27:40
Sheboygan, WI	87W45	43N46	5:51:00
Shelton, CT	73W05	41N19	4:52:20
Sherman, TX	96W36	33N38	6:26:24
Shreveport, LA	93W45	32N31	6:15:00
Silver Spring, MD	77W02	39N01	5:08:08
Simi, CA	118W47	34N16	7:55:08
Sioux City, IA	96W24	42N30	6:25:36
Sioux Falls, SD	96W44	43N33	6:26:56
Skokie, IL	87W45	42N03	5:51:00
Somerville, MA	71W06	42N23	4:44:24
South Bend, IN	86W15	41N41	5:45:00
South Euclid, OH	81W32	41N31	5:26:08
Southfield, MI	83W17	42N29	5:33:08
South Gate, CA	118W12	33N57	7:52:48
Southgate, MI	83W12	42N12	5:32:48
South Lake Tahoe, CA	119W59	38N57	7:59:56
South Pasadena, CA	118W09	34N07	7:52:36
South Saint Paul, MN	93W02	44N53	6:12:08
South San Francisco, CA	122W24	37N39	8:09:36
South Whittier, CA	118W02	33N56	7:52:08
Spartanburg, SC	81W57	34N56	5:27:48
Spokane, WA	117W24	47N40	7:49:36
Springfield, MA	72W35	42N06	4:50:20
Springfield, MO	93W17	37N13	6:13:08
Springfield, OH	83W49	39N55	5:35:16
Springfield, OR	123W01	44N03	8:12:04
Spring Valley, CA	116W58	32N45	7:47:52
Stamford, CT	73W32	41N03	4:54:08
State College, PA	77W52	40N48	5:11:28
Staten Island, NY	74W09	40N35	4:56:36
Sterling Heights, MI	83W01	42N35	5:32:04
Steubenville, OH	80W37	40N22	5:22:28
Stillwater, OK	97W04	36N07	6:28:16
Stockton, CA	121W17	37N58	8:05:08
Stratford, CT	73W08	41N12	4:52:32
Suitland, MD	76W56	38N51	5:07:44
Sunnyvale, CA	122W02	37N23	8:08:08
Superior, WI	92W06	46N44	6:08:24
Syracuse, NY	76W09	43N03	5:04:36
Tacoma, WA	122W26	47N14	8:09:44
Tallahassee, FL	84W17	30N27	5:37:08
Tampa, FL	82W27	27N57	5:29:48
Taunton, MA	71W06	41N54	4:44:24
Taylor, MI	83W16	42N14	5:33:04
Teaneck, NJ	74W01	40N53	4:56:04
Tempe, AZ	111W56	33N25	7:27:44
Temple, TX	97W21	31N06	6:29:24
Temple City, CA	118W01	34N07	7:52:04
Terre Haute, IN	87W25	39N28	5:49:40
Texarkana, TX	94W06	33N26	6:16:24
Texas City, TX	94W54	29N24	6:19:36
Thousand Oaks, CA	118W50	34N10	7:55:20
Titusville, FL	80W49	28N37	5:23:16
Toledo, OH	83W33	41N39	5:34:12
Topeka, KS	95W40	39N03	6:22:40
Torrance, CA	118W19	33N50	7:53:16
Torrington, CT	73W07	41N48	4:52:28
Town Of Tonawanda, NY	78W52	42N59	5:15:28
Towson, MD	76W36	39N24	5:06:24
Trenton, NJ	74W46	40N14	4:59:04
Troy, MI	83W09	42N37	5:32:36
Troy, NY	73W41	42N44	4:54:44
Trumbull, CT	73W12	41N15	4:52:48
Tucson, AZ	110W58	32N13	7:23:52
Tulsa, OK	95W55	36N10	6:23:40
Tuscaloosa, AL	87W34	33N12	5:50:16
Tustin, CA	117W49	33N44	7:51:16
Tyler, TX	95W18	32N21	6:21:12
Union, NJ	74W17	40N42	4:57:08
Union City, NJ	74W02	40N45	4:56:08
University City, MO	90W20	38N40	6:01:20
Upland, CA	117W39	34N06	7:50:36
Upper Arlington, OH	83W04	40N00	5:32:16
Upper Darby, PA	75W16	39N58	5:01:04
Urbana, IL	88W12	40N07	5:52:48
Utica, NY	75W14	43N06	5:00:56
Vacaville, CA	121W59	38N21	8:07:56
Valdosta, GA	83W17	30N50	5:33:08
Vallejo, CA	122W15	38N07	8:09:00
Valley Stream, NY	73W42	40N40	4:54:48
Vancouver, WA	122W40	45N38	8:10:40
Van Nuys, CA	118W26	34N11	7:53:44
Ventura, CA	119W18	34N17	7:57:12
Vernon, CT	72W28	41N51	4:49:52
Vicksburg, MS	90W53	32N21	6:03:32
Victoria, TX	97W00	28N48	6:28:00
Villa Park, IL	87W59	41N53	5:51:56
Vineland, NJ	75W02	39N29	5:00:08
Virginia Beach, VA	75W59	36N51	5:03:56
Visalia, CA	119W18	36N20	7:57:12
Vista, CA	117W14	33N12	7:48:56
Waco, TX	97W09	31N33	6:28:36
Wakefield, MA	71W04	42N30	4:44:16
Wallingford, CT	72W50	41N27	4:51:20
Walnut Creek, CA	122W04	37N54	8:08:16
Waltham, MA	71W14	42N23	4:44:56
Warminster, PA	75W06	40N12	5:00:24
Warner Robins, GA	83W36	32N37	5:34:24
Warren, MI	83W02	42N31	5:32:08
Warren, OH	80W49	41N14	5:23:16
Warwick, RI	71W28	41N42	4:45:52
Washington, DC	77W02	38N54	5:08:08
Waterbury, CT	73W03	41N33	4:52:12
Waterloo, IA	92W21	42N30	6:09:24

Longitudes and Latitudes of Major Cities

Watertown, MA	71W11	42N22	4:44:44
Watertown, NY	75W55	43N59	5:03:40
Waukegan, IL	87W50	42N22	5:51:20
Waukesha, WI	88W14	43N01	5:52:56
Wausau, WI	89W38	44N58	5:58:32
Wauwatosa, WI	88W00	43N03	5:52:00
Wayne, NJ	74W15	40N57	4:57:00
Webster Groves, MO	90W22	38N35	6:01:28
Weirton, WV	80W35	40N24	5:22:20
Wellesley, MA	71W18	42N18	4:45:12
West Allis, WI	88W00	43N01	5:52:00
West Babylon, NY	73W21	40N42	4:53:24
West Covina, CA	117W54	34N04	7:51:36
Westfield, MA	72W45	42N07	4:51:00
Westfield, NJ	74W21	40N39	4:57:24
West Hartford, CT	72W44	41N45	4:50:56
West Haven, CT	72W57	41N17	4:51:48
West Hempstead, NY	73W38	40N42	4:54:32
West Hollywood, CA	118W22	34N05	7:53:28
West Islip, NY	73W18	40N42	4:53:12
Westland, MI	83W23	42N18	5:33:32
West Memphis, AR	90W11	35N09	6:00:44
West Mifflin, PA	79W54	40N22	5:19:36
Westminster, CA	118W00	33N47	7:52:00
West New York, NJ	74W01	40N47	4:56:04
West Orange, NJ	74W14	40N47	4:56:56
West Palm Beach, FL	80W03	26N43	5:20:12
Westport, CT	73W22	41N09	4:53:28
West Seneca, NY	78W48	42N51	5:15:12
West Springfield, MA	72W38	42N06	4:50:32
Wethersfield, CT	72W40	41N42	4:50:40
Weymouth, MA	70W58	42N13	4:43:52
Wheaton, IL	88W06	41N52	5:52:24
Wheaton, MD	77W03	39N03	5:08:12
Wheat Ridge, CO	105W07	39N46	7:00:28
Wheeling, WV	80W43	40N04	5:22:52
Whitehall, OH	82W53	39N58	5:31:32
White Plains, NY	73W46	41N02	4:55:04
Whittier, CA	118W03	33N58	7:52:12
Wichita, KS	97W20	37N42	6:29:20
Wichita Falls, TX	98W30	33N54	6:34:00
Wilkes-barre, PA	75W53	41N15	5:03:32
Wilkinsburg, PA	79W53	40N26	5:19:32
Williamsport, PA	77W00	41N15	5:08:00
Willingboro, NJ	74W54	40N03	4:59:36
Willow Brook, CA	118W15	33N56	7:53:00
Wilmette, IL	87W42	42N05	5:50:48
Wilmington, DE	75W33	39N45	5:02:12
Wilmington, NC	77W55	34N14	5:11:40
Wilson, NC	77W55	35N44	5:11:40
Winona, MN	91W39	44N03	6:06:36
Winston-salem, NC	80W15	36N06	5:21:00
Woburn, MA	71W09	42N29	4:44:36
Woodbridge, VA	77W15	38N40	5:09:00
Woodland, CA	121W46	38N41	8:07:04
Woodside, NY	73W55	40N45	4:55:40
Woonsocket, RI	71W31	42N00	4:46:04
Worcester, MA	71W48	42N16	4:47:12
Wyandotte, MI	83W09	42N12	5:32:36
Wyoming, MI	85W42	42N54	5:42:48
Xenia, OH	83W56	39N41	5:35:44
Yakima, WA	120W30	46N37	8:02:00
Yonkers, NY	73W54	40N56	4:55:36
York, PA	76W44	39N58	5:06:56
Youngstown, OH	80W39	41N06	5:22:36
Ypsilanti, MI	83W37	42N14	5:34:28
Yuma, AZ	114W37	32N43	7:38:28
Zanesville, OH	82W01	39N56	5:28:04
Adelaide, Australia	138E35	34S55	-9:14:20
Agra, India	78E01	27N11	-5:12:04
Agram, Yugoslavia	15E58	45N48	-1:03:52
Ahmadabad, India	72E37	23N02	-4:50:28
Aleppo, Syria	37E10	36N12	-2:28:40
Alexandria, Egypt	29E54	31N12	-1:59:36
Algiers, Algeria	3E03	36N47	-0:12:12
Allahabad, India	81E51	25N57	-5:27:24
Amritsar, India	74E53	31N35	-4:59:32
Amsterdam, Netherlands	4E54	52N22	-0:19:36
Ankara, Turkey	32E52	39N56	-2:11:28
Antwerp, Belgium	4E25	51N13	-0:17:40
Athens, Greece	23E44	37N58	-1:34:56
Auckland, New Zealand	174E46	36S52	-11:39:04
Baghdad, Iraq	44E25	33N21	-2:57:40
Baku, USSR	49E51	40N23	-3:19:24
Bangalore, India	77E35	12N59	-5:10:20
Bangkok, Thailand	100E31	13N45	-6:42:04
Barcelona, Spain	2E11	41N23	-0:08:44
Belem, Brazil	48W29	01S27	3:13:56
Belfast, N Ireland	5W55	54N35	0:23:40
Benares, India	83E00	25N20	-5:32:00
Beograd, Yugoslavia	20E30	44N50	-1:22:00
Berlin, Germany	13E24	52N31	-0:53:36
Birmingham, England	1W50	52N30	0:07:20
Bogota, Colombia	74W05	04N36	4:56:20
Bologna, Italy	11E20	44N29	-0:45:20
Bombay, India	72E50	18N58	-4:51:20
Bonn, Germany	7E05	50N44	-0:28:20
Bordeaux, France	0W34	44N50	0:02:16
Bremen, Germany	8E49	53N04	-0:35:16
Breslau, Poland	17E00	51N06	-1:08:00
Brisbane, Australia	153E02	27S28	-10:12:08
Bristol, England	2W35	51N27	0:10:20
Brno, Czechoslovakia	16E37	49N12	-1:06:28
Bruxelles, Belgium	4E20	50N50	-0:17:20
Bucharest, Rumania	26E06	44N26	-1:44:24
Budapest, Hungary	19E05	47N30	-1:16:20
Buenos Aires, Argentina	58W27	34S36	3:53:48
Cairo, Egypt	31E15	30N03	-2:05:00
Calcutta, India	88E22	22N32	-5:53:28
Canton, China	113E16	23N06	-7:33:04
Capetown, S Africa	18E22	33S55	-1:13:28
Casablanca, Morocco	7W35	33N39	0:30:20
Catania, Italy	15E06	37N30	-1:00:24
Cawnpore, India	80E21	26N28	-5:21:24
Changsha, China	112E58	28N12	-7:31:52
Charkov, USSR	36E15	50N00	-2:25:00
Chemnitz, Germany	12E55	50N50	-0:51:40
Chittagong, Bangladesh	91E50	22N20	-6:07:20
Chungking, China	106E35	29N34	-7:06:20
Cologne, W Germany	6E59	50N56	-0:27:56
Colombo, Sri Lanka	79E51	06N56	-5:19:24
Cordoba, Argentina	64W11	31S24	4:16:44
Dacca, Bangladesh	90E25	23N43	-6:01:40
Damascus, Syria	36E18	33N30	-2:25:12
Danzig, Poland	18E40	54N23	-1:14:40
Delhi, India	77E13	28N40	-5:08:52
Dnepropetrovsk, USSR	34E59	48N27	-2:19:56
Dortmund, Germany	7E28	51N31	-0:29:52
Dresden, Germany	13E44	51N03	-0:54:56
Dublin, Ireland	6W15	53N20	0:25:00
Duisburg, Germany	6E46	51N25	-0:27:04
Durban, S Africa	30E56	29S55	-2:03:44
Dusseldorf, Germany	6E47	51N12	-0:27:08
Edinburgh, Scotland	3W13	55N57	0:12:52
Edmonton, Canada	113W28	53N33	7:33:52
Essen, W Germany	7E01	51N28	-0:28:04
Firenze, Italy	11E15	43N46	-0:45:00
Foochow, China	119E17	26N06	-7:57:08
Frankfurt, Germany	8E40	50N07	-0:34:40
Fukuoka, Japan	130E24	33N35	-8:41:36
Geneva, Switzerland	6E09	46N12	-0:24:36
Genoa, Italy	8E57	44N25	-0:35:48
Glasgow, Scotland	4W15	55N53	0:17:00
Gorki, USSR	44E00	56N20	-2:56:00
Goteborg, Sweden	11E58	57N43	-0:47:52
Greenwich, England	0W00	51N29	0:00:00
Guatemala, Guatemala	90W31	14N38	6:02:04
The Hague, Netherlands	4E18	52N06	-0:17:12
Hamburg, Germany	9E59	53N33	-0:39:56
Hamilton, Canada	79W51	43N15	5:19:24
Hangchow, China	120E07	30N15	-8:00:28
Hanover, Germany	9E44	52N24	-0:38:56
Harbin, China	126E41	45N45	-8:26:44
Havana, Cuba	82W22	23N08	5:29:28
Helsinki, Finland	24E58	60N10	-1:39:52
Hiroshima, Japan	132E27	34N24	-8:49:48
Hong Kong	114E12	22N17	-7:36:48
Hyderabad, India	78E29	17N23	-5:13:56
Hyderabad, Pakistan	68E22	25N22	-4:33:28
Ibadan, Nigeria	3E30	07N17	-0:14:00
Indore, India	75E50	22N43	-5:03:20
Istanbul, Turkey	28E58	41N01	-1:55:52
Jakarta, Indonesia	106E48	06S10	-7:07:12
Jerusalem, Israel	35E14	31N46	-2:20:56
Johannesburg, S Africa	28E00	26S15	-1:52:00
Karachi, Pakistan	67E03	24N51	-4:28:12
Kazan, USSR	49E08	55N45	-3:16:32
Kiel, Germany	10E08	54N20	-0:40:32
Kiev, USSR	30E31	50N26	-2:02:04
Kjobenhavn, Denmark	12E35	55N40	-0:50:20
Koln, Germany	6E59	50N56	-0:27:56
Konigsberg, USSR	20E30	54N43	-1:22:00
Krakow, Poland	19E58	50N03	-1:19:52
Kuybyshev, USSR	50E09	53N12	-3:20:36
Kyoto, Japan	135E45	35N00	-9:03:00
Lahore, Pakistan	74E18	31N35	-4:57:12
Lanchow, China	103E41	36N03	-6:54:44
La Paz, Bolivia	68W09	16S30	4:32:36
Leeds, England	1W35	53N50	0:06:20
Leipzig, Germany	12E20	51N19	-0:49:20
Leningrad, USSR	30E15	59N55	-2:01:00
Liege, Belgium	5E34	50N38	-0:22:16
Lille, France	3E04	50N38	-0:12:16
Lima, Peru	77W03	12S03	5:08:12
Liverpool, England	2W55	53N25	0:11:40
Lisbon, Portugal	9W08	38N43	0:36:32
Lodz, Poland	19E30	51N46	-1:18:00
London, England	0W10	51P30	0:00:40
Lucknow, India	80E55	26N51	-5:23:40
Lwow, USSR	24E00	49N50	-1:36:00
Lyon, France	4E51	45N45	-0:19:24
Madras, India	80E17	13N05	-5:21:08
Madrid, Spain	3W41	40N24	0:14:44
Madurai, India	78E07	09N56	-5:12:28
Magdeburg, Germany	11E38	52N07	-0:46:32
Manchester, England	2W15	53N30	0:09:00
Manila, Philippines	121E00	14N35	-8:04:00
Mannheim, Germany	8E29	49N29	-0:33:56
Marseille, France	5E24	43N18	-0:21:36
Mecca, Saudi Arabia	39E49	21N27	-2:39:16
Melbourne, Australia	144E58	37S49	-9:39:52
Mexico City, Mexico	99W09	19N24	6:36:36
Milano, Italy	9E12	45N28	-0:36:48
Monterrey, Mexico	100W19	25N40	6:41:16
Montevideo, Uruguay	56W11	34S53	3:44:44
Montreal, Canada	73W34	45N31	4:54:16
Moscow, USSR	37E35	55N45	-2:30:20
Mukden, China	123E27	41N48	-8:13:48
Munchen, Germany	11E34	48N08	-0:46:16
Nagoya, Japan	136E55	35N10	-9:07:40
Nagpur, India	79E06	21N09	-5:16:24
Nanking, China	118E47	32N03	-7:55:08
Naples, Italy	14E17	40N51	-0:57:08
Newcastle, England	3W06	52N26	0:12:24
Nice, France	7E15	43N42	-0:29:00
Nottingham, England	1W10	52N58	0:04:40
Novosibirsk, USSR	82E55	55N02	-5:31:40
Nurnberg, Germany	11E04	49N27	-0:44:16
Odessa, USSR	30E44	46N28	-2:02:56
Osaka, Japan	135E30	34N40	-9:02:00
Oslo, Norway	10E45	59N55	-0:43:00
Ottawa, Canada	75W42	45N25	5:02:48
Palermo, Italy	13E22	38N07	-0:53:28
Paris, France	2E20	48N52	-0:09:20
Patna, India	85E07	25N36	-5:40:28
Peking, China	116E25	39N55	-7:45:40
Perth, Australia	115E50	31S56	-7:43:20
Poona, India	73E52	18N32	-4:55:28
Porto, Portugal	8W36	41N11	0:34:24
Porto Alegre, Brazil	51W13	30S04	3:24:52
Portsmouth, England	1W05	50N48	0:04:20
Posen, Poland	16E55	52N25	-1:07:40
Praha, Czechoslovakia	14E26	50N05	-0:57:44
Rangoon, Burma	96E10	16N47	-6:24:40
Recife, Brazil	34W54	08S03	2:19:36
Riga, USSR	24E06	56N57	-1:36:24
Rio De Janeiro, Brazil	43W14	22S54	2:52:56
Rome, Italy	12E29	41N54	-0:49:56
Rosario, Argentina	60W40	32S57	4:02:40
Rostovnadonu, USSR	39E42	47N14	-2:38:48
Rotterdam, Netherlands	4E28	51N55	-0:17:52
Saigon, Vietnam	106E40	10N45	-7:06:40
Salvador, Brazil	38W31	12S59	2:34:04
Santiago, Chile	70W40	33S27	4:42:40
Sao Paulo, Brazil	46W37	23S32	3:06:28
Saratov, USSR	46E02	51N34	-3:04:08
Seoul, Korea	126E58	37N33	-8:27:52
Shanghai, China	121E22	31N07	-8:05:28
Sheffield, England	1W30	53N23	0:06:00
Sian, China	108E52	34N15	-7:15:28
Singapore, Singapore	103E50	01N17	-6:55:20
Sofia, Bulgaria	23E19	42N40	-1:33:16
Stalino, USSR	37E48	48N00	-2:31:12
Stettin, Poland	14E32	53N24	-0:58:08
Stockholm, Sweden	18E03	59N20	-1:12:12
Stoke On Trent, England	2W10	53N00	0:08:40
Stuttgart, Germany	9E11	48N46	-0:36:44
Surabaya, Indonesia	112E45	07S15	-7:31:00
Sverdlovsk, USSR	60E36	56N51	-4:02:24
Sydney, Australia	151E13	33S52	-10:04:52
Taipei, Taiwan	121E30	25N03	-8:06:00
Talien, China	121E35	38N53	-8:06:20
Tashkent, USSR	69E18	41N20	-4:37:12
Tbilisi, USSR	44E49	41N43	-2:59:16
Teheran, Iran	51E26	35N40	-3:25:44
Tel Aviv-yafo, Israel	34E46	32N04	-2:19:04
Thessaloniki, Greece	22E56	40N38	-1:31:44
Tientsin, China	117E12	39N08	-7:48:48
Tokyo, Japan	139E45	35N40	-9:19:00
Toronto, Canada	79W23	43N39	5:17:32
Trieste, Italy	13E46	45N40	-0:55:04
Tsinan, China	116E57	36N40	-7:47:48
Tsingtao, China	120E19	36N06	-8:01:16
Turin, Italy	7E40	45N03	-0:30:40
Valencia, Spain	0W22	39N28	0:01:28
Vancouver, Canada	123W07	49N16	8:12:28
Venice, Italy	12E21	45N27	-0:49:24
Vienna, Austria	16E20	48N13	-1:05:20
Volgograd, USSR	44E25	48N44	-2:57:40
Voronezh, USSR	39E10	51N40	-2:36:40
Warsaw, Poland	21E00	52N15	-1:24:00
Wuhan, China	114E17	30N36	-7:37:08
Winnipeg, Canada	97W09	49N53	6:28:36
Wuppertal, Germany	7E11	51N16	-0:28:44
Yokohama, Japan	139E39	35N27	-9:18:36
Zurich, Switzerland	8E32	47N23	-0:34:08

Let your computer look it up!!
PC ATLAS

The *American Atlas* and *International Atlas* for your PC

Accurate latitude & longitude information and time changes
on your computer with a few keystrokes.

Because so many of you have asked us for it, Astro Computing Services has prepared software for your IBM PC-compatible which enables you to have easy access to the comprehensive latitude/longitude information and time change tables from Tom Shanks' *American Atlas* and *International Atlas*. Your purchase of the software includes computer disks containing the encoded atlas information and the programs to access the information effortlessly from your PC. The Atlas data can either be retreived by a stand-alone program, accessed from another program by a resident pop-up program, or integrated into your Astrolabe software.

You key in the place name and a standard state or country abbreviation. The program immediately responds to your request with the coordinates of the location. If the look-up fails, you have the option of re-keying your name or asking for 'sounds-like' place names within the same state or country. For duplicate place names (eg, there are 17 Fairview, Tennessee entries) a menu screen provides you options for easy selection. Other pop-up screens provide easy selection of state and country abbreviations. After the location has been retrieved, you enter a particular date and time. The program responds with the correct time zone information for that date and place.

Machine requirements: IBM PC-compatible with hard disk. Suggested memory 640K or more for integrated software. 4MB of hard disk for either *American Atlas* or *International Atlas*, or 8MB of hard disk for both. Program adapts to variety of keyboards and monitors, and is mouse-capable.

Purchase Options:

ACS *American Atlas* Disk Files and Software (3 disks): $195

ACS *International Atlas* Disk Files and Software (3 disks): $195

Combined *American & International Atlas* Files and Software (6 disks): $295

Release scheduled for February 1990.

PRICES SUBJECT TO CHANGE

Also by ACS Publications, Inc.

All About Astrology Series
The American Atlas: US Latitudes and Longitudes, Time Changes and Time Zones (Shanks)
The American Book of Nutrition & Medical Astrology (Nauman)
The American Ephemeris Series 1901-2000
The American Ephemeris for the 20th Century [Midnight] 1900 to 2000
The American Ephemeris for the 20th Century [Noon] 1900 to 2000
The American Book of Tables
The American Ephemeris for the 21st Century 2001-2050
The American Heliocentric Ephemeris 1901-2000
The American Midpoint Ephemeris 1986-1990 (Michelsen)
The American Sidereal Ephemeris 1976-2000
A New Awareness (Nast)
Asteroid Goddesses (George & Bloch)
Astro Alchemy: Making the Most of Your Transits (Negus)
Astrological Games People Play (Ashman)
Astrological Insights into Personality (Lundsted)
Astrology: Old Theme, New Thoughts (March & McEvers)
Basic Astrology: A Guide for Teachers & Students (Negus)
Basic Astrology: A Workbook for Students (Negus)
Beyond the Veil (Laddon)
The Body Says Yes (Kapel)
The Book of Neptune (Waram)
The Changing Sky (Forrest)
Comet Halley Ephemeris 1901-1996 (Michelsen)
Complete Horoscope Interpretation: Putting Together Your Planetary Profile (Pottenger)
Cosmic Combinations: A Book of Astrological Exercises (Negus)
Dial Detective (Simms)
Easy Tarot Guide (Masino)
Expanding Astrology's Universe (Dobyns)
The Fortunes of Astrology: A New Complete Treatment of the Arabic Parts (Granite)
The Gold Mine in Your Files (King)
Hands That Heal (Burns)
Healing with the Horoscope: A Guide to Counseling (Pottenger)
The Horary Reference Book (Ungar & Huber)
Horoscopes of the Western Hemisphere (Penfield)
Houses of the Horoscope (Herbst)
The Inner Sky (Forrest)
Instant Astrology (Orser & Brightfields)
The International Atlas: World Latitudes, Longitudes and Time Changes (Shanks)
Interpreting Solar Returns (Eshelman)
Interpreting the Eclipses (Jansky)
The Mystery of Personal Identity (Mayer)
The Only Way to. . . Learn Astrology, Vol. I-III (March & McEvers)
    Volume I - Basic Principles
    Volume II - Math & Interpretation Techniques
    Volume III - Horoscope Interpretation
The Only Way to . . . Learn About Tomorrow (March & McEvers)
Past Lives Future Growth (Marcotte & Druffel)
Planetary Heredity (M. Gauquelin)
Planets in Combination (Burmyn)
Planets in Work (Binder)
The Psychic and the Detective (Druffel with Marcotte)
Psychology of the Planets (F. Gauquelin)
Secrets of the Palm (Hansen)
Seven Paths to Understanding (Dobyns & Wrobel)
Spirit Guides: We Are Not Alone (Belhayes)
Stalking the Wild Orgasm (Kilham)
Twelve Wings of the Eagle (Simms)
Tomorrow Knocks (Brunton)